GINSBERG
A BIOGRAPHY

BARRY MILES

SIMON AND SCHUSTER | New York London Toronto Sydney Tokyo

SIMON AND SCHUSTER
SIMON & SCHUSTER BUILDING
ROCKEFELLER CENTER
1230 AVENUE OF THE AMERICAS
NEW YORK, NEW YORK 10020

COPYRIGHT © 1989 BY BARRY MILES

DESIGNED BY BONNI LEON
MANUFACTURED IN THE UNITED STATES OF AMERICA

LIBRARY OF CONGRESS CATALOGING IN PUBLICATION DATA

Miles, Barry, 1943-
  Ginsberg : a biography / Barry Miles.
    p.   cm.
  Bibliography: p.
  Includes index.
1. Ginsberg, Allen, 1926-   —Biography.   2. Poets, American—20th
century—Biography.   I. Title.
PS3513.I74Z745   1989
811'.54—dc20
[B]   89-6422 CIP

TO ROSEMARY

CONTENTS

ONE | CHILDHOOD: PATERSON   9

TWO | A COLUMBIA EDUCATION: THE ORIGINS OF THE BEAT GENERATION   36

THREE | A STREET EDUCATION   62

FOUR | THE SUBTERRANEANS   117

FIVE | ON THE ROAD TO CALIFORNIA   139

SIX | "HOWL" AND THE SAN FRANCISCO RENAISSANCE   188

SEVEN | "THE CLASSIC STATIONS OF THE EARTH"   221

EIGHT | "KADDISH"   248

NINE | ADVENTURES IN PSYCHEDELIA   266

TEN | CUT-UPS   284

ELEVEN | INDIA   298

TWELVE | THE CHANGE   322

THIRTEEN | THE KING OF MAY   341

FOURTEEN | INTO THE VORTEX   369

FIFTEEN | PATERFAMILIAS   407

SIXTEEN | THE LION OF DHARMA   437

SEVENTEEN | EMINENCE GRISE   483

AFTERWORD   521

ACKNOWLEDGMENTS   535

CHAPTER NOTES   539

BIBLIOGRAPHY   563

INDEX   575

ONE | CHILDHOOD: PATERSON

The empty pond where I played, I will see it no more. The old house I cried to leave, the cats I cried to die. Childhood, the dresses I put on in front of the mirror. Those dreams of a magic spell, white-haired Norman . . . the tree in the empty lot, the meadow and the grass. The secret pathway through the woods.

—A.G.

THE SLASH OF PINK ABOVE THE DOWNTOWN SKYSCRAPERS WAS THE ONLY indication of daybreak when Allen Ginsberg left his friend Zev Putterman's apartment on West Fourth Street and walked toward Seventh Avenue. There was a whiff of wood smoke in the crisp subzero air as he hurried along the shadowless street, ghostly in the predawn light. Manhattan looked surreal, its sidewalks cracked and deserted at that silent hour, traffic signals clicking on and off for nonexistent taxis and trucks.

It was the winter of 1958–59. He was thirty-one years old and had just returned to New York City after eighteen months in Europe, living with fellow Beat Generation writers William Burroughs and Gregory Corso. The press had only recently taken to using that sobriquet to describe Ginsberg and the group of new American authors whose work was generating so much heated controversy. Burroughs's *Naked Lunch* was regarded by American publishers as too obscene to publish, and extracts from it published in the winter issue of *Chicago Review* led University of Chicago authorities to suppress the magazine. Jack Kerouac's *On the Road* had received a rave review from the *New York Times* but had been roundly condemned by Norman Podhoretz and other establishment critics. Corso's "Bomb" had caused supporters of nuclear disarmament to

throw shoes at him. Ginsberg's own "Howl" had been the subject
of a celebrated censorship trial in San Francisco, and his picture
had appeared in *Life* magazine. The landmark trial was won by his
publisher, and Ginsberg was now famous in literary circles as the
man who dared—in the middle of the McCarthy era and in the same
month that the American government was burning the books of sex
researcher Wilhelm Reich—to publish a book that revealed not only
his Communist upbringing but his homosexuality. America was not
used to that kind of honesty.

Ginsberg had spent the night talking with Putterman, who played
Ray Charles records for him. Ginsberg chanted passages from Shelley's "Adonais," and at about 3 A.M. they injected morphine and
methamphetamine. The drugs made him talkative, and Ginsberg
began to tell his friend the tragic story of his mother, Naomi, who
had died three years before in a state mental hospital. At her funeral, a *minyan* of ten Jewish men could not be assembled, so she
was denied the Kaddish, the prayer for the dead. Putterman found
his old bar mitzvah book of Jewish ritual and read aloud the central
passages of the Kaddish. Still thinking about Naomi and with the
powerful rhythms of the Kaddish ringing in his head, Ginsberg
walked toward his apartment on the Lower East Side, burning with
a tremendous desire to write.

As he crossed Seventh Avenue, he caught a glimpse in the distance of the high-rise buildings of midtown Manhattan. He recorded
every impression in the unreal early-morning gloom, and later that
day he wrote: "Look back over my shoulder, 7th Avenue, battlements of window office buildings shouldering together high, under
a cloud, tall as the sky." His route took him through the very heart
of Greenwich Village—Sheridan Square and Washington Square—
past all the familiar bookstores and corner groceries, closed and
shuttered. This was the neighborhood where, in the early 1920s,
Naomi and Allen's father, Louis, an aspiring poet, had moved on
the fringes of New York's avant-garde intellectual and bohemian
circles.

Ginsberg crossed Second Avenue, which in Naomi's day was the
Jewish Rialto. He passed the one surviving Yiddish theater on First
Avenue and reached the East Side area where, fifty years earlier,
Naomi, a frightened ten-year-old girl fresh off the boat from Russia,
had lived with her parents on Orchard Street. Finally arriving at his
apartment on East Second Street, he sat down at his desk, snatched
up a blue ballpoint pen, and began writing. He was filled with "a

kind of visionary urge that's catalyzed by all the strange chemicals of the City—but had no idea what Prophecy was at hand—poetry I figured."

From 6 A.M. that Saturday morning until 10 P.M. Sunday, he filled page after page with his unintelligible scrawl, writing nonstop except for trips to the bathroom, often moved to tears. His lover, Peter Orlovsky, brought him boiled eggs and cups of coffee, and Ginsberg took a few Dexedrine tablets to keep the creative energy flowing. He was writing what was to become his most celebrated poem: a Kaddish for his mother, Naomi.

"I began quite literally assembling recollection data taken from the last hours—'Strange now to think of you, gone without corsets and eyes while I walk . . .' etc. I wrote on several pages till I'd reached a climax, covering fragmentary recollections of key scenes with my mother ending with a death-prayer imitating the rhythms of the Hebrew Kaddish—'Magnificent, Mourned no more . . .' etc.

"But then I realized that I hadn't gone back and told the whole secret family-self tale—my own one-and-only eternal child-youth memories which no one else could know—in all its eccentric detail. I realized that it would seem odd to others, but *family* odd, that is to say familiar—everybody has crazy cousins and aunts and brothers.

"So I started over again into narrative—'this is release of particulars'—and went back chronologically, sketching in broken paragraphs all the first recollections that rose in my heart—details I'd thought of once, twice often before—embarrassing scenes I'd half amnesiaized—hackle-raising scenes of the long black beard around the vagina—Images that were central to my own existence such as the mass of scars on my mother's plump belly—all archetypes."

Naomi's parents were from Nevel, a small town on the main road between St. Petersburg and Odessa, about 120 kilometers north of Vitebsk in the middle of the Jewish Pale of Settlement. Her father, Mendel Livergant (his name was changed to Morris Levy at Ellis Island), sold American Singer sewing machines to the peasantry, the family business.

The Livergants were educated men, who spoke Russian as well as Yiddish. In those days, a sign of emancipation, whether one was Socialist or Zionist, was to shave off the traditional Jewish beard and to wear a Western suit rather than the shapeless clothes of thick brown linen woven at home. This Mendel did, but in other respects the country ways prevailed, and both he and his brother, Isser, married their first cousins from nearby Orsa.

Mendel's wife, Judith, gave birth to four children: Eleanor, Naomi, Max, and Sam. She and Mendel were both sympathetic to the anti-czarist revolutionary movement, so in 1904, when it seemed as if Mendel would be drafted to fight for the czar in the Russo-Japanese War, the family moved to Vitebsk to stay with Isser's family, while Mendel and Isser joined the stream of emigrants to the United States.

Naomi grew up speaking Yiddish. She learned to play the mandolin Russian-style and later told her children stories of seeing Cossacks riding through the village in carriages. Isser and Fanny's house in Vitebsk was a two-room wooden cabin. Judith and her four children squeezed in alongside Fanny and her seven children, waiting for Mendel and Isser to raise enough money for boat tickets, so their families could join them in America.

Vitebsk was a city of low, crudely built wooden buildings dominated by the shining domes of the Greek Orthodox church. It was illegal to build synagogues higher than the churches. The unpaved streets were ankle deep in dust in summer, mud in winter. Goats, chickens, geese, ducks, cows, cats, and dogs wandered everywhere. The painter Marc Chagall moved to Vitebsk when he was young, and his paintings of wooden houses, rabbis, and violin players floating over the rooftops reflect the town as it was when Naomi lived there. There was no Jewish ghetto, since Jews made up over a third of the population and owned more than a quarter of the town's businesses.

It was the second-largest city of the province and a center for the revolutionary ideas that spread into the Pale from Germany. Many of the Jews became Communists, whereas farther south, in the Ukraine, the revolutionary tendency was toward Socialism or Zionism, a division that was mirrored in the political opinions of Louis and Naomi Ginsberg when they met, years later, in Newark, New Jersey. The Vitebsk of Naomi Livergant no longer exists. It was destroyed completely by the Nazis, and after the war the Russians rebuilt it as the main industrial center for the area.

In 1905, the year of the first pogrom in the northern Pale, the two families left for the New World, Mendel's family heading for New York City and Isser's for Winnipeg. Mendel had settled on Orchard Street near Rivington, in the heart of the old Jewish section of Manhattan, where he had opened a candy store. Ginsberg described it in "Kaddish": "first home-made sodas of the century, hand-churned ice cream in backroom on musty brownfloor boards . . ." It was here that Naomi ate "the first poisonous tomatoes of America"; she later told her son that Eastern European immigrants thought tomatoes were poisonous. The family then moved to Newark, away from the slums and tenements of the Lower East Side. Naomi went to Barringer High School and, in 1912, met Louis Ginsberg. They were both seventeen.

Louis Ginsberg's father, Pinkus (Peter), who came from Lvov, Galicia, near the present Czechoslovakian border, was orphaned when young. He moved to Pinsk, a small industrial town about halfway between Kiev and Warsaw, but in view of the increasing political unrest in Russia, he decided that his prospects would be better in the United States. He made the crossing sometime in the 1880s and headed for Newark, where he had relatives. There he met Rebecca Schechtman. Rebecca's parents had come to the United States from the Ukraine in the 1870s, when she was very young. They settled in the growing Jewish community in Newark, where her father, Yossel, was able to make a living as a piece goods dealer and played an active role in the local synagogue.

Pinkus and Rebecca married and set themselves up in business, paying three hundred dollars for the horse, wagon, and goodwill of the West Side Laundry Company. The goodwill was not worth much, because the former owner immediately started a new company and poached back many of his old customers. However, the Ginsbergs had many friends and relatives, and for fifteen years they made a reasonable living washing clothes and stretching curtains. In 1895, their first child, Louis, was born. Peter was thirty-two and Rebecca twenty-six. Their family grew, and Louis was soon followed by Abraham, Rose, Clara, and finally, in 1912, Hannah.

At home, Louis grew up with the Socialist viewpoint of his parents, both members of the Yiddish Arbeiter Ring (Workmen's Circle). Pinkus took Louis to lectures by Eugene Victor Debs, a founder of the IWW and the Socialist presidential candidate from 1900 to 1920, and Louis quickly embraced his ideas. "He was magnificent," he later said. "All the ironies of the capitalist system came blazing forth. He was a brilliant man." Louis was so impressed that he named his first son after Debs.

Naomi, meanwhile, was a Communist. Her sister, Eleanor, who was five years older, was a Party cell member. Naomi felt torn between Louis's Socialism and the position of her family, but eventually she sided with her sister and joined the Party. Louis's family was disgusted, particularly his mother, Rebecca, who used to browbeat Naomi whenever she visited. The two women never got along.

The division between Socialists and Communists, always enormous, was exacerbated when war broke out in Europe. The Communists were in favor of America's entering the war, and the Socialists were against it, with Debs coming out strongly in favor of pacifism. Despite their political differences, Naomi and Louis continued to see each other. Both graduated from high school in 1914, and Louis went on to Rutgers, while Naomi attended normal school to train as a grammar school teacher.

Photographs from the period show Naomi as a pretty, vivacious young woman with large dark eyes, round cheeks, and a friendly smile. She was intelligent and self-confident. Her specialty became teaching educationally disadvantaged children, and she was very good at it: "teaching school, laughing with idiots, the backward classes—her Russian specialty," Ginsberg wrote in "Kaddish," and he went on to describe her students: "morons with dreamy lips, great eyes, thin feet & sticky fingers, swaybacked, rachitic—"

When the United States entered the Great War, Louis was drafted but was classified 4F because of his poor eyesight, and so avoided the conflict.

Naomi's mother, Judith, died in 1918, a victim of the influenza epidemic that swept Europe and the United States after the war. Not long after, in 1919, Naomi had her first nervous breakdown. She was teaching school in Woodbine, New Jersey, where she developed a condition in which light was painful to her and every noise came as a blow. She had to stay home from school and lie in a darkened room for three weeks. She knew something was seriously wrong with her, but no one was able to diagnose it. After she recovered, she refused to talk about her condition.

Naomi and Louis decided to marry. Both of his parents were opposed to the marriage. Rebecca, especially, did not like Naomi, partly because of her political opinions, partly because Rebecca was a strong, domineering woman and Naomi stood up to her. They argued constantly. After Naomi's strange illness, Rebecca was even more convinced the girl was not a suitable match for her eldest son. But Louis insisted he loved her, and he and Naomi were married in Woodbine in 1919. They settled in Newark, near his parents. They made an attractive couple: Naomi lithe, energetic, and with a good figure; Louis thin, dapper, with small round eyeglasses and his hair brushed back; both were socially concerned, determined to make the world a better place.

Louis had begun to write poetry in high school and had his first poem published in the Barringer yearbook. In 1920, when he was twenty-five, he wrote "Roots," which was to be the major poem on which his reputation as a poet rested. He and Naomi joined the Poetry Society of America, a meeting place for lyric poets, and they would go to readings in Greenwich Village with the poet Maxwell Bodenheim, with whom Naomi later claimed to have had a brief affair. Free love and a break with Victorian morality were vital aspects of emerging feminism, although in the United States at that time the "new women" were more or less concentrated in Greenwich Village. Vegetarianism and nudism were other parts of the ethos of modernity, and Louis and Naomi spent at least one vacation at a Marxist nudist camp in upstate New York.

In the early twenties, Louis was friendly with Lola Ridge, who ran the New York office of *Broom*, Alfred Kreymborg and Harold Loeb's literary magazine. Thursday afternoon was open house in Margaret Loeb's basement on East Ninth Street. In *Being Geniuses Together*, Lola Ridge's assistant, Kay Boyle, remembered: "I passed cups and plates to Marianne Moore; . . . John Dos Passos, who uneasily toasted the revolution in tea, and to Elinor Wylie; . . . I served them in silent awe: Jean Toomer, Waldo Frank, Babette Deutsch, Mary Heaton Vorse, Gorham Munson, Laura Benét, Edwin Arlington Robinson, Louis Ginsberg, Glenway Wescott, Monroe Wheeler, and countless others, listening when they read aloud their work, listening, listening, my critical faculties wholly numbed, believing that not one dispensable word could be spoken here."

Louis and Naomi also knew Joe Gould, then a protégé of Ezra Pound, and the anthologist Louis Untermeyer, who included Louis's work in his *Modern American and British Poetry*, *Modern American Poetry: A Critical Anthology*, and other collections. Later, in the thirties, Kreymborg published Louis's poems in *The Others*. Louis contributed to all the literary magazines of the day, including Max Eastman's *The New Masses* which, although it was the cultural organ of the Communist Party, published such non-Communists as Hemingway, Dos Passos, Mann, Cowley, and Anderson. *The New Masses* awarded Louis an important poetry prize. But the biggest event was always when he had a poem printed in the *New York Times* magazine. Then, particularly if it was a full page, everyone in the family would carry a clipping to show neighbors and friends.

Louis was a lyric poet in the Elinor Wylie–A. E. Housman mode and maintained that verse should rhyme. To him, free verse was anathema, and he simply didn't understand it. He was content to remain in the literary backwater of the Poetry Society, although when Naomi's sister, Eleanor, accused him of being a "bourgeois poet" he strongly resented it. Louis Untermeyer told him, "You have the lyric touch," and as John Hall Wheelock said on the dust wrapper of Louis's first book: "There is no other poet working in quite the same field that Louis Ginsberg has made so unmistakably his own."

Between 1921, when their son Eugene was born, and 1926, Louis and Naomi moved three times, finally settling at 163 Quitman Street in Newark, a few doors from Louis's parents. Their marriage seems to have been happy then, although the political tensions between them continued to rankle. On June 3, 1926, at 2 A.M., Naomi gave birth to her second son, in Beth Israel Hospital. He was named Irwin Allen Ginsberg, for his great-grandfather S'rul Avrum Ginsberg.

In 1929, Naomi underwent very serious pancreas surgery, during which she nearly died; it left her abdomen badly scarred. The family moved in with Eleanor and her husband, Max, in the central Bronx, near Jerome Avenue, so that Eleanor could nurse her sister and look after the children. Ginsberg has vague early memories of these days in the Bronx, images that appear in his poem "White Shroud."

After some six months in the Bronx, the Ginsbergs moved to Paterson, New Jersey, where Louis taught English at Central High School. Naomi was not with them when they moved. She had had another and much more severe nervous breakdown and was recuperating in the Bloomingdale Sanatorium, near Tarrytown, New York. Again light and sound hurt her, and she was disoriented and confused. Allen recalled visiting Naomi at Bloomingdale: dim memories of a big green lawn with croquet mallets, the patients dressed in white.

The apartment at 83 Fair Street, Paterson, was in a run-down Jewish neighborhood of shabby apartment buildings, wood-frame houses, warehouses, small workshops, and produce markets.

Bridge Street, a block away, led down to the Passaic River, where
the warehouses and factories gave way to slums, and black people
lived in old frame houses, their porches heavy with laundry hanging
out over the dirty water. The Erie Railroad crossed the street, and
beyond the tracks was a huge red-brick factory that produced silk
thread, one of Paterson's major industries. Its constant rattle was
heard in the Ginsberg apartment. Spools of defective silk and empty
cardboard cones littered the area; the children used them as play-
things.

A Bell Telephone building was constructed on the corner next
door shortly after the Ginsbergs moved in. Allen remembers playing
marbles on the sandy ground in front of it. In an alley that ran
between the telephone building and Allen's apartment house, he
was always scared of ghosts. This common enough fear of the shad-
owy figure, or boogeyman, gave rise to the image of the "shrouded
stranger" that was to occur in many of his early poems.

Allen attended kindergarten a block and a half away, at P.S. 1.
Since Naomi was still in the sanatorium, a family friend took him to
school on his first day. Allen, terrified of being left alone, yelled and
screamed so insistently that his father had to be called to take him
home. Louis's life was difficult. He was devoted to Naomi, and the
tragedy of her madness weighed heavily upon him. To pay for her
care in the private sanatorium, he had to borrow heavily from the
credit union, a worrying burden during the Depression, and he had
two growing boys to care for. He found solace in his poetry and
had a great deal published. Family and friends helped him with
the boys, and each weekend he would take them to a family get-
together in Newark.

Louis arranged with a neighbor to provide lunch for Allen and his
elder brother, Eugene, on school days, and in the evenings Louis
would either bring something home from the deli or take the boys
out to eat, usually to the S&Z, on River Street. Later, in his notebooks, Allen referred to eating at the S&Z, out in the grownup world
with his father and brother, as one of his "first experiences of reality." The S&Z also influenced his taste in food. To this day he
prefers inexpensive Eastern European cooking to all other and can
often be found eating borscht, kasha, and blintzes at the Kiev
Ukrainian restaurant on Second Avenue.

Allen played with his best friend, Danny Feitlowitz, who lived
next door, and with the boys and girls upstairs. The boys all dressed
in long stockings and woolen knickers. Allen was soon part of the

community of street children, who ran wild through the backyards and along the railroad embankment.

Naomi returned from the sanatorium not long after they moved to Fair Street. Allen's most vivid early memory is of a fire in his bedroom. Playing with matches, he ignited a rattan wastebasket that Naomi had made in an occupational therapy workshop. She was asleep in another room, tended by her nurse, and when Allen was unable to stamp out the flames, the apartment filled with smoke. Fire engines were called, and Louis was summoned from school. Allen denied everything.

Another memory, which recurs in his journals or dream records, is of an incident from 1931, when Allen was five. Louis sent him down to the corner candy store, where the big boys hung out, to buy a stamp and mail a letter. Allen bought the stamp but stuck it on the lower left side of the letter instead of the top right. No one had shown him how to do it. Everyone in the store laughed, and he felt such shame and humiliation that the incident remains one of the most persistent memories of his early childhood.

The family spent two summers at camp Nicht-Gedeiget ("No-Worry"), run by the Communist Party, near Monroe Lake in upstate New York. A beautiful wooded place, it had cabins and a few dormitories, and there was singing round the campfire in the evening. At the end of a huge meadow, an old Negro lived in a shack with a rain barrel outside. There were salamanders and fish in the streams. It was idyllic for city kids used to playing in the street.

Allen wrote of those halcyon days in "Kaddish": "holy mother, now you smile on your love, your world is born anew, children run naked in the field spotted with dandelions, / they eat in the plum tree grove at the end of the meadow and find a cabin where a white-haired negro teaches the mystery of his rainbarrel—"

Louis would come out and visit on weekends, but for him the camp was not so idyllic. In the mess hall there were big paintings of bloated capitalists and, such was the rift between the Communists and the Socialists in the thirties, there were also paintings of evil Socialists, their hands dripping with blood. This was the time of the Moscow purges, and the camp even had its own mock tribunal. Someone had made an improper remark to a woman who was bathing in the nude, and this minor domestic incident resulted in a full-scale trial before a big crowd in the mess hall.

As Naomi recovered from her breakdown, she became active in the local branch of the Communist Party, which met in a room over a pharmacy on Bridge Street. The group itself was quite small, five or ten members, but there was a large crowd for public meetings if someone famous, such as William Z. Foster, spoke. For a time, Naomi was the branch secretary. Louis felt this threatened his job; he objected further on political grounds, since he was a Socialist of the Eugene Debs–Norman Thomas school. Nevertheless, Naomi would sometimes take the boys with her to meetings, and the first songs Allen learned as a child were "The Red Flag" and the union song "On the Line." In his poem "America," he wrote: "America when I was seven momma took me to Communist Cell meetings they sold us garbanzos a handful per ticket a ticket costs a nickel and the speeches were free everybody was angelic and sentimental about the workers it was all so sincere you have no idea what a good thing the party was in 1835 Scott Nearing was a grand old man a real mensch Mother Bloor the Silk-strikers' Ewig-Weibliche made me cry I once saw the Yiddish orator Israel Amter plain. Everybody must have been a spy."

In 1934, when Allen was eight, the family moved to 155 Haledon Avenue, where they rented the whole house: two floors, a front porch, and a big backyard with a chicken coop. The two brothers shared a bed. Allen always wanted to cuddle up, but Eugene kicked and pushed him back to his side of the bed. Allen later commented, "Gene must have been sick and embarrassed at me hugging at him, pleading for physical love when we slept together as children." The brothers were close at Haledon Avenue, but they argued constantly, and Eugene teased Allen mercilessly.

The shared experience of Depression-era America was the radio, and Allen grew up listening to *Flash Gordon, Mandrake the Magician,* the *Amos 'n' Andy* show, and *The Shadow.* At the end of the weekly *Eddie Cantor Show,* the comedian sang, "I love to spend this hour with you, as friend to friend. I'm sorry it's through." Allen recalled later: "It was a really sad Jewish moment that was the high point of the week, I guess because he was Jewish and a national comedian, and everybody in the family identified with him."

Allen had difficulty at his new school. He was required to memorize his multiplication tables, which, though he was to develop a remarkable memory for long passages of poetry, he was unable to do. He was very self-conscious at school and felt like an outsider. He would awake suddenly from sleep into the silence of Haledon Avenue at night. The reflected lights of a passing bus would swing across the ceiling of his room as he lay thinking, in awe of the immensity of the universe. He would consider the inconceivable distances to the nearest stars and ponder the problems of infinity and the end of space. He was lonely.

Once, in an attempt to ingratiate himself with his schoolmates, he bought six baby chicks, placed them in the old chicken coop in his backyard, and invited the local kids to help refurbish the coop. The children took tiles from the next-door neighbor's garage roof to repair the coop. After the next rainstorm, the neighbor appeared at the Ginsbergs' door, absolutely furious. He and Louis stood talking on the stoop for an hour, and Allen was summoned to admit his guilt. Shamefully, it appeared to his brother that Allen had been trying to buy friendship. In the 1976 poem "Drive All Blames into One," he told the story in complete detail: "I had six baby chicks I paid for so I could attract / my grammar school boyfriends to play with me in my backyard . . . I'm mad at my boyfriends / for stealing that slate I took all the blame . . ." That night Allen had a dream that the boys caught him on the street corner by the candy store: "They got me bent over with my pants down and spanked my behind I was ashamed / I was red faced my self was naked I got hot I had a hard on."

A similar image occurred in an erotic fantasy from the same year. Allen had a preadolescent crush on a boy named Earl, the blond-haired leader of the local gang. Once Allen spent a whole afternoon on Earl's front steps, fantasizing how great it would be to have a magic spell that empowered him to do anything he wished: have millions of dollars, a white horse, a castle with a dungeon. Allen thrilled to the idea of the dungeon. Years later, in Saigon, he recalled his childhood fantasy: "I inspect my naked victims / chained upside down / my fingertips thrill approval on their thighs / white hairless cheeks I may kiss all I want / at my mercy / on the racks. / I pass with my strong attendants / I am myself naked / bending down with my buttocks out / for their smacks of reproval." Excited by thoughts of Earl, Allen stood behind the porch rail outside his house and pulled down his pants to expose himself to the passing traffic. No one noticed him. "dreamy Earl / you Prince of Paterson . . . / first dream that made me take down my pants / urgently to show the cars / auto trucks / rolling down avenue hill," he wrote in "Understand That This Is a Dream." These images of humiliation found their most famous form in Ginsberg's notorious poem of 1968, "Please Master":

please master order me down on the floor . . .
Master drive down till it hurts me the softness the
Softness please master make love to my ass, give body to
center, & fuck me for good like a girl . . .

Despite the images of punishment, Allen was disciplined rarely as a child. Though Louis would sometimes slap him, Ginsberg recalled, "There was a lot of screaming, but Louis actually was very gentle and it was more wounded pride than wounded body."

Naomi and Louis had frequent arguments, usually about money. When Naomi went into the Bloomingdale Sanatorium, Louis had borrowed money to pay for her care, and eventually he owed about $3,600, almost his entire annual income as a teacher. He eventually consolidated the debt with the Teachers' Credit Union, but it was still a great worry to him. During the Depression, teachers' wages were reduced, making things even worse. Naomi felt guilty about the debt and managed to convince herself that Louis had in fact given the money to his mother. Louis's family blamed Naomi for the debt, and it became a perpetual cause of familial bitterness.

Another cause of unrest in the Ginsberg home was Naomi's nudism. Louis upbraided his wife for parading naked in front of the boys, while he respected her belief in naturism (unfortunately, she had gained a good deal of weight from the medication she took and was scarred from her surgery). Naomi sometimes used her nudism to annoy Louis. He could never bring anyone home without telephoning first, and then she would argue vociferously for her right to be "natural." To Ginsberg, in retrospect, her nudism was more neurotic exhibitionism than a genuine belief in naturism. He said it did not bother him except when it upset Louis.

After her treatment in Bloomingdale, Naomi's mental health had remained stable for a number of years, and life was relatively normal. But in 1935, she suffered a relapse; the same symptoms reappeared: light pained her greatly, and she lay in a dark room in the house as the doctors ran tests. They gave her sedatives but were unable to diagnose her illness. After two months of agony, she came out of it and once again appeared to have recovered.

The illness returned a few months later in a much more severe form. Naomi paraded around the house naked, singing to herself. She began to display the classic symptoms of what is now known as paranoid schizophrenia: she heard voices, made grandiose statements, and displayed exaggerated suspicion. On one level, her thinking and behavior remained clear and ordered; she had no problems with her everyday work of cooking, cleaning, and bringing up the children, all of which made it almost impossible for Allen and Eugene to know when they could believe the things she said.

Louis came in for a great deal of hectoring. Naomi was convinced that he and his mother were plotting against her and that her mother-in-law was trying to kill her. As her voices and paranoia grew worse, Louis consulted her family in the Bronx and all the family friends, before he eventually made the painful decision to commit her. This time Louis simply could not afford to send Naomi back to Bloomingdale, so she was admitted to Greystone, a state hospital near Morristown, New Jersey.

It was quite different from the private sanatorium, where the patients had been treated with respect and their conditions referred to as "nervous breakdowns." Greystone was huge and had little therapy available other than insulin shock, Metrazol, and electroshock treatments. Naomi was given a complete course of forty shock treatments, which succeeded in diminishing her fantasies. Though she was severely traumatized, Louis felt he had no alternative but to trust the doctors.

Most weekends, Louis brought his sons to visit. The trip took two to three hours each way on a rattletrap bus, and Allen was frequently carsick. They rode past small towns and farms before they reached the big gray hospital, a landscape recalled with nostalgia in Ginsberg's poem "Garden State" and in "Kaddish."

Upon arrival, they walked down a seemingly endless corridor, past innumerable wards filled beyond capacity with patients. "It stank, sour smell of wards, disinfectant, vomit, piss, people incontinent," Ginsberg said. "And I remember walking down the wards, there were all these old people, and middle-aged people lined up, crooning to themselves, singing, talking to themselves, snapping their fingers, shadow boxing, usually in sloppy ill-fitting clothes. Some of them had been left there for years by their families."

In the visiting room there were bars on the windows, large institutional tables, and long wood benches like church pews. Naomi would be waiting there among the other patients receiving visitors. Haggard, she sat with her hands folded on the table, nodding her head, tearfully telling her family of her trials. She was convinced that wires had been planted in her head and that the doctors had shoved sharp sticks down her back. She was terrified of the shock treatment. She heard voices and complained about poison gas. She thought that the doctors were trying to kill her and begged Louis to take her home.

Sometimes the boys would visit her alone, taking with them a boiled chicken and some fruit. Naomi would tell them that Louis was plotting against her and they must help get her out. There was nothing they could do to relieve her suffering.

Naomi returned home in 1936, and that same year the family moved to a six-room apartment two blocks down the hill, at 72 Haledon Avenue. In the kitchen was an old-fashioned black coal-fired stove, where Naomi made borscht and chicken soup. Allen was transferred from P.S. 17, which he had now settled into, to P.S. 12, where he felt estranged. There, a schoolyard bully, much taller than Allen, taunted him with anti-Semitic remarks. Approaching to hit Allen, he was stopped in his tracks by a volley of long words.

But Allen wasn't always so lucky. There was a black boy named Joe who constantly taunted him, eventually provoking a fight—ten-year-old Allen's first—in which both were knocked down in front of their classmates. The contest was declared a draw, but Allen came home weeping to Naomi. After this, the two boys became good friends and played together in Allen's backyard. When the landlord, who lived on the ground floor, objected, saying he didn't want Negroes around, both Naomi and Louis, believing fervently in integration and equality, sprang to the boy's defense.

Many of the neighbors were anti-Semitic. In "Garden State," composed in 1979, Ginsberg wrote:

> *I was afraid to talk to anyone*
> *in Paterson, lest my sensitivity*
> *to sex, music, the universe, be discovered &*
> *I be laughed at, hit by colored boys.*
>
> *"Mr. Professor" said the Dutchman*
> *on Haledon Ave. "Stinky Jew" said*
> *my friend black Joe, kinky haired.*
> *Oldsmobiles past by in front of my eyeglasses.*

By now, Allen had acquired braces to straighten his teeth and eyeglasses to correct his vision. He was almost a teenager when sex became an issue in his life. One day, walking home from school along Haledon Avenue, he innocently told a girl, "My, what a big bust you have!" Her face red with anger, she hit him and broke his glasses, then chased him all the way home. Far from sympathizing, Eugene and Louis told him that it was his own fault. "Did you mean to insult her?" they asked. Allen did not understand what he had done wrong.

One day, his friend Morton said, "When I see girls in school, sometimes I want to rush right out and grab hold of them. Don't you feel that way?"

"I don't feel that way, no," said Allen. Later, Allen and Morton and two other boys went into the bathroom in Morton's house. Morton sat on the toilet seat, and one of the boys knelt in front of him and kissed his penis. "The amazing thing was that he didn't seem to be self-conscious about it," Ginsberg recalled. "Wasn't apparently afraid of what we'd think—that he was queer—being of an age when it was all new—and mysterious and forbidden."

Another time, during their play, a gang of children surrounded Morton and pulled his pants down. "I stood aside, not helping him for fear of getting my own pants pulled down," Ginsberg wrote later. "but enjoying Morton's humiliation and baring, the baring of his privates. This last phrase is particularly exciting to me—as perhaps my whole character is exhibitionistic and evidenced by 155 Haledon Ave fantasy and action on porch—slipping down pants for short time to traffic (unseen)—and dream of that time of getting turned over and spread by boys of my gang whom I feared."

Allen played with a group of street children, discovering secret paths through the woods on the vacant lot and exploring the pond by the silk factory: "The bathing pool hidden / behind the silk factory / fed by its drainage pipes; / all the pictures we carry in our mind . . ."

In 1937, Louis moved the family to 288 Graham Avenue, an ivy-covered apartment building on the corner of Broadway in downtown Paterson. Naomi began to get sick again—less than a year after she had been discharged from Greystone—and was often in such bad shape that Allen had to stay home from school to look after her. Naomi would try to get him to side with her in her delusional obsession that Louis's mother, whom the family called Buba, was the head of a spy network and was out to get her. Much of her paranoia focused on Louis's debt, the money that had paid for Naomi's first hospitalization. Naomi claimed Louis had given it to Buba. Allen, not yet eleven, was placed in a hopelessly confusing position between his two parents.

Naomi delighted in taunting Louis with allusions to her affair with Maxwell Bodenheim and did everything possible to cause him grief. but he refused to commit her again. Allen could not talk to anyone about the storm of emotions aroused by his mother's illness. Having just changed schools, he had no close friends who would understand, and his brother, at sixteen, busied himself with his own group of friends. Allen's diary from June 1937 is chilling in its casual depiction of an emotionally shattering event. Three weeks after his eleventh birthday, he wrote:

"June 19: My mother thinks she is going to die and is not so good . . . My brother is to graduate from high school soon, and will go to Montclair Teachers' College.

"June 21: . . . My mother is worse today.

"June 22: I stayed home to mind my mother. I got a haircut and two pairs of shoes and heard the 'Louis-Braddock' fight over the radio. Louis won and is now champion of the world.

"June 23: My brother graduated from high school today and we had a party. The party broke up about 12 o clock at night. We had an excellent time and my brother (for once) kissed my aunts goodbye. I stayed home from school to take care of my mother.

"June 24: I stayed home from school again only today I went to high school and saw my father teach. My mother locked herself in the bathroom early in the morning and my father had to break the glass to get in. She also went back to the sanatorium. I saw a newsreel of the Louis-Braddock fight, also 'Dangerous Number' and another picture in the movies. I also developed a sty below my eye."

As Louis Ginsberg later described the incident, Naomi, in a state of suicidal depression, had locked herself in the bathroom, refusing to come out. "Could hear her cough in tears at sink," Allen wrote in "Kaddish." When Louis finally broke the glass panel to open the door, she was standing with blood oozing from both wrists. "They were surface cuts," Louis said, "so I bandaged them and then put her to bed. The boys stood there, shivering in their night clothes, panic in their eyes. 'What traumas,' I thought, 'might sink into them and burrow into their psyches.' " The next morning, an ambulance arrived for Naomi, and Louis took Allen to work with him so that he could watch over him. Every hospitalization was a complete tragedy for Allen. "For years Allen could not understand why his mother had deserted them," Louis said.

Naomi's illness gave Allen an enormous empathy and tolerance for madness, neurosis, and psychosis. In his 1980 poem "After Whitman & Reznikoff," he wrote:

> *That round faced woman, she owns the street with her*
> *three big dogs,*
> *screeches at me, waddling with her shopping bag across*
> *Avenue B*
> *Grabbing my crotch. "Why don't you talk to me?"*
> *baring her teeth in a smile, voice loud like a taxi horn,*
> *"Big Jerk . . . you think you're famous?"—reminds me*
> *of my mother.*

According to his secretary, Bob Rosenthal, Ginsberg will go through the day's mail and, before dealing with the letters from academics and friends, instead read, with obvious relish and not a little anguish, one written in colored crayon on sixteen pages of torn notebook paper.

With Naomi again in the hospital, Louis reorganized the apartment. Eugene had his parents' old bedroom in the back, and Allen slept with his father in the front bedroom, where Louis had his big desk. Allen would lie in bed, dozing, while Louis graded English papers and wrote poems under a metal-shaded lamp. At night, Allen would snuggle up against Louis: "I was getting hard-ons, rubbing up against his leg, just pressing close and holding on to him as I couldn't with my mother or brother. And we neither acknowledged it." He was not conscious of anything unusual in this intimate relationship with his father, until he looked back on it.

As a baby, Allen had three good years of Naomi's sanity before she was taken away to Bloomingdale. Then, devastated by his mother's frequent absences at the hospital, he began to make constant demands of affection and love from other members of the family. "I must have been a sexpest to the whole family," he recalled, "even when sleeping with Louis. Gene was the only one who rebuked me, but without shame or guilt, just elastic rejection of elastic demand."

During his adolescent years, Allen avoided fears and unhappiness as he had in his childhood, by hiding out at the movies. In March 1938, he recorded in his diary: "Movies afford me great pleasure and are about the only relief from boredom which seems to hang around me like a shadow." He saw Fredric March's award-winning performance in *Dr. Jekyll and Mr. Hyde*, and at the hero's transformation to a hairy beast in the park, Allen ran from the theater and stood trembling outside, filled with "a nightmare vision of my own future." He wept copiously at a film that ended with the police taking a convict away to jail while his sad dog ran vainly after the police car alone; and when the Invisible Man was hunted down in the snow and died, pitifully transformed back to visibility. Allen wept for his soul.

With Eugene commuting each day to Montclair State Teachers College and Naomi still in the hospital, Louis became active in the New Jersey Chaucer Guild and the Manuscript Club. In 1937, he borrowed two thousand dollars to finance the publication of his first collection of poems, *The Everlasting Minute*, which consolidated his reputation as a poet.

When the family moved to Graham Avenue. Allen had transferred to P.S. 6, and he graduated on June 27, 1939. In his yearbook, he named Poe his favorite author, *Dr. Doolittle* his favorite book, and swimming his favorite sport. His motto: "Do what you want to when you want to."

Louis and the boys spent the summer at the shore in Belmar with the Ginsberg clan. On Labor Day weekend, 1939, all of them were sitting around a large wooden table in their rented house when they heard that the Germans had invaded Poland.

That fall, Louis brought Naomi home on the bus after three years in Greystone. She was nervous and shaky, standing in the doorway of an apartment she barely remembered, looking down the dark hall as her two sons rushed to greet her. The excitement proved too much for her, and she retired to the back bedroom to rest. After a while, Allen followed to keep her company. He told the story in "Kaddish":

> She went to the bedroom to lie down in bed and ruminate, or nap, hide—I went in with her, not leave her by herself—lay in bed next to her—shades pulled, dusky, late afternoon—Louis in front room at desk, waiting—perhaps boiling chicken for supper—
>
> 'Don't be afraid of me because I'm just coming back home from the mental hospital—I'm your mother—'
>
> Poor love, lost—a fear—I lay there—Said. 'I love you Naomi,'—stiff, next to her arm. I would have cried, was this the comfortless lone union?—Nervous, and she got up soon.

Naomi's arguments with Louis resumed. She took the Party line on the war with Finland in the winter of 1939 and supported the

USSR, so infuriating the family that even Allen would point to the map on his bedroom wall and yell, "But look, Mama, Russia's this big and Finland's so small. It can't be. It can't be!" Nevertheless, Ginsberg remembered this as a relatively happy time, and home life was mostly tranquil. They went to the New York World's Fair in June 1940 and to Belmar that summer. Every day Allen devoured the *New York Times*. He had compiled huge files of news clippings on Hitler and Mussolini and had been very emotional about the Spanish Civil War: "Lots of righteous wrath and self-righteousness," he later described it. Allen wanted the United States to join the war and was indignant about the isolationists. He and Eugene spent a lot of time at the campaign headquarters of Irving Abramson, a local CIO official who was running for Congress from the Eighth District of New Jersey. His opponent, Gordon Canfield, charged Abramson with being a "red," which unleashed a letter-writing campaign from the young Ginsberg.

Through Irving Abramson, Louis met Leo Perlis, publisher of the short-lived *Paterson Press*. Louis wrote some poems for the paper and Naomi had children's stories published every two weeks, small parables of friendship and fellowship in which Allen and Eugene often figured. As Allen referred to them in "Kaddish":

> *Naomi reading patiently, story out of a Communist fairy book—Tale of the Sudden Sweetness of the Dictator—Forgiveness of Warlocks—Armies Kissing—*
> *Deathsheads Around the Green Table—The King & the Workers—Paterson Press printed them up in the 30's till she went mad, or they folded, both.*

Allen had gone on to Central High in Paterson, where on May 9 and 10, 1940, he took part in the annual school show, All Central Night. He was in the chorus and acted in several sketches, but the high spot of the evening was clearly "Ballet Loose," which featured Allen as the *premiere danseuse*, with six of his schoolboy friends as ballerinas, all in tutus. Forty years later, he wrote in his journal: "Basil Battaglia, my old Central High School mate and chum who once kissed me in excitement the night of the high school play. I did the ballerina in tutu, bumping my ass at the football players in elephant costumes or drag, too, 1940 Central High School auditorium—I was thirteen that year hardly cognisant of my sex but sensitive to love and affection."

At Central High he excelled in English and took an interest in the school magazine, *The Spectator*, where his first two pieces appeared in print in the Easter 1941 issue. One was a piece of schoolboy humor called "On Homework in General," the other an interview with Canada Lee, the star of the Broadway production *Native Son*.

Sunday was the best day of the week at Graham Avenue. The *New York Times* was spread across the floor, and everyone would dip into it. Sometimes Louis would walk to and fro, quoting from Milton's poetry as they read. Later, when Allen was a well-known poet, Louis was led to ask, "Is he a poet by nature or nurture? I think both."

The more settled home life seemed to help Allen at school, and he became gregarious and popular with his schoolmates. He debated about Hitler in class and was very knowledgeable politically. Looking back, Ginsberg described himself: "Big eyeglasses and a thin face with buck teeth, going to an orthodontist to have them fixed. A kind of mental ghoul, totally disconnected from any reality, existing in a world of newspapers and aesthetics: Beethoven, Leadbelly, Ma Rainey and Bessie Smith." He had crushes on other boys, in particular one muscular young man who did a lot of weight lifting and exercises.

Across the street from the Ginsbergs' apartment house was a church and a funeral home, surrounded by a thick hedge. Ginsberg later described walking home from seeing movies at the Fabian Theater and passing the hedges with their mysterious shadows, "and my heart would ache and I would go into some kind of swoon thinking how mysterious the universe was and how lonely I was in it." The dark hedges were associated with his preoccupation with the end of space. "I kept trying to figure out what's infinity. At the end of infinity there must be a wall, maybe made of rubber." But even this flexible solution to the problem was inadequate, because something would have to be at the other side of the rubber wall.

The church was rebuilt and the hedges uprooted in the early fifties, but the image lived on for Ginsberg as a symbol of adolescent wonder and mystery. It inspired a number of later works: "Graham Avenue, the ugly church / nice steeple, cock atop / hedges—where I walked as a kid / hedges of melancholy / came home from the movies / Fred Astaire dancing / on black mirrors."

It seems that a bureaucratic mix-up had sent Allen to the wrong school, so in September 1941 he was moved from Central to East Side High. Yet again he had to start over and adjust to a classroom full of children who knew the ropes. Allen's knowledge of politics, his appalling jokes (which he collected in a special notebook), and his poetry, which he read aloud in English class, all helped him to be quickly assimilated as a member of the class of '43. He became president of both the Debating Society and the Dramatic Society.

It was Allen's English teacher Frances Durbin who introduced him to Walt Whitman. He has described how one afternoon she "read aloud verses from Walt Whitman's 'Song of Myself' in so enthusiastic and joyous a voice, so confident and lifted with laughter, that I immediately understood 'I wear my hat indoors as well as out . . . I find fat no sweeter than that which sticks to my own bones' forever, and still remember her black-dressed bulk seated squat behind an English class desk, her embroidered collar, her voice powerful and high, lilting Whitman's very words and shafts of sunlight through school windows that looked down on green grass."

That year Eugene decided he had chosen the wrong vocation and wanted to be a lawyer, not a teacher. He went to study law in Newark, where he took a small furnished room and worked as an elevator operator to pay his way through college.

In the winter of 1941, symptoms of Naomi's madness began to reappear. She accused Louis of poisoning her soup: Buba had bought the poison with money Louis had given her. Allen would drink the soup and say, "Look, Mama, it's not poisoned, see?" but to no avail. Allen again stayed home from school to look after her on her bad days, and one night she had some kind of seizure. Ginsberg described it in harrowing detail in "Kaddish":

> One night, sudden attack—her noise in the bathroom—
> like croaking up her soul—convulsions and red vomit
> coming out of her mouth—diarrhea water exploding from
> her behind—on all fours in front of the toilet—urine run-
> ning between her legs—left retching on the tile floor
> smeared with her black feces—unfainted—

Allen and Louis rushed to her aid and, holding her by the shoulders, tried to calm and comfort her. The attack was a mystery and seemed more like an epileptic seizure than a symptom of mental illness. Louis was always convinced that there was some chemical or biological explanation for Naomi's illness, but the doctors found nothing.

One day in the winter of 1941, Allen stayed home from school with her, sat her down, and demanded to know exactly what it was she was fearful of. She reiterated her problems: Buba had paid the doctors at Greystone to give her fifty electric shocks so that she would grow fat; they put poison in her food and had inserted three big sticks down her back. She sat stiffly in the chair. Allen, trying hard to understand, felt her shoulder where she said it hurt. According to his later account, she told him there were wires in the ceiling listening to every word she said and reporting them back to President Roosevelt.

"They're listening to everything we say," said Naomi. "I don't want to put you in danger."

"Who?" asked Allen, but Naomi wouldn't say. Allen gave her a pad of paper, and she scribbled the name of Allen's grandmother. "The wires are in this ceiling," she told him. "I could hear the crackling when you gave me the pencil. They knew it." Exasperated, Allen took the broom from under the bed and began thumping on the ceiling around the cracked paint by the light fixture, to prove that there were no wires, but Naomi insisted that they were inside the ceiling, embedded there and attached to the inside of her head. She said she could hear them talking. They were calling her names, saying she was a bad woman, a whore, and ordering their agent to kill her.

Then the voices told her that the agent was outside in the street. She jumped up and rushed to the window, closely followed by Allen. Across the street was the church, with its mysterious hedges. A few people were waiting on the corner for a bus. One of them looked a little like a banker and wore a smart hat. "That's him," said Naomi. "He's the one." She threw open the window and yelled, "Go away, you rotten thing!" before Allen could drag her back inside.

Naomi claimed she was ill and in need of a rest. She wanted to go to Lakewood, New Jersey, to a rest home. She had been there before and liked it. Allen said he couldn't take her to Lakewood unless her doctor approved. She insisted, so he phoned Dr. Hans Wassing and explained the situation. Perhaps Wassing believed he was talking to someone older or thought Allen was Eugene, because he unaccountably agreed. Allen wanted to call Louis, but Naomi persuaded him not to, saying it would disturb his work, and in any case Louis was one of the people plotting against her. Allen did not know what to do, but since the doctor had authorized it, he helped Naomi pack her suitcase, and they left.

"It was kind of dumb," he said later. "I was a prisoner in the house. I was smaller than she was and she was intimidating me to do this. She was splitting my mind because I didn't know if she was right or not. She said she was being persecuted and it didn't make sense but she was so insistent about it."

Naomi refused to go down in the elevator in case the elevator man informed "them" that they were escaping, so they walked down the stairs and into the street. Naomi held the collar of a large worn fur coat high to her nose as a gas mask against poison germs sprayed by Louis's mother in the downtown streets. A boy carrying his schoolbag came down the street toward them. Attracted by Naomi's furtive manner, he stared at them, then yelled, "Where are you going, lady? To death?" then he ran away, laughing. Allen shuddered.

At the bus terminal, Allen bundled Naomi onto the Newark bus and asked the driver if the bus continued on to Lakewood. The driver told Allen that they would have to change at Newark. Naomi immediately backed off the bus, whispering loudly to Allen, "We can't go on this bus. He's not going to Newark, can't you see? The bus is empty. He's going to kidnap us." She decided that they would go to Manhattan and take a Greyhound to Lakewood from there. At Times Square, they had to wait two hours for a bus, while Naomi fretted about "invisible bugs." The ride itself lasted three terrible hours, while Allen tried to stop her from making a scene. She argued with him, grew paranoid about the couple in the front seat, who were fortunately asleep, and looked surreptitiously at the other riders over the top of her turned-up coat collar like a "classical cartoon of a spy," as Ginsberg later described it.

He recollected the ride in a beautiful passage of "Kaddish": ". . . me tagging along, hoping it would end in a quiet room in a Victorian house by a lake. Ride 3 hours thru tunnels past all American industry, Bayonne preparing for World War II, tanks, gas fields, soda factories, diners, locomotive roundhouse fortress—into piney woods New Jersey Indians—calm towns—long roads thru sandy tree fields—"

It was late afternoon when they arrived in Lakewood. They straggled down the street, a large lady in a fur coat, peering anxiously over her shoulder, followed by a skinny youth who looked younger than his age, dragging a large valise. They reached the address, and the door was opened by an old man and a woman, wearing white coats. Allen stood in the hallway and asked their rates, while Naomi hid behind the door. Everything went well until Naomi came rushing out and demanded, "I'm weak, my blood spoiled by electricity. Can you give me a blood transfusion?"

"I'm sorry," said the woman, quickly ushering them out. "This place is for people who want rest and don't need continuous care." The long, quiet streets of Lakewood were filled with rest homes, but everywhere they went, they received the same treatment. At last Allen yelled at Naomi, "You won't get anyplace if you keep talking like that!" and they were able to find her a place. Allen gave the attendant a week's rent, but as the woman turned aside to write a receipt, Naomi began whispering urgently in Allen's ear. He clamped his hand over her mouth.

They trooped up the stairs to an old attic room with stained wallpaper, but there were lace curtains and a handcrafted rug on the floor. "Don't you *dare* say anything to them about your blood transfusion," warned Allen. "They'll kick you out. It's only a quiet rest home. Go lie down and rest. You're safe here. I'll go home and tell Louis."

This provoked a strong reaction from Naomi. "No, *don't* tell Louis where I am. . . . He'll send spies to watch me. He might poison me. The only reason he lets me live is he used to love me. His mother wanted me dead years ago." Allen pushed her down on the bed and told her to be quiet, fearful that if the attendant heard them arguing they might be thrown out. He calmed her and then left to take the long bus ride back to Paterson: "laid my head back in the last seat, depressed," he wrote in "Kaddish," "the worst yet to come?—abandoning her, rode in torpor—"

It was late when Allen arrived back at Graham Avenue, and Louis was waiting anxiously in the living room. He was horrified to hear what Allen had done and deeply worried by what he knew would happen next. The inevitable telephone call came at 2 A.M. Naomi had gone mad. She had run down the hallways barefoot, banging on all the doors, scaring the old ladies in their rooms. Then she had barricaded herself under the bed with her suitcase and was screaming about Mussolini, Hitler, poison germs, and calling out, "Help! Louis! Buba! Fascists! Death!" The frightened attendants demanded that Louis take her away at once, but since he had no car, there was no way he could get there until morning. He took the 6:30 A.M. bus to Newark and went from there to Lakewood.

All the attendants gathered on the porch as Naomi and Louis left the rest home; the old ladies peered from behind fluttering curtains. Naomi claimed there was a nail in her shoe and walked with one shoe in her hand, limping as Louis pulled her by the arm. It was only two blocks to the bus station, and Louis insisted that she could walk, but when a cab pulled up they took it. As Louis was paying, Naomi emerged from the cab and ran off, dropping her suitcase on the sidewalk. Louis snatched up the suitcase with one hand and caught Naomi with the other as she struggled into a pharmacy, yelling. The next bus to New York did not leave for two hours.

Naomi began to harangue the druggist, demanding a blood transfusion. Her voice rose as she became excited. Louis had no idea what to do and hovered near her, trying to calm her, asking her to please be quiet because she was attracting a crowd. Louis was humiliated. Naomi was triumphant. The bus finally arrived, but the driver refused to allow her aboard. In desperation, Louis telephoned Greystone Hospital. "Bring her here, Mr. Ginsberg," they said, as Naomi stood sniffing the air for germs.

Ginsberg used the scene, as told to him that night by his father, as a central passage in "Kaddish": "Naomi—sweating, bulge-eyed, fat, the dress unbuttoned at one side—hair over brow, her stocking hanging evilly on her legs—screaming for a blood transfusion— one righteous hand upraised—a shoe in it—barefoot in the Pharmacy—"

Louis had to pay thirty-five dollars for an ambulance to come from Red Bank to fetch her. The idea of returning Naomi to Greystone was so abhorrent that he took her instead to Hillgreen, a private rest home in Passaic. There, the admissions doctor would not accept her without a signed form from the county physician. He gave Naomi a sedative, but she and Louis had to wait in the ambulance until 6 P.M. for the forms to arrive by special messenger. Naomi was in Hillgreen for a week, but her condition was too serious for them to handle, and Louis reluctantly agreed to transfer her to Greystone, where she was to remain for the next two years.

Louis returned home exhausted. Eugene had no telephone and, visiting the next day, asked where Naomi was. "We had to send her back to the hospital," explained Louis. Ginsberg described Eugene's reaction in "Kaddish": "—his face perplexed, so young, then eyes with tears—then crept weeping all over his face—'What for?' wail vibrating in his cheekbones, eyes closed up, high voice— Eugene's face of pain."

That June, Allen turned sixteen. In Belmar, he watched the stars "from the Jersey shore all through one pitifully lonely summer

night." He continued his letter writing against the isolationists and
spent hours of his time listening to music. He listened to opera and
Gershwin and modern composers such as Aaron Copland and Eric
Coates. In October, Eugene went into the army and after basic
training was sent to Great Britain, where he remained for the duration of the war. Allen enrolled with Civilian Defense and spent some
of his evenings on patrol duty with two women wardens. From November 1942 until the following February, he worked as a page in
the Paterson Public Library, putting away books fifteen hours a
week for thirteen cents an hour. His journal later recorded that
while he was there, he sneaked into the office of the librarian and
looked up "homosexuality" in Krafft-Ebing. "Am I a homosexual?"
he asked himself, seeking an explanation for the crushes he was
always getting on other boys.

He liked one boy in particular. Paul Roth was a half year ahead
of Allen and got a scholarship to Columbia University. In "Kaddish," he was described as "my high school mind hero, jewish boy
who became a doctor later—then silent neat kid." "I was totally in
love," said Ginsberg. "I spent all the time I could with him, but in
a very shy way." Roth had no idea of Allen's feelings, though Allen
sometimes hinted at them; on one occasion, he remarked that
Roth's handwriting in a letter to him from Columbia was erotic.
Roth's reply was typewritten.

Allen was determined to follow his hero and applied to Columbia.
On his way to New York to take the entrance examination, he stood
on the prow of the Hoboken ferry in the cold air and made a solemn
vow that if he got into Columbia to be with Paul Roth, he would
devote his life to helping the working class. This was a serious vow,
not just the by-product of a schoolboy crush. It gave direction to
Ginsberg's activities over the years, and he used it as a benchmark
whenever he was confused by a choice of courses of action. Curiously, when Allen got to Columbia, he saw Roth rarely.

TWO | A COLUMBIA EDUCATION: THE ORIGINS OF THE BEAT GENERATION

When shall we go, over there by the shores and mountains, to salute the birth of new work, the new wisdom, the flight of tyrants, and of demons, the end of superstition, to adore . . . the first ones! . . . Christmas on Earth?

—Arthur Rimbaud

IT WAS SNOWING WHEN ALLEN ENTERED THE UNION THEOLOGICAL SEMInary a few days before Christmas, 1943. He climbed the stairs to his seventh-floor room and looked down the long wooden corridor. Most of the students had gone home for the holidays, and the transoms above the doors were dark, except for one at the far end, where a new boy had moved in. From behind this door came the sound of a clarinet and strings, playing music that Allen was unfamiliar with. He was intrigued and knocked on the door. It was answered by "the most angelic-looking kid I ever saw, with blond hair, pale and 'hollow of cheek as though he drank the wind and took a mess of shadows for his meat,' " Ginsberg said later, quoting Yeats.

"I heard the music," explained Allen.

"Did you like it?" asked Lucien Carr.

"I thought it might be the Brahms Clarinet Quintet," ventured Allen.

Carr seemed surprised and pleased. "Well, well! A little oasis in this wasteland." He invited Allen in. On his walls were prints of *The Bohemian Girl* by Franz Hals, Rousseau's *Sleeping Gypsy*, and a Cézanne landscape. The crowded bookcase held copies of Flaubert, Rimbaud's *Une Saison en Enfer*, and a criticism of Toulouse-

Lautrec, all in French. Allen also noticed *Jude the Obscure* and a worn copy of Spinoza's *Ethics*. Lucien produced glasses and a bottle of burgundy, and they began to talk.

Allen had arrived at Columbia University in September. He had book knowledge in many areas but no real experience in life; he had not traveled or had any kind of relationship outside his family. The only thing he knew a lot about was madness, which gave him a natural affinity with eccentrics and the rejects of society. His parents had each demanded that he accept their version of reality— diametrically opposed readings of the world: "I was putting on a stiff upper lip and trying to fulfill the obligations I thought were demanded of me, taking over my father's role of taking care of my mother . . . and having to be the recipient of her confessions and emotions but of a delusional nature. And that confused me, I didn't think I was confused but really I had a kind of split mind, of who I was supposed to trust. It left me in a kind of neutral limbo."

Since Allen was unable to trust anyone completely, and his parents were unable to provide what he called "empowerment or reassurance, that I was a nice man and could go out in the world," Allen had little self-esteem. He was ill-equipped to leave home.

At Columbia, he enrolled in a prelaw course, intending to become a labor lawyer to fulfill his vow made on the ferry. A scholarship boy, he was in awe of the confident, sophisticated Ivy League types he saw in the corridors, but he was determined to fit in.

The Columbia halls of residence had been taken over by wartime V-12 naval cadets, and the university found off-campus housing for its new students. When Allen arrived, he was given rooms with two other students, Jerry Rauch and Arthur Lazarus, in a large apartment at 50 Morningside Drive, half a block from the campus; by December, Allen and his two roommates had been moved to the Union Theological Seminary, at 122nd Street and Broadway, which was filled with Columbia students displaced by the cadets. It was there that Allen met Lucien Carr.

The Columbia English department was in those days one of the most famous and influential in the country. Allen's required courses were taught by such professors as Lionel Trilling, Mark Van Doren, and Raymond Weaver. Trilling was an elegant and learned literary critic, who, as Ginsberg later described him, "in a sense tried to revive the humanistic solidarity and good manners of mid-nineteenth-century England. Mahogany Matthew Arnold." Trilling was more concerned with a respect for boundaries than with breaking down barriers, always looking for "the best kind of truth." His class was filled with naval cadets, who would sit in the back and sleep, so Trilling concentrated his energy on the three or four students who paid attention, among them Allen, Herbert Gold, the future novelist, and Lucien Carr, who described Trilling as having pale blue, milky eyes, which made him look blind. Carr was very impressed by Trilling and thought, "This is the blind Homer teaching here."

Mark Van Doren was the literary editor of *The Nation* and a distinguished critic and poet. He was a close friend of the poet Allen Tate and wrote rhymed verse influenced by his friend Robert Frost. Van Doren had received the Pulitzer Prize for his *Collected Poems* in 1940. Among his more celebrated students were John Berryman and Thomas Merton.

Raymond Weaver, who shared an office with Van Doren, was the author of the first biography of Melville, *Herman Melville, Mariner and Mystic.* In the course of his research, he had discovered the manuscript of *Billy Budd* in a trunk in Melville's house on Twenty-third Street. "I mean, the man who discovered posthumous manuscripts of Melville. That's *really* a professor!" Ginsberg later commented. He was flattered and inspired to be working with men who had heretofore been only names in the *New York Times* or the *Herald Tribune*, and for his first year at Columbia he was a model student.

The amount of required reading during his first semester was prodigious. Allen made his way through Aeschylus, Herodotus, Thucydides, Sophocles, Aristotle, Euripides, Aristophanes, Plato, Virgil, Tacitus, Saint Augustine, and the Book of Job. By November he had moved on to Zola, Dante, Rabelais, Machiavelli, Montaigne, and Shakespeare. Despite this enormous work load, he found time to tentatively explore New York City, going to his first Japanese restaurant (still open, despite the war), visiting the museums, and walking the streets. He went often to the Metropolitan Opera, usually with Naomi, who had been released from Greystone earlier that year and was living in the city.

Though Naomi had recovered sufficiently to be allowed home, she was still convinced that Buba was persecuting her and that Louis had given Buba all his money. It was not long before their life degenerated into one continuous argument. Despite his deep and abiding love for Naomi, the twenty-two years of their marriage had finally exhausted Louis. His love was not reciprocated, the companionship, trust, and friendship had long gone, destroyed by Naomi's paranoia and delusions. She remained fixated on Louis's debt and the idea that Buba was plotting against her. Naomi was often abusive, and the arguments were so acrimonious that they sometimes ended with her moving to a local rooming house for a few days. One time, Allen followed her, and she made him swear to keep her address a secret from Buba and Louis.

When Allen moved to the city, Naomi was left with an empty nest. This enabled her to make the final break from Louis, and Louis let her go. He had done his duty and held the marriage together as best he could until his children left home. Naomi moved to New York, where she stayed with her sister Eleanor in the Bronx and took a job addressing envelopes at the Workmen's Circle. The nature of Naomi's illness was such that to most people she appeared to be a normal, cheerful, strong-willed, self-confident woman in her late forties. It was only when her delusions intensified and she began to hear voices that her behavior became noticeably aberrant. Through Eleanor she met Dr. Leon Luria, who, like herself, was a Communist. He was the official doctor for the National Maritime Union and had an office on West Eighteenth Street, near the NMU hall. Luria, whom Ginsberg described as a "bald and pudgy old doll," was attracted to her and offered her a job as his receptionist. It was not long before he became her lover and she moved in with him.

The break between Louis and Naomi had been coming for a long time, so Allen was not surprised. He continued to see them both and frequently visited his father in Paterson or attended the opera or a concert with him in New York, as well as visiting Naomi and her new lover. Louis had grown used to living without his wife and over the long years of her confinement had developed friendships with a number of women, though Allen and Eugene never knew how intimate those friendships were.

Soon after they met, Lucien Carr invited Allen to accompany him to Greenwich Village to meet some of his friends. Allen had not yet been to the Village and wrote excitedly to Eugene: "Saturday I plan to go down to Greenwich Village with a friend of mine who claims to be an 'intellectual' (that has a musty flavor, hasn't it?) and knows queer and interesting people there. I plan to get drunk Saturday evening, if I can. I'll tell you the issue."

Carr came from a well-known family in St. Louis, where his ma-

ternal grandfather was a successful dealer in jute and hemp fibers.
When Lucien was an infant, his father had walked out on the family
to become a sheepherder in Wyoming. Lucien was still a child when
his father died. At the funeral in Denver, where he was working as
a bank guard, the boy looked into the coffin and said, "I don't know
you, old man."

Lucien was two years older than Allen. A precocious, feckless
teenager, he had been expelled from Andover and sent to a special
school for difficult children, then to summer school at Bowdoin
College, Maine. He spent two semesters at the academically rigorous University of Chicago, then dropped out to bum around for six
months; he was admitted to Columbia in the fall. Since he had
already done his preliminary reading of the classics with Elder
Olson at Chicago, he was able to take it easy at Columbia and read
poetry and listen to music, while his fellow students sweated over
Thucydides.

Most of his problems at previous schools had been caused by a
tall, red-haired, bearded man named David Kammerer, who was
from a respectable St. Louis family and had supervised Lucien's
grade school play group. Kammerer had become obsessed with Lucien's beauty and followed him from school to school. Now he was
in New York, where he had taken a job washing dishes. Lucien
dealt with Kammerer's attentions by forming an uneasy platonic
friendship in which he had the upper hand, always telling Kammerer what to do and when he could see him. Kammerer would
obey meekly. It was an unhealthy relationship, but Lucien saw no
alternative.

Kammerer was not the only homosexual to lavish attention on
Lucien. His intense slanted blue eyes and tangled yellow hair attracted interest wherever he went, from women as well as men.
Vanity of Duluoz, by Jack Kerouac, describes Lucien arriving on
the Columbia campus one warm afternoon and going to the library
to play Brahms in a listening booth. As always, Kammerer follows
right behind, but Lucien makes him wait outside the booth while he
listens to the music undisturbed. A professor of French classics
comes by, takes one look at him, and bursts into the booth, exclaim-
ing, "Where did you come from, you marvelous boy?"

Lucien took Allen to visit Kammerer, who lived at 48 Morton
Street, just off Seventh Avenue. The street was littered with garbage cans and piles of dirty snow, but for Allen it was an enchanting
experience. "It was an uncharted, historic no-man's-land wilder-

ness to me, particularly entrancing as I was a closet queen and had not come out yet, so going down to the Village, where all the fairies were, but in disguise, with a beautiful friend, it was both romantically glorious and at the same time completely repressed, frightening, and frustrating."

Kammerer was asleep when they arrived, and Allen noticed a heavily penciled inscription, "Lu—Dave," written on the wall above his pillow, where a tear in the wallpaper revealed a patch of plaster. They headed out, treading carefully over the icy sidewalk to the Minetta Tavern.

On another excursion, a day or two later, Kammerer had a friend from St. Louis visiting when they arrived. William Seward Burroughs lived just around the corner at 69 Bedford Street. At thirty, Burroughs seemed awfully old to Allen, who was only seventeen. "[To me] anyone over twenty-two was superannuated," Ginsberg said later, "and Burroughs already seemed to have the 'ashen grey of an age-old cheek.' " He was tall and thin, with wispy, sandy-colored hair and thin lips, which he pursed in a nervous tic. He wore steel-rimmed eyeglasses and sat draped over a low settee by the fireplace.

Kammerer had a one-room apartment on the first floor, with French windows looking out over a garden. A lesbian named Louise lived upstairs, and Bill liked her because, in his words, she was "straightforward, manly, and reliable." These were the first words Ginsberg can remember hearing Burroughs speak.

Allen squatted on an upturned log that served as the coffee table and listened to Lucien and Burroughs talk. Lucien told the story of how, a few days earlier, he had drunkenly provoked a fight between Kammerer and a gay portrait painter he knew, which had demolished most of the painter's Greenwich Village studio. Lucien had bitten off part of the painter's earlobe and sunk his teeth into Kammerer's shoulder. Burroughs deplored the whole situation, saying, "In the words of the immortal bard, ' 'tis too starved a subject for my sword.' " Allen was amazed. It was the first time he had heard anyone casually quote an appropriate line of Shakespeare to voice an opinion.

Allen and Lucien swiftly developed a rapport. While Lucien mocked Allen's lack of worldly knowledge, Allen timorously criticized Lucien's degeneracy. Carr had this impression of the seventeen-year-old Allen: "Naive, he was incredibly naive! He was just an eager young Jewish kid from Paterson who wanted to know everything about books and writers and art and painting, who knew nothing about the serious things in life such as wenching and drinking!"

Allen and Lucien spent most of their time together talking about literature, challenging each other to spell difficult words, and trying to score intellectual points. To Allen, Lucien's little tests and arguments were often illuminating. In one typical bantering exchange, Allen used the quote "milk of human kindness" in something he said (he had just reread *Macbeth*). Lucien asked him to spell it. Allen was slightly put out at such an obvious spelling question, but Lucien showed him what he meant. They were standing at the urinal of the Minetta Tavern, and Lucien borrowed Allen's pen, then wrote on the wall "human-kindness" and "humankind-ness." "Macbeth is filled with the milk of humankind-ness," Lucien concluded.

"That still sticks in my mind," Ginsberg said. "It was a distinction I'd never thought about and was ultimately a real thing, between an idealist notion of human-kindness and humankind-ness, an odd little verbal thing that I hadn't examined, as if I had a portion of my unexamined life. I guess the word Lucien used at the time was 'jejune.' "

In October 1943, Allen began his first journal. On the front of it, he wrote carefully: "Being The Notebook of Allen Ginsberg; Now From the Cracked and Bleeding Heart, Triumphantly I fashion Art." It was the first of several hundreds of journals and notebooks he was to fill, a practice he has retained to this day. An early entry was from an old popular song Lucien liked to sing, headed "Carr's Melody": "Violate me / in violent times / the vilest way that you know / Ruin me / Ravage me / Utterly savage me / On me no mercy bestow."

When Allen first met him, Lucien had a girlfriend named Donna Leonard, whom he had known in Chicago; but he soon encountered Celine Young, a Barnard girl who could never decide whether she preferred intellectuals or football players. Celine and Lucien became inseparable, constantly kissing and holding hands, to the envy and disgust of David Kammerer, who disparaged her as a "bourgeois kitten."

Lucien and Celine, with Allen and Kammerer tagging along, could often be found sharing a booth at the West End Bar, just across Broadway from the Columbia campus. They were a distinctive group: Allen, with his thick horn-rimmed glasses, played the intellectual. Lucien, nonchalant, sporting a red bandanna, was the acknowledged leader. Celine, beside him, sensual and witty, mirrored Lucien with her long golden hair. Kammerer, for his part, focused solely on Lucien, as the group sat drinking Pernod, imagining themselves drinking absinthe in *fin de siècle* Paris.

Allen's late-night conversations with Lucien continued through the Christmas break. Ginsberg noted in his journal: "Know these words and you speak the Carr language: fruit, phallus, clitoris, cacoethes, feces, foetus, womb, Rimbaud." Rimbaud had come as a revelation to Allen: "The poet becomes a *seer* through a long, immense, and reasoned *derangement of all the senses*. All shapes of love, suffering, madness. He searches himself, he exhausts all poisons in himself, to keep only the quintessences. Ineffable torture where he needs all his faith, all his superhuman strength, where he becomes among all men the great patient, the great criminal, the great accursed one—and the supreme Scholar! For he reaches the *unknown*!"

Though immediately attracted, Allen still had doubts about *la vie de Bohème* to which he was being introduced. It held no place for the suffering masses to whom he had sworn to devote his life and in whose service he was studying to be a labor lawyer. Lucien openly ridiculed Allen's plans as naive, and one day, after the latest argument on the subject, Lucien stopped outside a rough-looking bar on 125th Street and pointed out that Allen would feel uncomfortable and embarrassed if he even went in there among the workingmen. "You want to be a labor lawyer?" he asked. "You've never worked a single day in your life!" Allen was reluctantly forced to agree.

Allen remained loyal to the West End Bar, with its mixture of seamen, naval cadets, and locals. Its proximity to the Columbia campus drew a large contingent of college kids, one of whom was Edie Parker, a birdlike, ebullient young woman from Grosse Pointe, Michigan. She and Lucien soon became good friends. Edie and her roommate, a journalism student named Joan Vollmer, lived nearby on 118th Street, and Lucien began to use their apartment as a place to escape from David Kammerer. Before long he brought Celine with him, sleeping with her on the couch in the living room.

Edie's boyfriend was a young seaman, an ex–Columbia football player named Jack Kerouac. He was away on a trip when Edie first got to know Lucien, but he soon returned. When Edie pointed Lucien out across the bar, Kerouac's response was: "Looks to me like a mischievous little prick," but he could see why Edie found him attractive. They became immediate friends and Lucien soon began to show up in class drunk or sleepless after an all-night session with Jack. Once Lucien put Jack in an empty barrel and rolled him down the sidewalks of upper Broadway; another night, they sat drunkenly in a puddle during a rainstorm and tipped ink over each other's heads, singing at the top of their voices.

Lucien enjoyed his talks with Jack about art and literature, and thinking that Allen would like to meet Kerouac, he gave him the address. Allen arrived one afternoon, probably in late May 1944. Kerouac described their meeting in *Vanity of Duluoz*, in which he calls Ginsberg by his first name, Irwin: "I was sitting in Edie's apartment one day when the door opened and in walks this spindly Jewish kid with horn-rimmed glasses and tremendous ears sticking out, seventeen years old, burning black eyes, a strangely deep voice."

Jack was sitting at the table having a midafternoon breakfast of bacon and eggs. He offered Allen a beer. Nervous and a little confused, he replied, "No, no. Discretion is the better part of valor." Kerouac's narrative continues: " 'Aw where's my food' I yelled at Edie, because that's precisely all I had on my mind at the moment he walked in. Turns out it took years for Irwin to get over a certain fear of the 'brooding football artist yelling for his supper in big daddy chair' or some such."

Jack Kerouac was four years older than Ginsberg. Born March 12, 1922, he was raised in Lowell, Massachusetts, then a dull industrial town, where his father owned a small printshop. The Kerouacs were a part of a large community of French Canadians who had immigrated to Lowell from Quebec, and Jack grew up speaking joual, the French of the Canucks, with English as his second language. Throughout his life he spoke to his mother in patois rather than English.

His mother, Gabrielle, a devout Catholic, made sure that Jack had a religious upbringing. Kerouac's friend Philip Whalen later described how it had affected him: "He'd go through these terrific changes where he'd suddenly be attacking you and saying everything was bad, everything was dirty, everything was ugly. You must remember that he'd been brought up in this very tough parochial school. He'd tell dreadful stories about the nuns who worked there. It must have been quite a harrowing experience. . . . American Catholicism is Jansenist, and it takes this tough line about how the body is evil. . . . So he had this trip about 'dirty me.' He had that going and this helped complicate his life and make him sad."

The death of his older brother, Gerard, after suffering two years with rheumatic fever, had wounded Jack deeply. He was only four, but throughout his childhood, Gerard was always held up by his mother and the nuns as an unattainable model of saintly perfection. From parochial school he went to Lowell High, where he became a football hero. He was offered a sports scholarship to Columbia, but first he spent a year at Horace Mann Prep to bring him up to the University's academic standards.

Once at Columbia, he fought with the coach and finally flunked out after injuring his leg. In December 1942, he joined the navy, but he did not fit in and feigned insanity to get a discharge. In the summer of 1943, he joined the merchant marine and crossed the U-boat-infested Atlantic to Liverpool on an ammunition boat. When Allen met him, Jack was still working as a merchant seaman.

Ginsberg later recalled: "I remember being awed by him because I'd never met a big jock who was sensitive and intelligent about poetry." Allen thought Jack was physically beautiful and admired his "sturdy peasant build." He liked his brooding Quebecois moodiness and described him as "Extraordinarily sensitive, very intelligent, very shrewd and very compassionate most of all. Compassionate toward the awkward kid. He was gruff but inquisitive." He looked like the stereotypical gay sex object, "the football player with a golden heart." Allen instantly fell in love with Jack, just as he had with Lucien.

Soon after they met, Allen and Jack took a walk together, and Allen was amazed and pleased at Kerouac's interest in him. They traversed the Columbia campus and got into a long conversation about the nature of phantoms and ghosts and, as Ginsberg described it, "the tearfulness of our own ghost presence."

Allen told Jack how he would stand in the shadow of the mysterious hedges on Graham Avenue and wonder how big space was and where the universe ended. Jack told Allen how he would stand in the backyard of his parents' house at night when everyone was eating supper and feel that everyone was a ghost, eating ghost food. Like Allen, he often looked at the stars and pondered the size of the universe. It was the first time Allen opened up and talked about such delicate subjective experiences; the conversation was quite different from the intellectual banter that characterized his talks with Lucien. Kerouac was curious and interested in what Allen was saying. "Gee, that's the way I think a lot too," he would say. "I have thoughts like that all the time."

Their walk had taken them to the Union Theological Seminary;

they stood on the corner of West 122nd Street and Broadway and looked down the hill to the gray spread of Harlem. Allen was moving out of the seminary and still had a few things to collect. He and Jack had discussed their admiration for Lucien, so there was a mutual understanding when Allen pointed out the door where he first heard the Brahms Quintet six months earlier.

Allen collected the few books and belongings he had come for, and as he turned from the dormitory suite he bowed to it, made a gesture of farewell, and said, "Goodbye, door." He continued down the stairs, saying goodbye to each step as he went. He bade farewell to the seventh-floor landing, the sixth-floor landing, and all the rest, like a poem, all the way down. Kerouac was struck by this: "Ah, I do that when I say goodbye to a place." They had a long, excited conversation about the recognition of each of the stairs as the final stair and about Allen's realization of the changes in himself since he first climbed them six months before.

"That struck him as an awareness of a soul in space and time, which was his nature," Ginsberg said later. Jack asked him if he knew any other people with the same awareness. Was it awareness? Was it poetry? They decided that everyone had it who was in any way conscious or sensitive. "Everyone has the same soul. We're all here together at once in the same place, temporarily, with a totally poignant tearful awareness that we're together," they decided. This recognition became the basis of their deep and lasting understanding of each other.

Allen was moving to the Warren Hall Residence Club, a small hotel on West 115th Street, where Lucien Carr now lived. He took a room on Lucien's floor and was delighted with his accommodation. For eight dollars a week, he had a small room with a bed, sink, closet, and hot plate. There was a telephone, connected to the lobby switchboard. He finally felt that he was out in the world.

It was a period of long, idealistic conversations. Allen and Lucien spent weeks, for example, arguing over a definition of art. Allen's position was that art had to be social and serve some purpose. Lucien maintained that art was "self-ultimate." The argument centered on the questions: "If someone carved a walking stick, was that art?" and "If he carved it and it was put on the moon and nobody ever saw it, would that be art? Did art need an audience in order to exist?" They asked Kerouac his opinion, but he didn't have one. Finally, they put the question to Burroughs.

"That's the stupidest question I ever heard of," Burroughs

sniffed. "It depends how you want to define the word 'art.' " When Bill was in Chicago, he had studied briefly with Count Korzybski, the founder of the theory of general semantics. Bill explained to Allen and Lucien that a word is not the thing it represents but whatever you use it to mean. "Words don't have a built-in definition. If you want to define this as art, then you define it as art. If you don't want to use that word for that situation, then you don't. But to argue whether the thing is art or not is obviously a confusion in terms." Ginsberg later recalled the occasion: "I laughed ever since on the naïveté of the discussion. Hung on words. Young kids. It was so embarrassing. It was a relief to hear such iconoclastic sense."

Long nights of conversation took place in the West End Bar, frequently degenerating into bouts of competitive drinking for Jack and Lucien. It was during this period that they came up with the idea of the "New Vision," the genesis of the philosophy of the Beat Generation.

Lucien Carr remembered: "In those years at Columbia, we really did have something going. It was a rebellious group, I suppose, of which there are many on campuses, but it was one that really was dedicated to a 'New Vision.' It's practically impossible to define. Maybe it was a term we just sold ourselves. It was trying to look at the world in a new light, trying to look at the world in a way that gave it some meaning. Trying to find values . . . that were valid. And it was through literature that all this was supposed to be done. And it was through Jack and Allen, principally, that it was going to be done."

The definition of "New Vision" in Ginsberg's journal reveals that Allen was soon converted to Lucien's viewpoint: "Since art is merely and ultimately self-expressive, we conclude that the fullest art, the most individual, uninfluenced, unrepressed, uninhibited expression of art is true expression and the true art."

After Allen and Jack had become good friends, they decided to pay a visit to Burroughs together and "investigate the state of his soul," since, as a result of many hours of intense conversation, they both felt that they had a very definite sympathetic understanding of the nature of their own souls.

Bill now lived in a small but rather grand apartment in one of the big buildings on Riverside Drive, overlooking the Hudson, which had been loaned to him by an ex–Harvard friend. Bill showed them his library. Most of the books they had never heard of. Bill explained that he had a scientific approach to reading, which was both functional and pragmatic: "I read each book for a special purpose," he told them. "For instance, I read Chas Jackson's *Lost Weekend* to see what alcoholism is like. I read for information." He told them he read Rimbaud for his description of the derangement of the senses, and both Rimbaud and St. John Perse for "the foreign perfume, the juxtaposition of strange experience and the images of cities glittering in the distance." Burroughs particularly liked the T. S. Eliot translation of St. John Perse's *Anabase*, which had a dry, St. Louis edge to it that he could appreciate.

Bill had books on parlor tricks, card games and formulas, boxing, jujitsu, an Egyptian grammar, Kovoor Behanan's *Yoga: A Scientific Evaluation*, a volume on hypnoanalysis, and Abrahamsen's *Crime and the Human Mind*, but the literature and poetry were what particularly interested Ginsberg. It was here that he and Jack discovered Kafka's *The Castle*, Cocteau's *Opium*, Louis-Ferdinand Céline's *Journey to the End of the Night*, Baudelaire's *Poésies*, and Blake's poems. Blake was not much studied in the United States at that time, but Burroughs thought him a "perfect poet."

There was a copy of the works of Shakespeare with marked passages; Burroughs was much given to quoting from him. Also on his shelves were a Louis Untermeyer poetry anthology, *The Ox-Bow Incident* by Walter van Tilburg Clark, *Nightwood* by Djuna Barnes, *The Folded Leaf* by William Maxwell, Gogol's *Dead Souls* and Nabokov on Gogol, Melville's *Moby Dick*, and *Maiden Voyage* by Denton Welch, who came to be Burroughs's favorite author, plus a number of John O'Hara novels and a collection of Raymond Chandler and other crime writers.

Burroughs's library was to have an enormous impact on both Allen and Jack. Allen went so far as to note down a list of titles on a yellow pad. When they left, Burroughs gave them each a gift. Jack received a copy of Oswald Spengler's *The Decline of the West*, and Bill gave Allen an old red clothbound Liveright edition of Hart Crane's *Collected Poems*. Allen had never heard of Hart Crane, but he was later to be one of the lesser influences on "Howl."

Burroughs had a curiously sinister reputation, even in those days, and Allen and Jack associated him with images of Berlin and Vienna before the war and the high camp culture of Proust and Gide. He was courteous and dignified, and they both came away with the image of Gainsborough's "Blue Boy," Burroughs as a perfect gentleman but very shy and sensitive. "Delicacy and melancholy, fragility and vulnerability, sweet and sad like a little boy," was how Ginsberg remembered him.

Bill's grandfather, William Seward Burroughs, had invented the adding machine and founded the company that became the giant Burroughs Corporation. A great inventor, he was a poor financier, and he was swindled out of most of the shares in the new corporation that bore his name. Later, in the Depression, Bill's side of the family sold off the remaining company stock for a fraction of its real worth. Bill's parents, Mortimer and Laura Lee Burroughs, lived a comfortable middle-class life in St. Louis with a cook, maid, and gardener, and a nanny to look after their two boys. Their youngest, William Seward Burroughs II, was born in 1914. As a child, he would go duck hunting with his brother, Mortimer, his father, and the chairman of the First National Bank. Bill became a good shot, and his consummate interest in guns later became a major theme in his writing.

In St. Louis he went to the John Burroughs School (named after the naturalist, who was no relation) and the Taylor School. When he developed asthma as a teenager, his parents sent him to the expensive Los Alamos Ranch School, in New Mexico, for his health. The school was later taken over by the Manhattan Project, and the atomic bomb was invented there. "It seemed so right, somehow," Burroughs commented later.

Burroughs studied English literature at Harvard and graduated in 1936. He did postgraduate work in anthropology, then studied medicine in Vienna for six months, before the rise of the Nazis led him to return to the States. He worked a year in New York as a copywriter for a small advertising agency, and in 1942, when America entered the war, he was drafted into the army but was soon released. In 1940, he had spent a month in Bellevue and Payne-Whitney after cutting off the last joint of the little finger of his left hand in order to impress a boyfriend. When his psychiatric papers came to light, he was given a civilian disability discharge.

Burroughs had various wartime jobs in offices and factories in St. Louis and New York. He even worked as an exterminator in Chicago. When Allen first met him, in December 1943, he was tending bar in the Village. With his Harvard background and his obvious intelligence, Burroughs could easily have found better-paid employment. He took dead-end jobs more for the experience than for the money, because he always had the security of the two-hundred-dollar monthly allowance sent him by his parents from the profits of a small garden-supply and gift shop they ran.

As the summer of 1944 wore on, David Kammerer became more and more obsessed with Lucien. Burroughs, who knew Kammerer from St. Louis, tried to convince him to go away, find another boy, go to sea, go to South America or even back to St. Louis, but to no avail. Kammerer also grew more antagonistic toward Celine Young. On one occasion, Kammerer and Burroughs called at Edie's apartment and, entering quietly, found everybody asleep. Lucien and Celine were curled up together on the couch. Kammerer commented, "Doesn't he look pale, as though he were being sucked dry by a vampire."

Another time, Kammerer climbed the fire escape behind Warren Hall and slipped in through Lucien's window, left open in the hot summer night. He stood over the sleeping boy, watching him silently in the moonlight for a half hour or so. As he climbed back over the fence, he was stopped at gunpoint by the hotel guard and questioned. The police were called, and Lucien was awakened to identify his visitor.

Early in the morning of August 14, 1944, Jack was awakened by someone shaking his arm. It was so hot that he and Edie were sleeping in the living room of her apartment, hoping to catch a breeze through the open windows. "I got rid of the old man," whispered Lucien, and Jack knew that David Kammerer was dead. Jack sent Edie out to get breakfast while he and Lucien talked.

Kammerer's unrelenting pressure had begun to unnerve Lucien, and he had again been considering ways to escape. He and Jack had recently seen Jean Renoir's *Grand Illusion* and had come up with the idea of imitating the escaped prisoners and fleeing to Paris. They envisioned signing on as seamen, jumping ship at Le Havre, and walking to Paris in order to be there for the liberation. At the union hall they found that a liberty ship, the *Robert Hayes*, was about to sail for France with supplies for the second front. At its dock, in Brooklyn, they found the crew swarming down the gangplank. "Don't go on that ship," they warned. "The mate is a son of a bitch!" Lucien and Jack boarded the deserted ship, chose bunks, and made themselves a meal. Then they encountered the mate, a huge redheaded, brutish-looking man, who demanded to know who they were. Explaining that they were able-bodied seamen, they told him they didn't want to sign on for France until they had made a trial run to Albany, where the ship was taking on supplies. "You didn't sign on?" asked the mate. They weathered his abuse, packed up their things, and returned dejected and embarrassed to New York, where they endured a ribbing from Edie and Celine.

They went to the West End Bar to relieve their sorrows, but Jack left at midnight in order to get a good night's sleep before trying for another ship the next day. As he walked home through the Columbia campus, he ran into David Kammerer, who as usual wanted to know where Lucien was. Jack said he had left him at the bar with Allen and a group of other friends. Lucien's attempt to escape to France brought matters to a head, and he and Kammerer got into a drunken argument. When the West End closed, the two of them went to nearby Riverside Park with a bottle and sat arguing and drinking, looking out over the Hudson in the hot summer night.

Kammerer made drunken threats against Celine. He claimed he loved Lucien and couldn't live without him. He would kill Lucien and himself if he couldn't have him, and he insisted that they have sex. Lucien resisted, and they began to struggle. Kammerer was a much larger, stronger man, and Lucien pulled his boy scout pocket knife to defend himself. He stabbed Kammerer twice through the heart, killing him. Terrified, his first concern being disposal of the body, he tied Kammerer's hands and feet with his shoelaces. Then, tearing the dead man's shirt into strips, he anchored rocks to the body, which he awkwardly rolled down the bank and into the water.

Lucien went straight to Burroughs, waking him at dawn. "I'll get the hot seat," Lucien said.

"Don't be absurd," said Burroughs. He advised Lucien to tell his family, get a good lawyer, and turn himself in. Despite his fear, Lucien retained a trace of his old bravado. He offered Bill a blood-stained pack of Lucky Strikes, saying, "Have the last cigarette."

"So this is how Dave Kammerer ends," Burroughs thought. Kammerer had been one of his oldest friends. Calm and efficient as always, Bill lent Lucien five dollars and sent him on his way. He shredded the pack of Lucky Strikes into tiny pieces and flushed them down the toilet.

Lucien went back uptown to see Jack. It was now about 6 A.M. He and Jack took a walk, and with Jack acting as lookout, Lucien dropped the bloody knife down a sewer grating near 125th Street. In Morningside Park, Jack pretended to urinate to distract any passersby, while Lucien buried Kammerer's glasses. They ate hot dogs in Times Square, had a few beers, saw Zoltán Korda's *The*

Four Feathers, and visited the Museum of Modern Art. With visions of "frying" in the electric chair at Sing Sing, Lucien was gathering his courage. He visited his psychiatrist on Park Avenue and borrowed some money, then went to an aunt who lived in Manhattan. She put him in touch with the family lawyers.

Lucien turned himself in on August 16 in the presence of his lawyer. At first, the police did not believe his story, but that same day the coast guard found Kammerer's body floating off 108th Street. Lucien was booked for murder, taken to the Tombs, Manhattan's jail, and detained without bail. Under the front-page headline "Columbia Student Kills Friend and Sinks Body in Hudson River," the *New York Times* of August 17 reported: "The fantastic story of a homicide, first revealed to the authorities by the voluntary confession of a nineteen-year-old Columbia sophomore, was converted yesterday from a nightmarish fantasy into a horrible reality by the discovery of the bound and stabbed body of the victim in the murky waters of the Hudson River." Lucien showed the police where he had buried Kammerer's glasses, and the *Daily News* ran a photograph of him pointing into the place in the river where he had dumped the body.

Burroughs and Kerouac were arrested as material witnesses. Bill's father bailed him out at once, and he left for St. Louis. Jack was not so fortunate. When he called his father to ask for bail money, Leo Kerouac roared, "No Kerouac ever got involved in a murder—you can go to hell!" Jack was forced to turn to Edie for help. Edie was due to inherit money, but her grandfather's will had not yet gone through probate, and her family lawyers would put up the $2,500 only if she was married to Jack. Jack and Edie had discussed marriage, but Jack had felt that she was pressuring him into it. However, seen from the viewpoint of the Bronx County Jail, where he was being held, it now seemed a more agreeable proposition. Wedding plans were quickly made.

A few days after Lucien's arraignment, Allen and Edie went down to Kammerer's room on Morton Street. "Lu—Dave" was no longer there. The landlord had already repainted the room, ready to rent it to someone new. Ginsberg wrote to Jack in jail, saying, "The sorrows of yesteryear seemed to have been cooled by equally white paint."

Jack and Edie married on August 22, 1944, the day Paris was liberated from the Nazis. Jack was taken from his cell by a plainclothesman, who drove him to City Hall and acted as best man;

Celine was maid of honor. The detective bought them all drinks at a local bar, then escorted Jack back to his cell to wait for his bail money to arrive, which it did a few days later. As soon as he was freed, Jack left town with his new wife, to live with her mother in Grosse Pointe.

Lucien, meanwhile, remained on the eighth floor of the Tombs, awaiting trial. He appeared in court on August 24 and was indicted for second-degree murder. He pleaded guilty to second-degree manslaughter and his plea was accepted. The issue of whether or not Lucien was a homosexual would play a large part in his trial. Celine, Edie, and Allen were all interviewed by the district attorney, and their assurances of his heterosexuality helped establish his case.

Lucien was found guilty, but his sentence depended very much upon an autobiography that his probation officer had him write for submission to the judge. "Had Lucien felt less pride in having Dave dog his footsteps he might have gotten rid of Kammerer before this and in a socially acceptable manner," Celine wrote Jack. She said that Lucien's probation officer was worried that Lucien's values were all intellectual ones: "If he persists in the idea that he has done a messianic service by ridding the world of Dave, he is becoming too presumptuous a judge. When he loses that pride in doing away with Dave, then I hope he is let out immediately. I know he is very remorseful at times."

Lucien was sentenced to an indefinite term in Elmira Reformatory in upstate New York, and his friends and family were told that with good behavior he would be free within eighteen months. A few days later, Ginsberg wrote to Eugene: "I got a long letter from Carr, who is somewhat sobered up from the decadent philosophic nihilism that used to be his attitude. He is reflective, more guilt, I suppose, and beginning to transvalue his attitudes and surrender to mores. After a long discussion of 'Jude the Obscure,' Tolstoi, and Spinoza, he concludes, 'as for prison life, I can't say I enjoy the discipline of steel bars, however it is a negative discipline and one can learn much under duress, esp in a society where one's confreres are all in the same boat. Amazingly strong animal—man.' "

Allen had been horrified by Kammerer's death and was awed to be involved in such momentous events. He did his best to help Lucien in his interview with the D.A., met with Lucien's mother, and attended to his minor affairs at Columbia. Celine Young and Allen were clearly sources of strength to each other during this difficult time. They were both teenagers, their newly constructed world in ruins. Their friends had all left town, and they were left to console each other over their loss. Ginsberg described her to Eugene: "Carr's girl, but I have taken her over now, in a small way, for the duration. She looks like Rossetti's Bless'd Damozel and writes very good short stories."

Though the summer break was a short one because of Columbia's accelerated wartime program, most of Allen's other college friends had also left the city. A week after Kammerer's death, Allen walked into the West End and found no one he knew. That summer's big hit, "You Always Hurt the One You Love," was playing on the jukebox—"That mawkish, accurate, melancholy air," as he described it in his journal. He had a beer and returned to his room. Under the heading "Like All Sad People, I Am A Poet," he wrote, just a little theatrically, "And now, this curtain has been rung down! Everything I have loved of the past year has fled into the past. My world is no longer the same."

This was true. Allen felt distanced from conventional society; the New Vision he shared with Jack, Lucien, and Burroughs was accentuated by the distorted news coverage and familial misgivings surrounding the death of Kammerer. The members of the inchoate Beat Generation experienced the inner workings of the law firsthand as Lucien's fate was decided by strangers in a faceless system of wheeler-dealer lawyers; they saw Columbia scrambling to defend its reputation and their families' overriding concern for respectability. It was all a great contrast to the actual human tragedy and confusion of the event itself and the youthful desire to rid the world of hypocrisy by revealing the tearful sensitivity and awareness that Allen and Jack recognized in themselves and their friends. Allen found himself unable to share the fashionable concerns of the wealthy Ivy League boys who had roomed on his corridor at the Union Theological Seminary, though even if he had aspirations in this direction, he could never have entered their world of sophisticated debauchery; he simply did not have the money.

Allen's crowd were all outsiders: Burroughs, the Harvard-educated intellectual with a private income, who was fascinated by low life and by the behavior of criminals; Kerouac, who had been discharged from the U.S. Navy for being of "indifferent character" and who saw himself as a writer with no responsibilities to anyone but himself; Lucien Carr, with his arrogant disdain for authority, wandering from one school to another, confident of his own intelli-

gence. Allen saw him as a romantic character in the French bohemian style, an image that was only enhanced by the death of
Kammerer. All three were older than Allen and considerably more
experienced. All three were essentially slumming, looking for their
education in the street rather than the classroom. Though he stood
alone in the summer of 1944 and thought that his bohemian world
had been destroyed, the principal players would soon return, and
their powerful influence would eventually win Allen over completely. Although Columbia had not provided the education he had
been expecting, it provided a sounding board against which he was
able to test his new ideas.

Jack felt completely out of place in Edie's high-society world in
Grosse Pointe, and early in October, when he had earned enough
money inspecting ball bearings at the Fruehauf truck plant to repay
the bail bond, he returned to New York City leaving Edie in Grosse
Pointe. Their marriage had been forged in exceptional circumstances, which had now changed. Shortly afterward Jack shipped
out on the *Robert Treat Paine*, but he was clearly ill-suited to life at
sea. He got on very badly with the bosun and jumped ship at Nor-
folk, Virginia, rather than make the crossing to Naples with a man
he felt sure was going to rape him. Jack returned to New York so
dejected that he didn't even tell his parents where he was, an unusual move, since he usually went home to his mother whenever he
was frustrated by the outside world. This time he stayed with Allen
at Warren Hall until he was able to get a room of his own there.

It was during this period, after many nights of frank discussion,
that Allen came out of the closet and told Jack he was homosexual.
He believed Jack's tolerance gave him "permission" to open up and
talk about it. "I knew he was going to accept my soul with all its
throbbings and sweetness and worries and dark woes and sorrows
and heartaches and joys and glees and mad understandings of morality, 'cause that was the same thing he had," said Ginsberg in
1972.

It was the middle of the night, but they were still lying awake,
Jack in Allen's bed and Allen on the mattress on the floor, when
Allen very timidly said, "Jack, you know I'm really in love with
Lucien. And I'm really in love with you. And I really want to sleep
with you."

Jack gave a long-drawn-out groan. "He suddenly saw this great
chasm of moral perplexity opening up in front of him for the rest of

our lives," Ginsberg said. "I remember his groan. It wasn't rejection. It was a groan of dismay. But he didn't want to make it with me. It wasn't for about half a year."

A room came up on the sixth floor of Warren Hall, and Jack settled down to write. In keeping with his somber mood, he lit a candle, cut his finger, and wrote "Blood" on a small calling card, which he then labeled "The Blood of the Poet" and attached to the wall to remind himself he was a serious writer. Kerouac burned most of his output so that his art would not appear to be done for ulterior motives, and each day he would smile to himself as the candle consumed his labors. Allen recorded in his journal, "Jeez, Kerouac is neurotic."

As the summer drew to a close and people returned from vacation, Allen was surprised to find just how many people he knew. He wrote to Eugene in October: "I am happy to say that, unlike Paterson, I have accumulated a modest number of close friends, some neurotic, some insane, some political." Indulging in his fondness for lists, he continued: "To categorize, I have three circles of acquaintance: first the madmen and artists from Greenwich Village and Columbia—Carr, formerly Kammerer (he had, as you may have observed, some limitations) and a novelist named John Kerouac. . . . Kerouac is one of the most interesting—he had a football scholarship to Columbia in 1940. But he left college when he couldn't stand the philistinism of Lou Little [the coach], the piggish priggishness of the football players and the restrictions of academic life."

Allen told Eugene that he was getting drunk with Kerouac twice a week. In the same first category, Allen included John Kingsland, "a prodigious 16 year old overdeveloped and worldly wise sybarite who has a marvelous irresponsible sense of humor." In his second category, that of "sensitive youths" and "young intellectuals," he placed Walter Adams. Adams was the son of Katherine Janverin Adams, who was in the Poetry Society and a friend of Louis Ginsberg's, so he and Allen had much in common. Ginsberg characterized him as a "literary anarchist" and saw quite a bit of him.

Also in the second category was Ted Hoffman, whom Allen regarded as a good poet, and Grover Smith, "a cheery medievalist who is translating Sir Thomas More's 'Utopia' from the Latin and writes sonnets that Lou likes." (Allen had shown Smith's work to his father.) According to one contemporary, Smith used to follow Allen and Lucien around, clicking his tongue in disapproval but anxious not to miss anything.

In Allen's third circle were his ex-roommate Arthur Lazarus,

William Woart Lancaster, whom Allen was planning to room with on campus the next semester, and Fritz Stern, later to become an eminent historian. "Voila!" Allen told Eugene. "It is well rounded, at any rate."

That November he began work on a novel for a creative writing course taught by Professor Harrison Steeves, chairman of the English department, taking the events of August as his subject for a romantic and awkward roman à clef. Shortly after he handed in a preliminary chapter, he received a letter from the assistant dean of Columbia, Nicholas McKnight, who asked him not to choose that subject; a matter of college policy was involved. Allen went to see McKnight and was told that his novel was "smutty" and his friend Kerouac was a "lout." The university did not want any more unfavorable publicity as a result of the Kammerer affair. Ginsberg later said that Columbia's instruction for him to stop writing his novel marked his first real shock of disillusionment with the university.

Burroughs arrived back from St. Louis and quickly put a stop to Jack's morbid candle burning and dripping blood. "My God, Jack," Bill cried in horror. "Stop this nonsense and let's go and have a drink."

Jack had not written to Edie for two months, but as the holiday season approached, he decided that his wife should be with him, and Edie came to New York to spend Christmas. They got on well together and decided to give their marriage another try.

Edie's old roommate Joan Vollmer returned to the city; she had missed all the excitement of the summer because she was away at her parents' place in Tuxedo Park, New York, having a baby. Her husband, from whom she was separated, was at the battlefront. Early in September 1944, she took a huge apartment on 115th Street and moved into it with her baby daughter. She began looking for roommates to help pay the rent, and since Jack's room at Warren Hall was tiny, he and Edie moved in with Joan.

Jack's return had unfortunate repercussions on Allen's status at Columbia. Johnny, the bartender at the West End, reported to the dean's office that Allen was staying there until the 3 A.M. closing time, drinking with Kerouac. Dean McKnight asked Allen's father to come in for a conference. Even though Allen read all his assigned books and had straight A grades, McKnight thought he was not benefiting fully from his experience at Columbia. He was very stern, and Louis left his office in tears. Since Allen was at Columbia on a scholarship, they had power over him and were prepared to use it.

Allen moved into Livingston Hall, on the campus, and it was

through his roommate, Bill Lancaster, that Louis learned that his son was a poet. Louis of course knew that Allen had written poetry at high school but hadn't realized that he continued to take it seriously. When Louis questioned him about it, Allen explained that he didn't think Louis would want yet another poet in the family. At that time, it was Eugene who was the most visible poet. He had often had poems in the *New York Times*, and on one memorable occasion he was in both the *Times* and the *Sun* on the same day. Louis had quipped to a friend that Allen was the only one in the family who didn't write and thus the only one who was "normal." Now he told Allen, "If you write poetry, I want you to do so only because you have an inner compulsion, because you feel you must write, and because you can't help but write poetry."

In fact it was only at the beginning of 1945 that Allen wrote his first serious poems. He kept a list of completed writings in his journal: "Jan–Feb: Started real poems—First poems of genius?" There were four poems listed: "He Who Walks Within the Womb," "I Have Been Unleashed," "This Stormy Foundation Bursts Upon the Air," and "Now in This Park, by This Lakeside."

Allen and Jack spent the early months of 1945 attempting to define their idea of the New Vision, a notion of the unity of being, taken mostly from William Butler Yeats's *A Vision*. Ginsberg and Kerouac were deeply influenced by the Romantic poets, particularly by Baudelaire's "Invitation to the Voyage" and Rimbaud's "Drunken Boat." Inspired by these nautical themes, Allen wrote his first long poem and called it "The Last Voyage"; its fifteen pages of rhymed couplets were later dismissed by Ginsberg as "jejune rhymed doggerel." In addition to his college curriculum, he was reading biographies of Verlaine, Baudelaire, Rimbaud, Cocteau, and Shelley, as well as the works of Coleridge, Fitzgerald, and the Marquis de Sade. He steeped himself in tales of *la vie de Bohème* and began to fashion himself after the classic image of the poet, complete with Lucien's red kerchief. When he delivered a paper to Trilling's English Romantics class comparing the early Shelley with Rimbaud, Trilling gave it serious consideration, just as he did Allen's early efforts at poetry.

Allen came increasingly under the influence of Burroughs, much to Louis Ginsberg's distrust. "He's dangerous," wrote Louis, "not because he rationalizes but because his end product of thought and attitude results, eventually, if carried out in action, in danger and disharmony and chaos. . . . I disagree with you—but definitely—

that an immoralist can confirm 'enduring human values.' . . . You're all 'wet' Allen. You simply have little experience in life. Where is your former, fine, zeal for a liberal progressive, democratic society? Your sophistry—for that is what it is—is a series of half-truths, verbal cleverness, and dangerous ideas expressed in specious and dextrous verbiage." As an afterthought, below his signature, Louis added, "What about a psychiatrist?"

On March 16, Kerouac paid Burroughs a visit at his room off Columbus Circle, over Riordan's, a local bar. They had a long conversation, in the course of which Burroughs told Jack bluntly that he would never free himself from his mother unless he made a proper break with her instead of running home every time he had a problem. Bill said, "The trouble with you is you're just tied to your mother's apron strings and you are going in a wide circle around her now, but it's going to get a narrower and narrower circle and sooner or later you are going to be right in there, unable to move away from your mother. That's your fate, that's your Faustian destiny."

This chilling prophecy disturbed Jack so much that he went uptown to Livingston Hall to talk about it with Allen. Struck by Burroughs's words, Jack acknowledged that he was too closely tied to his mother and that he had internalized many of her ideas. Allen was impressed by Burroughs's insight. Edie had moved back to Grosse Pointe, and Jack had been spending a lot of time in Queens with his parents in the last month, but Allen hadn't connected it with Jack's separation from Edie and his inability to commit himself to their relationship.

It got so late that Allen suggested that Jack stay over. Jack, of course, knew Allen's feelings toward him, but they slept chastely clad in their underwear. Allen was still a virgin, and though he was in love with Jack, he was afraid to touch him. At 8 A.M. they were awakened by the assistant dean of student-faculty relationships, who came bursting into the room.

Allen had been conducting a private war with the Irishwoman who cleaned his room. To draw her attention to the film of dirt on the windowpane, he had traced on the glass the words "Butler has no balls" (a reference to Nicholas Murray Butler, president of Columbia University). He suspected that the cleaning woman was anti-Semitic, so he also wrote an eye-catching "Fuck the Jews" and drew a skull and crossbones beneath it. The graffiti caught her attention, but instead of cleaning them off she had reported them to Dean Furman.

Furman had been one of Kerouac's football coaches at Columbia, so they knew each other, but Jack didn't stay to talk. He leapt from the bed and ran to Bill Lancaster's empty bed in the next room, pulling the covers up over his face and leaving Allen to face the situation alone.

Allen was made to wipe the offending words from the window, but he knew that Furman was thinking the worst. An hour later, when Allen went downstairs, he found two notes in his box. One charged him $2.35 for entertaining an unauthorized guest overnight. The other, from Dean McKnight, informed him that he was suspended and suggested that he spend the weekend with his father, "since the privilege of residence at Livingston has been withdrawn from you." Allen was forbidden to attend classes and told to abstain from all student activities. On the same day, McKnight wrote to Louis. The circumstances of Allen's suspension could not be reported in a letter, he said, but the two principal elements were obscene writings on his window and giving overnight housing to a person who was not a member of the college and whose presence on the campus was unwelcome.

On Monday morning, Allen put on his best clothes and a necktie and went to see McKnight. Kerouac had gone home to his mother, so he wasn't available to substantiate Allen's story. The dean ushered Allen in and invited him to sit down. He stared grimly across the desk and said, "Mr. Ginsberg. I hope you realize the *enormity* of what you've done!"

Allen thought of a scene near the beginning of Céline's *Journey to the End of the Night*. The narrator is standing in the middle of a World War I battlefield, with bombs bursting and bullets flying about him, and realizes that he is surrounded by dangerous madmen. "Had something extraordinary then come over these people? Something which I didn't feel at all? I must have failed to notice it," wrote Céline. "In this sort of business there's nothing for it; the only thing to do is to shove out of it."

Allen looked up at the dean, remembered Céline, and knew that the only way out was to humor him. "Oh, I do, sir! I do! I do!" he said. "If you can only tell me what I can do to make up for this . . ."

The punishment seemed unnecessarily severe for such a minor offense, and it seemed likely that other, unspoken factors must have contributed to the decision to suspend him. Bill Lancaster proved to be a stalwart friend and went to McKnight. "I understand there has been some difficulty," he said, "and I'd like to clear up the situation. I understand there are allegations of homosexuality. Is that what's at issue, when Kerouac and Ginsberg slept together?"

"No, no, no, no! Nobody said anything about it!" protested the dean. "Nobody has mentioned it. Nobody brought up the subject! I'm not accusing anybody of anything at all!"

But Allen's roommate continued to press his point. "Well, I can assure you that nothing of the sort went on, because the door was open and I was there all night and they're old friends and they just slept like college boys sleep."

Allen sought Lionel Trilling's advice. When Trilling arrived in McKnight's office to discuss the incident, McKnight was too embarrassed to quote the graffiti to the first Jew to penetrate the English faculty at Columbia, and he wrote the offending words on a piece of paper and passed it across the desk. Trilling and his wife were utterly unable to accept that Allen was simply goading the anti-Semitic Irish cleaner, and years later Diana Trilling was still using the incident as an example of Ginsberg's "Jewish self-hatred."

Mark Van Doren, who had often given Allen advice on his poetry, also petitioned on his behalf, but in the end McKnight decided that Allen was not to return to Columbia until he had worked at a job for a year and had seen a psychiatrist, who would submit in a letter that Allen was now mature enough to be a responsible member of the academic community. Allen told the story later: "So I was kicked out of Columbia, but the thing that rang in my ears was 'Mister Ginsberg. I hope you realize the *enormity* of what you've done!' because actually I hadn't done anything. I wanted to. I lay there longing all night!"

THREE | A STREET EDUCATION

"Everybody is going to fall apart, disintegrate, all character
structures based on tradition and uprightness and so-called
morality will slowly rot away, people will get the hives right in
their hearts, great crabs will cling to their brains . . ."

—Levinsky [Ginsberg], in Jack Kerouac, *The Town and the City*

ALLEN MOVED STRAIGHT INTO JOAN VOLLMER'S SUNNY, WELL-DECORATED
apartment at 419 West 115th Street. He shared a bedroom with Hal
Chase, a blond Columbia anthropology student from Denver, whom
Allen was immediately attracted to. Jack still had a room with Edie,
and Joan and her daughter, Julie, had the remaining two bedrooms.
Joan cooked simple, healthy meals, and they all contributed to the
eighty-dollar rent and food costs.

Allen took a job as a welder at the Brooklyn Navy Yard, working
for Eastern Gas and Fuel, the general agents of the U.S. War Shipping Administration. It was heavy work, but the money was good,
and he stuck it out until the end of April. Then he worked as a dish
washer and at the Gotham Book Mart for a few weeks, but Frances
Steloff fired him because he was too bemused and timid to do the
job efficiently.

Allen's swift and unexpected suspension from Columbia cast him
into limbo, with no plans and no idea when he would be permitted
to resume his studies. In the course of his two years at Columbia he
had grown up. He now knew his sexual inclination, though it was
still a closely guarded secret. He knew that he wanted to write; he
and Jack intended to write the New Vision into existence. He had
arrived at Columbia friendless. Now, though only eighteen, he was

a member of an adult group and had a number of close friends who gave him a level of emotional security he had not previously enjoyed. He loved them with a fierce loyalty, while deep down he still felt unloved and alone: the trauma of his childhood was lodged in his unconscious.

As long as he attended Columbia, his *nostalgie de la boue* was held in check by the authority of the English department and its celebrated professors. Now that he was out on his own, he looked for new teachers, and he turned naturally to William Burroughs. Together they explored the carny world of Times Square, of petty thieves and hoodlums, hustlers and prostitutes, cheap bars and rooming houses. Burroughs was engaged in a systematic study of the Eighth Avenue bars. Allen took his street education seriously and made a list, dividing the bars into nine categories: queer bars; gamblers' bars, which included those places where hoodlums and gangsters hung out; Bowery bars; old men's bars; intellectuals' bars; bars of chaos (such as the West End); dilettante rich bars, which included nightclubs; jazz bars, and Irish bars.

Burroughs was fascinated by criminals and sought out various underworld characters, mostly petty thieves. He explored their world even when it required breaking the law, usually by acting as an accessory or a receiver of stolen goods. He struck up a friendship with a small-time hoodlum called Bob Brandenberg, who had come to New York with the desperate desire to be a mobster but in the meantime worked as a soda jerk in a drugstore near Columbia. Bill liked to sit in the drugstore listening to Bob's stories about the underworld. One winter afternoon, Bill leaned across the counter conspiratorially and asked if Bob knew where he could unload a submachine gun and some boxes of morphine syrettes. Bob could only think of his two roommates: Herbert Huncke and Phil White. They had just returned from six months at sea, where they tried unsuccessfully to kick a junk habit. Phil ("The Sailor") White had been a messman and Huncke the second cook on a creaking tanker that delivered war supplies to Hawaii from New Jersey by way of the Panama Canal.

They had been back for ten days and sat around the apartment, on Henry Street beneath the Manhattan Bridge, waiting for Brandenberg to get home so they could borrow enough money from him to fill a prescription for morphine. The day Burroughs visited, he looked around a little disdainfully. He handed his snap-brim fedora, gray gloves, and fifteen-years-out-of-date chesterfield coat to Bob to put away. Bozo, the ex–show queen who rented the apartment, murmured apologies for the slummy surroundings, while Bill and White got acquainted. Herbert Huncke, a small man with an oval face, a weary expression, and huge, heavy-lidded eyes, reacted to Bill's presence with extreme paranoia. He stepped into the next room with Bob and told him he thought that Bill might be a plain-clothesman, possibly even FBI. If Bob didn't ask him to leave, then he, Huncke, would. Just then, in the other room, Phil White said, "What's that you said, Bill? You have morphine syrettes?"

Bill explained that there had been a drugstore stickup and that one of the men involved, a friend of his, had taken a gross of syrettes after cleaning out the register. Bill was trying to shift the goods. Huncke rapidly joined Bill and Phil at the living room table. Bill went on to explain that he wanted to sell all but one or two of the syrettes, which he wanted to try out himself. "Do you know this stuff?" he asked. "Do you know how it is taken?"

Phil laughed. They had been using identical syrettes for the last six months at sea. They demonstrated their use right away. After Phil, Huncke, and Bill had injected the drug, the conversation became much more animated. Bill had an enormous interest in drugs. Phil and Huncke told colorful stories of serving time for possession. Bill sold the remaining syrettes to Phil.

Bill saw a lot of Phil during the winter of 1944–45. After a couple of months he developed a small drug habit. Phil immediately coached Bill on how to persuade a doctor to write a "script" for morphine—"making the croaker," as the junkies called it. Bill took to it immediately. That spring, he also began working as a team with Phil, rolling drunks on the subway (the "hole").

Though he did not know it at the time, Burroughs was gathering material for *Junky*, *Naked Lunch*, and other works. *The Soft Machine* opens with the line: "I was making the hole with the sailor. . . ." In addition to his room over Riordan's Bar, he rented a small, fifteen-dollar-a-month railroad flat just down from Phil and Huncke's place on Henry Street. There was only occasional heat from the leaky radiator, and the windows were caulked with newspapers to keep out the cold. It was a classic seedy Lower East Side neighborhood, and few of Bill's friends would visit him there. Allen, however, shared his fascination with low life, and stopped by on Saturday afternoons to play Stravinsky and Prokofiev on Bill's phonograph.

One day, Bill took Kerouac down to Henry Street to score some morphine from Phil White, and the apartment door was opened by a tall, thin young woman with red hair. Vickie Russell was Bob's girlfriend and was the only one at home. There were no drugs in the house, but with Bill paying the cab fares, she was prepared to see if she could find something in Times Square for them.

She was speeding on a Benzedrine high and showed them how to crack open a nasal inhaler and extract the strip of Benzedrine inside. The inhalers were available anywhere for ninety-eight cents, and each one contained eight folds of blotting paper impregnated with the drug. One and a half strips could get a person extremely high, and two strips would last eighteen hours. The strips were rolled into balls and washed down with a cup of coffee. They were hard to swallow, and the taste was very unpleasant. Jack took too much the first time and thought he had overdosed, but Vickie looked after him and they wound up spending the night together at Bill's apartment.

Jack introduced Benzedrine to 115th Street, and soon Vickie herself started to visit. Jack liked taking it to write, because it enabled him to handle many complicated thoughts simultaneously. Bill and Jack were writing a novel together about the Kammerer affair, called "And the Hippos Were Boiled in Their Tanks," a reference to a fire at the St. Louis zoo. The person in the house who most appreciated the Benzedrine was Joan, and soon she was using it every day.

Jack's reconciliation with Edie had not lasted long, and she moved out of 115th Street early in 1945. Jack spent more and more time at his parents' house in Ozone Park, Queens, where his father was slowly dying of cancer. When Jack was in town, he stayed at 115th Street, where he and Allen spent much time discussing the New Vision. Ginsberg later described it as a matter of seeing "everybody lost in a dream world of their own making. That was the basis of the Beat Generation. That was the primary perception. The idea of transience of phenomena—the poignant Kewpie-doll dearness of personages vanishing in time. Not a morbid interest in death but the realization of the mortal turn . . . it's the sigh of mortality that Jack had."

Allen was still a virgin, his love for Jack unrequited. He discussed his sexual orientation with both Jack and Bill, but it remained hypothetical. Finally, he felt driven to sleep with just *anyone*. He went to the MacDougal Street Bar, a gay bar in the Village, and allowed himself to be picked up by a graying, forty-year-old sailor. He took Allen to a room in the Seamen's Institute, where he made Allen blow him. "He abused me, I thought, because he didn't entertain me, he didn't reciprocate and was a bit brutal," Ginsberg recalled. Bill told Allen, "The guy didn't treat you right." Allen felt the whole experience was inauthentic.

The next time was better. Allen had gone with Bill to the Museum of Modern Art, where he met a student his own age and went home with him. "I wasn't much taken with him emotionally, it was just a relief to have somebody physical," Ginsberg remembered. They spent a weekend together but quickly lost interest in each other.

Then, finally, Allen had his first sexual experience with Kerouac. They were walking by the waterfront where the elevated West Side Highway passed Christopher Street. The area beneath it was used as a truck park and would later become the center of the New York gay scene. They stopped between two trucks and jacked each other off. "I don't know why there should be some erotic spirit of a place," Ginsberg commented. "I think it was just the industrial isolation, and we were horny." However, the next time they walked through that area, they did it again, and it was not long before Kerouac allowed Allen to blow him. Allen fell completely in love.

Memorial Day came, and everyone left for the summer. Allen found himself in the empty 115th Street apartment with no money. At that time, the easiest way to make quick money was to go to sea, as Kerouac and Huncke had done. Allen enrolled in the U.S. Maritime Service, the fastest route to the coveted Seamen's Union card. On August 1, 1945, he presented himself at the U.S. Maritime Service Training Station in Sheepshead Bay, Brooklyn, and became Irwin Allen Ginsberg 4514-24594. His home for the next three and a half months was Bunk 6, Compartment H-44, Section 408. Ginsberg was in the navy. When he showed up in the city in his crisp uniform, short hair, and sailor's hat on his first leave, Celine hardly recognized him.

For the first few weeks, Allen spent his time buffing floors, washing dishes, and doing KP. The worst of the labors was night watch, which deprived him of sleep. He soon understood that the idea was to put in the hours at work or at classes but not to get anything done. In the end, he taught himself how to box a compass and to name the parts of a ship. Allen also learned how to swear. "It's sort of juvenile and overdone, but I got in the groove quick," he wrote

Eugene. His letter was filled with swear words, and he ended it, affectionately, "you old peckerhead!"

Allen was caught reading Hart Crane, and the navy mailman who delivered a postcard from Kerouac remarked suspiciously that it was in French, but Allen was accepted completely as "one of the boys," and they tended to come to him for advice and sympathy since, at nineteen, he was the oldest in his section.

"The boys here are all overgrown or warped adolescents, all screaming neurotics," he told Jack. "The petty officers are all fat buttocked marine sergeants with loud voices." Allen took none of it personally. He washed his clothes, stowed his gear neatly in his locker, and made his bunk, "giggling to myself unobtrusively," as he told Jack. Manhattan Beach was nearby, and on weekends he swam and lazed there in the sun. He found that he was quite enjoying himself.

However, it soon appeared that Allen was not cut out for the military life. He came down with a cold. He half-masochistically presented himself at the sick bay, only to be laughed at and told that he was goldbricking. He threw up in a toilet that was out of bounds to him and got in trouble; he had a nosebleed; and finally, the day after he reported sick, someone took his temperature. By this time he had developed pneumonia and was sent straight to a comfortable bunk in the sick bay, where he passed his time reading *The Way of All Flesh*, *The Bridge of San Luis Rey*, and *War and Peace*. He decided he preferred Dostoyevsky to Tolstoy.

From his sickbed, Allen wrote long, ruminative love letters to Kerouac. After a tentative comparison of Jack and Lucien to Tadzio, the beautiful boy in Thomas Mann's *Death in Venice*, and himself, even more tentatively, to Aschenbach, the self-conscious writer obsessed with the beautiful boy, Allen asked: "What am I? What do I seek? Self-aggrandizement, as you describe it, is a superficial description of what my motives are, and my purposes. If I overreach myself for love, it is because I crave it so much and have known so little of it. Love is perhaps opiate, but I know it to be creative as well."

He went on: "Well, these last years have been the nearest to fulfillment of my desires, and with full feeling I thank you for the gift. You were right, I suppose in keeping your distance. I was too intent on self-fulfillment, and rather crude about it, with all my harlequinade and conscious manipulation of your pity. I overtaxed my own patience and strength even more than I did yours, possibly.

You behaved like a gentleman, though I think that you did take me too seriously, assign too much symbolic value to my motion and friction."

Jack replied, asking Allen not to be so sophomoric and morbid in his criticisms and pleading for a little more finesse and, if possible, a dash of humor. Sometimes Jack experienced Allen's articulate affection as emotional pressure and tried to distance himself, but he always came back. Jack was finding life difficult. He was working on three novels simultaneously, keeping a large diary, and reading prodigiously; but he was living at home, and his mother was working in a shoe factory in order to support him. His dying father clearly thought Jack would never make anything of his life.

Jack was also upset by his homosexual tendencies; as well as fooling around with Allen, he had spent an evening drinking with Bill and some of Bill's friends, ending up as a participant in a drunken homosexual orgy, which he regretted the next day. "It automatically repels me," he wrote Allen, "thereby causing a great deal of remorse and disgust." However, it was also during this time that Jack went with Bill and Allen to the Everard Turkish Baths, where a group of French sailors blew him. "I think he just dug the idea of a bunch of French sailors," Ginsberg said. "He was quite sociable and happy. . . . He was very gay about it."

Until then, Jack only allowed Allen to blow him and did not reciprocate. "I was pulling him in different directions that were unnatural to him and difficult," Allen said. "He was bending and stretching quite a bit to accommodate my emotions. That's why I've always loved him, because I was able to completely unburden myself and express my deepest feelings and he could relate to them. Reject them, hear them out, reciprocate sometimes, actually go to bed with me sometimes, rarely. Get drunk with me, walk around, being there, hearing me through and giving me a reaction to bounce off against. So I was more intimate with him about my feelings than with anybody on earth. I bared myself to him and he was able to take it."

The letters continued back and forth, charting Kerouac's periods of closeness and distance. He claimed that the quality of his friendship for Allen was much purer than Allen's was for him, and that he was wasting his friendship on "a little self-aggrandizing weasel." But then, in another letter, he said he had grown fond of Allen again.

In November 1945, Allen graduated from MSTS and was released from active duty, having earned $103.79 in defense of his country. He used his new Seamen's Union card to ship out that same day, working as a messman on the Kearny-to-Norfolk run. Next, he joined a coal-carrying barge that made its way slowly down the coast to unload at New Orleans, where he smoked marijuana for the first time with some Puerto Rican sailors.

After Labor Day, the various inhabitants of 115th Street had drifted back to the city. Those actually sharing the rent were Joan, Hal Chase, Allen, and Bill. Jack stayed over two or three nights each week. Other frequent visitors were Celine Young, John Kingsland, Edie Parker, and Allen's brother, Eugene, who got out of the army in November 1945.

Allen and Jack had decided that Bill Burroughs and Joan Vollmer would make a great couple. They were both older than Jack and Allen, both witty and well-read. They had the same kind of sardonic intellectual sophistication. Bill and Joan hit it off right away. They were very amusing together and obviously enjoyed each other's company. Bill moved in, and they began sleeping together shortly afterward. They would spend hours sitting in Joan's room talking, high on Benzedrine. "We had all these really deep conversations about very fundamental things," Burroughs later recalled. "Her intuition was absolutely amazing." Though Burroughs was primarily a homosexual, they had an active sex life. Joan once told him, "Well, you're supposed to be a faggot. You're as good as a pimp in bed." Ginsberg remembered with nostalgia spending long hours in their room, Bill lying on the bed, propped up by pillows, with Joan at his side, her arm around him: "long conversation, night after night." Allen was fond of Joan and described her as "very beautiful: a moonlike oval face, very intelligent looking with a small and delicate cupid's bow mouth, fine eyes and nicely chiselled nose. She had a high hair line, similar to Bill."

"It was a year of evil decadence," said Kerouac in *Vanity of Duluoz*. Joan had a huge bed with an Oriental drape over it. Up to six people could sprawl there, taking Benzedrine and morphine and talking for days on end in an amphetamine haze. Jack took so much Benzedrine that his health began to suffer. His hair fell out (a symptom of excessive amphetamine use), and he looked pale and drawn. One day, Vickie Russell applied makeup to his face before she would go on the subway with him. Bill's day-to-day presence changed the atmosphere of the apartment. He began conducting experiments; the drug intake rose rapidly and conversations centered on the idea of expanding individual awareness.

Throughout one summer night, which came to be known to Beat Generation scholars as the Night of the Wolfeans and the Non-Wolfeans (after Thomas Wolfe), Allen lay in one bed with Hal, and Bill and Jack were in another. On the Wolfean side were the heterosexual all-American boys, Jack Kerouac and Hal Chase. On the other side, the non-Wolfeans, Burroughs and Ginsberg, held forth, "the sinister European fairies . . . who didn't believe in the wide open, dewy-eyed lyrical America" of the Wolfeans but were always trying to go to bed with them, nonetheless, as Ginsberg later summed it up. "Homosexuality was one of the attributes of non-Wolfeans, and among other things, intellectuality and fear of the body and manipulativeness and Jewishness. International concern rather than appreciation of America and homeyness and family and normal values."

Allen got very upset by the conversation that night. They were all coming down from a Benzedrine high and had the usual experience of exhaustion, depression, and dissociation from the world. Allen began to talk openly about how it felt to be a non-Wolfean. He used the image of a curtain of cellophane that separated him from his friends and from reality itself.

"I was trying urgently to break through and explain once and for all what I felt like, so as to appeal to them and win their sympathy and make them hug me and sleep with me. . . . I remember it being a reference point between us for many years. We came to try and define our roles and relationships, not intentionally, just to poetically find some image of how we were related. . . . If I had been the only non-Wolfean I would have felt like a jerk, but with Burroughs as one of us, I felt there was some dignity and possibility in the situation despite our deficiency in earthiness."

The experience of that night stayed with him always, and even in India, years later, he recorded in his journals: "Talking about transparent waterfalls of cellophane—pure synthetic abstraction making me groan with desire to be kissed on the mouth and held close to the breast of the fair boy's body I desired then and there, but it wasn't done, so I talked all night, explaining my delicate condition as hurt-voiced as I felt in my crying throat and sad warm 18 yr old breast."

That fall, the household began to play a complicated game of charades, inspired by Burroughs's attempts to psychoanalyze Allen and Jack. Burroughs had been in analysis for many years, first with Dr. Louis Federn, an old-time Viennese analyst who had been analyzed by Freud himself, and now with Dr. Leo Walberg, who used hypnosis to reach the different layers of the patient's personality. With Bill, he was able to find many different personality layers.

The top layer was Burroughs, the distinguished scion of an old St. Louis family. Below that was a nervous, possibly lesbian, English governess with a prissy, self-conscious, simpering personality. Below her was Old Luke, the tobacco farmer, who just sat in his rocking chair on his front porch with his shotgun over his knees, watching the catfish come down the river. Old Luke had the personality of a psychotic Southern sheriff. Beneath them all was an implacable, silent Chinaman, sitting starving, skull-headed, on the banks of the Yangtze, with no ideals, no beliefs, and no words, the ultimate Burroughs persona.

Bill liked to play out these characters in a form of charades that he called "routines." As an English governess he was very prim, always rapping people on the knuckles and serving tea, shrieking in a high voice, "My dear, you're just in time for tea. Don't say those dirty words in front of everybody!"

He could become quite terrifying as the old Southern sharecropper. He would slowly build his monologue: "See that catfish comin' down the river? Well, it's just one catfish after another going down. I jest sit an' watch 'em all day long. Once in a while I get out my fishing tackle and I catch me a catfish. *Ever gut a catfish?*" he would yell, and go mad with blood lust to gut a catfish in a truly psychopathic manner, while they all cracked up.

In Allen's favorite routine, he played the Well-Groomed Hungarian, while Jack would put on his father's old straw hat, which he had brought for the purpose, and play the innocent American bumpkin in Paris. Bill would don a wig and a woman's skirt and become a lesbian countess who acted as the shill for the Hungarian's art gallery. The countess bought naive Wolfean American tourists to buy the phony family masterpieces that Allen had supposedly taken with him when he fled Hungary during the war. Allen would rub his hands together and affect a thick Middle European accent. "Ah, my young man, you vant to buy some culture?"

"Aw, gee, fellers," said Jack. "I cain't; I got a girl. I have a date with my girl at the coffeehouse you got out there."

"You want to stay away from those, Jack," warned Burroughs.

"Those ladies got poison juices. Your cock falls off if you do that. Sometimes they got teeth up there."

Many years later, Bill recalled his role. "I was playing, er-hum, an Edith Sitwell part. I got in drag and I looked like some sinister old lesbian."

Hal Chase played the brash but innocent mountaineering Denver boy, Child of the Rainbow, "with pretty blond golden hair and good physique, an Indian hawk-nose and American boy State Fair fresh manners," as Ginsberg described him later.

Burroughs's "Talking Asshole Routine," "Dr. Benway," and "Blue Movies" from *Naked Lunch* all had their genesis in those routines and the definitions made during the Night of the Wolfeans and the Non-Wolfeans.

Burroughs's lay analysis continued until June 1946. Allen and Jack spent an hour a day free associating. Bill sat in a straight-backed chair like a proper Freudian analyst, while they lay on the couch. Allen found the sessions effective. He began to bare frail, sensitive, private fears. One day, he burst into tears and wailed, "Nobody loves me!" Bill sat impassively in the chair, friendly but impersonal, listening and commenting.

"It was kind of a breakthrough for me, a realization of my actual feelings," Ginsberg said. "Painful feelings I didn't want to admit to at that age, nineteen." These revelations, presumably connected with his mother's apparent withdrawal of love, left him naked and defenseless, and though Bill was not trained to help Allen to deal with them, he found the experience valuable. In a letter to Burroughs written from Sheepshead Bay, Allen discussed their latest session:

"Sunday nite was the first time I'd really been completely disintegrated and confused under analysis; it was not so much that 'resistance' was overcome, but that before my analysis I sensed that I could not regain my wits and perspective until I had set the specific paranoia in my mind straight, and, possibly, had 'confessed' it by way of grace." He went on to say the analysis "illustrated what I have dimly known, I feel more guilty and inferior by reason of faggishness than intellectualizations will admit is proper."

It was a very creative period for Ginsberg and Kerouac, as inspired by Burroughs, the teacher. Virtually everything they did was motivated by their newly discovered methods of concern for investigating, altering, and exploring the nature of consciousness. "The whole point of smoking grass or taking peyote was as a probe," Ginsberg recalled, "an examination of what is the alteration of consciousness caused by amphetamine, or morphine, or marijuana, or heroin, or peyote, or mescaline. At least that was my terminology then. Examination, like William James's experiments with nitrous oxide, very much in mind." It was a very scientific investigation; Ginsberg and Burroughs looked into hypnotism and made a few experiments together with cards, since they both had an interest in telepathy. They explored the sinister, the criminal, and the forbidden. They rejected the conformist, consumer society of America in the late forties but were not thinking in terms of rebelling against it. The Beat Generation began with personal exploration. "It wasn't a political or social rebellion," Ginsberg said. "Everybody had some form of break in their consciousness or an experience or a taste of a larger consciousness or satori." They had all read Spengler's *Decline of the West* and took it for granted that civilization was collapsing around them. The atomic bomb had just been dropped on Japan, and that, to them, was proof enough. The early Beats had no hope of trying to change society.

Herbert Huncke began dropping by with some regularity, until, in the end, he was there most days, sometimes staying over. At first, Huncke, as a junkie and a thief, felt his new friends were patronizing him. Joan was the exception. "She was in all probability one of the most charming and intelligent women I've ever met," he said. He grew very fond of her. "I think I fell sort of in love with her in a funny way. At one time I think she loved me in return." Huncke was surprised to discover that she and Burroughs had a sexual relationship.

Huncke's insecurity was completely unfounded. The group was charmed and fascinated by him. He was very well known on Forty-second Street, having been a male hustler there for about four years, so when Dr. Alfred Kinsey came to New York to conduct interviews for his massive study of the sexual habits of Americans, it was Huncke he approached when his research led him to the floating population of Times Square. Huncke introduced Kinsey to the whores, pimps, hustlers, and thieves of the neighborhood. Allen, Jack, Bill, and Joan all did interviews for the Kinsey Report as well. When the distinguished doctor asked Allen, "Did you ever 'brown' anybody?" Allen did not know what he meant.

Another person who began to come around was Bill Garver, an old prison friend of Huncke's, whom Burroughs liked, possibly because they had similar backgrounds. Garver, the son of an Ohio banker, was paid one hundred dollars a month to stay away from Ohio. He was tall and gaunt, with sunken eyes, graying hair, and loose features. It was only when he spoke that he betrayed his educated background. Garver supported a junk habit by stealing overcoats. He would sit in a cafeteria, nursing a cup of coffee until the coast was clear, then go to the coatrack and take the best coat there. He stole two or three a day and had to travel all over the city to pawn them without anyone's becoming too suspicious. Allen found him interesting and would sometimes go to Horn & Hardart and watch him at work.

Allen entered 1946 looking much as Kerouac described him in *The Town and the City*, written that year: wearing a belted raincoat, a paisley scarf, and dark-rimmed glasses, smoking cigarettes through a red cigarette holder and carrying the works of Auden and Rimbaud under his arm. In the book, Allen is called Leon Levinsky: "Levinsky was an eager, intense, sharply intelligent boy of Russian-Jewish parentage who rushed around New York in a perpetual sweat of emotional activity, back and forth in the streets from friend to friend, room to room, apartment to apartment. He 'knew everyone' and 'knew everything,' was always bearing tidings and messages from 'the others,' full of catastrophe. He brimmed and flooded over day and night with a thousand different thoughts and conversations and small horrors, delights, perplexities, deities, discoveries, ecstasies, fears. He stared gog-eyed at the world and was full of musings, lip-pursings, subway broodings—all of which rushed forth in torrents of complex conversation whenever he confronted someone."

This was Jack's idealized description of the persona Allen presented to the world, that of the moody, brooding intellectual. Allen was always attracted to beautiful youths, particularly those with great practical skills. He thought of himself as clumsy and unattractive, and in his love relationships he sought to overcome this by offering to share his scholarship. He did this with Kerouac, but Kerouac saw beyond to the anxious youth inside. It is a measure of Kerouac's friendship that he was prepared so completely to accept Allen's public face.

Allen was in constant correspondence with his father, on whom he tested most of his new ideas; not surprisingly, Louis often disagreed. Louis Ginsberg had the usual ambitions for his son; he wanted him to get ahead in the world. He hoped Allen would become a labor lawyer—a thoroughly satisfactory way of combining Socialist ideals and upward mobility. He was clearly concerned about Burroughs's influence. As far back as January 1945, Louis had cautioned Allen about Bill: "You don't know enough of life to separate his non-conformity from truth of realities. Frankly, I shall be disappointed in you if you persist in your intimate relation with him."

Louis, with the best intentions, was trying to steer Allen away from the madness and confusion of his youth, but for Allen, to reject madness meant to reject his mother. Naomi was the biggest influence on his life, and the great appeal of the bohemian life-style that Burroughs and Carr had introduced him to was its acceptance and approval of madness, since it gave Allen a framework within which he was able to accept her.

Twenty-year-old Allen was now pulled in two directions. On the one hand was Columbia and the ambition of his father. At the polar opposite was Rimbaud, poetry, and madness; drugs, criminals, and the underworld.

Louis was not trying to mold his son against his will. Although he had done his best, he still felt responsible for the trauma of Allen's childhood, and his main concern was for his happiness. When Allen was at Sheepshead Bay, he wrote, "I say, Allen, suspend your judgment, walk balanced between the seen world and the unseen one; and take care of your health! After the discipline or interlude of your merchant marine spell, get your A.B. degree and then find a job congenial to your nature." Louis ended the letter with a loving plea: "Don't grow away from me, Allen, as it will take you longer to find me again when you go in search of me."

However, Allen had no intention of growing away from or losing touch with any of his family. He loved the warmth and security of family life and always remained close to his relatives. He saw a lot of Naomi, and now that he was living in New York he was able to see more of his aunt Eleanor and uncle Max. Often he would spend Sunday at their house in the Bronx, eating a long, relaxed meal of lox and bagels, reading the papers, listening to music on WQXR, or playing Rosa Ponselle records on the phonograph.

Eugene was accepted into NYU Law School, and Naomi proposed that he come and live with her. He moved to New York at the beginning of 1946 and slept on the couch in Dr. Luria's office. Naomi and Dr. Luria lived across the street, but their relationship was becoming strained. Shortly after Eugene moved to New York, they broke up. Naomi found a furnished room in a brownstone on the West Side, and she and Eugene moved into it. It was a large room, crowded with furniture, with two windows overlooking the backyard. Eugene took jobs at Macy's and Schrafft's and spent the rest of the time studying his lawbooks, getting only six hours' sleep a night. Allen would often visit.

Naomi took to reading the Bible and told Allen, "I will think nothing but beautiful thoughts." In a long passage in "Kaddish," Ginsberg describes how, on one of his visits, Naomi told him that she had seen God:

> *"Yesterday I saw God. What did he look like? Well, in the afternoon I climbed up a ladder—he has a cheap cabin in the country, like Monroe, N.Y. the chicken farms in the wood. He was a lonely old man with a white beard.*
>
> *"I cooked supper for him. I made him a nice supper—lentil soup, vegetables, bread & butter—miltz—he sat down at the table and ate, he was sad.*
>
> *"I told him, Look at all those fightings and killings down there, What's the matter? Why don't you put a stop to it?*
>
> *"I try, he said—That's all he could do, he looked tired. He's a bachelor so long, and he likes lentil soup."*
>
> *Serving me meanwhile, a plate of cold fish—chopped raw cabbage dript with tapwater—smelly tomatoes—week-old health food—grated beets & carrots with leaky juice, warm—more and more disconsolate food—I can't eat it for nausea sometimes—the Charity of her hands stinking with Manhattan, madness, desire to please me, cold undercooked fish—pale red near the bones. Her smells—and oft naked in the room, so that I stare ahead, or turn a book ignoring her.*

To Louis's great relief, Allen applied for readmission to Columbia, and after some delay, a clearly uncomfortable Nicholas McKnight replied, saying that it was a difficult question for him to decide. He asked Allen to provide him with the professional opinion of a psychiatrist.

Allen contacted Hans Wassing, Naomi's old doctor, who signed the letter Allen wrote himself. The letter stressed Allen's emotional stability and even said: "I have noticed as well, that he takes good care of his personal appearance and shows adequate attention to the various necessary amenities of social intercourse. In my opinion, there is no question, that at present time he is psychologically pretty much as sound as they come." McKnight was satisfied, and Ginsberg was enrolled for the September 1946 term. Allen was glad to be returning to his studies. He genuinely wanted to complete his course before going off into the world and realized the practical necessity of the degree. He was also getting fed up with short-term jobs, the most recent of which had been checking coats in a nightclub.

The group in the apartment on 115th Street began to disintegrate. Bill had a morphine habit and was forging stolen prescriptions for drugs. His various Times Square hoodlum friends began to use the place to stash stolen goods. Allen, Jack, Joan, and Bill were all taking a lot of drugs; Joan, now completely addicted to Benzedrine, was using the entire contents of an inhaler in one day.

Joan claimed to have very acute hearing and said she could hear the old Irish couple talking in the apartment below. The others believed her reports of their conversations, chiefly quarrels over petty things and over the old man's sexual demands. Joan said the couple often referred to her as a whore and the others as dope fiends and debated whether they should tell the police about the goings on upstairs.

One evening, Joan reported that there was a bad quarrel in progress below. The man was threatening to stab his wife. Joan insisted they do something to stop it, so Jack and Allen ran downstairs and thumped loudly on the door. No one answered. There was no one at home. The whole five months of Joan's reported conversations had been auditory hallucinations caused by the amphetamine.

Joan displayed other symptoms of amphetamine psychosis. She and Huncke, who was also a heavy user, would spend hours talking about spores that they saw coming out of their skin. This was in keeping with the theory of radioactive disease Joan and Huncke had evolved: atomic testing was causing mutation and skin cancers, which would eventually affect everyone but could be seen most clearly among the inhabitants of Times Square. Under the bright neon and brilliantly lit all-night cafeterias, the diseased skins and other effects of molecular breakdown were immediately apparent.

Allen, mystified and intrigued by their hallucinations, was apparently oblivious of the disintegration of his friends. Phil White and Huncke took advantage of the situation and spent more and more time at the apartment, bringing in stolen goods, then spiriting them away a few days later. Sometimes they would borrow Bill's gun or blackjack to commit a robbery, and other times Phil stored his gun there. Huncke stole a prescription pad from an old doctor in Brooklyn, and Bill wrote up some phony scripts, which he filled, giving his real address, at a nearby pharmacy. Then one day in April, he sloppily misspelled Dilaudid, and the pharmacist informed the police. Bill was arrested at the apartment, and yet again his father flew into town to post bail.

In the two months between his arrest and his appearance in court, Bill remained in New York, "working the hole with the sailor"—rolling drunks on the subway with Phil White to finance his heroin habit. In June 1946, Bill's case finally came up; since he was a first offender, the judge gave him a four-month suspended sentence and sent him home to St. Louis with his father for the summer.

Allen was shocked and worried about Bill's arrest, but it didn't cause him to change his life-style. It was as if Allen was purposely rejecting his father's bourgeois values by letting his own life go to pieces. Joan reacted to Bill's arrest by taking more Benzedrine. Hal Chase was planning on living at a Columbia hall of residence and had already moved out and gone back to Denver for the summer. When he heard of the arrest, he broke off relations with all of them except Jack. Thus the division between the Wolfeans and the non-Wolfeans began to be played out.

Chase got a place in Livingston Hall on the campus. Huncke took over Hal's old room, and Phil White moved in. After Bill's arrest, Joan's behavior became more and more erratic. In the tape recordings that Kerouac made later of conversations with Neal Cassady, transcribed in *Visions of Cody*, he described the state of 115th Street at that time. Jack dropped by to see what was happening and found Joan out of her mind on Benzedrine. "She came in and she immediately stripped. I said, 'Joan, what are you doing?' She said, 'Who are you, strange man, get out of this house,' standing there."

Jack tried to remind her who he was, then Joan complained to Huncke that Jack was trying to rape her, but Huncke just lay in bed, saying, "Well ba-by, I don't know what to *do*" and "Well, I'm all hung up baby, I . . ." In the end, she went into Huncke's room to talk about it and closed the door. It was obvious from the way things were going that the apartment was doomed, but Allen didn't seem to notice; he sat typing a ten-page, amphetamine-inspired introduction to his epic poem "Death in Violence," as the place collapsed around him. ". . . who scribbled all night rocking and rolling over lofty incantations which in the yellow morning were stanzas of gibberish," he later wrote in "Howl," remembering the event.

Huncke was the next to be arrested and was sent to the Bronx County Jail for possession of drugs. It was only a matter of days before Joan cracked and was taken to Bellevue Hospital, suffering from acute amphetamine psychosis; she was the first female case they had on record and was kept there for ten days. Allen closed down the apartment. He went to stay with his father in Paterson until the Columbia term started, on September 20.

Allen got a room with an Irish family on West Ninety-second Street and prepared to become a student again. He had not lost touch with Columbia. Even though officially suspended, he had somehow remained the assistant editor of the *Columbia Review* and had poems, stories, and book reviews published in all four issues for 1946. He had been in correspondence and had meetings with Lionel Trilling, who encouraged him with his poetry, and he was still in contact with Weaver and Van Doren. However, Allen was no longer in awe of his professors. He had begun to realize that they were old-fashioned and closed to new ideas: Pound's mature work was dismissed, William Carlos Williams was raw and immature, and Walt Whitman was nothing but a provincial bumpkin.

Although he seemed to be fulfilling his father's expectations, Allen returned to Columbia in a daze. His attempt at psychoanalysis with Burroughs had revealed a deep pit of loneliness and loveless-ness; he was frustrated and confused sexually; he had no idea what he wanted to do after graduation; and he had not resolved his rela-tionship with Naomi. Part of him wanted to be like Trilling, but when he was with Trilling, it was Burroughs's ideas that they argued about, particularly when Allen tried to explain the subtle effects of marijuana.

Bill's life had taken a new direction. While in St. Louis, he had run into his old friend Kells Elvins, and he went into business with him as a citrus farmer in the Rio Grande Valley of East Texas. He wrote Allen to say that he was worried about Joan and had decided to bring her to Texas. She soon left for the citrus farm.

Lucien was released from jail that fall, having served just over two years. He returned to New York and his old friends, and one evening he asked Allen about his sex life. Allen told him he was "queer." Lucien was surprised: "So *that's* the setup!" Suddenly Allen's attitude toward him in 1943–44 made sense. "I had no idea that Allen was into homosexuality when I left New York," Carr said. "I thought he was just a shy little boy. I don't think anybody, myself, Kerouac, was aware of it any more than just hero worship." When he found out, he was saddened. "I remember thinking at the time that this is not the way to go, this is a lonely, sorry life, Allen, pull yourself together, man." At the time, Allen wrote: "The conversation was sort of a memorial landmark, after all these years, but I can't feel very historic about it." He thought Lucien's understanding of homosexuality was "technically naïve."

Jack had invited Hal Chase and other friends for Thanksgiving at his parents' home but did not invite Allen because his mother disapproved of their friendship. Allen, understandably upset, thought that Jack should stand up to his mother. Kerouac was spending most of his time in Ozone Park, working on *The Town and the City*. Huncke was still in jail, and Allen felt lonely. His journal entry for November 25 read: "Things going ill; poetry stopped, reading desultory, neurasthenic sleeping, loneliness, splenetic moods, boredom, fear, vanity." He overcame his self-pity by pursuing a relentless social life. He ran frantically from one apartment to another, from bar to bar, assignation to assignation, sleeping only when overcome by exhaustion. He was kept going, in large part, by pentaphon, an opium derivative, which gave him feelings of elation and confidence.

One evening, he and a friend, Walter Adams, went to see *Blithe Spirit* and afterward shot some pentaphon. Allen fumbled his vein shot and got blood everywhere. "I then set out to hypnotize him, and did poorly to be sure," he recorded. At the end of that session Allen took two goofballs (Nembutal) to put himself to sleep and slept for fourteen hours. At 2 A.M., he prepared to face the night with the aid of a strip of Benzedrine washed down with whiskey, four vitamin B tablets, and some fish oil capsules. He noted, "Much pleased with the benny, real zest in me now!"

The first time Allen got really high on marijuana was with Walter Adams. They were in Adams's car and got lost on Allen's block.

Eventually they parked the car, then went to a corner coffee shop. Allen ordered a huge black-and-white ice cream sundae. "Then halfway through I realized the whole place was swaying back and forth, and the lights were dazzling. The sky was infinitely extensive and spacious, the plate glass windows of the restaurant showed people walking back and forth with their dogs, smiling and chattering or weeping. And it was a grand moment of synchronicity; everything was joyful and gay, and it was the first and only ice cream sundae I've enjoyed in my life; everything else has been anticlimax."

One of the people on Allen's rounds was Vickie Russell, who had returned to New York and taken a tiny penthouse on West Eighty-ninth Street. When Huncke got out of jail in December 1946, he went to stay with her there. "Met Vickie again," Allen noted in his journal. "She's unattached and as attractive as any woman I know. Too bad I'm not ripe for one such as her."

Naomi stopped working for Dr. Luria and became a salad girl at a Horn & Hardart Automat, where she worked for about a year. Her mental health began to deteriorate, and she picked irrational arguments with Eugene. She walked around the apartment naked, her silhouette visible to neighbors. Her nudity disturbed Eugene, and her arguments disrupted his studies, so finally he moved out.

Allen was also distressed by her nudity, and there was one incident, described in "Kaddish," which he often cited as reinforcing his homosexuality. He had gone to visit her in her room:

> One time I thought she was trying to make me come lay her—flirting to herself at sink—lay back on huge bed that filled most of the room, dress up round her hips, big slash of hair, scars of operations, pancreas, belly wounds, abortions, appendix, stitching of incisions pulling down in the fat like hideous thick zippers—ragged long lips between her legs—What, even, smell of asshole? I was cold—later revolted a little, not much—seemed perhaps a good idea to try—know the Monster of the Beginning Womb—Perhaps—that way. Would she care?

Shortly after this, Naomi became convinced that Dr. Luria was in on Buba's plot to poison her. Her sister Eleanor, in the Bronx, took her in.

. . .

There was a new arrival in the city in the fall of 1946: a twenty-year-old friend of Hal Chase's from Denver. Neal Cassady came to New York with his seventeen-year-old wife, LuAnne. He and Allen met briefly at the West End, but it wasn't until January 10, 1947, that they met again. Allen was visiting Vickie Russell when Jack Kerouac arrived with Cassady. Kerouac described their meeting in *On the Road*, Ginsberg as Carlo Marx, Cassady as Dean Moriarty: "Two keen minds that they are, they took to each other at the drop of a hat. Two piercing eyes glancing into two piercing eyes—the holy con-man with the shining mind, and the sorrowful poetic con-man with the dark mind that is Carlo Marx. From that moment on I saw very little of Dean, and I was a little sorry too. Their energies met head-on, I was a lout compared, I couldn't keep up with them."

Neal was neatly dressed, muscular, and athletic, with a broken Roman nose and a wide, clear-eyed Western smile. He looked a lot like Kerouac. He could, according to Kerouac, run one hundred yards in ten seconds, pass a football seventy yards, do fifty chin-ups in a row, broad jump twenty-three feet, and masturbate six times a day.

Cassady had grown up in the long-lost world of pool halls and lunch carts, back alleys and freight yards echoing with the sound of steam locomotives. He was his mother's sixth child and his father's first and was born in Salt Lake City, in 1926, while his parents were driving from Des Moines to start a new life in Hollywood. His father, Neal Cassady, Sr., opened a barbershop at Hollywood and Vine, but the shop failed because of his drinking problem and the family moved to Denver when young Neal was two.

He was six years old when his parents split up, and he went with his father, to live in a series of flophouse hotels in Denver, finishing up in the Metropolitan, where they shared a room with a legless beggar known as Shorty. Neal and his father slept together on a dirty bed with no sheets, and in the morning the six-year-old would get himself off to school, while his father slept off the previous drunken night. Neal quickly became streetwise. His first appearance in juvenile hall occurred when his father was arrested for drunkenness as the two hitchhiked to California to pick fruit. Neal was seven. He stole his first car when he was fourteen, and by the time he was twenty-one he estimated that he had stolen over five hundred. He always took them for fun, never to sell or break up for parts, though sometimes he would change their appearance and keep them for a few weeks. He was arrested numerous times for auto theft and had done six stretches in the reformatory.

Neal's tremendous energy and enthusiasm, in addition to his physical beauty, attracted both Allen and Jack to him. He was another sensitive football player. For Allen, it was like meeting a second Kerouac. His conversations with Neal, in fact, were much like his early talks with Jack, exchanging the secrets and the fantasies of their youth: "What our actual fantasies had been as children, and later on, up to the present . . . We were really interested in what was going on inside, without regard to whether it was practical or real, but more interested in the charm and the absurdity that everybody was having such an amazingly naive secret life."

Neal was staying with the cousin of Jack's friend Alan Temko in Harlem. Allen and Jack walked him home that January night, but by then it was too late for Kerouac to travel to Ozone Park or for Allen to walk back to Ninety-second Street, so it was suggested that they spend the night and all have breakfast together in the morning. The problem was there were only two beds. Jack slept in the double bed with their host, Temko's cousin, and Allen and Neal took the cot. Allen lay with his back to Neal, balancing on the edge of the narrow bed, careful to keep his distance. But Neal stretched out his arm and pulled Allen to him, murmuring, "Draw near me." Allen lay trembling. They tentatively caressed each other and pulled off their shorts. A detailed description of what happened appeared in Ginsberg's poem "Many Loves":

> I lay with my hair intermixed with his, he asking me 'What shall we do now?'
> —And confessed, years later, he thinking I was not a queer at first to please me & serve me, to blow me and make me come, maybe or if I were queer, that's what I'd likely want of a dumb bastard like him.
> But I made my first mistake, and made him then and there my master, and bowed my head, and holding his buttock
> Took up his hard-on and held it, feeling it throb and pressing my own at his knee & breathing showed him I needed him, cock, for my dreams of insatiety & lone love.

Neal had been working at the parking lot of the New Yorker Hotel on Thirty-fourth Street, spending two nights a week studying writing with Jack out at Ozone Park and the rest of his time in bed with LuAnne in Bayonne, New Jersey, where they had found a cheap room. When Allen came on the scene, Neal reorganized his schedule to spend two nights with Allen at Ninety-second Street. Though LuAnne didn't know they were sleeping together, she recognized that she was getting a raw deal and returned to Denver within a week.

The new relationship with Neal had a profound effect on Allen. After their night together in Harlem, they spent the next two nights "staring into each other's eyes, finding out whether or not we bugged each other and what the limits were," as Ginsberg put it. Their love affair developed rapidly, and two weeks later Allen described in his journal what had happened to him after two whirlwind days with Neal. The entry for January 21, 1947, read: "Having spent a wild weekend in sexual drama with Cassady, I am left washed up on the shore of my 'despair' again. It is after such like pleasure that I get full knowledge of what I have closed myself off from."

Allen was aware of the potential problems of his growing entanglement with Neal but felt that Neal was "carefully considerate of all emotional angles and will do no wrong. I trust him." One reason he was not prepared to examine the advisability of getting involved with a married man was the possibility of good sex. Allen had had little sexual experience, all of it homosexual, most of it unsatisfactory, and was finally having a good time with Neal. He approached the matter of sex with Neal with his characteristic thoroughness and made a list:

"February 23rd, I will try to think on those sexual positions with Cassady which would please me. Try his laying me again. Try breast to breast position. Try 69 again, coming both at once. Try sitting on his chest and making him blow me. Try laying his mouth, French kissing, etc. Make him give me a trip around the world. Try (this requires real passion) browning him. Also a good massage. Laying his anus. Laying him backward thighs—kneeling and blowing, both ways. Wrestling—Whipping? Have I guts? Trip around the world, complete, winding up with blow job. No. I want some real hip sex. What is it?"

According to Ginsberg, Neal regarded sex as "a sort of joyful yoga, and transformed it into a spiritual social thing as well as a matter of esthetic prowess . . . an ultimate exchange of soul," a view in sharp contrast to that of many of Neal's women, who described him as a sexual sadist.

Allen's talks with Neal reached great depths of insight, yet frank as they were, they never seemed so convincing afterward, and Allen began to feel that he had learned all he could from Neal. "I think he *does* no longer excite me, I've almost used him up in a way," he wrote on March 2. He felt that he had "loved him as much as I can, to no end, except final loss of real feeling and love, and want no more of him." Later he said: "I realized then that it wasn't reciprocal."

Neal was due to return to Denver on March 4. Jack had been irritated by Allen's abduction of his new friend, but they had a long, sober talk the night before Neal left and achieved a rapprochement. Together, they saw Neal off on the bus to Denver. Neal was wearing a new thrift-shop three-piece suit and carrying a stolen portable typewriter, determined to make use of Kerouac's lessons on how to write. Allen said goodbye with no tears and then walked home. He felt empty but was comforted by the arrangement he had made to spend the summer with Neal in Denver when the Columbia term ended.

He initially worried about paying for the trip, since he was still trying to live on the fifteen-dollar weekly allowance his father gave him, but shortly afterward Allen won the first prize of $110 for his long poem "Death in Violence," in the biannual George Edward Woodberry contest at Columbia, a welcome surprise. Later in the year, he was to win second prize in the Columbia Philolexion Society contest, with his poem "A Lover's Garden," which was published in the August 1947 issue of the *Columbia Review*. This good news appeared in the Newark press and was dutifully clipped by all the relatives to show their neighbors. Allen's slight ambivalence toward Neal was dispelled by a series of breathless letters from Cassady, saying: "I need you now more than ever . . . every day I miss you more and more . . ." and: "Let us then find true awareness by realizing that each of us is depending on the other for fulfillment." Allen began to look forward to the summer.

Allen's plan to visit Neal underwent numerous modifications, beginning with Neal's confession that he disliked homosexual sex and continuing with his suggestion that he and Allen live with a girl. Neal wrote, "I *really don't* know how much I can be satisfied to love you, I mean bodily, you know I, somehow, dislike pricks & men & before you, had consciously forced myself to be homosexual, now, I'm not sure whether with you I was not just forcing myself unconsciously, that is to say, and falsity on my part was all physical, in fact, any disturbance in our affair was because of this. You meant so much to me, I now feel I was forcing a desire for you bodily as a compensation to you for all you were giving me."

Allen did not want to hear this at all, and from the force of Allen's replies, Neal obviously thought that his insistence that their relationship be entirely platonic would severely damage it, so he put off the day of reckoning with hints and suggestions that something might be worked out. Allen ignored Neal's disinclination to homosexual sex and clearly thought that he would be able to talk him back into bed.

In July, Allen gave up his room on Ninety-second Street and took the exhausting two-thousand-mile trip by Greyhound to Denver. Neal met him at the terminal and took him to the Colburn Hotel on Grant Street, where he had reserved a two-dollar room for him. Neal was living there with Carolyn Robinson, a Bennington graduate who was studying fine arts at the University of Denver. Neal introduced them, and Allen greeted her with a warmth that he wished he felt more deeply. Carolyn had white-golden hair wound in braids around her head and wore a blue dress. She was obviously in love with Neal, and Allen immediately sensed trouble.

Allen's money soon ran out, and Bill Burroughs sent him ten dollars to tide him over until he got a job. He was forced to move into Carolyn and Neal's room in the hotel. Sleeping there was a nightmare for him, because he could of course hear their lovemaking and all their whispered endearments. A terse note in his journal read: "Colburn Hotel Apt. Such terrible nights." It was not long before relations between Allen and Carolyn became strained. Unaware of Allen's sexual relationship with Neal, she had not considered that the cause of the tension might be intense jealousy, but she knew something was wrong.

On one occasion, Allen got her to do a drawing of Neal posing in the nude. The idea was presented as an objective artistic exercise, but Carolyn was embarrassed as Neal posed like a Greek statue while Allen sat watching from the window. Allen tried his best not to antagonize her and was sometimes able to be helpful. When she had to give an oral report, Allen coached her and edited her notes. Her talk was met with stunned silence, as Carolyn stood terrified before her art professors. Then they all rushed to congratulate her on the best performance the department had ever known.

Neal was driving a shuttle bus for the May Company department store, and Allen got a night job there, pushing a vacuum cleaner across the block-square second-floor sales area for twenty dollars a week. He moved to a damp three-room basement, sublet from friends of Neal's. It was in a red-brick rooming house on Grant Street, not far from the Colburn. The walls oozed water, and he had a small bed, a chair, and a candle. The small altar he built completed the impression of a monk's cell. Pigeons nested outside his window, and he awoke each day to their flapping and cooing.

Neal worked out a complicated schedule for himself that involved seeing his three great loves, Carolyn, LuAnne, and Allen, and a few other girls on the side. He and LuAnne had decided to get a divorce but, unknown to Carolyn, were still sleeping together. He would leave LuAnne's bed at 1 A.M. and go over to the Colburn. From there he went to see Allen, who had returned home from his night shift, and they would talk until 6 A.M.

The conversation was intense, a serious attempt, occasionally fueled by Benzedrine, to understand each other fully by analyzing every word and gesture. Sexually their relationship was not going well, as Neal had warned. The more Allen pressed him, claiming that this "sacramental" side to their relationship was of vital importance in their understanding each other, the more Neal withdrew. Neal was in the early days of his affair with Carolyn, and it was a fresh, exciting sexual relationship. He became more and more reluctant to leave her bed in order to spend the night fending off Allen's advances. He began to miss his meetings with Allen for days in a row, while Allen spent anxious nights waiting, unable to concentrate on anything but Neal's treachery. Some nights, he wept steadily for hours. He filled page after page of his big red journal with self-pitying prose about Neal and his own attempts to reach a "state of peace." Allen's only reason for being in Denver was to be with Neal. Allen had become obsessed with him, and his rejection hurt deeply.

The entry for July 28 revealed the depths of his despair: "My anxiety about the situation reached a peak of dragged hysteria at 8 o'clock this evening. All last evening at work and this evening even more so, I have been developing, quite out of my control, hallucinations about the telephone. The vacuum cleaner has a high singing pitch and I began last night, awaiting Neal's call, to confuse it with the dull ringing of the telephone. It reached such a point tonight, combined with an emotional exhaustion and an intellectual despair, that I was completely paralysed for minutes on end, stopping work turning off the motor, listening, half-hearing the phone. I had a vivid auditory sensation several times, that in the confusion, it really was the phone, and dropped my work, and ran over to the phone, and found it dead and silent. At one point I could not continue work and collapsed in a chair."

But unhappy as he was, Allen was not rendered totally immobile by the situation. On hearing of the birth of Bill and Joan's baby on July 21, he set out to write a birthday ode. It took him six days, working late at night on Benzedrine. Like much of his work in this period, it was an epic in many sections, written in highly artificial rhymed verse. A section on bebop began: "The saxophone thy mind had guessed / He knows the Devil hides in thee; / Fly hence, I warn thee, Stranger, lest / The saxophone shall injure thee."

He also wrote an entire sequence of poems that he called, collectively, "The Denver Doldrums," but the best thing to come out of his sojourn there was a prose sketch from August 23, his last day in Denver. Using Kerouac's "sketching" style, he described a bricklayer across the street. William Carlos Williams later suggested the poetic possibilities of his journal prose, and Allen altered the punctuation and line length, creating "The Bricklayer's Lunch Hour," one of his most successful early poems.

After a lot of intense talking, Allen persuaded Neal to accompany him to Texas to visit Bill and Joan. Neal finally told Carolyn about the plan and explained that he felt an obligation to try to be homosexual for Allen. She understood but said, "If that's the way it is, I don't want you. It's as simple as that. If you want Allen or something else, then go for it." Neal had little idea what he really wanted, and even Allen realized that his hero was not as organized as he had originally thought. He noted: "Neal strikes me sometimes as being even more simpleminded and confused than myself, except that may be the goofballs."

Carolyn made arrangements to go to California the next day to stay with friends, and took her things to the house of a teacher friend, where she spent the night, leaving Neal the Colburn room. The next morning, she returned to say a final goodbye to Neal. She opened the door and found him in bed, with Allen on one side and LuAnne on the other. She rushed out.

Neal was trying an impossible balancing act. Carolyn wanted him in San Francisco, LuAnne wanted him to stay in Denver, and Allen wanted to go with him to Texas. Neal had heard a lot about Bill and Joan from both Jack and Allen, and he wanted to meet them. He and Allen had always planned to go to Texas together after the summer, so in this instance Allen won.

Now that Joan was with him, Bill had taken a farm outside New Waverly, fifty miles north of Houston, where they planted marijuana as a cash crop. Kells Elvins remained in Pharr, Texas, tending the citrus groves. Bill's marijuana fields were set among oak and persimmon, several miles from the nearest road. The land sloped away to a bayou filled with Spanish moss, thick tropical vines, and vegetation.

The farmstead consisted of a few sheds, a collapsing barn, and a weathered silver-gray cabin, which had two enormous rooms, now divided into four. Bill had constructed a stand to hold a seven-hundred-gallon tank, which collected rainwater from the corrugated iron roof. He had ninety-seven acres, but the land was not suitable for anything other than subsistence farming or growing pot. He tried planting opium poppies, but it didn't work out.

Bill enjoyed his role as country squire. He cut wood, fenced in the property, and walked around with his guns, followed by a small hound dog. The sound of gunfire echoing through the forest was so common that local people asked if gangsters lived down there. Bill invited Huncke to join them, which he did, and for seven months Joan and her four-year-old daughter, Julie, Bill, and Huncke lived happily together.

Bill was still addicted to morphine, and Joan, who was pregnant, had doubled her Benzedrine habit to more than two inhalers a day. They soon cleaned out all the nearby towns of inhalers and had to make periodic runs to Houston, where Huncke made a contact who would sell them a gross every few weeks. He was also able to score there for pot and paregoric, which contained opium, so the farm was well stocked. They also cleaned all the local towns out of rum, tequila, and gin and had to drive twenty-five miles to the big liquor store in Conroe to stock up.

Conroe was where William Burroughs, Jr., was born. They had made no arrangements. At 3 A.M., Joan knocked on Bill's door and said it was time to go to the hospital. They climbed into the Jeep and drove off in the night. The next day she was back with her baby.

At ten-thirty each morning, Bill would emerge from his room, wearing a suit and tie, ready to go and get the mail and the local papers, which he would then sit on the porch and read. Joan looked after Julie and little Billie and cleaned the cabin, but she spent much of her time obsessively sweeping lizards off the tree in the yard. The moment she turned away, they would climb back. Huncke's job was to fetch firewood for the outdoor grill and cook the steaks. He also wound up the record player on the porch and changed the needle from time to time, to play Billie Holiday records and the Viennese waltzes that Bill loved.

As Allen hitchhiked toward Texas with Neal, the Rockies became a huge stage drop to the drama going on between them. It was a long, slow journey from Denver to Houston across the flat, unrelieved plains of Oklahoma and Texas, and they didn't get many rides. At one point in Oklahoma they found themselves at a crossroads at dusk, with no traffic in sight. They were in the middle of a deep conversation, and at Allen's instigation, they knelt in the road and made a solemn vow to own and accept each other's bodies and souls, and to help each other into heaven. "To accomplish a transfer of heart, and vow to stick with each other and be spiritual lovers, if not physical," Ginsberg explained. "He was going to teach me body and practical things, and I was going to teach him everything I knew intellectually and spiritually. Not that I knew anything."

It is a story told often in Ginsberg's writing. There is an account, written shortly after the event, in an unpublished story called "The Monster of Dakar," which captured the feeling of what happened: "He loved me, a big hustler, we kneeled together on the road in Oklahoma, in the middle of a four way cross of dirt roads, on an endless plain at night fall. I hadn't imagined such a place or such an eternal vow: fidelity, union, seraphic insight, sights of America, everything I could imagine. He accepted it all, just a poor lost soul, an orphan in fact, looking for a father seraph and I was looking for a seraphic boy."

It occurred again, in poetry, in "The Green Automobile":

> The windshield's full of tears
> rain wets our naked breasts,
> we kneel together in the shade
> amid the traffic of night in paradise.

Ginsberg later remembered it as a poignant moment, "although by hindsight I realize he was obviously just being nice to me, humoring me."

They arrived in New Waverly on August 30. Allen wrote: "When we got there, I expecting this happy holiday of God given sexuality, where was the royal couch?" Huncke was still trying to build it. He thought that Allen and Neal might like to have his room, since he slept on the screened porch. Huncke's bed would not hold two people, but there were some unused army cots and some boards around. "I conceived of getting these sideboards together in some kind of bed situation," explained Huncke. "The only place to work was dead in front of the cabin, everybody could see me working with that fucking bed. . . . I did work on it because I figured I had a practical idea. Unfortunately while I was working on it, they arrived."

Neal refused to help, so Allen and Huncke struggled with the cots. Huncke had taken one of the headboards off and they eventually got the other one off, so at least the bed was level on the ground. It sagged in the middle and was very uncomfortable, as well as being dangerous, since scorpions could reach it. "I was absolutely outraged with Burroughs for not having the sense to get a decent bed or make provision," Ginsberg remembered. "We didn't make out much, and that was the whole point of it. We were gonna go down there and I was finally gonna get satisfied for the first time." The tragic saga of the bed entered Beat legend as told by Cassady in Kerouac's *Visions of Cody* and by Huncke in *The Evening Sky Turned Crimson*.

Otherwise it was a pleasant visit. Neal busied himself putting up fence posts. It was quiet, and there was plenty of time for long talks with Bill, Joan, and Huncke. Ginsberg's strongest memory was of sitting on the porch in the evenings, talking by the light of the kerosene lamps, while little Julie ran around barefoot and Coleman Hawkins's "Low Flame" played on the Victrola.

Two days after they arrived, Allen finally accepted the fact that Neal was not interested in men. He wrote: "The sacramental honeymoon is over. I have a drag against turning my mind to a practical, non-romantic set of arrangements a propos Cassady. Since it has at last penetrated my mind and become obvious to me that, without angling, he means what he says when he says he can't make use of me sexually, it requires turn of mind."

It wasn't just Allen's physical demands that turned Neal off; it was the emotional ones as well. Neal told Kerouac: "I got so I couldn't stand Allen to even touch me, you know, see, only touch me. It was terrible. And man, I'd never been that way, you know, but, man, he was all opening up and I was all . . ." Yet despite

Neal's constant warning "It means nothing," Allen wrote quite seriously in his journal: "I am wondering what will happen to Neal if I really withdraw my active queer love and leave him alone emotionally."

Neal insisted they split up; there was no other way. As a consolation, he promised one final night together in Houston. Allen had decided to try and ship out from Houston on a boat to New York, to make some money for the fall semester. Neal was going to stay on and help with the marijuana harvest, then drive Bill back to New York, where he and Allen were to have another try at living together.

The night at the Brazos Hotel was a disaster. Allen, Huncke, and Neal drove into Houston, and Huncke went immediately in search of his drug connections. While Allen went to the NMU hall to look for a ship, Neal got high on Nembutals. He picked up a girl in the Jeep and drove back toward the hotel. Just as he approached it, the barbiturates hit him. He managed to steer the car into the no-parking zone in front of the hotel and stop it by hitting the curb. The girl, who had just been released from a mental hospital, dragged him up the stairs to his room. "And she went to bed with me and I tried to screw her and everything and I managed to finally even though I was high . . ." But then Allen came back and was furious. He felt betrayed, his fantasy once again shattered. And Neal was too high to do anything, even if he had wanted to.

Luckily, Allen had found himself a ship, a collier going to Africa. The trip was twenty days out, ten in port at Dakar, and twenty days coming back. It meant that Allen would miss the start of the Columbia term, but nonetheless he took it. He wrote to his father to reassure him that he really did intend to return to school, but not until January 1948, and that the money from the voyage would help him get psychoanalyzed. "I can't think really of going back to school and spending money on it till I have the psychoanalysis which I need much more."

The trip to Africa was uneventful. Dakar, once a major departure point for Africans being taken into slavery in America, was now the colonial headquarters of French West Africa and had the atmosphere of a French provincial town. A boy whom Allen employed to help him on board ship showed him the bamboo shacks in the poorer part of town, so he got some sense of Africa on his shore leave. He also smoked a lot of African marijuana. The best thing to come out of the experience was a story called "The Monster of

Dakar," an account of life aboard ship and the author's unsuccessful efforts to find a boy in port.

Neal finished the harvest and then drove Bill and the marijuana back to New York. Bill immediately set about selling the pot, then went into business with Huncke's old prison friend, Bill Garver, dealing junk, which they cut with milk sugar. Neal had nowhere to stay. He hung around the city for a week, hoping to hear from Allen, then left for California. Allen arrived a few days later, expecting a rendezvous, but all he found was a brief note saying that Neal had gone to marry Carolyn. Allen, stunned, wrote sadly to Neal: "I suppose I must say goodbye then. I don't know how."

Allen ran around New York, visiting his old friends, but his real desire was to be alone. He rented a small furnished room on West Twenty-seventh Street and sat there taking Benzedrine and writing rhymed couplets. One early morning at four-thirty, after writing a poem called "The Creation of the World," he finally wrote a long, sad letter to Neal, letting out his true feelings. "I have protected myself, armored, since I arrived, from grief or too much self pity and as a result I saw my mind turn more than ever . . . into isolation and phoney goodness." He confessed to Neal what Neal must have known all along, that his primary interest in him was sexual. "I must admit that I have known more or less consciously that all the 'purity' of my love, its 'generosity' and 'honor' was, though on its own level true, not at all my deeper intention toward you, which was and is simply a direct lover's."

In cramped, pinched, unhappy handwriting, he begged Neal to come back to him. "I am lonely, Neal, alone, and always I am frightened. I need someone to love and kiss me and sleep with me. . . . I have been miserable without you because I had depended on you to take care of me for love of me, and now that you have altogether rejected me, what can I do, what can I do?" He continued in the same vein, growing more maudlin and self-pitying with each page. Neal did not reply.

Allen's difficulties were compounded by Huncke, who stopped by one day and stole Allen's phonograph. He wrote, enclosing a pawnshop ticket and saying, somewhat prophetically, in his curiously formal manner: "I presume you have spoken of my pilfering to others—although it fails to bother me, it will place you in the role of being the proverbial sucker if you forgive me and continue allowing me parasitical advantages from my contact with you."

Allen was also concerned about his mother. After Naomi moved in with her sister, her state of mind had improved a bit and she even enrolled in the painting class at Bronx Adult High School. She painted Russian brides, saints with lugubrious faces, and the elevated trains running over the rooftops of the Bronx. There is a portrait of Allen from this period, naive but expressive. But then her symptoms began to return, stronger than ever. She got up at 6 A.M. to listen on the radio for spies. She thought she saw Buba on the fire escape with a bag of poison germs. She got angry and kicked Eleanor, who was already weak from a rheumatic heart. After that it was obvious that she could no longer stay. Her cousins Max and Edie Frohman, whom she had known since they were all children in Russia, lived in the same building, and they agreed to take her in.

Naomi would wake Edie in the middle of the night to tell her that she was a spy and Eleanor a rat. Edie worked all day as a union organizer, and in the end she could no longer take the strain of having Naomi there. She telephoned Allen and he went to see her. In "Kaddish," Allen wrote that Naomi's symptoms were worse than ever. She sang, she raged at Buba and Louis, complained of spies, Hitler, and the three big sticks down her back. Exasperated, Allen pushed her against the door and yelled, "Don't kick Eleanor!"

Naomi stared at him with contempt. "Eleanor is the worst spy!" she said. "She's taking orders!"

"No wires in the room!" yelled Allen. "You've been away from Louis for years already. Grandma's too old to walk!" But it was impossible. She had lost all contact with reality. While she raved at him about Eleanor being a spy, Allen called the police. The knock at the door when they arrived scared her, and she ran to the bathroom to hide from the spies. In "Kaddish," Allen described riding with her to the police station.

> *The ride then—held Naomi's hand, and held her head to my breast, I'm taller—kissed her and said I did it for the best—Eleanor sick—and Max with heart condition—Needs—*
>
> *To me—'Why did you do this?'—'Yes Mrs., your son will have to leave you in an hour'—The Ambulance came in a few hours—drove off at 4 A.M. to some Bellevue in the night downtown—gone to the hospital forever. I saw her led away—she waved, tears in her eyes.*

She was sent to Pilgrim State Hospital, out on Long Island. Allen, Eugene, and Louis all received pathetic, heartrending letters from her, asking to be released. "How I want you to know that I want to get out and cook for you and laugh and sing the rest of my life," she wrote Allen. But she added, "They found kerosene in my system in this hospital. These things make me delirious." She got worse, and on November 14, 1947, Allen received a letter from the senior director of the hospital, telling him that in the opinion of the doctors, Naomi's medical condition was serious enough to warrant a prefrontal lobotomy. She was hitting her head against the wall with such fury, working herself into paroxysms of fear, that the doctors felt she was likely to have a stroke unless she was stopped. Louis had divorced Naomi when she was living with Dr. Luria, so it fell to her sons to assume legal responsibility for her. Allen signed the forms.

Allen began to think that he was going crazy himself. He wrote Kerouac: "If you want to know my true nature, I am at the moment one of those people who goes around showing his cock to juvenile delinquents." This was the winter when Allen became "more actively queer," trying to drown out the memory of Neal by haunting the gay bars in Greenwich Village and Times Square and on Seventy-second Street. It was while he was living on West Twenty-seventh Street that he was sometimes able to persuade Kerouac to have sex: "I remember one particular time, he was high on Benzedrine and so extremely horny, as you get with Benzedrine, but at the same time he couldn't come for a long long while. One time there, he blew me."

Allen returned to Columbia and spent the winter of 1947–48 in a frenzy of activity, working at a part-time job, staying out late drinking and carousing, sometimes staying up all night on Benzedrine or morphine, writing poetry and playing records. He was aware that he was avoiding coming to terms with the facts about his situation but was hoping that a course of psychoanalysis he had undertaken would overcome his indecision. It had seemed to Allen that Reichian analysis would be the most suitable for his case, so he wrote to Wilhelm Reich, asking for his recommendation of a suitable doctor: "My main psychic difficulty, as far as I know, is the usual oedipal entanglement. I have been a homosexual for as long as I can remember, and have had a limited number of homosexual affairs, both temporary and protracted. They have been unsatisfactory to me, and I have always approached love affairs with a sort of self-contradictory, conscious masochism. . . . I have had long periods of depression, guilt feelings—disguised mostly as a sort of Kafkian sordidness of sense of self—melancholy, and the whole gamut I suppose."

He described his amateur analysis with Burroughs: "The inevitable and unfortunate effect was that it left me washed up on the shores of my neurosis with a number of my defences broken, but, centrally unchanged, with nothing to replace the lost armor." Reich's assistant replied with a list of three doctors recommended by Reich; Allen chose Dr. Allan Cott, who was based in Newark. Allen could combine the visits with seeing his father. He began the twice-weekly sessions as soon as he returned from his trip to Dakar.

It was impossible to discuss his analysis realistically with Louis without revealing that he was homosexual, so after careful consideration, he told him. The occasion was described in Ginsberg's poem "Don't Grow Old":

> A look startled his face, "You mean you like to take men's penises in your mouth?"
> Equally startled, "No, no," I lied, "that isn't what it means."

"I got very embarrassed," Ginsberg said later, "and said, 'It means that I can't be sexually aroused by women.' I put it into the traditional Jewish family terminology. I have the sense that he was reluctant to acknowledge that I was seriously disturbed and needed something as sophisticated as psychotherapy, because that put me more into the category of my mother—it meant trouble!"

The Reichian "vegetotherapeutic" system identifies repressed energies with "frozen" muscles and releases this blocked energy through body massage, including massage around the eyes and jaws. "It was really remarkable," Ginsberg said. "I felt this strange buzzing from disturbing the mouth area." As an orthodox Reichian, Cott would have had as his goal restoring Allen to his proper heterosexual genital potency, something that Burroughs, among others, was deeply critical of. "Frankly I don't trust that kind of genital Reichian. . . . Feller say, when a man gets too straight he's just a god damned prick," Burroughs wrote. But Cott clearly released some deep-seated unconscious material, because in 1960, writing about his experiences with the mind-altering drug ayahuasca, Ginsberg said: "A few times in psychoanalysis—with the Reichian Cott

—got to same depth of *significance* which was hard to bear, and drove me off."

Cott objected strenuously to Allen's smoking marijuana; he thought it might lead to a psychotic episode. He gave him an ultimatum, but Allen continued to smoke. Cott was true to his word, and after some three months he terminated Allen's therapy.

Allen was not smoking marijuana for kicks. "Our original use was for aesthetic study, aesthetic perception, deepening it. I was somewhat disappointed later on, when the counterculture developed the use of grass for party purposes rather than for study purposes. I always thought that was the wrong direction." Though it seems unlikely that Allen's use of pot was always so high-minded, he was certainly employing it to heighten his perception of art. He was writing a paper on Cézanne for Professor Meyer Schapiro at Columbia and would smoke a joint, then go to the Museum of Modern Art and look at Cézanne's watercolors. He became interested in the way that the artist juxtaposed two colors, so that the eye gave a little jolt in passing from one color to the next. "I got a strange shuddering impression looking at his canvases, partly the effect when someone pulls a Venetian blind, reverses the Venetian— there's a sudden shift, a flashing that you see in Cézanne canvases."

Ginsberg later characterized this shift as "eyeball kicks," and the last part of "Howl," Part I, contains a specific homage to Cézanne's method, which so influenced his own work: "who dreamt and made incarnate gaps in Time & Space through images juxtaposed . . . jumping with sensation of Pater Omnipotens Aeterne Deus." (The Latin quotes a letter from Cézanne to Émile Bernard.) A major element of Ginsberg's compositional technique was to be an attempt to find the equivalent in words of Cézanne's gaps, a choice of words that would create a *gap* between them, "which the mind would fill with the sensation of existence." Ginsberg's favorite example is a phrase from "Howl": "hydrogen jukebox."

By February 1948, Allen was living in a small room at 536 West 114th Street, facing the Columbia campus. That spring, with Mark Van Doren's encouragement, he assembled a book of poems called "The Denver Doldrums." He was still deeply depressed by the failure of his affair with Neal and was sleeping longer hours to avoid confronting his problems. A letter from Neal announced his marriage to Carolyn on April 1. Disgusted, Allen wrote, "Now, I suppose I should congratulate you on your marriage. So O.K. Pops, everything you do is great. The idea of you with a child and a settled center of affection—shit."

Neal replied angrily, telling Allen that he was "way, way, way off base." He opened by saying, "You and I are now farther apart than ever. Only with effort can I recall you." He was going through a psychotic period himself and felt nothing for anyone. He said he was only interested in one thing, and that was women, primarily whores. He concluded, "Let's stop corresponding—I'm not the N.C. you knew. I'm not N.C. anymore. I more closely resemble Baudelaire."

The weather improved, and Kerouac began to come into the city more frequently. He finished *The Town and the City* and gave Allen the manuscript to read. Allen was bowled over. "It is very great," he wrote Neal. He perceived in Jack's book that "all the turmoil and frenzy of the last years had somehow been justified—because I saw expressed in his novel a peace and knowledge and solidarity and, say, a whole creation, a true and eternal world—my world— finally given a permanent form. So I also felt my own failure as an artist to conclude a large, and, if not mature, at least complete and internally perfect work."

With Neal gone, Allen's gaze returned to Jack. Allen invited him to his father's house in Paterson for a Passover seder, but as they parted afterward at the 125th Street subway turnstile, Allen, frustrated by his intense desire, lost his composure and demanded that Jack hit him. Jack thought he had gone mad. Ginsberg later commented: "I wanted attention from him, *any* kind of attention!" Allen was losing control.

College ended in May, and Allen sublet an apartment from a friend, Russell Durgin, a theology student who was recuperating from tuberculosis. Allen owed Trilling a term paper, he had a gym requirement, which he had neglected, and he also lacked credits in math and science, which were giving him a lot of trouble, particularly organic chemistry, since he found it almost impossible to memorize chemical formulas in his fragmented state of mind.

The apartment was at 321 East 121st Street, in East Harlem. It was light and airy, with views out over the rooftops, and sufficiently far from Columbia and the West End Bar scene to allow Allen to concentrate on his work. He went to a class in the morning and worked part time as a file clerk. He idled around the house reading Durgin's books, which were kept neatly stacked in orange crates. These, and their owner, were later enshrined in "Howl": "who coughed on the sixth floor of Harlem crowned with flame under the tubercular sky surrounded by orange crates of theology." Allen dipped into Marvell, Saint Teresa of Avila, Plotinus, Martin Luther, and others. He was also reading a lot of William Blake and Saint John of the Cross, and was in a distinctly mystical mood.

All his close friends were away; Burroughs had sold his farm and moved with Joan to New Orleans, and Allen rarely saw Kerouac in Harlem. The apartment was too out of the way for anyone to drop in, and Allen had no telephone. Meetings had to be arranged by letter or by calling him at work. He took long exploratory walks in Harlem and wondered what to do with his life.

The summer heat was on. Allen lay on his bed by the open window, reading William Blake. The book was open to the poem "Ah! Sunflower," from *Songs of Innocence and Songs of Experience*. Allen had his pants open and was absentmindedly masturbating while he read; he had just come, when he heard a deep, ancient voice, reading the poem aloud. He immediately knew, without thinking, that it was the voice of Blake himself, coming to him across the vault of time. The voice was prophetic, tender. It didn't seem to be coming from his head; in fact, it seemed to be in the room, but no one was there. He described it: "The peculiar quality of the voice was something unforgettable because it was like God had a human voice, with all the infinite tenderness and mortal gravity of a living Creator speaking to his son."

> *Ah, Sunflower, weary of time,*
>   *Who countest the steps of the sun,*
> *Seeking after that sweet golden clime*
>   *Where the traveller's journey is done;*
>
> *Where the youth pined away with desire,*
>   *And the pale virgin shrouded in snow,*
> *Arise from their graves and aspire*
>   *Where my Sunflower wishes to go!*

He suddenly had a deep understanding of the meaning of the poem and realized that *he* was the sunflower. Simultaneous with the auditory vision came a heightened visual perception: The afternoon sunlight through the window took on an extraordinary clarity. The sky was ancient, the gateway to infinity, the same deep blue universe seen by Blake himself, and Allen knew this was the "sweet golden clime" itself. He was already in it. "I suddenly realized that *this* existence was *it*!" he said. "This was the moment I was born for. This initiation, this consciousness of being alive unto myself. The spirit of the universe was what I was born to realize."

Silhouetted against the bright living light of the sky he saw the grimy rooftops of Harlem. It was the first time he had looked carefully at the pressed metal cornices with their ornamental consoles and entablatures; he understood what human intelligence had gone into their creation, five decades before, so that they could stand there "like buttresses in eternity!"

Everywhere he noticed evidence of a living hand, even in the arrangement of bricks, and he was aware that each brick had been placed there by someone, that people had built the entire vast city, placing each stone and manufacturing each cornice and window frame.

"My body suddenly felt *light* . . . it was a sudden awakening into a totally deeper real universe than I'd been existing in." He looked further, to the clouds; they seemed signals of something vaster and more far-reaching than a workman's hand. He caught an understanding of the billions of years that the sea had been evaporating and forming into clouds, each one unique in shape, and of the vast complexity of nature. "I was sitting in the middle of an entire planetary solar system! . . . I had the impression of the entire universe as poetry filled with light and intelligence and communication and signals. Kind of like the top of my head coming off, letting in the rest of the universe connected to my own brain."

A few minutes later, the sensations began again, this time with the voice reading Blake's "The Sick Rose."

> O Rose, thou art sick!
>   The invisible worm,
> That flies in the night,
>   In the howling storm,
>
> Has found out thy bed
>   Of crimson joy,
> And his dark secret love
>   Does thy life destroy.

"I experienced 'The Sick Rose,' with the voice of Blake reading it, as something that applied to the whole universe, and at the same time the inevitable beauty of doom . . . it was very beautiful and very awesome . . . as if Blake had penetrated the very secret core of the *entire* universe and had come forth with some little magic formula statement in rhyme and rhythm that, if properly heard in the inner inner ear, would deliver you beyond the universe," Ginsberg said.

The third and final poem that brought on the sensations was "The Little Girl Lost," with its hypnotic repeating refrain:

> *Do father, mother weep?*
> *Where can Lyca sleep?*
>
> . . . .
>
> *How can Lyca sleep*
> *If her mother weep?*
>
> *If her heart does ache,*
> *Then let Lyca wake;*
> *If my mother sleep,*
> *Lyca shall not weep.*

"I suddenly realized that Lyca was me, or Lyca was the self," Ginsberg said. He understood that "If her heart does ache, / Then let Lyca wake" meant to wake up to the same realization he had just experienced, "the total consciousness of the complete universe. Which is what Blake was talking about . . . a breakthrough from ordinary quotidian consciousness into consciousness that was really seeing all of heaven in a flower."

He felt he must tell someone about his experience, and in a state of extreme elation, he crawled out onto the fire escape and tapped on the next-door window. "I've seen God!" Allen cried, startling the two young women inside. They slammed the window shut in his face. He crawled back to his apartment and began experimenting to see if he could reach the deeper levels of meaning in other texts. He found amazing images of horses in Plato's *Phaedrus*, dipped into St. John Perse, picked up Plotinus, but found him very difficult to interpret. "I *immediately* doubled my thinking process, quadrupled, and I was able to read almost any text and see all sorts of divine significance in it."

He wondered if he could retrieve the sensation at will, without the aid of Blake. He went into his kitchen. "I started moving around and sort of shaking with my body and dancing up and down on the floor and saying, 'Dance! dance! dance! dance! spirit! spirit! spirit! dance!' and suddenly I felt like Faust, calling up the devil. And then it started coming over me, this big . . . creepy feeling, cryptozoid or monozoidal, so I got all scared and quit."

The sense of supraconsciousness returned to him the next day in the Columbia University bookstore. He was standing in the poetry section, leafing through a volume of Blake, reading "The Human Abstract" from *Songs of Experience*. "I was in the eternal place *once more*, and I looked around at everybody's faces, and I saw all these wild animals!"

The familiar bookstore clerk had a long, thin face. Allen had not paid him much attention when he entered the store but now saw that he looked like a giraffe. As Allen studied the man's long nose, "I suddenly saw like a great tormented soul . . . I realized that *he* knew also, just like I knew. And that everybody in the bookstore knew, and that they were all hiding it! They all had the consciousness, it was like a great *un*conscious that was running between all of us, that everybody *was* completely conscious, but that the fixed expressions people have, the habitual expressions, the manners, the mode of talk, are all masks hiding this consciousness. Because almost at that moment it seemed that it would be too terrible if we communicated to each other on a level of total consciousness and awareness each of the other.

"The complete death awareness that everybody has continuously with them all the time [was] all of a sudden revealed to me at once in the faces of the people, and they all looked like horrible grotesque masks, grotesque because *hiding* the knowledge from each other. Having a habitual conduct and forms to prescribe, forms to fulfill. Roles to play. But the main insight I had at that time was that everybody knew."

It was an experience, a vision of himself and the world, that affected him deeply, but though many societies have respected and revered those who have visions, in postwar New York there was no one Allen could talk to about it. One of the first people he called was Allan Cott, his ex-analyst. "It happened," said Allen. "I had some kind of breakthrough or psychotic experience."

"I'm afraid any discussion would have no value," said Cott, and hung up.

Allen went out to Paterson to tell his father, but his wild talk about almost being swallowed by "God" only scared Louis and made him worry even more that Allen had the same fatal flaw that had driven Naomi mad. Louis was a confirmed agnostic, and they finished up arguing about God. Everyone around Columbia at that time was reading Santayana, William James's *Varieties of Religious Experience*, Buber, Donne, and books of Christian mysticism, and that was the only terminology Allen had to discuss his spiritual experience. Many of his friends advised him to see a psychiatrist, others just backed away. "I got very splenetic, angry and irritable, thinking that other people were resisting acknowledging what they themselves knew," he said. When Allen ran into the English department office, saying, "I just saw the light!" Mark Van Doren was the only professor who was sympathetic and asked him what he meant. Trilling and the others thought Allen had finally gone over the edge.

Ginsberg was staggered by the experience and said that his immediate thought was: "Now that I've seen this heaven on earth, I will never forget it. I will never stop considering it the center of my life, which is now changed into a new world. I'll never be able to go back, and that's great. From now on, I'm chosen, blessed, sacred, poet, and this is my sunflower, my new mind. I'll be faithful the rest of my life, and I'll never deny it and I'll never renounce it."

As the weeks passed, the vision faded. Allen kept trying to catalyze it by staring at cornices or trees or by reading Blake intensely. He looked to Blake for instruction on how to regain his visionary awareness. In the "Rossetti Manuscript" he found the lines: "To find the Western Path, / Right thro' the Gates of Wrath / I urge my way . . ." "I thought 'the path' was through the Gates of Wrath; Fear and Wrath, and Terror," Ginsberg said. "Cultivate the terror, get right into it, right into death. I said, 'Die, go mad, drop dead.' So I thought for many years that my obligation was to annihilate my ordinary consciousness and expand my mystic consciousness."

Thus he ultimately began a series of experiments with mind-altering drugs, which would continue for fifteen years. He took every powerful hallucinogen he could find, from laughing gas to mescaline; he sniffed ether and shot heroin. He disappeared into the upper reaches of the Amazon to take ayahuasca with the Indian witch doctors and smoked hashish all night with naked sadhus in the burning grounds on the bank of the Ganges. He virtually ignored everyday life in his concentrated effort to widen his consciousness. A little over a decade later, he discovered LSD, which did approximate the sensation of eternity, but "on acid, most of the time, I also got the horror trip, because I was trying so hard to get back to that eternity that I'd seen before; so every time I got high, when the first doubt came that I might not see 'Eternity' . . . or the fear came that I might get eaten alive by 'God,' then the trip immediately turned into a hell."

He did not get free from the desire to recreate his visionary experience until 1963, when he was living in India and met Dudjom Rinpoche, the head of Nyingma, the oldest of the various sects of Tibetan Buddhism, who, after Allen had presented him with his history of visions and drug experiences, advised him to stop clinging to the vision; to give it up. He told Allen, "If you see anything horrible, don't cling to it. If you see anything beautiful, don't cling to it." Allen had filled his head with so much thought about the vision that he had cut himself off from direct perception. "The remarkable thing is that I stupefied myself from 1948 to 1963. A long time. That's fifteen years preoccupied with one single thought."

Ginsberg never did renounce his Blake vision; even in 1986, he described it as "The only really genuine experience I feel I've had, something that seemed like a complete absorption of all my senses into something totally authentic as an experience."

He immediately tried to put the experience into words. There were eight poems in his early collection, *The Gates of Wrath*, that attempted to do this. "Vision 1948" reads:

> *I shudder with intelligence and I*
> *Wake in the deep light*
> *And hear a vast machinery*
> *Descending without sound,*
> *Intolerable to me, too bright,*
> *And shaken in the sight*
> *The eye goes blind before the world goes round.*

Many unpublished manuscripts also recalled the vision: "I stared into the sun and saw my city as it was: as real as a dream it rose on the horizon"; and over the years, he referred to it several times in his journals, including a 111-line poem about it, called "One Day," written in 1961:

> *That day I heard Blake's voice*
> *I say I heard Blake's voice . . .*

Other references were short and occurred among travel descriptions, such as an early draft of "Siesta in Xbalba," written in 1954 in Usumacinta, Mexico:

> I think in 1948: sitting in my apartment,
>   my eyes opened for an hour
> seeing in dreadful ecstasy
>   the buildings rotting
> Under the wide eternal sky

Louis was, of course, tremendously concerned. First Allen revealed that he was a homosexual; now he had seen God. His father was fearful of what might come next. But however worried and critical Louis was, he and Allen were still able to talk openly, and Allen was able to confide such intimate problems as his fixation on Neal. Louis's advice on this subject came in a two-word letter in July 1948: "Dear Allen, Exorcise Neal. Louis." They obviously discussed the matter further, because in October, over a year since Allen had last seen Neal, Louis wrote, "So, take my advice now, put a tourniquet knot around your affection for N.; tone your letters down properly."

Meantime, Neal was begging Allen's forgiveness and trying to become friends again. After a long reconciliatory letter at the beginning of August 1948, he wrote on August 20 to say that if he and Carolyn had a son, he would name it Allen Jack Cassady. "I anticipate him always signing his name thus: Allen J. Cassady," wrote Neal.

By September, Neal's letters had grown positively flirtatious, and he wrote, "I love all sex—yes all, all sex. Anyway I can get it. I need it, want it, shall *have* it—now. I wanta fuck—in despair I cry out, 'Allen, Allen, will you let me splatter my come at you?' "

Allen replied, humorously, "Fuck you, N.C. Next time you write send me some come so I'll know you're sincere."

Allen got a job as a copy boy at Associated Press Radio News Service in Rockefeller Center, working the midnight–8 A.M. shift. His last weeks in Harlem were not pleasant ones, as he wrote Jack. "Huncke moved in, yakked at me irritably for a week and a half, ate my food, took my last nickel and walked off with my last suits, a jacket, Russell's winter clothes (suits, coats, etc.) and twenty or thirty expensive books (hundreds of dollars worth of books) full of theological notes." Since he was the one who had allowed Huncke to stay in Durgin's apartment, Allen felt morally obliged to pay for everything. Huncke wrote Durgin to say that he would pay him back, but many of the books were irreplaceable, as were Durgin's annotations.

Naively, Allen wrote to Huncke, asking if he really intended to pay back the money. He mentioned the incident in a letter to Burroughs, who replied with a warning: "It seems very doubtful to me that Huncke will ever make any attempt to pay Durgin. I think that any policy of appeasement in that direction will be disastrous and can only lead to further imprudence and impositions." As was so often the case, Burroughs was right on all counts.

Among Ginsberg's new friends was Ed Stringham, a West Side literary type who worked at *The New Yorker*. Ginsberg, Stringham, and a young poet named Alan Ansen began a chain novel, writing a chapter each, which is as far as it got. Ansen had inherited his family's home in Woodmere, Long Island, where he lived in some splendor. Allen, Jack, and other friends would go out for weekends to listen to Wagner, bringing with them girls, boys, and grass.

Another new friend was a young, hard-drinking, ex-Harvard Italian lawyer named Bill Cannastra, whose exploits included lying down in front of the advancing traffic on an avenue crossing and dancing drunkenly along the parapet on the roof of his building. Through another young writer, Alan Harrington—whom Allen and Jack called "the faun"—Allen met the writer John Clellon Holmes, whom Harrington brought to Allen's Fourth of July party in Harlem. Holmes was the same age as Allen, and like Jack, he came from Massachusetts. He and Jack immediately took to each other, and Jack began to spend a lot of time at Holmes's apartment on Lexington Avenue at Fifty-sixth Street. Allen would often visit them there, and they would all stay up late, listening to Symphony Sid, the "all night, all frantic one," who played six hours of nonstop bebop, "at your request and in our groove," every night on WMCA. Allen even sent for a membership card in the Symphony Sid "Bop" Club, in recognition of the hours he spent listening to Lennie Tristano, Lester Young, Ben Webster, Charlie Parker, and all the other greats of forties bebop.

Allen's friend Walter Adams departed for France, leaving Allen his $14.95-a-month, three-room cold-water flat at 1401 York Avenue. In those days Lenox Hill was a drab neighborhood of cheap saloons, stables, thrift shops, and tenement blocks. It was October when Allen moved in with his orange crates of books. The bed, a gift from Kerouac, was the one his father had died in.

In December, Neal abandoned Carolyn and their three-month-old daughter in San Francisco and arrived in New York with his ex-wife, LuAnne, having used all his and Carolyn's savings to buy a brand-new maroon 1949 Hudson. They were accompanied by Neal's friend Al Hinkle, whose new wife, Helen, had been jettisoned along the way, when she ran out of money. The purpose of the trip was to collect Jack and drive him back to San Francisco, where he intended to stay for three days before returning to New York. It was the kind of pointless trip later celebrated by Kerouac in *On the Road*.

Allen took a few days off from Associated Press to drive around town with them and go to all the New Year parties, but during most of their stay he was still working the night shift. Neal and LuAnne slept in his bed, and he joined them there when he got in. Hinkle slept on the couch. Since they were all broke, Neal sent LuAnne out to work. Meanwhile, Neal, Al, and Jack sat up all night drinking, taking Benzedrine, and smoking pot. When she returned after a long day as a waitress in a Radio City coffee shop, LuAnne was expected to clean the apartment and cook the men's food. Jack was hanging around all the time, so she had to buy food for him as well. Allen bought his own.

Huncke was in the Rikers Island jail on a sixty-day rap for possession of marijuana. Allen wrote him to propose that he get a job and leave the world of petty crime; Allen would let him stay with him until he was set up and able to plan the future. The letter never reached Huncke, and fearful of Allen's anger over the theft of his typewriter and clothes and Durgin's books, he did not contact Allen when he was let out at the beginning of February 1949. The first person he moved in with attempted to kill him.

Having been ordered out of Times Square by the police, who accused him of being a "creep" unworthy to hang around its seedy streets, Huncke wandered homeless and coatless in the February cold and snow, until he finally presented himself at Allen's door at eight o'clock one morning, in the last stages of exhaustion. His feet were blistered and bleeding, and he was almost suicidally depressed. He had been living on Benzedrine, coffee, and doughnuts for weeks, bought by pawning the few things he had been able to steal at the Port Authority bus terminal.

Allen bathed and dressed Huncke's bleeding feet and gave him food. After a little conversation, Huncke fell back on the couch and slept. Huncke's arrival became a line in Ginsberg's "Howl": "who walked all night with their shoes full of blood on the snowbank docks waiting for a door in the East River to open to a room full of steamheat and opium."

Huncke spent most of the next two weeks sleeping. Allen wrote in his journal: "Huncke has been in bed on a couch in the living room for two weeks with the shades drawn. The most depressing thing is to get up to go to work, and wake him, and see him lift up his head, staring blankly, dumb, biting his lips, for half-an-hour at a time."

Gradually Huncke began to come to life, and Allen told him the content of the letter he wrote him in prison. Huncke listened carefully and seemed to agree. Allen felt that if he demonstrated sufficient interest in Huncke's welfare and showed him that someone cared, then "perhaps the spark of life would catch." As he recovered, Huncke began to make his presence known in the apartment, moving the furniture around until it was to his taste and burning incense.

Allen, meanwhile, was feeling a strong need to be more financially independent of Louis. He was earning $31.75 a week at Associated Press, but with Huncke living off him, he found that it didn't last out the week. Allen would work himself into a rage at Huncke's dependency and vow to get rid of him, but that only brought on guilt because he felt that the desire for financial stability came from a neurotic fear of flux and change, so he kept quiet and set out to enjoy Huncke's presence, planning to send him away when he could do it with a clear conscience. "And so my house and my belongings, wearily, painfully, anxiously, became his," Allen recorded. "He wore my suits, socks, shirts, even took over my bed, so that I sometimes, rather than selfishly claim possession, took over the couch to sleep on—sometimes."

Allen remembered Burroughs's warning of what would happen if he took Huncke in again, and he recognized that under Huncke's veneer of misery and impotence there was a calculating mind that would exploit Allen's every weakness. After the first two weeks, Allen gave Huncke a week's ultimatum to decide on his offer to find him a job and see that he kept it. However, Huncke conjured up a huge boil on his leg, which incapacitated him for another two weeks, during which time it was impossible for Allen to throw him out. Allen began to see him as "an actual damned soul living already in hell, aware of it, powerless to help himself and powerless to be aided." Burroughs liked Huncke for what he was, a petty criminal, whereas Allen had an idealized view of the criminal underworld and saw Huncke as one of Genet's criminal-saints.

Throughout this time, Allen was being warned by his father, Eugene, Lucien Carr, and Jack (who had returned from California) to get rid of Huncke. They saw him as a parasite, living off Allen and distracting him from any real creative activity. Louis was convinced that Huncke had some blackmail hold over Allen; he could see no other reason for their friendship. Eugene was also concerned for Allen's mental state. At one point he went to visit Allen, bringing with him an attractive young woman from his teachers' training college. "Allen immediately embarrassed me by urinating in the sink, so I was ashamed to ask her out again."

One day when Allen returned from work, Huncke told him that Vickie Russell and her boyfriend Little Jack Melody had visited. Allen had not seen Vickie for a year or so, and he knew Little Jack only by reputation, since, until recently, he had been in a federal prison for robbing a safe. Little Jack had helped Vickie kick a junk habit by taking her out to his family home in Long Island.

At the beginning of March, Vickie and Little Jack visited Allen. Vickie was as striking as ever—"a six feet marijuana smoking redhead," as the New York *Daily News* was to call her. Allen had been expecting Little Jack to be a big gangster type, but he was a half-bald, elfin, twenty-six-year-old Sicilian-American with "doe-like gentility and interest and sympathy with things and people around him," as Allen described him at the time. He and Allen got on well, and over the next few days Vickie and Little Jack spent a lot of time visiting, bringing marijuana with them and getting involved in long conversations about Cézanne, Spengler, and the nature of the universe. Little Jack often got pet ideas of a vaguely cosmic nature, which he found it difficult to express, and it became somehow embarrassing to disagree or not to show the appropriate amount of enthusiasm for what he was trying to say.

Toward the end of March, Allen had a recurrence of a bronchial illness that had bothered him on and off for about a year, so it was Huncke's turn to nurse Allen as he spent a few days in bed. Seeing that Allen had no music in the house (Huncke having stolen the phonograph from his previous apartment), Little Jack brought over his phonograph and some of Vickie's jazz records, including a set of Billie Holiday songs. There were other gifts, mostly books and food. Most nights were spent at the apartment. Toward dawn, Little Jack and Vickie usually went to sleep in Allen's bed. When Allen returned from work in the morning he would sleep on the couch, or on the floor if Huncke was on the couch. He worried about his inability to keep control of even his own bed but continued to say nothing.

Little Jack began to move in small items of furniture, including a painting he had done of Vickie, which made her look surprisingly savage. By this time there was a great deal of marijuana about the place; they smoked it in an opium pipe that was kept on the mantel. Little Jack and Vickie were feeling very much at home.

Kerouac was a regular visitor, and he and Allen spent hours walking around the city streets, discussing their work. Jack had revised *The Town and the City*, and it was through Allen that he found a publisher. Allen had pressured Mark Van Doren into reading the manuscript and set up a meeting between him and Jack. Van Doren was impressed and recommended the book to Robert Giroux at Harcourt Brace; it was accepted on his word. Jack received an advance of one thousand dollars against royalties and was overjoyed. Allen was pleased for him, but also envious and depressed.

Virtually all of Allen's poetry at that time was dense and abstract. But Kerouac understood and liked it and was genuinely convinced that it was the work of a genius. At parties and to new acquaintances, he and Allen promoted each other's work tirelessly. They were so close throughout this time that their conversation became quite hermetic, their numerous references to each other's work and to shared mystical understandings like a secret language that none of their friends could penetrate. Not all of Allen's work was filled with dense mysticism; in the spring of 1949 he started a poem:

> *I love the Lord on high*
> *I wish he'd pull my daisy . . .*

to which Kerouac wrote the refrain:

> *Pull my daisy,*
> *Tip my cup,*
> *All my doors are open.*

This collaboration grew in length and was the first thing Ginsberg would publish outside of college and the local New Jersey papers.

While Allen was in bed sick, he and Huncke had long talks. Huncke advised Allen to get out of his menial job at Associated

Press and plan for the future. The irony in this role reversal was not lost on either of them, but Allen realized that Huncke was right. He decided that teaching would give him enough money to be psychoanalyzed and enough time to write. Allen wrote to Lionel Trilling, who had once offered to help him get an instructorship at Cooper Union.

Having decided to leave Associated Press, he took up an invitation from Bill and Joan to spend the summer in New Orleans. He was concerned about the apartment, which he would need when he returned in the fall. However, he did not want to return and find Huncke still there. Little Jack had spoken to him about needing an apartment to "operate out of," but Allen had purposely not taken the hint and decided to let Eugene have it for the summer. There was a serious flaw with the New Orleans trip. Allen had no savings, and there were unpaid bills.

By now Allen was quite weary of Huncke's sponging, and there was constant tension between them, but even though he told Huncke how futile he thought their parasitical relationship was and how withdrawn from him he felt, he stopped short of telling Huncke to go, so of course Huncke stayed.

Little Jack and Vickie relieved the situation a little by suggesting that Huncke join forces with them on various projects, and Huncke again brought up the subject of Allen's subletting the apartment to Little Jack. Allen didn't want to, but Jack offered to do up the place, pay off all the bills, and give Allen the fifty dollars he needed to get to New Orleans. Allen accepted. In fact, they had already practically moved in. Little Jack and Vickie were using Allen's bedroom, and Vickie had brought clothes and makeup. Several weeks before, Jack and Huncke had cleaned up the apartment and rearranged the furniture. Allen had not minded; the old arrangement was what he had found when he moved in. The housekeeping and changing of the sheets was already done by Vickie, and Huncke was in charge of dishwashing.

Allen's possessions were gradually moved into a bureau drawer in the living room. He did not supervise this job, either, for Huncke, ever since he moved in, had been wearing Allen's clothes, and Allen was never sure where to find his personal belongings. Huncke had even appropriated a few drawers in Allen's desk in which to keep his own papers and trinkets. Allen's journal revealed his attitude at the time: "Didn't bother much about it. It saved me the trouble of thinking for myself on 'small' matters."

He was weary and complained that it was almost impossible to write in the chaos of the apartment, although many of the poems in *Empty Mirror* and *The Gates of Wrath*, such as "The Shrouded Stranger" and "Psalm I," date from this period. While he ruminated about "ghosts that stood in blood," Huncke and Vickie heisted automobiles. One evening in early April, Little Jack, Vickie, and Huncke asked Allen if he would like to come along on a job. He said yes. He was interested in seeing the gang in operation, just as he had previously watched Garver at work stealing coats at Horn & Hardart; he wanted no share of the spoils.

They cruised around midtown, stopping at one point for Huncke and Vickie to break into a car and steal a woman's coat. Next, they found a row of likely-looking cars. They parked around the corner and asked Allen if he would like to come and act as "lookout." He declined, and after a while they returned, empty-handed. He later wrote: "My feelings at the time were mixed. I had gone along with them on the ride, not knowing how I would react or what would happen. I thought, possibly, I might take part in a car haul. But I did not, when the opportunity arose, from a clammy feeling of fear and desire not to get involved in the actual operation. We had discussed my feelings in the car; they (especially Little Jack) were quick to defer and even sympathise with my desire to keep my 'cherry' as we referred to it."

The apartment gradually filled with stolen goods. One morning, Allen came home to find two huge sacks of rolls and bread in the kitchen. He ate some rolls and gave a loaf of bread to the old woman who lived next door. He was surprised to find an enormous cigarette machine in the kitchen, covered with a blanket. It stood there for several days, until Allen demanded that they get rid of it; Little Jack and Huncke broke it up and disposed of it.

On Easter Sunday, 1949, Allen watched the Fifth Avenue parade with Lucien Carr, then he went home to sleep before going to work. He spent Monday with his father and returned to the city on Tuesday, to find a letter waiting from Bill Burroughs and another from Joan. Bill had been arrested for possession of narcotics and his house searched. Among the items seized by the police were letters from Allen discussing the possibility of selling pot in New York. As the letter showed, and as Bill had told the police, the deal never went through, and Bill was sure that the FBI would not bother Allen, but just to make sure, Bill suggested that Allen keep his apartment clean. Huncke had opened the letter and shown it to

Little Jack and Vickie. They discussed the matter and reassured Allen that if the police came looking for drugs, they would not notice the stolen goods. Nonetheless, Allen grew more and more anxious and felt a growing sense of doom. He knew he was being used but felt incapable of doing anything about it.

That evening, Little Jack and Vickie pulled another robbery, arriving home at about 9 P.M. Allen helped them carry the loot, mostly clothes, up from the car, then went to find Lucien, who was working for UPI as a news reporter. Lucien was seeing an analyst and had been writing short stories. He had been released from Elmira on parole, and his freedom was dependent on his leading a blameless life. Although he still saw his old friends, like Allen, he could not afford to be associated with anything illegal. Lucien's shift ended at ten-thirty that evening, and he and Allen walked and talked all night. Allen showed Lucien Bill's letter, which provoked from Lucien a serious lecture, rebuking Allen for letting Jack, Vickie, and Huncke walk all over him. Carr remembered: "I told him, you better watch yourself, because these are a bunch of thieves you are dealing with here, and when the cops come down on them, they're gonna come down on you." He asked if Allen had disposed of papers, journals, letters from Neal, Burroughs, or any others that could possibly be incriminating. Allen admitted that he had intended to do so but had not; he felt ashamed.

For a long time, Lucien had asked Allen never to mention him, in even the most innocent of ways, in his correspondence and journals. Allen had ignored his warnings and kept Burroughs up to date on Lucien's activities and health, and these letters were now in the hands of the New Orleans police. Although there was nothing incriminating in them—Lucien was living an exemplary life—he was angry at Allen for endangering him. He was also horrified to find that even as they were walking around the city, Allen was "tempting fate" by leaving his journals and papers all over the house. Allen resolved to take care of the matter as soon as he got home. He returned at 6 A.M. Little Jack and Vickie were in his bed, Huncke was on the couch, so Allen slept on the floor.

Huncke was very resentful that day at not having been included in the robbery; he felt that he was not really a part of Jack and Vickie's team. He also resented doing the household chores. While Huncke complained, threatening to go away and live on his own, Allen sorted through his papers, taking out all the most sensitive material. He put about a hundred of his letters in a manila envelope, along with unsorted obscene autobiographical or confessional prose fragments that he did not want to get into the wrong hands. Then he returned the envelope to the drawer, intending to take it to Eugene's room and store it among a pile of old legal documents. Allen no longer felt secure about storing things in Paterson; the year before, Louis had started to read through his old homosexual love letters and writings.

Allen spent the next several hours assembling his poetry for a book, and he bound it all up together to take with him to work that night. In the evening, while Allen slept, Little Jack, Vickie, and Huncke pulled another robbery, returning to the house at about nine and waking Allen to help them unload the car. There were lamps, clothes, radios, cameras, and piles of pornographic books. The name written in the books was that of a high-ranking policeman; it was his Jackson Heights home they had just robbed.

That evening, Allen stopped off at John Clellon Holmes's place, looking for Kerouac; he was there. Allen had still not disposed of his incriminating papers and asked Jack if he was planning to stop by York Avenue later that night to see Huncke, because if he did, Allen would like him to take his journals and correspondence home with him to the safety of Ozone Park. Jack had not planned to visit Huncke and pointed out that since the New Orleans police also had his letters to Bill, his address was no safer than Allen's. "Yes, it's true," said Allen, disappointed at Jack's unwillingness to take the problem off his hands. Jack added, "Besides, if you really wanted to get them out of the house, you would have done so already yourself."

Allen felt such a twinge of remorse and anxiety at his inability to deal with the matter that he dropped the subject, after agreeing that his behavior had been confused. He later wrote: "But this agreement did not make amends for my lack of action. I felt even more the pressure of reality—a real world in which for some desperate reason of vanity or fear, I was manoeuvering myself, and everyone I knew, into some immediate catastrophe."

He got home from work just after nine the next morning, April 22. Allen pointed out to Little Jack that when he agreed to sublet the apartment, he had not intended that it be used as a center for burglaries. He asked them to clear all the stolen property out of the place. Little Jack agreed to remove everything by the next day. In fact, he had already planned to take the clothes out to an Italian friend on Long Island that morning. Allen still had all his letters and journals in his desk and asked if he could come along for the ride and be dropped off at Eugene's on the way back. That way he would be home by 2 P.M. and get some sleep before going to work at midnight. They loaded the car, and Allen sat in the back with the stolen clothes.

At twelve-thirty, they were driving along Northern Boulevard in Queens, Allen telling them about his trip to Dakar; Jack missed his turn and got off the highway to turn back. A patrol car signaled them to stop. They pulled over, and the policeman parked his car and began walking toward them. Jack was driving the wrong way up a one-way street. Patrolman McClancy pulled out his pad to write up a citation. Little Jack panicked. He was out on parole and forbidden to drive, so he couldn't show his license. Besides, he was driving a stolen car.

In a squeal of tires, he backed up, then U-turned, burning rubber, and sped off down Forty-third Avenue. The officer leapt back into his car with his partner and gave chase, siren blaring, and according to one newspaper report, he fired at the fleeing car with his revolver.

"We have to outrun them," yelled Little Jack. "We'll have to abandon the car." Vickie began to protest about leaving all the stolen goods. "Fuck the clothes!" yelled Jack. "We have to abandon the whole mess." By this time they were traveling so fast that Allen was too frightened even to look back to see if the police were on their tail. He sat, surrounded by stolen clothes, wondering if he should throw the manila envelope of letters out the window.

At first he had assumed that the seriousness of the situation was mostly to do with Jack's parole violation, then it quickly dawned on him that he was in serious trouble. "I began more clearly to see that the great horror had begun to descend at last," he wrote later.

After four blocks, Little Jack struck the curb, attempting to make a turn. Allen felt the car begin to turn over. He somehow relaxed himself enough to roll with it. He sang out, "Lord God of Israel, Isaac, and Abraham." His glasses flew off, and the stolen clothes and manuscripts tumbled around him in the car as it rolled over twice and came to rest upside down.

The next thing he heard was Little Jack's asking if everyone was all right and urging them to get out and run. The doors were all open, and Allen rolled out into the street. He stumbled about, looking for his glasses and papers among the heaps of clothes and broken glass, but all he could find was one unimportant journal from

1943–44. "I remember the horror of the scramble after them," he wrote. "And the sickening feeling of failure when I saw everything upside down and confused, including myself."

Incredibly, Allen escaped and was able to make his way back to the apartment. Then Vickie arrived and announced that Little Jack had been arrested. She and Huncke were planning an escape when the police knocked on the door and arrested all three of them. They had found the address in the papers left behind in the overturned car. Allen was kept behind bars at the Long Island House of Detention until his father got him out on bail.

FOUR | THE SUBTERRANEANS

We are healed of a suffering only by experiencing it to the full.

—Marcel Proust, *The Sweet Cheat Gone*

ALLEN SAT ON A CHAIR IN THE SIXTH-FLOOR WARD OF COLUMBIA PRES-byterian Psychiatric Institute, waiting to be shown his bed. He was joined by a tall, overweight Jewish boy in thick glasses, with a towel wrapped around his head. The young man was still shaky and re-covering his composure after an insulin shock treatment (patients were revived from the deep coma produced by insulin shock with intravenous injections of glucose). Seeing Allen, he inquired ami-cably, "Who are you?"

"I'm Myshkin," Allen said. (Myshkin was the saintly character in Dostoyevsky's *The Idiot*.)

"I'm Kirilov," came the reply. (Kirilov was the demonic nihilist in *The Possessed*.) Allen felt an immediate rapport with this new acquaintance, whose name was Carl Solomon, and began to tell him about his vision of William Blake. Afterward Allen wrote Jack: "It is very embarrassing, in a mad house, to do this. He accepted me as if I were another nutty ignu, saying at the same time, with a tone of conspiratorial glee, 'O well, you're new here. Just wait awhile and you'll meet some of the other (repentant) mystics.' "

Carl, two years younger than Allen, was born in the Bronx on March 30, 1928. Something of a prodigy, he had graduated at age fifteen from Townsend Harris High School for the gifted, then gone to City College, where he joined the youth branch of the Communist Party. When he was seventeen, he entered the U.S. Maritime Service and began to alternate a term in college with one at sea. In 1947, he jumped ship in France, joined the French Communist Party, and moved in with a Pigalle prostitute, Odette Belmaure. In Paris he became deeply involved with the European avant garde. He had read Artaud's essay on Van Gogh, *"Le Suicide de la Société,"* and one hot night in July he saw Artaud himself do a terrifying performance of "Ci-Git," trembling and screaming at the top of his lungs, an experience that had a profound effect on Carl's life.

Back in New York, he left City College for the more arts-oriented Brooklyn College and moved to Greenwich Village, where he hung out with Trotskyists and Reichians. When he heard that Wallace Markfield was to lecture on "Stéphane Mallarmé and Alienation" in a hall near the Brooklyn College campus, he and two friends, Leni Grunes and Ronnie Gold, decided to stage a Dadaist event. They bought potato salad at a delicatessen and threw it at the astonished lecturer, an event that Ginsberg later immortalized, with some poetic license, in "Howl": "who threw potato salad at CCNY lecturers on Dadaism . . ."

Carl later commented: "I gave Allen an apocryphal history of my adventures and pseudo-intellectual deeds of daring. He meticulously took notes of everything I said (I thought at the time that he suffered from 'the writer's disease,' imagined that he was a great writer). Later, when I decided to give up the flesh and become a professional lunatic-saint, he published all of this data, compounded partly of truth, but for the most part raving self-justification, crypto-bohemian boasting a la Rimbaud, effeminate prancing, and esoteric aphorisms plagiarized from Kierkegaard and others—in the form of 'Howl.' Thus he enshrined falsehood as truth and raving as common sense for future generations to ponder over and be misled."

"Howl for Carl Solomon" did contain many images taken from Carl's life story, though most of them were transformed or universalized. Carl had become interested in Gide's idea of *"le crime gratuit"*—gratuitous crime—and committed one in his own small way. He stole a peanut butter sandwich from the Brooklyn College cafeteria and showed it to a policeman. He was sent to a psychiatrist. He was in a very negative mood, and as his twenty-first birthday approached, he and Ronnie Gold began to talk a lot about the validity of suicide. Finally, on his birthday, Carl presented himself at the Psychiatric Institute, demanding a lobotomy, a symbolic suicide—or to be "suicided," as Artaud put it. This, too, was enshrined in "Howl": ". . . and subsequently presented themselves on the granite steps of the madhouse with shaven heads and harlequin speech of suicide, demanding instantaneous lobotomy." He was admitted.

Allen's tenure at the Psychiatric Institute was the result of the combined forces of Columbia University, Lionel Trilling, and his father. After his arrest he was forbidden to have any contact with Huncke, Little Jack, or Vickie. Trilling took him to see Professor Herbert Wechsler at Columbia Law School, who told him to commit himself voluntarily to a mental hospital and plead guilty, and that he would then get off. Trilling recommended a psychiatrist, Dr. Fagin, who said that in his opinion, for the immediate future, Allen was too sick to do anything except go to a psychiatric hospital. He was sicker than he, or anyone, knew, Fagin told Allen darkly. Allen breathed a sigh of relief. He wrote Jack: "I have manoeuvred myself to a position I have always fancied the most proper and true for me. . . . I really believe, or want to believe, really I am nuts, otherwise I'll never be sane." He described his position as quite serious. "I've gotten so hung up on myself now it isn't funny anymore. I stop in the middle of conversations, laughing shrilly—stare at people with perfect sobriety and remorse, and then go on cackling away."

Van Doren told Allen that he had to choose between criminals and society. "If you do believe that Huncke is some sort of criminal saint or illuminated being, then you have to follow through with your choice and perhaps even go to jail for your beliefs, although some of us here have been thinking that it might be a good thing for you to hear the clank of iron." Allen asked if there was a middle choice, and Van Doren insisted there was not. He said that Allen had exaggerated and romanticized Huncke. This was certainly the view of Allen's lawyer, who met Huncke and described him as a "filthy stinking mess. One look at him and you can tell he's no good." Meyer Schapiro was the only one at Columbia with a more open and sympathetic attitude. He invited Allen over, and they had a long talk about spiritual matters and vagrancy. Schapiro recounted that he had been arrested and put in jail for being a "stateless bum" in Europe as a young traveler, which made Allen feel a little better.

Louis had remarried; his new wife was an attractive, vivacious younger woman named Edith. She was from Paterson, and they were house hunting together in order to start their new life in a new home. Allen lived quietly at home with them and heard no news of the case until the beginning of June, when he was told that he had been cleared by the grand jury but that the other three were to go to court. Allen had not known that Dr. Allan Cott, Mark Van Doren, Lionel and Diana Trilling, and Dean Carmen would all attend the hearing and testify on his behalf. He wrote Jack: "I don't know any details. But I must say that's mightily cricket of them all. I was really worried last month. . . . I feel grateful. . . . That's what Van Doren means by society I suppose, people getting together to keep each other out of trouble (or away from tragedy) till they get an inkling of what they're getting into." His legal costs were one thousand dollars, which were paid by Louis and Eugene. It was arranged that he would go to Columbia Presbyterian Psychiatric Institute on 168th Street but would continue to spend his days in Paterson until a bed became vacant.

Most of his news from the outside world came through Kerouac, who was very supportive through this difficult time. He kept up a stream of letters discussing poetry, his new novel (*Dr. Sax*), and the latest gossip, using pseudonyms for their friends—e.g., Huk for Huncke, Dennison for Burroughs—because Louis was now opening Allen's mail.

In addition to his remarriage, Louis's life had been changed by Naomi's release that spring from Pilgrim State. Although recovered sufficiently to be discharged, she was not well enough to look after herself or get a job, so she moved back in with Eleanor, becoming a financial drain on Louis, Eleanor, and Eugene. Allen was all the more guilt-ridden about his own financial imposition on Louis and Eugene. He felt close to his mother, particularly now that he was officially "mad" like her, and his sympathy was shown in a journal entry from that period: "That night at Eleanor's, I suddenly became angry at Eleanor, and inwardly sickly at my brother because they so patronized and baffled and fogged the natural exuberance and innocent perception of Naomi; however, Naomi too started compulsively blindly questioning me in repeated monotones, about my travels, which she's half forgotten, till I became weary of all. . . . I feel I could half start a conspiracy of the insane with her, underground—but she goes blank and mechanical often."

Two and a half months after his arrest, the day after his birthday, Allen entered the Psychiatric Institute. The previous day, he wrote reflectively in his journal: "I have been wrathful all my life, angry against my father and all others. My wrath must end. All my images now are of heaven. I dream of incomprehensible love and belief. I think always that I am about to put an end to my life, only now there is no worry as to how I will do it, as last summer after the vision. In the hospital I hope to be cured. My images tell me that the hours of truth are at hand. I am not going to die, I am going to live anew. My thought has been peaceful all week. I have been reading *The Possessed*. My devils have been cast out." The entry is strikingly similar to Naomi's saying, "I will think nothing but beautiful thoughts."

Another birthday journal entry revealed the extent of his feeling of isolation. "Tonite all is well . . . what a terrible future. I am 23, the year of the iron birthday, the gate of darkness. I am ill. I have become spiritually or practically impotent in my madness this last month. I suddenly realized that my head is severed from my body, I realized it a few nights ago." This sad passage was later transcribed almost verbatim to become the second poem in his collection *Empty Mirror*.

There had been a bureaucratic mix-up, and on June 6 he recorded: "Back home. Hitch in madhouse venture." The hitch was only temporary, however, and on June 29, 1949, he was installed in the sixth-floor ward of the P.I., overlooking the Hudson River. Jack, who was in Denver for the summer, wrote an encouraging letter, but warned Allen to be careful, when he was trying to convince the doctors he was not crazy, that he also didn't convince himself.

Allen spent a lot of time sunning himself on the roof, looking out at the George Washington Bridge and the boats plowing up the Hudson. Under the influence of the doctors, he began to question the significance of his Blake vision, and he wrote Kerouac: "The people here see more visions in one day than I do in a year." The P.I. was doing its work. Having been convinced that he was sick, he was now encouraged to reject madness and return to the fold. In so doing, he drew away from Naomi. He ended the same letter to Kerouac: "I am beginning to hate my mother."

For Allen to be "cured," he also had to reject Burroughs. Bill made this easier for him by launching into one of his tirades against liberals. Bill had been appalled that Allen had allowed himself to be told what to do by his father and the Columbia establishment instead of fighting the case himself. He wrote Kerouac: "If I was in Al's place I would say, 'Go ahead and place your charges, if any.' His present position is insufferable. Imagine being herded around by a lot of old women like Louis Ginsberg and Van Doren. Besides I don't see why Van Doren puts in his 2 cents worth. Sniveling old liberal fruit."

Kerouac reported Bill's views to Allen, who replied sadly: "I have discovered that I have no feelings, just thoughts, borrowed thought taken from someone I admire because he seems to have feeling." Allen began to question his whole relationship with Bill, and in particular all the insights of his year of amateur analysis with him. "O Bleak Bill," Allen wrote Jack. "He is afraid that I will find out that he is crazy, that his analysis of me was a tragic farce—not an absurd farce, but a tragic real one—that he has led me astray." Allen told Jack: "Reality, as [Bill] well knows, is that familial and social community which we, as madmen, have discontinued."

For the next seven months Allen tried hard to get back to "reality," but it was not as easy as he thought. He was given no drugs or shock therapy. He saw a psychiatrist two or three times a week and during his stay there had four different doctors, all of whom thought their job was to make Allen conform and fit into a *Saturday Evening Post* view of society, with a wife and an ordinary job. But Allen said he wanted life to be "a sweet humane surprise." When he looked at himself he saw a miracle, and he thought others should see miracles in themselves as well, but the doctors didn't understand. "Do you still think you are superior to other people and different?" they asked. Finally, to please them, he said no, but the lie upset him. "I think if I had argued a lot I could have got myself into a lot of trouble," he said later.

Allen tried to cooperate and get some good out of his hospitalization; he even thought that perhaps the doctors had a secret knowledge. He kept expecting miracles to happen in return for agreeing and conforming, but they were raw young interns, who were unable to find the underlying causes of his anxiety or his real feelings and needs. They discouraged all talk of visions, and most displays of individuality by their patients were dismissed as "ward nuttiness." One time, as a joke, Allen and Carl began banging on the piano and yelling as if they were crazy, and the doctors came running in horror —the "catatonic piano" in "Howl."

Allen quickly adapted to the routine. There was a time to shave (after which all the razors were locked up), a time to eat, and a time to sleep. He was allowed out daily from four until seven in the evening and from 4 P.M. on Friday until Sunday night, provided someone took responsibility for him, so his social life was not too

disrupted. Jack returned to New York from Denver in late August
with Neal, and Allen spent most weekends with them. Neal had
again abandoned Carolyn, who was now pregnant with their second
child and demanding child support for their first. Neal took a job
parking cars and moved in with a girl named Diana Hansen, whom
he also made pregnant. Since she was the only one with an apartment, she found herself playing host to both Allen and Jack most
weekends, one of them taking the spare bed and the other sleeping
in the armchair.

Allen's ideological dispute with Burroughs intensified. He wrote
Bill that he was considering returning to his old idea of being a labor
leader when he got out of the P.I., an idea calculated to enrage
Burroughs. "I hope you are not serious in this labor leader idea,"
he ranted. "My opinion of labor leaders and unions is very close to
the views so ably and vigorously expressed by Westbrook Pegler,
the only columnist, in my opinion, who possesses a grain of integ-
rity." Both Kerouac and his father had always loved Pegler's column—ultra-right, fanatically anti-Communist diatribes typical of
the cold war period. "That was one of Kerouac's ways of making
fun of me, because he knew I hated Westbrook Pegler," Ginsberg
later said. He was less sure of himself in the P.I. and wrote to ask
Lucien's opinion of Pegler. Lucien replied in classic hipster argot,
characterizing Pegler as "a mouldy fig with nuts."

Meanwhile, Burroughs fulminated to Kerouac: "I fear the U.S. is
heading for Socialism. . . . Allen, by the way, has been utterly corrupted by those liberal psychiatrists. He talks of becoming a labor
leader! I wrote him what I think of labor leaders, unions and liberals. Perhaps I should have restrained myself, but I am a plain blunt
man who speaks right on. Allen is aligning himself with a cancerous
element that will stifle every vestige of free life in the U.S." Allen
wrote Bill: "Really, dearie, we know so little about home economics
that all this b.s. about Stateism . . . and welfare state is just a
W. C. Fields act. Vow for my part, it would make things no worse
for me if we had socialism. Trouble with you is you never had to
work for a living." He ended, "As for me, I have nothing better to
do than to help those less fortunate than myself. . . ."

Carl introduced Allen to the work of Jean Genet, Henri Michaux,
and Antonin Artaud, writers whose works were later cited by Ginsberg as influences on the composition of "Howl." Carl bought an
under-the-counter copy of Genet's *Our Lady of the Flowers* at the
Gotham Book Mart and smuggled it into the P.I., and he showed

Allen the April 1949 issue of *Partisan Review*, which contained a long article about Genet. He also had a copy of *Tiger's Eye*, containing Artaud's article on Van Gogh, and the Samuel Putnam anthology *The European Caravan*, which contained Artaud's "To Be Done with the Judgement of God." All this work impressed Allen enormously and, to an extent, counterbalanced the efforts of the doctors to turn him into their conception of a well-adjusted American.

Allen reciprocated by telling Carl all about Kerouac, Cassady, and Burroughs. They spent their afternoons sitting in the dayroom and arguing over Walt Whitman and what it meant to be a poet. When Carl first met Allen, he called him a "dopey daffodil," a reference to Wordsworth, because Allen saw the poet as a "sensitive soul," whereas Carl preferred Artaud's concept of the poet as a brute. After reading Genet and Artaud, Allen began to come around to Carl's point of view.

As the months went by, the doctors at the P.I. convinced Allen that his only hope was to return to Paterson, get a job, find a girl, and try to fit into society. Allen recognized that there was a tremendous gulf between him and ordinary people, and after eight months of treatment he believed the doctors when they said that once he closed this gulf, he would be cured. He was told that he would be released in February 1950, and he set about trying to get a job in Paterson.

He applied to the *Morning Call*, the *Evening News* and the Passaic *Evening News*, but to no avail. His luck in finding a girl was no better. He wrote Kerouac: "I wish I could meet a really gone sweet girl who could love me, but I guess a really gone sweet girl is too much to expect. Why is everything so hard?" At this time Kerouac was the only person Allen could really open up to, and he responded as a true friend. On January 13, 1950, Jack wrote to him at the P.I. to tell him that he admired him, loved him, and considered him a great man. Such valuable friendship helped Allen to bolster his shattered ego and take charge of his life again.

On February 27, Allen left the P.I. and moved in with his father and stepmother at their new home at 416 East 34th Street, Paterson. He had his own room, and there was a big, dry attic where he could store all his papers and books. There was no need for Allen to hide his manuscripts anymore; there were hardly any secrets left. Besides, he was now a heterosexual, albeit a virgin one. The doctors at the P.I. had cured him, or at least convinced him to give heterosexuality a try for his own good. His doctor had met with Allen,

Edith, and Louis to talk things over, then Allen left the room. Edith later told him that the doctor said, "You want to have a close relation with your son. He is partly homosexual. If you really want to have a close relation, you have to accept that, even to the point of receiving his lovers in your home, and if you want a really close relation, of allowing them to stay over." Ginsberg later said, "This did a world of good, because my father believed in authority, and if that was the word, it relieved him of the necessity to come down hard and worry and be scandalized." But it would be quite a while before the time came to test their tolerance, because for the next five years, Allen was to have a series of apparently satisfactory heterosexual relationships. As he wrote to Jack on the day he was released: "A turning point has been reached in that I am no longer going to have homosexual affairs: my will is free enough now to put this in writing in a final statement."

Although to the people of Paterson, Louis Ginsberg was their most famous poet, largely through his weekly column of puns in the local press, their city was also under scrutiny from a quite different artistic eye, that of the poet William Carlos Williams, writing from nearby Rutherford. Williams's five-book epic *Paterson* was a mixture of poetry and prose, quotations from newspapers and letters, idiomatic fragments of everyday American speech and chunks of stodgy local history. Williams was the first poet since Whitman and Dickinson to find a distinctly American voice. Half British on his father's side, he spent his life battling against the European influence of his fellow Americans T. S. Eliot and Ezra Pound. Pound was an old friend; they first met when Williams was studying medicine at the University of Pennsylvania in 1902, and it was through Pound that he met the poet Hilda Doolittle (H.D., as Pound subsequently named her).

Williams led a double life. An overworked local doctor, making house calls, delivering babies, prescribing medicines to his mostly impoverished patients, he was also the prolific author of plays and stories, poems and essays. Although he traveled to Paris and met most of the leading lights of modernism, he preferred the obscurity of Rutherford, where he lived and worked throughout his life.

On March 2, 1950, Williams gave a reading at the Guggenheim Museum in New York. Allen attended and afterward went backstage to meet Williams, but he changed his mind and waved to him instead. Two days later, he wrote Williams a long letter.

"Dear Doctor," he said. "In spite of the grey secrecy of time and my own self-shuttering doubts in these youthful rainy days, I would like to make my presence in Paterson known to you, and hope you will welcome this from me, an unknown young poet, to you, an unknown old poet, who live in the same rusty county of the world. Not only do I inscribe this missive somewhat in the style of those courteous sages of yore who recognized one another across the generations as brotherly children of the muses (whose names they well knew) but also as fellow citizenly Chinamen of the same province, whose gastanks, junkyards, fens of the alley, millways, funeral parlors, river-visions—aye! the falls itself—are images white-woven in their very beards. . . .

"I envision for myself some kind of new speech—different at least from what I have been writing down—in that it has to be a clear statement of fact about misery (and not misery itself), and splendor if there is any out of the subjective wanderings through Paterson. This place is as I say my natural habitat by memory, and I am not following in your traces to be poetic: though I know you will be pleased to realize that at least one actual citizen of your community has inherited your experience in his struggle to love and know his own world-city, through your work, which is an accomplishment you almost cannot have hoped to achieve."

He enclosed nine poems, the best of his total output, including "Ode to Sunset," which he spent many months writing at the P.I., and a recent "Ode to Judgement." The sixty-six-year-old Williams was amazed and delighted to receive such a letter, which must have seemed a response to his work from the streets of Paterson. The combination of the arrogance of youth and an obvious poetic vision charmed him so much that he included the entire letter, and a subsequent one, in Part Four of "Paterson." He was less delighted with Ginsberg's poetry. He replied, saying that the poems were not very good. "In this mode, perfection is basic," he wrote, referring to rhymed verse, and Allen's poems were imperfect. Ginsberg later said, "I took this to mean that there was very little concrete detail in them, it was all a sort of refining of the imagery of roses and light and mystical references—rehashing of it over again. I'd thought maybe if I could concentrate all my mind's focus into these few symbols and juggle them round a couple of times, make some crystal-like perfect symbolic statement that would turn other people on and catalyze the same vision in them. But it didn't work."

Williams, as an imagist, believed "No ideas but in things," a basic rule that, when he finally applied it, totally transformed Ginsberg's poetry. Williams wanted to "Get form without deforming the language," and by language he meant everyday American speech, not the carefully pronounced British diction of formal poetry. In *I Wanted to Write a Poem*, Williams explained: "The rhythmical construction of a poem was determined for me by the language as it is spoken. Word of mouth language, not classical English." Allen had to get rid of his "thee"s and "thou"s before his work would be acceptable to the doctor.

Allen's uncle Leo got him a job as a reporter on a labor newspaper, the *Labor Herald*, the official journal of the New Jersey AFL. It was published in Newark, so Allen had to rise early to make the fifteen-mile trip to work each day, but in other respects the job was ideal, combining his ill-defined desire to become a labor leader and his vocation as a writer. He became more involved with life in Paterson, walking the streets, investigating the area around River Street, near where he grew up, with the same determination with which he had explored the bars on Eighth Avenue in Manhattan five years before. He wrote Williams: "Do you know this part of Paterson? I have seen so many things—negroes, gypsies, an incoherent bartender in a taproom overhanging the river, filled with gas, ready to explode, the window facing the river painted over so that people can't see it. I wonder if you have seen River Street most of all, because that really is at the heart of what is to be known."

Allen still went to the city every weekend to attend parties or just to hang out at the San Remo. The San Remo bar, at the northwest corner of Bleecker and MacDougal streets, was the center of the bohemian life of Greenwich Village throughout the late forties and early fifties. Among its regulars were James Agee, Larry Rivers, Paul Goodman, John Cage, Merce Cunningham, Chester Kallman, Harold Norse, and virtually everybody associated with Judith Malina and Julian Beck's newly launched Living Theater. These were the people whose stories Allen would tell in "Howl."

Allen's crowd included Carl Solomon, Lucien Carr, Jack Kerouac, the young poet Philip Lamantia, and Bill Cannastra. Russell Durgin also turned up there, though they saw less of him after he got married that June. Alan Ansen was a regular whenever he was in town, and John Kingsland was often seen in the company of an attractive young woman called Dusty Moreland. Allen had had his eye on her before he went to the P.I., and now that he was looking for a girl, he paid her special attention. Allen referred to the people at the San Remo as the "subterraneans," a name that Kerouac used later for his book about them. In it he gave Allen credit: "The subterraneans is a name invented by Adam Moorad [Ginsberg's name in the book] who is a poet and friend of mine who said, 'They are hip without being slick, they are intelligent without being corny, they are intellectual as hell and know all about Pound without being pretentious or talking too much about it, they are very quiet, they are very Christlike.' " Even if the quote sounds more like Kerouac's voice, the sobriquet at least was Ginsberg's.

Another term for this group had already been coined, but it had been all but forgotten. "Beat Generation" was a phrase discovered by Jack Kerouac and John Clellon Holmes in the fall of 1949, while Allen was in the P.I. Their accounts differ as to what occurred.

"We were talking about the Lost Generation and what this generation would be called," said Kerouac, "and we thought of various names and I said, 'Ah, this is really a Beat Generation!'—and he leaped up and said, 'You've got it!'—see, just like that."

Holmes said, "Jack and I never talked about the Lost Generation particularly. You see, when Jack used that phrase, we certainly didn't say 'That's it! That's it!' and make a big issue out of it."

Either way, three years went by before anyone used it again, and it was only when Holmes's book *Go* was published by Scribner's in 1952, with the line: "You know, everyone I know is kind of furtive, kind of beat . . . a sort of revolution of the soul, I guess you'd call it," that the *New York Times* grabbed hold of the catchy phrase and asked him to write an article about it. Holmes's piece, "This Is the Beat Generation," appeared November 16, 1952, and the Beats were defined as a public phenomenon, long after the fact. The word itself came to them from Huncke, who had been using it, long before he met any of them, to describe the condition he was usually in—beat.

Another of the subterraneans at the San Remo was Jay Landesman, the editor of a popular psychiatric magazine called *Neurotica*. Notable in the Spring 1950 issue were Carl Solomon's powerful "Report from the Asylum—Afterthoughts of a Shock Patient," which he published under the name Carl Goy, and four verses from Ginsberg's "Pull My Daisy," published as "Song: Fie My Fum." Allen wrote to Jack: "I went down on my knees (practically; took me days to recover from the fury) to Landesman to get him to publish 'Pull My Daisy.' He finally agreed but I had to chop the poem down to half its size so he could squeeze it in; it still looks good." It was Allen's first appearance in a commercial magazine.

At the end of May, Allen's life entered a new phase, and he wrote excitedly to Jack from Provincetown, Massachusetts: "If you are in any ennui or doldrums, lift up your heart, there IS something new under the sun. I have started into a new season, choosing women as my theme. I love Helen Parker, and she loves me, as far as the feeble efforts to understanding of three days spent with her in Provincetown can discover. Many of my fears and dun rags fell from me after the first night I slept with her, when we understood that we wanted each other and began a love affair, with all the trimmings of eros and memory and nearly impossible transportation problems."

In his 1955 poem "Transcription of Organ Music," Ginsberg wrote: "I remember when I first got laid, H.P. graciously took my cherry, I sat on the docks of Provincetown, age 23, joyful, elevated in hope with the Father, the door to the womb was open to admit me if I wished to enter."

Allen's life as a heterosexual got off to a wonderful beginning with Helen Parker. She had impeccable literary credentials; older than Allen, she had once been engaged to John Dos Passos, and through him had met Ernest Hemingway and other luminaries. Allen entertained her in his best Well-Groomed Hungarian manner and played the "mad hipster with cosmic vibrations," but also, to his delight, he was able to just be himself and talk seriously and intimately, without recourse to irony, about a gamut of subjects, from obscure metaphysics to everyday problems. "Then we screw, and I am all man and full of love," he told Jack. "The first days after I lost my cherry—does everybody feel like that? I wandered around in the most benign and courteous stupor of delight at the perfection of nature; I felt the ease and relief of knowledge that all the maddening walls of heaven were finally down, that all my aching corridors were travelled out of, that all my queerness was camp, unnecessary, morbid, so lacking in completion and sharing of love as to be almost as bad as impotence and celibacy, which it practically was anyway. And the fantasies I began having about all sorts of girls, for the first time freely and with the knowledge that they were satisfyable. Ah, Jack, I always said that I would be a great lover some day. I am. I am at last."

Allen asked Jack, who was staying with Neal in an apartment next door to Bill and Joan in Mexico City, to "tell me what weary, skeptical comments Bill comes on with." Bill had written him a month before, on May 1, saying: "I am more than a little dubious of a program to overcome queerness by 'attentive work like studying for a job.' I think you will find it is not as simple as that." But for once Bill was wrong. Allen's heterosexual bliss was quite genuine. A picture of the continuing efforts of Allen's P.I. analyst to keep him on the straight path emerged from Bill's letters. Bill wrote: "I simply do not recognize such an entity as a 'neurotic heter with strong queer leanings.' For the Cris sake do you actually think that laying a woman makes some one heter? I have been laying women for the past 15 years and haven't heard any complaints from the women either." (Here Joan annotated Bill's letter with the word "Correct!") Bill continued: "What does that prove except I was hard up at the time? Laying a woman, so far as I'm concerned is O.K. if I can't score for a boy.

"As for this normal man of yours who isn't sexually mature until he is thirty," Bill continued, "I don't buy him. I say he will never be mature, which I can say about 90% of U.S. males. And another thing, I am dubious of these slow changes. *Any basic change is sudden.* Like me getting off junk. I suspect this slow change routine is an analyst alibi." But Allen's affair continued. Helen wrote him in July: "How I miss you—you boy of repressed delight!"

There were some practical problems: She had two children, young boys aged five and ten, who needed a father, something Allen felt sure he could not be. Helen suggested that they set up house-keeping on Cape Cod and that Allen stay at home and write, while she went to work. She also tempted him with the idea of spending the winter in Key West, but Allen's need to continue seeing his analyst and his desire to become financially stable precluded this.

In the middle of May, Neal returned to New York from Mexico City, where he had gone to get a cheap divorce from Carolyn. He and Diana Hansen were already estranged but were getting married to legitimize her forthcoming child. Neal had lost his job parking cars but had been offered a job with the Southern Pacific Railroad, and in typical Cassady fashion, two hours after getting married he set out for California, using his railroad pass; he promised to save money and return as soon as he could. His new wife was left with the uncomfortable suspicion that he was going back to Carolyn and the kids, which of course was true.

At the end of September, Allen received a nasty blow to his pride when he was fired from his job on the *Labor Herald* for incompetence. He was very conscious of his lack of aptitude in practical things, so he decided to rectify this with manual labor. He got a job in a Paterson ribbon factory, at the very good pay of $1.25 an hour. His function was to pick up all the broken threads and tie them back into the loom. He became so self-conscious and stricken with anxiety that he found it impossible to tie the tiny threads at all. He told Neal: "my eyes unfocussed, I would daydream, I lost track of how to do the simplest things and wandered around embarrassedly trying to fit in." They fired him after two and a half weeks. "Truly the real world is my downfall," he complained to Neal.

The logistical difficulties involved in getting to Provincetown meant that Allen was unable to see Helen as often as he would have liked, and in the meantime he began going with a girl in New York called Rayanne. He told Neal that she was "sharp, a real NY 'on the town' pro type." He called up Jack to tell him to come over and meet Rayanne, but Jack said, "I only fuck girls and learn from men, so why should I come up?" Allen, annoyed by his misogyny, wrote him a poison-pen letter and said: "That's why you're so dumb!" Eventually Allen dropped Rayanne, and she had a short affair with Jack.

That summer of 1950, Allen saw a lot of Bill Cannastra, who lived in a loft three doors down from Lucien Carr on Twenty-first Street. Cannastra was a regular at the San Remo, and both he and Lucien gave a lot of parties. Although his sexual preference was for men, Bill was living with a young woman named Joan Haverty, who regarded him as something of a father figure. They played pranks together, creeping down fire escapes and peering into apartments. Cannastra, fond of spying on people, had drilled peepholes in his bathroom wall so that he could watch his guests. He was a heavy drinker "who . . . danced on broken wineglasses barefoot smashed phonograph records of nostalgic European 1930s German jazz finished the whiskey and threw up groaning into the bloody toilet . . ." ("Howl").

One night in October, Bill Cannastra and a group of friends on the town ran out of money, and around midnight Cannastra decided they should take the subway to go and borrow some from Lucien. As they reached the Bleecker Street station, someone mentioned the Bleecker Tavern. The train began to pull out of the station, and Bill, as a joke, leapt up and lunged at the open window, as if he were going to the bar. He misjudged his leap and found himself hanging too far out of the window. The others rushed to pull him back as he struggled to regain his balance, but his coat ripped away in their hands. The train gathered speed, and he began to scream for help. As the train entered the tunnel, he ducked his head to avoid the pillars. There was a thud, and he was torn from their hands, out of the window and onto the roadbed, where he was dragged for fifty-five feet before the train stopped. He was rushed to Columbus Hospital but died on the way.

Joan Haverty now became the subject of much attention. With Lucien's encouragement, Allen began leaving notes, arranging meetings, and showing interest in her. When he finally made his move to sleep with her, however, he failed by being overbearing and impatient with her "sentimental enshrinement of Cannastra's image."

Kerouac had better luck. He had returned from Mexico City and was living at his mother's house in Queens, where he was working on a new book. He moved in with Joan, then they surprised all their friends by getting married. The wedding was one month after Cannastra's death. Allen and Lucien were the best men.

Allen wrote to Neal the next day, describing Joan as "a tall dumb darkhaired girl just made for Jack. Not dumb really, since she's 'sensitive' and troubled." Joan earned her living making dresses. She was only twenty years old and didn't know what she was getting into by marrying Kerouac. The next day he moved in his desk and began writing. The marriage was doomed from the start. Although he was only twenty-seven, Jack held the same old-fashioned, provincial views about marriage as his father; Joan was forbidden to hold any views that differed from his and was not allowed to accompany him when he went out with his buddies, which was much of the time. She had to clean the loft, do the shopping, cook the food, and earn the money to keep them both while he wrote.

One of Jack's reasons for getting married was to find someone to look after his mother, and it was not long before he insisted that they move in with her in Queens. Joan had to hand over her wage check each week to Jack's mother, who treated her as little more than a slave and made her do all the cooking and cleaning. Joan quickly realized that she was being used, and she moved out. She took a downstairs brownstone studio apartment on West Twentieth Street and told Jack he could move in with her if he wanted to; otherwise she would live alone. He moved in, and it was in that apartment, in April 1951, that he wrote the first draft of *On the Road*, while Joan continued to provide for them.

Allen's romance with Helen Parker did not go well, and that fall she left him for the folk singer Ramblin' Jack Elliott. Allen's next affair was with a girl called Mardine, whom he eventually left for her roommate. Dusty Moreland had come to New York from Wyoming to study painting. She had an oval face, with dark hair, slanting eyebrows, large eyes, and full lips. Allen had known her for several years, and she appeared to be the "really gone sweet girl" he was looking for. He began to spend his nights with her instead of returning to Paterson.

One day that winter of 1950, Allen stopped off for a drink at the Pony Stable, a lesbian bar on Third Street at Sixth Avenue. There, at a table, sat a twenty-year-old boy with dark brows, tousled black hair, and bright flashing eyes. Allen was immediately attracted to his classic Italian features and youthful energy. The boy had a thick sheaf of poems with him, and announced that he was a poet, but unlike many of the self-proclaimed poets of Greenwich Village, he had his work professionally typed, which immediately made Allen take him more seriously. He read the poems and was surprised to find that they were good; one in particular stuck in his mind; it began: "The stone world came to me, and said Flesh gives you an hour's life."

The boy's name was Gregory Corso, and the images of classical antiquity that filled his poems had been acquired in jail, where he spent many of his teenage years. The old-timers there told him, "Don't serve time, let it serve you," and he took this good advice and embarked on a course of self-improvement. Not knowing where to begin his studies, he started with Greece and Rome, and by the time he was released he had a thorough grounding in classical culture.

Corso never knew his mother, who was from the mountains of Lombardy and may have taken the boat back there shortly after his birth. He was born above the funeral parlor across the street from the San Remo, in what was then part of Little Italy. He had lived with eight sets of foster parents in different parts of the city until he was about ten years old; then his father took him, thinking, incorrectly as it happened, that to have a child would keep him out of the war. His father went into the navy, and Gregory lived on the streets.

On one occasion when he was twelve years old, he was so hungry that he kicked in the window of a restaurant; caught on his way out, he was sent to the Tombs. Fortunately, he was streetwise enough to avoid being raped, and he learned fast from the other prisoners.

He was released a year later, with no money and nowhere to go. After walking the streets, he broke a window at a youth center to get in and sleep. Discovered by a night watchman, he was sent straight back to the Tombs. There he fell ill and was transferred to Bellevue, which, in wartime, was overcrowded and understaffed. One day in the dining room, he flicked a piece of bread and hit one of the mental patients in the eye, and in the uproar that followed he was put in a straitjacket and carried out. He spent the rest of his time at Bellevue on the fourth floor, with the seriously mentally ill. By the time he got back on the streets he was fifteen and very tough.

After pulling off several robberies, Gregory was caught again, and the judge gave him three years. He was in Clinton Prison in Dannemora, up by the Canadian border, from 1947 until 1950. He got out of jail just before his twentieth birthday, and shortly afterward he met Allen.

Gregory and Allen discussed poetry that night and told each other their life stories. Finally, Gregory told Allen about a fantasy he had. Gregory had a furnished attic room on West Twelfth Street, and from his window he could see everything that went on in the fourth-floor apartment of a girl who lived across the street. Every night Gregory would masturbate while watching her take a bath, use the toilet, undress in front of a mirror, and make love to her boyfriend. He told Allen he dreamed of crossing the street, knocking on her door, and introducing himself. As Gregory told the story, Allen realized, with growing amazement, that the girl was Dusty Moreland, who lived on West Twelfth Street, and that the boyfriend was himself. "You want me to introduce you?" Allen asked. "I have magical powers!" And the next day he took Gregory to meet her.

Over the Christmas break, Dusty went back to Wyoming to see her family, and Allen resumed his affair with Mardine. He saw a lot of different girls, and the rumors began to spread. Bill wrote to him on the first of the year: "Lucien tells me you are a virtual satyr—a mythological Greek creature characterized by insatiable lust I mean, not Jean Paul Satre [sic] the existentialist—Well stick with it and no backsliding."

That December, Allen took a job as a market researcher with National Opinion Research Center, asking members of the public their feelings about the Korean War. In May 1951, he moved on to Doherty, Clifford and Shenfield, a market research company on the fifty-second floor of the Empire State Building. He spent his days worrying about toothpaste. Ipana toothpaste was about to launch a million-dollar advertising campaign. But first they had to decide whether to put their million behind the slogan "Ipana makes your teeth sparkle" or "Ipana makes your teeth glamorous." Tens of thousands of dollars were spent on a research project to test people's reactions to these slogans, and Allen sat in his office drawing a graph of all the answers and writing a report. The entire project was designed to find out just which words and images would convey a particular idea, useful work for a poet.

Allen had been employed as a free lance, and when summer came, he found himself broke and out of work. He lost weight and was having dreams in which he became a giant blue skeleton, starving to death on the city streets. Lucien had planned to go to Mexico City that August to attend the wedding of a friend who worked for UPI. He invited Allen to join him, and they planned to stay with Burroughs. Having failed as a pot farmer and been arrested for indecent behavior in Texas, then for possession of drugs in New Orleans, Bill had taken his family to Mexico City.

They drove in Lucien's old Chevrolet, with Lucien's little dog in the back and a goodly supply of bottles in the front. In Texas, they encountered a terrible heat wave, which caused the car's thermometer to explode. That June, Burroughs had moved his family to a tiny apartment at 210 Orizaba Street, near the center of Mexico City and the university, but when Allen and Lucien arrived, they found that Bill was away in Ecuador with Lewis Marker, looking for land.

Joan and Lucien immediately paired off in a protracted drinking contest, while Allen looked around the city. Joan's fine features had been eroded since Allen and Lucien first met her, seven years before. She had caught polio when she and Bill were living in Texas, but she'd refused to see a doctor. "I have polio," she said, "I'll have polio." The disease had withered her leg, and she walked with a limp. Benzedrine had blackened her teeth, and alcohol had ravaged her good looks. She was drinking two bottles of tequila a day, trying to take care of her son, Billy, who was now five, and her daughter, Julie, who was seven. "Julie's getting really pretty," Allen told Joan. "She's gonna be some competition for you!"

"Ah, I'm out of the running," Joan replied.

Allen had been making small talk, but Joan meant what she said. Still only in her twenties, she had more or less given up. She was an alcoholic, stuck in a Mexico City slum, with two children, a

Benzedrine habit, and a boyfriend who was away on a trip with *his* boyfriend. When Bill had a boy, he had no use for women. Her prospects did not look good, although Bill took his family financial responsibilities very seriously.

Lucien got very drunk at the wedding. After driving the bride and groom to the airport, he was arrested when he ran into a few cars while trying to get the Chevrolet out of the airport parking lot. He spent the night in jail with a large drunken Indian.

Joan had a pot connection in Guadalajara and suggested a trip there. Lucien and Joan sat in the front, passing the Quinebra gin bottle. Allen, Julie, and little Billy cowered, terrified, in the back, as Lucien skidded around the hairpin bends on the mountain roads, while Joan yelled, "How fast can this heap go?" Much of the time Lucien was too drunk to drive, so Joan would take over. Lucien lay on the floor pushing down on the gas pedal, while she steered and used her one good leg on the brake as they screamed around corners. The two of them enjoyed themselves enormously. Ginsberg's memory of the trip is of "great kicks and torment of continual threat of death." He thought Joan was trying deliberately to get them all killed.

Their car got stuck in an attempt to ford a river, and the Mexicans who appeared out of the night to help them stole Allen's pants; he had taken them off so that they wouldn't get wet while he helped push. Lucien couldn't stop laughing. The trip wasn't all terror and alcoholic frenzy; they had magnificent views of jungle-covered mountains and the Pacific. They spent some time in Mazatlán. On the trip back, they saw the active volcano Paricutin and drove onto its lava field at night. The car kept falling into crevices, and Lucien used the jack to get it out. Joan urged him on: "Go on! Go on! Let's get to the volcano!" Molten lava and rock shot into the air. A mile from the rim, the smoking rocks showered all around them. Allen was vastly relieved when they got back to the city.

They dropped off Joan and the kids in Mexico City and prepared to leave. Lucien and Joan had become very close; in fact, Billy had bitten Lucien in the leg for paying too much attention to his mother. Joan looked so mournful when they left that Lucien was of half a mind to stay. "There was something, in a wistful way, tremendously compelling about Joan," Lucien said. "She was very very bright and very exciting, very much in command of the various tight situations she got into. She was in command of everything but herself!"

They began the long drive back to New York City, and had

reached Galveston when the car broke down. Lucien had to return to work, so he flew on to New York, leaving Allen with the car and the dog; he would fly back in a week to collect Allen and the repaired car. Allen rented a shack overlooking the Gulf of Mexico. He spent his time swimming, sitting on the beach, and walking around Galveston. He did a lot of sleeping.

On September 7, he read in the evening paper: "An American tourist trying to imitate William Tell killed his wife while attempting to shoot a glass of champagne from her head with a pistol, police said today. Police arrested William Seward Burroughs, 37, of St. Louis, Mo., last night after his wife, Joan, 27, died in the hospital of a bullet wound in her forehead received an hour earlier."

Allen, completely shaken, wrote to Neal that night: "My imagination of the scene and psyches in Mexico is too limited to comprehend the vast misery and absurdity and sense of dream that must exist in Bill's mind now."

Thirty years later, in a television documentary on his life, Burroughs recalled that Thursday night in Mexico City. Bill had just taken a knife he had bought in Ecuador to be sharpened. "That day I knew something *awful* was going to happen," he said. "I remember I was walking down the street and the tears started just streaming down my face. Of course, if that happens to you, *watch out!* You see, I've always thought myself to be controlled at some times by this completely malevolent force which Brion Gysin described as the Ugly Spirit. But my walking down the street and tears streaming down my face meant that I knew that the Ugly Spirit, which is always the worst part of everyone's character, would take over and that something awful would happen."

He had gone to a friend's apartment on Monterrey, where he had arranged to meet Joan and Marker. When he got there he began tossing back drinks in order to release himself from the terrible depression he felt. He had eight or ten drinks, then said to Joan, "It's about time for our William Tell act." Joan put a six-ounce water glass on her head, and Bill pulled out his Star .380 automatic and fired one shot. The report was deafening. The glass fell to the floor, where it spun in concentric circles, unbroken. Joan's head slumped to one side; she began to slide toward the floor. Marker, the one nearest to her, saw the trickle of blood and gasped, "Bill, your bullet has hit her forehead." Bill leapt across the room, shouting, "No!" He knelt at her side in tears, calling out her name.

Taken from the Red Cross Hospital to police headquarters, Bill had not been there more than five minutes before his lawyer, Bernabé Jurado, arrived. "Don't say anything, Bill," he advised. "This is a shooting accident." The next day, Bill appeared before a criminal judge. He was questioned for ninety minutes, then held without bail in "formal prison" to await trial. Jurado believed Bill's story, but he didn't think it would look good in court. He decided to tell the judge that the gun had gone off accidentally when Bill pulled back the slide to see if it was loaded, and this was demonstrated in court, using one of the policemen's .45s. John Healy, Lewis Marker, and Ed Woods, who had witnessed the shooting, all corroborated the statement in court, and the judge decided that Bill should be charged with *imprudencia criminal*, which had a maximum sentence of five years. Bill pleaded guilty as charged and on September 21 was released on bail, after his brother Mort arrived from St. Louis with the $2,312 bail money. Jurado was very proud that Bill had been held only thirteen days; the average for a homicide was two months. Bill thought that Jurado was worth every cent of his $2,000 fee. The sentence was not due to be delivered for a year; meanwhile, Bill had to sign in at Lecumbere prison each Monday morning, or his bail would be revoked.

Bill's brother arranged Joan's burial, then took Billy back to St. Louis to live with his grandparents. Joan's parents flew in, barely able to conceal their distaste for Bill, to collect Julie and return with her to Albany. Bill remained in Mexico City, his wife dead, his family dispersed. Joan's death caused him to face up to his demons; it compelled him to become a writer. In 1985, he stated in the introduction to *Queer*: "I am forced to the appalling conclusion that I would never have become a writer but for Joan's death, and to a realization of the extent to which this event has motivated and formulated my writing. I live with the constant threat of possession, and a constant need to escape from possession, from Control. So the death of Joan brought me in contact with the invader, the Ugly Spirit, and maneuvered me into a lifelong struggle, in which I have had no choice except to write my way out."

It is the poet, Allen Ginsberg, who has gone, in his own body, through the horrifying experiences described from life in these pages. . . . Say what you will, he proves to us, in spite of the most debasing experiences that life can offer a man, the spirit of love survives to ennoble our lives if we have the wit and the courage and the faith—and the art!—to persist.

—William Carlos Williams, introduction to "Howl"

ALLEN SPENT THE NEXT TWO AND A HALF YEARS IN NEW YORK CITY, during which time, under the influence of William Carlos Williams, he made radical changes in his writing style, adopting the open form, with syllable count and variable breath-stop length for verse measurement, that enabled him to write "Howl." His life was much more under his control; as a free-lance market researcher, he had a reliable and undemanding way of making money that gave him the time he needed to write and enough cash to enjoy a full social life in the bohemian circles of Greenwich Village, where he was still meeting the characters who would populate the poem.

In the fall of 1951, Allen was again staying on and off in Lucien Carr's spare bed, but at the beginning of December, he found himself a dark eighteen-dollar-a-month two-room attic apartment, lit by dormer windows, at 346 West 15th Street. He furnished it very simply, with a table, a chair, and a bed, and a radio on which he would play classical music late at night until the neighbors beat on the wall. Some evenings Allen would sit on the small stoop, watching the stars "roll over the walls of the warehouse" across the street. He wrote a number of good poems about the place, including one dedicated to Alan Ansen, "Cockroach at My Door." "Walking Home at Night," which he included in his early collection *Empty*

Mirror, ended: "Remembering / my attic I reached / my hands to my head and hissed, / 'Oh, God how horrible!' "

A huge combination New Year and wedding party celebrated the arrival of 1952 and the marriage of Lucien Carr and Francesca Van Hartz. Allen had immersed himself in a frenzy of social activity during the holidays. Dusty was visiting in Wyoming, and Allen saw a number of girls from Barnard College. When Dusty returned, she was accompanied by her mother, and together they set up an apartment in the Village. Allen told Neal: "I dream of marrying her but don't have the force or money, and we don't love each other. We are great tired friends now. We talk a lot, sleep once in a while, but never screw." Allen asked her to marry him, but she turned him down. Allen wrote Neal that he was tired of sex.

He was also feeling guilty about it; that January he wrote Neal that he had seduced young Gregory Corso and worried about the reemergence of his gay leanings for weeks afterward. Gregory traveled to the West Coast almost immediately afterward, and Allen did not see him before he left. Corso denied that the seduction ever took place: "That Ginzie, he'll say anything." But he confirmed that he and Ginsberg had become good friends before his departure for San Francisco.

Allen missed Jack and Neal, but when Jack wrote and suggested that he join them in San Francisco, Allen explained that he did not want to interrupt his analysis. He was even able to resist Neal's tempting offer: "Why don't you come out here? Nice place if one likes it. Be brakie and make lots money. Or write in attic and make love to wife and me." However, the idea was planted, and Allen did eventually take him up on it, with the predictable disastrous results.

Allen saw some of his old criminal friends again but with more detachment than before, having opted to join "society." In the aftermath of the overturned car episode, Huncke was still in jail, but Little Jack had managed to fake insanity and served only one year. Bill Garver, the overcoat thief, told Allen that Phil ("The Sailor") White, Burroughs's old friend, had hanged himself. Phil had been held in the Tombs on three separate charges and tried to get out by informing on an old heroin dealer he knew. The dealer was caught and sent to Rikers Island, but the police reneged on their deal with Phil and dropped only two of the charges against him. There was a third, non-narcotics charge, which would have put him on Rikers too. Phil knew what they did to stool pigeons on the island, so he took the only way out.

Garver told Allen, "I never thought he had much character, but what else could he do? He was washed up as a junkie in New York." Burroughs was astonished when Allen told him the news. "I was sincerely shocked to hear about Phil," he wrote Allen. "He was so uncompromising and puritanical about stool pigeons. He used to say, 'I can't understand how a pigeon can live with himself.' I guess Phil couldn't after what he did." It was only after White's death that the facts began to emerge about him. Phil White was a psychotic killer; fueled by a mixture of Tuinals and heroin, he would get into murderous rages, walking into a store and shooting before anyone had time to sound the alarm. He hit liquor stores and fur shops and killed one man because he didn't have enough money on him. "He was quite a guy," said Huncke later.

In addition to Dusty, and Lucien and Cessa Carr, Allen's friends at that time included his ex-Columbia classmates Richard Howard, John Hollander, and Hollander's wife, Ann; his old friend from the Psychiatric Institute, Carl Solomon, and his wife, Olive; and Alan Ansen, all of whom he saw about once a week. He was also in close touch with Eugene, Louis, and Edith. He had made many new friends at the San Remo, and wrote Neal: "I love a great new group of subterraneans." It was one of these, Bill Keck, who gave him his first peyote, in April 1952. Allen stayed overnight in Paterson and got up early to take it. He swallowed three buttons, gagging on the bitter metallic taste. Nauseated, he lay down on the bed and the sickness passed, though he continued to feel empty-headed. He noticed the beautiful pattern on the pillowcase and the intense color of the cherry blossoms in the garden. Taking his notebook, he went out to sit under the cherry tree. "Heavens the universe is in order," he wrote. It was a beautiful day, with a few puffy clouds floating peacefully across a deep-blue sky. A bee dropped onto the open page of his journal, and butterflies and flies danced by his head. He began to think of space as a solid form between him and the clouds. He could hear the neighbors going about their Sunday morning chores, clanking garbage pails.

He recorded all his observations in his journal. Everything took on a superreal quality. Looking at a rock, he began to think about its great age and how it would outlast him. He went into the house and talked to his relatives in the kitchen, but all the time he wanted to get back to the rock. "I have been going around grinning idiotically at people," he wrote, back under the cherry tree, "almost afraid they'll ask, 'What's the matter with you this minute?' but they seem to me also—so strange in their momentary consciousness." He settled into his seat and wrote: "Rock. Serried and worn by years, so old, a huge stone tear. I can't even see you under your shroud of dirt. A bird just shat on me! It must have been on purpose." Louis came to the back door and looked out. "Imagine being in the literal presence of one's own father," wrote Allen, clearly moved by seeing Louis standing there.

Some laundry fell from the washing line and a voice from the house called out, "Please, Allen, will you hang that up?" then he heard Louis say, "He's busy with himself." Allen wondered if he was attracting too much attention to himself, just sitting in the backyard writing. He decided that probably only William Carlos Williams and himself in a radius of fifty miles could see the world in such terrible detail and were so conscious of the open sky and the solidity of the transparent air.

He drifted through the day, listening to family arguments, playing jazz records, and admiring the cherry blossoms. Later that evening, he began to come down from the twelve-hour trip. He wrote: "Glad I sailed through this peyote test without any of the mental imaginables—the horror of accidents, I didn't cut my thumb or bite anyone or tip my mit." But the peyote did cause a shift in consciousness, which he sought; though not as extreme as his Blake experience, it indicated that he was on the right path.

In the summer of 1951, Joan Kerouac had found that she was pregnant. Though they had earlier tried hard to have a child, Jack now felt utterly unable to accept the responsibility of a family, and despite his Catholic upbringing, he tried to get her to have an abortion. She refused, and he pretended the child was not his. Their marriage now broke down completely, and Joan went to stay with her mother in Albany. Jack refused to pay for prenatal care, and Joan got a court order. He eventually coughed up four payments of five dollars. That fall, after swearing his friends to secrecy, he left New York to stay with Neal and Carolyn in California. Neither Allen nor Lucien Carr approved of his behavior, and by the time he left he was on bad terms with both of them.

Neal, meanwhile, was taking his responsibilities seriously. Working seven days a week to earn money for a family vacation, he did a daytime shift as a brakeman on the Southern Pacific, and in the evenings he recapped tires. Jack couldn't understand this commit-

ment to family and complained about Neal's "materialistic attitude." This inevitably led to problems. Neal grew increasingly
irritated by Jack's failure to contribute enough toward his upkeep
and for the household pot, which he smoked continuously. Jack's
parsimony was legendary; he never even shared his cigarettes with
his wife.

On February 16, 1952, Janet Michelle Kerouac was born, and the
Brooklyn Uniform Support of Dependents and Abandonment Bureau began searching for Jack. Meanwhile, he was worried, not
about his wife and their newborn child but that he might not be able
to live safely with his mother again without being sued for mainte-
nance. Burroughs's grim 1945 prediction that Jack would eventually
be strangled by his mother's apron strings was already coming true.

John Clellon Holmes's *Go* was published at the beginning of 1952,
and Allen was shocked to read Holmes's vision of him. John Hall
Wheelock, the book's editor, claimed that Holmes had depicted a
real poet and that the poems in the book—which were imitations of
Allen's—were profound mystical works. Allen wrote Neal in February: "But I say Wheelock is a fool, and Holmes, because he talks
nice and treats self badly in book, as badly as me or you, is not so
much of a fool." He thought the treatment of his Harlem vision of
Blake was crude and vulgar.

"You haven't really caught the way it felt," he told Holmes, referring to the Blake experience, "but you've caught something else.
You've caught the solemn funny little kid I guess I must have been
in those days." When in 1976 he was asked, in his role of elder
statesman, to write a preface for a new edition of the book, Ginsberg
had to refuse. He had not looked at it in twenty-four years, but on
rereading it he was dismayed by it all over again. "I was too
ashamed of the prose to write a preface," he said, "so Holmes,
whom I love, got mad at me."

Kerouac also disliked the book, but his problem was mostly one
of frustration and jealousy at seeing Holmes get an astonishing
twenty-thousand-dollar advance, when Allen, who was acting as
Jack's unofficial agent, trying to place *On the Road*, had only been
able to secure an offer of one thousand dollars from Carl Solomon,
who was working as an editor for his uncle, at Ace Books, publishers of cheap pulp paperbacks. Allen was also working on Bill's
behalf, toting the manuscript of *Junky* from publisher to publisher.
Although he didn't think of it in these terms, this was the beginning

of Ginsberg's self-appointed Ezra Pound role, which resulted in so many of the Beats' getting published.

In May, Jack took a bus to Mexico City to stay with Bill Burroughs, who had often invited him. Jack finished his revision of *On the Road* in Mexico City and mailed it to Carl Solomon. The manuscript was mostly material that finished up as *Visions of Cody*. Carl read it and passed it on to Allen, who read it and passed it on to John Clellon Holmes. On June 12, 1952, Allen wrote to Jack: "I don't see how it will ever be published, it's so personal, it's so full of sex language, so full of our local mythological references, I don't know if it would make sense to any publisher—by make sense I mean, if he could follow what happened to what characters where. The language is great, the blowing is mostly great, the inventions have fullblown ecstatic style. . . . Where you are writing steadily and well, the sketches, the exposition, it's the best that is written in America."

Allen told Jack he was concerned. "Ace I'm positive won't take it now. I don't know who will. . . . Will you be revising it at all? What are you trying to put down, man? You know what you done?" In his opinion, it had to be pulled together; otherwise it would never be published. Allen's assessment of the book's reception by publishers was accurate, and *Visions of Cody* was not published until Kerouac had died, and even then only after considerable pressure from Ginsberg.

Allen had better luck with Burroughs. Bill had been sending him sections of prose ever since Allen got out of the P.I. *Junky* was a controversial autobiographical account of his life as a heroin addict in New York and Texas, beginning in 1944, when he met Phil the Sailor and Huncke. There were two related texts, called "Junk" and "Queer." "Junk" was the more complete of the two, and it was this that Allen took on his rounds. Carl Solomon decided to publish it, paying a thousand-dollar advance. Bill wrote to Allen: "You really are a sweetheart. I could kiss you on both cheeks. We should get used to calling each other sweetheart, I understand it is the standard form of address between agent and author but this time I mean it."

In 1952, Allen made an abrupt change in his writing style. For some time he had been trying to find a way to speak naturally in his poems. The two major influences upon him at the time were William Carlos Williams and Jack Kerouac. Two years earlier, shortly after the publication of Kerouac's *The Town and the City*, he had written Jack: "I have to learn how to talk naturally in verse again; find out how to say great things or beautiful things naturally." One of Kerouac's influences was his technique of sketching. Jack's architect friend Ed White had suggested, "Why don't you just sketch the streets like a painter, but with words?" Jack gave it a try and was amazed by the results. The idea was, of course, not a new one, but to Kerouac it was a great innovation, and his enthusiasm rubbed off on Allen.

Allen went back through his old journals, which had many passages just like that: straightforward prose sketches of what he saw before him, written in a clear, detailed style, with no attempt to be poetic or "break everybody's mind open." He took a couple of paragraphs containing word pictures out of the journals and arranged them on the page in lines like Williams's. Sometimes he arranged them by counting the syllables, sometimes by the breath lengths, and sometimes he just balanced the lines visually on the page. Years later, he told a class of literature students, "These were just the ordinary, unselfconscious notebooks, prose, and I took the nuts out of it, the intensest moments of prose, pushing everything else aside, isolating it, framing it on the page." He was quite pleased by the results, which looked like Williams's work, but unaccountably, he didn't realize the importance of what he had.

In January 1952, he dug out the poems and sent a group of them to Williams, because "I had nothing else to send and felt washed up as a writer." He told Williams that they were "Fragmentary notes I picked out of a journal and put in lines just as experiment about a year ago. I gave up then, thinking they were nothing, thinking also that I was aimlessly trying to make poetry out of prose scraps." He could not have anticipated Williams's reaction.

Writing from the Hotel Weston in New York City, where he was taking a few days' vacation, Williams wrote: "Wonderful! . . . How many of such poems as these do you own? You *must* have a book, I shall see that you get it. Don't throw anything away. These are *it*." Allen, deliriously happy, wrote immediately to Jack and Neal in San Francisco. He enclosed copies of ten poems and said, "Now you realize you old bonepoles, the two of you, whuzzat means? I can get a book out if I want! New Directions (I guess). Whew! An you realize further, Williams is also nutty as a fruitcake. It also means we can *all* get books out (just you and me and Neal). . . . I have a new method of Poetry. All you got to do is look over your notebooks (that's where I got those poems) or lay down on a couch, and think of anything that comes into your head, especially the miseries, the mis'ries, or night thoughts when you can't sleep an hour before sleeping, only get up and write it down. Then arrange in lines of 2, 3 or 4 words each, don't bother about sentences, in sections of 2, 3 or 4 lines each. We'll have a huge collected anthology of American Kicks and Mental Muse-eries. The American Spiritual Museum, A gorgeous gallery of Hip American Devices." It is entirely typical that Ginsberg's first thought was to find a way for his friends to share in his good fortune.

The earliest poem composed by this method was "The Bricklayer's Lunch Hour," which Allen had written as a prose sketch in his journal while looking out of Carolyn's hotel window just before he and Neal left Denver for Texas in 1947. In it, a young bricklayer sits on a ladder on top of a wall, eating a bag lunch, and plays with a cat. Allen typed it out as lines of poetry without changing a word and had a poem. "This is probably the earliest text I published which makes real sense," Ginsberg later told a class of literature students, and quoted the three final lines: "it is darkening as if to rain / and the wind on top of the trees in the / street comes through almost harshly." He discussed the lines with his students: "Without even intending it, there is that little shiver of a moment in time preserved in the crystal cabinet of the mind. A little shiver of eternal space. That's what I was looking for."

Inspired by Williams's letter, he began reading furiously through all his old journals, searching for the poems hiding there. Two weeks later, he was able to tell Jack: "I have been working steadily at typewriter, piecing together mad poems—I have already 100 of them. I'm jumping." These he winnowed down to eighty or so and sent off to Williams.

This was to be the beginning of an association that lasted for the rest of Williams's life. Allen had finally found a poetry teacher able to show him the craft. That March, Williams took Allen to a small cocktail party, and afterward they sat in the car in his garage. "Get locale, local speech, accents and rhythm," he told Allen. "Write in that idiom." Williams took up the offer in Allen's letter that they explore the River Street section of Paterson. They went to the old swimming hole of Allen's youth, behind the silk factory; picking up a handful of trash at the riverbank, they made up a poem on the spot about what they had found. Allen wanted to take Williams on to the bars of River Street, but he said he was too old and wanted to go home. Allen later recorded their conversation.

They sat in the car in the darkness. Williams said, "What's it all for?"

"Why?" said Allen.

"I'm getting old," Williams said. "Two years more and I'll be seventy."

"Are you afraid of death?" asked Allen.

They sat in the car, looking at the asphalt suburban street, and he said, "Yes, I think that's it."

Allen's friends were astonished by his new poetry. John Hollander thought that he had burst forth like Rilke. He stared at Allen in amazement and suggested he give them Greek titles so that they would look like poems. Lucien liked the "amusing ones" best, whereas John Kingsland preferred the "recherché ones about Marlene Dietrich." Allen told Jack: "Dusty liked (eek!) the metaphysical ones best."

On April 4, Allen delivered a copy of the manuscript of his book, now called *Empty Mirror*, to Williams, who had agreed to help him make the final selection of poems. Williams wrote an introduction, in which he stressed how Allen used the language of the crowd to reach the crowd: "what can he do, in the end, but speak to them in their own language, that of the daily press?" Allen dedicated the book to Huncke.

Allen sent copies of his manuscript to *Partisan Review*, *Hudson Review*, *Commentary*, and *Poetry Chicago*, with no luck, and in May he showed it to Van Doren and Random House and sent a copy to Kenneth Rexroth, who was a reader for New Directions, but all to no avail. *Empty Mirror* was not published until 1961, by which time Ginsberg was well known.

Bill Burroughs was pleased when Kerouac arrived to stay with him in Mexico City; he was lonely and still badly shaken by Joan's death. Bill's pleasure was short-lived, however. The Mexican authorities had just begun a crackdown on marijuana, and foreign residents were obvious targets. Bill was still out on bail and wanted to maintain a very low profile, so he was particularly annoyed by Jack's daily habit of smoking three very large joints, the pungent smell of which lingered in the small apartment. Then he discovered that Jack had allowed a drug dealer to hide pot in the apartment. Had this been found in a police raid, Bill's bail would certainly have been revoked, and it would have weighed heavily against him when he was sentenced.

Bill's problems did not end there. Jack was very tight with his money—"Like pulling an impacted molar," Bill told Allen—and he had rapidly depleted his resources. After living off Bill for two months, during which time he wrote most of *Dr. Sax*, Jack left for his sister's place in Rocky Mount, North Carolina, borrowing Bill's last twenty dollars for the trip, on the condition that he would repay it the day he reached his family. Two months went by, and Bill received nothing, not even a postcard. He protested to Allen: "To be blunt, I have never had a more inconsiderate and selfish guest under my roof."

Jack's sister felt that Jack should contribute his share of money for room and board, so his stay in Rocky Mount was a short one. He made a brief trip to New York, where he had a bad argument with Carl Solomon over the manuscript of *On the Road*, and decided to return to California to live with Neal and Carolyn. Neal wired him twenty-five dollars, and in September he left for the Coast, traveling by bus since he was dubious of the rail pass Neal had sent him.

Back in New York, Allen's grand plan to publish Burroughs, Kerouac, Alan Ansen, Jean Genet, and various others through Ace Books was upset. In June, he reported to Bill that Carl had broken up with Olive, stopped traffic on Eighth Avenue by throwing his shoes and briefcase at passing cars, smeared paint on the walls of his apartment and flooded it, attacked his books with a knife, run screaming in the streets, and been in and out of Bellevue. "This has been going on for two weeks and I can't get anything done at Ace till he calms down. Gad."

Dusty Moreland was living with Allen in his attic room, so he had little time to himself, particularly when Dusty's cat died, an event she took very badly. Everyone Allen dealt with seemed to be behaving strangely. Carl was going through an emotional crisis; Jack was paranoid that his wife might find him and angry that his book was not being hailed as a masterpiece; and Bill was planning a strange jungle expedition, in search of the hallucinogenic drug yage. "Everybody seems off their heads, blowing tops around me," Allen wrote Bill. "I don't have a moment's peace from these people with their cats and yages and wives and voids and anger at the universe, why can't everybody calm down, I always say, like the nice people in the boobyhatch."

Allen had been collecting unemployment compensation; when it ran out in October, he took a job with George Fine Market Research, on Forty-second Street, as a market analyst on cosmetics, deodorants, and other commercial accounts. With a regular income coming in again, he arranged to move to a better apartment: 206 East 7th Street, on the Lower East Side of Manhattan, an area he would live in for the next thirty-five years.

He and Dusty had decided to separate. He told Neal: "With Dusty I seldom lay and it's no good really though I like her alright." When the time came to move to the new apartment, Dusty had nowhere to go, so she moved with him. Allen tried to get her to go to work and help out financially; he wrote Jack what happened: "She got totally annoyed," Allen wrote Jack, "had a phase of insisting she was hot for me. We finally had one great sweet screw full of innocence and hotness on both sides, then she disappeared up Third Avenue." Dusty didn't contact Allen for months, though all her clothes and furniture were in the apartment. "She's mad at me," Allen wrote Jack. "Thinks I betrayed her—and I did because I came on real stern and annoyed after a while . . . I didn't want chaos, it was unsettling my mind."

Jack, meanwhile, was brooding in San Jose, where Neal and Carolyn now lived. No publisher was interested in *On the Road*, and Jack looked for the villains of the piece and saw them all in New York. In a three-page temper tantrum, fueled by his wounded pride, he directed his resentment and anger at all those who had dared criticize his book. The letter, dated October 8, 1952, was addressed to Allen, but it was John Clellon Holmes who bore the brunt of the attack: "The smell of his work is the smell of death. Everybody knows he has no talent. . . . His book stinks, and your book [*Empty Mirror*] is only mediocre, and you all know it, and my book is great and will never be published. Beware of meeting me on the street in New York."

To Allen, he raged: "And you, who I thought was my friend—you sit there and look me in the eye and tell me that 'On the Road' I wrote at Neal's is 'imperfect' as though anything you ever did or anybody was perfect? And don't lift a finger or say a word for it . . ." Jack declared dramatically: "I shall certainly never find peace until I wash my hands completely of the dirty brush and stain of New York and everything you and the city stand for." He reviled everyone who had tried to help him get his book published: Allen, Lucien, Solomon, and Holmes.

Allen had had a great deal of experience with paranoia. He gave Jack time to cool off, and less than two weeks later, he received the manuscript of *Dr. Sax*, which Jack wanted him to place. They were reconciled, but Allen retained the uncomfortable knowledge of

Jack's true feelings about his friends. When Jack returned to live with his mother that winter, the old intimacy between them was tarnished.

In January 1953, Allen visited Naomi at Pilgrim State for the first time in many months. He took the elevator to the women's ward, and two buxom nurses in white uniforms led her out. Allen gasped, horrified at how much his mother had changed. She had had a stroke. The flesh on her face was wasted and lined with age. She had lost a lot of weight and no longer had the robust, healthy look of past years:

> Too thin, shrunk on her bones—age come to Naomi—
> now broken into white hair—loose dress on her skeleton
> —face sunk, old! withered—cheek of crone—
> One hand stiff—heaviness of forties & menopause re-
> duced by one heart stroke, lame now—wrinkles—a scar
> on her head, the lobotomy—ruin, the hand dipping down-
> wards to death—

There was another change. Even when raving, she had always had self-confidence; now Allen saw "pitiful batbrained hysterical fright and lack of sureness." She was out of her mind. "Are you a spy?" she asked. "Who are you? Did Louis send you?" Allen's eyes filled with tears as he sat at the small table. Naomi weaved back and forth to the door of the visiting room, asking why he was crying, then ordering him to get out before he was struck down. "You're not Allen," she said. After a few minutes a nurse came and led her away. Allen staggered into the men's room, "sobbing, saying 'Horror, the horror of it,' and groaning with grief at the reality of her death's hand."

That winter Allen became very fond of three young women who were known around the San Remo as the Three Graces. They had long hair, sometimes rolled into buns, wore small round wire-framed glasses, granny dresses, and old beads that they found in junkshops. They were pioneers of the hippie look of the next generation.

Sheri Martinelli was a painter, at one time Ezra Pound's girlfriend at Saint Elizabeths Hospital. Pound wrote the introduction to a small book of reproductions of her work. Iris Brody was also a painter. She did mystical landscapes, which Allen liked so much that he took a group of them to Columbia to show Meyer Schapiro, his old art professor. "They are obviously exquisite," Schapiro agreed. "The difficulty of the painter is that the materials she's using indicate some tragic direction, partly carelessness of materials, careless with her own beauty. So the question is, not only will the canvases survive rather than disintegrate, but will she survive to continue painting?" It was a prophetic remark. Iris Brody died in the mid-sixties of a heroin overdose, and the paintings Allen had collected flaked off the canvas and disintegrated in Eugene's cupboard.

The third grace was Ruth Goldenberg, a silent madonna type, who frequented Louis' Bar and the San Remo. One day, to everyone's astonishment, she began talking. Years of pent-up experience and opinions came out. She talked nonstop through the next day and the next, finally finishing up at Bellevue. Ginsberg devoted five stanzas in "Howl" to her: "who talked continuously seventy hours from park to pad to bar to Bellevue to museum to the Brooklyn Bridge . . ." Her parents came and took her away to "nowhere Zen New Jersey," and that was the last anyone saw of her.

In the spring of 1953, Allen met a girl named Elise Cowen. Joyce Johnson, then Joyce Glassman, wrote movingly about their relationship in her autobiographical volume, *Minor Characters*. She pointed out the strong resemblance between them: "They could have been born into the same family, brother and sister, they looked so much alike. Their broad foreheads and somewhat heart-shaped faces, the vulnerability at the corners of their mouths, their same darkness. They even wore nearly identical black-rimmed glasses, through which their large brown eyes absorbed the world nearsightedly."

Allen saw a lot of Elise, and she told Joyce, "He seems to think I'm very deep." But Allen did not invite her to move in with him. She became a part of Allen's circle of friends. Lucien Carr always called her Elipse: "She was a sweet girl. I was very fond of her. She was very shy and like a wounded bird. You couldn't help feeling sort of protective about Elipse." Joyce Johnson succinctly summed up Ginsberg's relationship with Elise when she said: "Elise was a moment in Allen's life. In Elise's life, Allen was an eternity."

Ace planned to publish *Junkie* (as they spelled it) in the spring of 1953. Bill had decided to use the nom de plume William Lee, in case his parents saw it. They had been very critical after reading his thinly disguised exploits in Kerouac's *The Town and the City*, and since they were bringing up his son and still providing him with an allowance, he did not want a repeat performance. It was curious, therefore, that he chose Lee—his mother's maiden name—as his new surname. To publicize the book, Allen had provided material for David Dempsey's "Literary Notes" column in the *New York Times*, but Jack refused to allow his name to be used there, since Bill was publishing under a pseudonym. In a February 21, 1953, letter addressed to Allen, Jack, referring to the Dempsey article, also said that he did not want *The Town and the City* mentioned in connection with *Go*, and denied permission to put his name next to Clellon Holmes's as an expert on the Beat Generation. Had Kerouac not been so jealous, this would have been the first article on the inchoate literary movement. Curiously, Jack still regarded Holmes as a friend; he continued to stay at his apartment and go drinking with him.

Ace aimed *Junkie* strictly at the newsstand market. They printed up 100,000 copies at thirty-five cents, with a lurid cover that showed a man and a woman struggling to get possession of a hypodermic syringe. To cover themselves against any suggestion that they might be advocating the use of drugs, Ace added a publisher's statement disassociating themselves from Burroughs's views on drugs and published the book as a double volume with *Narcotic Agent* by Maurice Helbrant—"a gripping true adventure of a T-man's war against the dope menace." Thinking that some of the slang used in *Junkie* would be incomprehensible to their readers, they added a glossary, partly compiled by Allen, which included such esoteric terms as "yen pox," "flop," and "mud."

Despite his refusal to help publicize Bill's book, Jack wrote to Allen on May 7 to ask if he would act as his agent again and try to place *Dr. Sax* and his *bildungsroman, Maggie Cassady*, because his agents, MCA, had found no takers. *Dr. Sax* was one of Allen's favorites, but it was still incomplete. When Jack returned to the city, he and Allen walked around Greenwich Village in the spring sunshine, trying to find an appropriate end. As the text then stood, a great black snake, hundreds of miles long, was just emerging from the deep. Allen suggested a Shakespearean-style ending: "Ah! 'twas a husk of doves," meaning that the snake, representing all the evil in the world, was just a dead outer skin, within which was a flock of doves. Jack went home and finished the book, saying that Satan was enamored of doves and that "his Snake would not destroy the world but merely be a great skin of doves on coming-out day."

. . .

At the end of April, Allen discovered Chinese painting and spent days in the Fine Arts room of the New York Public Library, poring over books of reproductions. He wrote Neal: "You begin to see the vastitude and intelligence of the yellow men, and you understand a lot of new mind and eyeball kicks." He also said that he had "begun to familiarize myself with Zen Buddhism through a book by D. T. Suzuki, *Introduction to Zen Buddhism*." This was typical Ginsberg understatement. He had embarked on an ambitious study plan and took out more than seventy books on the subject from the Columbia University library alone. In one of the artbooks, he found a scroll painting by Liang Kai called *Sakyamuni Coming Out from the Mountain*, which showed Buddha exhausted after his enlightenment. Allen sat with the book open before him, entranced, and wrote a poem with the same title, using a long line and Williams's triadic form, breaking each line into three:

> *He drags his bare feet*
> > *out of a cave*
> > > *under a tree.*

It was the beginning of a new form of writing for him. Pleased with the results, he immediately set out to write something more ambitious: to set his feelings about Neal Cassady down on paper once and for all. He called the poem "The Green Automobile," a private homosexual reference to the green robes of the *galabanti,* male whores of imperial Rome, to whom Oscar Wilde paid homage with his green carnation. Ginsberg later described the poem as his "first breakthrough as a poet. First time I let my imagination and desire dominate over what, in the mental hospital, I had been taught to accept as an adjustment to reality, to limit my demands of the external world to what could be workable so as to avoid excess suffering."

It was a joyful poem, celebrating his love and friendship for Neal. It was written in very long lines, each one broken into quatrains:

> *He'd come running out*
> > *to my car full of heroic beer*
> > > *and jump screaming at the wheel*
> > > > *for he is the greater driver.*

Allen wrote Neal: "In new poem I am beginning to explore some of the uncharted verbal rhetorical invented seas that Jack (& yrself) sail in. . . . After my 'Empty Mirror,' which for me strips yakking down to modern bones, I would like to build up a modern contemporary metaphysical yak-poem, using the kind of weaving original rhythms that Jack does in his prose, and the lush imagery. I been dry too long. The Green Automobile . . . does this, at least begins this." He let his imagination run wild:

> *This time we'll buy up the city!*
> *I cashed a great check in my skull bank*
> *to found a miraculous college of the body*
> *up on the bus terminal roof.*

It was a long poem, of thirty-four such stanzas, and he was still working on it in September. He told Neal: "The point of this poem is to rewrite history, so to speak, make up a legend of my poor sad summer with you, and try to create some recognizable human-angelic ideal story, too." The whole poem was a "legend of love," idealized, as only then, six years after that painful summer, he was able to do.

In the summer of 1953, Allen began work as a copyboy at the New York *World-Telegram,* where he had short, sociable hours for a change. Gregory Corso was more or less living with Allen, supported by Allen's forty-five-dollar weekly salary, an echo of the Ginsberg-Huncke situation. Early photographs show Corso looking a lot like the young Frank Sinatra, with classic Italian features, and Allen enjoyed having an attractive "soulful" poet around. All this would change when Burroughs came.

Bill wanted to leave Mexico City; a year had passed since Joan's death, but he still had not been sentenced. Then in November, his lawyer was involved in a car crash. A seventeen-year-old driver sideswiped Jurado's Cadillac, damaging one of its fins. During the ensuing argument, Jurado shot the boy in the leg. He died in the hospital of tetanus, and Jurado left immediately for Brazil.

Jurado's partners began demanding more money to keep Bill out on bail, so though it meant forfeiting his bail bond, Bill followed his lawyer's example and skipped the country.

He visited his family, then spent most of the spring and summer traveling in Ecuador, Colombia, and Peru in search of the legendary hallucinogenic drug yage.

Bill arrived in New York in the middle of August, intending to stay for one month en route to Tangier. He and Allen had not seen each other for six years, not since Allen and Neal visited him in New Waverly, Texas, but they had been in continuous correspondence, particularly over the publication of *Junkie*. Allen found Bill changed. He told Neal: "He is really exciting to talk to, more so for me than ever. His new loquaciousness is something I never had the advantage of. I'm older now and the emotional relationship and conflict of will and mutual digging are very intense, continuous, exhausting and fertile. . . . One of the deepest people I ever saw." Bill decided that he was in love with Allen, and as he slowly and methodically used his machete to chop up the two suitcasefuls of dried yage he had brought back from Peru, he would give Gregory bloodcurdling looks. Gregory prudently decided to spend his time elsewhere.

Allen got home from work at 4:45 P.M., and he and Bill would talk continuously from then until 1 A.M. or later. Allen was not getting enough sleep and couldn't concentrate on his work. "I'm all hung on a great psychic marriage with him," he wrote Neal. Thirty years later, Ginsberg recalled the time: "Burroughs fell in love with me and we slept together and I saw a soft center where he felt isolated, alone in the world and he needed . . . a feeling of affection, and since I did love him and did have that respect and affection, he responded. I kinda felt privileged."

Many of the ideas that appeared later in Burroughs's *Naked Lunch* had their genesis in this period. The futuristic vibrating city of Interzone, with its levels connected by a web of catwalks, was inspired by the fire escapes and washing lines in Allen's backyard. Another, more sinister, idea to emerge that fall was "schlupping," Burroughs's proposition that he and Allen should become soulmates and somehow merge into one entity. Bill kept making up weird routines about parasitic symbiosis, like Bradley the Buyer in *Naked Lunch*, who "schlupps up" the District Supervisor in some unspeakable manner. Bill was hoping to amuse and please Allen, but in fact he was sending chills down Allen's spine.

It seemed that Bill was serious. He wanted an ultimate telepathic union of souls. Ginsberg explained: "Schlupp for him, was originally a very tender emotional direction, a desire to merge with a lover, and as such, pretty vulnerable, tenderhearted and open on Burroughs' part." Allen's uneasiness grew. Part of the reason was sexual. They slept together a lot, and Allen did everything he could to please Bill, even though he preferred younger men. "But I thought he was my teacher, so I'd do what I could to amuse him," Ginsberg said. "In bed, Bill is like an English governess, whinnying and giggling, almost hysteric. . . . He liked to come while being screwed."

Allen tried hard not to reject Bill or withdraw from him emotionally, but the intensity of the affair frightened him. At one point they were discussing the future, and Bill told Allen that he wanted him to come to Tangier with him. The idea of the situation continuing indefinitely so shocked Allen that he blurted out, "But I don't want your ugly old cock." Years later Ginsberg recalled, "It wounded him terribly because it was like complete physical rejection in a way I didn't mean. Like a heart blow that severed the trust, because I'd freaked out for that moment, and regretted it ever since."

In December 1953, Bill left New York by boat for Tangier. Allen prepared to go in the opposite direction. In November, when things had been at their most intense with Bill, Allen had arranged to visit Neal and Carolyn in California. His plan was to send a trunk of books and papers on ahead and hitchhike there via Mexico. Allen began to close down the apartment. He borrowed money from Eugene and various friends, and the *World-Telegram* owed him back wages. There was a security deposit on the apartment, and he was able to sell the refrigerator for thirty-five dollars. The biggest problem was trying to get rid of the ungainly Reichian orgone accumulator that Bill had built in the bedroom.

In the end, Allen's plans changed. He decided to go first to the Yucatán and see the ancient Mayan ruins, before traveling on to Los Angeles by bus. He told Neal: "This is a rare and marvellous trip I need to feed (and free) my soul from ten years of NYC which I can afford to make—and as you must agree, should make, so when I see you I'll be able to talk for hours, not only about NYC intellectual beauties, but also manly savage solitude of jungles we've never seen—will add to our stores of souls."

Allen hitchhiked to Florida and spent Christmas with Bill's family who had moved to Palm Beach, then he flew from Key West to Havana, his first plane ride. Havana was a big disappointment. Instead of the wild sex orgies he had heard about, he found only a shabby city run by gangsters. He reached Mexico in time for the New Year celebrations. Before he left New York, Allen had been to the Museum of Natural History, where he was given the name of the director of archaeology at Chichén Itzá. As a result, he was given a pass to stay, free of charge, in the archaeological camps in

that part of Mexico. At Chichén Itzá, he slept in a large square
concrete room with a dusty floor, right next to the late-eleventh-
century pyramid known as El Castillo. On his first night there, high
on paracodin, he climbed the ninety-one steps to the top of the great
pyramid, hung his hammock in front of the main entrance to the
summit chamber, and lay for an hour in the tropical night. Bats flew
around the ruin, and the forest seemed to close in on him. A creak
in the stone rooms below, which encased an earlier Toltec-Maya
castillo, startled him. After an hour, he saw Naomi, young and
dark-haired, seated at the piano at a party, close up, facing him,
svelte and enjoying life.

> *So spent a night*
> > *with drug and hammock*
> *at Chichén Itzá on the Castle . . .*

Before supper he would go to the tourist hotel, the Mayaland, for
a drink, but at night he was the only living person in the dead city.
A single clap of his hands in the Court of the Thousand Columns
would echo back from a half-dozen structures before the sound was
absorbed into the forest filled with night birds and chirruping insects. He would light his old Coleman lantern and wander through
the great stone portals of the Temple of the Warriors, examining
the wall of the skull-rack platform in the moonlight. He sat before a
death's-head and wondered about the unknown artisan who carved
it, seven centuries before.

On January 12, 1954, he set off for the ruined city of Uxmal.
Uxmal was the crowning achievement of the Mayan builders, a huge
complex of large quadrangles with a palace on each side. There
were a number of pyramids and ancillary buildings, all covered with
low reliefs and sculptures, the enormous structures connected by
vast plazas; and when Ginsberg was there, just after the excavations
and restorations of Alberto Ruz in 1951–52, the cleared area extended for more than a mile.

The main ruins were surrounded by unexcavated mounds in the
jungle, which could be reached by winding mule paths. Dressed in
army pants, walking shoes, and a sun hat, Allen strolled along the
crisscrossing paths, watching the ants on the cracked dried mud
surface, inspecting the huge orange fungi and the fan-shaped banana plants. He was surrounded by the constant twitter of birds in
the tall trees, and the paths would pass overgrown, unexcavated

houses and walls of the ancient city. The paths were littered with potsherds, and periodically he would come upon a pile of carved stone pediments, stelae, and serpent heads gathered from the jungle.

After walking for several hours, he would emerge suddenly at a building he had previously seen only from afar, across the green forest canopy. He climbed the tree-covered pyramids and found beautiful pottery shards. From the top he could see twenty miles across the jungle to distant blue mountains in the brilliant sunshine. At nightfall, the mosquitoes were very troublesome. All beds in the Yucatán were equipped with nets, and Allen bought one for his hammock. When the light faded and the chorus of chattering insects and bat squeaks began, he would go to the bar and restaurant to eat his evening meal and listen to the manager complain about his life. At night, alone in the moonlit ruins in his archaeologist's hut, he often felt lonely. "Worrying about my fate again," he wrote. "That a small breeze of nostalgia fluttered in my heart, thinking a moment past I had someone in the room I loved with me—no ghosts —a man of flesh to talk to and hug."

Allen arrived in the state of Chiapas in a bad temper. He had had a persistent head cold for several weeks and a touch of dysentery, and he had run out of water on an expedition through thornbushes and mud, trying to get a particular jungle view. He was already low on money, and his faulty command of the language meant that he often lost his temper with the bewildered Indians when he tried to buy something.

At the Palenque ruins, Allen stayed as usual in the archaeologist's hut. Palenque lay on a small tributary of the Usumacinta called the Otolum. The ceremonial buildings were all built on high ground at the foot of the hills that rose to become the Sierra Madre. It was a very old site. Palenque was at its apogee between the sixth and eighth centuries A.D., before it was abandoned to the macaws and monkeys.

The small area that had been cleared when Allen visited was dominated by the palace, with its three-story astronomical observation tower, and by the Temple of Inscriptions, where only two years before, in June 1952, Ruz discovered an underground crypt containing a giant carved sarcophagus and the remains of a priest-king wearing a jade death mask. In his thirteen-hundred-year-old tomb were the Mayan inscriptions that led eventually to the decipherment of Mayan glyphs. Most of the buildings and pyramids were still overgrown with thick jungle cover, and the forest was loud with bird song and the buzz of *chicharras grandes*, locusts, and crickets; the distant roar of jaguars could be heard in the deep forest. Allen's visit to Chiapas was transformed by a chance meeting in the Palenque ruins with the "White Goddess."

Her name was Karena Shields. She was about fifty years old and had been brought up in Palenque. She learned about the Maya from the Karivis Indians, their direct descendants, and had studied their metaphysics, symbolism, and history. The ruins of Palenque stood on her land, but she had discovered lost cities and explored sites all over Chiapas and neighboring Guatemala. She had written various scholarly papers and a popular book, *Three in the Jungle*. Shields had been educated in the United States and had played Jane in early Tarzan movies. She lived on a cocoa *finca* (plantation), which she ran, single-handed, deep in the forest. She was just the sort of person Allen needed to meet in order to see the real Mexico, and when she invited him to visit her *finca*, he readily accepted.

In Palenque, Allen had a series of vivid and melancholy dreams in which he embarked for the "ancient parapets of Europe." He dreamed of closing down his apartment and making arrangements with his family. He heard the foghorns sounding in the mist of New York harbor and dreamed of ships' captains, bunks, and cabin lights. After a particularly powerful dream of being with Burroughs on an Italian train, Allen decided that he must, as soon as possible, go and live for a time in Europe. The Mayan ruins had invoked a desire to see the antiquities of his own culture.

> *Yet these ruins so much*
> *woke me to nostalgia*
> *for the classic stations*
> *of the earth,*
> *the ancient continent*
> *I have not seen . . .*

On January 19, Allen, Shields, and three others set out on the seven-hour journey to the *finca*. They took a Jeep as far as the jungle track, then continued on horseback. This was a new experience for Allen, but he acquitted himself satisfactorily. Karena Shields had lived at the Finca Tacalapan de San Leandro since she was three years old, when her parents moved from Ohio to manage a rubber plantation in Chiapas. There was a large, open-sided shelter with a thatched roof, and a fire burned constantly at one end for coffee and the tortillas and frijoles they ate at every meal. They slept in hammocks slung across the room from tree trunks. Behind the house were six native huts for the families who worked the plantation. In front was Mount Don Juan, densely covered by trees that obscured Mayan ruins. Legend had it that craftsmen came back to a large tree on the summit, to complete work left unfinished at their death. The area was called Xibalba (pronounced Chivalva), and the Mayans believed it to be a region of limbo or purgatory.

Allen went fishing by flashlight at night with the Indians, carrying a long pronged stick to spear crawfish as big as lobsters. He rode horses and took long walks through the jungle, often wading up the rocky bed of the San Leandro River in the midday sun, wearing just his shoes, and surrounded by giant mahogany trees filled with monkeys. He could choose to wade ankle deep or, if he got hot, walk neck deep on the sandy bottom. There were clear rock pools surrounded by great ferns, ideal for swimming, and farther upstream he discovered a deep canyon with rapids and waterfalls. He washed away ten years of New York soot in a tropical paradise.

From logs, Allen built himself a set of drums ranging in size from three to seventeen feet, suspending them by vines from a wood support. He tapped a rubber tree to get the proper hard black tops for his foot-long drumsticks. He played several times a day, especially at dawn and in the evening in front of the fire. Usually he played with a very soft beat, but sometimes, when a file of Indians rode through, he would break into wild rhythms that could be heard for miles. He wrote Lucien Carr: "People come from miles around to listen to me play my drums. It really goes over big: this because I can actually bong out a variety of interesting African type rhythms, and because their own native drumming is so awkward and inept . . . my smooth easy-to-dance-to style is a great wonder."

The weeks passed. Allen grew a goatee and mustache, which made him look like a German professor. He tried his hand in the banana groves, and worked at most stages of cocoa production. He particularly liked standing in the river with the Indians, each with a woven basket of the beans, swishing them around in the water. On February 5, there was a meteor so bright that it illuminated the whole sky in brilliant red and blue, and on the same day they felt an earth tremor strong enough to shake the house and make the hammocks swing. A few days later, a rumor reached them that the earthquake was the result of a volcanic eruption at Acavalna, which had killed eight people in the town of Yajalon and toppled its four-hundred-year-old church. The population was said to be fleeing en masse.

After weeks of rumors but no hard facts, Allen decided to investigate. From Salto de Agua, the settlement nearest the *finca*, he hitched a ride to Yajalon with a reckless American pilot who flew a 1914 biplane over the jungle. A two-day trek by mule through the mountains, it was only fifteen minutes by plane. In Yajalon the old church still stood. Allen started the journey to the volcano on foot. Halfway there, he met a rancher, who loaned him his mule. Two men from Yajalon caught up with him, wanting to join the expedition, and at each village Allen passed through, his party grew larger. The first night was spent at Zapata, a small coffee-producing village.

At dusk, Allen heard what sounded like a colossal subway train passing beneath him. The sound shuddered. The village dogs began to bark. He was told by the villagers that they felt twenty such tremors a day; sometimes they were stronger. A hollow drum summoned everyone to the little thatched church at seven-thirty. The women sat in a circle on the floor and the men on logs against the walls. Each woman held a long wax taper, the only illumination in the room. The prayers were in Tzeltal, the native language, and the responses in Latin. After a silence, the boy next to Allen produced a bamboo flute from inside his shirt, another produced a small drum, and they began to play. A half hour later, they were joined by two guitarists. Suddenly the mountain roar began again, this time much louder. As the room began to shake, the women shrieked and ran for the door. Lumps of adobe began to crack from the walls, plaster fell from the beams, the roof creaked ominously. The whole mountain seemed to shake, and the roar became deafening. Pieces of adobe the size of tortillas were falling all around, grazing Allen's shoulders. Just as it seemed as if the church must surely topple, it was suddenly quiet. Allen stood trembling, regretting the stupid arrogance that had brought him to this dreadful mountain. He began to have second thoughts about the expedition he was to lead the next day.

When they set off in the morning, Allen's party numbered fifty-four. They climbed steadily. Everywhere was evidence of the tremors, and the path was strewn with rocks and rubble. At the summit, they found no sign of volcanic activity. The whole mountain, in fact, looked like a gigantic pile of ancient volcanic rocks rather than a dormant volcano. They looked out over the surrounding mountain ranges. A thin layer of smoke haze hung in the valleys, as all over the countryside Indians were burning the *milpa* for maize fields. The Indians pointed out the various villages below, and they watched a coffee company's plane enter the other end of the huge valley. Suddenly Allen heard the crackle and roar of flames. The Indians had set fire to a large dead tree and were jumping about in front of it, warming their hands in the cold mountain air. The fire caused clouds of smoke to billow from the top of Acavalna. The Indians were much amused. They knew that as soon as the people below saw the smoke, they would abandon their village. Satisfied that Acavalna was still extinct, the expedition set off for Zapata.

They got back in the late afternoon, and Allen prepared a report to be sent to all the nearby towns and villages to calm people's fears. They made a copy for the Instituto Geologica and for the government. Allen spent the night at a *finca* halfway down the mountain. The next morning, he rose early and went to the gate to look at the view of the Hunacmec valley. There at the gate he found about forty Indians from the town of La Ventana. They had trekked to the *finca* at dawn and waited patiently for him to finish breakfast. The Indians wanted him to come with them to the east side of the mountain, where there was a huge cave. Two of the men had been there many years before, and they wanted to know if the earthquake had destroyed it.

The new expedition set off at eight-thirty, with twenty men going on ahead of Allen to open up an old path through the *milpa* with their machetes. Eventually the men at the front began yelling that they had found something. When Allen reached the head of the column, he found all the men lined up on stones and rocks in front of a drop. Above them towered the huge arched entrance to an immense cavern.

Allen reported to Neal: "When I came out in the clearing, I saw a hole in the side of the mountain as big as St. Patrick's Cathedral, entrance to the great legendary cave—first stranger other than Indians ever there—solving riddle of the name of the mountain—House of Night—dark cave. Indians have great poetic imagination for names—a mountain anciently named house of night & forgotten why except for one or two who nobody believes centuries later."

The morning sunlight illuminated the great cathedral space. The floor near the entrance was carpeted with moss. Part of the roof edge had collapsed in the earthquake, bringing with it boulders and trees, which now littered the floor, their leaves still green. They all stood in awe for a while, then Allen, feeling obliged to take the lead, climbed down ten feet or so of rock and went in first. "I had to do something brave to justify the honor," he told Neal. Most of the Indians followed him. To their left was a great hole, its upper levels hung with stalactites. They could hear the steady drip of calcareous water.

Some of the stalactites were connected to stalagmites, to form columns. There was rubble everywhere, caused by the tremors. They heard a distant rumble and felt a movement deep in the mountain, but nothing fell from the roof. Afraid to venture too far within, they spent an hour climbing among the stalagmites nearest the entrance. Allen collected some fragments and they left. As they filed into the intense green light of the jungle, they heard the rumble of rocks falling deep in the cavern, though they neither heard nor felt a tremor.

On his return to Yajalon, he wrote Kerouac: "It was a real great Life Magazine intrepid American adventurer situation, I really was a great hero and nobody knew except in Yajalon where I lived in the Presidente's house and strode the streets in my beard and all the Indians saluted me respectfully and asked me for volcano advice (they were all terrified) and all the merchants invited me in back of their shops for coffee and the priest and I had many long afternoons over beer and theology and geology and I ate in the restaurant every evening and dined with the pilots of the crazy air service, heroes of these mountains (my friend who piloted me around was killed 2 weeks later with 4 passengers in the mist), and my restaurant bills went to City Hall, and everybody in town loaned me mules and guides for further exploration, other caves came to me, I went to Petalcingo, Chillon, all the little villages and towns in central Chiapas." He sent to Salto de Agua for his camera, and together with some officials from Yajalon, he returned to the cave to take photographs and explore some more.

Down to his last ten pesos, Allen decided not to wait until his welcome grew thin, and returned to Karena Shields's *finca*. In response to the information provided by Allen, a team arrived from the Instituto Geologica with generators and equipment to measure the cave, which turned out to be one of the largest in the Western Hemisphere. Allen and the Indians who had accompanied him became local heroes, and their picture went on sale all over central Chiapas.

Allen had been writing regularly to his family and friends, but
unknown to him, the Mexican postal service had lost all but a few
of his letters. Bill Burroughs in Tangier wrote to Jack: "Allen's
neglect will drive me to some extravagance of behavior. I don't
know what I will do, but it will be the terror of the earth. You must
remonstrate with him. I didn't expect him to act like this (not a line
in four months) and I didn't expect I would feel so deeply hurt if he
did." He asked Jack to write to Allen and tell him of the pain he
was causing.

In the last letter to reach Bill from Mexico, Allen had told him to
write him care of American Express in Mexico City. This Bill had
done, but his letter was returned unclaimed. "I don't mind he
doesn't write if he wants to feel completely free for a while," Bill
told Jack, "but he could have spared me all this hurt—(which I am
not playing up, which is worse than I describe in my letters to him)
—by simply dropping me a line (as he apparently did to you) saying he would be out of touch for a while. . . . P.S. No matter what
Allen says I want to hear it understand? If he says something
that you know would hurt me, please don't keep it from me. I want
to know. Nothing is worse than waiting like this day after day for
a letter that doesn't come. . . . THIS IS SERIOUS JACK, DON'T let me
down."

Unaware of the great drama unfolding in Burroughs's mind, Allen
remained at Karena Shields's *finca*. He spent most of April and the
beginning of May working on an eight-page poem, "Siesta in
Xbalba" (misspelling "Xibalba"). He told Neal: "I seem to be back
on ball, art *developing* and real serious. All old forms of 'Empty
Mirror' poems now falled together and synthesized in such a manner that the casual fragments of thought utilized for short poems
before are now linked together in a natural train of thought or images, very much paralleling the development of an intense meditation lying in a hammock just thinking along." He told Neal that he
wanted to make something sublime out of his visit to Chiapas and
described the central passage of the poem as a "meditation on a
carving of a skull I saw in Chichen Itza months ago":

> *In front of me a deathshead*
> *half a thousand years old . . .*

Allen could not continue his journey until money arrived; Karena
Shields was also broke, waiting for her book royalties. Storms

washed out the track from the *finca* to Salto de Agua and made the rivers impassable. When they were finally able to make the trip, Karena found the Mexican postal authorities had returned her royalty check to Harcourt, Brace the day before she and Allen reached town. They spent most of the time lying in their hotel rooms with nothing to do but wait. Eventually twenty dollars arrived from Eugene, and Allen was able to repay Karena and pay his hotel bill, but this left him almost completely broke again. He had to wait for Karena's check so that he could borrow enough to get to Mexico City, where money from Neal and, he hoped, his back wages from the *World-Telegram* were waiting.

Bill Burroughs, meanwhile, had become sick with worry. Allen had written Neal on April 6, urgently requesting money, which Neal had sent at once. The reply came from Salto de Agua that the funds were "unclaimed." Bill asked his parents to cable Allen thirty dollars from his next month's allowance, which they did, but the money disappeared en route. Bill deluged Jack with letters to forward to Allen. He wrote to Louis Ginsberg, suggesting that he make inquiries at the U.S. embassy in Mexico City, and asked Lucien to contact the Mexican branch of UPI. Bill told Jack: "I am afraid he may be in serious trouble, perhaps held incommunicado in jail. To stupid people he *looks* like a communist." He concluded: "I don't know what I would do if anything happened to Allen. I guess you have seen the letters I wrote to him and have some idea of how much he means to me."

Neal was also getting concerned; three letters in a row had been returned. Allen, of course, was happily writing letters to his family, Bill, Neal, Lucien, and Jack, but they were all lost. Then a letter from Yajalon, telling Bill about the volcano expedition, finally got through to Tangiers and calmed him down.

The intensity of Bill's feelings began to worry Allen, and he wrote Neal: "He sure is lonely or imagines himself such and I guess it drives him off the road at times. . . . This kind of need, with which I cannot but sympathize & try to do something real about . . . will be a real problem. But of our friendship, so complicated now & in some ways difficult . . . I hardly know what to do to straighten out and think probably the loco elements too deep to resolve and so must be put up with—too ingrained with the genius. My confidence to Bill always—though was relieved leaving New York to have his intensity off my back for a period. However a creative intensity which catalysed me to where I am now—much better off."

• • •

Karena Shields's check finally arrived, and Allen was able to set out for legendary California, having built up high hopes of renewing his love affair with Neal.

He found Neal, Carolyn, and the children living in San Jose in a nine-room wood-frame house with a large porch, its yard filled with every variety of fruit tree. In the front was a gigantic palm. Roses thrived in the constant sunshine, as did the pot plants in the adjacent vacant lot. The mountains of the Diablo range loomed to the east. Allen's room had French windows and an oversize desk. Neal provided him with a typewriter and a clock radio and even put his tape recorder at Allen's disposal. Allen unpacked the box of books and papers he had shipped from New York and made himself comfortable.

The balmy climate of that part of California had over the years attracted a considerable number of eccentrics, followers of fringe religions, and cranks, and the ground was thick with phrenologists, Theosophists, Rosicrucians, Reichians, flying-saucer spotters, flat earthers, Kirlian photographers, Vedantists, vegetarians, vegans, and nudists. It had also been a center for the late psychic theurgist Edgar Cayce. Both Neal and Carolyn had become followers of his philosophy. Cayce would go into a trance state and prescribe medications and treatments for the sick. He knew nothing about medicine, and his cures were usually herbal or homeopathic. A believer in the lost kingdom of Atlantis, Cayce was also a traveler on the astral plane. He made predictions and gave "life readings," going into a trance and revealing his followers' previous incarnations.

Neal was told that he had been a famous general and a champion charioteer in ancient Egypt. Unfortunately, he had cut down his children with blades attached to the axle hubs of his chariot. Neal, still working as a brakeman, took all this very seriously. Since Allen had last seen him, he had grown cold and emotionless. His passion for life had soured and become a series of obsessions: for driving, sex, marijuana, chess, and the philosophy of Cayce. His driving was faster and more frantic. Whereas he used to take pleasure at being at the wheel, now he was filled with hatred for everyone else on the road. He and Carolyn were having personal problems and were no longer having sex. Carolyn later said: "Neal never enjoyed it unless there was violence. He couldn't manage it any other way. The only times he was ever not able to do it was when I was offering or willing. It had to be rape. Until finally I only submitted because

I was afraid of him. At last, then, I said, 'I can't stand it anymore, kill me or whatever,' and much to my surprise he was very nice about it, he seemed to understand."

Neal spent a lot of time hunting down new sex partners and even seduced a seventy-year-old spiritualist masseuse. On the railroad, he was caught masturbating by the conductor when he was supposed to be on duty. He would smoke too much pot and then get into a rage over his inability to connect with what was going on. He played endless, robotic games of chess with his neighbor Dick Woods, and in the evenings he and Carolyn attended Cayce meetings, where they sat and discussed Gurdjieff, Atlantis, and the Akashic records.

Kerouac had stayed with Neal and Carolyn earlier in the year, expecting to meet up with Allen, but when Allen was delayed at the *finca*, Jack had returned home to his mother. Jack had also found Neal to be very cold and had been irritated by his blind allegiance to Cayce. Unable to understand how Neal, his all-American hero, could fall for something so anodyne, Jack began to look up the original Oriental texts the Cayce people drew on, in order to undermine Neal's credulity. In particular, Jack studied Dwight Goddard's *Buddhist Bible*, an anthology of most of the standard Buddhist texts, including the Diamond Sutra. He and Neal argued furiously, Cayce versus the Buddha, and in the process, Jack became a Buddhist. He submerged himself in the Buddhist texts and wrote a dreamy letter to Allen in Mexico professing his love and asking to hear about his Mayan discoveries and poems. But he warned Allen not to expect him "to get excited by anything anymore."

When Allen arrived, he was soon given the word on Cayce, and though skeptical, he read Cayce's *Extracts from Readings* and Gina Cerminara's *Cayce System Book*. He concluded that Cayce was a "crackpot," which didn't help his relationship with Neal. No matter what subject they discussed, Neal seemed to have memorized Cayce's views, and once those were announced, no further discussion was possible. Allen reluctantly concluded in a letter to Jack that Neal "really is suffering some incipient insanity." The emotional closeness Allen had been hoping for, the main reason for his trip, was lacking. Allen put this to Neal, and he agreed. "I have no feelings, never had," he said. It was a far cry from Allen's idealized dream fantasy of the situation, set down in his "Love Poem on Theme by Whitman," which opened with Whitman's line "I'll go into the bedroom silently and lie down between the bridegroom and the bride, / those bodies fallen from heaven stretched out waiting naked and restless . . ."

Allen's occasional sex with Neal was aggressive, harsh, and frantic, and his enormous desire was frustrated night after night by Neal's indifference. His journal records the unhappy catalog of his frustration: how he arranged the shades, turned down the lights, and waited for Neal to finish seven games of chess with his neighbor. But then, instead of joining him, Neal suddenly retired to his own bed without a word. "Once again, I've manoeuvred myself into a frustrating idealistic situation where I'm reduced to pathetic beggary," he recorded.

The Cayce people had told Neal to stop writing. "I was writing about sex, you dig, it's sinful, I know . . . ," he told Allen, and Carolyn agreed: "What good is that sort of thing? You call that art? It's just dirt!" Allen lamented the pages and pages of Neal's manuscripts that had been thrown in the trash. Neal hardly talked to Allen, except in a dissociated way. Allen thought that Neal probably hated Carolyn but felt trapped by the children and, in any case, had nowhere else to go. Earlier in the year, Kerouac had been horrified when Neal knocked his daughter Cathy clear across the room. When Allen tried to talk to him about it, Neal just said that there was "No way out for me," and he drove even faster, played chess with even more maniacal intensity, or just went blank. Allen wrote Kerouac: "Everything seems *impossible* as far as any real contact —he really gets no kicks from me."

Carolyn, meanwhile, had withdrawn protectively into herself and was grimly devoting herself to her three children and trying to save her marriage. She had asked the Cayce people for advice on how to live with Neal, and Hugh Lynn Cayce told her, "All you have to do is keep your mouth shut." Allen completely misunderstood her plight and complained to Jack: "She doesn't dig new things (statues or paintings when pointed out)—I mean she has no active curiosity or aesthetic or kicks interests and lives by this ruinous single-track idea of running the family according to her ideas strictly, ideas which are mad copies of *House Beautiful* and are really nowhere."

Allen thought Neal had been unfair to invite him to come out and then reject him, "making things unclear, leaving me hung up when he knows my habit so well." The situation brought out the masochistic side of Allen's character, and he began to record sex fantasies in his journals: "I want to be your slave, suck your ass, suck your cock, you fuck me, you master me, you humiliate me—humiliate me, I want to be tied and whipped, spanked on the behind over knees, want to be made to cry and beg and weep for love."

But Neal simply said, "Do what you want." The situation was frustrating and painful. Unfortunately, Allen was trapped by poverty; Neal was paying for his upkeep. Allen wrote: "I feel like a strange idiot, standing there among wife & children all to whom he gives needs of affection and attention, aching for some special side extra sacrifice of attention to me—as if like some nowhere evil beast intruding I were competing for his care with his children & wife & job."

Early one morning in August, Allen was in his room reading as Neal prepared to go to work. Somehow Allen enticed him into his room. Carolyn burst in and caught them. She screamed in horror and revulsion, then recovered herself enough to order Allen from the house. Neal went blank and ran off to work, leaving Allen and Carolyn to work it out.

"You've always been in my way since Denver," Carolyn accused him. "You're trying to come between us." Allen went cold with horror and felt "steeped in evil." The same tired despair and hopeless futility he had felt when, as a teenager, he had taken Naomi to Lakewood returned now as Carolyn raged at him. Allen did not sympathize with her plight, nor did he see himself as in any way responsible for, or contributing to, the shaky state of her marriage. He was focused on Neal, and on his own desire.

Allen said nothing in reply to her accusations, just "went blank with a kind of hopeless feeling she was mad . . . I didn't come to screw her up." But Carolyn was adamant. She forbade Allen ever to see Neal again. She drove him to Berkeley and lent him twenty dollars. The ride was tense, but she asked Allen to try to understand and forgive her. He wrote Jack: "I know what I was doing with Neal sounds on the surface like a monstrous thing, as Carolyn, with some justice, suddenly exploded out with, but that is not the cause of their woes."

Bill Burroughs, for one, was not surprised at this turn of events. He wrote to Kerouac: "[Allen] wrote me about he had been throwed out of the Cassady house. Hardly surprising. You know how women are. Come on broadminded and understanding. . . . I knew a woman once in Chi, a German, said she was emancipated and didn't mind her husband going with other women until he did it, then she attacked him with a carving knife, called the cops and attempted suicide. Well I guess Caroline [sic] has what she wants now. What

every U.S. bitch of them wants. A man all to herself with no perni-
cious friends hanging about."

After Allen's departure, Carolyn and Neal finally had some serious talks and decided that they both should take the Rorschach
inkblot test, a personality and intelligence test, very popular at the
time, used in determining levels of clinical insanity. Neal's test
showed that he was sexually sadistic; that he was prepsychotic; that
he had a "delusive thought system"; and that he was intensely
anxiety-prone. Allen, who had previously not believed in the idea of
"clinical insanity," now began to think there might be something in
it, certainly as far as Neal was concerned.

In San Francisco, Allen looked up Al Sublette, who had received
him with great civility when he visited a few months earlier. Sublette, a friend of Kerouac's, was a black seaman with an ear for
good jazz and an eye for women; he lived at the Hotel Marconi.
Allen checked in, and that night he met a girl in Vesuvio's Bar and
fell in love.

Her name was Sheila Williams Boucher, and he described her
excitedly to Kerouac: "A *great* new girl who digs me, I dig—22,
young, *hip* (ex-singer, big buddy of Brubeck, knows all the colored
cats, ex-hipster girl), *pretty* in a real chic classy way, . . . she has a
wild mind, finer than *any* girl I met—really, a real treasure—and
such a lovely face—so *fine* a pretty face—young life in her—and
real sharp." He continued to extol her virtues, particularly the fact
that she wasn't crazy. "What a doll. *And* she's not a flip thank God.
Not a stupid square in any way but *not* a flip . . . instant digging
each other—how wild and great."

Sheila was small, with short blond hair, and when Allen met her
she was not yet divorced from her husband. She had a job writing
advertising copy for the May Company on Market Street and tried
to get Allen a job there. For the first week they did nothing but talk
and neck, spending most of their time wandering around the streets
of San Francisco in the warm evening air or sitting drinking coffee
in her apartment on Nob Hill. She liked Al Sublette and was quite
familiar with marijuana from her days as a singer in roadhouses.
Allen was especially pleased at her appreciation of particular lines
in his poetry, rather than just expressing approval of the poems in
general. The only drawback was that she had been married at eighteen and had a four-year-old son, Michael, living with her. Allen
was now prepared to be paternal.

Neal, meanwhile, out of either guilt or sheer perversity, suddenly wanted sex with Allen. Whenever his railroad job brought him to San Francisco, he would stay with Allen. "I had a torrid romance then with Neal while I was at the Marconi, some really wild sex scenes," Ginsberg remembered later. On one occasion Allen and Neal went to bed with Sheila. They both made love to her, and while she slept, Allen and Neal crept out of the room, "went into the bathroom and started screwing. That was probably the dirtiest we ever got."

Allen found himself a job with the market research firm of Towne-Oller. His hair was close-cropped; he was clean shaven and wore a good tweed suit. He seemed to enjoy his transformation, as described in an unpublished poem, "In Vesuvio's Waiting for Sheila," which opened: "Here at last a moment / in foreign Frisco. / Where I am thoroughly / beautiful / Dark suit—dark eyes / no glasses, / Money in my wallet— / Checkbook abreast— / Toward an evening / of fucking and jazz . . ."

Shortly after Allen's arrival in California, Neal had driven him into San Francisco, where he visited Kenneth Rexroth, who, at forty-eight, was already the doyen of the Bay Area literary scene. He held weekly seminars at his house, in which political, religious, and literary subjects were discussed. Rexroth was an old-time anarcho-pacifist, with an interest in Oriental mysticism. He translated from the Greek and Latin, Chinese and Japanese, in addition to writing his own open-form poetry. Allen came armed with a letter of introduction from William Carlos Williams and had with him the manuscript of *Empty Mirror*. He had also corresponded with Rexroth in 1952, at Williams's suggestion, so Rexroth knew who he was. Rexroth had a reputation for being prickly, but Allen found him very easy to get along with. Now that he was living in San Francisco, Allen naturally renewed the acquaintance and began attending Rexroth's literary salon.

He got to know Robert Duncan, seven years Allen's senior, who, together with the poet Jack Spicer, had his own literary circle. Although Allen liked Duncan as a person, he found his poetry too aesthetic and precious. There was always a slight distance between them. Allen began to meet the local North Beach characters. Peter DuPeru, a sensitive, curious, and intelligent soul, reminded Allen of Carl Solomon because he had received shock treatment. DuPeru wandered the streets without socks, looking at San Francisco's baroque architecture, which was his great love. "He has the best mystic mind I've met here," Allen reported to Kerouac. "Digs me too." In the first draft of "Howl," several lines were devoted to the Peter DuPeru story: "Who limped over the city hills with half a mustache growing on the sinister side of his lip, looking for an example of baroque architecture carrying Butler's Analogy." Allen also met Kenneth Patchen, the author of *The Journal of Albion Moonlight,* who lived a few blocks away on Telegraph Hill. Patchen lent him a rare Black Sun edition of the Dos Passos translation of Blaise Cendrars' *Transsiberian Voyage,* a long poem which later served as one of the models for Ginsberg's travelogue-style works, *The Fall of America* and *Iron Horse.*

It was only a matter of weeks before Allen moved into Sheila's Pine Street apartment, on Nob Hill. Three decades later, Ginsberg recalled that it was a "deep affair, really fell in love and wanted to fuck and could get hardons. It was the first time I'd had a balanced heterosexual life, to the point where I really wanted to get married and have kids and settle down to a life in advertising."

Burroughs was horrified; he had been planning to move to San Francisco and live with Allen. He wrote to Kerouac: "Now Allen is talking about making it with a chick, and I am really upset and worried. If I get out to Frisco and he is making it with a chick I might as well turn round and start back. You know how U.S. chicks are. They want it all. It would be the end of my relationship with Allen. At this point I couldn't stand to be around him all the time with no sex. It would be too much strain on me."

Bill's idea of joining Allen in San Francisco was partly Kerouac's fault. Bill's fear for Allen's fate in the Mexican jungle and his extravagant expressions of love had led Jack to ask: "If you love Allen, why don't you return and live with him?" Bill replied from the male brothel where he lived in Tangier: "You are right, I will, unless he can arrange to come here very soon. One basic fact I have learned on this trip, is how much I need the few friends I have." Bill had clearly not regarded Cassady as much of a problem, but Sheila was definitely a threat.

Burroughs left for the States from Gibraltar in September 1954, and Allen grew increasingly worried. "God knows what will happen," he wrote Jack. "The impossibilities of his demands are ultimately inescapable unless I let him carry me off forever to Asia or something to satisfy his conception of his despair and need. . . . I do like him and would love to share a place with him here, if it could be done, which it will be—but he is going to be frantic and possessive you know. . . . The situation with Sheila will be a madhouse. I don't know how to manage it. . . . It's a real bitch, man."

Allen's visit to Neal had been in some ways a flirtation with danger; though he had had high hopes for a renewed emotional relationship, Neal's rejection hurt him most in terms of sexual frustration, and he was able to retain his composure. Dealing with Burroughs's infatuation was an altogether more difficult task. It meant finally rejecting his teacher. It was also a big test of his hard-won independence. His choice was either to surrender himself to Bill, thereby losing his own identity, or to reject Bill and continue to build his independent new life. Although it worried him enormously, he knew it was only a matter of time before he had to make the break.

Allen had settled into an approximation of a comfortable middle-class American life. He was earning $250 a month and lived in an elegant large apartment on Nob Hill with a beautiful woman, a child, and a friendly cat. He worked all day at the advertising agency, where he had two secretaries, and in the evenings he and Sheila entertained.

Neal, no longer feeling any emotional pressure from Allen, began to drop by once or twice a week to deliver or borrow pot, sometimes bringing his pusher with him. Often Neal would sit on the floor of the living room with his pot spread out on a newspaper in front of him, chopping and cleaning it, blowing the seeds to one side, while Allen busied himself around the apartment, collecting the child's toys, tidying up, and taking out the garbage. One evening Neal settled himself on the white shag rug, smoked a joint, and began to read aloud from Marcel Proust, just as he used to in New York back in 1947. "A quiet sweet nite," Allen called it in a letter to Kerouac.

But Allen soon began to feel the strain of his middle-class lifestyle. He hadn't written anything since he was in San Jose, because he never had any time alone, and he was very worried by Burroughs's impending arrival. He began to find fault with Sheila, complaining to Kerouac that she was "younger and more prey to girlish psychological semi-dramatizations (I'm an old man, tired sort of, I can't make the flux of love illusions) and undoubtedly the seeds of dissolution of this affair have already set in, now that we are established." But later in the same letter, he confided: "Sheila hates me because I am a stuffy old nag—saying [I'm an] abstractionist and not a Dostoievskian lover. I screw for the first time regular these days, by the way, what a relief to come home to." By the middle of October he found time to continue work on "The Green Automobile" and began to thumb through his full notebooks for other passages that showed promise as raw material for poems.

Truly dreading Bill's arrival on the Coast now, fearing an inexorable involvement, Allen told Jack: "There would be a bust with the cops ultimately, and I'd be coming late to work, and I'd have to sit and listen to him and routines mercilessly applauding and so on. . . . I lack solitude here and Bill is a power of solitude—got to give him *all* attention." Allen tried to let Bill down gently and kindly, pointing out all the many problems, but Bill simply interpreted this as Allen being coy. Unfortunately, the situation was exacerbated by Kerouac, who, feeling sorry for Bill in his misery, told him a white lie: that Allen secretly wanted to be with him, otherwise he wouldn't have talked about it so much. Eventually Allen screwed up his courage and wrote a severe, stiff letter of rejection, which finally brought home the truth of the situation to Bill. Burroughs was absolutely shattered. "I think I'm responsible for single-handed destroying Bill's belief in love," Ginsberg said later.

Bill gave up the idea of moving to the Coast, and it was to be another twenty years before he saw California. He went instead to see his parents in Florida, where he received more bad news. The garden center they operated was not profitable as before, and they had to halve his allowance to one hundred dollars a month. Since he was broke and owed Jack money, he wasn't even sure that he could make it back to Tangier.

Allen was annoyed with Jack for giving Bill encouragement, and it took several letters to straighten out matters between them. When Allen was staying in San Jose, he and Jack began to exchange letters about Buddhism, and Allen asked Jack to be his teacher. Jack had made a thorough study of the material available in the San Jose public library when he was there but had not made contact with any Buddhist teachers or groups. Nevertheless, he was prepared to go along with Allen's request. He sent him a "correct bibliography" and rather pompously instructed Allen to listen to him, for his beginning studies in Buddhism "as tho I was Einstein teaching you relativity or Eliot teaching the formulas of Objective Correlation on a blackboard in Princeton." Allen did not tell him that he had already read a massive amount of material on Zen Buddhism when he was studying Oriental art in New York City.

Jack's understanding of Buddhism, however, seemed to be basically theistic, since he never gave up his Catholic faith. As Lucien Carr mentioned in a letter to Allen later that year: "The old kannuck bean peddler; eye think he thinks Buddha is the pope." In fact, Allen apparently was the only one of Jack's friends who took his Buddhism seriously.

Meanwhile, Allen's Nob Hill life continued. Neal spent more time in San Francisco and taught Al Sublette and half of North Beach how to play chess. To Allen's constant irritation, Neal was even more deeply involved with Edgar Cayce and brought him up at every possible moment. His work on the railroad was deteriorating because he was high on pot all the time. The other railroad workers were complaining about him, and he had come up before three company investigations. To bring them nearer to San Francisco, Carolyn sold the San Jose house and moved the family to Los Gatos.

Allen's relationship with Sheila hit serious trouble when he finally told her about his long sexual history with Neal. He had decided to begin analysis again, and a factor in his decision to reveal his homosexuality to Sheila may have been so that he could talk to her about everything that came up. Looking back, Ginsberg said, "We had developed a tremendous trust and I felt that she accepted me for myself and I no longer had to hide anything from her." But homosexuality was not spoken about casually in 1954, and for Sheila it may have been an unknown, terrifying, and revolting thing. "She threw a big fit and apparently it destroyed our relationship at least for the time being," Ginsberg said, recalling the situation years later. "She didn't want to sleep with me anymore, so I went through all sorts of masochistic tortures, with a girl this time for a change, which was a relief, a break in my pattern."

Ever since Allen arrived from Mexico he had been under stress, first from Neal, then from Carolyn and Bill. On November 10, he went for his initial one-dollar-an-hour therapeutic session at the Langley Porter Clinic, a division of the University of California at Berkeley Medical School. Allen's doctor was Philip Hicks, but he was pleased to find another psychiatrist there who was an old friend from Columbia, Steven Schoen. They had long talks, and Allen felt reassured by Schoen's sensitive approach to his problems.

Allen continued to live with Sheila, and though she wanted him to move out, life in many ways continued normally. Allen entered into a very productive correspondence with Bill, who returned to Tangier in December. Burroughs sent long "routines," flights of imaginative writing three or four pages long, with virtually every letter he wrote. These routines were destined to become part of *Naked Lunch*. Allen resumed his role as Bill's agent and took some of the pieces to Kenneth Rexroth, who was a reader for New Directions.

Allen showed him the "Roosevelt After Inauguration" routine, written the previous May in Lima, in which (among other things) Roosevelt replaces members of the Supreme Court with purple-assed baboons. Rexroth grimaced and said, "I don't think that's funny." Bill was incredulous at Rexroth's response. "It's not supposed to be *accurate*. Does he think it has anything to do with Roosevelt?" A series of incidents such as this gradually brought Bill and Allen back together as old friends doing battle against the philistines.

At the end of November, Al Sublette shipped out to Chile. Allen helped him carry his precious collection of jazz records on board, and as they stowed his things, Allen suddenly got a tremendous desire to ship out again and make enough money to fulfill his dream of going to Europe.

He continued his extensive correspondence with Kerouac. It was for the most part concerned with spiritual matters, though by the end of the year, Jack had reconsidered his "Einstein" role as Allen's teacher of Buddhism. He decided that he was too ignorant to be a master and told Allen that they were "fellow disciples before the Awesome Law." Their other discussions were usually political. Kerouac had become a great supporter of Senator Joseph McCarthy's crusade against communism and began to rail against old friends like Al Hinkle, whom he labeled a "commie," criticizing Allen for defending him. It has been suggested that Kerouac shifted to the political right sometime in the sixties, but in fact he had always retained the reactionary political values of his parents.

Allen and Sheila argued constantly about their affair and the reasons why Allen didn't really love her deeply. Perhaps he loved men too much, though he wasn't sure if that was still the case. He did still have an idealized fantasy of a boy lover, but "What would I do with a pilgrim soul if I did find a real one here in San Francisco?" he asked her in the middle of one argument.

At the beginning of December, Allen was walking alone through the nighttime streets after yet another row with Sheila. He wandered aimlessly, a little drunk, and came to Polk Gulch, which was then a bohemian neighborhood. Entering Foster's Cafeteria, he looked for Peter DuPeru, who lived nearby, but no one he knew was there.

There was a table of young artist types, and Allen went up to the one who had a beard and looked the most interesting. He was a twenty-six-year-old painter named Robert LaVigne. Allen introduced himself, and they talked about art. Allen soon impressed him with stories about Franz Kline, Willem de Kooning, and Larry Rivers, whom he knew from New York. LaVigne invited Allen to come back with him and see his paintings. He lived only a few blocks away, in a large apartment on the first floor of a wooden Victorian house on Gough Street.

Allen was at once enthralled by a large oil painting of a naked boy with yellow hair and a frank youthful expression, who looked right out of the canvas at him. He felt his heart leap and asked who the boy was. "Oh, that's Peter," said LaVigne. "He's here. He's home." And into the room walked Peter Orlovsky, with the same youthful innocent expression on his face, only a little shyer. He was twenty-one years old, a tall, silent, gentle Russian youth.

They invited Allen to return, which he did, about a week later, bringing Neal Cassady with him. Another of LaVigne's paintings was a nude study of an attractive red-haired girl. Neal reacted as Allen had to the painting of Peter; he fell in love with her. The woman also lived in the apartment, having moved in about three months before. Her name was Natalie Jackson.

LaVigne had an exhibition opening in San Diego and told Allen that once the show was over, he intended to leave town to paint. He asked that Allen see as much of Peter as possible, because Peter "needed a sweet companion." Allen shuddered. He felt doomed. He could already feel his heart melting toward Peter. "Oh God, not again!" he exclaimed. "Lord, what are you asking me for?" LaVigne was being very mysterious. He clearly felt that his own season with Peter was terminating, and he wanted Peter to be looked after. It seemed to Allen that LaVigne was behaving like a *shadchen*, an arranger of marriages.

Allen spent a night at Gough Street with Peter. He wrote Jack: "Real sweetness in my breast, too much, I'd almost cry, but it's such a poor pitiful fleeting human life, what do I want anyway? Nature boy—to be loved in return. So followed a night of embraces, not sex."

Allen had to leave the city for a few days. His brother Eugene was getting married to Connie Herbert, a minister's daughter. On December 14, 1954, Allen flew to New York, still a major trip in the early fifties, involving stopovers in Los Angeles and Chicago. The wedding was a big, happy family occasion, marred only by Buba's annoyance that Eugene had chosen a girl who wasn't Jewish. She took Eugene aside and pinched him viciously on the arm. Before the wedding, Allen went out to visit Naomi. She was quiet and tearful, and she looked very old. She complained about the wires in her head and asked to be taken home. It was the last time Allen saw her.

Back in San Francisco, Allen found that there had been a number of changes during the five days he was away. Neal was living with Natalie in LaVigne's apartment and had introduced the household to pot. Neal's friend Al Hinkle and Sheila had started sleeping together. This pleased Allen, because when he returned, LaVigne and Peter asked him to come live with them. "Good, that's what you deserve," was Sheila's response. "Get out of here."

Ginsberg described his first sexual experience with Peter in some detail:

"I went to Peter's room. We were to sleep together that night on a huge mattress he had on the floor. I took off my clothes and got into bed. I hadn't slept with too many people. Never openly, completely giving and taking. With Jack or Neal, with people who were primarily heterosexual and who didn't fully accept the sexualization of our tenderness, I felt I was forcing it on them; so I was always timid about them making love back to me, and they very rarely did very much. When they did it was like blessings from heaven. If you get into it there's a funny kind of pleasure/pain, absolute loss/hope. When you blow someone like that and they come, it's great! And if they touch you once, it's enough to melt the entire life structure, as well as the heart, the genitals and the earth. And it'll make you cry.

"So . . . Peter turned around (he was in his big Japanese robe), opened up the bathrobe—he was naked—and put it around me and pulled me to him; and we got close, belly to belly, face to face. That was so frank, so free and so open that I think it was one of the first times that I felt open with a boy. Then, emboldened, I screwed Peter. He wept afterwards, and I got frightened, not knowing what I'd done to make him cry, but completely moved by the fact that he was so involved as to weep. At the same time, the domineering, sadism part of me was flattered and erotically aroused.

"The reason he wept was that he realized how much he was giving me, and how much I was demanding, asking and taking. I think he wept looking at himself in that position, not knowing how he had gotten there; not feeling it was wrong, but wondering at the strangeness of it. The most raw meat of reasons, for weeping. Then Robert hearing, seeing the situation, came in to comfort Peter a little bit. I was very possessive and I pushed Robert away. That got me and Robert into a funny kind of distrust that lasted for a year or two. . . . Peter was primarily heterosexual, and always was. I guess that was another reason he was shocked—the heaviness of my sadistic possessiveness in screwing him. For the first time in my life I really had the opportunity to screw somebody else!"

Allen wrote the poem "Malest Cornifici Tuo Catullo" and addressed it to Jack:

> *I'm happy, Kerouac, your madman Allen's*
> *finally made it: discovered a new young cat,*
> *and my imagination of an eternal boy*
> *walks on the streets of San Francisco,*
> *handsome, and meets me in cafeterias*
> *and loves me. . . .*

Allen liked the Gough Street apartment, with the smell of oil paint from Robert's front-room studio. The big messy rooms and the kitchen where everyone met and talked reminded him of 115th Street, New York. Peter's room was in the middle and Natalie's was in the back. Neal was constantly rushing in and out like Oliver Hardy, happy, pulling off his pants as he ran down the corridor to make it with Natalie, giggling. He and Natalie played games together and sometimes wore each other's clothes while they sat and smoked pot in her room. One day Allen and Neal met at the door and nodded to each other in agreement; they had both "gained so much tender youth kicks in the last two weeks entering the apartment," as Allen wrote Jack. "So sweet and promising . . . tender joy entering the house again for me and Neal feels the same."

Despite these enormous changes in his personal life, Allen continued his market research with Towne-Oller and his analysis with Dr. Philip Hicks at Langley Porter. He confided all his fears to Hicks: "You know, I'm very hesitant to get into a deep thing with Peter because where can it ever lead? Maybe I'll grow old and then Peter probably won't love me—just a transient relationship. Besides, shouldn't I be heterosexual?"

"Why don't you do what you want?" asked Hicks. "What would you like to do?"

"Well," said Allen. "I really would just love to get an apartment on Montgomery Street, stop working and live with Peter and write poems!"

"So why don't you do that?" asked Hicks.

"What happens if I get old or something?"

Hicks laughed. "Oh, you're a nice person. There's always people who will like you." Allen was amazed. At last, an authority figure had given him permission to be completely free.

Robert LaVigne had second thoughts about giving up Peter. After a few weeks of emotionally stormy weather, during which Allen and Peter lived in separate hotels, Allen took an apartment at 1010 Montgomery Street. A week later, in mid-February, Peter moved in. Allen proposed that he and Peter take a marriage vow, similar to the one he had persuaded Neal to take at the rainy crossroads in Oklahoma. Sitting in Foster's Cafeteria one morning at 3 A.M., "We made a vow to each other that he could own me, my mind and everything I knew, and my body, and I could own him, and all he knew, and his body; and that we would give each other ourselves, so that we possessed each other as property, to do everything we wanted to, sexually or intellectually, and in a sense explore each other until we reached the mystical 'X' together, emerging two merged souls. We had the understanding that when our (my particularly) erotic desire was ultimately satisfied by being satiated (rather than denied), there would be a lessening of desire, grasp, holding on, craving and attachment; and that ultimately we would both be delivered free in heaven together. And so the vow was that neither of us would go into heaven unless we could get the other one in."

As with Cassady, the vow was very much an attempt by Allen to formalize and make permanent their erotic relationship. It was also similar to Burroughs's "schlupp" proposal. In a long soliloquy in his journal addressed to Peter, Allen wrote: "So I don't care who else you screw, make it with girls, only to be sure to keep compassion for me, answer call when I break down to need of love moment— initiate my liberation and sexual revelation of self. Far as I know I want to be tied to bed and screwed, whipped, want to wrestle and blow and come in unison, sexual ecstasy. . . . In return . . . my role as teacher already well defined but also promise to deliver with two special talents—creative sense & literary craft kicks. . . . Which amounts to exchange of souls and bodies. . . . So in this, you be master in bed, and I be master in book. . . . Peter, I feel as if I'm in heaven. If this works out, I could end notebooks here and go on to impersonal existence. I'm on the verge of a great discovery. And the poems to write . . ."

Though Allen and Peter's relationship was to last for more than thirty years, it had within it the fatal flaw of Peter's heterosexuality. Over the years, he had a number of long-term relationships with women, creating more than one ménage à trois of unusual complexity, which caused a great deal of tension and strain.

Peter's family history would add another complexity to the relationship. His father, Oleg, was a cadet in the czar's army in St. Petersburg. During the Revolution, he narrowly escaped death while guarding the Winter Palace. He was captured, escaped, and eventually made his way to the United States, arriving in New York City in 1921. There he met Katherine Schwarten, born in Yonkers, who had left home at seventeen and moved to the Lower East Side to become a writer. They were married in 1926, and Peter, born July 8, 1933, was the third of their five children—Nicholas, Julius, Peter, and the twins, Lafcadio and Marie—born between 1927 and 1941.

Katherine and Oleg were dogged by ill fortune. In 1927, a mastoid operation performed by an incompetent doctor left Katherine deaf and with a partially paralyzed face. Oleg's business did badly; he ran a silk-screen shop in what is now SoHo, in Manhattan, where his sons were pressed into working long, exhausting hours, but he was put out of business at the end of the war by cheap imports from the Far East. Oleg began drinking and released his disappointment and frustration through violence toward his family. Eventually he and Katherine separated. Katherine took the children and moved to Queens, where Peter went to school. His mother made him drop out when he was seventeen because she said she was too poor to continue feeding him. He remembered the occasion. She walked around him a couple of times and said, "You're a big handsome boy with strong hands. You'll have no difficulty in getting jobs in your life." By this time Peter's brother Julius had been sent to Central Islip Mental Institute, suffering from catatonic schizophrenia.

Peter took a menial job at a hospital in Queens, washing dishes for seventy-five cents an hour. He worked twelve hours a day, six days a week, then got a better job at a state mental hospital, where he worked a forty-hour week tending senile patients. He changed their sheets, mopped the floors, and fed them. He attended night school and finished the requirements for his high school diploma.

The job depressed him, and sometimes, while he was on ward duty, he cried at the bleak, hopeless lives of the patients.

In 1953, during the Korean War, he was drafted into the army. Peter had always been quiet and dreamy, and at boot camp in West Virginia he spent his spare time thinking or reading, until one day a lieutenant found him reading a book by Erich Fromm and demanded to know if he was a Communist. "An army is an army against love," Peter told him. They sent him to work as a medic in the army hospital in San Francisco for the duration of his military service. He was very lonely and took long, solitary walks around the city on his weekends off. It was during this vulnerable time that he met Robert LaVigne.

LaVigne was very friendly. Peter was still a virgin, though he felt attracted to girls. However, he desperately needed friendship and human contact and allowed himself to be seduced by LaVigne. "I was very scared. I was trembling all over. He was showing me these big thick artbooks. I knew something was going on. I don't remember too much after that," Peter said. "I was young. I've always liked girls, but I couldn't make it with them yet. I didn't know how to do it. I was a dope, a creep, a hermit, a moron. I was going to spend the rest of my life by myself unless I had a brainstorm. But Bob LaVigne came along and there was a whole new friendship, exciting sexual knowledge facts."

On Montgomery Street, Allen and Peter each had his own room, separated by a hallway, so they both had privacy. Turkish rugs covered the living room floor; there was a large fireplace and a soft armchair to read in. Allen bought a three-speed phonograph from a pawnshop. He happily unpacked all his books, records, and papers and arranged them on his big work desk. In addition to his own journals and poetry, he had manuscripts by Kerouac, Burroughs, and Cassady that he was still trying to place with publishers.

Peter spent a lot of time brooding. He would go into dark Russian moods, lock himself in his room, and weep for days on end, then emerge cheerful and friendly, as if nothing had happened. Allen soon learned that it was best not to interfere. Kerouac wrote reassuringly about Allen's friendship with Peter. This was a time of great closeness between Jack and Allen, though they were on opposite coasts, and their letters grew intimate. Jack wrote to say that he loved getting letters from "my fine sweet Allen," called him a saint, and swore that he would never get mad at him again.

Allen was doing his best to place Jack's *Visions of Cody*. He gave it to Kenneth Rexroth, who showed it to Robert Duncan. Allen respected Duncan's high literary standards, so he was delighted when Duncan said it was obviously a work of genius: "Any man who can write fifty pages of description of reflections within a polished car bumper is a great genius in the tradition of Gertrude Stein consciousness prose," Duncan told Allen. Rexroth, on the other hand, was not impressed.

Allen was surprised by the amount of literary activity in the Bay Area. Duncan ran his poetry workshop at San Francisco State College, and at the end of 1954, Ruth Witt-Diamant founded the San Francisco Poetry Center. The inaugural reading was by W. H. Auden; Allen first met the poet Michael McClure at the reception afterward. Neither of them was impressed by the reading, and as they talked, they discovered a mutual interest in William Blake. McClure remembered, "One of my first memories of Allen was how different his idea of Blake was from mine. How profoundly both of us resonated with the work of Blake, yet how extremely different our views were. It was almost as if there were two Blakes." For McClure, Blake was the liberator, whereas for Allen, he was a prophet.

The City Lights Bookstore was an extraordinary mecca for poets. Peter Martin, an instructor at San Francisco State College and the son of the Italian anarchist Carlo Tresca, had started a popular culture magazine called *City Lights* (named after the Chaplin film); a paperback bookstore was to pay the rent for the magazine's editorial office upstairs. He asked Lawrence Ferlinghetti, a local poet of nominal reputation, to go in with him on the venture, and they each put up five hundred dollars. The magazine lasted only five issues, and Martin left for his hometown, New York (where he later opened the New Yorker Bookshop), selling half the store to Ferlinghetti for five hundred dollars.

The City Lights Bookstore, opened in June 1953, was America's first bookstore devoted to quality paperbacks. Though Avon and Pocket Books published an enormous number of titles, they were purely commercial ventures, sold at drugstores and newsstands. "One of the original ideas of the store was for it not to be an uptight place but a center for the intellectual community," said Ferlinghetti, "to be nonaffiliated, not tied up with, not belonging to any official organization." The store was an immediate success, and they literally had a hard time closing their doors. The manager, Shigeyoshi Murao, kept the store open until midnight during the week and till 2 A.M. on weekends. "We seemed to be responding to a deeply felt need," Ferlinghetti said. City Lights became a regular late-night destination for the local poets.

Ferlinghetti had always wanted to publish books through the bookstore, but Martin had not thought it would work. As sole owner, Ferlinghetti began a paperback series called the Pocket Poets, beginning with his own *Pictures of the Gone World*, which he published in August 1955. Ginsberg became friendly with Ferlinghetti. Their student days at Columbia had overlapped (both studied under Lionel Trilling and Mark Van Doren), though they had never met there. Ferlinghetti got his M.A. in 1947 and went to France; he attended the Sorbonne on the GI Bill until 1951, getting his doctorate. Writing poems and a novel, he lived on the Left Bank, where he met Seldon Kirby Smith. They returned to the States in 1953, married, then moved to San Francisco, becoming part of its artistic community. Ferlinghetti worked as an art critic for *Art Digest* and was the poetry reviewer for the *San Francisco Chronicle*.

Born in March 1919 in Yonkers, New York, he was the youngest of five sons. His father died of a heart attack before he was born, and his grief-stricken mother was committed to the State Mental Hospital in Poughkeepsie before Lawrence was a year old. The baby was taken in by his mother's uncle Ludwig and his wife, Emily. Ludwig and Emily split up almost immediately, and Emily took young Lawrence home with her to Strasbourg, in northern France. When Lawrence was five, Emily returned to the States and took a job as the live-in French tutor to the daughter of Presley and Anna Bisland, in Bronxville, New York. Then one day Emily simply did not return after her weekend off, leaving Lawrence with the Bislands, who decided to keep him with them.

In World War II, Ferlinghetti served as the commander of a subchaser in the North Atlantic. After VE day, he was transferred to the Pacific theater and arrived in Nagasaki six weeks after the bomb had been dropped. Seeing the ruins reinforced Ferlinghetti's deep-seated hatred of war. "You'd see hands sticking up out of the mud—all kinds of broken teacups—hair sticking out of the road— a quagmire—people don't realize how total the destruction was." His experiences led him to develop his lifelong commitment to left-leaning, libertarian, anarchistic political philosophy.

Spring came. Allen and Peter bought a used car and went on weekend excursions to Monterey, Point Lobos, and over the Golden

Gate to Mount Tamalpais, Muir Woods, and Stinson Beach. There were lots of visitors at Montgomery Street: Neal and Al Hinkle would spend afternoons playing chess by the sunny front-room window, and Neal and Natalie sometimes spent whole weekends camped out in Allen's bed. Later that spring, Neal and Carolyn decided to split up. Neal arrived in San Francisco with his typewriter and his clothes and took a room in North Beach. He had a telephone installed so that the railroad could contact him if they needed a brakeman, and leaving his typewriter with Peter, told him that he was going to "do nothing but fuck and play chess."

Allen still saw a lot of Sheila, though their friendship had been severely strained by his declaration of homosexuality. Once, she appeared drunk at Montgomery Street and caused a scene, demanding to know why Allen had left her. "You can fuck *me* in the ass if *that's* what you want!" she yelled. "If *that's* what it's all about!" and she broke his fireplace.

Although leading a settled life with Peter and making good money, Allen was persistently reminded of his past insecurities and worries by the letters he received from Naomi. "The wire is still on my head, and the sunshine is trying to help me. It has a wire department, but the wire that's outside of my head the sun doesn't touch, it is connected with the inside of me," she wrote from Pilgrim State. She told him that she was taking Thorazine, and added, "If I were home I could be out in the sunshine. It doesn't cost anything. When are you getting a regular sweetheart?"

On May 1, Towne-Oller closed down their San Francisco office. Allen wrote Jack: "I'm being replaced by a mechanical brain." In fact, it had been Allen's idea that an IBM computer could do his job more efficiently, and he spent two months correlating the information for transfer to the machine. Allen was delighted and looked forward to six months of thirty-dollar-a-week unemployment money. He could now relax and spend his time writing. He celebrated by spending thirty-five dollars on Bach recordings.

On his twenty-ninth birthday his love life was in one of its pen- ~~1949~~ *1955* dulum swings, and he was gloomy because Peter was refusing to sleep with him. He wrote to Jack: "I am passing, like all others, out of youth, into the world . . . faced with financial problems that must be solved. How the hell are we going to get the $s to get to Europe, and when that $s gone, what are we going to do? How can we live with no future abuilding? That's what's bothering me." That night he made love with the girl downstairs and felt a little better.

He was still recording his dreams, and his "Record of a Dream-Vision Night 8 June, 1955," which was later reworked and published as "Dream Record," was an early appearance of the famous Ginsberg long line: "—I revisited Mexico City and saw Joan Burroughs sitting at ease in a garden, clear eyes and ironic smile as eternalized in my imagination, her face restored to a beauty tequila and salt had made strange before the bullet in her brow." He worked hard on the poem, perfecting every line, then sent it to Burroughs, who was startled by it. "About your poem on Joan," he wrote, "I think it is completely successful. I experienced a distinct shock at the end, I could see the picture of her talking and smiling so clear and precise like a telepathic image. I *knew* that I was seeing exactly what you saw."

Allen also sent a copy to Rexroth, who said: "You went to Columbia University too long. You're too old to be going on with all this formal stuff like that. What's the matter with you?" Allen accepted Rexroth's criticism, but at the same time he knew he was on the right track. The year before, in San Jose, he had written "In Back of the Real," which was composed in a mode of variable measure following the later Williams. Williams himself had praised the poem, and Allen thought it was his best so far. In "Dream Record," Allen used a system of relatively even syllable count, with a squarer line. Working out of William Carlos Williams, he evolved a style in which he would write "Howl," a variable system of measures adaptable to long free-verse lines by dividing them into three.

For some time, Peter had been concerned about his younger brother, Lafcadio, who was now fifteen. Peter thought that he would be better off with him in San Francisco and decided to take on the responsibility of looking after him. At the end of June, Peter set out, hitchhiking, for New York to retrieve him. Allen accompanied him as far as Reno and they spent a few days sightseeing in the Sierras before Peter continued on to New York.

On July 28, Allen enrolled at the University of California at Berkeley to complete his English M.A., a decision that cheered his father. Due to start college in September, Allen found a one-room garden cottage on a side street six blocks from the university.

He knew that he would have to get a job to support himself at college, but the unemployment money was still coming, so he settled down to assemble a collection of his work from the past four years and continue his reading: the Latin translations he had been studying since 1954—he was deeply immersed in Catullus—and modern Spanish and French poetry, particularly Lorca and Apollinaire.

One afternoon early in August, he sat at the typewriter in his large front room on Montgomery Street, with the intention of writing whatever came up. He had taken Rexroth's criticism to heart and decided that his poetry was too formal and too tight, so instead of sitting down to write a poem, he tried for something looser, more like prose, which would give him more freedom. "I thought I wouldn't write a *poem* but just write what I wanted to without fear, let my imagination go, open secrecy, and scribble magic lines from my real mind—sum up my life—something I wouldn't be able to show anybody, writ for my own soul's ear and a few other golden ears." He began to write about his life, again using William Carlos Williams's triadic verse form, only with the lines extended out to his own long breath length—each line a single breath, like blowing an extended cadenza on a saxophone:

> *I saw the best minds of my generation*
> *generation destroyed by madness*
> *starving, mystical, naked,*
> *who dragged themselves thru the angry streets at*
> *dawn looking for a negro fix . . .*

SIX | "HOWL" AND THE SAN FRANCISCO RENAISSANCE

I began typing, not with the idea of writing a formal poem, but
stating my imaginative sympathies, whatever they were worth. As
my loves were impractical and my thoughts relatively unworldly,
I had nothing to gain, only the pleasure of enjoying on paper
those sympathies most intimate to myself and most awkward in
the great world of family, formal education, business and
current literature.

—A.G.

ALLEN SAT AT HIS DESK IN THE CORNER BY THE FIRST-FLOOR WINDOW,
overlooking the street. Afternoon sunlight filled the room as he fed
more paper into his big black secondhand office typewriter. He
wrote using the rhythms of speech from the American street—black
speech, phrasings overheard on street corners and in bars—and the
rhythms of bebop and jazz, of sports commentators and the cool
DJs on the all-night jazz programs. It had a new rhythm and used
new language. It was "a tragic custard-pie comedy of wild phrasing,
meaningless images for the beauty of abstract poetry of mind, running along making awkward combinations [of images] like Charlie
Chaplin's walk, long saxophone-line chorus lines I knew Kerouac
would hear *sound* of—taking off from his own inspired prose line,
really a new poetry."

He depended on the anaphoric "who," that opened each line to
keep the beat. It was the base to which he would continually return
before taking off on each long flight of the imagination: "who sat in
rooms naked and unshaven listening to the Terror through the
wall, / who burned their money in wastebaskets amid the rubbish
of unread Bronx manifestos." As he piled line upon line, he grew
exuberant: "continuing to prophesy what I really knew, despite the
drear consciousness of the world," as he later described it. He was

writing the tale of the tribe, "Ten years' animal screams and suicides!" and the characters in his life appeared to take up their
positions on the page.

He described Herbert Huncke's first appearance at York Avenue
in 1947: "who wandered all night with their shoes full of blood on
the snowbanks of East River looking for the door in the river to open
on a roomfull of steamheat and opium, picking his scabs saying who
is my friend?" and remembered the story of his friend from the San
Remo bar, Tuli Kupferberg, "who jumped off the Brooklyn Bridge
and walked away unknown and forgotten into the ghostly daze of
Chinatown soup alleyways & firetrucks." Overcoat thief Bill
Garver: "who pondered his cherries in longchamps waiting to kidnap an overcoat on a coat hanger, apparition of a week's rent,"
appeared alongside Russell Durgin, in whose apartment Allen had
his vision of William Blake: "who coughed up celluloid balls in
Harlem with their lungs full of sixth floors of tubercular sky and
orange crates of theology."

He wrote of Ruth Goldenberg, one of the "Three Graces" from
the San Remo: "who talked continuously seventy hours from park
to pad to bar to Bellevue to Museum to Long Island to the Brooklyn
Bridge . . ."; of Peter DuPeru; and of course of Neal Cassady, who
was very much on his mind: "N.C., secret hero of these poems,
cocksman and Adonis of Denver . . ." But he made only oblique
references to his oldest friends, Jack and Bill. They didn't really fit
in the poem; they had not been destroyed by madness, and their
stories lacked the raw power of Solomon's shock treatment,
Huncke's despair, or even the saga of Louis Simpson, "who threw
their watches out of the windows in the ballot of eternity." To have
described his relationship with Jack or Bill would have required a
very different poem.

Recalling the stories of the "best minds" of his generation, he
paraphrased incidents from his own life: "who were expelled from
colleges for printing obscene odes in the dust of the sexless windows
of men's dormitories and burned alive in bloody flannel suits of
innocence amid the cannon blasts bestsellers and shrapnels of
leaden verse and nitroglycerine shrieks of fairies and mustard gas
of sinister intelligent editors." He referred to his wait for a ship in
Houston after the failure of his season with Neal in Denver: "who
lounged hungry and lonesome thru Houston seeking jazz or soup; &
ate candy for six days and followed the brilliant Spaniard to con-
verse about America & Eternity a hopeless task," and of the part-

time cleaning job he had taken to supplement his unemployment money: "who mopped all night in desolate Bickfords listening to the crack of doom on the hydrogen jukebox."

He wrote solidly, with copious x-ing out, until he had filled seven pages. He quickly found that the theme he kept returning to was the story of Carl Solomon: "who threw potato salad at dadaist lecturers at CCNY & subsequently presented themselves on the granite steps of madhouses with shaven heads and harlequin speech of suicide, demanding instantaneous lobotomies, and who were given the concrete void of insulin metrosol electricity hydrotherapy psychotherapy occupational therapy pingpong & amnesia and who in protest overturned one symbolic pingpong table."

Recognizing that the poem was about Carl, he began a second section, specifically addressed to him:

> Carl Solomon! I'm with you in Rockland
> where you're madder than I am
> I'm with you in Rockland
> where you must feel very strange . . .

Ginsberg later wrote: "The rhythmic paradigm for Part III [which this section later became] was conceived and half-written same day as the beginning of 'Howl.' I went back later and filled it out."

Allen went through the manuscript of the first section, labeling all those lines that belonged together A, B, C, or D. Those about Neal were "A," those about Carl were "C," and so on. He made a few vital tonal changes to the text, such as "mystical" to "hysterical" in the first line, then retyped the lines in their new order, so that the poem now led up to the long climactic passage of Carl in the madhouse. He ended the first section on a positive note by heralding the "madman bum and angel," as these were most likely to have visionary awareness, and listing practical methods of attaining the widened field of consciousness that he had experienced through the use of art: "the use of the ellipse the catalog the meter and the vibrating plane"—a reference to Céline's use of idiomatic staccato ellipsis, to Walt Whitman's extended catalogs, to William Carlos Williams's meter, and to the hot advancing colors and cold receding colors that create Cézanne's "shimmering space."

With a pink editing pencil he wrote across the top of the page, "Howl for Carl Solomon": not a poem dedicated to Carl but an empathic howl of grief and rage for Carl's plight and the plight of all the others like him he had known. As Ginsberg later described it, "A lament for the Lamb in America, with instances of remarkable lamb-like youths." He bundled together the first six pages of the manuscript and sent them off to Jack Kerouac in Mexico City. (The seventh page of the manuscript had so much x-ing out on it and was so messy that he did not think Kerouac could make any sense of it.)

Jack, instead of recognizing the great breakthrough that the poem represented for Allen, responded on August 19 to say that "Howl for Carl Solomon" was very powerful, but that he wanted "spontaneity or nothing." Kerouac did not like the x-ing out in the poem and wanted Allen to stick to his first thoughts, not make corrections as he worked.

Allen misunderstood him and replied: "The pages I sent you of Howl (right title) are the first pages put down, as is. I recopied them and sent you the 100% original draft. There is no preexistent version. I typed it up as I went along, that's why it's so messy." Allen also misunderstood Jack's use of the title of the poem; Jack was not suggesting a title for it, he was quoting the title Allen had already given it. But Allen had clearly forgotten that he had titled the poem before sending it to Jack, because from then on, he always believed that Kerouac had suggested the title "Howl" to him and even thanked him for it on the poem's dedication page. Ginsberg didn't see the original manuscript again until it turned up among John Clellon Holmes's papers in 1980. (In any case, Kerouac was unlikely to have suggested a title that dedicated the poem to Carl Solomon, since he and Solomon had argued badly over *On the Road*.)

Peter returned from the East Coast. He had hitchhiked with Lafcadio, a copy of Rimbaud's *Illuminations* in his pocket. He walked into 1010 Montgomery at 3 A.M. and threw his arms around Allen. It had been a traumatic trip for Peter. His two older brothers, Nicholas and Julius, sat mute in the Central Islip madhouse, and he had seen that Lafcadio was heading in the same direction. But now that he had Lafcadio with him, he sat scratching his head over his new responsibility. Lafcadio spent six hours a day in the bathroom and talked incessantly about striking it rich and making twenty million dollars. Allen found living with Lafcadio very difficult and wrote to Jack, "I am trying to shepherd 15 year old Orlovsky around thru life, like being married and having overgrown problem child crazy kicks pathos of real life."

One of the biggest problems was that Lafcadio ate everything in the icebox. Allen would shop for groceries, but by mealtime he would find that Lafcadio had eaten all three steaks intended for supper. Allen complained to Burroughs, who suggested an obvious solution: "In your place I would take a firm stand with Peter's brother and his appetite," he wrote. "Sounds to me like he needs a boot in the ass figuratively and literally. I mean, why kowtow to an obnoxious young punk?" Clearly the problem did not improve, because two months later Bill wrote again: "Why do you take all this crap from Peter's brother? People are better off if they don't get all they want to eat. It's been proved with rats."

A few days after Peter returned, he and Allen took peyote. It was Allen's second time: a very disturbing experience. They stood on the corner of Broadway and Columbus Avenue in front of City Lights: "I looked into Peter's eyes, and I couldn't find anyone there," Ginsberg said. "He looked into mine and couldn't find anyone there. There was a total absence, a vacancy and emptiness. It was a shock when we looked at each other and perceived two phantom ghosts with empty eyes, laughing fiendishly. I got scared, thinking 'Oh, oh, it's all empty.' "

They went out in the nighttime streets. "We wandered on Peyote all downtown, P&I, met Betty Keck & saw Molock Moloch smoking building in red glare downtown St. Francis Hotel, with robot upstairs eyes & skullface, in smoke, again," Allen wrote Jack. The word "Moloch" came to Allen on the clanging Powell Street cable car, and he sat muttering it till, seated in the cafeteria at the foot of the hotel, he wrote the opening stanzas of "Howl," Part II: "Moloch! Moloch! Whose hand ripped out their brains and scattered their minds on the wheels of subways? / Molloch! Filth! Ugliness! Ashcans and unobtainable dollars! Beauties dying in lofts! Harpsichords unbuilt! . . ."

He was continuing in the same vein as "Howl," Part I, opening with a reference to Bill Cannastra's death and following it with a reference to his friend Bill Keck's passion for harpsichords (he had just met Betty Keck on the street), but then he changed and became less specific in his metaphors: "Children! children! The very children breaking their backs under the subways. Breaking their backs trying to lift the Whole City on their backs—Pavements! Buildings! Trees Rockefeller Center Tons . . . " It would go through nineteen separate drafts before he was done with adding to it and shaping it, but he now had the beginning and end of "Howl," Part II.

Allen had for some time been negotiating with City Lights to publish *Empty Mirror,* his book of Williams-inspired poems, but Ferlinghetti had rejected it. However, when Allen showed Ferlinghetti "Howl," his response was much more positive, and Allen wrote Jack: "City Lights Bookstore here . . . will put out 'Howl' (under that title) next year, one booklet for that poem, nothing else, it will fill a booklet."

Peter and Lafcadio stayed on at Montgomery Street when, on September 1, 1955, Allen moved to 1624 Milvia Street, Berkeley, a one-room rose-covered Shakespearean cottage in the backyard of a larger house. He spent his first night there alone: "home at night to pancakes high and Jupiter symphony and garden and moonlight and loneliness—the huge horror of Berkeley ahead—it could be nice, but ugly forebodings all day, job worry and study fears and the million books of scholars unreadable." His first poems written there were "A Strange New Cottage in Berkeley" and "Supermarket in California," written on the same day. This time he used the long line to write short, quiet, lyrical poems.

Allen began his studies. To support himself, he washed dishes and read examination papers for the American Literature course. The twenty or thirty dollars a week he made were sufficient for his modest needs. His studies, homework, and part-time jobs meant that he had time to see Peter only on weekends.

One day early in September, Allen ran into Michael McClure, who had been asked to organize a poetry reading at the Six Gallery but didn't think he would have time. Allen had been contemplating putting on a reading featuring Jack, Neal, and himself, so he immediately volunteered. He consulted Rexroth, who recommended Gary Snyder, a young Berkeley poet. Allen went over to see him at once.

Snyder had been intending to go to the state fair in Sacramento that day to see the long-haired angora goats, but in the end he stayed home to work on his bicycle. He had it propped up in his backyard when Allen arrived. Thin and wiry, with blond hair and a little goatee, Snyder had slanting, almost Oriental-looking green eyes, and his face was creased with laugh lines. He was twenty-five, a graduate student of Chinese and Japanese at Berkeley, who planned to go to Japan to study on a grant from the First Zen Institute of America the next spring.

He had been studying Buddhism since the late forties, when he was at Reed College, and did Buddhist meditation practice with the Berkeley Young Buddhist Association, which had published a number of his poems in their magazine, *Berkeley Bussei*. He was muscular and tanned from spending the summer working with a trail crew in the Sierra Nevada. His cottage was tiny and had a monastic look. Ice axes and climbing ropes hung from the walls, and orange-crate bookcases housed a valuable collection of books on the Orient, many of them in Japanese and Chinese, as well as a good collection of modern poetry. His table was also made from orange crates. There were no chairs, just straw mats. In the yard was an almond tree, and Gary had arranged a few rocks and boulders to make his own Zen garden.

There was an immediate rapport between the two men. Gary had been very impressed by William Carlos Williams when Williams spent a week at Reed College in 1950 and had been influenced by him ever since. Gary brought out some of his own poems, which Allen liked. Gary also told Allen about a poet friend of his, Philip Whalen, also from Reed College, who was arriving the next day from the mountains. Allen, in turn, told Gary about his friend Jack Kerouac, a great poet, who was arriving any day from Mexico City. They discussed the upcoming reading, and it was dark by the time Allen walked home through the warm night air.

As Allen and Gary talked, Kerouac came hitchhiking into town. He found Allen's cottage and, high on Benzedrine, sat and played the *Saint Matthew Passion* at full volume until Allen returned.

Philip Whalen had spent the summer fire-watching from a lookout tower on Sourdough Mountain in Washington's High Cascades. Before arriving in Berkeley, he had stopped off with friends in Seattle and taken his first peyote, a subject of great interest to Allen. He and Allen quickly became friends. Whalen, a big, gentle man with a wide, easy smile, was studying Zen Buddhism (eventually he became a Buddhist monk, after studying in Japan). He was born three years before Allen, in 1923, in Portland, Oregon. A wartime job in a B-17 aircraft factory delayed his entry to Reed College, but once there, he became close friends with two other young poets, Gary Snyder and Lew Welch. The three of them shared a house at college, and then all moved down to the Bay Area. Kerouac described Whalen in *The Dharma Bums* as "Booboo big old good-hearted Warren Coughlin a hundred and eighty pounds of poet meat." Allen quickly put Whalen's name down for the reading.

Philip Whalen and Gary Snyder now joined Peter, Neal, and Jack in the inner circle of Allen's friends. The San Francisco chapter of the Beat Generation was getting under way. Allen busied himself organizing the reading. The poets decided that the readers would be Allen Ginsberg, Michael McClure, Gary Snyder, Philip Whalen, and Philip Lamantia. Carl Solomon had introduced Allen to Lamantia in the San Remo in 1948. He was a year younger than Allen and had gone to New York when he was sixteen to present himself at the office of the Surrealist journal *View*, in whose pages André Breton subsequently hailed him as an authentic Surrealist.

Snyder suggested that Rexroth be the master of ceremonies. Rexroth, delighted, went to a thrift shop and bought a pin-striped cutaway for the occasion. Allen disseminated a postcard to advertise the reading. He listed the poets and the date, October 13, 1955, and continued: "Six poets at the Six Gallery. Kenneth Rexroth, M.C. Remarkable collection of angels all gathered at once in the same spot. Wine, music, dancing girls, serious poetry, free satori. Small collection for wine and postcards. Charming event."

The Six Gallery was a converted auto-repair shop at Union and Fillmore. At one end was a small stage, on which they arranged six large chairs in a semicircle. Jack and Allen arrived with Lawrence Ferlinghetti and his wife, Kirby, to find over a hundred people squeezed into the small space. The whole bohemian poetry intelligentsia of the Bay Area appeared to be gathered together in one room for the first time, and there was an atmosphere of great gaiety and excitement. For most of the poets, including Allen, it was their first public reading.

Rexroth made a short speech and introduced Philip Lamantia, who chose to read the posthumous poems of his friend John Hoffman. Hoffman was also a friend of Carl Solomon's and an acquaintance of Ginsberg's; he was rumored to have died in Mexico City of a peyote overdose.

Lamantia was followed by Michael McClure, who, at twenty-three, was the youngest poet there. McClure's lifelong involvement with the ecology movement and its new emphasis as a motif in American poetry was prefigured by his reading of "Point Lobos: Animism" and "For the Death of 100 Whales," the latter being his response to the news that bored GIs at a NATO base in the Antarctic had destroyed a pack of killer whales. This was McClure's first meeting with both Gary Snyder and Philip Whalen. Whalen read next and took the reading up to the ten-thirty break with his "Plus ça Change . . . " lines of American speech, as suggested to him by Williams.

Jack had refused to read, claiming that he was too shy, but he wanted to share the excitement. He collected money for wine, then rushed out and bought gallon jugs of California Burgundy, which the audience passed around. He sat, with his own bottle, on the edge of the stage. Ruth Witt-Diamant, who was to play an important role in promoting the new San Francisco poetry, was shocked by the wine and the irreverent tone of the meeting but enjoyed herself.

Then, with the wine circulating freely, Allen made his way to the front of the room, nodding to his many acquaintances, and as the lights dimmed for the second half, he began the first public reading of "Howl": "I saw the best minds of my generation destroyed by madness, starving hysterical naked, dragging themselves through the negro streets at dawn looking for an angry fix, angelheaded hipsters burning for the ancient heavenly connection to the starry dynamo in the machinery of night . . . "

He was nervous and had drunk a great deal of wine. He read with a small, intense voice, but the alcohol and the emotional intensity of the poem quickly took over, and he was soon swaying to its powerful rhythm, chanting like a Jewish cantor, sustaining his long breath length, savoring the outrageous language. Kerouac began cheering him on, yelling "Go!" at the end of each line, and soon the audience joined in. Allen was completely transported. At each line he took a deep breath, glanced at the manuscript, then delivered it, arms outstretched, eyes gleaming, swaying from one foot to the other with the rhythm of the words. Rexroth sat with tears in his eyes and ignored Ruth Witt-Diamant's gestures to him to tone it down. Allen continued to the last sob, the audience cheering him wildly at every line.

Afterward Jack said, "Ginsberg, this poem will make you famous in San Francisco." Rexroth corrected him: "No, this poem will make you famous from bridge to bridge." Michael McClure, in *Scratching the Beat Surface*, wrote: "Ginsberg read on to the end of the poem, which left us standing in wonder, or cheering and wondering, but knowing at the deepest level that a barrier had been broken, that a human voice and body had been hurled against the harsh wall of America and its supporting armies and navies and academies and institutions and ownership systems and power-support bases." McClure later told Ginsberg that he thought "Howl" was "Allen's metamorphosis from a quiet brilliant burning bohemian scholar, trapped by his flames and repressions, to epic vocal bard."

Gary Snyder was left to follow Allen, and sensibly let the clamor fade before reading "A Berry Feast," his poetic invocation of the first-fruits festival of the Indians of Oregon. He read well, in a deep, resonant voice, and was able to capture the attention of the excited audience. Afterward the poets and their girlfriends and boyfriends all went to Snyder's favorite Chinese restaurant to discuss the remarkable evening, and thence to the Place, a favorite poets' bar on Grant Avenue. And after that there was an orgy.

When Lawrence Ferlinghetti got home, he sat at his desk and, paraphrasing the message sent by Ralph Waldo Emerson to Walt Whitman on receiving *Leaves of Grass* a century before, sent Allen a telegram: "I greet you at the beginning of a great career. When do I get the manuscript?"

The Six Gallery reading catalyzed the Bay Area literary community, and all who had taken part in it became local celebrities. With the success of the first part of "Howl" at the Six Gallery, Allen set to work to complete the other sections of the poem. One afternoon, he sat at his typewriter, looking out at the garden bushes, and filled page after page with suggestions for the middle section of Part II, the naming of "the monster of mental consciousness that preys on the lamb." Gary Snyder was sitting cross-legged, Japanese-style, before a writing frame on the rug, translating Han Shan from the Chinese. Allen was muttering and sometimes laughing out loud in his trancelike self-absorption as he thought of more and more outrageous verbal associations to go with "Moloch," and Gary called out, "Moloch who reaches up through the toilet bowl and grabs my pecker every time I try to crap." It was not long before the middle section of the poem was more or less complete, but the fine-tuning of the lines and phrases went on for months.

Allen began working on Part III, some of which he already had. It had a fixed base in the phrase "I'm with you in Rockland," which was followed by a graduated longer response, just made for reading aloud:

> *I'm with you in Rockland*
> > *where we are great writers on the same dreadful*
> > > *typewriter*
> *I'm with you in Rockland*
> > *where your condition has become serious and is*
> > > *reported on the radio*

Ginsberg took the form of this section of the poem from Christopher Smart, the eighteenth-century English poet, whose "Jubilate Agno" ("Rejoice in the Lamb") he had been familiar with since the forties. Each line of "Rejoice in the Lamb" is a statement, opening with the word "Let," followed by a counterstatement, opening with "For":

> Let Nahshon rejoice with the Seabreeze—the Lord give the sailors of his Spirit. For he that walked upon the sea, hath prepared the floods with the Gospel of peace.
> Let Helon rejoice with the Woodpecker—the Lord encourage the propagation of trees! For the merciful man is merciful to his beast, and to the trees that give them shelter.
> Let Amos rejoice with the Coote—prepare to meet thy God, O Israel. For he hath turned the shadow of death into the morning, the Lord is his name.

Allen used "I'm with you in Rockland" as the statement and opened his counterstatement with "where":

> I'm with you in Rockland
>   where there are twentyfive-thousand mad comrades
>   all together singing the final stanzas of the
>   Internationale
> I'm with you in Rockland
>   where we hug and kiss the United States under our
>   bedsheets the United States that coughs all night
>   and won't let us sleep

The final section of the poem (called "Footnote to Howl" rather than "Howl," Part IV, because it was a variation on "Howl," Part II, with "Moloch!" replaced by "Holy!") was written as Allen sat weeping on the Kearny Street bus in San Francisco. The manuscript was hastily scribbled in ballpoint on a page from a notebook and needed very little work:

> Holy the groaning saxophone! Holy the bop apocalypse! Holy the jazzbands marijuana hipsters peace peyote pipes & drums!

> *Holy the solitudes of skyscrapers and pavements! Holy*
> *the cafeterias filled with the millions! Holy the mysterious*
> *rivers of tears under the streets!*

After a few weeks, Allen gave up his attempt to get an M.A. at Berkeley and settled down to enjoy his new fame. His friendships with Gary and Phil grew deeper. With Gary he spent pleasant afternoons gardening, carving poems into tree trunks, or watching Gary prepare his esteemed horse-meat sukiyaki with sweet and sour sauce. He learned an enormous amount about Zen Buddhism. There were also discussions of Zen with Philip Whalen, as well as long talks about Williams and Gertrude Stein, whom Whalen had been studying since he was in the army. On Thursdays, Gary would appear at Allen's cottage with a slim, gray-eyed girl, and he and Allen would practice "yabyum" with her. It was an Oriental form of sex based on the mystical formula: "Om, the thunderbolt in the void." They were the "thunderbolt," and she, of course, was the "void." Jack was initially upset by this. He had been brought up to think that nakedness was a sin and had also been celibate for a year, in keeping with his attempt to become a Hinayana Buddhist. Gary sometimes tried to get Kerouac to meditate, but Jack had wrecked his knees when he was a football player and couldn't sit still very long. "He was too jumpy," Whalen said.

A year before, Peter had been a virgin, too shy to approach a woman. Now Allen wrote to LaVigne: "Peter and I wandering around finding, finally, various pretty girls to make it with menage-a-trois." He told LaVigne about one girl they had been seeing together: "finally, I screw dog her and she kneeling blows Peter, then we change around. She shy at first but after a while we all began goofing happily with our cocks and cunts and everybody woke up pleased." Allen and Peter took their clothes off every chance they got. Peter particularly liked orgies. Philip Whalen remembered the parties: "Allen got a kick out of seeing who was there, and sometimes deciding to upset them and get them going by disrobing. I remember a number of parties at Berkeley, as far as I was concerned at the homes of complete strangers, many of them academics, and Allen thought he could loosen them up by saying, 'Let's all get naked!' He would remove his clothes and everyone would say, 'How interesting,' or 'My goodness,' and some would leave. Very funny reactions. It happened a lot."

Allen was interested in seeing people's reactions: "In Frisco when Peter and I and Gary and Jack, and everybody would go to parties, if we got drunk enough, because we were all feeling very happy at the time, feeling that it was a real renaissance of naked poetry, and feeling the beauty of the world and the beauty of men, almost, so we would take our clothes off. And everybody liked it really, nothing wrong with it."

One afternoon, Allen, Jack, and Philip Whalen were strolling around the railroad yards in south San Francisco, when Allen made a strange discovery and asked Philip what it was.

"It's a sunflower," said Whalen. Allen had never seen one before. It had gone completely to seed and was all black and sooty from the locomotives. "He was completely enthralled and really went into it," Whalen remembered. That evening at the cottage, just as they were preparing to go out to a party, Allen had an idea for a poem. "Just give me a minute," he said, "I'll write this down," and as Jack waited by the door, Allen quickly scribbled a poem using Jack's sketching style and his own long lines. In twenty minutes he was done, and they left for the party. The poem was "Sunflower Sutra," with its famous long final line:

"We're not our skin of grime, we're not our dread bleak dusty imageless locomotive, we're all golden sunflowers inside, blessed by our own seed & hairy naked accomplishment-bodies growing into mad black formal sunflowers in the sunset, spied on by our eyes under the shadow of the mad locomotive riverbank sunset Frisco hilly tincan evening sitdown vision."

Late in October 1955, Jack, Gary, and their friend John Montgomery, a librarian from Berkeley, went mountain climbing in Yosemite. They returned at the end of November, and Jack went immediately to see Neal. Natalie was acting crazy. Neal had persuaded her to forge Carolyn's signature on bonds worth ten thousand dollars so that he could pursue his "system" at the racetrack. He lost all the money. Natalie's guilt at stealing from Carolyn precipitated a nervous breakdown. She took enormous amounts of amphetamine and within days became skeleton thin, with huge, terrified eyes. She was convinced that the police were coming to arrest them and tried, unsuccessfully, to cut her wrists. Neal's friends began seriously to recommend that she be hospitalized. Neal asked Jack to look after her while he went to work.

Jack tried to calm her with his Buddhist homilies: "Why don't you relax and enjoy God? God is *you*, you fool!" When she refused to listen, Jack got angry and went out to buy wine, bringing back with him the musicians who lived in the apartment below, whom he had met in the street. Natalie's paranoia about the police subsided, and she seemed to quiet down, but the next morning, November 30, 1955, just before dawn, after Jack had gone back to Allen's cottage and while Neal slept, Natalie went up to the roof in her bathrobe and broke the skylight, to cut her wrists with the jagged glass. A neighbor saw her sitting on the roof bleeding and called the police. Thinking they had come to arrest her, she ran away terrified. Despite the efforts of one of the policemen to tackle her, she fell six floors to her death.

Allen had been worried by her paranoia but hadn't realized how serious it was. In an unpublished poem he wrote:

> *Your truthful eyes troubling me too late.*
> *In the car coming over for Thanksgiving*
> *You gave me look so tearful I knew it was death,*
> *or thought so . . .*

Natalie's death threw a pall over the community. Long-suffering, all-forgiving Carolyn took Neal back, and Allen joined them for a quiet Christmas in Los Gatos. Jack decided to spend Christmas with his mother and hitchhiked to Rocky Mount, North Carolina, where she was living with his sister.

That December, Allen concentrated on making final revisions to "Howl" and sending copies to family and friends. On December 9, he mailed it to William Carlos Williams, along with "A Strange New Cottage in Berkeley," "A Supermarket in California," and "Sunflower Sutra." "Look what I have done with the long line," he wrote. "In some of these poems it seems to answer your demand for a relatively absolute line with a fixed base, whatever it is . . . all held together within the elastic of the breath, though of varying lengths. The key is in the jazz choruses to some extent; also to reliance on spontaneity & expressiveness which long line encourages; also to attention to interior unchecked logical mental stream. With a long line comes a return, (caused by) expressive human feeling, it's generally lacking in poetry now, which is inhuman. The release of emotion is one with the rhythmical buildup of long line."

He sent copies of some of the poems to his father; "Howl" he thought too revealing. Louis responded enthusiastically: "Read with interest your 'Sunflower Sutra.' I did not like the dirty words dragged in, nor the long long lines. However it had feeling and fervor and good concrete details. The ending builds up well. . . . Bet you're making a literary reputation! Keep it up! You'll land somewhere in time!''

Louis was not so positive about all Allen's activities. In their correspondence, Allen continued to test his ideas. He engaged in a spirited defense of the values of the "Beat Generation"—complete openness, free love, marijuana, etc.—which Louis looked upon with distaste. "All your vehement, vaporous, vituperations of rebellion move me not one jot," he told Allen. "Your attitude is irresponsible—and it stinks!''

Allen was taking concrete steps toward getting to Europe. The recently passed Taft-Hartley Act had opened up the shipping unions, and he thought that a three- or four-month stretch at sea would give him enough money for seven or eight months in Europe. In December, he began applying for ships. One finally came up in May.

Jack was intending to return to the Coast to work as a fire-watcher that summer, and when he heard that Gary Snyder had moved to a cabin where there would be room enough for him, he immediately hitchhiked west. Shortly after Jack arrived, a huge poetry reading was presented at a theater in Berkeley. Robert LaVigne, back in town, had made a seven-foot-high Lautrec-like poster for the reading and decorated the hall with pen drawings of Allen and Peter making love. Onstage there was a row of thronelike wooden chairs left over from a stage set, one for each poet. It was the same lineup as the Six Gallery reading, a repeat by popular demand for Berkeley, and the audience knew by now what to expect. Kerouac passed the hat for wine and kept the bottle moving. Allen, wearing an unraveling, crumpled sweater, stood beneath the brilliant white spotlight and delivered his lines like a saxophone solo, putting everything he could into it. He read "America" and gave the first public reading of "Howl," Part II, and the audience booed and hissed at each "Moloch!" The excitement was tremendous. As Allen finished, there was a triumphant burst of light as the colored stage lights were turned on. All the other readers jumped to their feet to hug and congratulate him.

Everyone was aware that something special was happening. Rexroth told Allen that his presence was the catalyst for a major poetry renaissance on the West Coast, and Rexroth's wife later informed Allen that Rexroth had been waiting all his life for a situation like this to develop. Photographers had come from as far away as Vancouver, and the entire reading was professionally recorded. Rexroth wanted to form a poetry-jazz combo with Allen and a group of local musicians, and another group of jazz musicians proposed writing a musical setting for "Howl" and touring the West Coast with Allen, performing "Howl" as a "Jazz-Mass." Fantasy Records, the Berkeley jazz label, also wanted to record him with a jazz backing. Literary magazines were eager to publish Allen's work, and three separate organizations had sprung up to organize poetry readings, so that there was now at least one a week. Robert Duncan was leaving town for Europe, and Ruth Witt-Diamant arranged for Allen to take over his poetry workshop one evening a week at San Francisco State. Allen told Louis, "You have no idea what a storm of lunatic-fringe activity I have stirred up."

The influential literary critic and poet Richard Eberhart arrived in San Francisco and was the guest of honor at a party at Ruth Witt-Diamant's house, where Allen gave him a private reading of "Howl." They got along well, and Eberhart took Allen with him to visit the poet Karl Shapiro, who was teaching at Davis College. This visit further confirmed Ginsberg's dim view of the establishment. He described Shapiro to Louis as "blank eyed, dull, acts like advt. executive and about as sympathetic." They talked about Shapiro's trip to India.

"India was nasty," said Shapiro.

"Karl didn't like it at all," said his wife.

Shapiro said that the only way to deal with the suffering there was to ignore it. "There was no light in his spirit at all, just money," Allen told Louis. "The theme of his poems is moderation and the virtues of middleclass existence, which is for him a refuge from experience. And HE teaches a creative writing course, and is admired by a flock of dull-eyed professors."

Allen set himself a deadline of the end of April 1956 to finish revising "Howl" and selecting poems for the book. When he handed in the final version of the manuscript, Ferlinghetti was so pleased that he decided to give him royalties. Robert Creeley made Ditto copies of the poem for use in Duncan's poetry workshop, and Allen sent copies to Eliot, Pound, Van Doren, Trilling, Eberhart, Meyer Schapiro, William Faulkner, and other literary celebrities, with a long letter requesting the reader's reaction. He also sent copies to Louis, Eugene, Naomi, Lucien, and other friends. Louis's reaction to the complete poem was positive: "My first impression at first blush, is that it is a wild, volcanic, troubled, extravagant, turbulent, boisterous, unbridled outpouring, intermingling gems and flashes of picturesque insight with slag and debris of scoriac matter. It has violence, it has life, it has *vitality*. In my opinion it is a one-sided neurotic view of life, it has not enough glad, Whitmanic affirmations." But Louis also conceded: "The poem should attract attention and perhaps be a sensation. You will hear defenders and detractors. But it should give you a name." His immigrant aspirations for his son to be a success were being fulfilled in an unexpected way.

Allen had sent William Carlos Williams the completed manuscript in March, and a month later he received a strange Introduction from him. It read almost as if he were confusing Allen with someone else, except that he recalled Allen's father and background. He described Allen as "physically slight of build and mentally much disturbed by the life which he had encountered about him after the first world war as it was exhibited to him in and about New York City. . . . Now he turns up fifteen or twenty years later with an arresting poem." Williams had had a stroke, which may have made him forgetful. But he understood the poem well and sympathized. He clearly enjoyed the power of it and ended his Introduction: "Hold back the edges of your gowns, Ladies, we are going through hell."

Allen was determined to wrest a response from Ezra Pound, and wrote to him a second time, enclosing poems. "Please READ at least one page of the enclosed ms. Or 1 line for that matter so long as you can judge the rhythm," he demanded, but Pound wasn't having any of it. Allen mentioned in his letter that William Carlos Williams had written the Introduction to the book, so Pound mailed the letter and the poems to Williams with a note: "You got more room in yr/ house than I hv/ in my cubicle. If he's yours why don't yu teach him the value of time to those who want to read something that will tell 'em wot they don't know." Pound had been judged insane and sent to Saint Elizabeths mental hospital in Washington, D.C., in order that he not be put on trial for treason, a charge stemming from his wartime broadcasts on Radio Rome. Living in a madhouse himself, he was already quite familiar with "best minds . . . destroyed by madness."

On May 19, 1956, Eugene's wife, Connie, gave birth to Alan Eugene Brooks (Eugene had changed his name when he became a lawyer; now he used the English spelling of Alan). Allen was very touched: "Thanks for naming the baby after me. It'll be an illustrious name (but perhaps temporarily in disrepute when my poems are published). I almost cried thinking you cared that much to name it Allen." In addition to celebrating the new birth, there was much discussion in the family about Naomi. Allen thought that if she was well enough to leave the hospital, she could be boarded with Peter's mother in Northport, Long Island, but when Eugene visited the hospital to make inquiries, he was told that Naomi was in no condition to leave. A letter from Naomi to Eugene, written that spring, showed how sick she was. Eugene passed the letter on to Allen, who later used the phrases in "Kaddish." Naomi wrote: "God's informers came to my bed, and God, himself, I saw it in the sky— it was after Jan 1, 1956. The sunshine showed it too, a key on the side of the window for me to get out. The yellow of the sunshine, also showed the key on the side of the window. I'm begging you to take me out of here."

In May, Allen joined the USNS *Pvt. Joseph F. Merrell* as a yeoman-storekeeper, at $5,040 a year. He walked around San Francisco with a military haircut, wearing a leather jacket and khaki shirt and pants, and carrying a leather suitcase filled with poems. Moving his things to Peter's apartment, he left Philip Whalen in sole charge of the Milvia Street cottage.

On Saturday night, June 9, a telegram arrived. Allen was in 1956 Berkeley, but Peter was home and accepted it. It read: "Allen Ginsberg, care Orlovsky, 5 Turner Terrace, San Fran. Naomi Ginsberg died suddenly Saturday afternoon. Would appreciate your communicating this to Allen Ginsberg. He may call me at Hotel Regent. Eugene Brooks."

Knowing that Allen would stay over at Milvia Street, Peter set off for Berkeley. Allen was not at home when he arrived, so Peter scribbled on the envelope: "I got this at 7:30pm, and here at 10:45pm. Out to find you. Be back soon. She's in the sunshine now. Love Peter."

In "Kaddish," Ginsberg wrote:

> *Returning from San Francisco one night, Orlovsky in my room—Whalen in his peaceful chair—a telegram from Gene, Naomi dead—*
> *Outside I bent my head to the ground under the bushes near the garage—knew she was better—*

Allen did not go to the funeral, for reasons he can no longer remember. He knew it was not going to be a big family gathering, and the journey from coast to coast in those days was a long and difficult task, not undertaken easily. Eugene and Louis both provided descriptions of the service. There were only seven mourners. "I guess it was the smallest funeral on record," said Eugene. They were driven to a funeral parlor in Hempstead, Long Island, where they had a brief view of the body. "She was quite recognizable," said Eugene. "Her face was perhaps a little sad, though in repose." A sexton muttered a few prayers in Hebrew. He had to stop and ask her name in the middle of the short service and still did not get it right. The cortege went to Beth Moses Cemetery in Farmingdale, Long Island, where Eugene shot a few minutes of movie film. It was a spacious cemetery, with low headstones and a few pine shrubs. "It has a rather pleasant look and not crowded, and there is a lot of blue sky," Eugene told Allen. As the casket was lowered, the sexton prayed again but would not say the Kaddish because a quorum of ten males (a *minyan*) was not present, as required by Jewish law. Louis stood blinded by tears, recalling his happy early days with Naomi, the pathos and tragedy of her well-meaning life, and the constant struggles she had within her. "As I saw her coffin lowered into the hospitable earth, I thought that now she would at last have peace and rest, something I had struggled all my life to give her," he wrote Allen.

Afterward they visited the grave of Naomi's sister, Eleanor, one hundred yards away. They had not told Naomi of Eleanor's death, some months earlier. "Well, today the world is inexorably evil," Eugene wrote. "I suppose tomorrow it will be better." Naomi's wedding ring was given to Eugene, who gave it to Connie. Allen received one thousand dollars. He wrote his father a long letter and received a tear-stained reply. "It is difficult to write you and tell you in a few words a life full of love for Naomi," Louis wrote. "Though fate had removed her physically from me for the last few years, I confess she was in my heart always. There was no day during which I was in a crowd or happy that thoughts of Naomi, torn within herself and cooped up in a desolate room, did not invade my mind."

A few days after Naomi's death, Allen sat on the dockside in San Francisco and wrote: "Everything changes toward death. My mother. Myself . . . My childhood is gone with my mother. My memory becomes less clear. My body will go. There is no me left.

Naomi is a memory. Naomi is a memory. My 30 years is a memory to me." Eugene was also moved to write about his mother's death, and his poem "To My Mother" appeared on July 25 in the *New York Times*.

Knowing that Naomi had been denied the Kaddish at her graveside, Allen attempted to get one said for her. He, Peter, and Jack were taking one of their long walks around San Francisco, when they found themselves in the old Jewish neighborhood between Fillmore and Buchanan. Seeing a synagogue, Allen suggested that they go in and say a Kaddish for Naomi. "I showed the letter saying there was no Kaddish said, and talked with some of the fellows there," Ginsberg remembered. "They asked Peter, 'Are you Jewish?' 'No.' Kerouac, 'Are you Jewish?' 'No.' They were friendly, I was a nice little Jewish boy whose mother had died so they tried to get a *minyan* together, but they couldn't come up with enough Jewish men. I remember Kerouac was very sweet about it, very accommodating." Finally, Allen decided to write a Kaddish for Naomi himself and asked Louis to get him a copy of the prayer. Louis replied that he would, and commented: "Those chants therein have a rhythm and sonorousness of immemorial years marching with reverberations through the corridors of history . . . laden with the tears of things." Several years would pass, however, before Allen completed his task.

Allen joined a new ship, the USNS *Sgt. Jack J. Pendleton*, taking with him the proofs of *Howl* from City Lights, which Villiers Press in London had begun typesetting at the beginning of June. The long verse line breaks of the poems were very poorly set. "This being my first book I want it right if I can," Allen wrote Ferlinghetti on July 3. "It looks as if the whole book will have to be reset practically," and he offered to pay up to two hundred dollars for the cost of resetting. In his anxiety to extend his good fortune to his friends, Allen devised a dedication that managed not only to proclaim Neal Cassady's unpublished *First Third* and Burroughs's *Naked Lunch* but to name all eleven of Kerouac's unpublished manuscripts. Lucien he congratulated on being appointed night bureau manager of United Press, a compliment Lucien could have done without. Allen was still thinking of the book as a slim volume of obscure verse published in the provinces.

Allen's ship was on its way to the Arctic Circle to deliver matériel to refurbish the Distant Early Warning line radar system, and weeks were spent assembling the cargo from military depots in Portland, Seattle, and Tacoma. Philip Whalen forwarded mail to Tacoma. One of the letters came as a shock. It was from Naomi. It had been mailed by the hospital two days after her death, but unlike her other recent letters, it was quite lucid. She congratulated Allen on his birthday and talked about the mimeographed copy of "Howl" he had sent her. "It seems to me your wording was a little too hard. Do tell me what father thinks of it," she said. She worried about Allen's prospects and continued:

"You know you have to have a good job to get married. I wish you did have a good job. What did you specialize in when you went to college? This going to the North Pole, who supplies the wearing material? They say when you visit the Eskimos you need a double coat of fur. Are you fit for that flying job? Don't take chances with your life! I wish you get married. Do you like farming? It's as good a job as any. I hope you behave well. Don't go in for too much drink or other things that are not good for you. . . . As for myself, I still have the wire on my head. The doctors know about it. They are cutting the flesh and bone. They are giving me teethache. I do wish you were back east so I could see you. . . . I am glad you are having your poetry published. I wish I were out of here and at home at the time you were young! Then I would be young. I'm in the prime of life now—Did you read about the two men who died at 139 and 149 yrs of age? I wonder how they lived. I'm looking for a good time. I hope you are not taking drugs as suggested by your poetry. That would hurt me. Don't go in for ridiculous things. With love and good news. (mother) Naomi."

Allen was comforted by the thought that she had seemed to be in calm spirits before her death, and he forwarded the letter to Eugene, asking him to show it to Louis. "I've been thinking a lot," he told Eugene. "We all die, life's a short flash. Standing on prow of ship with roaring ocean and stars and force of wind in sleeves, great majesty and tenderness to life, at its heart, a kind of instantaneous universal joy at creation, and everything in the ocean moves."

Seven days out of Puget Sound, they sailed through the Bering Strait, but it was foggy and Allen could see only white-breasted birds flying from Alaska to Russia. He wrote a haiku: "One fingernail dirty and the Bering Sea," and threw it in the water along with the seven cents in his pocket as a tribute to Naomi, being so near to her Russia. The ship followed the Alaska coast to Icy Cape, where, along with forty other ships, they had to wait for the ice to break up farther north before they could continue. The sky was filled with clouds, and sometimes the ship was buffeted by rainy wind. They could see ice floes in every direction but no icebergs, nor was land in sight, though a radio antenna rose from an invisible beach just over the horizon.

Allen had access to the ship's mimeograph machine, and on the weekend of July 26–27, he made copies of his poem "Siesta in *1956* Xbalba," which he stapled into a twenty-two-page booklet, dedicated to Karena Shields. He sent copies to Ferlinghetti and to Louis, who responded encouragingly: "It's very interesting with cinematic flashbacks of scenes and people. There is entangled in your lines a nostalgia for the past and for ruins that make a pulpit for mortality. Congratulations!"

The ship moved slowly up the coast and by August 4 was anchored off the Eskimo trading-post town of Wainwright, but the crew were not allowed ashore lest they infect the Eskimos with measles. A few days later, they completed their journey and arrived at Point Barrow, 340 miles north of the Arctic Circle and the northernmost point of the United States.

In early August, the mail brought Allen a package from City *1956* Lights Books, and he saw for the first time the stark black-and-white cover of *Howl and Other Poems*. He was pleased by the way the type had been reset and happy that it cost him only twenty dollars to have it done. He wrote to Ferlinghetti: "Received the copy of the book you sent me promptly and was excited to see it. . . . I shuddered when I read the poetry tho, it all looks so jerry-built sloppy and egocentric most of it. 'Greyhound' looks fine, I'm glad you told me to put it in. Reading it all through I'm not sure it deserves all the care and work you've put into it and the encouragement you've given me, in fact, to tell you the truth, I'm already embarrassed by half of it but what the hell. . . ." He thanked Lawrence for publishing it and asked, "I wonder if we will actually sell the thousand copies."

Allen was in the land of the Midnight Sun. He described the scene to Kerouac: "Dread ghastly pallor all night through clouds, and this week fantastic burning iron sun going down at edge of horizon for a few hours, clear weather. The water always moving, clouds always moving, birds same, clouds and me same, like a transparent shifting layer everywhere changing." The *Pendleton* spent a month in the Arctic and delivered goods to various camps and bases during the week of midsummer when the sun never fully reached the horizon.

For the first time in his life, Allen read the Old Testament of the

Bible. He began with Genesis and by mid-August had read four hundred pages. He was amazed by it, and wrote Kerouac: "I never understood Jews or Christians before, it's all explained in the Book. . . . The Bible is fantastic, complete history of the Jews from Adam, to God speaking on Sinai, telling them they are chosen people, and the building of holy empire of seed of Abram Isac and Israel, all forefathers to whom God prophesied—with Jews always violating the covenants they made with God in Moses' time when he first laid down permanent Law for them to live up to. Then the culmination of peaceful holy land in wise Solomon's time, the building of the Temple and after that, Spenglerian degeneration, all told in detail, whoring and queerness and worship of moloch, till God finally gives up and breaks down the walls of Jerusalem and disperses them all into captivity, Babylon and elsewhere. It's a huge vast Shakespearian tragic cycle book, fantastic consistent plot. I am beginning to see how important Christ is in relation to old Testament—he just turns it upside down, revokes the old God-spoken holy laws in person."

Coming directly after the death of his mother, the trip to the Arctic was mostly a period of solitude and contemplation. Ginsberg was unable to relate to his Jewish heritage but was moved by an as yet undefined spiritual quest. He had long talks about Muhammad with two black shipmates from the mess hall and gave them his copy of the Diamond Sutra (the Bible was not the only holy book he had with him). He told Kerouac: "I spend a lot of time on the prow at night, often on my knees praying, but don't know to who or what." He was still searching.

1956

Back in San Francisco at the beginning of September, Allen immediately set to work sending out his book. Copies went to Carl Solomon, still in Pilgrim State, to Charlie Chaplin, Henry Miller, Robinson Jeffers, Louis Zukofsky, W. H. Auden, T. S. Eliot, Louise Bogan, Marianne Moore, Ezra Pound, Kenneth Patchen, e. e. cummings, and the celebrated lesbian Natalie Barney, as well as to Burroughs, Kerouac, Holmes, Carr, and all his friends. Lucien wrote Allen: "I was touched at being included in your dedication. But I value a certain anonymity in life and it always jars me when my friends, of all people, find it desirable to include mention of me in their works—dedication page as well as text." He asked Allen to remove it from subsequent editions of the book, which he did.

Allen mailed out over one hundred review copies of *Howl*, but the review that mattered most had already been written. Richard Eberhart's long serious article, "West Coast Rhythms," appeared in the *New York Times* on September 2, 1956, and though he mentioned *1956* Snyder, McClure, Whalen, and the benevolent influences of Patchen, Jeffers, and Rexroth, the article was centered on Allen, whom Eberhart identified as a major young poet. "The most remarkable poem of the young group, written during the past year, is 'Howl' by Allen Ginsberg." After describing Ginsberg's background, Eberhart went on to say: "After years of apprenticeship to usual forms, he developed his brave new medium. This poem has created a furor of praise or abuse whenever read or heard. It is a powerful work, cutting through to dynamic meaning. Ginsberg thinks he is going forward by going back to the methods of Whitman. My first impression was that it is based on destructive violence. It is profoundly Jewish in temper. It is Biblical in its repetitive grammatical build-up. It is a howl against everything in our mechanistic civilization which kills the spirit, assuming that the louder you shout the more likely you are to be heard. It lays bare the nerves of suffering and spiritual struggle. Its positive force and energy come from a redemptive quality of love, although it destructively catalogues evils of our time from physical deprivation to madness."

Eberhart went on to point out the humor in Ginsberg's work, citing the line, in "America," "Asia is rising against me / I haven't got a Chinaman's chance," and he mentioned "Sunflower Sutra" as "a lyric poem marked by pathos." Allen could not have asked for more.

Louis was overjoyed by the article: "I was happy to see it. Edith keeps a copy in her purse and shows it to all and sundry. I have passed it around the Newark folks. I rejoice that your book is coming out. I predict it will make a name for you. You may wake up one morning and find yourself famous. I hope so."

Allen was now famous enough for him to write to Kerouac: "Agh! I'm sick of the whole thing, that's all I think about, famous authorhood, like a happy empty dream. . . . How beautiful tho," Allen continued. "I guess I really feel good about it. It's assuming proportions of an 'it' in my life."

Allen and Peter saw a lot of Gregory Corso, who had moved to San Francisco and was staying in North Beach with a Frenchwoman. Gregory, with his spiky New York humor and paranoia, antagonized both Michael McClure and Neal Cassady, causing difficulties within the group, which Allen took it upon himself to smooth over—a role in which he would frequently find himself with Gregory over the decades. Allen's tremendous loyalty to his friends meant that he would do anything to keep peace among them and maintain a working poetic relationship.

Allen single-handedly *willed* the Beat Generation into being by his unshakable belief that his poet friends were all geniuses. Without Allen, Burroughs would almost certainly never have published *Junkie* and would not have continued his writing career. Without Allen, it is unlikely that Kerouac would have published anything other than his first book, and even that was done with Allen's aid. Over the years, he devoted an enormous amount of his time to promoting Kerouac, Burroughs, Corso, Snyder, Whalen, Orlovsky, and the other writers loosely known as the Beats, as well as promoting post-Williams poets he was less close to, or didn't know personally at all, such as Levertov, Oppenheimer, Marshall, Zukofsky, and Niedecker. In *Jack's Book*, Robert Duncan was quoted as saying: "Ginsberg always lived in the romance that he was going to know overwhelming writers. Allen came to San Francisco because of Rexroth and Patchen. Even meeting me, and I was nothing, was to him overwhelming, as Kerouac had been and Burroughs was. He invented the sky with new stars in it, and his invention of it was a poet's."

Allen had his reasons. He viewed the literary establishment of Trilling, *Partisan Review, Kenyon Review,* and the Southern School as ultimately reactionary: "They were liberal but in the long run they would go along with a police state if it happened—they wouldn't go to jail." They seemed preoccupied with fighting communism and Stalinism. To Allen, theirs was "cultural resistance to communism . . . so I was reacting to that conservative group with a hip shot. The reason I was so eager to ally with Rexroth and Duncan and the old San Francisco renaissance was because we basically had the same politics—which was like philosophical anarchism. I thought it was urgent for the poets to make a united phalanx: Black Mountain, North West, San Francisco, Renaissance, Beat, and New York School, to try and correlate our efforts and publishing. Because to me, Williams's 'open form' meant 'open mind' . . . I wasn't just plugging and promoting my friends, I had a much larger agenda."

McClure said, "The group that Allen was trying to get together smacked of New York, of homosexuality, and on the other hand, something I admire very much, a social commitment that I did not have within myself. As a matter of fact, the thing that I've learned from Allen is social commitment." At the time, however, Allen denied he was consciously trying to form a group. "We're all friends," he told Lawrence Lipton later that year, "but not organized as a literary movement."

Not all the poets liked the idea of the "San Francisco School," as Eberhart had called them, and preferred jealously to guard their own individualism. Robert Duncan in particular felt that his work was being overlooked, and McClure wanted to keep his identity very much separate. Squabbles were inevitable. "The lines were drawn, the battles were horrific," said McClure. "We were pretty macho, but we really didn't want to do any damage to each other. I mean, there were only about a dozen of us. No matter how territorial we were or how ferocious our internecine wars might be, we had a lot more in common with each other than with anybody else out there. So there was probably some yelling and name calling, but only once or twice." One thing that highlighted the factionalism of the poets was an article in *Mademoiselle* magazine on the San Francisco scene. Allen, Jack, Gregory, Peter, and the others wanted a group photograph to accompany the article, but Duncan and McClure insisted on having their photographs taken separately. Allen could simply not understand competitiveness among poets and rather naively, but genuinely, wanted everyone to be friends and unite against the philistines.

That September, Allen decided his season was coming to an end. 1956 The inner group was beginning to split up and it was time to move on. Gary Snyder had already left to live in Japan. Allen was ready for his European trip.

He had achieved a lot in San Francisco. He arrived unknown and unpublished, and in three short years he found himself at the center of a dynamic new literary movement, the famous author of a powerful and critically acclaimed work. He was now able to view himself as a poet and to see a future for himself in literature. It would have been easy to remain in San Francisco and be a big fish in a small pond, but he knew that if he stayed he would become more and more embroiled in the social scene and never get any work done. Success and local fame had given Allen confidence and stability, and he now wanted, more than anything, to help Bill Burroughs with his writing. "The Beat Generation was just beginning to burgeon, and I was very conscious of leaving the scene to do something more serious and steady," he said. "I already thought Bill a genius writer teacher, so I thought that was important and it was dramatically interesting to be involved with something onward going rather than the past."

Between himself and Peter, he thought, all of Bill's needs could be met. He felt protected by his relationship with Peter, which was working out well, and would perhaps have been less eager to go to Tangier alone. Allen had promoted a great growth in Peter. His sympathy and encouragement had enabled Peter to become much more self-confident, and by setting up orgies and threesomes, Allen had enabled Peter to conquer his shyness as well as staving off any problems arising from his preference for women. However, it was Allen who dominated the relationship. Allen always needed to be in charge, even if his role was sometimes a masochistic one; this Neal had only occasionally acquiesced to and Jack hardly ever allowed. In Peter he seemed to have found his ideal lover.

The European trip was something Allen had been planning ever since Mexico. His original idea had been to continue on to Russia, but it was to be another eight years before he achieved this. He intended not just to see the sights of Europe as a tourist but to settle down, living and working in one place.

It had been three years since he last saw Burroughs, and in his letters Bill sounded a little miserable. Peter had never met him, but, as Ginsberg said, "Peter and I decided that since he was so lacklove, the two of us would take him on and do anything he wanted. Satisfy him. So we went to Tangier to fuck him—to exhaust his desires." Bill, delighted, replied that he expected Allen and his entourage in January 1957. He went on to extol the beauty of Tangier: "This place relaxes me so I am subject to dissolve. I can spend three hours looking at the bay with my mouth open like a Kentucky Mountain Boy." Allen had been a bit worried that Bill would want him all to himself, but Bill said: "By all means bring Jack and Peter. I assure you I will not be jealous, in fact, jealousy is one of the emotions of which I am no longer capable. Self-pity is also impossible for me."

Jack then revealed his worries about going to Morocco. Writing from Mexico City, he told Allen he wanted to go to Europe, but was afraid the Arabs would kill them if they went to Tangier. Bill scoffed at Jack's fears, and told Allen: "Jack must not be afraid of Arabs, I am in a position to officially abolish fear." He also mentioned that he had recently acquired a large machete.

Plans were made. Allen, Peter, Lafcadio, and Gregory would go first to Mexico City and stay there for a few weeks with Jack, who had gone on ahead, then proceed to New York to make preparations for a long sojourn in Europe. Allen had not seen his father or brother since Naomi's death and wanted to spend time with them before leaving again for a long spell. They expected to arrive in Mexico City by November 7 and asked Jack to look around for somewhere they could all live for a few weeks.

Allen and Gregory set out to hitchhike to Los Angeles, on the first leg of the journey, leaving Peter and Lafcadio to close down the apartment. Allen had sent advance warning of their arrival in Los Angeles. A consummate publicist for the group, he wrote to Anaïs Nin, whom he did not know, asking her if she could organize a reading for them and invite Christopher Isherwood, Aldous Huxley, James Dean, and Marlon Brando. "I don't know what you can do with us," he wrote, "but if you can figure anything you're welcome; and the occasion, whatever it is, will not, please understand, be just a big nowhere bore. I mean our poetry swings and is literate & OK. . . ."

Allen and Gregory got to Los Angeles on October 30, intending to *1956* stay only a week. Lawrence Lipton had arranged a reading for them on Saturday night. Allen and Gregory arrived drunk, Allen carrying an open bottle of wine. Anaïs Nin came with a group of friends, though not the ones Allen had requested. He gave an inspired, drunken reading of "Howl," addressing his delivery exclusively to her, and in his enthusiasm he knocked over his bottle of wine, spilling it on himself. As it happened, someone in the audience, who had also been drinking, began to heckle. Allen politely asked him to hear out the reading and said that he would be pleased to hear his opinions afterward. This stopped the heckler for a bit, but when Gregory stood up to read, the drunk interrupted. "What are you guys trying to prove?" he demanded. Allen immediately yelled out, "Nakedness!"

"What do you mean, nakedness?" asked the drunk.

"I meant spiritual nakedness," Ginsberg explained later, "poetic nakedness—candor. Then I suddenly realized what I had said. Inspired, I just started taking off my clothes." "All right," Allen challenged the drunk. "You want to do something big, don't you? Something brave? Well, go on, do something *really* brave. *Take off your clothes!*" The man was speechless. Allen advanced on him, tearing off his shirt. "Come and stand here, stand naked before the people. I dare you! The poet always stands naked before the world." Allen threw his shirt and undershirt at the man's feet, and he began to back away. "You're scared, aren't you?" asked Allen. "You're afraid." Allen kicked off his shoes and socks and pulled down his pants. Doing a little hopping dance, he kicked them off and followed them with his shorts. He was now completely naked. The drunk had by now retreated to the back of the room. The audience sat in stunned silence.

Suddenly the room exploded in cheers, jeers, applause, and angry argument. The drunk was booed and hissed until he left. Anaïs Nin was impressed and wrote in her journal: "The way he did it was so violent and direct, it had so much meaning in terms of all our fears of unveiling ourselves. . . ." Gregory wanted to leave at once and take Anaïs Nin with them, but Lipton restored order and Gregory was persuaded to finish his reading. Allen took his time in putting his clothes back on, smiling quietly to himself through half-closed lids. He finished the reading with "Sunflower Sutra" and "A Supermarket in California." He wrote to Ferlinghetti: "Reading we gave in L.A. was the most wild ever. I disrobed finally. Been wanting to onstage for years." Burroughs got to hear of it in Tangier and wrote: "What's with you? You wig already and remove your dry goods inna public hall?"

Peter and Lafcadio soon joined Allen and Gregory, and they headed south to Tijuana. In Guadalajara, they stopped to visit the young British poet Denise Levertov. Allen told Ferlinghetti: "She was nice to us, we liked her a lot. I was surprised how much a good Joe she was. . . . Levertov is a good poetess, certainly. I read a lot of her work there." Allen added a folio of her poems to the collection of manuscripts he carried with him to show editors and publishers wherever and whenever he found them.

During their two-week stay in Mexico City, some Mexican boys took Allen, Peter, and Jack home with them to play spin the bottle. They all took off their clothes and had a gay orgy. Jack took Allen to meet Esperanza, the young prostitute who inspired him to write *Tristessa.* She was thin and weak from morphine addiction, and it was clear to Allen that Jack had a hopelessly sentimental view of her. Gregory saw nothing romantic in the poverty and filth of Mexico City and wanted to leave as soon as possible. He moved to an expensive tourist hotel to wait for his girlfriend to cable him the airfare back to the States. Allen, Jack, Peter, and Lafcadio took an expense-share car ride to New York City through a newspaper ad. It was a very uncomfortable trip.

• • •

The news that Allen and Jack were back in town traveled fast. *1956* No one was more thrilled to see Allen again than Elise Cowen, who was living with her friend Sheila in Yorkville. Allen and Peter found Lafcadio a place in a rooming house, then moved in with Elise and Sheila in their sixth-floor walk-up. They dragged another mattress into the bedroom, and all four of them slept together. Allen had a lot of catching up to do, visiting his father and stepmother, in Paterson, and Eugene, who had moved to Hicksville, Long Island. Eugene drove him to the snow-covered cemetery where Naomi was buried. Crows circled the graves.

Allen met Peter's family in Northport. Peter could not decide whether to accompany Allen to Europe. Allen and Peter had hired a lawyer to organize the release of Peter's brother Nicholas from the mental hospital, and Peter knew he was the only one in his family capable of handling matters if anything went wrong. He felt torn between nursing his brothers and living his own life.

Allen, meanwhile, ran around town, visiting. He had arrived in New York with manuscripts and books by Gary Snyder, Philip Whalen, Robert Duncan, Ed Dorn, Robert Creeley, Philip Lamantia, Denise Levertov, Michael McClure, and Charles Olson, determined to extend the San Francisco Poetry Renaissance to New York. He threw himself into the task with enormous energy. He presented himself at the *New York Times* and asked them to review *Howl*. He was interviewed by Harvey Breit, whom he inundated with material. Breit wrote an informative, though unenthusiastic, piece as a follow-up to Eberhart's earlier *Times* article. *Mademoiselle* printed Denise Levertov's poems and also some Burroughs material. Allen was interviewed, at his insistence, by a cynical feature writer from the New York *World-Telegram*, where he once worked as a copyboy, and Allen, Gregory, and Jack were interviewed by the *Village Voice*.

Allen approached *Time, Life, Esquire*, and the *Hudson Review*. *Partisan Review* and the *Kenyon Review* agreed to review some of the books he left with them. He persuaded James Laughlin, at New Directions, to include some San Francisco material in the upcoming *New Directions Annual*, and gave John Clellon Holmes's editor at Scribner's a big pile of books and manuscripts to look through. At *The New Yorker*, Louise Bogan agreed to review *Howl* and other San Francisco publications. Allen gave Louis Simpson an enormous selection of material to consider for the anthology he was editing with

Donald Hall, *New Poets of England and America*. The fact that Simpson rejected them all is a measure of how conservative the New York establishment was. Allen's best reception came from editor Don Allen at newly founded Grove Press, where *Evergreen Review* was in the works. It was decided that the entire second issue of the magazine be devoted to the San Francisco scene.

One of the poets Allen visited was Diane di Prima. Ginsberg remembered his first meeting with her: "She sent a bunch of funny poems, and then, when we went back to the East Coast, Jack Kerouac and Peter and I all got into bed with her and a couple of dancer friends she had, and we all had a big all night orgy—she and Jack and me sucking the cock of this really pretty looking dancer boy fellow." Ginsberg joked about orgies in the narration for a film sound track in 1979: "Yes, we did quite a few. Peter would always get the girls and I would always get the guys, or we'd get a guy and a girl and take them home with us. I would make it with the guy if I could, and Peter would make it with the girl. Sometimes they were fifteen-year-old boys and sometimes they were sixteen-year-old girls. Good times. Fun."

When Allen was away in Paterson or out in the literary jungle, Elise washed and ironed, made soup, took endless telephone messages for him. The fact that Allen was with Peter didn't seem to bother her unduly. Allen encountered Salvador Dali at a gallery opening and introduced himself as a poet. "Do you know the poet Lorca?" Dali asked.

Allen took two steps back and began reciting: "Not for one moment beautiful aged Walt Whitman / have I failed to see your beard full of butterflies . . ."

"But do you know his 'Ode to Salvador Dali,' " he asked, but Allen had never heard of it. "It is a beautiful poem, one of his best," said Dali. "What is your address? Do you have a group? I am interested in meeting the young poets." They had a short, intense talk about Surrealism, then Dali, returning to the subject of his old friend Lorca, said, "Ah, 'The Poet in New York,' that is not the great Lorca. It is too Surrealist. The early gypsy ballads are more solid." They arranged to continue their conversation another day at Dali's hotel.

Allen, Peter, Jack, and Gregory arrived at the St. Regis dressed so badly that Dali's wife, Gala, took one look at them and postponed the meeting for a week. Allen reported their initial encounter to Robert LaVigne: "It was all very weird to have contact with dream-like Dali. . . . He seems intelligent and more serious than I'd have imagined." Gala arranged Sunday lunch for them at the Russian Tea Room, and Allen, Peter, and Jack dressed as well as they could for the occasion. Jack wore a huge vicuña coat that reached the ground, and he had a ski cap pulled over his ears to protect him from the vicious cold. Dali and Gala were waiting, Dali leaning forward on his cane. He ordered "One grapefruit . . . *peenk.*" Allen explained his vow of poverty; he had decided never to read for money. Dali disagreed completely. "The measure of genius is gold!" he told them. Allen said that they wanted to meet Marlon Brando, who they knew ate in the Russian Tea Room. Dali pointed at Jack and said, "He is more beautiful than Marlon Brando." They asked about his politics, and Dali said, "As a politician I am a Royalist. I would like to see the Throne of Spain return, Franco and the others out." He told them, "Last night I finished my latest painting, using a pubic hair for the last final touch." Peter explained rock 'n' roll to them and offered to take them to one of the big concerts at the Paramount. The Dalis went on their own and later marketed a "Rock and Roll" perfume.

Allen, Peter, Jack, and Gregory visited William Carlos Williams in New Jersey. He was then seventy-three, but youthful and alert. They all read their poems, while he stared out the white-curtained windows at the traffic plowing through the slush and snow. Sometimes he seemed somewhat bored. They stayed all afternoon and into the evening, drinking the cheap wine they had brought with them, until Flossie, Williams's wife, went to the cellar and brought up something better. Williams liked Peter's poems (he had written two), but most of the time it was Ginsberg and Williams talking. As they left, Kerouac asked, "Before we go, Dr. Williams, do you have any wise words for us?"

Williams stared out the window, "There's a lot of bastards out there!"

"They were dressed as bums, they were bums," Williams said later, and remembered that they had smoked some funny-smelling stuff while they were there, but he was enthusiastic about the younger poets, and after their visit, he wrote Theodore Roethke: "I think you've heard of Allen Ginsberg and his gang, Karuak and Corso. What does it mean? At least we live in an age where anything goes and I for one welcome it." Williams, like Richard Eberhart, considered this group to be Ginsberg's creation.

• • •

Jack was the first to go. Allen lent him $225 and on February 15 he sailed for Tangier. Ten days later, Gregory left for Paris, to meet up with his girlfriend Hope Savage. Peter finally made up his mind. He and Allen each paid $185 one-way passage, and on March 8 they kissed Elise and Sheila goodbye and set sail on the *Hrvatska*, a Yugoslavian freighter headed for Casablanca.

1957

| "THE CLASSIC STATIONS OF THE EARTH"

It was a magical interlude, and like all such interludes, all too brief: "The things we have never had remain: it is the things we have that go. . . ."

—William S. Burroughs, 1983
Foreword to Harold Norse, *Beat Hotel*

BILL BURROUGHS HAD BEEN IN TANGIER SINCE DECEMBER 1953 AND HAD lived in a number of places, including a celebrated male brothel. After a spot of trouble with his most recent landlady, who objected to the constant flow of Arab boys, Bill found "the original anything-goes joint," Villa Muniriya (or Villa Delirium, as it came to be known), in the old French quarter. It was owned by an aging Frenchwoman who had an "in" with the authorities and had previously run a whorehouse in Saigon. The ex-madam poked Burroughs in the ribs and said, "You can be *free* here, you understand." Bill's room was small and damp, but he liked it because the door opened out onto a garden, where he was able to grow some roses and play with the housekeeper's two cats. Most of the occupants were prostitutes, and the biggest excitement was the screaming match that ensued whenever Joselito, the Spanish houseboy, tried to waylay one of their clients.

Bill's room was painted white, and he had covered one wall entirely with snapshots, mostly from his 1953 expedition to the South American jungle in search of yage. Another wall was his shooting gallery, pockmarked with bullet holes. As usual, Bill was heavily armed. He had an assortment of razor-sharp knives, including a meat cleaver and a machete. When Kerouac was in Tangier, Bill scared him by producing a rifle and waving it drunkenly over Jack's head.

In the corner of the room stood a homemade orgone accumulator, in which Bill used to sit, doubled up, smoking kif. He had his own little stove, on which he made hashish candy, or majoun, of which he was very proud; finely chopped kif was mixed with caraway seeds, ground nutmeg, cinnamon, and honey, then heated until it became the "consistency of sticky shit," as Ginsberg described it. One tablespoon of Bill's majoun would see you through the night.

The floor was littered with bottles that once contained eucodal— a morphine-based painkiller—and with pages and pages of type-writing, which lay thickly around the legs of Bill's desk and which the sea breezes would blow out the open door and into the garden. Bill would sit hunched over his portable, sometimes chuckling to himself, mopping his brow, hair awry. He would tear a page of manuscript from the machine and scribble on it in his spidery cal-ligraphy, before throwing it over his shoulder to join the pile. Some-times he found his routines so funny that he would roll on the floor, doubled up with laughter. The manuscript had the working title "Word Horde." It was later published, much revised, as *Naked Lunch*.

When Kerouac arrived in Tangier in late February 1957, Bill got him a rooftop room in the Villa Muniriya. A tiled patio looked out over the topsy-turvy rooftops and palms to the tower of the Catholic church and the bright green water of the bay. In the distance could be seen the coast of Spain and the mountains farther inland, and sometimes Gibraltar was visible in the bright Mediterranean haze, a small bump of coastland to the northeast.

Burroughs led a very orderly life in Tangier. Each morning he would row, like a gondolier, in the harbor, and at 4 P.M. he would get out the cognac. His neighbor Eric, an old Etonian, would stop by for a snifter and reminisce about his experiences in Burma and the Far East. Through the open garden door the sun would set purple over the bay.

One evening, Bill treated Jack to an excellent meal, complete with fine wine and liqueurs. Back at the hotel, they collected Bill's binoculars and went to Jack's rooftop patio to look at the breathtak-ing nighttime view. Brilliantly lit boats were arriving in the harbor from Casablanca, and the stars hung in the clear night sky. Bill stared out to sea. "When will Allen get here?" he asked. They stood against the parapet looking across the strait to the distant twinkling lamps of Tarifa, listening to the cicadas and the far-off whoosh of the ocean. Bill began to cry. Still obsessed by Allen, after three and a half years, he missed him dreadfully. He leaned on Jack's shoulder, sobbing.

Jack's rooftop room cost him only twenty dollars a month. The sweet Malaga wine he liked was only twenty-eight cents a liter, and a meal at the local Arab café cost thirty-five cents. He could have afforded to stay there indefinitely, but within a month he was homesick for America and missed his mother. He began complaining about the high cost of whores (three dollars). He had a bad experience with opium, and became violently ill after smoking hashish that had been cut with arsenic. Burroughs himself began to scare Jack. Jack couldn't understand Bill's obsession with Allen, nor could he relate to Bill's ordered European ways. He described his feelings in *Desolation Angels*: "On the opium overdose I had snarling dreary thoughts about all Africa, all Europe, the world—all I wanted somehow was Wheaties by a pine breeze kitchen in America. . . . So by the time Allen and Peter finally arrived for their big triumphant reunion with us in Africa it was too late." Jack had already made plans to move on.

On March 19, Allen and Peter docked in Casablanca, where they *1957* spent three exciting days. Disregarding Burroughs's grim warning never to enter a Muhammadan establishment, they headed straight for the Medina, with its narrow streets and archways. They wandered down a dark alley and found an Arab café, where they were given the national drink of sweet mint tea. Someone produced a long-stemmed kif pipe and passed it to Allen. He spent the afternoon high, looking at the veiled women and at the Arab men in their hooded robes seated in dim cafés drinking tea. Beggars crouched in doorways and an old palsied Jew in a black hood and skullcap stood in the sunlight, one palm outstretched, a few brass coins clutched in his bony fist. Allen was struck by how clean the streets and alleys were, "spotless and bright in the sun." After their three days in the capital, they continued their voyage around the coast, and as their boat pulled in to dock, they saw Bill and Jack waving to them from the sunny harbor wall.

The excitement of seeing Allen was too much for Bill, who got very quickly drunk. He waved his machete about until Allen told him to stop frightening everyone. Allen wanted to do everything: hike to the countryside, go swimming in the harbor, explore the Medina and the Kasbah, visit the circus, go inland to Fez by train, sit in outdoor cafés sipping mint tea and smoking kif. Bill's orderly life was thrown into chaos.

They rolled Bill's majoun into balls and chewed on it for hours, washing it down with hot plain tea. After an hour or so it produced a slow, strong marijuana high that was like peyote. Allen and Bill would stay up half the night talking, Bill stumbling around the room, endlessly stirring his drink with his index and middle fingers, visiting the two or three kif joints that he had burning in various ashtrays around the room, his voice sometimes raised high in protest as Allen gleefully proposed one contentious idea about art or literature after another for the sheer pleasure of watching Bill attempt to shoot it down. The fights were good-natured and stimulating.

Jack left for France in April, and Allen and Peter immediately moved into his wonderful rooftop room. Kerouac later regretted leaving; he accused Allen and Peter of putting pressure on him to go, so that they could have his room. With a room of their own, Allen and Peter settled into more of a routine. Allen got up at dawn and wrote on the patio, watching the sun rise, then spent five or six hours working on Bill's manuscript.

Each day, the Chinese maid brought a delicious lunch to Allen and Peter's room as they lay reading or writing. Cigarettes cost twelve cents a pack, Egyptian hashish was plentiful, and opium was fifty cents a gram, enough to keep one awake for twenty-four hours. They spent a lot of time on their patio, looking out at the harbor and the boats or leaning over the concrete parapet to watch Bill putter about in the garden with the cats. The warm Moroccan nights were spent in conversation with friends.

By late May, there were over two hundred pages of finished manuscript. They were approaching the harder task of going through Bill's letters to Allen from 1953 to 1956, pulling out biographical material, routines, and narrative fragments to add to the main text. As the work progressed, Bill experienced liver trouble and had to stop drinking. He also cut out majoun. The manuscript gradually took shape, and Allen wrote Lucien: "It's quite a piece of writing—all Bill's energy & prose, plus our organisation & cleanup & structure, so it's continuous and readable, decipherable."

Peter was unhappy in Tangier and wanted to go to Europe so he could meet some Western girls. He was getting on badly with Bill, who, despite regarding himself as incapable of jealousy, constantly teased Peter and put him down. Bill's condescending attitude toward Peter also offended Allen, who had hoped, perhaps naively,

that Bill would like Peter and accept the situation. One evening
when they were all high on majoun, Allen could not take Bill's
mockery any longer. He leapt up and ripped open Bill's khaki shirt
with a hunting knife. Peter, for his part, was glad when Allen began
reading guidebooks to Spain.

They left Tangier in June 1957, bound for Granada. Allen was *1957*
astounded by the exotic rambling Spanish and Arab battlements of
the fourteenth-century castle, the Alhambra. Nothing had prepared
him for such a sight. Its palatial Arabian halls, decorated from floor
to ceiling with the most intricate and sophisticated arabesques and
mathematical patterns, fascinated him. To Eugene he wrote: "Only
a people inspired by hashish would have taken trouble with such
detail—you can sit in the room and get high by osmosis contemplating the infinite structure of the human imagination."

From Granada they took the train to Seville, where they stayed
for two days, exploring the enormous black cathedral and getting
lost in the winding streets and narrow alleys, which were covered
with white canvas sun awnings. They zigzagged back to the ancient
university city of Córdoba, arriving late at night and taking a cheap
room in a narrow winding street. The next day, they investigated
the Great Mosque, with its hundreds of Arab pillars and colored
arches.

They arrived in Madrid on the overnight train, took their travel-
stained clothes to be cleaned, and rested up. They ate mostly as the
Madrilenians did, standing at bars and stalls, dining on delicious
small portions of lobster, crab, and prawns, yogurt or fresh fruits.
They ate small but tasty steaks for eight cents in the overcrowded
student bars and strolled in the thronged evening streets.

Allen, naturally, headed straight for the Prado, where he was
astonished by the vibrant color and intricacy of detail in the paintings of Brueghel and Bosch, El Greco, Goya, Velázquez, and Ru-
bens. He spent an hour examining the details of Hieronymus
Bosch's *Garden of Earthly Delights*. *The Annunciation* by Fra Angelico was, he thought, simply the greatest painting he had ever
seen. In it, the dove descended to Mary on rays of pure gold, still
bright after seven centuries. The faces were delicately drawn on
ivory white, and Mary was sheltered by a blue dome supported by
golden pillars. A guard noticed Allen's preoccupation with the
work, and confessed that he, too, thought it was the best piece in
the museum.

Allen wrote Kerouac: "At that instant I got Europe hungry and museum hungry and realized all the treasures of Europe all over, in Italy & Spain & Moscow & Paris, all the vast collections of infinite pictures." Allen's hunger for museums and cathedrals and works of art remained with him, and over the decades he managed to visit virtually every collection of significance throughout the world.

Allen and Peter liked Madrid and made an effort to find work in order to stay the summer, but no job materialized. They made arrangements to spend the summer with Alan Ansen in Venice instead, and meanwhile concentrated on seeing as much of Spain as they could.

For Allen, the greatest thing in Barcelona was Gaudí's magnificent Sagrada Familia. He and Peter climbed its towers and also visited Gaudí's Park Güell. They walked on the Ramblas and explored the dim alleys and high, dark fortresslike stone tenements of the Barrio Gótico. They visited Jean Genet's Barrio Chino—a cheap slum, half medieval, half rebuilt after Franco's bombing during the Spanish Civil War—filled with whorehouses, artists' bistros, and workingmen's cafés. They took a large garret room, high in the rooftops, with a small window through which the setting sun turned their bed sheets first orange, then pink. They wandered the streets, looking for the life Genet had described, but it was long gone.

They arrived in Venice on July 1, having taken a train along the Côte d'Azur in a heat wave and spent a day and a night in Milan. Allen and Peter stayed up all night talking with Alan Ansen and at dawn watched the sun rise over the lagoon. They settled into Ansen's apartment on the Calle delle Carrozze. Allen could put his head out the window and see the blue water of the Grand Canal, a half block away, with the gondolas bobbing past and the water taxis leaving wakes that slopped against the striped mooring poles, as in a Canaletto painting.

Each day, like most tourists, Allen was drawn inexorably to the Piazza San Marco, the vast colonnaded plaza fronting the cathedral, where the orchestras of the outdoor cafés battled with each other, playing Italian light opera, Strauss, and gypsy dances, as great flocks of pigeons whirled and swooped among the tourists. Allen never grew tired of visiting the basilica, its five Byzantine onion domes fronted by a group of giant bronze horses looted from imperial Rome. He found the edifice even more impressive inside, where the warped mosaic floor tiles rose and fell in waves and curves, the ancient wooden piles beneath having settled unevenly into the mud of the lagoon. The walls and ceilings were covered by thousands of square feet of delicate mosaic, the famous "golden gloom" of ninth- and tenth-century Byzantium. This was the Old World of Europe that Ginsberg had dreamed of in Chiapas and California, and he was utterly enthralled.

On May 21, 1957, acting on orders from Captain William Hanrahan of the San Francisco Police, Juvenile Division, two police officers went to City Lights Bookshop and bought a copy of *Howl*. The officers then obtained a warrant for the arrest of Lawrence Ferlinghetti as the book's publisher and as owner of the bookstore, and a John Doe for Shigeyoshi Murao for selling the book. Shig was taken the three blocks to the Hall of Justice, where he was fingerprinted and photographed, then locked in the drunk tank, which smelled of piss. Two hours later, an ACLU lawyer bailed him out. Ferlinghetti arrived not long after with his lawyers and was also fingerprinted and photographed but not detained. The *Howl* trial was under way.

Two months earlier, U.S. Customs had confiscated 520 copies of *Howl* arriving in the United States from the English printer. Ferlinghetti had immediately referred the matter to the American Civil Liberties Union, whose lawyers said that in their opinion the book was not obscene and they were prepared to fight the seizure. At this, the U.S. Attorney in San Francisco backed down, and the books were returned. Now that the police had decided to prosecute, the ACLU again stepped in.

They planned a defense based on the first amendment rights of freedom of speech and press, and assigned one of their best lawyers to the case, J.W.K. ("Never Plead Guilty") Ehrlich. Opposing him was Ralph McIntosh, who had a long history of prosecuting nudist magazines and "pornographic" films. The trial was a great cause célèbre for the Bay Area literary community. Kenneth Rexroth rose up in arms; Robert Duncan, Ruth Witt-Diamant, and dozens of others offered assistance; and it was to be the main topic of literary discussion that summer. The trial date was set for August 22.

With all the heavyweight literary support on his side, Allen didn't foresee any trouble in winning the case. There was Richard Eberhart's article in the *New York Times*; William Carlos Williams's introduction to the book; the moral support of Louise Bogan, Randall Jarrell, James Laughlin, and Grove Press. "The literary backup was impeccable," Ginsberg later said. "You couldn't possibly lose the case, so I didn't take it seriously as a threat, and Ferlinghetti in his letters didn't sound too threatened." The trial, of course, gave enormous publicity to the book, and Kerouac wrote Allen to complain that everywhere he went he was introduced as the guy *Howl* was dedicated to, and now he couldn't be famous on his own.

1957

After a month in Venice, Allen and Peter made their first big sightseeing trip to the Italian mainland, first to Florence and then on to Rome, where, in the Protestant Cemetery, Allen plucked a clover from Shelley's grave to send to Corso in Paris, and took another to send to his father. He was overcome by emotion at seeing Keats's grave. The rest of the day they spent on the beach at Ostia (where twenty years later they would read poetry to audiences of thousands at open-air festivals).

A visit to the Vatican Museum confirmed Allen's anti-Catholic sentiment. He found that drapery had been painted all over the naked bodies of Michelangelo's *Last Judgment* and fig leaves fixed to all the torsos in the Vatican's great collection of classical statuary. Allen expressed his indignation to his father: "I never saw the Church in such vulgar and ugly relief. After Florence and its classical openness and after seeing statuary in the Forum and various State museums, to go to the Vatican and see them desecrating the very significance and point of ancient sculpture—idealized human beings, but real ones . . . It stands out like the piece of dirtymindedness that it is."

They took a train to Assisi, the beautiful mountain town overlooking the Umbrian valley. On the train, Allen noted in his journal: "Great landscape full of castles and cities on hills." He and Peter arrived in the town dirty and unshaven and footworn, with Allen wearing a broken straw hat, much as Saint Francis himself must have appeared in his tattered cloak, begging and singing in the streets. They presented themselves at the Franciscan monastery, but the monks first refused them refuge, then solicited donations. They toured the churches, saw the tomb of Saint Francis, his relics and robes. They climbed the mountainside to visit the secret hermitage where Francis spent his winters, and Allen tried out his bed. Some of the monks spoke English, which gave Allen a chance to vent his anger about the fig leaves in the Vatican.

Since the monks would not provide shelter, Allen and Peter unrolled their sleeping bags and slept on the monastery's front lawn. The monks were much put out. It was a beautiful warm night, and the experience moved Allen so much that when he wrote his "His-

tory of Visions—A List" in Peru three years later, he included that
night among them: "With Peter in Assisi, the clouds afright over
the Umbrian plains in moonlite; cocksucking in the darkness on the
grass in front of the cathedral doors." They awoke early the next
day to see the rising sun illuminate Giotto's frescoes in the church.
Allen was in fine form and ready to continue his arguments with the
monks. He read them his poetry and disturbed their whole routine.
They showed him the bed of roses into which Saint Francis had
thrown himself, which thereafter had grown no thorns. Allen could
see the thorns as clear as day and took pains to point them out. The
monks regarded him with even greater suspicion as a hell-bent
atheist. Allen concluded that the Catholic Church was nothing more
than a "vast nasty thought control organization." He thought that
the monks walked, talked, and prayed like zombies, and that their
arguments were crude, flat, and pseudological. "I never was struck
by what a bunch of namby pamby amateurs they were before," he
wrote his father. And to his brother he wrote: "Close up, in Rome
and in the great Franciscan center of Assisi they're nothing but a
bunch of hard up, fig-leaving, psychotic politicians." He had been
hoping to find a deep understanding of mystical experience and
possibly a model beatific life-style among the Franciscans but was
sadly disappointed. Allen and Peter spent a second night on the
monastery lawn, then hitchhiked back to Venice. He had not found
the answer to his spiritual quest but had had one of the best times
since their arrival in Europe.

   Time magazine telephoned from Rome, wanting to interview ~~1957~~
Allen about the upcoming trial. Short-staffed because of the summer vacation, the editors readily agreed to Allen's proposal that
they pay his way down there and give him two days' living expenses.
They sent him a round-trip air ticket and thirty-five dollars. The
interview itself was a depressing experience—the *Time* reporter
accused him of being insincere—but Allen was able to stretch the
money to last two weeks, enough for him to make a trip to Naples
and Ischia, where he hoped to find W. H. Auden.

   After making the rounds of the Rome bars, Allen rose the next
day at noon and took a train down the coast to Naples, where he did
the usual tour of museums and saw the collection of art from Pompeii, including the famous room of Roman pornography. On the
second day, he climbed Mount Vesuvius and spent an hour sitting
and watching the steam oozing from the walls of the great crater.
He walked around the rim, looking out over the Gulf of Naples to

Capri and beyond. Then he slid and ran, arms outstretched to the sun, scattering powdered black lava sand, all the way down the side, running and walking through the lava fields until finally he came to beautiful vineyards, where he picked delicious blue grapes as he walked to the ruins of Pompeii. There he spent the afternoon in the strange deserted streets. A lot of statuary and painting remained, including a number of naked Venuses, satyrs, and drunken Bacchuses, which pleased him. He also discovered the priapic illustrations on the walls of the ancient ruined bordello, before returning, exhausted, to his youth hostel in Naples.

Allen found a fisherman to take him to the isle of Ischia, where Auden had spent his summers for the last decade. Auden disliked sunshine and only came out in the evenings. Allen located him at Marie's Bar, where he was sitting with a group of friends, "a tableful of dull chatty literary old fairies," as Ginsberg later described them. They were probably not at all pleased to have Allen intrude upon them, since he spent the evening drinking copious amounts of wine and arguing furiously and angrily with them on the merits of Walt Whitman. Allen found Auden's approach to the argument long-winded and rationalistic. Writing to his father the next day, he described the conversation:

"I doubt if Auden respects his own feelings anymore. I think his long sexual history had been relatively unfortunate and made him very orthodox and conservative and merciless in an offhand way. He sounds like an intelligent *Time* magazine talking, approaching such questions as capital punishment and literary censorship as if they were complicated bureaucratic problems, as if they have no right to have private feelings but only a series of pseudo-factual logical considerations—a sort of fetish of objectivity—which strikes me as no objectivity at all, but a sort of abject distrust of people and their loves. . . .

"I quoted the first line of Whitman, 'I celebrate myself,' etc., and Auden said, 'Oh but my dear, that's so *wrong,* and so *shameless,* it's an utterly bad line. When I hear that I feel I must say "Please *don't* include me" ' (Re: 'What I shall assume, you shall assume'). Said he was an orthodox Englishman, not a democrat (in this context). It all boils down to some sort of reactionary mystique of original sin.

"Auden is a great poet but he seems old in vain if he's learned no wildness from life. Said he 'intensely disliked' Shelley. He thought my own book was 'full of the author feeling sorry for himself' and saw no vitality or beauty beyond that as far as I could see. All this strengthens the conviction I have had, that the republic of poetry needs a full-scale revolution and upsetting of 'values' (and a return to a kind of imagination for life—in Whitman's 'Democratic Vistas' that I have been reading in Venice).''

By the end of the evening, Allen was drunk, and as he left he called them all ''a bunch of shits.'' He woke the next morning, breakfasted on a huge peach, half a quart of milk, and a large sugar bun, then went swimming before settling down with a lemonade at a shady café table to write a long report of his encounter. Actually Auden liked Ginsberg's work and often defended him in private, so the incident was probably more an example of Auden's having fun with an uninvited guest than a record of his real opinions.

Summer was coming to an end, and Allen and Peter began preparing to move on to Paris, where they intended to spend the winter. In order to see as much of Europe as possible, they traveled via Austria and Germany, stopping off in Vienna to see the museums, and then in Munich, where they visited the Dachau crematorium. *1957*

Allen's expectations of Paris had been high, but still it amazed him. He wrote Louis: ''Paris is beautiful. The only city I've seen so far that would tempt me to expatriate and settle down . . . Paris has universal interest and permanent charm as a living place. I'll try to stay here half a year and then come home.'' It was to be almost a year before he left. Allen headed straight for the Louvre to see the Mona Lisa and spent several afternoons there. He and Peter took the creaking old elevator to the top of the Eiffel Tower, which was much bigger than he had expected. ''Very vast, like dream machinery in the sky,'' he wrote Louis.

Most of all, Allen and Peter enjoyed ambling through the ancient twisting streets and alleys, and sitting in outdoor cafés on Haussmann's grand boulevards. ''Everything as charming and arty and free and grotesque as advertised,'' Allen told Louis. ''The very faces on the streets look like they've stepped out of paintings by Lautrec and Van Gogh. The streets look like impressionist streets . . . and all the millions of Hemingway and legendary café and boulevard and movie recollections of Paris I've stored up since I got to college.''

Kerouac's *On the Road* had been published that summer, and *1957* Allen, in Paris, read Gilbert Millstein's laudatory review in the *New York Times*. ''So fine and true,'' he wrote Jack. ''Well, now you don't have to worry about existing only in my dedication & I will have to weep in your great shadow."

After Carl Solomon had rejected *On the Road*, Jack touted the manuscript around New York. He was urged by Allen to show it to the celebrated editor Malcolm Cowley, at Viking Press. Cowley was interested but thought that it needed some revision—in particular, that the endless confusing cross-country car rides should be condensed into three or four trips. Cowley was only an adviser at Viking and had not yet found an editor there who liked the book. He recommended that Jack publish excerpts, which would generate interest in the book, and suggested *New World Writing* and *Paris Review*. Extracts were published in both, and Cowley finally found an editor at Viking, Keith Jennison, who shared his opinion of the book. Several more years were to pass, however, before Viking finally published the book, in 1957.

Allen heard in October that Judge W. J. Clayton Horn had pronounced *Howl* to be not obscene. Judge Horn's handling of the case was exemplary. He read all the relevant case histories, including the trial of *Ulysses*, and identified the constitutional aspects of the case: that to be considered obscene, a book had to be shown to have no redeeming social importance. He announced: "I do not believe that 'Howl' is without redeeming social importance. The first part of 'Howl' presents a picture of a nightmare world; the second part is an indictment of those elements in modern society destructive of the best qualities of human nature; such elements are predominantly identified as materialism, conformity, and mechanization leading toward war. The third part presents a picture of an individual who is a specific representation of what the author conceives as a general condition. 'Footnote to Howl' seems to be a declamation that everything in the world is holy, including parts of the body by name. It ends with a plea for holy living. . . . The theme of 'Howl' presents 'unorthodox and controversial ideas.' Coarse and vulgar language is used in treatment and sex acts are mentioned but unless the book is entirely lacking in 'social importance' it cannot be held obscene." The judge concluded: "In considering material claimed to be obscene it is well to remember the motto: *Honi soit qui mal y pense*." He found the defendants not guilty.

The trial had generated tremendous excitement in San Francisco, with letters to the *Chronicle*, mimeographed public statements circulated to the press, round table discussions on the radio, and statements of support streaming in from editors and publishers.

Barney Rosset and Donald Allen gave the most dramatic support by publishing the full text of "Howl" in their special San Francisco issue of *Evergreen Review*. All the press attention resulted in terrific sales of the book; by the end of the trial, more than ten thousand copies were in print.

Allen and Peter found a room in a cheap residential hotel in rue Git le Coeur, a tiny medieval lane in the Quartier Latin. Number 9 had forty-two rooms, which were always full. Residents' guests slept on the floors and sometimes out in the hallways. It was a big event if the sheets got changed. There were no carpets or telephones in the rooms, and the toilets consisted of a French-style hole in the floor on each stair landing. The building was over three hundred years old, and the floors sloped crazily. The plumbing was subject to backups, fierce loud vibrations, clankings, and leaks. One had to give advance notice of the desire to take a bath, so that the water could be heated. Naturally, there was a surcharge for this service. The electrical system was extremely sensitive and plunged the house into darkness whenever someone overloaded the circuit by plugging in a tape recorder or another such device. Small, blue-haired Madame Rachou, who bought the hotel in 1933, could tell by consulting her electrical switchboard if anyone had smuggled in an illicit hot plate or even a radio.

Hookers, shopping-bag ladies, and a giant black man from French Guiana lived side by side with jazz musicians and poets. Artists painted over their ceilings and walls, there was a photographer in the attic who had spoken to no one for two years, and one artist filled his room with straw. Rooms were 120 francs a month (thirty dollars), but Madame Rachou sometimes allowed her guests to pay with paintings or manuscripts, none of which she kept, not for a moment considering that they might someday be valuable. Madame treated her tenants as she would her own children, and so, as Burroughs noted, she "was very mysterious and arbitrary about who she would let into the hotel."

Madame Rachou presided over a small bar, which served coffee, beer, and wine and closed at ten-thirty. Next to the bar was a dining area, where she would cook huge cheap lunches of cassoulet or rabbit stew and would sit talking endlessly to her tenants over cups of watery espresso. Madame gave lunches to the local police inspectors, with whom she endeavored to maintain very good relations.

The hotel had a separate entrance for residents, and this door was never locked, but Madame had an uncanny clairvoyant knowledge of everything that went on in the hotel and in the street and was able to materialize at the door to protect her residents from con men, occasional police visits, creditors, and sometimes from themselves.

Allen and Peter were given a small furnished room with paper-thin walls, a roof that leaked when it rained, walls of discolored plaster, and a small round table covered with oilcloth. Madame Rachou promised that a cheaper room, in which they could make as much noise as they wanted, would become free in a week or so, and it did. They moved to chambre 25, third floor front. Their new room was much better. It had whitewashed walls and French windows with long drapes. There was radiator heat all week and hot water on Thursday, Friday, and Saturday. They had a two-burner gas stove, on which Allen cooked lentil soup, beef stew, and mussels, which he bought at the magnificent open-air market on the nearby rue de Buci. Before moving into the hotel, they visited with Gregory Corso in Amsterdam. He returned with them to Paris, and Allen, Peter, and Gregory all slept together in a big, sagging bed. Allen unpacked his red portable Royal typewriter from its carrying case and set his papers out on the worktable. For the next ten months, this was to be his home.

Back in the States, *Life* magazine ran a big article on *Howl* and the trial. Soon the book was a best-seller. The subsequent publication of *On the Road* led to enormous interest in the "Beats," and Allen began to consider that he might actually be able to live off his literary activities. Royalty checks were arriving with regularity. *Howl* was in its fourth printing, and sales showed no signs of abating. Grove Press had issued a record of modern poets, including Allen, reading their work, and Fantasy Records in Berkeley proposed that he record an album of his own in a Paris studio. *Evergreen Review* and *Partisan Review* bought some poems, and Citadel Press wrote asking to include "Howl" in an anthology of "Beat" writing they were assembling.

Things were not going as well for Peter, who had received disturbing news from his mother about Lafcadio. When Allen and Peter left for Tangier, Lafcadio had gone back to Northport to live with Mrs. Orlovsky, who was finding it difficult to cope with him. During one argument, Lafcadio hit her, and she in turn threw a can opener at him, which cut his arm to the bone. Peter decided that he should return to the States to protect his family and get his brother Julius out of the Central Islip hospital, where he had been for years.

Peter applied to the U.S. Embassy to get a Veterans Administration loan, since neither he nor Allen had enough money for his fare. Allen was hoping Kerouac would repay the $225 he owed him, since Jack knew about Peter's situation and was making a lot of money from *On the Road*. Although Jack kept promising, he never sent it, much to Allen's frustration. It wasn't until the next year that the V.A. finally loaned Peter the passage money.

Allen soon found that the heroin in Paris was much cheaper and better than anything he had ever taken with Burroughs or Bill Garver. Sniffed, it had an effect that was longer lasting and stronger than when shot in the vein, and the initial hit was almost as strong. Marijuana was also cheap and easy to get, and he liked to smoke it before visiting the Louvre: "stared back at the Mona Lisa high on T."

Now that he was settled, Allen began to write poetry again. The six months of running around Europe had been too frantic for him to do much more than write letters. He had, in the meantime, concluded that he needed to change his writing style. He found himself addressing his mother's death.

In November 1957, he wrote Jack Kerouac: "I sat weeping in Cafe Select, once haunted by Gide and Picasso and the well dressed Jacob, last week writing first lines of great formal elegy for my mother—

> *Farewell*
> *with long black shoe*
> *Farewell*
> *smoking corsets & ribs of steel*
> *Farewell*
> *communist party & broken stocking . . .*
> *with your eyes of shock*
> *with your eyes of lobotomy*
> *with your eyes of stroke*
> *with your eyes of divorce*
> *with your eyes alone*
> *with your eyes*
> *with your eyes*
> *with your death full of flowers*
> *with your death of the golden windows of sunlight . . .*

"I write best when I weep, I wrote a lot of that weeping anyway and got idea for huge expandable form of such a poem, will finish later and make a big elegy, perhaps less repetitious in parts, but I gotta get a rhythm up to cry." The poem was to be "Kaddish."

Winter came but no snow. Although a vicious wind cut down the Seine, the narrow alleys were sheltered. Allen would get up around noon and spend the afternoon walking the gray streets alone. He took long strolls by the river beneath the gray branches of the plane trees and bought the unexpurgated Olympia Press editions of Henry Miller, Jean Genet, and Apollinaire's pornographic novels from the bookstalls there.

The evenings were spent cooking supper, then reading or writing; there were visits to movies, to the Chinese ballet. The first local French people they got to know were a pair of shopgirls, one of whom, Françoise, was very attracted to Allen. "She was really hung up on me. I didn't realize the consequences. I didn't take it seriously. I didn't realize it was real," Ginsberg recalled, and said that his reactions were the same whenever that situation arose. "I keep thinking it's my mother whenever a woman gets emotional over me. It's apparently a big neurotic problem of mine, not recognizing genuine affection. I thought anybody in love with me must be crazy! Since I'm gay anyway, and I've been living with Peter, if anybody gets fixated on me there must be some misjudgment of some sort. I didn't see it, as I might now, as an indication for an open situation, more as a fixed obsession on her part. So I probably hurt her a great deal, being so closed off. She was very young. I was thirty by then." Allen and Peter both made love to her, and when she was not around, Peter would go to visit the whores in the truck warehouses near the Gare de Lyon. Later, a girl named Joy Ungerer became a good friend of theirs. She was half French, half Malaysian, very cheerful and friendly. She grew quite attached to Peter but was happy to sleep with both of them.

People stopped by Allen's room all the time for supper, marijuana, or whatever was on the menu. Strange beat characters wandered in and out, and Gregory Corso later came up with a name for Madame Rachou's establishment; he called it the Beat Hotel (a sobriquet Allen never liked).

They continued to explore Paris. They visited the catacombs, walking a mile underground in the eerie haunting dampness and the sickly-sweet odor of millions of human skulls and bones, stacked like fire logs along the sides of the tunnel. Gregory stole a legbone, which they displayed on their hotel wall alongside a portrait of Rimbaud. Peter and Gregory spent a lot of time painting. Peter did strange red angels sitting in red trees, while Gregory, who was an accomplished artist, painted sparkling abstracts on canvas paper tacked to the wall. Allen was too shy to take up a brush, though his journals often contained line drawings.

Letters arrived from Bill, sometimes several a week. He appeared to have resolved his feelings for Allen and no longer thought they would ultimately be together. Allen wrote to Lucien, saying that Bill "seems unhungup on me now, which is a relief, relations turning to normal again. It always made me nervous." Allen was being deluged with fan mail, in addition to the copious correspondence he received from family and friends. He wrote Louis: "Spend, or waste, a lot of time answering strange letters, everything from Jesuit appeals to Christ to young poets who write in on toilet paper."

The letter on toilet paper came from a young poet named LeRoi Jones, who had just moved to Greenwich Village. He had read "Howl" and was very moved by it. In his autobiography, Jones later said: "Wanting to be as weird to him as I thought he was to me, I wrote him a letter on toilet paper, sent to the 9 rue Git le Coeur address, asking was he for real. He sent me back a letter, also written on toilet paper, but the coarser European grade that makes better writing paper. He told me he was sincere but he was tired of being Allen Ginsberg. (The notoriety was just starting.) He signed the letter and had a drawing under his signature of a lineup, a parade of different beasts and animals, all with halos over their heads in some weird but jolly procession." Allen sent Jones poems, some of them Gregory's, for the magazine he was just starting, *Yugen*, and suggested that he contact Whalen, Burroughs, and Kerouac. He particularly tried to get Jones to publish Kerouac's poems, because Lawrence Ferlinghetti had just rejected Jack's *Mexico City Blues* poetry collection.

Allen was too broke to celebrate New Year's Eve, 1958. He wandered around the Place Pigalle in Montmartre all night, "under the noisy stars," walking back at midnight through the Les Halles red-light district, where the drunken celebrants staggered in the street. His lack of money was serious. He didn't even have enough to pay his grocer's small bill for milk and eggs. He wrote again to Jack, pointing out his dire straits and asking him to pay his debt.

Allen had been encouraging Burroughs to visit Paris for some time. In January, a flurry of letters announced his imminent arrival.

Allen rented a room for him in the hotel. Bill flew in from Tangier on January 16, the day before Peter left for New York. Both Allen and Peter were apprehensive. As they parted, they kissed and waved goodbye awkwardly, filled with doubts and worries about the future of their own relationship and, especially, Bill's intentions. Bill behaved at first as he had in Tangier—poker-faced and impassive, mocking and distant—but this didn't last. Something had happened to Bill, as Allen was to find out a few days later.

The evening after Peter left, Allen fell into a deep depression. He sat sobbing on his bed, then took some heroin. He had sex with Bill for the sake of their old friendship, then they started arguing and misunderstanding each other, according to their old pattern. Allen smoked some pot, but that only made matters worse, giving him an anxiety attack. Françoise came in and tried to climb all over him. Feeling paranoid and at his wits' end, he fell silent and terrified on the bed. There was a knock on the door, and it was Gregory, back from Germany, where he had been trying, unsuccessfully, to sell encyclopedias to GIs. Allen was enormously pleased to see him. He was so familiar and reassuring, a solid connection to the happy days he and Peter had spent living in the room together. "I also thought he would save me from sordid sorrows with Satanic Bill," Allen wrote Peter.

The next night, Bill and Allen sat facing each other, eye to eye, across Allen's kitchen table and had a serious talk. Allen confessed his doubts and misery, and Bill revealed what had been happening to him in Tangier. As Bill spoke, he was transformed in Allen's eyes. In the last months of 1957, Bill had stopped drinking and stopped writing. Every afternoon, he sat on his bed, thinking and meditating, working things through slowly, until he finally became conscious of what he called "a benevolent sentient center to the whole Creation." He had apparently had, in his own way, a vision of what Ginsberg called a "big peaceful Lovebrain." It had given him the courage to look at his whole life, and his relationship with Allen, more dispassionately, he said; his trip to Paris was not to claim Allen but just to visit; he wanted to see a psychoanalyst to clear up the unconscious blocks that remained.

He and Allen talked late into the night, finally establishing a rapport so exquisite and delicate that Allen trembled. It was a closeness similar to the one he shared with Peter, only it was not sexual. Bill even began to recognize that while Allen was willing to have sex with him, he didn't really want to, so he stopped putting pressure on Allen. Allen wrote Peter: "He no longer needs me like he used to, doesn't think of me as a permanent future intimate sex schlupp lover, thinks even he'll wind up maybe after difficulties with women." Allen's dread of Burroughs cleared up overnight, and he awoke the next morning with "a great bliss of freedom and joy in my heart." He wrote Peter: "Bill's saved, I'm saved, you're saved, we're all saved, everything has been all rapturous ever since. . . . I cried the other night realizing you'd gone, thinking that love would go away with you and I'd be alone without connection—but now I see Bill is really on same connection and I begin to feel connected with everything and everyone, the universe seems so happy."

The new rapport was real. Bill and Allen began to discuss the means of extending "Love bliss" to others and spreading the connection between them without sacrificing intimacy, which was what Allen and Peter had been trying to do in San Francisco, New York, and Tangier by bringing other people into their relationship, and bed, but with little success. Allen now felt confident. "We'll solve that problem too before we're done," he wrote Peter. It took them a few years, but by the mid-sixties, their ideas of love and peace, open sexuality, and the use of consciousness-expanding drugs had reached hundreds of thousands of people worldwide. The hippie movement, in this respect, had its roots directly in the Beat Generation.

Thomas Parkinson, Allen's English professor from Berkeley, invited him to visit London. Parkinson was preparing a series of programs for the BBC and hoped Allen would record his poetry. Allen crossed the Channel on February 2, 1958. On the ferry, he cried at the thought that he would soon see the "sad fogs of the land of Blake" and wrote a small poem. His first view of Britain was of the white cliffs of Dover, stretching away in the mist. In London, with his pack still on his back, he spent several hours mingling with the Saturday night crowds in the West End. He saw Piccadilly Circus and the winter moon over Big Ben before finally taking the tube to Parkinson's house in Hampstead.

He spent the next day in the National Gallery, where he delighted in the Rembrandts and Vermeers, but he wrote Peter: "The greatest here is *Turner*. The only British painter and great genius like Van Gogh." He saw many Blake works and spent hours examining the Elgin marbles, writing Peter: "Elgin Marbles Naked Love in British Museum. Greatest thing in Europe."

Allen began to record his five-minute contribution to Parkinson's series on American poetry, but the program director rushed in excitedly to ask him if he would record both the complete "Howl" and "A Supermarket in California." Feeling confident, Allen began again and gave a slow, sorrowful reading, gradually building up the tempo. He almost broke down in tears, dreaming that he was talking through the huge BBC microphone to the "Soul in the Fog"—that he was reading to Blake himself. Parkinson called it a great reading, and afterward Allen went out drinking with the program director, who drunkenly promised to record Jack and Gregory and everyone. Allen spent a night in Oxford, where he gave a small informal reading. He read Creeley, Whalen, Levertov, and "Howl." The students responded with enthusiasm. Allen wrote Peter: "I feel great again, communicating and crying in public—in front of the mild withdrawn English." Parkinson drove Allen to Salisbury Plain to see Stonehenge and to visit Salisbury Cathedral, "a big sweet cathedral looks so calm on the huge green lawn, big as daytime." Back in London, he sat up all night talking to Kerouac's school friend Seymour Wyse and met a few English poets. He climbed to the Whispering Gallery in the high dome of Saint Paul's to look out over the city. London was then the largest city on earth, a sprawling dirty metropolis. Signs of postwar reconstruction were everywhere, men clearing bomb sites and the skeletons of new buildings going up. Allen wrote a long prose sketch of the scene from his high perch in the pale winter sunlight.

He arrived back in Paris, to find Bill gloomy and with a light paregoric habit. Paregoric, an elixir of opium, could be bought cheaply in any drugstore in France. Bill claimed that he was making experimental use of it in his analysis, but Allen took him to a doctor and got him some apomorphine, and he began withdrawing. "He was glooming about the state of the world, all them armies and armories," Allen wrote Peter.

Bill began to mix with the younger crowd who hung out at the Café Monaco, and he made friends with a bearded folk singer named Darryl Adams, who wore a ring through his ear, an unusual adornment for a man in the 1950s. Allen saw a lot of a big, tough-looking American with wild black hair and a strange look in his eye, who called himself B.J. Bill had positive feelings about this new American generation. He thought they would be hip and would slowly transform things, that the laws and attitudes would change and there would be some redemption for America. America would find its soul. Allen wasn't so sure but hoped Bill was right. These were the new beatniks, many of whom were still around seven years later to begin the hippie movement of the mid-sixties.

The first warm day of spring came at the end of March, and Allen and Bill were able to go for a walk without their topcoats. They ran into Gregory and a young French girl, and also met the novelist Iris Owens, who wrote pornography for Olympia Press under the name Harriet Daimler and had just published her erotic classic, *Innocence*. Farther along the street they were joined by the drummer Al ("The Shades") Levitt and his black friend Money. They all drifted down the street toward the Jardin du Luxembourg, where they met Ramblin' Jack Elliott, the folk singer, who was out for a stroll with his wife. Ramblin' Jack had stolen away Allen's first girlfriend, Helen Parker, but that was long forgotten. They saw John Balf, then came across Mason Hoffenberg, who had just collaborated with Terry Southern on writing *Candy* for Olympia. The whole group stopped for ice cream cones, and Bill entertained them with stories of man-eating piranhas and sharks. Two days later, it was April in Paris. Madame Rachou celebrated by changing the curtains in the rooms and washing the bedspreads.

The painter Larry Rivers arrived in Paris, and Allen spent a wonderful week drinking with him in the spring afternoons, sitting in outdoor cafés, watching the passing show. Allen and Gregory were walking down Boulevard Saint Germain one day when someone hailed Allen. It was Dom Moraes, a young Indian poet from Bombay, whom Allen had met in London. They joined him and his girlfriend at a table and immediately got into a deep discussion about God. Allen and Gregory began to see a lot of them, taking them sightseeing, driving around Paris in a convertible, and making spontaneous poetry tapes. They introduced Moraes to Larry Rivers, who had a young American woman with him. In his autobiography, Moraes said: "They leapt at her, suggesting that we all strip and make love on the pavement, 'Like William Blake and the angels, man,' cried Corso. The girl became very upset and burst into tears and the poets were much concerned, petting her with repentant hands, and offering her poems and candy which Corso pulled from his pocket."

Moraes liked them, and he offered to arrange readings for them in Oxford if they visited England that summer. Gregory did not want to wait, and the next week they were in London, looking at the sights. One evening, after a round of Soho pubs, they wound up broke and hungry at midnight on the pavement in Piccadilly. The book dealer David Archer came and rescued them after an emergency phone call from Allen; he fed them and gave them a little money, "for poetry's sake." Archer had had a legendary bookshop in Holborn in the thirties and had published the first books by Dylan Thomas, George Barker, and David Gascoyne at his Parton Press. Through him, they met Barker and caught a glimpse of the remnants of the Dylan Thomas era of literary London, mostly in the pubs of Soho and Fitzrovia.

Dom Moraes, who came down to London to get them, was surprised to find that they had already met up with his friend David Archer. Archer was delighted with Allen and Gregory. "Charming chaps, what? And really talented," he told Moraes. Their first reading in Oxford was at Jesus; Allen did a fiery rendition of "Howl." At University College, they demanded to know where Shelley's rooms were. Moraes, not having the slightest idea, vaguely indicated the nearest door. Gregory flung it open and fell to the ground, crawling over the carpet, kissing it reverently, while the occupant of the room, who had been making himself a pot of tea, stared at him in horrified silence.

W. H. Auden had forbidden Moraes to bring any Beat poets near him, but Allen and Gregory had already found out where Auden's rooms were. Auden, taken by surprise, was noncommittal about their remarks on poetry, but later he warmed to them and took them to tea. Gregory asked him, "Are birds spies?"

Startled, Auden said, "No, I don't think so. Who would they report to?"

"The trees," said Allen. Allen had heard that Auden regretted his aloof behavior in Italy, so he brought him a volume of Artaud as a gift. It was unclear what Auden really thought of Ginsberg's poetry at the time, but Charles H. Miller, in his account of Auden, recalled a heated discussion of "Howl" in which Auden defended the poem against Chester Kallman's negative appraisal. Auden also announced, in Miller's hearing, sometime in the late sixties, "Of course Allen *has* contributed to literature. 'Howl' *does* have much to say, and Allen may well grow to even larger achievements. Give him time."

Auden showed them around Christ Church Cathedral. They described this as the high spot of their visit, despite having been around it themselves with a guidebook the previous day. To Auden's acute embarrassment, they attempted to kiss the hem of his garments, but he swiftly moved his trouser cuffs out of range and said goodbye. Moraes commented: "This curious mixture of true innocence combined with a sharp eye for the main chance was very attractive."

Dame Edith Sitwell arrived in Oxford for a performance of her "Façade" at the Town Hall. Allen and Gregory were taken to the afternoon rehearsal and introduced to her. Allen told Dame Edith that he was editing an anthology of poetry, to be illustrated with photographs of the poets in the nude, and invited her to contribute. The seventy-year-old Dame Edith declined gracefully.

Allen and Gregory's reading at New College was invaded by a large number of home-grown Beats and was the cause of some controversy. New College was the main Campaign for Nuclear Disarmament stronghold in Oxford. Gregory's lighthearted approach to the subject of the H-bomb in his new poem "Bomb" was regarded as outrageous. "O Bomb I love you / I want to kiss your clank, eat your boom . . . ," Gregory read. The members of the New College Poetry Society threw shoes, accusing the poet of being a fascist. Allen wrote to Peter: "The students got mad and attacked him for being, they thought, anti-social."

Gregory responded by calling them a bunch of creeps. Allen tried to explain the poem, but they argued back with politics, so Allen called them a bunch of assholes. Tight-lipped and silent, Allen and Gregory hastily packed away their poems. They, Moraes, and several friends left New College for a party of their own, which ended the evening on a high note. "Big funny time," Allen wrote Peter. They liked Oxford, saw all the sights, and went punting on the river, stopping beneath the historic Magdalen Bridge to smoke a joint.

Edith Sitwell invited Allen and Gregory to luncheon at the Sesame Club in London. She made a reservation in her club's inner dining room, "So that the old ducks would not have so much to quack about." Dame Edith, wearing a tall, wimple-like conical hat, a long satin dress, and a fur coat, led the way past the expensively dressed diners, leaning upon her ebony stick. She was escorted by Quentin Stevenson from Oxford. Her secretary, Elizabeth Salter, followed with Allen and Gregory, who were wearing turtleneck sweaters, jeans, and sandals. Sitwell later described Allen as having the "look of a starved wolf." Allen sat to her left and Gregory to her right, and they slowly ate their way through a specially ordered meal of smoked salmon, lobster Thermidor, and, possibly as a discreet literary reference to Gregory's Oxford reading, the club's specialty, an ice cream "bombe à l'américaine."

Dame Edith opened the conversation by praising American

poetry for its vitality, saying she particularly liked the work of Jose Garcia Villa, e. e. cummings, and Marianne Moore. A discussion of Aldous Huxley's experiments with mescaline led to the subject of drugs, the use of which the Americans defended on the grounds of "heightened sensibility." Dame Edith's position was that "no poet should need a drug to produce extreme sensibility, which must be, if he is any good, a part of his equipment." A report in *Life* magazine suggested that at this point, Allen offered Dame Edith some heroin, which she refused on the grounds that it brought her out in pimples. When she read the account afterward she was most offended, not only by the suggestion that she had used heroin but by the allegation of spots. "I'm hardly the spot queen," she said. They talked for hours, and she told them that she liked their work and that they were the hope of English poetry.

The Algerian war had polarized the French population, and the arguments and accusations, political moves and repercussions, changed constantly. Back in Paris, Allen followed events with interest, and the war was the subject of a long correspondence with his father. There was a huge anti–de Gaulle march and demonstration at the Place de la République. Silver-helmeted riot police waited down the block, but there was no violence. It was the first large political demonstration Allen had seen since his childhood days handing out leaflets against Mayor Hague in Journal Square, Paterson. These were the same types of people, arms upraised in comradely salutes, shouting "Vive la République" and "Front Populaire." Allen almost cried, imagining that he saw Naomi and his aunt Eleanor among the marchers.

The news coming in from the States looked bad. Neal had been busted and was put in the San Bruno County jail to await trial for selling pot to a narcotics agent. In the course of their investigation, the police had found that Neal was Dean Moriarty of *On the Road* and were, as Allen wrote Eugene, "apparently doing all they can to be evil about it." Allen was very worried and wrote asking Kerouac what was to be done. Allen proposed getting people such as Kenneth Rexroth and Ruth Witt-Diamant to write letters as character witnesses, saying that Neal was a writer, but Jack wasn't prepared to do anything at all to help the hero of his books.

Herb Caen, in his San Francisco *Chronicle* column, said that the smell of marijuana was now stronger than that of garlic in North Beach, and there were other newspaper stories about the area. The resulting publicity brought in the police and attracted outsiders. People were arrested and violent crime began to occur. Everywhere "beatniks" (as Caen dubbed them) gathered, the police did too. Poetry-jazz bars were raided, and life became difficult. Allen wrote Eugene thankfully: "I'm glad I'm not there and got out in time."

Early in June, Allen, Bill, and Gregory went to a big party on Avenue President Wilson, where they met Marcel Duchamp, Man Ray, and Benjamin Peret. They got tipsy and talked with Duchamp. Allen kissed him and made him kiss Bill. They all wound up absurdly drunk, crawling along the floor after Duchamp between the legs of the elegantly attired guests. They felt up his pants leg and begged him for his blessing. He took it all very well, giggled, and tried to explain that he was only human.

The day before the party they had run into Tristan Tzara, the Dadaist poet, at the Deux Magots restaurant. Allen thought that his "Dada Manifestos" were very good poetry and had always liked the line "Dada is a virgin microbe." Allen began reading Robert Motherwell's *The Dada Painters and Poets* and went to see a few Surrealist movies, including the famous *Un Chien Andalou*, made by Luis Buñuel and Salvador Dali in 1928. The shock scene of an eye being sliced by a razor, which had been censored in the United States, was not as horrifying as Allen had expected.

Allen and Bill visited Louis-Ferdinand Céline, the author of *Death on the Installment Plan* and *Journey to the End of the Night*. Céline and his wife, Lucette, lived in a large house with a mansard roof on a cliff in Meudon, a southwest suburb of Paris, with a view overlooking the Seine and the city's spires. Céline was dressed almost as a *clochard*, in three moth-eaten sweaters. He had long hair, and there was brown mold under his fingernails. Ferocious dogs were barking when they arrived, but Céline assured them the animals were just noisy and not dangerous. Bill, who hated dogs, was not so sure.

"I keep them for the *noise*," said Céline. "I take my dogs to the village because of the *Jews*. The postmaster destroys my letters. The druggist won't fill my prescription. . . ." The dogs continued to bark and howl in their compound.

Rusty bedsprings stuck up from the overgrown lawn near the gate, and they sat outside at a rusty garden table. Madame Céline brought them tea and wine. Céline was friendly, and the visit lasted for several hours. Allen got the impression that Céline did not get many visitors. They spoke in broken French and English, but his

English was no longer very good. Céline and Bill discussed the various prisons they had been in, and Céline said that one could know a country only by seeing its prisons. Bill told him about his days as a morphine addict, which prompted Céline to recall the time when he was a ship's doctor and had calmed panic on a sinking ship by injecting all the passengers with morphine. He still practiced as a doctor, but said, "All the young women want a young doctor to look at them, and all the old women want to stand naked in front of a young doctor," so what could he do? "It's too filthy here to practice." He showed them around the house, through huge messy downstairs rooms and up to the cluttered study where he wrote his books. Allen and Bill were very respectful, and Céline appreciated it. They gave him copies of *Howl*, *Junkie*, and Gregory's book, *Gasoline*. As they left, Allen said, "We salute you as the greatest writer in France!" to which Lucette playfully added, "In the universe!"

Allen had been abroad eighteen months and was feeling homesick. He began to consider ways of raising the funds to buy passage back to New York. Louis offered to loan him the money, but Allen first tried to get hired on a New York–bound ship, to no avail. He made a few calculations to see if he could sell enough poems to pay his way but found that he could not. That spring, Kerouac had finally repaid the $225 he owed Allen, but the money had been very quickly used up. Allen hinted heavily in a letter to Kerouac that he was in need of ticket money, but Jack, despite his earnings from *On the Road*, was as tightfisted as ever; anyway, his mother would never have allowed it. In the end, Allen accepted Louis's offer.

Allen tried to persuade Bill and Gregory to return with him. Gregory had no one in New York to go back to, could live more cheaply in Paris, and was scared of the police in the United States. Bill was not interested. He told Allen simply, "I have told no one to wait."

Allen met one final literary celebrity before he left. He had written a drunken postcard to Henri Michaux to say that he would like to meet him. A few days later, Allen was sitting in his room, naked and without his eyeglasses, washing his feet, when someone knocked on the door. As usual, he sang out "Come in," and there was Michaux, waving Allen's postcard. He hardly ever came out, he said, but was on vacation and wanted to make the most of it. He promised to return, and later that evening, Allen, Gregory, Bill, and Michaux got into a long conversation about mescaline. It seemed that they had had similar experiences, and they agreed about everything. They became immediate friends, and Michaux arranged to come back the next night, which was Allen's last in Paris, and bring a chicken for dinner. They had a wonderful evening. Allen explained the structure of "Howl," Part II, to him and translated Gregory's poem "Lost Watches," which Michaux laughed over.

Allen sailed for New York on the *Liberté* the next morning, July 17, 1958. Bill was in tears when he left, and Allen wondered if he would ever see him again. A few months later, when Allen was in New York, Gregory wrote to complain: "Did you pee in the sink when Michaux came to visit? One of us did and what's wrong with that? But rumor has it that Michaux told people about it and thought that we were trying to impress him, really, so fucking European to even detect such an action."

EIGHT | "KADDISH"

O Naomi, the photographs I have of 1920, you sitting on the
grass, with long black hair, a mandoline upon your knees
    O beautiful Garbo of my karma, then, lovely young woman,
Communist beauty . . .

—A.G., "Kaddish" (early draft)

THE WINKING NEON AND FLOODLIT TOWERS OF THE MANHATTAN SKYLINE
loomed through the mist as the *Liberté* pulled in to dock. "Like all
the spires and architecture and cathedrals of Europe all put together on one shelf and more massive height," Allen wrote Gregory.
"You get a sense of eternity looking at Manhattan from a boat
arriving—the buildings look as if they were manufacturing cosmic
jazz."

For the last two years, Allen had managed to live entirely on his
poetry and his literary skills. He had emerged from the *Howl* trial a
famous literary figure, and upon his return to the States, the press
seized upon him as the leader and spokesman of the scene. Despite
his tag as "King of the Beats," Jack Kerouac was now little more
than a right-wing alcoholic, hiding at home with his mother and in
no condition to give interviews. With Bill and Gregory still in Paris,
the mantle of leadership fell on Allen. He organized poetry readings, pressured editors to publish the new work, and lobbied the
press on a variety of issues, from legalized marijuana to free love.
He took pains to show the difference between the Beat Generation,
with its philosophy of love and tenderness, and the beatniks, who
were mostly weekend bohemians out for a good time, but the press
generally blurred the distinction, and the public perception was that

Allen was the progenitor of all the bearded young men who wandered around Greenwich Village in handmade leather sandals, carrying bongos and a bottle of Chianti. Certainly they all had a copy of *Howl* in their jeans pockets.

When Peter had arrived back in New York six months earlier, he had an unexpected reunion with his father, Oleg, whom he had not seen in five years. They rented a large room together, and Peter took a job as a nurse on the night shift at the Psychiatric Institute, where Ginsberg was a patient in 1949. Peter checked out armfuls of books from the library and was usually able to read for five hours each night, when the patients were asleep. He spent a lot of time with his brothers; Lafcadio was at home in Northport with his mother, and Julius was still in the hospital, where Peter visited him every week. Julius now recognized him. Peter wrote Robert La-Vigne: "It's gotten to now where he imitates me, like flicks his ash from cigarette when I do, he puts his hand on his hip when I do. At least he notices me. Kind of a social thinking in his mind. Seems he wants to be close to me. . . . There are few people in whose eyes have I seen such constant fear, as if Julius were continually looking over a battle field like in Bosch's Hell painting." Peter wrote sadly: "Seems I am married to my sick brothers."

When, on his return, Allen arrived at Lucien's with his brother Eugene, Kerouac was there, already a little drunk, and he insisted on picking Eugene up, saying, "I want to lift the Ginsbergs." He was bloated from alcohol and had grown heavier since Tangier. Jack told them he was a Republican—no surprise, since he had always been a supporter of Senator McCarthy and his anti-Communist witch hunts. Jack may have been feeling guilty about certain letters mailed to Allen in Paris, which Allen had not yet seen. Jack did not mention them.

Jack's mother had read a long letter Allen wrote Jack when he was high on cocaine, and her immediate reaction had been to fire off a hate letter to Allen in Paris, warning him not to write to Jack or try to contact him through other people. Not realizing that extra postage was required to send letters abroad, she put a six-cent stamp on it; it went sea mail and didn't reach Paris until after Allen had left. It was a masterpiece of the genre, calling Allen an immoral lout not fit to associate with Christians like Jack and herself. She said that her husband, on his deathbed, had made her promise to keep Allen away from Jack, and she swore that she would honor that promise. She had given Allen's and Bill's names to the FBI.

"You miserable bums all you have in your filthy minds is dirty sex and *dope*." She warned them: "Don't ever mention Jack's name or write any more about Jack in your 'dirty' 'books' I'll sue you and have you in 'jail' . . . We don't want sex fiens or dope fiens around us."

Allen had asked Bill to open any mail that came after his departure, and Bill's initial reaction was to dismiss her. "A stupid, small-minded vindictive peasant incapable of a generous thought or feeling," Bill wrote, upon forwarding the letter. "I mean, she really is evil in her small way. In your place I would show Jack the letter. If he is content to be treated like a child and let his mother open his mail and tell him who to see and correspond with, he is a lost cause."

Jack *was* a lost cause. When his mother told him what she had done, he quickly wrote to defend her actions. Bill's reaction to Jack's letter was more extreme: "I herewith forward Jack's weak and cowardly letter, like some cat explaining to a former friend how he can't have him to the house anymore because of the little woman don't like Jews and after all I am out of 'all that' now. Not that we can't meet now and then (not too often) for a glass of beer someplace maybe, etc. Weak and cowardly, 'and of course you understand I can't help out with Neal or Julius. After all why should I involve myself. Must consider Mother first. She is easily upset you know, and I *did warn* him after all.' And a *Catholic-Buddhist* yet, My god! She really has him sewn up like an incision."

Bill asked Allen to tell Jack from him that no one could achieve the fence straddle he was attempting. "No one can simultaneously stand behind those filthy letters of Mrs. Kerouac and be in any meaningful sense a friend of the person to whom those letters were addressed. Jack has reaped fame and money telling Neal's story, recording his conversation, representing himself as Neal's lifelong friend. Maybe the fuzz got onto Neal through Jack's book. In any case he sold Neal's blood and made money. Now he will not lift a dollar to help. I don't see it, Allen."

Bill brooded over the matter and the next day added a postscript: "He seems to forget all your hours of work getting his manuscripts before publishers, agents, etc. I don't like the way he shrugs off the horrible injustice of Neal's imprisonment. All he wants is *security for himself*. A weakling and a coward who cannot be trusted under any pressure. He doesn't want *his name* mentioned. What about *your* name and *Neal's* and mine in his books??" Meanwhile, Mrs.

Kerouac continued to bombard Bill and Allen with letters in Paris; Jack had not told her that Allen was back in New York. The last letter Bill received he burned in his bidet, then he wrote to her, saying he would not forward any more of her insane letters to Allen but would destroy them unopened.

Allen went to visit Peter's family in Northport. The Kerouacs lived only two blocks from the Orlovsky household. While Allen and Lafcadio hid from Jack's mother in the bushes, Peter asked him to come out for a visit, but Jack refused. He told Peter he was afraid his mother would know if he saw his forbidden friends, and anyway, "What good would it do?" As they waited, Lafcadio, in the bushes, was confiding to Allen that a rocket from Mars had flown low over Northport and signaled to him as he ran naked out of the house to hide in the woods. They were coming back for him because he was the one perfect man, and they were going to save him from the coming apocalypse. Allen, realizing that Lafcadio was crazy and that Kerouac and his anti-Semitic mother were both crazy, wondered what strange chain of events had led to his hiding in the bushes like a ten-year-old, waiting for the King of the Beats to come out to play.

However, Allen had no intention of abandoning his friendship with Kerouac, and eventually his perseverance paid off. Within a few months, he had managed to drag Jack a little way from his mother's apron strings, and that fall and winter they saw quite a bit of each other.

Toward the end of August 1958, Allen and Peter found an apartment at 170 East 2nd Street, overlooking an all-night Jewish bakery. Noisy trucks came and went all night, and the bakery had a big clock in its front window, which was useful since Allen didn't own a timepiece. The apartment had four medium-sized rooms; there was steam heat, hot water, a shower, a refrigerator, and a new stove, all of which seemed quite luxurious after Paris. The rent was sixty dollars a month, which Peter paid until Allen had money. Allen's room in the Beat Hotel had become like a railroad station, with a constant stream of people sleeping on the floor and visiting, making it very hard for him to get any work done. With his new East Village apartment, he was determined to stick to a policy of no visitors. "It's a silent castle for sleeping, balling, cooking and writing," he told Kerouac—whom he invited to come and stay anytime. He and Peter bought a pallet for the spare room.

They quickly developed a routine. Allen saw Peter off to work at eleven every night, then toured the bars. He would go down to the Five Spot, where a waiter he knew let him in free. Thelonious Monk was the resident musician, so Allen heard hours of magnificent jazz. He would often go to Lucien's after midnight and watch the *Late Show* with him and talk politics. Then he would go on to the San Remo or the Cedar Street Tavern, to see if any of his old friends were there. Allen wrote Jack: "I visit them all, sneak up like a ghost and spend all evening talking about what happened to them. Then I go home." There was eighteen months' worth of gossip to catch up on. "I am slowly going round digging every one of the multitude of people that I know, or knew, sneaking silent thru the streets and surprising them in their lives. No big mad scenes."

He finally got to meet LeRoi Jones, to whom he had been writing from Paris, and went to big parties at his apartment, where the painters Willem de Kooning and Franz Kline and the Cedar Street Tavern art crowd mingled with black jazz musicians. "An acme of good feeling," Ginsberg later called it. "A lot of mixing, black white hip classic." Jones was publishing *Yugen* magazine and in 1960 began editing for Totem Corinth a series of books by Snyder, Whalen, Kerouac, Joel Oppenheimer, and Ginsberg (his early poems, *Empty Mirror*), many of which Ginsberg had originally tried to get City Lights to publish. Jones also edited the anthology *The Moderns*, which did for contemporary prose what Don Allen's *New American Poetry, 1945–60* did for poetry.

Sheila Boucher, Allen's old girlfriend from 1955, showed up. Running away from her husband and children, she had crossed the country in true Beat style, spending four days in jail for vagrancy somewhere in the Midwest. She met up with a young painter on the road, and they arrived in New York together. She got an advertising job in the Empire State Building, but since they had nowhere else to go, she and the painter took over the spare room in Allen and Peter's apartment. Allen felt guilty for resenting it. He really wanted to be alone to work, but there seemed to be no way that he could ever manage it.

One night, Allen went on an FM talk show, where he drunkenly and enthusiastically explained why marijuana should be legalized. The producers were horrified, thinking that they must surely be breaking the law. Afterward, still elated, Allen showed up at the Five Spot at 3 A.M. and read Gregory's "Bomb" to the musicians and the handful of remaining customers.

He gave a copy of *Howl* to Thelonious Monk, and a week later ran into him standing outside the Five Spot. He asked him if he had read it.

"Yeah, I'm almost through," said Monk.

"Well?" asked Allen.

"It makes sense," replied Monk.

Allen spent a lot of time in New Jersey, visiting his relatives and having heart-to-heart talks with his cousins, who all seemed to have grown up, married, and had children since he went to Europe. He had supper with William Carlos Williams and Flossie. They told him that Ezra Pound had stayed with them after he left Saint Elizabeths and showed him a snapshot of Williams sitting, looking sad, with wire-haired, bare-chested Pound standing behind him, staring into the camera. They had thought Pound was "wacky."

Sheila Boucher and her boyfriend stayed on at Allen's apartment. Her job hadn't lasted, and now they spent all day sleeping, then got up and vanished into the nighttime streets. Sheila Plant, a San Francisco girlfriend of both Peter's and Lafcadio's, came to stay while she prepared to return to the Coast. She had been in and out of mental institutions since Peter last saw her.

The apartment threatened to grow even more crowded. Carl Solomon was getting out of Pilgrim State soon, and his mother wanted him to live near Allen. Robert LaVigne wrote from San Francisco to say he wanted to visit New York and asked if he could stay. Allen could not bring himself to refuse, but told him: "Now I want, weep for, need, prolonged solitude. I've come to the wrong place for it but I'm hung up with Peter and his brothers' problems, which is so much to handle. I dread what's to come."

Allen had a meeting with James Laughlin, owner of New Directions, and collected a copy of William Carlos Williams's *Paterson*, in which Williams had reprinted portions of Allen's letters. He talked at length to Laughlin about unpublished works by Philip Whalen and Gary Snyder and discussed "Ferlinghetti's blindness" at not seeing how good all these new authors were. Allen believed so strongly that Ferlinghetti should publish Jack's book of poems, *Mexico City Blues*, that he had offered to pay the costs out of his own future royalties, but City Lights finally turned it down, as well as rejecting an anthology of Buddhist poems by Kerouac, Snyder, and Whalen. Ferlinghetti was also uninterested in Burroughs, though Allen still had hopes of persuading him to publish a short, ten-to-twenty-thousand-word Burroughs pamphlet. "You make a big mistake to pass him up," he wrote Ferlinghetti. "DIG BURROUGHS

HE'S A BIG GENIUS." Allen was also trying to get Ferlinghetti to publish a second book by Gregory Corso, who was now penniless in Greece. New Directions eventually became publishers of both Corso and Snyder, and their books sold in large numbers throughout the sixties.

By now, Allen was well aware of the problems of being published by a small press. He kept reporting to Ferlinghetti that New York bookstores were out of stock of *Howl* or had written repeatedly for copies, which had not been supplied. Nevertheless, he remained loyal and continued to press Ferlinghetti to publish his friends. In the end, he took the manuscript of *Mexico City Blues* to Don Allen, and Grove published it in October 1959.

Kerouac's *The Dharma Bums* was published by Viking Press in October 1958. Allen sat down with an advance copy and read it through. He wrote Jack: "The whole thing's a great piece of religion testament book, strange thing to be published. . . . You settling down in simpler prose, or just tired like you said? Montgomery is great in there, and Gary is fine too. I don't dig myself (too inconsistent mentally) (in the arguments). It is a big teaching book which is rare and spooky." Although he didn't regard the book as up to Kerouac's usual standard, this didn't stop him from promoting it for all he was worth.

Allen was concerned that Kerouac's publishing career was going astray and did his best to intervene. Jack had a number of good unpublished manuscripts, among them *Mexico City Blues, Dr. Sax,* and *Visions of Cody.* However, his agent, Sterling Lord, had persuaded him to write a follow-up to *On the Road,* continuing the adventures of his characters—*The Dharma Bums.* Now Lord wanted him to write a travel book about Paris for Viking. Meanwhile, Grove Press was clamoring to be allowed to publish *Dr. Sax.* They had been promised it long before and had signed their side of the contract, but Lord had still not returned it. Grove editor Don Allen met with Allen to see if he could influence Jack, pointing out that Grove had done well for him with *The Subterraneans.* Allen wrote to Jack: "I say, perhaps Viking and Lord are neglecting your good books and trying to get you to write 'potboilers' according to their idea of what your writing career should develop like." It made no sense to Allen for them to put off the publication of *Dr. Sax,* which in his view was one of Kerouac's best books. In another letter he spelled it out: "My opinion—don't let Madison Avenue try water you down and make you palatable to reviewers Mentality by waiting on Wildbooks and putting out commercial travelogues (however good)—Sax is logical next book and you're in a position to do what you want now." Allen's pressure made Jack act, and Grove published *Dr. Sax* the next April.

Allen began a long-delayed course of dental treatment. The dentist had no idea that the nitrous oxide he administered as a painkiller would have a profound effect on his patient. As the office Muzak receded into the distance, Allen had a glimpse of another area of consciousness. "Kerouac, Snyder and Whalen are all correct as far as I can see," he reported to Ferlinghetti. "The whole fabric of existence is illusion. If you can get the kind of explicit Nirvana thru meditation as you can thru Nitrous Oxide, Contemplation here I come. I never saw anything like *that* before—whole friggin cosmos slipped into the void like lizard's tail into crack in black wall. Sort of immense obvious cosmic joke." He began work immediately on the poem "Laughing Gas."

> Stepping outside the universe
> 　By means of Nitrous Oxide
> anesthetizing mind-consciousness . . .

Delighted, he wrote Kerouac: "Dammit it's all a big cheat—great universal razz like ridiculous woody woodpecker disappearing laughing into the receding eyehole of cosmic cartoon, all the universes disappearing all at once. I'm sorry I was so deaf, I was hung on Harlem God—I still don't understand how both absolute impressions can exist without contradictions in same universe."

For the past year, Allen had been reading Keats, Shakespeare, Crane, Thomas, Mayakovsky, Esenin, Artaud, Christopher Smart's "Rejoice in the Lamb," Lorca's "Poet in New York," and after finally succumbing to eight years of pressure from Gregory, he was now reading through Shelley for the first time since his childhood. He found a similar rise to rhythmic and poetic ecstasy in Shelley's "West Wind," "Adonais," and "Hymn to Intellectual Beauty" and in Crane's "Atlantis." Both poets rose to wild heights of prophecy that interested him greatly, "Like the earth opening up and you see all creatures moving around at once in eternity." It was a poetic form that he was trying to attain in his own time. He wanted to write something that he would himself regard as "awesome." Weeping as he read Shelley's "West Wind," he knew that he wrote best himself when he cried; he hadn't wept over his typewriter in a year.

One night, Allen sat up until dawn with his friend Zev Putterman, playing Ray Charles records. He injected morphine and methamphetamine, and chanted passages from Shelley's "Adonais." Put-terman found his copy of the Kaddish, and they read aloud from the central passages. Allen returned to his apartment, and with the rhythms of the Kaddish echoing in his head, he began to write his own prayer for his dead mother.

He scribbled in blue ballpoint and, when that ran out, continued in red. He sat at his desk from 6 A.M. that Saturday until 10 P.M. Sunday, concentrating totally on the one theme of his mother and the history of his family. He was sustained by a combination of heroin and liquid Methedrine injected in the vein, and as the night wore on, he took a few Dexedrine tablets to keep the flow going. After the twentieth hour, his attention began to wander, and the writing became more diffuse. He found it harder to hold together the associations, but he persevered until he had completed the whole chronology of Naomi's sad life, ending in a prayer: "Blessed be death in us all!" He had written fifty-eight pages.

Allen used a new measure in the poem. Whereas he had previously followed Williams and looked for his measure in everyday American speech, he now observed the fixed rhythms of deeply emotional expression: wailing, crying, the moaning at a deathbed or in states of extreme stress, on which he thought he could build huge poetic structures, as he had tried and succeeded in "Howl," Part III.

The only way he knew to build a mighty rhythm was through repetition and syntactical parallelisms, repeats and litanies, because these were all present in natural speech. The hysterical screaming of a twenty-year-old boy from the Bronx stuck in his memory of the Psychiatric Institute. The boy had had an attack of hysteria in the shower and was dragged off to a padded cell in a straitjacket, yelling: "All you patients on the eighth floor, all you patients on the seventh floor, all you patients on the sixth floor, everybody on the fifth floor, doctor, nurses, all you attendants, YOU'RE ALL GONNA DIE!"

The boy had drawn his breath out like the howl of an agonized dog at the end of each line until he was winded with the force of it, then he inhaled enormously. He screamed the last line at the top of his voice. Here was everyday language under great emotional stress. Allen used the same repetition in "Kaddish":

> with your sagging belly
> with your fear of Hitler

> *with your mouth of bad short stories*
> *with your fingers of rotten mandolins*
> *with your arms of fat Paterson porches . . .*

He repeated it thirty-eight times over, each line change like a sob.

The final section of "Kaddish" came to him later when he was standing on a street corner at dusk. He realized that the alternation of "Lord, Lord" with the "caw caw" of the crows that circled over his mother's grave would make a powerful rhythm. At home, he began typing rapidly:

> *Caw caw caw shriek the crows in the white sun over the*
>   *grave stones in Long Island*
> *Lord Lord Lord time breaks me down to this my*
>   *mother's tomb & piece of grass . . .*

He built on this litany, until he reached the final lines:

> *Caw caw all years my birth a dream caw caw New York*
>   *the bus the broken shoe the vast high school caw*
>   *caw all visions of the Lord*
> *Lord Lord Lord caw caw caw Lord Lord Lord caw caw*
>   *caw Lord.*

It was mid-November 1958. The poem was complete. The bulk of it, the first two sections to the end of "Hymmnn," had been written in the one mammoth forty-hour session, the fourth part he had done in Paris, and the short third part was provided as a link to the main text. It was not until January that he began the massive job of revising the text.

Filmmaker Robert Frank and painter Alfred Leslie were making a low-budget, fifteen-thousand-dollar movie, based loosely on the third act of Kerouac's play, *The Beat Generation*. In it, Neal Cassady came home from the railroad, bringing with him a group of friends, the Bishop stopped by to visit, and eventually Carolyn threw them all out. Neal was played by painter Larry Rivers; Kerouac was played by Gregory Corso, who had now returned to New York; Richard Bellamy, who ran the Green Gallery, was the Bishop; David Amram, who wrote the music, played a cowboy. Allen and Peter played themselves.

At one point, Kerouac tried to bring in a bum to drink with him; the man was so filthy that Al Leslie banned Jack from the set for the remainder of the shooting.

Allen, Peter, and Gregory thought it was wonderful to be paid eighteen dollars a day to clown around. They just sat drinking wine, pouring water on each other, taking off their clothes, juggling, and performing circus tricks. Allen refused to put his clothes back on during one of the scenes, and Larry Rivers shouted that Allen was stealing the scene from him. "*Anyone* can draw attention to themselves by being nude in a movie!" he yelled, but Allen still refused to cooperate. Rivers began to march around the studio playing his saxophone. Al Leslie stood in the middle of the room, shouting futilely at the top of his voice.

The shooting started in January 1959 and lasted six weeks. Robert Frank shot thirty hours of film, which was edited down to twenty minutes. Then it was found that MGM had cunningly copyrighted the title "The Beat Generation," so they used *Pull My Daisy* instead, after the ditty Allen and Jack wrote in the forties. The film became a classic of the new American cinema and the forerunner of the underground film movement of Andy Warhol and Jonas Mekas in the early sixties.

On the literary front, Allen made a last attempt to get Ferlinghetti to publish Whalen and Snyder, using both flattery and financial inducement. He offered to pay the cost of printing both books and said: "They are so historically important for S.F. Muse and you are the historically important S.F. pioneer so it would work out madly great if you'd relent." But there was no relenting. Ferlinghetti turned them both down. Allen had also been trying to help the Living Theater raise money to put on William Carlos Williams's play *Many Loves* and gave a benefit reading. The play opened in January. Allen's next mission was to go to Chicago.

Irving Rosenthal and Paul Carroll had been printing much of the new Beat writing in *Chicago Review*. They published numerous pieces by Kerouac, Ginsberg, and Burroughs. Then the review was attacked by Jack Mabley, a gossip columnist for the Chicago *Daily News*, who, under the headline "Filthy Writing on the Midway," ended his column: "But the University of Chicago publishes the magazine. The trustees should take a long hard look at what is being circulated under their sponsorship." The trustees did take a long hard look, and they decided that the chapters from *Naked Lunch*, Kerouac's "Old Angel Midnight," and a prose piece by Edward

Dahlberg would all have to be dropped from the forthcoming winter issue. Dean Wilt told Rosenthal that the issue had to be "completely innocuous," and he wouldn't even allow an article on German Expressionism. Rosenthal resigned as editor, and so did Carroll, the poetry editor. They formed a nonprofit trust to publish the suppressed winter issue in a new magazine to be called *Big Table*. Allen and his gang flew into town like the Lone Ranger, to help fight the forces of reaction and to do benefit readings that would raise money toward the printing bill.

With the suppression of the winter issue of *Chicago Review*, Allen, Gregory, and Peter became big news. The Chicago *Sun-Times* devoted half its front page to their arrival. They met Rosenthal and Carroll and were taken to a welcoming party given by socially prominent Mr. and Mrs. Albert A. Newman in their Lake Shore Drive apartment. There, photographers from the local press and reporters from *Time* and *Life* interviewed them in front of works by Picasso, Monet, and Jackson Pollock. Each day, the gossip columns detailed their every move. It was the Beats' first big-time news coverage. *Time* devoted almost a whole page to them, including a photograph. On January 29, despite a winter rainstorm, nearly eight hundred people made their way to the Sherman Hotel, where, in the Bal Tabarin Hall, Allen read from "Kaddish" and did a powerful reading of "Howl." It was the recording made that night that Fantasy Records finally released as an album.

On February 5, Allen, accompanied by Gregory and Peter, made a triumphal return to Columbia to read at McMillin Theatre. The moderator was F. W. Dupee, a founder of *Partisan Review*, who placed the event in historical perspective by pointing out that the last poetry reading he had attended in McMillin was by T. S. Eliot. But even Eliot had not been able to pull the crowds Allen commanded. Fourteen hundred people managed, after some scuffling, to get into the hall, while a further five hundred were turned away at the door by the police. Allen was in his element, and even dedicated "The Lion for Real" to Lionel Trilling. Trilling was not there, but his wife, Diana, was, which caused some embarrassment later, when she wrote a long patronizing account of the evening for *Partisan Review* and misinterpreted "The Lion for Real" as a love poem to her husband. In fact Ginsberg's ironic dedication to Trilling referred to the line "a lion myself starved by Professor Kandinsky, dying in a lion's flophouse circus."

Allen described the reading to Ferlinghetti, who had also gone to

Columbia: "It's my old school I was kicked out of so I suppose I'm hung up on making it there and breaking its reactionary back. In fact I almost went mad on the stage weeping over a poem ('Kaddish,' and my Pop in the audience) and denouncing the English faculty as a pack of ignorant amateurs. Gave long lecture on Prosody etc and we answered questions, even Peter read two poems. Strange night. . . . God, reporters all over, all asking the same questions and no end in sight, it's getting stranger and stranger, life. Beginning to get invites from TV programs but have been holding out for scene where I can read poetry rather than discuss Beatnikism. The world is really mad."

They began to take their poetry out on the road. Allen and Gregory read at Harvard, and Allen, Gregory, Peter, Ray Bremser, and LeRoi Jones read at Howard and at George Washington University in Washington, D.C. Allen read at Brooklyn College and gave impromptu readings at the Gaslight Café on MacDougal Street, which was the first of the coffeehouses springing up all over Greenwich Village that had poetry readings.

Allen made plans to spend the summer in San Francisco. Thomas Parkinson offered to fly him out and pay him one hundred dollars to read at UC, Berkeley, and Ruth Witt-Diamant offered him the same amount to read at San Francisco State. Philip Whalen wrote to say that he would have a place to stay, "enormous bathtub, huge orgy bed, Mike Nathan painting. Kirby Doyle's old apartment," so he was all set. Allen and Peter flew out in April.

A research experiment on the effects of LSD 25, or lysergic acid, was being conducted by Gregory Bateson at the Mental Research Institute in Palo Alto. Bateson invited Allen to participate, and he jumped at the chance; he had been trying to track down some LSD since hearing of its existence in 1957.

Allen described his first trip to his father: "It was astounding. I lay back, listening to music and went into a sort of trance state (somewhat similar to the high state of Laughing Gas) and in a fantasy much like Coleridge world of Kubla Khan, saw a vision of that part of my consciousness which seemed to be permanent and transcendent and identical with the origin of the universe—a sort of identity common to everything—but a clear and coherent sight of it. Rather beautiful visual images also, of Hindu-type Gods dancing on themselves. This drug seems to automatically produce a mystical experience. Science is getting very hip."

Allen read the later parts of "Kaddish" in Berkeley, with one surprising result. Stephen Spender was in the audience and afterward objected to the intrusion of personal material in the poem. A few days later, Spender stopped by Thomas Parkinson's office and said that he had not been able to forget the reading and had begun writing poems again after several dry years, this time using personal material. A few days after that, he visited again and asked if Parkinson could get Allen to send "Kaddish" to *Encounter*, which he edited, but Allen had already promised it to *Yugen* and *Big Table*.

Allen was still wrestling with the first long part of "Kaddish," but he sent the rest of it to his father. Louis wrote back immediately: "I like it very much; it is nostalgic and poignant; some lines are heart-wrenching, what with not only you but me being at that time in the middle of the anguish. Some of the lines are poetically magnificent and imaginatively vivid. I do object to one line: about the 'beard about the vagina.' It's bad taste and offends my sensibilities. Alas, to a lesser degree, I have reservations about all those 'caw caw's though you might have something there."

Allen replied: "The line about the 'beard around the vagina' is probably a sort of very common experience and image that children have who see their parents naked and it is an archetypical experience and nothing to be ashamed of—it looks from the outside, objectively, probably much less shocking than it appears to you I think—it's a universal experience which almost everyone has had tho not many poets have referred to it but it can do no harm to be brought to consciousness.

"Caw Caw I still rather like since it's the climax of a sort of musical form—two themes (Caw Caw and Lord Lord—representing realistic bleakness-pain-materialism, versus Lord Lord which is mystical aspiration) that alternate and in the last line merge into one *Cry*. I've read it aloud here and it sounds alright."

Louis changed his mind about the "caw caw"s, but not about the vagina. "I think on reconsideration, that the lines 'Caw Caw and Lord Lord' are good; the unity of the assonance and the contrasting implications of the two names do hover over the grave. However, I still have reservations about 'the beard . . .' It still offends my taste, and I object to it. But the decision is yours. . . . In words begin responsibilities."

Allen received a flood of letters from Gregory in New York, begging for money, and Barney Rosset and Lawrence Ferlinghetti reported the same. In the end, Allen wrote to say he was tired of trying to hustle money for Gregory and refused to ask Jack for any more on his behalf: "It's too much, trying to pull loot out of Jack's teeth." Earlier, when Gregory was still in Paris, Allen had started a Gregory Corso Fund, which he announced in the *Village Voice*, and actually received some contributions. On May 15, Gregory revealed in a letter that he had just lost four hundred dollars at the Belmont racetrack.

There was more sad news from New York. Sheila Plant, one of the two Sheilas who had stayed with Allen and Peter on East Second Street, committed suicide by pill overdose. She left a note: "I am disillusioned but have found the beauty of love and am returning to the womb."

From Kerouac there was good news. The publication of *Dr. Sax* in April 1959 cheered him up considerably, and he was grateful to Allen for urging him to publish it. Jack had announced, to Lucien's dismay, that his next book was to be about Lucien and the death of David Kammerer. Allen told Jack: "Don't write the book. He really doesn't want it and I accept his wishes and feelings here." Jack was persuaded to hold off for a while, and his account of the affair, *Vanity of Duluoz*, was not published until 1968.

Allen and Peter were both on the "bored of directors" of *Beatitude*, the Beat literary magazine, founded in May. It was one of the liveliest of all the small mimeo magazines of the period, and the list of contributors over its sixteen issues was a catalog of the San Francisco Poetry Renaissance: Kerouac, Corso, Whalen, McClure, Brautigan, Lamantia, Persky, Kaufman, Ferlinghetti, and, of course, Allen and Peter. Ferlinghetti published an anthology of its best work.

Allen took more of the little LSD pills at Palo Alto and wrote to his father, exhorting him to try the drug: "You would enjoy it and it's not exhausting. Good as a trip abroad."

Back in New York, meanwhile, Gregory realized that his return to the States had been a mistake and sold enough things from Allen's apartment to enable him to take off for Greece. Gregory wrote to Allen asking him to set up another Corso fund, and, in August: "Sorry about the cats, the bed, the chair, the TV but I had to get away from the USA." Gregory's check to the shipping line somehow bounced, and apparently he was put off the ship before his intended destination.

Summer came, and Allen and Peter prepared to travel, to "swing into the west and wander hand in hand in small towns by deserts and forget the world a while," as Allen wrote Kerouac.

It was the middle of the August heat when they finally reached New York. The Lower East Side's hydrants were all on, flooding the potholed streets, making pools among the rubble and the over-flowing garbage cans. Allen slept through the day and lived mostly at night, when it was cooler.

The publicity surrounding the beatniks continued unabated. Greenwich Village was filled with tourists, and weekend beatniks in beards and berets packed the new coffeehouses.

On Avenue C, near Allen's apartment, the Scottish writer Alexander Trocchi had his "Methedrine University," where the lights burned all night and every meth head on the Lower East Side assembled to take drugs and do garbage art. They would find interesting pieces of wood in the street and spend hours cleaning them, as only a speed freak can, then they would paint them with shiny enamel in savage, totemic, clashing colors. At night, when the whole street was dead and quiet, Trocchi's place stood out like a beacon, with its bare high-intensity light bulbs shining into the street.

One evening after midnight, Allen took Norman Mailer, Carl Solomon, and a few others over to visit. It was like entering a blazing-white universe. About thirty people sat around mumbling to themselves, scrubbing little bits of wood and painting in intricate detail. Sometimes one of them would go over to the table and help himself to another shot of speed to provide the concentration needed for the task. Trocchi beamed all over his bony face as Allen's group came in, and he tried to find something for them to sit on. The University couldn't last; it was eventually closed down by the police after one of the regular students, a thin girl called Tessa, discovered that Trocchi had all along been listening to her brain and called the cops.

Meanwhile, big things had been happening in Paris. Maurice Girodias read the ten chapters from *Naked Lunch* in the first issue of *Big Table* and told Bill that he wanted to publish the book immediately. Bill signed a contract with Olympia Press. *Naked Lunch* was published in late August. Allen read it straight through and was astonished. "Burroughs gave me a gasp," he wrote in his journal. "I shivered in my room on East 2nd Street, seeing suddenly a flash out of nine years work with Burroughs on 'Naked Lunch.' He delivered. I grasped what was beyond (us) in the living grave."

Allen attended a reading by T. S. Eliot at the Ninety-second Street YMHA in October 1959. Eliot was heavier, fatter, and older than Allen had expected. He spoke hypnotically into the silent hall.

Allen fixed his eyes on him, staring so hard that the air around him seemed to vibrate with moving colors.

Herbert Huncke was out of jail, broke and homeless as usual, and he turned again to his old friends. Jack sent a small check in care of Allen, to whom he wrote to say he wasn't Frank Sinatra and wanted to be repaid, making the transaction somehow Allen's responsibility. (Jack had just spent $2,500 fixing up the attic in the house he bought in Northport.) Three days later, Allen received one of Gabrielle Kerouac's letters: "I want this to be the last time I have to tell you to leave Jack alone and don't you ever again ask him for money for Bums."

Lawrence Ferlinghetti wrote to say that he and Allen were invited to a literary conference in Chile in January 1960. Allen began to plan a big South American trip, which would include Bolivia and Peru.

He continued his heavy schedule of readings, including an East Coast tour with Michael McClure and Philip Whalen that was organized by Elsa Dorfman from Grove Press—one of the first big poetry tours. Allen was also handling Burroughs's affairs in New York, arranging for the Grove edition of *Naked Lunch*. He was advising *Big Table*, *Evergreen*, and *Yugen* and circulating manuscripts to many other magazines. Allen spent a good deal of time helping editors and anthologists with collections of "Beat" writings. Kerouac, on the other hand, was constantly making their lives difficult and undermining Ginsberg's work by demanding exorbitant fees. He justified his position to Allen in a letter: "Sterling [Lord, his agent] only claims that in every beat anthology I shd get 'premium' payment because they cant make it without my name. That's all."

Allen saw Jack one last time before leaving for South America, and it was not a pleasant encounter. Peter's younger sister, Marie, who was training to be a nurse, was staying with them. Jack arrived wildly drunk in the middle of the night and stormed into her room, giving her a bad fright. Allen described it as "Some great traumatic boogie-man shot, which he thought was funny, being drunk, which scared her back to the bug house." As he pointed out later, Kerouac would have been quite annoyed if anyone had visited his home and behaved badly—or if any of them had visited his house at all—yet he felt free to cut loose in other people's households. So Allen lost his temper and yelled, "What are you doing in my house, at this hour, at four o'clock in the morning?"

Kerouac collapsed on the kitchen floor, laughing, and with a disdainful look on his face said, "Ginsberg, you're a hairy loss." At the time, Allen resented Kerouac's arrogance and was hurt by it. However, on reflection, he came to regard his remark as something profound and significant, which he cited in lectures as an example of Kerouac's Buddhist insight.

NINE | ADVENTURES IN PSYCHEDELIA

I will have to accept women
if I want to continue the race . . .
Between me and oblivion unknown
woman stands . . .

—A.G., "This Form of Life Needs Sex"

IN JANUARY 1960, ALLEN MADE AN EXHAUSTING TWENTY-FOUR-HOUR flight from the sleet and snow of Newark Airport to Los Carrillos Airport in Santiago, Chile. It was the beginning of six months of solitary exploration of volcanic peaks, Inca ruins, and Amazonian jungle. The most unexpected and astonishing experience he was to have, however, was an overwhelming desire to love women and have children, an insight that came to him through the drug ayahuasca.

Not until their arrival in Chile did Allen and Lawrence discover that the literary conference was sponsored by the Communist Party, though as Ferlinghetti said, "It didn't make any difference, because at that time, being Communist down there was the only thing to be if you were humanitarian at all. It wasn't like Stalinism. Most of the intellectuals and poets in Peru and Chile were Communists."

Twenty-seven writers from fifteen American countries had come to the conference, at the University of Concepción. There was a lot of debate and argument, particularly over the recent events in Cuba, where Fidel Castro had led a socialist, but at that time non–Communist Party, revolution into power.

Allen gave his speech in a mixture of Spanish, French, and English. He read from John Wieners's *Hotel Wentley Poems*, Philip Lamantia's *Narcotica* and Gregory Corso's *Bomb*, as part of a long lecture on prosody, jazz, drugs, and the soul. "It was a big mad speech and they dug it," he wrote Peter. "I think it was probably the best of the speeches." The San Francisco *Chronicle* reported: "Ginsberg was liked both as an artist and as a melancholy, black-bearded Boy Scout in exile. He talked in Spanish, made numerous speeches, danced and asked questions."

The Communist Party organized a trip for the delegates to the coal mines at Lota, a few miles south of Concepción, to see what conditions were really like for the working class in that part of the world. The mines extended out under the sea, and miners worked a ten-hour shift for one dollar, under the most primitive conditions. Allen described them in his journal: "The miners scrambling in and out of the dripping black iron elevator like dirty animals—crouched together while the different stages of the elevator are unloaded—a platform of miners substituted for a platform of coal on the elevator."

The extreme contrast between rich and poor in South America, the excitement generated there by the Cuban revolution, and the ongoing Marxist debate among the intellectuals, writers, and poets from the South American countries made it inevitable that Allen should try to figure out just where he stood on the political spectrum, and for the next six months his journals were to contain his ruminations on the subject. It was the only time that overtly political material appeared in his journals on a regular basis. He wrote: "I live as if indifferent to the suffering of animals and men who die and groan to feed me and make my houses warm and bright—as if shielded from their sufferings, from knowledge and share of theirs by my tricky beard and wit. So that my poetry is all a half-celestial con, worth nothing to the bloodshot eyes of Physical sufferers in the mines and factories and fields. My original vow to help mankind in its sorry world-fate, on the boat to Columbia, is now being tested. Can I, as the Marxists claim [I do], remain aloof from the 'final conflict' to bring bread and love to the masses?"

Allen's mail arrived from the States. He read Peter's letters and felt "a little sweet pain around my heart that Huncke screwed Peter." Gregory reported from Milan that translator Nanda Pivano was trying hard to get everyone published in Italy; Gregory had asked Willem de Kooning for airfare back to New York. A later letter reported that Gregory had received a grant and was offering to pay for everyone to go to India. It was tempting, but Allen wished to continue his exploration of South America. He had already made a long trip to the southern half of Chile; his next destination was Bolivia, where he planned to take cocaine with the Indians.

He spent three weeks in La Paz. The market was the most fantastic he had ever seen. It was an enormous web of streets, and he explored them all. The old Indian ladies in their brightly colored scarves wore colored bands over their noses and brown bowler hats. Allen sat and chewed coca leaf with them, but he found it only mildly stimulating. After a few days of chewing, the corners of his mouth were stained green, and he was nauseated by the smell of coca on his breath. He strolled through the market in a black hat and dungarees, buying little silver flies, spiders, and butterflies, and green and purple women's shawls. The poverty was so extreme that he felt out of place.

He continued on to Peru, Allen and fifty Indians crammed together in the back of a truck with nowhere to rest their feet as they bounced along the dirt road for twelve hours in the rain. At Puno, Allen took a train to Cuzco, to see the Inca ruins of Machu Picchu. His health was beginning to suffer from the privations of his travels. He had not been able to take a bath for two months, and the prolonged lack of toilet facilities had aggravated an anal fissure, which caused him discomfort.

A week later, Allen was still in the Machu Picchu area, following the Inca trails and staying in rough *pensiones*, living on *asado*, eggs, and rice, and writing in his journal by kerosene lamp or candlelight. He had arranged to spend a night in the ruins. The mountainside was loud with the chirruping of crickets, and butterflies danced over the eroded brown soil as he climbed the treacherous rocky path to the fourteenth-century Inca city. He watched the sunset from the Intiwatna Stone. The mossy green stones blackened as dusk fell, and when darkness descended, the last tourist bus was halfway down the mountain. The Temple of the Sun, the Royal Tomb, and the more than three thousand stone steps were all his to explore in the moonlight, just as he had done in the Aztec cities in the Mexican jungle.

The next day, he climbed to the highest rock in Machu Picchu and lay in the hot sun, staring with half-closed lids at the smoky Andean peaks, letting the sun warm his naked belly. "Then descending, an area of terraces below a ruined empty gate, thru which I see the blue clouds—burst into a Millennium chant and song," he wrote. "Resurrection—seeing the colossal high terraces in total ruin, the classical jungle overgrown, and cleaned away again to reveal the dirt striven rocks of the terrace walls, steep down in a crevice open on the top of the sky—Total ruin—Though of what music I might hear in a dream seeing the ruins of New York after a millennium."

The writer Peter Matthiessen had arranged for Allen to receive a half gallon of ayahuasca, or yage, the powerful hallucinogen used by the Amazonian Indians, which supposedly enabled them to see wonderful cities and tell the future. Allen took it for the first time as he lay in his hotel room in Lima. After drinking the strange-tasting liquid, he noted the results in his journal: "Slowly drifting away but still thinking in my body, till my body turned to passive wood and my soul rocked back and forth, preparing to slide out on eternal journey backwards from my head in the dark. An hour, realizing the possible change in consciousness, that the Soul is independent of the body and its death, and that the Soul is not Me, it is the wholly other 'whisper of consciousness' from Above, Beyond."

On ayahuasca, he wrote: "I have come home, I am the God, and I demand admittance thru the door." But he knew that the drug he was able to get in Lima was nothing compared to that used by the *curanderos* in the jungle and that he would have to follow in Burroughs's footprints to track it down.

Three days later, on May 31, he left Lima at dawn, by train, heading to Pucallpa in quest of yage. By the end of the day he had reached Cerro de Pasco, a dirty little town 14,350 feet up in the Andes, full of Indians and with a good market, which sold the traditional white-and-orange-striped *mantas* blankets. His journey took him through Huánuco and Tingo María, on toward Pucallpa. He made the final stretch lying in the back of a creaky old truck covered with spiderwebs, on top of sacks of sugar. It bumped through the jungle at seven miles per hour, giving Allen time to look at every tree he passed, all of them hung with orange orchids. As night fell, he watched the stars and moon, feeling quite solitary as he passed the unrelenting jungle, mysterious in the darkness. He felt "as if I had really left all behind and were now a permanent traveller in a world with no return to Peter or home—that pure solitude which makes the stars sharper and life seem more new strange dream, all universe an *old familiar* phantom." He had been traveling alone for six months.

In Pucallpa, he was introduced to a *curandero*, called Maestro, a mild, unassuming man of about thirty-eight, who lived with a wife and children on the outskirts of town, at the edge of the jungle. An apprentice *curandero* is trained by a witch doctor, who takes him into the jungle and gives him ayahuasca day after day, until he has explored every facet of it and been to every place that the people in his future care could possibly go to. Only then is he ready to be a *curandero*.

On a moonlit night in June, Allen took his first Pucallpa ayahuasca, which was drunk like beer. Maestro had prepared it from fresh young *Banisteriopsis caape* plants that grew in his backyard; they were mixed half and half with a catalyst, the *mescla*, which was a leaf called *chacruna*. The two leaves were cooked all day and the liquid strained off. The resulting brew was served with full ceremony.

Allen lay on the ground in a robe and "entered the great being again." It was much stronger than the fermented drug he had taken in Lima. At first, he saw a spectrum of different-colored designs, similar to the pottery and blankets at the local market, then the bands of color took on an organic form: Flies, bees, golden bugs, and serpents appeared and eventually became a seething fabric before his eyes. In the center was a small black hole, and it was through this that Allen went. His concentration had been disturbed at first by the mosquitoes that buzzed around and bit him, but finally, accepting their high-pitched whine as part of the jungle music of locusts, frogs, and distant dog barks, he lay still and allowed them to buzz and bite, all part of the same universe.

Allen lay there for several hours. Later, he went into the house where the four other people who had taken the yage were. He experienced "a great feeling of communal fraternity and a sharing of a realization of Infinite Intimacy."

Allen became obsessed by ayahuasca. He lay in bed all afternoon to escape the sun, waiting to go again to the *ayahuancero* at night and writing the long poem "Magic Psalm," about his experience of the previous night, which would appear, much abbreviated, in *Kaddish and Other Poems*. Allen approached his next session with fear and anticipation but soon found himself experiencing the "great squid of Eternity opening and closing its mouth in vast slow motion in the inner phantasmal recesses of imagination during hallucinated state—with undersea fringed labia."

His third session took place the following night. There was a bright light at the *curandero*'s door, and thirty or so men and women sat around on the wooden porch or squatted under nearby trees, slapping mosquitoes. Maestro was distracted; his wife was in the final stages of labor in the next room. After the baby was born, the *curandero* came out carrying a flashlight and stood staring into the darkness. He lit a cigarette and announced that the ceremony would begin soon. Allen saw a meteor, with a red and blue glowing center, arc through the black sky near the full moon.

Maestro dipped an enamel cup into the green-brown liquid and held it in front of his mouth. He inhaled on his cigarette and blew the smoke over the lip of the cup, whistling a sad little tune through the smoke. Then, after more puffs, he hummed the same tune straight down into the cup. He passed the cup to Allen, who had to light a cigarette, blow smoke on the surface of the brew, and drink it straight down. He wrote Burroughs what happened:

"Lay down expecting God knows what other pleasant vision and then I began to get high—and then the whole fucking Cosmos broke loose around me, I think the strongest and worst I've ever had it nearly—(I still reserve the Harlem experiences, being Natural, in abeyance. The LSD was perfection but didn't get me so deep in, nor so horribly in)."

He felt that he was confronting death itself. He became nauseous and staggered out on the porch and into the garden to vomit. He was all covered with snakes. Brightly colored serpents wrapped themselves around his body. He felt he was a snake, vomiting out the universe. In the trees around him he could hear the other drinkers vomiting in the night, "all around the noise of vomit, of the universe vomiting up parts of itself—the snake that eats itself, vomiting back forth into Being—I was a vomiting snake, that is, I vomited with eyes closed and sensed myself a serpent of Being, or Serpent of Isolation, the Serpent of Allen, covered with Aureole of spikey snakeheads miniatured radiant and many colored around my hands and throat—my throat bulging like the Beast of Creation, like the Beast of Death—to vomit forth my physical misery to Be— I heaved it out four or five times and remained standing in a trance, horrified at my Serpent Self."

As he walked home in the moonlight, one of his new friends told him that the more you saturate yourself with ayahuasca, the deeper in you go, until you "visit the moon, see the dead, see God, see the Tree Spirits." Allen was worried, wondering if he had the nerve to go back, let alone go upriver six hours to drink with an Indian tribe, as he had planned. He was afraid of real madness, of entering a permanently changed universe, from which there was no way back.

Knowing that Bill had been there before him and would be able to advise him, he wrote telling Burroughs his worries about going mad and of the drug's permanently changing his consciousness. He said that he was now concerned about bringing the drug back to New York as he had originally planned, in case it drove Peter crazy. Bill would reply mysteriously: "There is nothing to fear. . . . Your Ayahuasca consciousness is more valid than Normal consciousness. . . . Why are you surprised to see me? You are following in my steps. I know the way. And yes, know the area better than you think. Tried more than once to communicate what I know. You did not or could not listen. 'You can not show to anyone what he has not seen.' " The quote was from Hassan i Sabbah, the old man of the mountain and founder of the Hashshashins, the original Assassins.

The next day, Allen examined his situation. He found that the right lens of his eyeglasses was cracked, probably broken while he was vomiting in the jungle. He began to record his experiences in his journal. Terrifying as the ayahuasca experience was, he felt that he was now reaching into a forbidden area of such fundamental importance that it was worth the fear and risk involved. In his quest to enlarge his field of consciousness, he had finally come upon a drug that enabled him to encounter at first hand the great cycle of birth and death; to understand his mother's death and the future deaths of Louis and Eugene. He felt his own acute fear of death and had a realization that the escape from the inevitable is to reproduce. This insight made him confront his homosexuality.

"Naomi dead, in madhouse," he wrote. "My mother who I am afraid to (be) return to in sex—all Mother the same—Birth—yet what was she, and what am I that I am her product and continue to live in the world of her madness? Is that my curse, which forbids me to live or die, to give birth, but be neither man nor woman, fucked in the ass, or fucking poor Peter—I resolved to bear babe, to bear Women, learn women—again."

He recalled all the women he had rejected—Natalie, Elise, Aileen, Dusty, Françoise. "Horror! They maybe are sent to save me, and I, not knowing in my pride, act Prophet over them and withdraw from their embrace and copulation and vomit of new birth."

He realized that for all those years he had clung to Peter, Jack, Lucien, and Bill as family, because he was afraid to be alone with the knowledge of death, with no one to love him, "no soul to *sign* to me what is the way of life, no seraph to be my father and protect me—afraid to be born the lone seraph of Existence—which each man is? The lone and Final seraph of Being. *The seraph that is alone, and dies into the void, not knowing the next transfiguration if any, to come*—leaving a part of Babe Angel behind in human children to guard the garden of Existence?"

It rained all day, and the streets of Pucallpa turned into brown mud. Colorful parrots stretched their wings and screeched over his door. He slept until four in the afternoon, feeling lazy, defeated by the rain and the tropical heat. He began to weep, afraid of what might happen that evening, feeling the death of his family and the "vast Wheel of Time turning invisibly."

And so Allen went back. About ten people were already gathered there when he arrived. He again took the brew and lay down on the porch, afraid to close his eyes as he felt the intoxication stealing over his senses. He vomited and found himself back in the familiar ayahuasca universe, "with snakescales gleaming all over, hat of feathers and savage grass, and a look of skull-trance on my visage, a Devil worshipper. A snarling, savage cat, at bay." Again he found himself, "a self condemned to worry about its extinction." He realized that God is death itself, and as the *curandero* hummed a strange tune, and the toads croaked in the mud, and distant tom-toms echoed from the huts on stilts down the track, and a thousand locusts whistled in the vegetation, he had a long conversation with God.

"What should I do about women?" Allen asked God.

"Make love to them," came the answer.

He returned to Lima by air from Iquitos, flying over the Amazon jungle. He had gathered samples of the various elements of yage— the leaves and the different catalysts—to take home. In Lima, he spent long hours meeting with government officials, getting proper authorization to carry bottles of the drug to the States.

During the flight home, Allen assessed his months of solitary travel and learning. "I'm a poet," he wrote. "I've striven to record Beauty, and now my memory is going to be grabbed from me—all gone—yes, let this life pass. I hope I give up my memory without screaming."

Allen devoted much of the next six months to further drug experiments, ranging from the ayahuasca he brought back from Peru to the magic mushroom drug, psilocybin, which he took at Harvard.

Drugs seemed to be a method of achieving an approximation of the expanded consciousness he had glimpsed with his Blake vision. His experiences with LSD, ayahuasca, and various other hallucinogens convinced him that drugs were possible means of altering public consciousness, a way of introducing ideas of a life-style closer to the Beat ideals of spontaneity, sexual openness, literary honesty, and spiritual liberation. He lobbied extensively for the legalization of marijuana and gave much thought to methods of introducing psychedelics to the general population.

Meanwhile, in his own apartment, he was surrounded by speed freaks and heroin addicts and was engaged in a constant battle to keep the hard drug pushers away from his door. The spiritual questions thrown up by his drug experiments caused him to begin planning another long quest, this time with Peter, to India.

Allen had brought back a gallon of ayahuasca, for him and Peter to experiment with. Even in New York, Allen had the horrifying black hallucinations. He read all he could find that related to the experience, including Robert De Ropp's *Drugs and the Mind*, W. Y. Evans-Wentz's translation of *The Tibetan Book of the Dead*, and Alexandra David-Neel's various books on Tibet. He found the section on "Centering" in Paul Reps's *Zen Flesh, Zen Bones* to be useful.

Allen continued his work on "Kaddish," but the August heat filled him with depression and lethargy. In September, fueled by Benzedrine, he finished "Kaddish" in a characteristic thirty-one-hour marathon session. He wrote various hymns in a sob-racked trance state and completed the final draft of the long first section. This he sent to Ferlinghetti and, still unsure about the poem, said in his covering letter: "I don't know what it'll look like to you, poetry or not—huge white elephant maybe—you figure out what to do with it. . . . Let me know what it looks like to you—I have lots of doubts." But Allen need not have worried. Ferlinghetti was enormously impressed. On October 11, Allen sent him the final version. Without breaking stride, he immediately began assembling poems for a subsidiary volume, since *Kaddish* only covered 1958–60. He thought of the title "Hiccup, Poems 1955–58," but fortunately he changed it to *Reality Sandwiches*, a quote from one of the poems.

When Fidel Castro visited New York in September 1960 to appear before the United Nations, his party stayed at the Hotel Theresa in Harlem. The Fair Play for Cuba Committee arranged a reception for them in the hotel, and Allen, Peter, LeRoi Jones, and other friends were among the invited guests. Allen and Peter pushed their way through the assembled FBI men to shake Castro's hand.

There was a press conference, and Allen astonished the gathering by saying, "Marijuana is revolutionary, but the imperialists have invented all kinds of stories about it just so no one will smoke it and rebel. What does the Cuban revolution think about marijuana?" The Cubans were surprised by the question, since it was not something the revolutionaries had any position on. There had been clandestine farmers in the Sierra Maestra for whom marijuana was second only to coffee as a cash crop; at first, Castro had turned a blind eye to them, but then he began to crack down. At the time of the press conference, marijuana was illegal in Cuba, just as it had been before the revolution. With so much work to be done, the Cubans clearly didn't relish the thought of people sitting around stoned.

Allen wrote Gregory about Castro's visit: "N.Y. horrible with U.N. hysteria and Americans acting like a bunch of jerks, I am losing my sense of humor and having stomach trouble I get so mad. Went to reception for Fidel who's an honest rat, now my name in the paper as pro-Fidel. Which I am."

Allen's political uneasiness was not helped by his watching the first of the four Nixon-Kennedy television debates at Lucien's house. That night, still angry, he amused himself by rattling off a letter designed to irritate Kerouac: "This country is Evil and Whitman and I now spit on it and tell it to be nice or die, because that's what's coming. I HATE AMERICA! Ugh. And Nixon and Kennedy combine all that's most obnoxious, but Nixon does take the cake."

Kerouac left his mother and came to town in mid-October for a drinking binge. Allen noted in his journal: "Jack in for three days, finally ending in bed w/me & Peter like Silenus nekkid—his big thighs and belly."

That November, Allen took one of his first steps toward active political involvement. He was listed, together with Seymour Krim and Noel Parmentel, Jr., as a press secretary to Norman Mailer, who, at the height of his fame and notoriety, was running for office as mayor of New York. Mailer announced his candidacy on November 22, but that night, after the celebration party, he stabbed his wife Adele and was arrested for the third time that year. She refused to press charges, but Mailer's mayoral campaign was stillborn.

At a "Beat Generation" symposium organized by the Group for the Advancement of Psychiatry, Allen learned that Harvard University was conducting experiments with psilocybin, the magic mushroom drug. Asked to participate, Allen needed little convincing, and a few days later, he, Peter, and Lafcadio were on a plane to Boston, where they would stay with Dr. Timothy Leary at Harvard. The atmosphere seemed very academic, with a small cocktail party for them when they arrived at Leary's comfortable house on Beacon Street in Boston, but Leary's infectious grin and Irish gift of the blarney soon relaxed everyone.

Leary at forty was six years older than Allen and at the height of his career. He had spent a decade as the director of the Kaiser Foundation for Psychology Research in Oakland, then in January 1960 joined the Department of Social Relations at Harvard, where he taught a graduate seminar entitled Existential Transactional Behavior Change. Each year, Leary had taken his son and daughter to a villa near Cuernavaca, and it was there, in 1960, that he had his first experience of the hallucinogen extracted from the fungus *Psilocybe mexicana*. When he returned to Harvard that fall, he received permission to begin a research project on the behavioral effects of the drug.

Though the drug experiments had Harvard's written seal of approval, it was completely against Leary's contract that he take his research home with him. But Leary had little regard for Harvard's scientific traditions; that evening, he gave Allen a large 36-milligram dose, eighteen pills, of psilocybin. Allen bustled around his room, preparing for the trip. Leary had given him his daughter Susan's record player, and Allen had selected Wagner and Beethoven from the record library in the study. Once he was ready, he took off his clothes, turned off all the lights, and lay on the bed, listening to the music. Peter lay down naked next to him. Leary said that he would check on them every fifteen minutes. Downstairs, a friend of Leary's was beginning a trip.

The drug took effect, and Allen saw himself lying on the bed with two choices: he could either withdraw into mystical introspection and vomit, or he could swallow back the vomit and live in the present universe. "I felt intimidated by the knowledge that I had not reached yet a perfect understanding with my creator, whoever he be, God, Christ, or Buddha, or the figure of octopus as before [in Pucallpa]. Suddenly, however, realized they were all imaginary beings I was inventing to substitute for the fear of being myself—that one which I had dreamed of."

When Leary checked on Allen, he was lying on top of the blanket with his glasses off and his pupils completely dilated, feeling scared, unhappy, and nauseous. Peter lay next to him with his eyes closed, sleeping or listening to the music. Allen asked Leary what he thought of him. Leary later wrote: "I leaned over and looked down into the black liquid eyes, faun's eyes, man's eyes, and told him he was a great man and that it was good to know him. He reached up his hand."

Ginsberg would write: "Professor Leary came into my room, looked into my eyes, and said I was a great man. That determined me to make an effort to live here and now." He swallowed back the vomit.

Suddenly, out of the window, Allen saw a flash of light, which reminded him of the Star of Bethlehem, and as the music of Wagner's *Götterdämmerung* thundered in the room, "like the horns of judgement calling from the ends of the cosmos—calling on all human consciousness to declare itself into the consciousness," it seemed to Allen as if all the worlds of human consciousness were waiting for a Messiah, "Someone to take on the responsibility of being the creative God and seize power over the universe. . . . I decided I might as well be the one to do so—Pronounced by nakedness as the first act of revolution against the destroyers of the human image. The naked body being the hidden sign."

Allen thought of Milton's Lucifer and wondered why Milton sided with the rebel in Heaven. He got up from the bed, put on his eyeglasses, and walked downstairs naked, closely followed by Peter. They headed for the study, where Frank Barron, Leary's co-worker, who shared the house, was sitting at his desk. They stopped in front of him. As Leary came into the room, having ushered his young daughter up to the safety of the third floor, Allen raised his finger in the air and waved it. "I'm the Messiah," he said. "I've come down to preach love to the world. We're going to walk through the streets and teach people to stop hating."

"Well, Allen, that seems like a pretty good idea," said Barron.

"Listen," said Allen to Leary. "Do you believe I'm the Messiah? Look, I can prove it. I'm going to cure your hearing. Take off your hearing machine. Your ears are cured. Come on, take it off. You don't need it."

Barron sat smiling, and Peter looked on earnestly as Leary took off his hearing aid and placed it on the desk.

"That's right," said Allen. "And now your glasses. I'll heal your vision too."

Leary took off his glasses, and Allen beamed around for approval of his healing abilities. Then Leary made a good point. "But, Allen, one thing . . ."

"What?"

"Your glasses. You're still wearing them. Why don't you cure your own vision?"

Allen was surprised at his oversight. "Yes, you're right," he said, and he took off his glasses and put them on the desk next to Leary's. "Come on," he said. "We're going down to the city streets to tell the people about peace and love. And we'll get lots of important people on a big telephone network and settle all this about the Bomb once and for all."

"Fine," said Barron. "But why not do the telephone bit first?"

"Who we gonna call?" asked Peter.

"Well, we'll call Kerouac on Long Island, and Kennedy and Khrushchev, and Bill Burroughs in Paris, and Norman Mailer in Bellevue . . ."

"Who we gonna call first?" asked Peter.

"Let's start with Khrushchev," Allen said.

"Why don't you start with Kerouac?" suggested Barron. "In the meantime, let's pull these curtains. There's enough going on in here so I don't care about looking outside."

After some squinting, Allen found the white telephone and dialed the operator. "Hello, operator, this is God. G-o-d. I want to talk to Kerouac. Try CApitol 7-0563, Northport, Long Island." There was a pause, then the operator could be heard telling Allen something. "No such number? Oh, right. That's the house in New Jersey where I was born. Look, operator. I'll have to go upstairs to get the number, then I'll call back." Allen, looking a little sheepish, explained what had happened, then skipped upstairs to get his huge address book. He reappeared moments later and this time was able to get through. He began to shout at Kerouac to come to Boston.

"Take a plane up here immediately. The revolution is beginning. Gather all the dark angels of light at once. It's time to seize power over the universe and become the next consciousness!"

Kerouac laughed and said, "Whazzamatter, are you high?"

"I am high and naked and I am King of the Universe. Get on a plane. It is time!"

"But I got my mother . . ." Kerouac protested.

"Bring your mother!" Allen commanded, serious.

"Aw, I'm tired," Kerouac complained, but he remained interested. It was the first time Allen had ever dared to challenge Mrs. Kerouac's control.

"What do you want to do?" Allen asked.

"Lay down and die," Kerouac said.

"What's the matter with you?" Allen shouted. "Are you *afraid?*" Allen told him that he was afraid of God, that he didn't realize that he already *was* God! Kerouac was surprised to hear such authority and conviction in Allen's voice. It was the first time Allen had spoken to him like that in years. "Who else but us is *it*, the life force, is God?" thundered Allen, and Jack had to agree. Allen was rapturous and made Jack promise not to die. Allen began to think that he could save everyone, take over the universe and freeze it into a permanent eternal present. He decided that William Carlos Williams should not be allowed to die and began to look up his number. Wagner's horns surged from the loudspeakers, inspiring him: "Da dam, da dam, da da Dee!" "Revolt in Paradise, the Messiah had broken loose!" Allen could see all the population of earth linked by radio, television, telephone, computer, into one simultaneous transmission of consciousness, which would *turn on the universe!*

Finally, Leary and Barron prevailed upon Allen to lie down on the couch and stop running up their phone bill. They put on a recording of James Joyce reading from *Finnegans Wake*, and as he listened, Allen realized that the drug consciousness would sooner or later wear off. "[I] saw control of the universe slipping out of my hands," he wrote. Eventually, in a dressing gown and over a cup of hot milk, Allen began to describe what he had seen. The psilocybin had reinforced the revelations of the ayahuasca and finally opened the door for him to women and heterosexuality. He could see a womanly body and family life ahead, a view confirmed a few days later when he wrote to Neal Cassady and Carolyn and told them the news: "I will have babies instead of jacking off into limbo. . . . All's well . . . we're starting a plot to get everyone in power in America high. . . . Hurrah!" The latter proved easier to accomplish than the former.

Allen and Tim Leary began plotting the psychedelic revolution. To Allen, it was simple and egalitarian, an example of his deep belief in American democracy. Everybody should be allowed to have the mushroom drug and explore his or her own mind; it should not be reserved for an elite of professors and experimenters. But Allen knew that there would be a problem if it was introduced suddenly. It would get outlawed, and there would be horror stories in the newspapers. The correct way to introduce it was to get a series of respectable people to endorse it, and to talk about the experience, so that by the time the authorities found out what was happening, there would already be a solid body of reputable opinion in favor of the drug. He felt that he should not campaign too much himself but was prepared to do a lot of the legwork. "Big serious scientist professors from Harvard" should do it, he said "I can't do it. I'm too easy to put down."

He produced his big address book and began to compile a list of people to be turned on: Robert Lowell, Jack Kerouac, LeRoi Jones . . . He listed painters, editors, publishers. The plan was that Allen would make the initial approach, and if the people were interested, Leary would write to them and send them research papers to sign. Allen would then make the arrangements, and Leary would come down to New York on weekends and run magic mushroom sessions with them. The program aimed to discover various reactions, to test the drug's limits, and to find out from serious, thoughtful people what could be done with the drug. "These people will have more confidence in you than in me," Allen said. Within seven years, over four million Americans would have taken LSD. "Allen Ginsberg came to Harvard and shook us loose from our academic fears and strengthened our courage and faith in the process," Leary later wrote in *High Priest*.

In January 1961, Allen wrote to Leary with the addresses of the first four people who had agreed to take psilocybin pills as part of the Harvard Behavior Study Project. They were Willem de Kooning, Franz Kline, Dizzy Gillespie, and Thelonious Monk—two painters and two jazz musicians. Allen would convey the pills and the report to be returned to Harvard. Monk was given fifteen pills to swallow in the security of his home. Allen called him after five hours, and he said he felt fine. A few weeks later, Allen went to Monk's apartment on West Sixty-third Street to find out what had happened and to write up the report. Monk said, "Well, I took 'em, but ain't you got nothin' stronger?"

Leary came to town one weekend for a series of sessions that Allen had set up. The first was with Jack Kerouac. Jack was already drunk when Tim got to Allen's apartment. "So what are you up to, Dr. Leary, running around with this Communist faggot Ginsberg and your bag of pills?" Jack demanded. "Can your drugs absolve the mortal and venial sins which our beloved savior Jesus Christ, the only Son of God, came down and sacrificed his life upon the cross to wash away?"

"Why don't we find out?" suggested Allen, getting out the pills.

Kerouac continued to behave like a small-town drunk, stamping around the room and standing on chairs. He climbed on Allen's couch and declared, "I'm the King of the Beatniks." All three took the pills, and Leary, who had experienced mushroom sessions with over a hundred people, found himself propelled by Kerouac's behavior into his first bad trip. He curled up in a fetal ball in the dark bedroom. Allen found him and played the role of the soothing *curandero*. Kerouac was in the other room, still yelling, red-faced, drinking wine, smoking cigarettes, and telling stories. Allen and Tim attempted to explain the philosophical implications of altered mind states, but Kerouac, unconvinced that enlightenment could be attained that easily, replied, "Walking on water wasn't made in a day."

Leary later analyzed the session with Kerouac in *Flashbacks*: "Throughout the night Kerouac remained unmovably the Catholic carouser, an old-style Bohemian without a hippie bone in his body. Jack Kerouac opened the neural doors to the future, looked ahead, and didn't see his place in it. Not for him the utopian pluralist optimism of the sixties."

Allen, Tim, and Peter went uptown to visit Robert Lowell and Elizabeth Hardwick at their Riverside Drive apartment. On the way there, Allen told Leary, "We're not dealing here with a Dionysian fun lover. He's a good guy with a psycho streak. We should be cautious about the dose."

"Why are we giving psilocybin to Lowell?" asked Peter.

"We hope to loosen him up, make him happier," said Allen. "And on the political front, if Pulitzer Prize–winner Robert Lowell has a great session, his product endorsement will influence lots of intellectuals."

While Allen guided Lowell through the experience, Peter and Tim talked with Hardwick in the kitchen. Three hours later, Lowell was beaming. According to Leary, he shook his hand and said, "Now I know what Blake and St. John of the Cross were talking about. This experience is what I was seeking when I became a

Catholic." Allen, however, remembered a less enthusiastic reaction. At the door, leaving, he said, "*Amor vincit omnes*," to which Lowell replied, "I'm not sure."

Once they were out of the apartment, Leary said he wasn't sure that the dose was anywhere near large enough to have produced a transcendental result. "Maybe we should have given him the option to have a heavy-dose experience and go all the way."

"That could have been risky for us," Allen said. "I wouldn't want to be known as the guy who put America's leading poet round the bend."

Their next visit was to the elegant town house of the publisher of Grove Press. In Allen's opinion, if Barney Rosset had a good trip, the news would be all around town in no time, and everyone would want to try it. But Rosset's trip was not a success, and he complained that this was precisely the kind of anxiety that he paid his analyst seventy-five dollars an hour to avoid. Furthermore, Rosset's girlfriend also participated, and a few days later she moved in with Leary.

But psilocybin was not the only new drug around. Methedrine was everywhere on the Lower East Side, and particularly in Allen's apartment. Huncke, Elise, Peter, and his girlfriend Janine were all taking it. At that time, before he saw what terrible damage it caused, Allen's attitude was benign. "All the young kids are shooting (needle) a drug called methedrine," he wrote Leary in February. "An amphetamine semi-hallucinogen—haven't tried it yet. It's all the vogue." Allen took it for the first time later that month, mixing it with heroin and some psilocybin pills as a writing cocktail. From 8 P.M. until noon the next day he wrote a ten-page, single-spaced, clearly Methedrine-influenced poem, which was eventually published in a shorter version as "Television Was a Baby Crawling Toward That Deathchamber."

For some time, Allen had been planning a trip to join Gregory in Athens and get a little peace. The situation in the apartment had become so crazy that he found it very hard to get any work done. Peter was on junk. He, Janine, Lafcadio, Huncke, and Allen were all crammed together in the small tenement, and Elise was next door and visiting all the time. Allen often found complete strangers taking a bath or making themselves tea in his kitchen. He couldn't wait to get out. The plan developed that Peter and Allen would visit Bill in Paris, where Gregory would join them, then they would continue on to India.

Jack was around a lot, very frequently drunk. He was obsessed with the idea that the New York Jewish intelligentsia were out to get him, and Allen, typically, tried to use reason against his irrationality, pointing out that many of the people who had helped him were Jewish: Allen himself, Seymour Wyse, Gilbert Millstein at the *New York Times*, whose rave review launched *On the Road*. "The lineups are too mixed to categorize your 'enemies' as Jewish," Allen wrote Jack. "You could make similar lineup of Catholics, Protestants. You are talking Jewish to annoy me, and it does because you think I am a *Jewish* Truth Cloud. Are you a *Catholic* Truth Cloud? You may be too drunk to remember you were screaming how Hitler was right—and your mother was too."

Had Allen not persevered, there is no doubt that his friendship with Jack would have terminated long before this. Lucien Carr, speaking about the friendship, said, "On Allen's part, it was one of real devotion. On Jack's part, it was sort of a love-hate thing. One moment Allen was his oldest truest friend and the next moment Allen was nothing but a Jewish schemer. But Jack was funny that way. He never turned on me, but then, providentially, I wasn't Jewish."

Allen and Peter were to leave New York on March 23, 1961, and Peter managed to kick his heroin habit just in time. Allen made complex arrangements for Lafcadio, Huncke, and Janine. He paid the rent on the apartment until the end of March and gave Janine and Huncke letters of authorization to get back the deposits on the utilities. He left money for the outstanding bills, but, as was to be expected, without Allen there to take charge, everything fell apart the moment he left. Huncke and Janine were both injecting Methedrine into the vein, and Allen's money simply disappeared. Marie Orlovsky came from Northport and rescued Lafcadio. Janine and Huncke got themselves a place with Elise in a renovated tenement building. Bill Heine moved in with them, and his speed freak friends began to hang out there. Alexander Trocchi and his wife, Lynn, who had both been shooting speed for years, moved in, and the apartment became a shooting gallery. Janine's weight dropped to ninety-five pounds. One day she came home to find Huncke and Heine gone. They had both been arrested. Elise was carried away to Hillside mental hospital, diagnosed as acutely schizophrenic. The terrors of the Methedrine plague were beginning to be seen.

TEN | CUT-UPS

I kiss his dirty shoe, and from my heart-string
I love the lovely bully.

—Shakespeare, *Henry V*

A SMALL GROUP GATHERED AT THE DOCK TO SEE ALLEN AND PETER LEAVE on the S.S. *America*. The Empire State Building was wrapped in mist, and though it was the end of March, snow lay on the ground. Eugene and Louis, Carl Solomon and LeRoi Jones, were among those who came to see them off, knowing it would probably be years before they returned. Elise stood on the dock, peering over her eyeglasses. Janine, white-faced and blond-haired, wearing a black jacket, waved her scarf. Lafcadio gestured with a straw hat, a half-smile on his face, as the huge ship pulled away. Peter stood at the rail in a Russian fur hat, waving, his other hand over his heart. Allen was at the bow. "And when I called their names I saw them, drifting away with their skulls," he wrote. He got his feet wet in the sleet.

"I hope America will still be there when we get back," said Peter.

In Paris, they went straight to the Beat Hotel, expecting a grand reunion with Bill Burroughs. But Bill had checked out, leaving no forwarding address. Allen was stunned. Why hadn't Bill waited for them to arrive, or at least left a message to say where to meet him? The answer, as Allen quickly found out from Bill's friend Brion Gysin, was that Bill had left to avoid seeing Allen. Gysin also mentioned in passing that Bill was an assassin and was responsible for

various deaths, including those of Cannastra, Kammerer, Joan Vollmer, and Phil ("The Sailor") White. Allen decided that he had
better be nice to Gysin and try to figure out what had been going on
in Paris in the three years since he left.

The root of the problem lay in cut-ups, a literary technique that
Bill had first written to him about late in 1959. Cut-ups were invented that September, when Gysin was cutting a mount for a drawing and sliced through a pile of old newspapers and back issues of
Time and *Life* with his Stanley blade. He noticed that the sliced-up
strips of newspaper made new texts when a piece of one article
overlapped another and was read across. He was delighted with his
discovery. He was literally reading between the lines: "Cut through
the word lines to hear a new voice off the page." When Burroughs
returned from lunch, Gysin ran to show him. Bill immediately
recognized the potential of the method. He looked serious and
prophesied, "A project for disastrous success." Cut-ups were to
preoccupy Burroughs for most of the next decade.

They showed their discovery to Gregory Corso and Sinclair
Beiles, who were living in the hotel, and soon everyone was doing
it. The first cut-ups were juxtapositions of random newspaper and
magazine articles, but soon printed books were used and new
poems made from the cut-up words of Rimbaud and Shakespeare.
These initial cut-ups by Burroughs, Gysin, Corso, and Beiles were
published as *Minutes to Go.*

Soon Burroughs began to cut up his own texts, and it was here
that he parted company with Corso and Beiles, who believed
that inspiration and imagination were essential ingredients in all
forms of literary and artistic activity, no matter how depersonal-
ized the work. To Burroughs and Gysin, fighting subjectivity, cut-
ups meant that anyone who owned a pair of scissors could write
poetry. Corso and Beiles were not going to let the poetic muse die
that easily. The ensuing arguments got so bad that Beiles had a nervous breakdown. Then Burroughs cut up some of Corso's poems.
Corso was furious and dissociated himself totally from cut-ups,
and when *Minutes to Go* was published, he refused to sign copies. Throughout 1960, Burroughs produced literally thousands of
pages of cut-ups.

Burroughs came to believe that the only way to find out what
people were *really* saying was to cut up their words and get at the
meanings hidden inside. He extended his method. With the aid of
his English friend Ian Sommerville, he began work on a series of
tape recorder experiments in which the spoken word was subjected

to the same technique, enabling him to use the further dimension of time. With Sommerville, he worked on various photographic collages, endlessly rephotographing an image, then collaging it in. He was cutting up the word in time and space.

Finally, Burroughs applied his technique to people, metaphorically dissecting his friends and acquaintances to "see who was inside," who they *really* were. His training as an anthropologist at Harvard enabled him to be quite unsentimental about this, regarding old friendships as simply more encumbrances that had to be cut through in order to reach the reality of the person inside. This was the stage he had reached by the beginning of 1961, when he heard that Allen and Peter were coming to Paris. He left for Tangier, taking his entourage with him. Allen wrote to him there, and eventually Bill replied, encouraging Allen to visit. With Gregory Corso, Allen and Peter made their way slowly to Tangier, stopping off at the Cannes Film Festival and St. Tropez en route. They arrived in Tangier early in June.

They expected to find Bill waiting at the dock with his binoculars, as before, since they had wired their arrival time and written several letters telling him their plans, but he was nowhere to be seen. He was in fact at home, ignoring their arrival. When finally they met, Allen was delighted; Bill, however, had changed. He was strangely distant and very suspicious, asking Allen who had sent him.

His cut-up experiments had led him to conclude that everyone had been conditioned by language and that all apparent sensory impressions were in fact illusory. He was now attempting to trace back along the word lines, to find out when and where the programming had taken place and who was responsible. He suspected that the entire fabric of reality was completely conditioned and that someone was running the universe like a sound stage, with banks of tape recorders and films. He was determined to find where the control words and images were coined and to locate the image bank. He thought that *Time* magazine's newspaper clipping morgue controlled the lives of millions of Americans, telling them what to think, believe, eat, and behave. The image banks of the FBI and the CIA were also prime suspects. However, with the aid of a great deal of marijuana, Bill had finally determined that everybody was in fact an agent for a giant trust of insects from another galaxy.

In Allen, Bill could detect certain parts of Louis Ginsberg and traces of ancient Jewish culture; in the intonation of Allen's voice and in his choice of words he identified aspects of Columbia University's English department: "If we cut you up, who would we find inside? Lionel Trilling!"

Bill was encouraged by two young Englishmen, Ian Sommerville and Michael Portman, with whom he was living at the Villa Muniriya. "My feeling was that they had replaced us in Bill's affections and intimacy," Ginsberg said later. Very protective of Burroughs, they dictated his social life. In a letter to Kerouac, Allen described them as "scampering and skipping behind his elbows like demons, simpering at us all." There was certainly a lot of simpering going on, and women were definitely excluded from the scene.

Ian Sommerville, Bill's new boyfriend, was a thin, almost gaunt, nervous mathematician. He had recently graduated from Cambridge and had been in Paris on a small scholarship when Bill met him in George Whitman's bookshop. Bill was attempting a self-administered apomorphine cure for his heroin addiction and hired Ian as a nurse. Ian quickly became more than that. His expertise in science and mathematics made him an ideal collaborator for both Bill and Brion Gysin, who were just then embarking on the great cut-up experiment.

"Mikey" Portman was a scion of the Portman family, which owned a large chunk of London's West End. He was young and angelic-looking, arrogant in an English public school way, and obsessed with Bill. Allen found it increasingly hard to relate to Bill because Mikey was always there, interrupting and making facetious remarks. Allen wrote Lucien: "Bill's all hung up with 18 yr old spoiled brat English Lord who looks like a palefaced Rimbaud but is a smart creep—Apparently Lady Portman his mother gave him into Bill's hands to look after here—platonic anyhoo—But Bill got some kinda awful relation with him and the kid bugs everyone so intimacy with Bill is limited and Bill absentminded all the time—however very busy with his cut-up experiments and applying it to pictorial collages and taking brownie photographs and very busy and creative—also did new book in cut-up method, very pure experiments and strangely good reading tho oft toneless, 'The Soft Machine.' "

The Villa Muniriya had become too expensive for their budget, so Allen, Peter, and Gregory took two rooms around the corner at the Hotel Armor. Allen and Peter had a tiled room on the roof, which led to a glassed-in conservatory and terrace with a spectacular harbor view. Paul Bowles often visited them there and recalled Allen's conservatory: "I have an acoustical memory of the clicking of Allen's typewriter accompanied by the ceaseless rattling of the windowpanes as the *levant* roared outside."

From the moment they arrived, Peter was given a particularly hard time by Bill and his boys. This was a time when Burroughs seriously considered women as perhaps not human at all, having been sent from outer space as agents for the insect trust that was manipulating the planet. Burroughs proposed that all women should be exterminated just as soon as males had found some form of parthenogenesis. Peter, instead of accepting these discourses as Swiftian routines, always argued back in favor of love and sex and women, which of course only encouraged Burroughs and his entourage to come up with even greater outrages to upset him. Peter would get hoarse from the arguments, and Allen would become upset at seeing Peter so pained by it all. The boys felt threatened by Peter's ebullience and energy, and his openness and vulnerability made them deeply paranoid. Their reaction was to either ignore Peter or put him down. "What if we cut up Peter? Peter likes girls, so we'd probably find a Venusian inside," cackled Burroughs, and Mikey Portman chimed in, "That's right! Peter's a Venusian!"

Bill was now so inhuman that Allen was worried and frightened. He tried to get Peter to ignore the put-downs, but Peter preferred to confront them, so Allen and Peter wound up quarreling as well. The argument went right to the heart of Allen and Peter's relationship. Although the fundamentally heterosexual Peter had become inextricably involved in a homosexual relationship with Allen, he was not prepared to sit back and let Burroughs and a couple of neurotic kids attack the things he held most dear, and he argued forcefully on behalf of women and normal sex. But he was no match for their combined cynicism and sophistication, and each argument left him more frustrated.

Allen felt trapped by the situation, because he was unable to display the same indifference toward Bill that Bill felt toward him. Bill criticized Allen's attachment to Peter and to himself, and was scornful of Allen for depending so much on the brotherhood of old friends, which Bill dismissed as sentimental.

The conflict between Peter and Bill was exemplified in a series of mutual interviews conducted for a magazine Ferlinghetti was starting. Allen and Gregory interviewed Bill, who said such things as: "I feel like I'm on a sinking ship and I want off," and Gregory interviewed Allen. Peter chose to emphasize his commitment to love in the face of Bill and his gang by transcribing a lovemaking session between Allen and himself. The results were awkward but strangely powerful, particularly in Peter's unique spelling:

AG: "Kiss me?"

PO: "I do for a short wile & then get back to"

AG: "Why dont you put the typewriter on my back then I can blow you directly?"

PO: "He now is in my ear—& has his hand on my head"

AG: "Does that feel good or am I just bugging you? . . ."

Allen didn't think that the transcripts were suitable for Ferlinghetti's magazine. "At the time I was ashamed of it. We were supposed to be interviewing each other on world politics for City Lights' *Journal for the Protection of All Beings*, and I thought Orlovsky was being irrelevant," Ginsberg said later. "However, now I see he had the right heart: bringing everything mental right back down into the body and disclosure of the secrets of the body's feelings. . . . Orlovsky's humanity was waked while I was in the power of my spectre —thinking I could make great angry pronouncements about the universe. All I wanted was love. All anybody wants."

Another of Peter's transcripts conveys the tensions between Allen, Peter, and Bill:

AG: "After all the tender lovings we've given to each other."

PO: "Well, thank God I didn't charge you anything. That is, I wasn't. I wasn't a whore boy!"

AG: "Yeah, well I guess it's all lost now. I'm getting older and creepy middleage looking. I guess you get disgusted when you realize what male potbellied being you wound up with for wife. But that's inevitable. I guess it's time we started out toward female, or me started, and see how that feels again. I still have that nightmare emptiness from someday when I'm dying and I've left no me behind, or child. Whole sisters and full sons to futurity, perpetuate this being. Awful if we didn't have a chance to settle down and get married and issue new Ginsbergs and Orlovskys before, Wham, the Bomb falls and ends that whole ecstatic story. That's the last moment fantasy I was telling Gregory about. I had it in Peru when I was high on Ayahuasca. It was so real it made me vow to get married and die papa, not even thinking of Bomb! . . . But that's what I mean, a specific example of widening area of consciousness. The drug trance opened my soul and made me aware of the whole void side of my life and tenderized me to all the girls I'd ever had romance with and denied. So I'm talking about something real now that general men and women can dig. . . ."

PO: "I didn't want to do it. You made me queer. It had to be you. Big cocky you. But you pulled me so and then I knew. I tried hard to fight it."

AG: "That's right you did. You always did keep telling me at the beginning you just wanted to be friends and you were afraid I was just acting nice so I could get in your ass. And now look at us."

PO: "But now I'm a bonefide queer on the witness stand."

AG: "Did I make that come true?"

PO: "Make it? You hypnotized it true."

AG: "And now the dehypnotization is begun. I'm getting old and you're realizing you're no longer in my power. . . ."

WSB: "Yeah, man. It's best for you to be away from him now. I mean now." Bill staggers drunkenly to his feet and knocks over his chair.

AG: "Oh really Bill! Don't wimper like that to me. I mean, I'm feeling something right now. Don't you realize I have to sooner or later find a girl and get married so I got a junior?"

WSB: "Take a tip from me, kid, and steer clear of 'em. They got poison juices dripping all over 'em. Fishy smell too. Down right pornographic. Up a stretched asshole, that's where they make ya look. Wise up Allen and picture yourself right for once in a while can't you?"

PO: "I know there's a lot of love to go around. And a lot of people are missing the ball. For me? I want to stop smoking and breathe some starry air."

AG: "Well, let's go in the room and make love again. Is that the answer to the World Question?"

PO: "Yup. No, because I can't give you a baby."

AG: "I didn't want to stop coming with you just on account of that."

Peter had mild jaundice, dysentery, and a cold, and spent much of his time in bed, brooding. After a week in Tangier, he finally had enough of the pressure and the put-downs and announced his decision to leave for Istanbul alone, breaking up their seven-year marriage. He refused to be moved by any of Allen's tearful arguments. Depressed, Allen recorded in his journal: "July 9. Yesterday in the Socco, sitting at the Cafe Fuentes table overlooking the street filled with passing Arabs and ill dressed youths, while Peter was visiting the whorehouse for half an hour, I wept, thinking of all the happy and past years we had lived together—how with this departure the sense of assurance and unity I enjoyed would be gone—and the sense of purpose to seek love—for what to seek now? As I am 35 and half my life now past, I have no sure road ahead, but many to choose from, and none seem inevitable."

Timothy Leary arrived in Tangier at the end of July. At Allen's suggestion, he had corresponded with Burroughs and had invited him to Harvard to take part in a symposium on psychedelic drugs that he was organizing for the September 1961 meeting of the American Psychological Association. Burroughs had agreed, and Leary flew down from Madrid to discuss the arrangements with him, as well as to visit with Allen. He was surprised to run into Peter, passing through customs in the other direction.

Allen wrote to Peter in Greece, which was his first stop. "Beautiful to see you ride off and I felt good that you were off into World alone, just tearful that we had been quarreling with each other and separating in soul, but that will be ok I hope next time we meet—I felt lost when you said 'years' but if years alas, then years alas. I'll still cry to see yr old eyes." He wrote to Ferlinghetti about Peter's leaving: "We had big arguments about future of universe in Tangier. He wanted it to be sex-love, Burroughs wanted it to be unknown Artaud mutation out of bodies. I was undecided, confused. I still am except Burroughs seems to have killed 'Hope' in any known form. The Exterminator is serious. Peter wanted innocence and sex apocalypse. It got very serious. I was vomiting."

Bill's attack on word and image, supported by Leary, had confused Allen completely. He thought that maybe poetry was redundant and found that he could write only journals and letters. In a letter to Gary Snyder, he said: "Harvard opinion is that 'arbitrary conceptualization' is located in a specific brain area—cortex—and that drugs knock out cortex activity and leave open brain. Thus the present world psychic struggle is a war over Control of the nervous system. I see no way of writing at the moment since my original interest was something like mind transmission and present scientific research techniques have made great leap forward and perhaps now obviated words. At least that's Burroughs/Leary's opinion. That is, any aesthetic thrill or awareness a poem can bring can be catalyzed by wires and drugs, much more precisely." Although there was, and is, no evidence that science is yet able to achieve this, Allen was so shaken by the idea, and so trusted the opinions of his friends, that he developed a block against writing poetry. It lasted for several years.

A few days after Peter left, Allen wrote him a long letter, covering most of the areas of their arguments and discussions: "Leary told me he agreed with Bill that poetry was finished. Because he felt the world was really moving on to a new super consciousness that might eliminate words and ideas. It's just this point that had bugged me with Bill and hurt my pride—so I realized that at any rate part of my pride was hurt—or better dependence for security on my identity as a poet and my life work as a poet.

"I told Bill I wanted to see him alone and he said yes, and then we began a rapport again—I think aside from my own vanity pride (which his basic ideas were attacking and so it hurt me temporarily) —and aside from his carelessness and vanity and sloppiness because he is so busy—that Michael has been in the way. He kept hovering around the door when we were talking inside, and when Bill and I went out for lunch he said, 'I guess I'll come along,' and intruded on us. Bill said while he was gone for a second, 'He is *too* dependent on me, that's his problem'—so Bill sees that—I see it *less* as a conspiracy of Bill and Michael now—Bill does want everybody included—or thinks he does—probably truly does—but the basis of *inclusion* must be that we drop our minds. i.e. my mind says I am poet and Orlovsky's lover, so when I got high I vomited with anxiety when I realized I was not that separate self but the same as everybody else.

"I guess your leaving must have robbed me of last prop, and it was courageous of you to do the same thing for yourself and take off and be a cloud and no more part of the *idea* we had together which was partly beautiful idea, but an idea doomed to fail after Zen-cut-up-loss of role-identity. The beautiful shiver tho always remains.

"As to sex, talked with Bill about that—his objection is to the use of sex as part of idea of identity, as part of re-affirmation and support of *me*-ness and ego—he admitted that sex might be a way of merger of souls on ego-less basis like we have had it,—and so he doesn't put it down, finally, in itself, but only where it is corrupted especially in civilized countries where it is part of power ego-grab. There is no *real* argument between you. . . .

"I think one trouble here was you were isolated, I was confused and since I was clinging to my identity with you I could not see thru your identity to your heart, and I think you wound up over-affirming your identity and pressing down harder on it while it was under attack, instead of just giving it up and coming out free. . . .

"All in all I think our idea of sex was right and beautiful and led us (or me) forward and I thank you Peter. . . . Anyway it's worked out magically for the best and you and I are both free now so forgive me and take me in thought hello and I'll see you soon whenever we both can on free basis, I hope sooner than ten years because that would mean it would take ten long years for both of us to be really free."

The scene began to break up. Leary went to Copenhagen, promising he would send Gregory and Allen the rail fare to join him once he reached Paris. He said that there were lots of girls in Denmark, and Allen was tempted to go and have another try with women. Alan Ansen, who had been visiting, returned to his house in Venice, leaving only Gregory and Allen in their hotel and Bill with the boys in the Villa Delirium, with a strange sort of cold war between them. Bill, Ian, and Mikey prepared to go to London, and Gregory decided to go with them. So Allen was left alone in Tangier to mop things up. He was almost broke; ever since Paris, he had foolishly lent Gregory money, all of which Gregory lost at the casino. They arranged that Gregory would repay the money as soon as he reached London, sending it to American Express in Athens so that Allen could collect it on his arrival.

Allen left Tangier on an August afternoon in 1961. Standing on the ship's deck, "alone, solitary, hopeless, tranquil, still with knapsack," he watched the familiar church spire, the hillside cluttered with Arab houses, and the white apartment blocks disappear into the blue sea haze. His only plan was to meet Gary Snyder in India on New Year's Day.

Allen arrived in Athens in the evening and immediately went out exploring. He stayed up all night talking to people he met in cafés and in the morning set out to collect the money Gregory was to have sent. As he left his hotel, he caught a glimpse of the Parthenon and was all prepared to spend a pleasant day sightseeing, but at American Express he was brought down with a jolt. Despite all his promises, Gregory had let him down. Allen wrote angrily to him: "So now I have about three bucks left and am totally bugged. . . . Will you please send me what you said you'd send me which is $120 borrowed plus the $70 earlier. . . . It's all a big fat stupid fucked up drag." Gregory wrote back to say that he felt guilty; he enclosed five pounds, about fourteen dollars.

Allen was also owed money by *Show Business Illustrated* for an article he had written on the Cannes Film Festival, and fortunately this check arrived the next day. The magazine objected to his use of the word "shit," which he quoted from the film *The Connection.* Despite his desperate need, Allen wrote back and said that he would repay the money if necessary, but they could not censor his text. The article was never run, nor was the $450 payment reclaimed.

Allen liked Athens. "It's like a small town and very cute and toylike," he wrote Gregory. His travels around Greece produced many beautiful pieces of descriptive prose, which would be published in *Journals Early Fifties Early Sixties.* He visited Delphi, drank from the Castalian Spring, and explored the Cave of the Muses. After three days in Hydra, he crossed to the mainland to spend a night at Melana on the isthmus and visit Epidaurus. In Mycenae, as the full September moon appeared yellow between the two volcanic peaks above his hotel, he took his flashlight and set off to explore the famed ruins. Far below in the valley, he could see tiny auto lights moving along the road from Argos. Easily vaulting the fence, he entered the ruins in brilliant moonlight and descended the steps into the tomb of Agamemnon. As he turned off his flashlight to experience the total darkness, he felt a twinge of fear, remembering Henry Miller's reaction in *The Colossus of Maroussi:* "I don't believe any civilized being knows, or ever did know, what took place in this sacred precinct. . . . Here at this spot, now dedicated to the memory of Agamemnon, some foul and hidden crime blasted the hopes of man."

"Where there is nothing, there is nothing to fear," Allen said aloud, and he lay down on the stairs at the bottom of the pit to get the feel of the place. He wandered all over Mycenae, then settled himself under the Lion Gate to make notes in his journal. In the distance he could hear the tinkle of the goat bells on the mountainside.

Back in Athens, he spent an evening with Leslie Fiedler, the literary critic, who later recounted how "surprised and shocked" he had been at Allen's melancholy. Allen was walking around Greece in a daze, still not entirely sure what had happened to him in Tangier. From Athens, he wrote to his friend Howard Schulman and told him the story: "We looked into Bill in Tangier and I met *someone I didn't know;* who rejected me, as far as Allen and Bill were concerned and all previous relationships they built up. And if I don't know Bill I sure don't know myself because he was my rock of Tolerance and Friendship and true Art." He told Schulman about the cut-ups, then said:

"He was cutting up his own consciousness and escaping as far as I can tell outside of anything I could recognize as his previous identity. And that somewhat changed my identity since that had been something built, I had thought, and permanently shared with him. And Peter and I suddenly broke thru the automaton Love-Faith habit we were junked-up and comfortable in, and looked in each other's eyes—and nobody was there but a couple robots talking words and fucking. So he left for Istanbul and I stayed in Tangier and vomited off the roof.

"Now the serious technical point that Burroughs was making by his cut-ups, which I resisted and resented, since it threatened everything I depend on—I could stand the loss of Peter but not the loss of Hope and Love: and could maybe even stand the loss of them, whatever they are, if Poesy was left, for me to go on being something I wanted, sacred poet however desolate; but Poesy itself became a block to further awareness. For further awareness lay in dropping every fixed concept of self, identity, role, ideal, habit and pleasure. It meant dropping language itself, *words*, as medium of consciousness. It meant literally altering consciousness outside of what was already the fixed habit of language-inner-thought-monologue-abstraction-mental-image-symbol-mathematical abstraction. It meant exercising unknown and unused areas of the physical brain. Electronics, science fiction, drugs, stroboscopes, breathing exercises, exercises in thinking in music, color, no thinks, entering and believing hallucination, altering the neurologically fixated habit pattern Reality. But that's what I thought Poetry was doing all along! *But* the Poetry I'd been practicing depended on living inside the structure of language, depended on words as the medium of consciousness and therefore the medium of conscious being."

All these methods, of course, achieved widespread use as the sixties continued, being applied in a variety of art forms, from underground rock music to the theater. In 1961, however, this was a forbidding and unknown area, and it was Burroughs, Ginsberg, and a few other pioneers who first mapped it out, albeit at some personal cost to themselves, as Allen went on to tell Schulman:

"Since then I've been wandering in doldrums. . . . I can't write, except journals and dreams down. As the next step if any for Poetry I can't imagine. . . . I also stopped reading newspapers two months ago. Also the paranoid fear that I'm a degenerate robot under the mind-control of the mad spectre of Burroughs. Except that it finally seems (after dreams of killing him) that he has only taken the steps, or begun to take, steps toward actual practice of expanded consciousness that were on the cards for me anyhoo, since the first days of mind break up with Blake, and of which direction I was repeatedly reminded in drug trances."

Feeling desolate, Allen decided to try and meet up with Peter in Haifa, where, by Allen's calculations, Peter's mother would be forwarding his next V.A. check. Allen arrived in Haifa in October but found no sign of Peter. Allen was not overly impressed by the place. He wrote Kerouac: "Haifa is like a ratty looking Bronx, amazingly full of Jewish people who all think they're Jewish, under a Jewish sky with Jewish streetcars and Jewish airplanes and armies and Jewish speeches and dances and theaters and Jewish newspapers, so after a while I felt like an Arab. Except like being surrounded by millions of relatives from Newark, so I felt lost and lonely."

Ten days later, Allen and Peter had a joyful reunion on a street corner in Tel Aviv. Peter had grown long hair and was very tanned. After Greece, he had gone all through Turkey to Aleppo in Syria, then to Damascus and Beirut, where he took a boat down the coast to Port Said and Cairo. He was so broke at one point that he had to sell his blood in order to eat. In Egypt, he climbed the Great Pyramid and looked the Sphinx in the eye. He took a boat back to Beirut, and went from there to Jordan to explore Jerusalem and finally to Tel Aviv to find Allen.

Allen and Peter visited Jerusalem for a week and met Martin Buber there. Looking like the classical image of a wise man, with his mouth hidden in his long white beard, he gave them a very friendly reception. Peter asked him what kind of visions he had had, and he told them that he had seen ghosts coming in through his bedroom window when he was younger but was not interested in visions like that. Allen tried out Burroughs's theories on him, saying he thought that loss of identity and confrontation with the nonhuman universe was the main problem—that man had to evolve and change, and maybe become nonhuman in order to "melt" into the universe. Buber disagreed vigorously. He was interested in human-to-human relationships, for it was a human universe that we were destined to inhabit. "Mark my words, young man," he said. "In years to come you will realize that I was right!"

Peter was uncertain about continuing on to India. He had received some distressing news from home. Lafcadio had not left his mother's Main Street apartment in Northport ever since Marie came and rescued him from the amphetamine freaks on the Lower East Side. He had let his hair grow down past his shoulders and grown a full beard. He sat in his room all day and howled like an animal, until the neighbors called the police. He was to be committed to Central Islip Hospital, but his mother, Kate, objected strenuously. She had managed to line up a job for herself and was sure that this would put an end to it. Thinking Lafcadio had destroyed her last hope, she became hysterical; she concealed a kitchen knife under her coat and went to the police station to "put Lafcadio out of his misery," as the doctor quoted her afterward. The police jumped her before she could inflict more than a superficial wound. Lafcadio received two stitches, and Kate was committed along with her son.

Allen's brother Eugene had taken on the case, and he wrote to say that there was nothing Peter could do. Marie still had the apartment, and the neighbors were helping her out. When Peter's mother was released from the hospital, she would probably be booked on second-degree assault. If the grand jury decided to take it to court, nothing would happen until the next year. Eugene assured Peter that the courts would be helpful rather than punitive. Since there was really no purpose in his returning, Peter took Eugene's advice, and he and Allen made plans to continue on to India.

ELEVEN | INDIA

Allen Ginsberg to Kushwant Singh: "Do you know any nice young poets?"

Peter Orlovsky to Kushwant Singh: "Can ya introduce me to some drug addicts?"

ALLEN AND PETER LANDED IN BOMBAY IN MID-FEBRUARY 1962 WITH exactly one dollar. Fortunately, Lawrence Ferlinghetti had forwarded Allen's royalties. They changed their money on the black market, getting seven rupees to the dollar. At this rate, a meal cost them about fifteen cents. In Tangier, Paul Bowles had issued dire warnings about staying only in good hotels and eating only in the best restaurants, but Allen and Peter were delighted to find that neither the water nor the one-rupee vegetarian meals upset their stomachs. Since they were hoping to live on twenty rupees a day between them, this meant they could stretch their money a long way.

Their original arrangement had been to meet Gary Snyder in Bombay on January 1. They were almost two months late, but there was no message waiting from him at American Express. They spent two days looking around the city, taking fifteen-cent rides in the horse-drawn carriages through the incredibly crowded streets. Then, since there was still no message from Gary, they took an all-day, all-night third-class train to Delhi. They had air mattresses, so they spent the journey lying comfortably, watching India flow past their window, a panorama of huge plains and distant brown mountains, of palm trees and cows and people in loincloths tending water buffalo in muddy rivers.

In Delhi, they stayed at a Jain dharmashala on Lady Hardinge Road. Dharmashalas are big hostels near the temples, established in all towns and cities to provide free lodging and cheap or free food for anyone on a pilgrimage or visiting on business. They were introduced to the dharmashala by a businessman from Jaipur, whom they met on the train. His name, like that of a great many Jains, was Mr. Jain. The Jain sect was founded by Mahavira, a contemporary of Buddha, who believed that the universe is an infinite repetitious cycle of Kalpas, or ages, all practically identical. Allen explained the system to Kerouac: "Nobody ever gets out—except 24 Tirthankars or Pure Ones each Kalpa who rise to the top of the universe and float free because they're so light and pure on account of not eating onions and many prayers and some even starve themselves to death suicide. They're supposed to be naked and chaste and most of them are in the jewelry business."

Mr. Jain was in the jewelry business, and he took them around the alleyways of old Delhi and introduced them to a lot of his jeweler friends. One friend was able to get them morphine and opium, which was surprisingly cheap and good. He said he was a brahmachari, one who had renounced sex, because, "You see, you must not give away your jew-els, you must retain your jew-els!"

Despite his having read so much about India, the enormous part played by religion there still came as something of a shock to Allen. He told Kerouac: "Everybody in India is religious, it's weird, everybody ON to some Saddhana (method) and had family guru or Brahmin priest who knows all about how the universe is a big illusion; it's totally unlike the West—it really is another Dimension of time-history here. . . . It's assumed that all Gods are unreal so one should respect all Gods as purely subjective forms of meditation to fix the mind on one image and still it down and be peaceful—the Gods are all interchangeably friendly—Saraswati for people hung on music and learning; Lakshmi for people hung on moviestars beauties and loot; (Rhada for young lover devotees); Krishna for cocksmen-coyote types; Ganesha the elephant head god of prosperity and slyness for the Jerry Newmans and Peter Orlovskys of the universe (Peter has become a Ganesha devotee), Buddhas for the Jacks, Kalis and Durgas for Bill and ilk, anything you want—a huge cartoon religion with Disney Gods with three heads and six arms killing buffalo demons—everybody so gentle about it all it's unbelievable—except the Moslems swept down in the 12th century with their One Allah like a bunch of hysterical Jews and smashed all the pretty Walt Disney statues before they calmed down and got happy like the Hindus. Weird thing is we met hundreds of retired house-holders (sunyassis) all over, they really do retire from the world—Imagine my father wandering around New Jersey in orange robes with big serious expression—it's like that."

Gary Snyder finally arrived in Delhi, with Joanne Kyger. Allen had not seen Gary in six years; he and Joanne had been living in Japan. Allen noted that he had aged and lost his baby looks. After a joyful reunion, they spent a week sightseeing in Delhi, visiting the Red Fort, the mosques and temples, and the old walls and gate-ways.

Now that the team was together, they set off on the road, heading first for the foothills of the Himalayas, where they were to visit the ashram of Swami Shivananda. It was a jumble of half-finished brick buildings surrounded by groves of mango trees in a gorge on the banks of the Ganges, at the edge of the Siwalik mountain range. They were shown into a large basement filled with people sitting cross-legged on the floor for the evening *darshan*, or "presence." The swami was a large man in his eighties, well over six feet tall. He lay on a couch with his head propped up, his head and face completely shaven, and wearing a large camel-hair coat. American ladies wearing saris were asking him questions about the nature of duality. His answer was always "Om!" Cutout cardboard pictures of him were stacked in boxes around the room. After *darshan*, everyone was served hot milk and fried chickpeas. "Do they have chickpeas in the United States?" Shivananda asked Allen, who told him that they did.

They were given a dusty room in a building on a hill overlooking the main complex. They ate in the dining hall, where they received unusually small portions of vegetarian food. They washed their clothes and bathed in a stream that came tumbling from a spring in the woods, to empty into the Ganges. The Ganges was filled with big friendly fish that crowded to the banks. No one ever caught or ate them; instead they fed them bread crumbs, rice, and tomatoes. It was regarded as a particularly holy spot for bathing.

That afternoon, they had a private yoga lesson on the roof of their building. The ashram's yoga teacher, a young Indian called Shiva-lingum (Phallus of Shiva), showed them how to roll their eyes and exercise their mouths, tongues, and lips, and demonstrated many other yoga positions.

At the evening meeting, a series of swamis got up and read or recited inspirational works, until Shivananda got tired of them and cut them off with an "Om." Joanne had to sit with the women on one side of the room, while the men sat on the other. There were about five Western women, dressed in saris. Shivananda asked Allen, "How many of you are there?"

"Four," he replied.

"That's an auspicious number," and Shivananda winked at Allen as he passed along, supported by his two assistants. He gave the four of them each an envelope containing five rupees, and sitting on his padded chair, he directed his assistants to place a wreath of flowers around Joanne's neck. To Allen he gave a small book called *Raja Yoga for Americans*. Shivananda had been a very energetic man in his youth. He had founded hospitals as well as the ashram and had written 386 books. "I write with electric speed," he told them.

It was at Shivananda's ashram that Allen learned the Hare Krishna mantra, in which the various names of Vishnu are repeated. "Hare Krishna, Hare Krishna, Krishna Krishna, Hare Hare; Hare Rama, Hare Rama; Rama Rama, Hare Hare." Ginsberg was the first to introduce this to the United States and chanted it at readings and public meetings throughout the sixties. Now it can be heard on the streets of most big cities in the United States and Europe, chanted by the devotees of the late Sri Bhaktivedanta. Bhaktivedanta arrived on the Lower East Side of New York from India in 1965 at the age of seventy and received enormous help and encouragement from Ginsberg in getting his first center started.

Allen had an audience with Shivananda, which he described to Kerouac: "[He's a] charlatan of mass-production international nirvana racket—but actually quite a calm holy old man. . . . I rather liked him. I asked, 'Where can I get a guru?' and he smiles and touches his heart and says, 'The only guru is your own heart, dearie' or words to that effect, and adds, 'You'll know your guru when you see him because you'll love him, otherwise don't bother.' Well, not quite that funny but that was the message. Which made me feel quite good after all that Tangier austerity and loveless gurus."

Ginsberg found this message very reassuring, as he told Tom Clark in a 1965 *Paris Review* interview: "That is the sweetness of it I felt—in my heart. And suddenly realized it was the heart that I was seeking. In other words, it wasn't consciousness, it wasn't *petites sensations*, sensations defined as expansion of mental consciousness to include more data—as I was pursuing that line of thought, pursuing Burroughs' cut-up thing—the area that I was seeking was heart rather than mind." The meeting with Shivananda set him on a new direction.

They had to move from the ashram the next day because a large crowd was expected for Shivaratri, the Night of Shiva, but they were directed to another ashram, just across the Ganges. A free rowboat service connected the ashrams. They walked along the glittering white sand on the banks of the Ganges and did their washing and bathing in the cool, clear water. They spread their clothes on the rocks to dry and dozed in the sun. The woods around were filled with the little white huts of hermits, and farther upriver they came across a group of Shiva-worshiping sadhus, sitting motionless under trees, deep in meditation. They had bloodshot eyes and long matted hair, and their naked bodies were smeared with ashes. They sat on deerskins, and had small tridents stuck in the ground around them. One had a pet cow. Allen could not understand how they sat so still and was surprised when Gary said he could also sit like that. Gary had learned Zen sitting in Japan, and during the course of their travels in India he taught Allen how to do it.

The next day, they took a walk on the hill behind the ashram to see the hermits' huts and the cow pastures. A teenage youth with long hair, wearing orange brahmachari's robes, was sitting on a big swing that hung from a flowering tree with a mass of fresh banana fronds beneath it. He spoke English. He told them he was on his way down from the Himalayas for spring and invited them to an "astral lunch." Allen asked him about the red-eyed sadhus in the valley below, and he dismissed them with a laugh. "Ah, they're just the advertisement posters for the real yogis whom you can't see, way back in the mountains." India was proving to be everything Allen had hoped for.

March 4 was the opening of the Kumbh Mela, a congress of holy men that takes place in Hardwar every twelve years and lasts for two months, filling the small town with two million people. The festival opened with a parade of sadhus marching through the town to the Ganges. There they bathed, purifying the river of all the filth accumulated in past years from laymen washing away their sins. The parade was led by a large, muscular naked sadhu, who hopped and danced in the road, swinging a sword and leading an elephant in full caparison. Behind the elephant came five hundred or more naked men carrying swords or Shiva tridents, all of them bearded and with long hair, their bodies smeared with white or blue ash. The townspeople lined the streets and threw flowers in their path, for these were the naga sadhus, the snake sadhus. There was a naga sadhu who lived in Hardwar under a tree, and as his brothers marched past he gave triumphal honks on a conch trumpet, before joining them for a dip in the river.

After the naked men came a long line of women in orange robes, with shaven heads, some of the older ones staggering and supporting each other in the gusts of rain and whirls of dust, singing as they passed. After the holy women came everybody else. At the Ganges, the man with the elephant was the first to enter and bathe. He washed away his ashes and was followed by the other sadhus. From the river they walked back through the town to the temple, where they smeared themselves with fresh white ashes. Allen was so fascinated that he wanted to stay on for the whole two months, but this would have disrupted their travel arrangements. As they took the rowboat back across the river, a storm broke overhead and they were completely soaked. The thunder rattled around the hills, and lightning flashed over Shivananda's ashram. It was Shiva's night.

They continued their sightseeing with trips to Almora, where they enjoyed spectacular views of the Himalayas, and to the maharajas' palaces in Jaipur, which Allen found terribly dull. The long overnight train rides, the nights on the floor, sometimes four to a room, began to take their toll. Gary and Joanne argued frequently, and Joanne became irritated by Allen and Peter. In a letter quoted in her journals, she said: "Peter Orlovsky locks himself in the bathroom all night and smokes opium and then vomits all the next morning so we travel slowly." In the same letter she described Allen and Peter's appearance: "Allen Ginsberg is running around in an unwashed white Indian (grey) pajama outfit with flapping arms and legs, or else very short shorts from Israel, and a Greek shirt and red nylon socks. He is balding on top, his curling hair down his neck. But if you think his hair is long, you should see Peter Orlovsky whose hair actually falls over his face to his nose in front (but that's all right because he can take drugs behind it easier) and down to his shoulders in back and a tee shirt that doesn't quite cover seven inches of his stomach in front and some tennis shoes full of holes without any shoelaces. The Indians for their own perverse reasons seem to adore him."

India had permitted the Dalai Lama to set up his Tibetan government in exile in the hill town of Dharmsala. Allen and Peter, Gary and Joanne, took lodgings at a tourist bungalow and ate in the Lhasa Hotel, where the food was Tibetan and consisted of noodles with scraps of meat, the first meat they had eaten in months.

They made arrangements to stay in the Triund Forest Bungalow and set out the next day to hike the seven miles up the hill to the ten-thousand-foot level with their rucksacks. They passed the Dalai Lama's headquarters and stopped to make an appointment to meet him the next afternoon. They had been unable to telephone; his line was out of order.

Next day at noon, they saw the Dalai Lama. His compound was guarded by armed Indian troops, as it had been since he fled Tibet in 1959, aided by the CIA. The four Americans were quickly cleared through security and taken to a waiting room in a group of low wooden buildings. Tibetan prayer flags were strung like wash on lines between deodar trees and fluttered constantly in the breeze. An interpreter, Sonam Kazi, came to talk with them while they waited for an audience. The Dalai Lama was delayed because the king of Sikkim, who was about to marry Hope Cooke, an American college girl, had dropped in unexpectedly.

Eventually they were shown into the chamber where, dressed in red-and-black robes, the Dalai Lama reclined on a velvet couch surrounded by colorful Tibetan tankas, or painted scrolls. Gary prostrated himself, and the others greeted him more conventionally. He was then twenty-seven years old and looked to Joanne like a "gawky adolescent." His interpreter was with him, though he spoke English well.

Allen described his many experiences with drugs and asked about their relationship to the spiritual states reached in meditation. Gary recorded the conversation in his journal: "The Dalai Lama gave the same answer everyone else did: drug states are real psychic states, but they aren't ultimately useful to you because you didn't get them on your own will and effort. For a few glimpses into the unconscious mind and other realms, they may be of use in loosening you up. After that, you can too easily rely on them, rather than undertaking such a discipline as will actually alter the structure of the personality in line with these insights. It isn't much help to just glimpse them with no ultimate basic alteration of the ego that is the source of lots of the psychic-spiritual ignorance that troubles one."

Allen asked him if he would like to take LSD, and the Dalai Lama said: "If you take LSD, can you see what's in that briefcase?" He said he would be interested in taking psilocybin to see what Westerners were always talking about, and Allen said that he would arrange for Timothy Leary to send him some from Harvard. Allen was hogging the conversation, and eventually Gary said, "Really, Allen, the inside of your mind is just as boring and just the same as everyone else's. Is it necessary to go on?" Gary proceeded to discuss Zen meditation techniques. The Dalai Lama asked how he sat, where he put his hands, how he arranged his tongue, and what sort of breathing he did.

Asked by Allen how many hours a day he meditated, the Dalai Lama replied, "Me? Why, I never meditate. I don't have to!" which prompted Joanne to write in her journal: "Then Ginsberg is very happy because he wants to get instantly enlightened and can't stand sitting down or discipline of the body. He always gobbles down his food before anyone else has started. He came to India to find a spiritual teacher. But I think he actually believes he knows it all, but just wishes he *felt* better about it." She asked the Dalai Lama if it was necessary for Westerners to sit in the full lotus position in order to meditate, since it was so uncomfortable for them. He replied, "It's not a matter of national custom." It was dark when they walked back to their bungalow, and the mountainside was illuminated by occasional flashes of lightning.

Next, they took the famous Pathankat Express to see the stupas at Sanchi. The huge stone domes with elaborately carved walls and gateways dated from the second century B.C. and were among the oldest Buddhist monuments in India. The smaller stupa had beautiful bas reliefs on its posts and rails; Joanne spent a whole day making rubbings of the carvings.

From there they continued to Faridpur, where the Ajanta caves were cut deep into the cliffside where a river made a great bend in a steep gorge. There were five temple caves and twenty-four monastery caves, the oldest dating from the first century B.C. and the most recent from the eighth century. Some were as much as seventy feet deep, and a few still had painted walls and ceilings, though the colors had faded and were eroded and stained. Gary discovered that the caves had wonderful acoustics and chanted the Prajnaparameta Sutra in one, his voice echoing through the caverns and little side rooms of the complex. Allen was impressed and wrote Kerouac: "He knows how to chant sutras in Japanese Sanskrit with big Tibetan Noh play sepulchral voice reechoing in caves and syncopating jijimuje syllables.'' Allen learned the words from him and later added the sutra to his repertoire of chants for public readings.

The Ellora caves at Aurangabad came next: more than thirty caves, all painted, about half Buddhist, half Hindu, and some Jain. They were astonishing. Cave number 16, Kailasa, was not a cave at all but a full-size Hindu temple carved from the living rock. Allen described it to Kerouac: ''The great rock cut cave temples of Ellora where the great GLORY of Indian art really is, makes Michelangelo's renaissance look Western little. I mean, they got great dancing shivas balanced with ten arms doing cosmic dances of creation 20 feet tall, and fantastic skully Kalis invoking nightmare murders in another yuga, thousands of statues dancing all over huge temple built like Mt. Kailash the Himalayan abode of Shiva—And Ganesha with fat belly and elephant head and snakehead belt and trunk in a bowlful of sweets riding on his vehicle a mouse—How can DaVinci beat an elephant on a mouse?'' To Gregory, he raved: ''The sculpture at Ellora, the missing noses (Moslems knocked off all the noses in this part of Earth) is greater than anything in Greece—Mount Kailash Temple Ellora, cyclopean bas reliefs of six armed five headed wildhaired sex goddesses, demons shaking mountains where Gods are playing dice.''

Their travels led eventually back to Bombay, where Radhika Jayakar, an elegant young Indian woman Allen knew from New York, invited them to stay in her large, comfortable house on Malabar Hill. The luxuries there contrasted vividly with their recent traveling experience. Each morning, Bhima, the barefoot servant, brought them tea and eggs as they lay in beds with fresh white sheets and pillows. Huge shade trees grew in the garden.

They collected their mail. Allen was shattered by news of Elise Cowen's suicide. Released after her amphetamine breakdown from Hillside Hospital into her parents' care, she had been taken to their apartment in Morningside Heights, where she sat and brooded. One cold February day she leapt from the living room window into oblivion. Allen wrote Gregory: ''That really gave me a turn. I had felt a little responsible for her welfare and hadn't been much help to her when I was around, always felt revulsion for the deathsmell in her hair and so always held myself distant from her, and then she lived upstairs in East 2nd Street. . . . Everyone that took amphetamines regularly wound up a thinfaced paranoiac nervous wreck like Elise.'' The news depressed Allen for a long time.

There was other bad news from New York. Gregory reported that Harry Phipps, who had befriended them in Paris in 1958, died of an amphetamine overdose at the age of thirty, leaving a wife and a two-year-old child. Gregory also said that Kerouac was in bad shape: "He is not so fine, drunk, and can't talk straight with him, wanted to, he just cares about his self and demands I respect that self, but I can't if he just sits there bubbling drunkenly how great he is and how bad who else is, so unreal, unrelated, that he truly bored me."

Peter also received grim news. Lafcadio was causing trouble at Central Islip Hospital, and his mother, hospitalized after her attempt to stab him, blamed it all on Allen. She wrote to Peter that it was Lafcadio's "getting fucked up the ass and choked and beaten up" by Allen that had driven him crazy. Peter replied that he didn't think Allen desecrated Lafcadio that much; whatever happened occurred when Lafcadio had a "general love" for Allen. Allen had worried and asked Peter if he should have sex with Lafcadio; Peter said it was all right where friendship and love existed, and it didn't seem to upset Lafcadio. "But it's not that sex cock play with Allen that sent Lafcadio back to Bughouse," Peter wrote. "It was me and my stupidness making bad arrangements for him when I left NYC and also my leaving him." Peter told his mother that he was considering coming home to get Lafcadio out of the hospital and take an apartment with him.

Allen spent much of his time sitting around reading hymns to Kali, the classic poetry of Kabir, Ganeshwar, and Ghalib, and other Indian texts. He gave a reading with Peter and Gary, and over a hundred people came to sit in the warm evening air and hear their controversial poetry. The American consul was in the audience. Peter read first, loud and brash, warming up the audience for the others. Allen used the occasion to give one of his rare readings of "Kaddish." A few days later, Gary and Joanne took the boat back to Japan.

Now that he was settled in one place for a few weeks, Allen gradually began to connect with Indian intellectuals. He was interviewed by the *Illustrated Weekly of India*, which treated him and Peter like visiting saints, and they met a group of five young poets who were very interested in the Beats and were translating Beat texts into Marathi, the language of Bombay. Allen took them to literary tea parties where Indian critics sat around discussing Robert Graves in Oxford accents, and they, in turn, took Allen and

Peter to the Bombay opium dens. They spent hours walking in the red-light district. There were houses full of hermaphrodites and transvestites; on one block, eunuchs lived on part of the sidewalk, their charpoy cots arranged neatly with their cooking stoves and other goods. The eunuchs were mostly middle-aged, with brightly rouged faces and bald spots; they sat combing long black hair that fell to their waists, as they camped it up for passersby. A policeman sat at the corner in his hut, peacefully surveying the scene and keeping everyone from harm.

The enormous tolerance in India for every possible form of eccentric behavior and religious excess made Allen feel that most of his friends in North Beach and the Lower East Side would be better off here. The pressures that drove Elise Cowen out of her window just did not exist in India. He felt that even his mother would have been able to live happily in a tolerant society where everyone was accepted as a sadhu, following his or her own path, and there was an elaborate support system of ashrams and free lodgings and food. Allen wrote to Paul Bowles: "Indians really sophisticated as far as letting everybody be as crazy as they want and taking it as formal personal method of relating to Gods, all very proper and dignified. The Moslems and Jews and Christians seem really mean and stinky in this respect, the more I think of it."

One small example of this tolerance was the way the Indians took to Peter. Friendly and open, they clearly related to him as some kind of American sadhu, with the result that Peter became expansive and talkative, in direct contrast to his misery in the uptight atmosphere of the Burroughs circle in Tangier, or in middle-class America. Peter strode through the streets in a flowing silk shirt, humming Bach, on his way to visit the opium den, or sometimes he just ambled after the white cows in the street, talking to the cow girls—*gopi* girls, whom he called goopy girls. No one gave a second thought to his long hair and his clothes. As Allen wrote to Kerouac: "Everybody, workers, walk around in the streets in underwear, regular striped Hollywood nightmare shorts with open flies like Americans have nightmares being caught in the streets in."

India was slowly working its magic on them, changing and relaxing them both. After eleven weeks in the country, Allen was able to tell Kerouac: "The subjective result on me of India has thus been to start dropping all spiritual activity initiated since Blake voice days and all mental activities I can discard, and stop straining at heaven's door and all that mysticism and drugs and cut-ups and gurus and fears of hells and desire for God and as such, as result, in sum, I feel better and more relaxed and don't give a shit and sometimes sit in cafe downtown Bombay and my brain does get empty and filled with big thrilling cosmic Indic Persian Gulf sunset XX Century."

Allen now attempted to dissolve his writer's block by embarking on an ambitious "Hymn to Kali," based on a classical hymn that he read in translation. The result was "Stotras to Kali Destroyer of Illusions," which appeared in *Planet News*.

Allen and Peter began to feel they were overstaying their welcome on Malabar Hill, so on May 11, 1962, they said goodbye to Radhika and boarded the train for the long journey across the subcontinent to Calcutta.

In Calcutta at the end of May, Peter had to take his Veterans Administration examination to verify that he was still crazy enough to merit his pension. He passed easily and had guaranteed funds for the next two years. Allen meanwhile went on an expedition to the Himalayan foothills in the north. In Kalimpong, he visited many monasteries, and the head of one lamasary offered to get him a boy; Allen didn't take him up on it, because he was too busy trying to find a tantric lama who would give him initiation. An old English lama with blackened teeth gave him the name of Dudjom Rinpoche, the head of the oldest school of Tibetan Buddhism, the Nyingma sect. Allen saw Dudjom on his thirty-sixth birthday, June 3, 1962.

Dudjom was suffering from asthma. He looked strangely like a woman, with his hair in a bun, his smooth round face like an American Indian's, and his Tibetan skirt. Allen talked with him about his fear of the hallucinations caused by LSD and ayahuasca. Dudjom sucked in the air between his teeth and advised, "Watch the wheels within wheels, but don't get attached to anything you see. Let it pass into you but be inactive and not grasping nor rejecting. If you see anything horrible, don't cling to it. If you see anything beautiful, don't cling to it." Allen did not immediately grasp what Dudjom had told him. Only later did he achieve the realization that he was hopelessly attached to his Blake vision and the idea of a widened consciousness. When he finally severed this attachment, it transformed his life. Then he took Dudjom's advice to heart, and he quoted it often in interviews, lectures, and readings.

Next, Allen took a Jeep to Gangtok, the capital of the tiny Himalayan state of Sikkim, to visit the Karmapa, head of the Kagyu sect

of Tibetan Buddhism. Gyalwa Karmapa was recognized by his followers as an incarnation of a line of lamas that stretched back to
the yogi poet Milarepa, who founded the sect in the eleventh century A.D. A jolly fat man with a baby face, Karmapa was very interested in what Allen had to say about drugs and claimed that he
would like to try mescaline. He called Allen a manjusri, a bodhisattva of wisdom and learning, and told him there was something
definite he could teach if Allen could spend a week there. But Allen
had been given only a three-day pass to Sikkim and had to leave the
country the next day. He felt extremely frustrated.

Back in Calcutta, Peter had found them a place to live on the top
floor of a third-rate Muslim hotel called the Amjadia, in the downtown bazaar district. They had a small whitewashed cell-like room
with a ceiling fan, two beds, and creaking green shutters. Everywhere there were people sleeping on the sidewalks and in doorways,
and the streets were filled with lepers, beggars, and holy men with
ashes in their hair.

Calcutta is the center of Kali worship in India, and October 8–10
were the Durga Puja holidays. In all the Hindu quarters of the city,
huge papier-mâché statues were set up in big tents, and the streets
were filled with people drinking bhang—a legal infusion of marijuana and almond milk—banging on drums and cymbals, smoking
ganja—high-grade marijuana—singing and swaying in their rags in
honor of the goddess of destruction. Ginsberg described her as
"The official traditional dignified image of the nature of the universe
here, representing what IS, like, power, electricity, force, being—
all that is created, preserved and then destroyed." Allen mingled
with the crowds, smoking ganja and sitting in the tents with the
half-naked, ash-smeared sadhus under the giant iron Howrah
Bridge that spanned the Hooghly River (as the Ganges is called
when it reaches Calcutta). The sadhus passed the pipes around and
sang mystical songs to Shiva and Krishna. Allen soon learned the
rituals: A devotional heap of flowers was placed in the middle of the
circle and special incense lit. The devotees would raise the clay-
bowled ganja pipe to the sky and shout, "BOOM BOOM MAHADEVA,"
before blasting on it. Allen was soon behaving like a professional
and became very good at yelling the invocation.

He went to the Nimtallah Ghats, where, on the steps leading
down to the river, bodies were burned according to traditional
Hindu funeral rites. To Allen, it was like entering a strange Bosch-
like visionary world. Fakirs and sadhus sat in circles of five to

twenty men, passing the ganja pipe. The mourners, groups of respectable white-robed men of all ages, smoked ganja and sang
hymns. Sadhus with long, matted hair and beards danced with rolling hip movements to the drumbeats of blind beggars. The smoke
from the funeral pyres rolled through the trees and swirled around
Allen's head as he watched the show.

One of the pyres was for a three-year-old boy, and Allen looked
on as his body was oiled to make it combustible. On the next pyre
was a lawyer; his abdomen was already consumed, but attendants
were still poking sticks at his chest and half-burned head. Allen
stared at the puffed and blackened eyes, with the skull showing
where the skin had burned away, and thought: "There's nobody
inside his head anymore. They're burning an old pillow. It's all
okay." Tantric ascetics in red robes and white beards sat around in
alcoves facing the six corpse fires. One white-robed ascetic sat right
in the ashes of the dead.

Allen decided to spend a night there alone with the sleeping
sadhus. He bought two packages of ganja from the pipe shop on the
main street and sat on a bench by the first ash pit to smoke and
watch a body burn: "Pile of wood and the head slowly bubbling up
around mouth and nose—Cheeks blackened with sheets of flame
clasping the volume of the face—splitting, and pink underskin siz-
zling open . . . " After five minutes he moved on to the Mandir,
where he bought food for one of the dancing sadhus and drank tea.
He wandered around the pyres as the sadhus were quieting down
for the night, though a few still sat chanting. Back in the Mandir,
he settled himself next to a handsome sadhu, and one of the attendants gave them a pipe. "I blasted enough till my throat dry and
panicky—then walked up and down, my body trembling, my neck
constricted, till I peed, and still the trembling wait, as if I vomit or
Ramakrishna appear in the river—or Krishna in every animal eye
all around, each of the beggars—lay down to sleep finally on a
marble bench in inner waiting room with rows of Baul singers and
rags sadhu buttocks sheeted on the floor." He took off his rubber
sandals and put them under the bench; in the morning they were
gone, and he had to walk barefoot for tea, puris, and potatoes before
hopping on the number 19 tram to go home to the hotel and Peter.

Allen began spending nights regularly at the burning ghats,
usually Tuesdays and Saturdays, the nights of the biggest ganja-
smoking rituals. One day while he was there, the attendants placed
a young woman on the pyre, but she was not dead and fortunately

awoke before the wood ignited. Allen spent long nights walking the Calcutta streets, looking at the thousands of homeless people murmuring in their sleep on the roadsides and sidewalks, scattered everywhere like bodies on a battlefield. In his journal he wrote: "It isn't enough for your heart to break because everybody's heart is broken now."

Calcutta became Allen's home. The painting of dancing skeletons on the wall of their room, Peter's cracked brown guitar, their knapsacks stacked neatly against the wall, the crude green shutters, the red paper kites fluttering outside in the hot air, the constant rickshaw bells, the bearded groceries seller wailing to Allah, the transvestite singing on the corner—all became familiar. The cool marble tables of the Hotel Amjadia's restaurant, the Baul saints in their strange waistcoats and skirts, the lepers and beggars, became everyday sights. He got to know the tram system and the lamplit stalls at Burrabazaar, where he drank bhang. He sat regularly beneath the mile-long black iron Howrah Bridge, listening to the roar of traffic and watching the tidal bore surge by.

On December 10, 1962, Allen and Peter took the Doon Express third-class sleeper to Benares. The Hindu equivalent of Mecca or Rome, Benares is an ancient city, built on the banks of the River Ganges at the time of Thebes, Babylon, and Nineveh. At the water's edge is a cliff face of ancient maharajas' palaces, temples, dharmashalas, and worn cracked steps leading down to the river: a jumble of masonry and turrets and narrow crooked alleys, all teeming with people. It was on one of the narrow streets that Allen and Peter found a room, "a few steps from Ganges near main mangy dog leper sadhu bathing ghat," where they would live for the next five months.

The room, on the third floor of a house on Dasaswamedh Ghat, overlooked a market square on one side and the steps of the ghat on the other. French windows opened to a balcony, which encircled the room as on a Parisian *rond-point* and from which they could see the Ganges flowing by and the pointed turrets of the temple across the street. Chicken-wire grilles over the windows stopped monkeys from coming in and stealing bananas from the table.

There was a desk and plenty of shelves for Allen's books and manuscripts. They bought a hundred-watt bulb to prevent eyestrain when they worked at night; straw mats for the floor; clay pots to store water; and a big pail for cleaning. They arranged their blankets on the charpoy, a rope bed on a wooden frame, and bought a kerosene stove for a dollar. It looked and felt like home. Allen would tune his portable radio to Radio Peking, take a shot of morphine-atrophine, and lie back on the charpoy, relaxed and happy.

There are four miles of bathing ghats in Benares, and each morning before dawn, thousands of pilgrims made their way through the narrow streets to the steps leading down to the Ganges to greet the sun. Pandits, the Brahmin priest caste, had already set up their mushroom-shaped sun umbrellas. They wore little strings looped from ear to belt, and placed third-eye red dots of incense paste on the foreheads of the bathers. Their job was to guard under their umbrellas the clothes and wristwatches of the bathers who walked into the river as the sun rose and offered cupped handfuls or small copper bowlfuls of water to Surya, the sun god. Small votive candles surrounded by marigold petals were set adrift in the river, in boats made from leaves.

The street below Allen's house was constantly noisy with women vegetable sellers calling their wares and lepers and beggars catching the bathers on their way to the river and back. Sacred cows and monkeys roamed at will, and all the marriage or first haircut or special funeral processions came past the house, often two or three each day, a small gang of drummers preceding them, sometimes with eunuchs dancing ahead or with camels and elephants leading, "a great surf of noise from dawn to midnight, statues of Gods passing on litters and holymen and attendants coming to take a bath."

Allen spent a lot of time at the Manikarnika burning ghat, the holiest in all India, which he regarded as the "best show here." Geese and swans pecked among the leaf boats and marigold petals at the ash-blackened water's edge, boats with rectangular sails floated past downstream, "the air above the pyre curling in the heat, like a transparent water veil between my eyes and the green fields and trees along the horizon on the other side of the Ganges—and the embankments, red temples, spires, toy mosques, trees and squat little shrines walling in the bend of the river upstream to the long red train bridge at Raj Ghat an inch high."

Two weeks after settling in Benares, Allen and Peter took a trip to Agra, about 350 miles away, toward Delhi, to spend Christmas at the Taj Mahal. Christmas was the anniversary of the death of Shah Jehan's wife, for whom the tomb was built, and the hereditary Muslim guards held a two-day festival of Urdu singing and poetry. The monument was open forty-eight hours for the celebration, and Allen and Peter bedded down in a marble alcove screened from the light as the amplified Urdu voices echoed and reechoed around the vast dome, "Great waves of sound frothing out of the arch." Allen wrote Paul Bowles they had "lots of ganja to make the symmetries more awesome." He was deeply impressed by the building and rhapsodized to Lucien Carr: "Taj Mahal an awesome surprise—the picture postcards don't tell the Vibrational story—it really is a sublime joint—like being inside a perfectly symmetrical 3-D DeChirico canvas—you get that particular infinity sensation around it—like a time machine—Fortunately we *lived* in it for three days so we got quite an exposure . . . Friendly atmosphere . . . most stupendous motel in Universe I'm sure—Worth a trip to India just for that." In his journal he wrote:

> *O glorious bulge, marble filled with eyes,*
> *   balloon moving the sky apart*
> *Help whistle the trees in your path*
> *   from the mouth of the Moghul moonbeam.*

They spent the next week in Brindiban, Lord Krishna's home and the center of bhakti yoga, whose cultists offer their gurus devotion, faith, and love. There, in his quest for gurus, Allen met Srimata Krishnaji, and Bankey Behari, who told him to "Take Blake as your guru," to practice bhakti to Blake, obviously Allen's guru, and stop looking for a living one. When Allen returned to Benares, he tacked a postcard of Blake's death mask, from the National Portrait Gallery in London, on the wall between the windows.

Allen gave a free reading at the Benares Hindu University. At the end, the head of the English department, a professor O'Brien, stood up and said that the poetry was obscene and vulgar. Allen looked him coldly in the eye and said, "Not half as vulgar as the speech you're making now."

O'Brien, who was clearly used to everyone deferring to his opinion, got angry. "You have the nerve to make us sit here and listen to that obscene 'poetry' and won't even listen to our criticisms?"

To which Allen replied sarcastically, "Must you make a *speech*?"

The professor exploded. "You'll never be invited to Benares Hindu University again!"

"Oh, come now!" said Allen, bored. He later realized that instead of insulting O'Brien and undermining his authority, he should have neutralized his hostility and given him a way out. But the damage was done, and the professor's acolytes, members of the Indian Communist Party, turned on Allen: "You wouldn't have talked to him that way if his skin was white. You Americans with your airplanes and your rotten wheat. Now you come here with your filthy fucks to corrupt our pure Hindi poetry!" They sent a copy of *Howl* with all the dirty words underlined to the Criminal Investigation Department of the local police, requesting that Allen be run out of town.

The CID was already investigating Allen and Peter: why would Americans want to stay in India so long and mix with such low-class people? India was in a state of emergency: there was a border dispute with China. Allen and Peter might be spies, possibly from the CIA. What had really focused CID attention on them was the arrival, in February 1963, of Pete Turner, a photographer from *Esquire* magazine, whom the Indian Tourist Bureau had commissioned to do a photo essay on Allen and Peter in Benares for an *Esquire* special issue on tourism in India. Allen and Peter took Turner out on a boat at dawn to photograph sunrise on the Ganges and showed him the city.

Then began a period of harassment. The next day, an arrogant young CID man walked unannounced into their room. He refused to identify himself and demanded to see their passports. He asked what Allen did, and Allen said he was a poet. To Allen's surprise, he asked to see Allen's writing, so Allen showed him a copy of *Howl*. The man left, and later that day Turner flew off to his next assignment.

The CID man hung around all the next day, talking to the neighbors and spreading lies. He told Pandit, their landlord, that Allen and Peter were immoral foreigners and that he would get in trouble for renting them a room. This upset Pandit, who knew them well and thought they were some new sort of American sadhus. The CID man shocked the dentist downstairs by saying that they had been buying whiskey from the liquor store across the street. In fact, the bottles he had seen contained apple juice, bought for Turner, who could not drink the water.

All of this was guaranteed to cause suspicion, generate more rumors, and sour their previously good relations with their pious neighbors, but before Allen could do anything about it, he was visited by Mr. Singh from the Foreigners' Registration Office. Allen complained to him of the harassment, and Singh said he knew nothing about it. No one but his office had the right to ask for papers, and the CID man was possibly a fake; if he came around again, they should seize him and send for the police. He said that they were living quite within their rights and departed, leaving Allen and Peter puzzled and confused.

The next morning, the CID man could be seen sitting in the shop across the street, questioning the local tea sellers about them. Allen went down and asked to see his identification papers. When he refused, Allen insisted on taking him to the police station. There, Singh took the man into a side room and returned to say that the man was from the CID but working under secret orders, so his identity could not be given. However, said Singh, the man apologized for spreading rumors. Allen, angry, said the damage was already done in the neighborhood.

He took the matter to Singh's superior, who didn't see what all the fuss was about, so Allen demanded to see *his* superior. In the end, Allen went to the Special Police, and eventually the CID man, and his boss, came to reassure the landlord that everything was all right and that it had been a mistake.

Singh was the next to harass them. A few days later, he walked into their room without even knocking, and when Allen asked him why he was there and if it was an official or an unofficial visit, he said that he was just passing and that he was their friend, "or take it any way you wish." Singh continued to come around late at night on "social" visits, which clearly disturbed and worried the landlord.

An *Esquire* reporter was arriving on February 26, so Allen went to the Tourist Bureau and asked if they could make discreet inquiries into the reason for the harassment, which, he pointed out, hardly made for good tourist publicity. The reporter, Alice Glaser, arrived and stayed in Benares for a week, taking a lot of notes. Allen and Peter liked her even though her high heels prevented her going with them to the burning ghats or walking by the river. The day after she arrived, a clerk from the Foreigners' Registration Office delivered a visa denial and an expulsion order, which said that Allen and Peter had to leave India at the "earliest possible time." In a typical Indian bureaucratic slipup, the denial was for the August 1962–February 1963 visa, which had already expired. The clerk said they should come to the office the next morning to make another application, but he took the landlord and the dentist aside and told them that the application would be denied.

That evening, only Peter was in when Singh made his usual nine o'clock harassment call and said that Allen and he had two to three days to leave India, otherwise they would be arrested and given a five-month jail term and fined five thousand rupees. Peter said they couldn't leave because they were waiting for money and that if they were put in jail, "Thousands of journalists will come to visit us in Benares in our jail cell. There'll be stories in the paper about what's happening."

"Let them come," Singh replied. "India's in a state of emergency. In these times there are more important things."

There was nothing for it but to go to Delhi and try to find someone who understood the situation. They left immediately. Allen began at the top, with a telegram to Pandit Nehru, asking him to invite them to tea so they could explain the situation. He didn't get the interview. Allen reported to the Home Ministry bureaucracy, until at last he found an official who understood their reasons for wanting to stay. "Oh, you're here on an intellectual level," he said, and stamped their visa applications for another six months.

Back in Benares, the Communist Party had learned about its members who had sent the marked copy of *Howl* to the CID; they were ordered to apologize. Singh stopped his visits, and the landlord was again a happy man. It was later revealed that the Benares CID had been acting on orders from Delhi and that a fifteen-page report had been filed, detailing everyone Allen and Peter knew and everywhere they went. The report had been requested because certain respectable people had made complaints about them and their "immoral" poetry.

All this led Allen to the conclusion, as he wrote Kerouac, "that I really should treat people gentler and not insult and drive them into a corner so they claw out in self defence. I have a tendency to flip into heroic outrages, Jeremiah-like, but aside from letting off my steam that generally complicates the situation rather than resolves it in understanding. . . . So my Peace Program is to pacify myself to begin with."

Allen continued his search for gurus. He visited Kali Pada Guha Roy and told him his doubts about poetry as a discipline fit for the void. The reply: "Poetry is also a Sadhana, and Yoga also drops before the void." Ninety-year-old Citaram Onkar Das Thakur told Allen that if he really wanted to find a guru he should not eat meat, fish, eggs, or onions. He should stop smoking and masturbating, say, "Guru, guru, guru, guru . . ." under his breath for a week, and then come back to see him. Allen kept it up for two days on the principle that anything was worth trying.

Allen did seem to give some credence to the notion that he take Blake as his guru. From that time on, there were frequent references to Blake in his journals:

> *Blake on the wall last week*
> > *eyes closed frowning on my*
> > > *insults to the Professor*
> *I skipped in the room ashamed & fluttered*
> > *my face with my fingers—*

The weather grew warmer, and it was soon hot enough for Allen to bathe in the Ganges again. Whenever he felt too hot and sweaty, he would grab his red towel and, wearing just his pajama bottoms, walk the few feet from his house to the steps of the river. A collection of holy men in orange robes were always gathered there, sitting on platforms under their umbrellas, gossiping with each other and smoking ganja. One had no arms, just tiny flippers, and wrote with a pen held in the toes of his left foot. Lepers sat under the trees in a little park, surrounded by dogs and cows. Rowboats and flowers crowded the water's edge where Allen washed his underwear on the wet steps with hard red soap.

He spent much of his time at the ghats, watching the corpses burn. He told Gregory that it "ended a lot of my anxiety about dying, especially always getting high with naked holymen in burning ghats, watching the roast." He gave Gregory a graphic description: "Yesterday I sat all afternoon writing random free little notebook pages. They were burning a woman and after an hour her thighs and arms were burnt and half her head. They pushed the armless legless face and chest upright over the fire and flopped it face down in the orange colored flames—I got up close and saw blood dripping through the nose hole burnt away—one time I saw brains afire—anyway, nobody left inside to feel it."

Allen was walking across the campus of Benares University on the night of March 20, talking to a professor of German, when the man turned and told him that William Carlos Williams had died. Allen stopped under the trees and, wide-eyed, asked, "Williams is dead?" The instructor had *Time* magazine with him, and together they stood on the porch of the International House Annex bungalow, so that Allen could read the obituary under the electric light. As insects buzzed around the bulb, the news sank in. He looked up at the night sky. "I saw the Big Dipper in the sky, that's all," he wrote to Gregory the next day. He went home, smoked a little ganja, and wrote lines in his journal that were later published, unaltered, as the poem "Death News":

> *Williams is in the Big Dipper. He isn't dead*
> *as the many pages of words arranged thrill*
> *with his intonations the mouths of meek kids*
> *becoming subtle even in Bengal. . . .*

Many beggars lined his street, but Allen couldn't help noticing one who, particularly hideous, crouched in a fetal position, naked, against a urinal, looking like one of the skeletal survivors of Buchenwald. He was covered with loose brown feces, and huge festering sores on his hips and elbows crawled with flies. He was obviously dying. Somewhat fearfully, Allen gave him some milk, but he was too weak to take the rupee that Allen put in his hand. The pathetic creature was a deaf-mute. There was yellow pus in his eye, and old curry stains dribbled down his chin. One hand was withered to a paw, and his swollen, shiny-skinned feet looked overlarge at the end of his thin stick legs. One toe seemed to be leprous, and there were maggots coming out of his ear. Flies covered his eyes and his ass. That night, Allen heard him screaming a piercing high-pitched wail. The next day, the beggar gurgled heavily as he breathed.

Allen and Peter knew an orphan boy who lived in the small leper park where the ghat met the river. The boy's parents had died, and he grew up there serving the beggars. Allen, Peter, and the boy carried the man-corpse with his few rags to the Ganges to bathe, and Allen went for a doctor. The diagnosis was that nothing was wrong except starvation and its complications, so Allen and Peter began to feed him milk and fruit and bought him a mattress to lie on. Peter put hydrogen peroxide in his ears to kill the maggots and sterilize any infection. He put penicillin powder and afterward talcum powder on the open wounds, demonstrating for the boy, whom they hired for fifty cents a day to feed him and to wash him in the river every day at noon. They bought the beggar white pajamas and a sheet, and propped him in the shade of the bo tree in the leper park, where he sat stupefied.

He was incontinent, and every day they took his mattress to the river to wash the shit off and dry it in the hot sun. Slowly, he began to stir, and one day he wrote in the dust, "dood," the word for milk. Allen brought him a notebook and a pencil and he began to write in broken English: "Sir I want to die because Hearing anybody magi saying to me he is thief Hardwar." This was followed by some scrawls in Urdu and Hindi and a couple of Sanskrit letters. Then he wrote: "I want to go to my house where my family is I want to go to Hardwar I want my bed and clothes."

Allen had planned a visit to the ruins of the Buddhist university of Nalanda, which took him out of Benares for a few weeks. When he returned, he found that the sick beggar was a little stronger. Peter had been looking after him, administering the medicine and paying the boy. One day, the beggar spoke to them in a high, squeaky, piercing voice. His tongue had been cut out by Muslims during the partition of India, and he had been repeatedly stabbed, which had crippled him. Another day, as they were crouched, attending to him, a Hindu postal clerk came over and took down the man's name and address, offering to write to his family. Shortly afterward the clerk came with the family's reply. He had disappeared six months before, and his mother had been crying every day since, thinking him dead. His brother was traveling to Benares from the Punjab, a thousand miles away, to get him. In the meantime, Allen had managed to get the man admitted to a hospital, where his health improved immediately.

Allen found that the hospital was free, but patients weren't admitted unless someone important or a foreigner brought them in. It was an attitude Allen found hard to believe. When he had first gone to the Municipal Health Bureau, which was only a few hundred feet from where the man lay dying, he was told to return the next day, because the official there would have to consult with his superior. Allen made a fuss, but it was still some time before he was able to get the beggar admitted. Having once achieved success, he returned to the hospital the next day on behalf of a dying woman and eventually got her admitted as well.

Now that he was involved, Allen went to the top, the mayor of Benares, to complain about the situation, but the mayor just gave him a polite runaround. It took Allen a week to corner the bureaucrat in charge at the hospital. The facilities to treat sick and dying beggars were there, but the bureaucrats were so self-centered and lazy that they would rather allow people to die in the street than stir themselves. Allen described his experience in a letter to Paul Bowles: "We got another into hospital and tended a few others, so got inside the beggar starvation decor. . . . Everybody afraid to bother for fear of getting inextricably involved in insoluble problem. . . . I've seen four people die on the street downstairs in last month." With the thousands of people on the streets, he could not do much, but instead of trying to ignore the starvation and squalor, he confronted it, and in doing what little he could, he understood it and experienced a side of India that most people preferred to pretend did not exist.

Allen accepted an invitation extended by Robert Creeley to come and teach poetry for three weeks at Vancouver University in July and August 1963, which offered a round-the-world ticket as payment. Peter had been opposed to the idea, but Allen wanted to go. Peter became surly and incommunicative. They had developed separate sets of Indian friends and had not done much together in Benares. Peter had been taking a lot of drugs: in Calcutta he had smoked opium and in Benares he shot up morphine. Now they lived together in silence, broken only by Peter's curt answers to Allen's questions. Neither of them raised his voice with the other, Allen containing his sadness and Peter his irritation. One night, on morphine, Peter revealed that he thought Allen was washed up; by going to teach at Vancouver University he had broken his vow never to read poetry in public for money. Peter obviously felt that Allen was abandoning him and perhaps truly realized then that with Allen's ever-increasing fame, they could never be equals in the relationship. Allen had no reply for him. He felt desolate and empty.

Allen left Benares by train for Calcutta. Peter saw him off. "That was a nice look you gave me at the RR station," Allen wrote him from Calcutta. "I always feel bad to part from you if we're cold to each other, and I feel happy to be alone when I know there's still a little tender look between us left in eternity. For no matter what happens, I always *want* to love you—I don't feel good with the barren-ness of kissless silent hopeless goodbye." Years later, Ginsberg confessed that he had never really noticed Peter's excessive use of drugs; he was so used to being surrounded by crazy and eccentric behavior that it seemed quite normal. He was prepared to let their relationship drift, confident that they would reconcile back in the States. Allen's plan was to visit Gary and Joanne in Japan on his way to Vancouver and to stop off in Thailand, Cambodia, and Vietnam en route. On May 26, he flew from Calcutta out across the Bay of Bengal and the Andaman Sea to Bangkok.

TWELVE | THE CHANGE

I believe sexuality is the basis of all friendship.

—Jean Cocteau

In Bangkok, Allen ate the cheap Chinese food and drank the delicious iced sodas. He visited the museums, guidebook in hand, and saw the sights, the Dawn Temple and the huge golden reclining Buddha, "big as a ship."

In the park at night, rock 'n' roll boys in blue pants and neat lightweight shirts lounged on the grass or on the steps of the statue of King Rama VI, while music was piped through loudspeakers. In his one week there he twice took boys back to his hotel, but as he wrote Peter: "Only trouble is they stick to me like adhesive tape afterwards." One of them was able to supply him with some morphine. On June 1, he left for Saigon.

The United States had been involved in the war in Vietnam ever since September 1945, when Ho Chi Minh, Communist leader of the Vietnam Independence Movement (the Viet Minh) proclaimed the former colony independent of France at a huge rally in Hanoi. Fearful that if Vietnam went Communist, neighboring countries would follow, the United States provided over $2 billion in financial and military aid to France in its fight to regain the colony. France was defeated at the battle of Dien Bien Phu in 1954, and a Geneva conference forced the victorious Viet Minh to agree to a "provisional" division of their country into north and south until free elections could be held in the newly independent state. The United States quickly recognized the puppet state set up in Saigon by France and its premier, Ngo Dinh Diem, a Catholic protégé of Cardinal Spellman from a powerful mandarin family. When it became apparent that free elections, to be held in 1956, would result in a landslide victory for Ho Chi Minh, President Eisenhower refused to allow them and pledged American support for Diem's regime in the civil war that followed. By 1960, there were 900 American "advisers" in South Vietnam, trying to prop up Diem's corrupt regime, which by this time had lost nearly all the countryside to the Viet Cong insurgents, bent on overthrowing him. To try and salvage America's position, President Kennedy increased the number of American military advisers to more than 16,000 by the end of 1963, in direct violation of the Geneva accords. In 1962, armed "strategic hamlets" were introduced in the Viet Cong–controlled countryside, and the U.S. Air Force began flying "training missions" (over 8,000 in 1961–63). Washington pressured Diem to make political and social reforms to give the regime a more palatable image, but Diem ignored them. Diem's brutal suppression of Vietnamese Buddhists demonstrating against religious persecution ultimately led to his downfall.

Buddhist protests against Diem were continuing when Allen arrived in Saigon. He was in Saigon for four nights and spent most of his time hanging out at Neal Sheehan's office at United Press, where all the U.S. newsmen socialized. There he met reporters from *Time, Newsweek*, the *New York Times*, and the agencies. He wrote Peter that he "got the whole story of Vietnam war gossip from them—EEEEK—it's like walking around in a mescaline nightmare— I can arrange to fly inland and see 'model hamlets'—battles, but decided no and am scairt. . . . The war is a fabulous anxiety bringdown. It's *awful*."

Allen allowed himself a week to visit the ruins of Angkor Wat in central Cambodia. The ruins were huge, much larger than anything he had seen in India. "Very extensive like secluded vast park full of old stone Coney Island ruins," he wrote Peter. Angkor Wat was surrounded by and often encroached upon by thick forest and jungle. Great roots curled over the carved stone heads, slowly dislodging the nine-hundred-year-old masonry. Bas reliefs were just visible behind barriers of vine and creepers. Snakes and insects lived in the rooms and cavities beneath the statues. Allen took photographs and wrote extensive journal notes about the ruins, which were published as *Angkor Wat* by Fulcrum Press in 1968: "The huge snake roots, the vaster / serpent arms fallen / octopus over the roof . . ."

It rained much of the time he was there, silencing the parrots and filling the jungle with the sound of millions of raindrops dripping through the leaves and pouring over the statues, deepening their colors; nonetheless, he wandered among the buildings for hours.

It was night when he arrived in Tokyo. Hotels were all five or ten dollars a night, so he slept on a sheet of cardboard in the station, waking at dawn to catch the early train for the seven-hour journey to Kyoto, where he was to stay with Gary and Joanne. The top of Mount Fuji was cloud-covered as the train sped by; still Allen wept at the sight, so familiar from Hiroshige prints.

The Snyders' little Japanese house reminded him of Mill Valley, California. A rock garden with moss and leafy trees was visible through the open screen walls and glass door of the main mat room, where Allen sat at the floor desk to write. He liked the Japanese food Joanne prepared—fish and bean-curd soup—and the neat, clean feel of the country, which was the height of civilization after the countries he had been in for the past two years. In Japan, girls were free to travel by themselves without a chaperone, teenage couples walked together on the streets and sat together in buses, and there were no starving beggars—all in stark contrast to India, where kissing in public was illegal and the image of death lined the streets.

Gary was in the middle of a Zen meditation week, so Allen signed up for four nights and sat cross-legged next to him for several hours each night. His ankles hurt after the first session, but he realized that the position kept him naturally balanced, his back straight. He found the Japanese style of sitting much simpler than the complicated Hindu style and the meditation much easier: breathing deeply into the stomach naturally and exhaling slowly and easily, keeping mind and thoughts on the feeling in the stomach. Whenever his mind wandered, he just went back to the feeling in the stomach.

The monks wore black robes, and everything was very formal and silent, like a ballet. It was so still that Allen could hear the fish plashing in the pond outside. He learned more about "sitting" in those four days than in the previous year and a half. It was all in great contrast to the noisy religions of India.

He began to get into the swing of things and did a tour of the queer bars and latrines of Kyoto. Impressed by how neat and sexy all the Japanese boys and girls looked in their tight-fitting drip-dry pants, he bought himself a pair of permanent-press pants and a drip-dry shirt for five dollars. He wrote Peter: "Japan first place I seen where modern radios clothes cameras are all nice toys everybody got."

He began to feel different, lighter, less death-haunted. He told Peter: "Maybe it's the change from gaunt ascetic India sorrows." He realized that India had depressed him. "The depressed humanity brings down the atmosphere, it's real, but it's the Indian universe. Japanese universe much *funnier* and more cheerful." The poverty in India had been "man-made in a way—you can see it here in Japan—It's also overcrowded but everybody's neat and clean." Allen was happy. With the weight of India off his back, he could begin to understand what he had learned there, "the sweetness of all those gurus sinking into me."

He was sorry to leave, but on July 17 he boarded the Kyoto–Tokyo Express, to spend a few days in Tokyo before flying on to Vancouver. As the train pulled away from Kyoto, everything seemed gray: the river, the bridges, the stonework, the train itself. In the distance, the brilliant neon of downtown Kyoto snapped on and off. By the side of the track, lanterns hung in rows under the damp eaves of the houses. The railroad followed a gray river with a surface like plastic.

He looked back over the events of the past two years. A great deal had happened since he and Peter boarded S.S. *America* and stood in the snow flurries, waving at the little group of family and friends on the dock. At that time, Allen had painted himself into a corner with drugs. After his Blake vision, he had vowed to widen his area of consciousness and had systematically explored his mind, using stronger and stronger drugs: heroin, mescaline, peyote, LSD, psilocybin, ayahuasca. But with the more powerful hallucinogens he encountered an inhuman serpent monster, a vision of death, and it got so that if he took drugs he would start vomiting with anxiety. Yet he still felt it his duty to take them, for the sake of an expanded consciousness. He felt compelled by his Blake vision to break down his identity and seek a "more direct contact with primate sensation, nature."

All through India he asked the holy men and gurus for their advice on how to deal with this problem, and they all, in one way or another, pointed him straight back to his own body: from Swami Shivananda's "The only guru is your own heart," to Dudjom Rinpoche, whose advice was for Allen not to cling to visions, be they horrible or beautiful. Allen realized he was clinging to his Blake vision. He was hung up on the memory of an experience and trying to reproduce it.

The gurus all told him to get *into* his body, to live in and inhabit the human form and not try to escape it with drugs or other methods. Allen had thought he had to break out of his body if he wanted to attain complete consciousness; that if he wanted to attain God, he had to die. Now he felt that he had been wrong, that maybe he had even misunderstood Blake and that Blake's "Human form divine" meant living completely *in* the human form.

All through India he had questioned the validity of his search for a means to higher consciousness, and by the time he reached Japan he had already changed his position a good deal. Joanne Kyger, in her journals, noted that Allen no longer spoke about the significance of his drug visions when he stayed with them in Kyoto. Removing himself from the weight of the Indian experience permitted what he had learned there to come through, and as the train sped toward Tokyo, Allen realized that he did not want to be dominated by the inhuman serpent drug experience anymore, or even dominated by the moral obligation to enlarge his consciousness, or to do anything except *be* in the present, accepting himself for what he was.

"I had a very strange ecstatic experience then and there, once I had sort of gotten that burden off my back, because I was suddenly free to love myself again, and therefore love the people around me, in the form that they already were. And love myself in my own form as I am. And look around at the other people and so it was *again* the same thing like in the bookstore [in 1948], except this time I was completely in my body and had no more mysterious obligations. And nothing more to fulfill, except to be willing to die when I am dying, whenever that be. And be willing to live as a human being in this form now. So I started weeping, it was such a happy moment."

Between the tears, he scribbled in his notebook the long poem later published as "The Change": "In my train seat I renounce / my power, so that I do / live I will die." Abandoning the quest for immortality and cosmic consciousness that would live forever, he returned home to his own body. In renouncing visions, he had of course renounced Blake as well. He was amazed to find himself free at last. He now knew that in order to attain the depth of consciousness he had experienced back in 1948, he had to cut himself off from the Blake vision, otherwise he would be perpetually hung up on its memory. He said later, "The remarkable thing is that I stupefied myself from 1948 to 1963. A long time—that's fifteen years preoccupied with one single thought."

Allen arrived at the University of British Columbia, jubilant in the knowledge of his new realization and clearly in a delicate emotional state, crying all the time and fondling people, demanding to be loved for what he was and loving everyone in return. He was treated with the utmost tenderness, particularly by Creeley, who recognized the change in him. Allen was to teach poetry with Robert Creeley, Charles Olson, Robert Duncan, and Denise Levertov, and it seemed that they were all talking about the same thing and must have had the same realization as he, Olson saying, "I am one with my skin" and Creeley talking about "The place we are." Allen and Duncan were even able to get over their mutual paranoia and make up their differences. One of the first things Allen did was persuade Creeley that Philip Whalen should also be there. Creeley agreed, and he and Allen sent Whalen money to fly up to Vancouver.

Allen in fact caught, or created, the mood of the entire conference. The students all appeared to be lovelorn, and it was a period of change for many of the poets. It turned into what Allen described to Lucien Carr as "three weeks teaching poesy, free love and belly sighs to lots of unhappy students who want heaven." The poets all lived together, and many of the students spent nights with them. Allen was in ecstasy and wrote Peter: "I'm telling you, the Cold War's over. Hurrah, all we gotta do is really love each other." Allen had written a similar letter to Peter from Paris in 1958 when he and Bill first proposed the idea of a "love generation," but such an idea was premature in the Eisenhower era. Now, as the sixties got under way, with Kennedy in the White House, it was an idea whose time had come.

It was not until the third week of the conference that Allen began to come down from his elated state, but as he wrote Peter: "Can open up at will and cry for love anywhere—even to police—*everybody* gotta be included, you were always right. Burroughs trouble is he cutting up his feelings as well as mind. Mind needs cut ups to release feelings." Allen had brought an Indian harmonium back with him from Benares and used it to accompany himself in singing the Hare Krishna mantra. "He drove us all mad with that," Whalen remembered. "It meant a lot to him. He actually was singing, which he loved to do anyway, but he was singing this thing and getting

into, for all practical purposes, a bhakti yoga, a devotional yoga.
. . . He was just beginning to get into the idea of using music and
chanting for part of his poetry reading."

Allen practiced what he preached, as usual, in the extreme,
whether it was the chanting of Hindu mantras or his new-found
acceptance of his own body as a love center. He could be very
persuasive. On August 16, the poetry conference ended with a huge
party, during which Allen sat on the floor and chanted "Hare
Krishna," weeping and ecstatic, kissing everyone and feeling everybody's stomach.

Allen arrived in San Francisco in August 1963 and stayed in the
roomy attic of Lawrence and Kirby Ferlinghetti's rambling Victorian
house. He ran around town visiting all his old friends. Allen thought
Michael McClure looked older and even more handsome, and was
pleased when for the first time McClure gave him a kiss, their old
differences settled. McClure thought Allen had changed for the
better. Whalen found him more mellow, with less "hopping around"
than usual. However, not everyone was pleased with Allen's new
message. Jack Spicer's poetry circle was very suspicious, of both
his new interest in Oriental religion and his attitude to sex. Poet
Larry Fagin, who had met Allen in Paris in 1961 and was living in
San Francisco in 1963, remembered, "He was put down by Spicer's
circle. . . . Zen was okay, but this smearing your eastern goo on
everyone was unheard of." As for Allen's new message of free love
to save the world, Fagin said, "Spicer found the orgy scenes utterly
repulsive." Just as in 1956, "Allen wanted everyone to be one big
happy family."

A surprise visitor to San Francisco that August was Lucien Carr,
bringing some of the original 1940s Beat Generation spirit to the
West Coast. His wife was away in the country, and he had got drunk
one night with a girl named Lois and just taken off on the spur of
the moment. "I said, 'Let's go to San Francisco!' " They arrived
drunk and practically penniless. Lucien remembered Allen's saying
that North Beach was the place to be, so they went there and
checked into a cheap Chinese hotel. They sat in their room with a
box of saltines, a couple of cans of sardines, two quarts of gin, and
no money. Lucien called City Lights and spoke with Ferlinghetti.
Identifying himself, he asked, "Is there anyone in town I know?
And if there isn't, can you lend me fifty dollars?"

"As a matter of fact," Ferlinghetti said, "Ginsberg's just come to
town."

"Ginsberg came and somehow found us in this rabbit warren,"

Lucien remembered. "And we'd been locked in there for two days with nothing but all this gin and saltines. Anyway, he rescued us and took us to Ferlinghetti's attic. . . . Allen was conducting all sorts of poetry business at one end of this attic and we were at the other end, but the stairs that you got up to the attic were in such a place that you had to step over the mattress that Lois and I had, to get down to have your poetry discussions with Allen. And there we were constantly drunk, constantly fucking, people stepping over us, until Ferlinghetti finally told Allen, 'You've got to get your fucking friends out of here!' "

Allen made arrangements for them all to move down the hill to a house owned by an eccentric doctor. "It was the same situation," Lucien remembered, "one great big room with Allen conducting his business at one end, and Lois and me at the other. But this crazy man had two big apes, in a cage that was half outside the wall and half in the living room, and the apes would go into an absolute frenzy when they watched all this screwing going on." After about a week Lucien decided that it was time he returned to face his wife. Allen had just received royalties from Scandinavia and gave them to Lucien to get himself and Lois back to New York.

There was a spare room at 1403 Gough Street, Robert LaVigne's old apartment, where Allen had met Peter, eight years before, so he moved in. To complete his sense of déjà vu, Neal Cassady also moved in, with Anne Murphy, his girlfriend of the past eighteen months, just as he had joined Allen to live with Natalie in Gough Street all those years before.

Neal's arrest in 1958 for offering a couple of joints to undercover agents in trade for a ride to work had resulted in two terms of five years to life. In actuality, he spent two years in jail—three months in Vacaville and the remainder locked in San Quentin. There he became a devout Christian, memorizing the names of all 262 popes and devising prayers to be said at different times of day. He was released on July 4, 1960, and took a job changing tires—his good railroad job was gone forever. He began to violate his parole by hanging out in North Beach and down in Palo Alto, where a new friend lived, the writer Ken Kesey who had a place in the woods where a permanent party seemed to be going on, celebrating the joys of LSD. Neal had a string of girlfriends, many of them coeds from Stanford, then settled down with Anne Murphy. For the sake of their three children, Carolyn had waited for him when he was in jail, but since it was clear that nothing had changed, she filed for divorce in the summer of 1963. When Allen met up with him again,

Neal had given up work and was living on unemployment, most of which he lost at the racetrack, trying to prove his "system."

On October 28, Madame Nhu arrived in San Francisco to address a gathering of businessmen and civic leaders at the Sheraton Palace Hotel. After Buddhist monks in Vietnam had died and been injured in clashes with Diem's police and soldiers, a number of monks immolated themselves in an effort to draw world attention to the religious policies of Diem and his fiercely Catholic sister-in-law, the beautiful and sinister "Dragon Lady," Madame Nhu. To try and counter this, Diem sent Madame Nhu on a coast-to-coast tour of the United States to give his side of the story, which was: "There is absolute religious freedom in Vietnam." Married to Diem's brother, Ngo Dinh Nhu, the chief of the secret police, Madame Nhu did not help her cause by telling reporters she enjoyed the monks' "barbecues." Everywhere she went, she was met by student demonstrations, and it was only at the Roman Catholic Fordham University in New York that she spoke without interruption and received enthusiastic applause.

Over five hundred people held a protest rally and formed a picket line outside San Francisco's Sheraton Palace Hotel, Allen among them. It was his first political demonstration, and he approached it with characteristic individualism. He made a placard. On the left side, he carefully painted a three-fish "Buddha's Footprint" symbol, using patriotic red, white, and blue fish tails with gold and silver scales. On the right, he printed a poem:

> War is black magic.
> Belly flowers to North and South Vietnam
> include everybody.
> End the human war.
> Name hypnosis and fear is the
> Enemy—Satan go home!
> I accept America and Red China
> To the human race.
> Madame Nhu and Mao Tse-tung
> Are in the same boat of meat.

He held the placard aloft for fourteen hours, singing various Hindu mantras. He told a local journalist, "I'm here today on the picket line trying to be tender to Madame Nhu and Mao Tse-tung.

Or better, asking them to be tender." He explained his political philosophy: "Anger and fury of left wing will only drive the humanoid bureaucrats and cops into deeper humanoidism. Be kind to cops; they're not cops, they're people in disguise who've been deceived by their own disguise." It was pure hippie rhetoric, enunciated for the first time—the direct result of his experience on the train in Japan.

Allen now looked the way most people remember him from the sixties: black curls to his collar, hair thinning on top, wise rabbinical beard, and large sad brown eyes magnified by thick-framed glasses. He was already a public figure, as he found out one day while strolling through North Beach. He came upon a fight between groups of black and white youths and watched as the police arrived with sirens blaring and red lights flashing. It seemed to Allen that the police were being unduly rough on the black youths, so he walked up to one of the officers and began to stroke his face. "You should be more understanding," Allen told him. "You must learn to love, not hate."

The officer pulled back, aghast, flung open the back door of the police car, and yelled, "Get in, you're under arrest." Allen climbed in, and they drove off.

As they rode along, the officer said, "Say, you're Allen Ginsberg, aren't you?"

Allen nodded modestly.

"The poet?"

Allen nodded again.

The cop got furious all over again. "Now why would a famous man like you, a man who knows so much about life, want to get mixed up in a street fight?" he asked. "Now get out and be a good boy." He stopped the car and Allen climbed out.

On November 22, 1963, Allen was sitting at the kitchen table eating some eggs, when Neal rushed in and yelled, "Kennedy's been shot!"

"What? Where?"

"In Texas. He's dead. What do you think will happen?" asked Neal.

"The country will go into a tailspin," Allen replied.

They turned on the television and watched as Lee Harvey Oswald was described as a pro-Castro leftist. The assassination was called a Communist plot, and even the liberal Fair Play for Cuba Committee was dubbed a violent organization. There was an orgy of anti-left feeling propagated by television and the media, which went on for weeks, most of it having no bearing on the killing at all. The outpouring of hate, represented by the assassination itself and the media reaction to it, strengthened Allen's desire to get his message of love and peace across before the country was consumed by a wave of neo-McCarthyism. Many people found his views shocking.

His vision of universal love applied to every area of politics, including his views on Israel and the Jews. Although normally reluctant to appear in anthologies of Jewish poetry or to be interviewed by Jewish magazines, he spoke four days after the assassination of Kennedy to Leland Meyerzove, the editor of the Jewish magazine *The Burning Bush*. With Kennedy's death and the burgeoning civil rights movement very much in mind, Meyerzove asked two questions: What should be the Jew's relationship to the Negro? What was Allen's opinion about American and Israeli Jews?

"I think Jews should start making it with Negroes," Allen said. "My Jewish family in New Jersey doesn't have any Negro friends—and they think they are big liberals—and they really would get upset if one of their daughters married a Negro. . . . When my brother brought home this Southern Baptist minister's daughter as a bride, then my grandmother, God rest her soul, took him aside into the bathroom and started pinching his arm in anger. In other words, Jewish race consciousness is built upon the same stuff that killed President Kennedy, to the extent that it excludes other human images as clan to its family consciousness. . . .

"And the trouble with the Israelis is that they are *Jewish*, they were hypnotized by the Nazis and all the other racist magic hypnotists of previous eras. Astonishing mirror image resemblance between Nazi theory of racial superiority and Jewish hang-up as chosen race. They didn't desire it—any of them. Any fixed categorized image of the Self is a big goof. Open wide the doors of the future! Hurrah! Messiah has come!"

Needless to say, his position did not endear him to his family or to some of his friends, particularly during the various Arab-Israeli wars, but he always stuck to it, refusing to make racial distinctions or to take sides just because of his Jewish ancestry.

Allen returned to New York in December of 1963. He was met by Eugene at La Guardia Airport and driven out to Long Island to stay awhile with his brother's family. It had been almost three years.

Eugene and Connie now had five children, including their new baby, Anne. Allen also spent a few weeks in Paterson, telling Louis and Edith his traveler's tales and catching up on their news. While Allen was in San Francisco, Peter had hitchhiked at remarkable speed through the Middle East and Europe to London. He reached New York in November, a month before Allen got there.

Allen made an attempt to see Kerouac during a visit with Peter to the Orlovsky clan in Northport. Allen hid in the bushes, as before, while Peter knocked on the door, but Jack's mother turned him away. Allen telephoned Jack four times in one week, but no one answered. He decided that Jack must have a signal system, so he phoned, let it ring three times, then hung up and dialed again. Kerouac's mother answered and said that Jack was not home. Allen asked her to give Jack his number, but she refused and hung up. Exasperated, Allen wrote to Jack: "I think she's carrying things too far. Goddamit what's the matter at your house?" Kerouac methodically labeled and filed the letter but did not reply.

Allen and Peter stayed with Ted Wilentz and his wife. Wilentz had handled many of Allen's affairs while he was in Europe and India and had published *Empty Mirror* under his Corinth Press imprint in 1960. He also published Kerouac's *Scripture of the Golden Eternity* and books by LeRoi Jones, Gary Snyder, Philip Whalen, and Diane di Prima, as well as *The Beat Scene*, a heavily illustrated poetry anthology, which spread not only the new poetry but images of the Beat life-style around the world. Allen and Peter occupied the room of Wilentz's daughter, away at college. One of their first visitors was the journalist Al Aronowitz, who showed up one day with his friend Bob Dylan.

Dylan's career was taking off; his *Freewheelin' Bob Dylan* had sold so well that Columbia Records took him back into the studio that September and rush-released the results: *The Times They Are a-Changin'*, the ultimate protest album of the period. Dylan himself was also changing—his CORE worker girlfriend left him and he met Joan Baez. He was distancing himself from the civil rights movement and the folk circles surrounding Woody Guthrie, where he got his start. Leaving Greenwich Village, he moved in with his manager, Albert Grossman, in Woodstock, New York.

Dylan was familiar with Allen's work and that of the other Beat writers, and Allen, in his turn, was interested in the author of "A Hard Rain's A-Gonna Fall" and "Masters of War." They talked about poetry and got along very well. Dylan was about to play a concert in Chicago and invited Allen to fly out with him, but Allen was too busy looking for an apartment and getting back into New York, and also too proud. "I thought he was just a folksinger, and I was also afraid I might become his slave or something, his mascot."

The meeting with Bob Dylan had a curious outcome. Dylan owned the manuscript of a group of Allen's rhymed poems from 1948 to 1952, which Allen had assumed was lost forever; he had neglected to make copies of many of the poems before he let the folder out of his hands. He had been unable to get the poems published in New York, so when a friend left for London, Allen gave her the manuscript on the off chance that she might meet someone who would be interested in publishing it there. The manuscript passed from hand to hand, and when Dylan was in London, someone gave it to him, knowing his interest in Allen and the Beat Generation. He returned it when Allen went to visit him in Woodstock. *Gates of Wrath* was published by Don Allen at Grey Fox Press in 1972.

Shortly after they met, Allen went with Dylan to a concert in Princeton. Photographs taken backstage appeared on the sleeve of Dylan's album *Bringing It All Back Home*. Allen was shown clean-shaven and wearing a smart top hat. Filmmaker Barbara Rubin was in one of the pictures, ruffling Dylan's hair. Allen had been introduced to Barbara by Jonas Mekas. Barbara had short dark hair and big eyes that seemed always to be darting around the room, checking who was there. The way she held her jaw suggested that she was impatient for you to finish speaking. Much of her time was spent trying to figure out how she could fit people into her various schemes. Barbara took enormous quantities of acid. When they met, Barbara at once took Allen to Mekas's Film-Makers Cooperative nearby, to see her experimental film *Christmas on Earth*. Allen was very impressed by it.

"It was a lot of porn, beauty, in which she made an art object out of her vagina. I thought that was in the right spirit. We got into a very funny rapport, we were just there alone, and we actually ended up screwing on the floor that very night. She was really young and pretty and I liked her." Her method of filmmaking consisted largely of swinging the camera around her head. She superimposed the film strips on each other to make flowing, abstract images, so it didn't really matter much what the raw material was.

In the first week of 1964, Allen and Peter moved to 704 East 5th Street. Their apartment was very light, and they could see the towers of Wall Street over the rooftops from the back windows. They bought a rug and found furniture on the streets; Allen made himself a sawhorse desk. Their Chinese scrolls and Tibetan tankas were hung on the freshly painted white walls.

In San Francisco, Allen had begun work on a movie script of "Kaddish" with Robert Frank, but the writing had not gone well. Now he spent most of his time with Frank, blocking out the script and elaborating on all the details about Naomi. Allen became part of the new underground film scene. He wrote Ferlinghetti: "The Lower East Side movie world here is really thrilling, like a poetry renaissance, excitement, parties, tragedies, masterpieces in lofts, etc. Best thing in NY."

Films were being made everywhere, but Andy Warhol's silver-lined Factory was the most prolific studio of them all. Warhol had made his first films in 1963: *Kiss, Haircut, Eat,* and the eight-hour *Sleep.* They were followed by such as *Blow Job* and *Tarzan and Jane Regained . . . Sort Of.* Warhol filmed every day. Whoever dropped by was the star of that afternoon's film. Many of the films were never screened, many were never even given a title. Reels got lost or stolen or borrowed. He made one of Allen, Jack Kerouac, and Gregory Corso, in his "Couch" series, three-minute silents of people sitting on the Factory couch, but perversely he shot it from the side, so that it was difficult to see what was happening or who was who.

Allen usually went to the Factory with Barbara, who was very involved with Warhol through her film work. Allen renewed his friendship with Warhol's assistant, the poet Gerard Malanga; in 1958, Malanga had organized a poetry festival at Wagner College on Staten Island, in which Allen took part. It was Malanga's job to silk-screen the paintings of Marilyn and Elvis, the car crashes, and the flowers that became Warhol's most famous images. When Allen met him, Warhol was working on his giant Elvis Presley images and paintings in the "Car Crash" series. Allen could see certain parallels between Warhol's Factory and his own place. Despite the drugs and sex and madness, there was always work going on. Describing the Factory years later, Ginsberg said, "There were people taken in to work with them, to work with their neurosis and work with their colorfulness and maybe turn it to artistic advantage and value, and maybe get therapy that way. I always thought it seemed like a good project."

Allen did not get very involved in the Warhol scene, in part because of the pervasive amphetamine use; Allen had already seen its destructive effect on his friends. Half the people hanging around Allen's apartment were taking Methedrine, and it would have been foolish to expose Peter to even more at the Factory. "I was interested in the films, the civil liberties, and the beautiful boys he had," said Ginsberg. "But they were unobtainable or in another realm of some sort. I didn't find any serious Angels there to talk to who wanted to know about poetry." Over the next several years, Warhol invited Allen to screenings and his parties, but Allen mostly saw him in the back room at Max's Kansas City, which opened early in 1966 and was virtually the private club room of Warhol and his so-called superstars.

Two big legal campaigns preoccupied Allen in the spring of 1964. The city was insisting that in order for coffeehouses to hold poetry readings, they should meet cabaret standards, with sprinklers, fire exits, and kitchen flues; since most of their customers bought only one coffee a night, this was clearly uneconomic. It meant the end of the free readings at Le Metro and other popular haunts. In a model lobbying campaign, Allen and ACLU lawyers petitioned the various politicians involved and won the case.

Simultaneously he was testifying, along with Susan Sontag, in defense of Jonas Mekas, who was charged with obscenity for screening Jack Smith's *Flaming Creatures* and Jean Genet's *Chant d'Amour*. He spent hours on the phone with lawyers and journalists, concerned poets, filmmakers, and coffeehouse owners. His telephone rang continuously.

He also engaged in a frenzy of literary activity, self-publishing Burroughs's *Roosevelt Routine*, which had been censored from *The Yage Letters*, editing Huncke's stories, writing introductions, and pestering editors. He went on TV shows and revised foreign-language proofs of his books. He got no poetry written but enjoyed himself enormously.

Allen still saw Jack from time to time and continued to behave as if there were a real friendship between them. He listened to Jack's late-night drunken anti-Semitic phone calls, trying to reason with him. Sometimes, however, he just hung up on him: A journal note of May 12, 1964, read: "I had cut him off the phone yesterday dawn when he began repeating some accusations against Jews—'All the bureaucrats of Soviet Hungary are Jewish'—called drunk, I was sleepy." Most people would have written Kerouac off long before

their relationship reached this stage, but Allen's enormous tolerance and understanding of madness enabled him to persist and still
find value in their friendship. Ginsberg described their relationship
in a lecture: "So, from 1963 on, the relationship was—contentious,
sometimes close, odd, occasionally he'd come by, really drunk, and
want me to blow him, and get very insistent. 'Nobody loves me,
c'mon, give me a blow job! You're a fairy, give me a blow job!
Nobody loves me, I'm too fat and old and redfaced. I'm lonesome!'
Careless. He didn't give a shit anymore, what I thought or what
anybody thought."

Spring came, and Gregory Corso arrived from Cleveland with his
wife, Sally, and their baby girl. They moved in with Allen. Robert
LaVigne was also staying. The days grew warmer, then turned hot
and muggy. There were riots in Harlem. Cassius Clay took the
world championship from Sonny Liston. *Dr. Strangelove* was released, and Rudy Gernreich marketed topless bathing suits. The
sixties were getting into their stride. Allen moved into high gear,
answering letters and writing poetry, mostly at night when the other
people in the house were asleep and there were fewer telephone
calls. He would often finish up watching the dawn break over the
city, the saffron-colored drapes blowing out of the window in the
summer breeze, as the first gruff Puerto Rican voices of the day
drifted up to him from the street below. He wrote: "How I love the
poetry of the lovely roofs, the city purring muffled in the cars."

He and Peter took Peter's brother Julius out of Central Islip
Hospital, where he had been living for the previous twelve years,
and brought him back to live on East Fifth Street. After a few weeks
of silence, Julius began to talk nonstop. "Do you want to live or
die?" Allen asked him.

"I don't know," said Julius.

Allen began to visit the Kerista collective, a Lower East Side
commune of about eighteen people living in a storefront on Ludlow
Street, described as "a sort of benign Manson family" by Rosebud
Felieu, who lived there. She described Allen's first visit: "He was
always hot for whatever was new on the scene and this was one of
the first weird drug sex communities around at that time. Everyone
there was very odd, like very skinny or fat or nervous. They all
thought Allen was bad news because he had an ego or something
but I thought he was amazingly funny and kind." She didn't know
who he was when he arrived, but he looked very sweet, so she sat
on his lap, tickled him, and asked him his name. "Allen was pretty

surprised I think that some school girl liked him just for being a fine guy." He told her if she ever needed a place to stay, to come over to his place; she did.

Allen and Peter had big orgies with Rosebud and with Ann, who lived next door, the English poet Harry Fainlight, a local poet named Szabo, and many others. Ann would drag her mattress across the hall to Allen and Peter's floor. Allen wrote Charles Olson: "Been making it with some nice young girls and boys—what a pleasure to be a clean old man—More I see it I think there is a big sex upsurge revolution which will alter and enlarge family unit—long house—with everybody making it like on the bed in Vancouver. Huge pot-love circle here in Lower East Side busted this week."

It was also in 1964 that Allen met Maretta Greer, a painfully thin blond mendicant, who had just returned from India. She presented herself at his door and said that she had heard of his interest in Eastern philosophy and wanted to meet him. "She needed a place to stay," said Ginsberg, "and she was mystical and pretty and we immediately got on." She was to be his girlfriend on and off for a number of years, whenever she was not in India. There was always room for another young person in the apartment.

Sally Corso returned to Cleveland with the baby, leaving Gregory in New York. In September, he cracked up and had to be taken to the hospital, "raving on goofballs, screaming about the baby," Allen noted. Gregory calmed down, visited his family in Cleveland, then went to stay with friends in Buffalo.

Haydée Santamaría, the Cuban minister of culture, invited Allen to attend a writers' conference in January 1965 at the Casa de las Americas in Havana. The Cuban government would pay all expenses. He could fly there from Mexico City, but because of pressure from the United States, Mexico would not give reentry permits to travelers from Cuba, so he would have to return via Prague. Allen accepted the invitation with alacrity, and was even pleased by the cumbersome travel arrangements, because he thought that he stood a very good chance of finally reaching Moscow if he got as far as Prague. The State Department initially refused to issue him the required travel permit, but Allen's lawyer threatened an injunction, and the State Department gave in.

Ken Kesey and his Merry Pranksters arrived in New York in November, with Neal Cassady at the wheel of their famous bus. They immediately telephoned Allen, and he and Peter went to see them at the luxurious Park Avenue apartment in the Eighties where they were staying. Allen and Peter got there at about 1 A.M. The psychedelic bus, with its "Further" destination sign, and its ad, "A Vote for Goldwater Is a Vote for Fun," was parked across the street. In the elegant apartment, the Pranksters were jumping all over the furniture, filming each other to the rhythm of the Grateful Dead. They were smoking a lot of pot, and several were high on acid. Although Neal was completely exhausted from his driving, he continued out to Northport to collect Jack. Kerouac was unwilling to come, but Neal cajoled him and he finally relented.

It was a tradition with the Merry Pranksters to celebrate the American flag; they wore stars and stripes on their shoes, on their teeth, and on their faces, so in honor of Kerouac's arrival they draped a huge flag over the couch for him to sit on. Jack picked it up and carefully folded it. Allen took note: "He very carefully folded up the flag as an object lesson, how to treat the flag and respect it, which I thought was a bit reactionary. After all, he didn't have to go to that length." Jack was withdrawn and silent. He occasionally slugged from a wine bottle, but he turned down all offers of pot or acid.

It was Neal's big moment, introducing his new hero, Ken Kesey, to his old hero, Jack Kerouac. It was almost impossible for them to talk in that atmosphere. The situation must have been particularly confusing to Kerouac, who, apart from a few drinking buddies at the local bar, was isolated and had no idea what was going on with young people in the sixties. He didn't know who the Merry Pranksters were or their orientation or philosophy. Kerouac didn't say much. Ginsberg thought later: "To Jack, when he came in, it must have looked like a bunch of weirdo apes jumping up and down in a cage."

On November 11, Allen and Peter flew to Boston as guests of Harvard, where Allen was scheduled to give four readings. These were the first public readings in which he sang as part of his performance. He and Peter chanted mantras, using Peter's harmonium as accompaniment. At Brandeis University, Allen gave a seventy-minute ecstatic, tearful reading of the whole of "Kaddish," which astonished the audience and moved many of them to tears. Fortunately, it was recorded, and in January 1965, Allen signed a contract with Jerry Wexler at Atlantic Records to release it as an album. Allen and Peter spent long evenings visiting old friends and drinking at the Harvard Tavern, and they slept with so many people, male and female, that they were banished from Harvard's Lowell Hall by their hosts and had to stay with friends for the remainder of their visit. After three weeks of poetry and orgies, they returned to New York to find that local Methedrine freaks had broken into the apartment and stolen all of the Tibetan tankas and scrolls they had collected on their travels. Many books were missing and also Allen's typewriter.

For years, Allen had been speaking out in favor of the legalization of marijuana; now he got together with the poet Ed Sanders and others and founded LeMar, whose aim was to legalize marijuana. On December 27, 1964, they staged their initial demonstration, probably the first of its kind. The nearest piece of federal property they could find was the Department of Welfare building on the Lower East Side. Here, nineteen men and women gathered to demonstrate in favor of legalization. Allen carried a sign that read "Smoke Pot, It's Cheaper." Two bored policemen and a handful of puzzled local people looked on, but it was too cold for a big crowd to gather. Interviewed by the New York *Herald Tribune*, Allen said that he thought marijuana would be legalized in the United States within five years.

On January 11, he flew to Boston again, this time to testify along with Norman Mailer and John Ciardi at the obscenity trial of *Naked Lunch*. Eloquently, he praised Burroughs's ear for common speech, quoted lines of pure poetry from the text, and pointed out the high moral tone of the book. He expressed admiration for Burroughs's courage to make such a total confession and said that the book had influenced him greatly, "particularly because it was such an enormous breakthrough into truthful expression of exactly really what was going on in his head, with no holds barred. He really confessed completely, put everything down so that anybody could see it." They lost the case, but Grove Press appealed, and on July 7, 1966, the Massachusetts Supreme Court finally declared *Naked Lunch* not obscene, reversing the earlier decision by the Superior Court of Boston and removing the threat of a nationwide ban on the book.

THIRTEEN | THE KING OF MAY

It's another universe here, rather a shock in fact—not much place for a dribbling subconscious to sit down.

—A.G.

GINSBERG WAS UNPREPARED FOR CUBA. HE HAD NOT STUDIED THE HIS-tory of the country or the revolution and could not adjust to the radically different life-style the people there were forging for them-selves. He appeared unaware of the pressure being put on Cuba by the United States. The U.S. had tried to invade the country and had set up an economic blockade, which was very damaging to the Cuban economy, making it more reliant on the socialist countries than Castro would have liked. Cuba was struggling to build enough schools and hospitals to educate and provide medical care for its people, while developing its industry to self-sufficiency in the face of the American deterrent.

The delegates to the writers' conference were put up at the Ha-vana Riviera, a luxury hotel built by Meyer Lansky and the mob during the corrupt regime of Fulgencio Batista. Now it was one of the few hotels where foreign visitors could stay. Allen was given a huge room overlooking the Caribbean.

During his first foray to explore Havana's nightlife, he was ap-proached by three youths, who asked whether he was Allen Gins-berg. They had been trying to reach him all day at the hotel. The youths published a literary magazine called *El Puente* (The Bridge) but said that the people responsible for funding were conservatives and didn't give them much financing.

They all went to a nightclub, where the youths got tipsy and complained about the crackdown on homosexuals by the special police division Lacra Social and about arrests in the street of "Sick" types, a term derived from the "sick" jokes and cynical Beat Generation humor associated with the comedian Mort Sahl. However, they told Allen, they supported the revolution. They spoke quite freely and openly about the situation in Cuba. When Allen said that he thought Cuba should put an end to capital punishment, they told him to tell Fidel his views. Allen had not realized that he might actually meet Castro, but they said, "Sure you will."

Havana had a very Mediterranean feel to it. Since the revolution, all available resources had been channeled into the countryside, so Havana looked like a shabby, sleepy Spanish city, with peeling paintwork and potholed roads. Yet there were sudden views of the intense blue Caribbean, and palm trees waved lazily over the rooftops. Each morning, Allen woke to the sounds of crowing roosters: chickens were kept on the rooftops. Then came the deep-throated roar of the Havana rush hour, as thousands of ancient American cars chugged through the streets, emitting clouds of black smoke.

On his second day in Havana, Allen met the assistant editor of *Cuba* magazine. Although he had been in Cuba less than forty-eight hours, Allen began complaining about Lacra Social, saying that its policies toward homosexuals, marijuana, and the "Sick" youths of La Rampa Street had led to the arrest of a number of people, many of them teenage poets from the Writers Union, wrongly suspected of being homosexuals just because they wore tight blue jeans and beards. That was the beginning of Allen's troubles.

Naturally, the man from *Cuba* was very interested to hear Allen's views and told them to his colleagues. Allen had not realized that in a country with a population about as big as that of New York City, gossip, personal contacts, and meetings often constituted the social debate. In fact, two of Cuba's leading poets had already visited the minister of the interior and complained to him about the persecution of homosexuals on La Rampa. Not only was the persecution stopped; Lacra Social was dissolved. That was how things were done.

After dinner that second day, Allen was interviewed by a well-dressed, bearded reporter from *Hoy*. They were interrupted by a telephone call from the lobby. Two youths from *El Puente* had brought their translation of "Kaddish" but had been prevented from going up to his room. Allen rushed downstairs in anger, dragging the reporter with him as a "witness." The hotel officials directed Allen to the official government guide, who explained that hotel rules forbade visitors to the rooms because of the large number of whores hanging around and also because visiting farmers had a habit of bringing chickens and even cows with them, which they tried to put into the elevator. However, in this case, the boys would be allowed up, "as long as they can identify themselves."

The guide was clearly embarrassed by Allen's anger; many European hotels had the same rules. One of the youths, José Mario, had his Writers Union identification with him, but Manuel Ballagas had nothing but his manuscript of "Kaddish," which Ginsberg clumsily seized and thrust in front of the guide's nose, saying, "That's *his* identification. He translates some texts of mine." Then Allen, realizing that he had overreacted and that the boys had already been given permission to go up, added, "Besides, the doctor told me to stay inside and not go out [he had flu] . . . so obviously I have to receive people upstairs, journalists, poets, et cetera." The situation was saved.

They sat talking in Allen's room until midnight. Allen corrected the seventeen-year-old Ballagas's translation of "Kaddish" and quizzed him about the persecution of homosexuals. He dictated to the *Hoy* reporter a page-long appreciation of the revolution, which was mostly sympathetic but complained about the persecution of homosexuals by Lacra Social, and ended by quoting Voznesensky: "Communism comes from the heart." What would Allen ask Fidel Castro if he met him? the reporter asked. He would ask about the persecution of "Sicks" and homosexuals, ask why marijuana was not legalized, and suggest that Cuba end capital punishment. Rather than execute bomb-throwing terrorists, Allen said, they should give them magic mushrooms and jobs as elevator men at the Havana Riviera Hotel.

Since these remarks seemed unlikely to get into print, Allen tried to put crude pressure on the reporter by saying that if Blas Rosa, the editor of *Hoy*, wouldn't publish the interview, Allen would write about it in *Evergreen Review*, and his article would be translated into French and seen by Jean-Paul Sartre and other supporters of the Cuban revolution.

His flu was better next day. He had been invited to dinner by María Rosa Almendres, the head of Casa de las Americas. In conversation, her husband agreed with Allen that there was no free press in the American sense: "But so what? Everybody knows everybody! You can always complain to Fidel, or take up a grievance with someone in power."

That night, Allen watched Castro on television: "A real hairy creature for president," he wrote in his journal. "Ten times more natural than Johnson, in fact human . . . One finger up—talks rapidly like Cassady." Allen completed the night's journal entry with the line: "Communism / Socialism / Revolution, constantly under discussion. I'm obsessed with Lacra Social."

The next day, a nineteen-year-old youth, Reglo Guerrero, brought a handwritten poem for his opinion. They were interrupted by Nate González Frere from *Revolución*, come to interview him. Both had been prevented from going up in the elevator without permission, but the Cultural Friendship Office gave it immediately. Allen got angry when the journalist said the policy made sense because of the whores, the farmers with their cows, the thieves, and especially the counterrevolutionaries, who might seek publicity by attacking a foreign visitor. As one of the few places where visiting government officials and foreign guests stayed, the hotel was a terrorist target. But it was no use; the elevator, along with the disbanded Lacra Social, became something of an idée fixe for him during his stay in Cuba.

In his interview with Frere, he discussed the changes in American poetry caused by William Carlos Williams and described the Lower East Side scene. He explained Indian mantras to her and then spent an hour complaining about Lacra Social. She told him that she couldn't report his views on that because her interest was in literary matters, and in any case, Lacra Social, which she agreed had been terrible, had been dissolved. "Oh, no!" said Allen, relying on the street gossip of his teenage informant. "They arrested a boy on La Rampa last week."

The conference got under way with a big meeting at Casa de las Americas. Haydée Santamaría explained the rules of the poetry competition they were to judge: "Give the prize to the best work outside of politics and go talk to anyone you want."

Allen's complaint that *Hoy* wouldn't publish his interview on the "socialist acceptance of homosexuals" had repercussions. *Hoy* sent another reporter, who wanted to know why Allen had proposed such a strange subject. Was he serious? Was he saying it to shock? The Cubans genuinely could not understand what he was talking about. Even in the United States, his views were controversial, but at least his fellow Americans could understand them. To the Cubans, whose primary concerns were building hospitals and schools and teaching the mostly illiterate population to read and write, Ginsberg's preoccupation with homosexuals, Lacra Social, and the legalization of marijuana was incomprehensible.

He noted in his journal: "Having had this interview already over and over, it's become an obsessional subject of explanation, like I'm sick of it and my own opinions, except the whole lack of communication on the subject indicates either I'm neurotic special case out of step with the universe, or they're just plain insensitive—So I have to go into long painful explanations of why I lust for boys and men and that gets sticky. Wound up trying explaining my early image of women was affected by my mother died in a bughouse. The journalist was very sympathetic but altogether the point was lost."

He got down to the serious work of reading the submissions for the competition. He was faced with ninety-one manuscripts, all carbon copies and all in Spanish. He was pleased when the young poet Manuel Ballagas came by to help him out.

The next morning, Ballagas telephoned Allen with the news that when Allen's limousine dropped him off the previous night, Ballagas had been taken to the police station and questioned. Ever since the Bay of Pigs, the police were paying particular attention to anyone consorting with foreigners, particularly with Americans. Ballagas was taken home, and his mother had to sign a paper promising that she would bring him to the station if they ever wanted to see him. It was not a serious matter.

Two more reporters from *Hoy* interviewed Allen that day. Allen gave them a long literary interview about exploring consciousness by association rather than by metaphor. He told them that he was gay but liked girls and that he smoked pot, then asked them about the persecution of gays in Cuba. They responded, "You must understand the Revolution is more concerned with basic issues like raising production, feeding and educating the people, cutting sugar and defending ourselves from US pressure. Later on these aesthetic issues can be discussed."

That evening, a large group of delegates went to hear the new "feeling" music. Allen sneaked Ballagas and a few other young writers into the delegates' free box. Afterward, as he sat writing in his hotel room, he received a call: Ballagas and another poet had been arrested as they left the theater.

María Rosa Almendres tried to explain the situation to Allen. "Perhaps you don't understand how hard we have to struggle to keep the Revolution clean. You have to understand that the stupid ones, the squares here, think it's bad for us to have the young ones washing our dirty linen in public, discussing problems with foreigners. After all, *we* have to struggle with the conflicts, and worse, with threats from outside, not you!" She was obviously irritated by Allen's lack of understanding.

Allen had an appointment to see the minister of culture the next morning. He described her in his journal: "Looks about 45, Russian, blonde buxom, talks like a woman making a speech to high school girls, too rapidly and with too much authority, as if her words were some kind of governmental policy, which it is, which is dangerous, since she doesn't know much more about psychic life than my Aunt Clare."

Allen's harsh assessment was not shared by the Cubans, who held her in high regard. Haydée Santamaría was a great hero of the revolution. She took part in the famous raid on Moncada barracks with Castro in 1953. Captured and jailed, she was forced to watch as her brother and his fiancée were tortured to death by Batista's troops. When she was released, in 1955, she joined Castro and the rebels in the hills and was later made a member of the Revolutionary Council. She could have had virtually any high position in the government, but her passion for the arts led her to choose the Ministry of Culture.

Explaining to Allen the need for society to deal with homosexuals who made a spectacle in public and seduced unformed young people, she told him that the *El Puente* youths were filling his head with gossipy complaints. Allen interrupted to ask about the problem of the boys in jail (they had been held only three hours, but he didn't know that at the time). They talked at cross-purposes for a while, but Santamaría promised to investigate how such a mistake could have been made and told him the boys would be released.

As she left the room, Allen reached over and gave her a slap on the backside. Within an hour, ten people had come up to ask Allen what he had done to insult her so. It was almost as if he *wanted* to be deported.

Allen began to feel nostalgic for his New York City scene and wrote: "All these people, even old Paris fairies here, all going around saying that they don't think it's right elders seduce the young. They have absolutely no idea what goes on—Oh for my New

York bed full of teenage boys and lost wandering Tibetan / Amphetamine girls of 20." Rather than meet Castro and the others who made the revolution, to find out about it firsthand, Allen preferred to hang out with the *El Puente* crowd. Certainly much of his time was spent trying to seduce one of the *El Puente* youths, with eventual success.

The next evening at dinner, he overheard criticism of the *El Puente* boys for complaining to Allen. Apparently, gossip about them was everywhere. Allen now became paranoid, fearful of the situation he had created. His own gossip was coming back to him, fifth hand, transformed almost beyond recognition, undoubtedly partly as a result of his faulty Spanish. In his journal for February 7, he wrote: "Total collapse today—woke totally isolated, didn't know who to talk to to confide in. . . . Entering Orwellian dreamworld—Total suppression of conscious and unconscious fantasy everywhere. . . . Can't trust anyone. Like having a nervous breakdown, 'I got the fear.' "

Another of the boys who had shown Allen his poems was taken in for routine questioning, detained for several hours, then released. A group that had invited Allen to read his poems at the university had the reading canceled by the rector, and the students were advised not to have private meetings with Ginsberg. Allen was asked not to go with the rest of the delegates to a meeting with Prime Minister Dorticos. María Rosa Almendres had a long meeting with Haydée Santamaría and reported that Haydée was very angry with him. Had he said that Raul Castro was a fairy and that he wanted to sleep with him? Allen had said it, but he couldn't remember to whom. There was also a lot of gossip around the Casa because Allen had told a reporter that he had had a sex fantasy about Che Guevara. In a country that was 85 percent Catholic, such statements were bound to be controversial and offensive, particularly to people who had fought alongside Raul or Che, and most particularly coming from an American.

At the conference, Allen gave a slow, deliberate explanation of poetry as an exploration and expansion of consciousness. Speaking in Spanish, he explained the technical means that he had adopted for this purpose: dreams, waking fantasies, marijuana, mushrooms, peyote, spontaneous composition. He explained meditation, yoga, and mantra singing by comparing them to the trance state induced by the dancing and chanting in Santeria ceremonies of the African Elequa cult, which in 1965 had a million adherents in Cuba. He amplified his explanation with a lengthy catalog of antibrainwashing techniques that could be used for combating universal sloganism, dogmatism, and mass-media hypnosis, concentrating on an explanation of the cut-up technique of William Burroughs. This part of his lecture was probably not understood by most of his audience, and he was hampered by not having the appropriate texts. Out of concern for the Casa, he did not speak about any controversial subject.

On February 3, Allen was wakened by a phone call from a professor at the University School of Letters, canceling his Walt Whitman lecture. That day, the delegates were all taken in cars to a luncheon at the Old Country Club. Waiters circulated with ice-cold rum drinks. When Haydée Santamaría arrived, she went up to Allen, shook hands, and launched into a long monologue that he was unable to follow because her Spanish was so rapid. He calmed himself by inwardly repeating a mantra a couple of times. She was telling Allen the facts of the revolution: "We have established 20,000 schools, and we need more cement. Work and cement is our need. Afterwards will come other matters." After a while, Allen shifted the conversation.

"There's one thing I want to clear up," he said. "Perhaps you misunderstood. You see, when I left you last time, I was quite happy and relieved at the rapport we had and felt so good I slapped you. Sort of exuberant and affectionate. I hope you didn't misunderstand. In my country . . ." He had trouble pronouncing the words, because he had already consumed three of the delicious iced rum drinks, and they seemed to be affecting his command of Spanish.

She tried to explain to him that he had formed his bohemian ideas in another country and that they didn't apply in Cuba. She mentioned his use of marijuana, which was illegal in Cuba. "It has always been a crime and it's definitely a crime and that's how it must be for the time being. That's the policy we've adopted." Allen said that he was aware it was illegal and was only trying to introduce some legitimate information into the discussion of marijuana as a social problem. He reported the conversation in his journal:

"She replied, leaning now against the piano and apparently willing to talk to me for a while—which surprised and excited me and I began to relax—getting into it—huge room full of artists and functionaries all dressed up and she the chief personage there, and here I was all involved alone talking to her—a kind of egotistical amazement at the position I found myself in, being such a serious / embarrassing problem for her to handle—'Yes, but we have work to do and cannot afford these extra luxuries which impede the senses. . . . We have to raise the young children here with revolutionary ideals . . . the Revolution is for them, the life, the reason for being. . . . Though you may discuss such matters [as marijuana] with people on a high level or mature officials, you understand we cannot have you spreading such ideas which are against the laws of our country and our policy among the young people. They are too young, too impressionable. You came as a foreigner and invited here by us as a great poet of fame, and we cannot support that you spread ideas to the young against our own policies that we have arrived at. . . .' "

Tom Maschler, the chief editor of Jonathan Cape in London and a close friend of Allen's, strolled by, and Allen introduced him. Maschler, who had just published John Lennon's *A Spaniard in the Works*, suggested that the Cuban government invite the Beatles as a gesture of world harmony and as a propaganda gesture. Allen excitedly seconded the idea, saying how well loved the Beatles were by the youth in the U.S.

Santamaría replied that very few people in Cuba knew who the Beatles were, and besides, they had no ideology. "Yes," said Maschler. "But they're like Frank Sinatra, the young girls swoon over them and weep. If you want to attract the young, invite the Beatles."

Santamaría patiently explained that they wanted to build something permanent: a life and a hope for the future; the revolution wasn't a marketing exercise. "Without a true ideology, a true understanding of life, there can be no future for the young. . . . The Beatles will come and it will be like our Fiesta. Everybody will be excited for a few days and then that will be the end of it. We want to give our people something *more*. Some truth and work and food."

Allen and Maschler explained that it would change U.S. State Department policy and end the cold war if Cuba and the Beatles accepted each other joyfully and that it would cause the brainwashed children of the States to see Cuba in another, friendly light.

The music of the Beatles and their iconoclastic personalities had catapulted them to superstardom by 1965. Their film *Help!* had recently been released, and they were about to record *Rubber Soul*, a radical departure in pop music, which pointed the way to *Sgt. Pepper*, recorded two years later. The idea that a Beatles concert in

Havana would improve U.S.-Cuban relations illustrated the lack of comprehension between Allen and Haydée Santamaría. To the Cubans and their supporters, one of the most important points of the Cuban Revolution was that a Latin American country had removed itself from the American sphere of influence.

Despite his misgivings, Allen still felt able to enter in his journal for February 4: "They obviously do have a tough struggle to survive, that their defiance and resentment of US obnoxious intrusion and blockade is understandable completely, and even their blank dumb miscomprehension of my own queer rare literacy extravaganza, and they do suffer too much to take it easy." He began teaching American poetry informally at the Writers Union, reading from Creeley's *For Love* and Williams's *Collected Poems*. He felt that things had lightened up and people were getting used to him.

Allen had arranged to visit Yves Espin, an architect who knew and liked his poetry. He had been educated at MIT and was Raul Castro's brother-in-law. Picking Allen up at the hotel, Espin drove him to his fine apartment on the Vedado, where a group of his elegantly dressed friends had gathered and were drinking rum and ice water. Allen was the center of attention, and they asked him many questions, including, inevitably, what did he think of the revolution? Allen liked the look of them, so he answered honestly.

"Too much suppression of communication of unconscious content, dreams, fantasies, intuitions and jokes here. Actually too much fear. Everybody in Cuba secretly thinks they're anti-revolutionary in *one* part of their soul, so everybody's afraid. Actually the words 'revolutionary' and 'counter-revolutionary' have lost their meaning and are just a fear stereotype now. How could an artist sit down and write blind poesy and know in advance if it would be categorized as pro or anti? If he thought about it he'd be paralyzed. If a big Dostoyevsky, with no sense of guilt, and a huge brown humor, wrote a novel here about Lacra Social and terrible in-group club and art-school, and everybody's sex lives and Marxist dogma and gossip, could it be published here? Nobody here wants that kind of genius art!"

Espin laughed and agreed with him: "They'd never publish it here." Allen, relaxed, sat on the floor and talked about magic mushrooms, Tim Leary, and Hitler's sex life with Eva Braun. He drank and sang the Shiva mantra with his finger cymbals. Espin and his wife were charming, friendly, and relaxed, and the party went on into the night. It was 2 A.M. when Espin drove Allen back to his hotel. Just as he was going to bed, Caballo, a Mexican dramatist, telephoned and said, "Ginsberg! We're all here having a party. Come and join us!" Allen immediately pulled on his white Indian pajamas, donned both sets of his Chango beads, put finger cymbals and cigarettes in his pockets, and walked barefoot to the room.

For the first time, all the *invitados* were gathered in one small room, happy, drinking. They shouted greetings and applauded Allen's late arrival in costume. Songs were sung, and the party eventually disintegrated into a drunken political argument. Allen got back to his room at 5 A.M. and fell into a deep sleep.

Three hours later, he awoke to a sudden knock on his door. Scrambling into his pajamas, he opened the door to someone from ICAP, the cultural organization. The man was accompanied by three soldiers in neatly pressed olive-green uniforms. Allen was told to dress immediately and bring all his belongings. They were going to the immigration department, where the chief wanted to see him.

"I realized the jig was up," Allen wrote later that day, "and got a cold chill thru my back—adrenalin panic—more like a cold fear thrill—everything sharp and clear as in a dream." The soldiers began looking around the room. Allen stumbled about sleepily, trying to wake up, looking for his underwear. He suddenly remembered that the black notebook on his bedside table contained a detailed description of his making love with one of the *El Puente* boys. He had used only initials, but it would have been easy enough for them to discover the boy's identity.

"Have you called the Casa de las Americas?" he asked. They told him that it was not usual to call them. "I think you should call Haydée Santamaría," said Allen, "and check out if this procedure is regular." He dressed laboriously and went to the bathroom to brush his teeth. One of the soldiers remarked on his electric toothbrush. Allen began emptying his drawers. "I want to call the Casa," he said, but they told him he was not allowed to make any calls.

He packed his knapsack, sliding the incriminating notebook under his jeans at the bottom. He stuffed the masses of papers he had accumulated into some large envelopes and put them in the knapsack. It was now full, and he still had a big pile of Cuban books and newspapers. One of the soldiers loaded them onto a handcart.

They took him to the old immigration building and put him in a room to wait. He found his finger cymbals and began chanting very slowly and quietly, so as not to disturb anyone. After a while he was taken to a small room with a large barred window, a chair, and a bed. One of the soldiers brought him cigarettes and a copy of *Hoy*. Allen flipped pages nervously.

Another uniformed man appeared and said, "We have arranged your departure this morning on the plane to Prague, London, and New York."

"Fine, but if I may ask, what is this all about? Have you not made a mistake? Have you consulted the Casa de las Americas?" Allen asked the man's identity. He was the head of Cuban immigration, Carlos Varona.

They got back in the car with the soldiers and drove off along Malecón, passing the ships in the harbor. One cargo boat had the name *Mantric*, which prompted Allen to pull out his finger cymbals and begin a low chant: "Ooom Oom Oom Sarawa Buda Dakini . . ." which he followed with the Hare Krishna mantra. "It cleared my senses a bit," he wrote, "very useful and good steadying influence." Varona reached for the car radio, and Allen put his cymbals away. He asked yet again why he was being kicked out.

"Respect for our laws, compliance with our laws."

Allen wanted to know which ones, but Varona was not specific. "Just general immigration policy . . . also a question of your private life, your personal attitudes."

"What private life?" Allen laughed. "I haven't had much of that since I've been here." Varona laughed with him. "Are you sure you're not making a mistaken judgment on the basis of gossip?" continued Allen. "I mean, Havana is a small town and full of exaggerated gossip."

"Havana has more work to do than gossip," said Varona. "Havana is a serious place. Do you understand?"

"Yes, certainly, but are you sure you're not mistaking rumor for real acts and kicking me out for nothing serious?"

"We may be making a mistake."

"Then why not take your time and discuss it with Haydée Santamaría?"

"I have called her," said Varona. "I am sure she will accept our decision. I have an appointment with her at noon."

"What time does the plane leave?"

"Ten-thirty."

Outside on the strip stood a huge silver jet with CESKOSLOVENSKE painted on it. Allen shook hands with Varona and the soldiers and walked out to the waiting plane. Before boarding, he turned and waved goodbye. The soldiers waved back.

Louis Ginsberg, poet, teacher, socialist, married Naomi Levy in 1919. Both their families had emigrated from Russia to New Jersey; both families opposed their marriage. [GINSBERG COLLECTION]

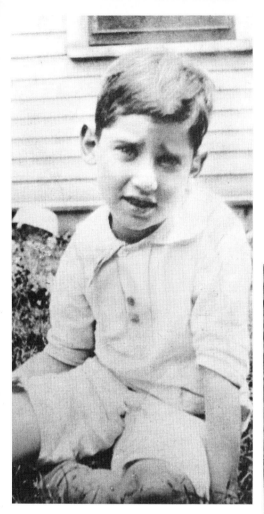

Eugene Ginsberg (above), named in honor of Eugene Debs, was born on June 3, 1921. Irwin Allen Ginsberg (r.) was born exactly five years later. Their lives took dramatically different courses—Eugene became a lawyer and a respectable family man —but the brothers would always remain close. [GINSBERG COLLECTION]

Allen with his mother Naomi at the New York World's Fair in 1940. Tormented by bouts of paranoia and severe depression, Naomi was in and out of mental hospitals all through Allen's childhood. He wrote one of his most powerful poems, "Kaddish," in her memory. [GINSBERG COLLECTION]

Allen at sixteen in his yearbook picture from East Side High School in Paterson, New Jersey. Admitted to Columbia, he made the solemn vow to devote his life to helping the working class. [GINSBERG COLLECTION]

Jack Kerouac (l.), ex-football player, college dropout and aspiring writer, with Lucien Carr on the Columbia campus in 1944. Through Carr, Allen met Kerouac and the curiously sinister William Burroughs, and together they formulated their "New Vision" of art and literature, the genesis of the philosophy of the Beat Generation. *[GINSBERG COLLECTION]*

Allen as a merchant seaman in 1945, after the shocking death of David Kammerer and Allen's suspension from Columbia. "Everything I have loved of the past years has fled into the past," he wrote. "My world is no longer the same." [GINSBERG COLLECTION]

Back in college, Allen's writing attracted the notice of the Columbia literary establishment. He graduated in 1948, but in his poetry and his explorations of the tawdry world of drugs and petty crime, he proclaimed rebellion.

[GINSBERG COLLECTION]

Newfound friend Carl Solomon, whom Allen met at Columbia-Presbyterian Psychiatric Institute where he had voluntarily committed himself after his arrest in the company of his underworld companions. Solomon would later become the publisher of William Burroughs' first book. [GINSBERG COLLECTION]

In 1950, Allen met Gregory Corso (l.) at a lesbian bar in Greenwich Village. A self-educated poet, fresh out of prison, Corso completed the quartet of original Beat writers: Ginsberg, Burroughs, Kerouac and Corso. [GINSBERG COLLECTION]

Heir's Pistol Kills His Wife; He Denies Playing Wm. Tell

Mexico City, Sept. 7 (AP).—William Seward Burroughs, 37, first admitted, then denied today that he was playing William Tell when his gun killed his pretty, young wife during a drinking party last night.

Police said that Burroughs, grandson of the adding machine inventor, first told them that, wanting to show off his marksmanship, he placed a glass of gin on her head and fired, but was so drunk that he missed and shot her in the forehead.

After talking with a lawyer, police said, Burroughs, who is a wealthy cotton planter from Pharr, Tex., changed his story and insisted that his wife was shot accidentally when he dropped his newly-purchased .38 caliber pistol.

Husband in Jail.

Mrs. Burroughs, 27, the former Joan Vollmer, died in the Red Cross Hospital.

The shooting occurred during a party in the apartment of John Healy of Minneapolis. Burroughs said two other American tourists whom he knew only slightly were present.

Burroughs, hair disheveled and clothes wrinkled, was in jail today. A hearing on a charge of homicide is scheduled for tomorrow morning.

No Arguments, He Says.

"It was purely accidental," he said. "I did not put any glass on her head. If she did, it was a joke. I certainly did not intend to shoot at it."

He said there had been no arguments or discussion before the "accident."

"The party was quiet," he said. "We had a few drinks. Everything is very hazy."

Burroughs and his wife had been here about two years. He said he was studying native dialects at the University of Mexico. He explained his long absence from his ranch by saying that he was unsuited for business.

Wife From Albany.

He said he was born in St. Louis and that his wife was from Albany, N. Y. They have two children, William Burroughs Jr., 3, and

William Seward Burroughs in Mexico City prison.

(Associated Press Wirefotos)

The late Mrs. Joan Burroughs— killed at party.

Julie Adams, 7, who he said was his wife's daughter by a previous marriage. The couple had been married five years.

She had attended journalism school at Columbia University before her marriage to Burroughs.

Burroughs, who also had been married before, formerly lived in Loudonville, a swank suburb of Albany. He is a graduate of Harvard University and worked for two weeks in 1942 as a reporter for the St. Louis Post-Dispatch.

His paternal grandfather laid the foundation of a fortune when he built his first adding machine in St. Louis in 1885.

ALLEN GINSBERG

The death of Burroughs' wife, Joan, was ruled an accident, but the tragedy drove him into self-imposed exile from America and to "a long struggle in which I have no other choice except to write my way out." [NEW YORK DAILY NEWS, SATURDAY, SEPTEMBER 8, 1951]

WILLIAM BURROUGHS

Burroughs (l.), Ginsberg (above) and Kerouac (r.), briefly reunited in New York at Allen's East 7th Street apartment in the summer of 1953. Both Kerouac and Burroughs had published early works. Allen, who was "all hung on a great psychic marriage" with Burroughs, was still searching for his poetic voice. [GINSBERG COLLECTION]

ALLEN GINSBERG

Looking like "a German geologist," Allen spent five months exploring Mayan ruins in the jungles of Mexico in 1954, the first of his many exotic travels in the years to come. [GINSBERG COLLECTION]

Peter Orlovsky at 1010 Montgomery Street, San Francisco, in 1955, standing in front of one of Robert LaVigne's many portraits of him. Allen fell in love with a full-length portrait and then with Peter. [ALLEN GINSBERG;

GINSBERG COLLECTION]

Neal Cassady rejoined his old friends Ginsberg and Kerouac in San Francisco in 1955 and would soon find himself celebrated in their work as the quintessential Beat rebel. [ALLEN GINSBERG: GINSBERG COLLECTION]

Allen made a brief stab at middle-class respectability in San Francisco, until the publication of "Howl" in 1956 brought him both fame and notoriety.

[GINSBERG COLLECTION]

Bob Donlin, Cassady, Ginsberg, LaVigne and Lawrence Ferlinghetti in front of the City Lights Bookstore in 1956, when the celebrated San Francisco Renaissance was in full cry.

[PETER ORLOVSKY: *GINSBERG COLLECTION*]

The expatriate wing of the Beat Movement was centered in Paris in the late 1950s and early 1960s, where Allen lived at the dilapidated "Beat Hotel," 9 rue Git le Coeur.

[HAROLD CHAPMAN: *GINSBERG*
COLLECTION]

Burroughs in Paris at the Beat Hotel in 1960, shortly after the publication of *Naked Lunch*. Allen had worked with Burroughs in assembling and editing the manuscript, and was instrumental in getting it published. [BRION GYSIN: *MILES COLLECTION*]

Orlovsky, Burroughs, Alan Ansen, Corso, Paul Bowles and Ginsberg in 1961, in the garden of Burroughs' villa in Tangier. [*GINSBERG COLLECTION*]

Allen and Peter went to India in 1962 in search of spiritual enlightenment. Living in Benares among the outcasts of Indian society, they aroused the suspicions of the Indian authorities. [GINSBERG COLLECTION]

Back in San Francisco, welcomed by Neal Cassady, Allen had assumed the beard and long hair that became his trademarks. His rebellious lifestyle and his experimentations with drugs and oriental mysticism would be widely imitated by the hippies of the **1960s.** [GINSBERG COLLECTION[

An international celebrity, recently expelled for his dissident activities by the governments of both Cuba and Czechoslovakia, Allen sat at Shakespeare's feet in London in 1965, dined with prominent literary figures and partied with the Beatles. [JOHN HOPKINS, LONDON]

• • •

Allen had very few contacts in Czechoslovakia. One of them was the writer Josef Skvorecky, who had written to Allen asking him to explain some of the references in "Howl" in order to help his friend Jan Zabrana, who was translating it into Czech. Allen found Skvorecky's number and phoned him. Skvorecky, astounded when Allen said he was calling from a phone booth in the Prague airport, immediately drove out to collect him. That evening, they went to Zabrana's apartment; they talked late into the night. The next day, Zabrana took Allen to the Writers Union.

It turned out that Allen had royalties due him for a book of poems, and back money for publication of his work in *Literarni noviny*, the foreign-literature magazine. He also had two years' back royalties for performances of his poetry at the Viola poetry café. In addition, invited to stay in Prague as a state guest of the Writers Union, he was given seventy-five dollars spending money in crowns and a free hotel suite at the beautiful nineteenth-century Hotel Ambassador, in the center of town. There he had a large sitting room to work in and a bedroom with a huge bathroom. His windows looked out onto the tramcars and black cobblestones of the main street of the old city. Outside, snow was falling.

Allen loved Prague, with its blue-gray stone buildings and the ancient stone bridges over the Moldau, or Vltava, its royal statues and red tramcars. "Over the river again today in Breughel's winter city, / the snow is white on all the rooftops of Prague," he wrote in "Message II." He told Ferlinghetti: "Prague is lovelier in miniature than Paris almost."

Allen worked with Jan Zabrana on translations of his poems for a forthcoming book and gave him "Message II" to translate for the Writers Union literary weekly. When Zabrana saw the lines "I lie / with teenage boys afraid of the red police," he said, "Allen, you know you can't publish this, 'afraid of the red police,' because it wouldn't pass the censor." Allen thought awhile, then crossed out "red" and inscribed "pink." Zabrana told him, "This doesn't really help."

With all his Czech money, Allen found that he had enough crowns to live well in Prague for a month and also take a train to Moscow, to return via Warsaw. He wrote to Peter apologetically: "Forgive me for setting foot in Russia without you, but I am so near, so eager! And the money's got to be spent here too!"

Allen was very well received in Prague, particularly at the Viola poetry and jazz nightclub, in the center of town. The café was decorated with huge blowups of Fred McDarrah's photographs from the anthology *The Beat Scene*, featuring Allen and Peter. Here, where poetry and jazz were combined, as on the records of Patchen, Rexroth, and Kerouac performing to jazz, jazz musicians would gather after gigs for jam sessions.

When Allen was taken there, on his second day in Prague, the beautiful young poet Vladimira Cerepkova was sitting at the bar, talking with a friend. She exclaimed, "My God, every bum nowadays looks like Ginsberg!" and Allen, recognizing his name, said, "That's me!" No one had known he was in Prague, and to the regulars of the Viola it was as if the pictures on the wall had come to life. Even Allen felt it a little incongruous when, a few days later, he sat in the audience as "Message" was performed onstage with a musical accompaniment.

The Czechs were amazed not only at Allen's being there but at his life-style. It was February, and yet all he wore on his feet in the snow was a pair of thin Cuban tennis shoes. On the other hand, he had with him an electric toothbrush, something no one in Prague had even heard of in 1965, which to them was the height of bourgeois luxury. Sadly, it broke down before he was able to demonstrate its abilities.

Within a few weeks, Allen was the best-known member of the Prague underground scene and the hero of the student dormitories. One night, a gang of kids took Allen back to their place to drink, and at the end of the evening one nineteen-year-old boy crawled into bed with him. Homosexuality was quite legal in Czechoslovakia, and by March 12, Allen was able to write to Peter: "I'm having a ball here, as long as I don't open my dirty mouth like in Cuba—in public. . . . I'm making it with teenage kids in orgies and going to wild Turkish baths and screw boys by the Moldau River and blowing in dark alleys."

He gave a big poetry reading at Charles University, the oldest in Europe, before an audience of five hundred students, who overflowed the hall. He read the whole of "Howl" and his new Prague poems, including "Message II" with its line about the red police. He wrote: "They let me loose, I talked freely, the walls of the State didn't fall."

He also spent time with Skvorecky and with Igor Hajek, the editor of *Literarni noviny*, who was preparing a major article on Allen and his poetry—which he had no intention of publishing until

Allen was safely out of the country. Having seen Allen in action the year before in New York, he feared that the visit to Prague might end abruptly and with a scandal. He waited until Allen left for Moscow, not realizing that he planned to return to Prague before going on to London.

Warm March sun was melting the heaps of snow on the black cobbled streets of Prague as Allen began the two-day train journey to Moscow. "Trembling at the Railway Station, amazed at the great red train *Moscoka–Prague*," he wrote. He had paid Intourist in advance for four days in Russia and was also invited for one week as the official guest of the Writers Union. He was equipped with a small English-Russian dictionary and some strong new shoes for Red Square.

As the train approached the Carpathian Mountains, Allen scribbled excitedly in his notebook:

> *My Slavic Soul, we are coming home again—*
> *once more on Red Square by Kremlin wall*
> *in the snow to sit and write Prophecy—*
> *Prince-Comrades of Russia, I have*
> *come from America to lay my beard*
> *at your beautiful feet!*

At dawn they arrived at Chop, just over the Russian border. The train rolled on, past villages of thatched houses surrounded by pink mist, through snow patches and black fields, horses in the distance drawing sleighs through the mud. They passed isolated dwellings, where figures in black clothes could be seen trudging up snowy lanes, and came to Lvov, with its onion-domed cathedral and its police in long nineteenth-century coats with epaulets. It was in Lvov that Allen's grandfather Pinkus was born a century before. All Allen's paternal ancestors came from the towns and villages of this part of the Ukraine.

Ylena Romanova, the head of the Western Literature department of Moscow University, met him at the station. He was taken to the modern glass-and-brick Minsk Hotel and given a small room, then they went to the Writers Union to meet Frieda Lurie, who was to look after him. The Writers Union was an enormous building from another age. There they took a table in the restaurant beneath carved mahogany balconies and great chandeliers and were served a classic Russian meal of borscht, smoked salmon, caviar, steak, and vodka. Allen explained at once what had happened in Cuba and told them he had no intention of voicing such opinions to reporters in Moscow.

"You will stay here awhile," said Frieda Lurie, "but let me advise you that we have an experience, the war, and a different life to you, so that certain things are best not spoken about, especially to journalists. People don't and won't understand. We hope you'll come to see our point of view." The subject of homosexuality was raised. "We all have a normal love life here," she explained. "Russians may not appreciate your interests, though possibly you may have some truth or some valuable opinion; still, your proposal to be silent and watch is best."

Allen went straight to the Kremlin, which, he found, was not one building but a great collection from many different ages, all gathered within the huge Kremlin walls. He wrote his first impressions: "Then walking in thru Kremlin estate—the surprise of the 16th century vastness—the medieval fortress still in postatomic operation, offices and central bureaus there with the formal front of the old Feudal shield and wall and turret and clock and gold onion dome and peaked gate keep solid as Bronx Park Zoo right in the middle of Moscow—and the spaciousness—as if all the steppes of a Siberia and 'Asiatic vague immensities' were on display in the Central Powerhouse Castle—Capital of the Future Spacy Universe Nation— huge walks in thru gates, fields with palaces and old cathedrals, a 16th century iron-embroidered cannon—I felt like a provincial from Pinsk or Magnitogorsk, seeing the Worlds Fair Ancient Center."

After dining on smoked salmon and sturgeon and milk, he went at midnight to Red Square. Saint Basil's Cathedral was almost as beautiful as the Taj Mahal; with its great roof of domes and cones, each one a different shape and color and pattern, it was set at the end of the square, with the huge Gum department store to one side and the Kremlin on the right. The giant red electric stars on the gatehouse towers of the Kremlin glowed deep ruby in the dark night, the ancient golden clock moved slowly, the two soldiers guarding Lenin's black and white marble mausoleum slowly goosestepped the length of the Kremlin wall and back again. Allen crossed the "vast black lawn of cobblestones" and sat on a wooden plank to write, in awe of the size and age of the place.

The next day he arranged to meet his relatives. Joe Levy, seventy-two years old, came into the hotel, hesitated a little, then

walked up to him. Allen said, "Joe?" They had last met when Allen
was five years old, before Joe and his wife decided to return to
Russia to live. They sat and talked, and Allen finally got straight
the story of his mother's family's emigration to the United States.
Then Joe took him home, where his wife, Anne, was preparing
supper.

Joe was Naomi's cousin; his father, Isser, and Naomi's father,
Mendel, were brothers. In 1931, a group of thirty friends and relatives from Newark went back to visit Russia. Joe and Anne were so
impressed that they decided to stay. Anne returned to Newark
alone to pack up the furniture and ship it all to Moscow. It was still
there, including a 1922 Victrola with Caruso records and a big
American bed.

Anne produced the photograph album: Allen's aunt Eleanor with
her husband, Max, smiling on the beach, Naomi and her girlfriends
staring at Allen through time. Allen found a photograph of himself
as a cute four-year-old in shorts, with a thin belly. It was all too sad:
Eugene staring painfully at the sky through spectacles; Louis and
Naomi in the twenties, Louis with his teacher's mustache; Naomi
in the thirties, wearing tennis clothes; Allen and Eugene, Newark
1933; Edie and Aunt Rose; and pictures of other cousins, still alive
in Russia, some who never left. Then came the sixties photographs,
in color: pictures of weddings and grandchildren in a land almost
forgotten. "The expression, the sad tragic aloneness never changes
in half a century, surviving them the unknown descendants," Allen
wrote. "Anne and I were sad and tears rolled down our cheeks as
we came to the end, the last pictures of the unknown newly grown
children in America." Joe and Anne had no children.

When he arrived in Moscow in 1931, Joe had taken a job as an
electrician on the Moscow subway; after the anti-Jewish campaign
began under Stalin, he was transferred to a job stuffing horsehair
into sofas. He had a nervous breakdown. "It wasn't Stalin," he said.
"Beria misled him! Beria was working for Scotland Yard. It was all
Beria's fault."

Anne sighed. "Oh, Joe, you still believe that?" But Joe had to; he
had staked his life on it. "The collective heart is the most important
thing about communism," he affirmed to Allen, but Anne seemed
dubious. Allen sang them the Hare Krishna mantra and Hare Om
Namo Shiva, but when Joe took Allen back to his hotel by subway,
he said tentatively, "That kind of singing doesn't seem to have
effect here." Allen wondered what he meant.

Allen was drunk when he met Yevgeny Yevtushenko, Russia's most famous living poet and literary activist. Accompanied by the interpreter provided by Frieda Lurie, Allen had been to dinner with two members of the Writers Union. On the restaurant stairs, he encountered a tall, thin, handsome, bright-eyed man, dressed in a striped suit, who said, "Yo soy Yevtushenko." Allen drunkenly knelt to touch his knees, but Yevtushenko stopped him. This was Yevtushenko's first day out of bed after a bout of pneumonia, and he was still suffering from vertigo. He wore his thin blond hair brushed forward over his brow. "I love you," said Allen, impressed by the Russian poet's good looks. Allen kept touching and saluting him, and in Cuban Spanish tried to get him to understand that he admired his nose and hair and mouth. Yevtushenko arranged a meeting for the next night.

Yevtushenko lived in an area of unfinished streets where a few old wooden buildings remained. He took Allen's coat, gave him a bowl of soup to warm him, and told him, "You were very drunk last night." In fact Allen remembered very little about their conversation of the previous evening. Yevtushenko continued, "I saw you were a good man. Here, we hear many bad things about you, that you are a pederast, scandals, but I know it is not true."

"It's all true," Allen said. Through his interpreter, he explained to Yevtushenko, in some detail, his Blake vision and said, "As for homosexuality, that's my experience and that's the situation I'm in. So the scandal comes from talking openly about it."

"I know nothing of such matters," said Yevtushenko. "It is a private affair of yours." Next, Allen began a long explanation of the uses and qualities of different drugs. Yevtushenko seemed restless and asked, "But why are you interested in such matters?"

Allen tried to explain, citing the use of ganja in Shivaite sects in India and of LSD in the U.S. Allen was in the middle of trying to explain what the unconscious felt like, when he finally lost Yevtushenko, who said, "Please, Allen, I like you. I like you as a poet, but these are your personal problems. Please don't speak to me about them. They are not interesting to me. I respect you as a great man, a great poet, but these two subjects, homosexuality and narcotics, are not known to me, and I feel they are juvenile preoccupations. They have no importance here in Russia to us. It only disturbs my impression of you. Please don't talk about these two matters."

"I feel rejected," said Allen.

"I have problems more important than these," said Yevtushenko.

"Okay," said Allen. "Tell me all your problems, and tell me the problems of Russia."

Yevtushenko told him of the twenty million people who had been arrested during the era of Stalin. He said that as many as fifteen million may have been killed or died in prison. Yevtushenko's own grandparents both disappeared. "But after all, we believe in Russia and in our system," he said, and tried to explain. "What would it mean to be anti-Communist? To go back to monarchy or capitalism? Nobody, very few people, want that in this country, so we have to work our problems out. It's slow. It's terribly slow, but I think we'll win."

He told Allen of his difficulties with the censors. His last major long poem had been ready in proof for a year but not published. He had to make four hundred fifty changes to get it passed, but he thought it was worth it because the magazine had a circulation of more than a million. He said that he once read to fourteen thousand people, in Moscow. He played Allen a recording of himself reading in Paris. Talking about his work had cheered him. He stood up, hugged Allen, and kissed him on the mouth. Allen, unused to Russian customs, was embarrassed.

They went to a Georgian restaurant to meet Yevtushenko's wife, Genia. Allen tried to explain Kerouac's spontaneous prose style, but Yevtushenko couldn't accept it as a valid method. Allen felt the cultural gap between them was immense, and the next day he woke up depressed, convinced that they had achieved no real communication. He wrote Peter: "Saw Yevtushenko. He nice but square—couldn't talk deep soul—*another* kind of poetical soul. I'm lonely." Allen may not have realized, possibly because of faulty translations of their conversation, that he had already made an impact on the Russian poets. In a conversation in 1986, Yevtushenko said that in the fifties, issues of *Evergreen Review* were eagerly passed around and Ginsberg's work was given very careful study. "You know, in the late fifties, you were my idol," he told Allen, "my idol!"

Allen visited virtually every museum in Moscow. At the Pushkin, one of the world's greatest collections, he finally saw Cézanne's *Harlequin*, which he knew from a reproduction in Bill Cannastra's loft. There were many Cézannes there, as well as magnificent Gauguins, sunny Matisses, and beautiful dark golden Rembrandts, all of which he meticulously noted in his journal. He spent a morning at the Dostoyevsky Museum, examining the great novelist's desk and inkwell, photographs, and first editions of his works; he also visited the Mayakovsky Museum.

Ylena Romanova had arranged another week for him at the Writers Union's expense. He took the train to Leningrad, where he spent two intense days at the Hermitage, shuffling across the huge parquet floors of the royal palace, stopping at Rembrandt's *Prodigal Son* and Titian's *Danaë*. He found a whole room of Cézannes; the old woman attendant pointed out the worn top and bottom of a canvas of Mont St. Victoire that Cézanne had rolled up to throw away. Allen lingered long in a room containing fourteen Gauguins that he had never even seen in reproduction.

Back in Moscow, Allen finally met Andrei Voznesensky, the other Russian poet whose work bore some resemblance to that of the Beats. They spoke in English, and Voznesensky invited him to his home. There, Voznesensky sat relaxed, in an armchair, and both he and his wife were very friendly. They discussed poetry, Allen saying, "Yes, sometimes I think in rhythm," and Andrei replying, "Yes, *I* think in rhythm!"

Allen was excited; it seemed that they were making real contact.

Andrei asked him, "Does rhythm come to you, and do you carry it around for several days?"

"No," Allen told him, "the first draft is the last, ideally. That is the ideal, not to touch the composition. So the rhythm comes as an impulse to writing. Or comes *during* the composition. Sometimes, maybe two or three times in my life, I've had the full rhythm, a complete rhythm from my whole body, when the whole physiology moved in one strong rhythm, a sort of cosmic rhythm. I never know when that will happen. I sometimes get minor rhythms, but those are beautiful too."

"Cosmic rhythm." Andrei translated it to his wife. "That's good. Here's a toast first to cosmic rhythm!"

Allen gave a long discourse on different drugs, but Andrei, like everyone else in Moscow, could not understand his interest in them. Andrei asked if Allen's strongest rhythm came with or without drugs, and Allen said both. Once with, once without, and once half and half. Then Andrei asked him to read from his work, and he read, softly, Parts II and III of "Howl," for him to hear the rhythm. Voznesensky said afterward, "I don't fully understand the words, but I was with you in the sound."

Later, Allen chanted mantras, then it was time for Voznesensky to attend a performance of his poems set to music. Allen accompanied him, and in the car he began to weep. Andrei told him, "You look beautiful now." Allen, a little drunk, said, "This may be the only time we see each other. You have no idea the trouble I went through to get here. It was very difficult, and I am unhappy that I can't stay more than a few days." His visa was due to expire shortly.

Andrei told him, "I am glad to see you. We are both poets above all else. We are together, that's supreme."

The train journey to Warsaw passed less than fifty miles south of Naomi's hometown, Vitebsk. Allen arrived in Warsaw just as the sun was setting behind the peaked roofs of the old town. He checked into the Europeski Hotel and went to walk the wide streets. There were construction sites everywhere; Warsaw was still rebuilding the city the Germans razed at the end of the war. The old town was being lovingly restored to its former glory.

Allen went to the Writers Union, which welcomed him as a guest of the Ministry of Culture, arranged to pay one week of his hotel bill, and gave him one hundred zlotys spending money. He ran into Dan Halberstam, whom he had last met in Saigon. "It's a goddam police state," Halberstam said. "Never saw a country like this, where there's a total split between populace and government."

Halberstam gave Allen a tour of the city, which ended at the site of the Warsaw ghetto, now a vast stretch of greensward surrounded by new apartment projects. Children were playing on the stone steps of a large bronze commemorative monument. Allen recorded his impressions: "I started crying—whatever happened was completely invisible—a whole new universe had emerged in the same place in space—nothing left of all that ruin and suffering except the monument and a few visitors."

In a café he wrote: "old buildings rubbled down, gaiety of all night parties under the air bombs, / first screams of the vanishing ghetto—Workmen step thru prewar pink-blue bedroom walls demolishing sunny ruins," lines that would become part of the poem "Café in Warsaw."

Voznesensky arrived in Warsaw and demanded to know what "Wow" meant. Allen had left him a note at his hotel: "I'll wait for you. Wow." So he shouted, "Wow!" and Voznesensky laughed. He had to leave the next day, but Allen was able to dine with him and exchange a little gossip. Voznesensky's most amusing story was that Khrushchev, now in retirement, had revealed to a Western journalist that he had become a poet. "In his spare time he writes poetry for his family and friends," said Voznesensky, laughing. "He reads it aloud to them. It is Surrealist."

1965

Allen returned to Prague and checked into the Merkur, a cheap hotel. The next day was May Day. Traditionally, a medieval festival, Majalis, was celebrated; students elected a May King and held a beauty contest to find him a queen. They paraded them through the streets and held a mock wedding ceremony. The festival had been suspended for twenty years, since the Communists came to power. Instead, students had begun rioting against the police in a small wooded park on a hill near the river. Allen had made sure that he returned to Prague in time for May Day.

That year, 1965, with the growing liberal climate, the authorities had decided to let the students revive their Majalis festival and have their own parade in the afternoon. Each school of the university had nominated its candidates for May King and Queen, who would be paraded through the streets from their school to the Park of Culture and Rest, where, in the exhibition hall, the winners would be chosen.

Josef Skvorecky had been nominated as May King by the Engineering School of the Polytechnic, but he had come down with influenza. Told by Jan Zabrana that Allen was back in town, Skvorecky called him at his hotel and asked, "Allen, would you like to be the King of Majalis?"

Concerned that he would attract too much attention, Allen asked, "Is it political?" Skvorecky assured him that it was just a student affair of no significance, so Allen agreed. The afternoon of the parade, Allen was met at the hotel by a large delegation of students dressed in 1890s costumes: men in top hats and waistcoats, carrying canes, women in hoop skirts with parasols, surrounded by jesters, who burst into the room blowing trumpets. "Mr. Ginsberg, we have the honor to beg your presence in procession to the crowning of the King of May, and to accept our support for your candidacy of Kral Majalis, and we humbly offer you crown and throne." They placed a gilded cardboard crown on his head and a scepter in his hand and sat him in a chair covered with red drapes. He wrapped himself in an old chamois coat, got out his finger cymbals and a statue of Ganesh, the elephant god, that he happened to have with him, and was borne unsteadily down in the elevator to a waiting flatbed truck.

The streets were filled with students drinking wine and beer as

the parade commenced. They reached the courtyard of the Polytechnic, where a huge crowd of students had gathered to greet their
candidate for king. There, a bigger truck awaited him, garlanded
with roses, with a Dixieland band playing on the back and five pretty
female attendants. It was piled high with crates of beer, and a sign
on the front read, in Latin, "Ginsbergum Krale Majalis."

Allen drank a beer and made his first speech: "I'll be the first
kind King and bow down before my subjects. I'll be the first naked
King." They lurched off into the streets of Prague, Allen drinking
beer and wine. Whenever someone put a bullhorn or microphone to
his lips for a speech, he sang a mantra, "Hare Om Namo Shiva" or
"Om Sri Maitreya." No one was expecting the huge crowds that
lined the streets. Following the truck were several thousand students, singing and chanting, "Long Live Majalis!"

The parade wound its way through the old town. It reached
Staremeskaya Nameska Square, and Allen made another speech:
"I dedicate the glory of my crown to the beautiful bureaucrat Franz
Kafka, who was born in the building around the corner here." Then
the procession, fifteen thousand strong, moved on past the House
of the Golden Carp, where Kafka wrote *The Trial*. Allen excitedly
pointed it out to the crowd: "On your left, comrades, is the actual
house where saintly Kafka lived and cleaned his teeth, and wrote
his huge novels which your comrades have not even published!"

Allen drank more beer and wine and sang louder and louder.
Finally, the procession passed over the old stone bridge across the
Vltava. Townspeople sat on the riverbanks, leaned from windows,
and waved from the rooftops. A crowd of 100,000, excited and
happy, filled the Park of Culture and Rest; a half-dozen rock bands
were playing. The organizers were amazed, and just a little worried,
because they had expected only ten or fifteen thousand people that
afternoon.

They gathered in the huge exhibition hall, and the election of the
King of May began. There were four or five candidates besides
Allen, dressed as kings or clowns. The medical school candidate,
wrapped entirely in bandages, made an eloquent speech in Latin.
The law school candidate, in kingly robes, spoke entirely about
fornication. The Engineering School candidate, in dirty Levi's and
a work shirt, sang "Om Sri Maitreya" for five minutes and then sat
down. He had a landslide victory: 100,000 people elected Allen Kral
Majalis, the King of May!

All that afternoon, he ran around with his gang from the Polytechnic, exercising his kingly powers by fondling everyone within reach, listening to the bands, and drinking. At midnight, the people would choose a queen for him. It grew late, and the students finally reassembled in the hall to begin the beauty contest. Allen sat on his throne, looking out at the crowd, the footlights dazzling him a little. As the selection went on, he spent a quiet fifteen minutes writing a poem in his notebook.

Jiri Hendrych, the Party Secretary for Cultural Affairs, was not pleased to find 100,000 drunken citizens in the Park of Culture and Rest at midnight. He had been expecting to see the harmless drunken revels of a few thousand students. When he entered the hall and found that they had elected an American as King of May, he was horrified. He turned white with rage. "This is impossible! You have to get rid of him immediately!"

The student organizers had little choice but to obey. The students had a security force, dressed as American military police, in uniforms left over from a film that had recently been shot in Prague. As Allen sat musing on his regality, a line of ten American MPs appeared in front of his throne. The master of ceremonies spoke a few words into the microphone, saying that Allen had been deposed and made prime minister and that a Czech student was to be king in his place.

The "MPs" lifted Allen from his throne and sat him on the side with the May Queen judges, while a drunken Czech student, who had no idea what was happening to him, was put on the throne, where he sat, blinking, looking confused and embarrassed.

Allen, cheated out of the two hundred dollars he was supposed to receive as May King, grumbled in a letter to the poet Nicanor Parra: "The May Queen was elected but I didn't get a chance to marry and sleep with her as was tradition for the night. In fact, I was supposed to have the run of Prague and do anything I wanted and fuck anybody and get drunk everywhere as King."

Allen spent all night singing and talking with a group of students in the dormitory, undeterred by the presence of two middle-aged business-suited men with a tape recorder and a supply of Scotch. They welcomed the men, knowing full well they were secret agents. The Prague newspapers played down the extraordinary events as much as they could, but the authorities had been alerted. They took a dim view of Allen's disruptive presence and decided to get rid of him.

For the next two days, Allen wandered around Prague making a movie with some filmmakers, singing "Hare Krishna," and tape-recording interviews with student magazines on the evolution of consciousness, sex logic, and space-age feeling. He went to rock concerts, wrote poems, slept with boys, and kept his journals. Then, on May 3, he found that his notebook was missing. It contained the usual things: six poems, including the one that he wrote under the spotlights while on his throne; politics, and gossip: "All the capitalist lies about communism are true and all the communist lies about capitalism are true." It included descriptions of a few orgy scenes with students and gave a detailed account of masturbating in his room at the Hotel Ambassador, kneeling on the bathroom floor with a broomstick up his ass.

He went to the Viola café and saw the two men in business suits, who gave him vodka until he was drunk and reeled out into the street at midnight, singing "Hare Om Namo Shiva." A police car stopped and asked him for his identification, which he did not have, as his passport was being held at his hotel. They took him to the station, where he explained that he was the May King, and a tourist poet, and not really drunk, just happy. They let him go. From this time on, he was openly followed by plainclothes police. He decided to keep sober. His plans were to continue to travel in Europe, and he didn't want to leave Prague until his travel arrangements were complete.

On May 5, at midnight, he left the Viola with a young couple. As they turned onto a lonely street, a man came around the corner, saw Allen, hesitated momentarily, then suddenly rushed toward him, yelling, *"Bouzerant! Bouzerant!"* ("Homosexual!") He punched Allen in the mouth, knocking him down and sending his glasses flying. Allen scrambled to his feet, grabbed his glasses, and began running. Allen's companions tried to hold his assailant back, but he pulled free and gave chase. He caught up with Allen outside the post office and knocked him to the ground.

A police car arrived almost at that moment, and Allen looked up from the sidewalk to see four rubber clubs held menacingly over his head. "Om!" he chanted, then stayed quiet. Allen, the couple, and Allen's assailant were all bundled into the police car and spent the night at the station. The stranger maintained that they'd been exposing themselves on the street when he passed by and that they had attacked him. Allen demanded a lawyer and to be allowed to speak to someone at the American Embassy. At this, the police decided to let them all go.

Allen concluded that it was definitely time to leave Prague. He consulted with his friends at the Writers Union and at *Literarni noviny*, and they agreed with him. He had only one remaining appointment, a radio interview on May 6. Afterward, he went with friends to a remote café on the outskirts of town, where he was approached by plainclothesmen. The police had found Allen's missing notebook. "If you'll come with us and identify it, we'll return it to you and you'll be back here in half an hour."

Allen went apprehensively with them to the station and identified his notebook. As soon as he signed for it, one of the detectives said frostily, "On sketchy examination we suspect that this book contains illegal writings, so we are holding it for the public prosecutor." Allen was free to go.

The next morning, May 7, the same plainclothesmen appeared and took him back to the station. In an upstairs room, Allen was seated before five pudgy-faced bureaucrats at a polished table. "Mr. Ginsberg," they said. "We immigration chiefs have received many complaints from parents, scientists, and educators about your sexual theories having a bad effect on our youth and corrupting the young, so we are terminating your visa." They told him that his notebook would be returned to him (it never was). Allen explained that he had a plane ticket to London and would leave on his own, with no fuss, the next day. He pointed out that letting him leave voluntarily would be more diplomatic and would spare them the embarrassment of exiling the May King.

His views seemed to have no impact, and he was taken to his hotel to pack his things. He ate lunch in his room with a detective. He was not allowed to telephone the U.S. Embassy, the Writers Union, or any of his friends. They escorted him to the airport. Allen sank into his seat on the BEA jet and sighed, kicked out of a Socialist country for the second time in four months.

In the opinion of Igor Hajek, of *Literarni noviny*, Allen brought a lot of the trouble on himself by his provocative behavior. He mixed with people in Prague that most individuals in literary circles would have avoided. As a foreigner unfamiliar with the norms of the country, he stirred things up more than could be tolerated, even in those comparatively liberal times.

Ginsberg's deportation served as a pretext for the Stalinist element to attack the Writers Union and its rather liberal weekly newspaper. Since Hajek had written the original "Introduction to Ginsberg" article, he also came under fire. *Mlada fronta*, the Communist Youth Organization daily, ran a full-page article, written by its editor on the orders of the Ideological Department, attacking the Writers Union, *Literarni noviny*, and Hajek. The CIA-front Radio Free Europe issued a summary of the Prague press coverage on May 17:

"Czechoslovakian Communist Party daily *Rude pravo* had accused American beatnik poet Allen Ginsberg of having abused Czechoslovakian hospitality and grossly violated the norms of decent world behavior. The accusations were made one day after *Czedeka* [the Czechoslovak Press Association] reported that Ginsberg had been expelled from the country because of his negative influence on young people. Last Sunday *Czedeka* also had quoted Communist Youth Organization daily *Mlada fronta*, which printed excerpts from his personal diary. *Rude pravo* claimed that the documents printed by *Mlada fronta* testified to the fact that Ginsberg is a person with a sexual deviation and a narcotics addiction. They alleged that in his notebook Ginsberg described *in detail* sexual orgies he staged in various places with young men. Ginsberg's character is completed by the notes in which he speaks with disdain of our Republic and of the citizens whom he met and with whom he talked. The number of those who had taken their guidance from Ginsberg has not been negligible, the paper said, adding that after the publication of the facts about his moral character all have the opportunity to correct their own critical feelings. . . . *Mlada fronta* says that in his diary we find insults to representatives of our State, our Party, and our people. The diary was found by a citizen and handed over to the police."

Czechoslovakian president Anton Novotny himself went on the air and attacked Ginsberg, explaining the official reasons for expelling him. A June 2 news dispatch from a Vienna newspaper was headlined: "Deliberate Corruption of Czechoslovakia's Youth Is the Latest Charge Made Against the West by Czech President Anton Novotny."

Much was made of Allen's deportation from both Cuba and Czechoslovakia, and he himself described his eviction from Cuba as "one of the best things I've done." His attempts to explain his behavior in these countries were usually dismissed as "unbelievable political naïveté"; certainly, as a result, a number—possibly dozens—of people were interviewed by secret police. In Cuba, Allen genuinely thought that his views—that homosexuality should not be persecuted and that marijuana should be legalized—were "revolutionary" (as he had stated at the Cuban press conference in New York three years before). That was his yardstick, and when Cuba did not manifest his particular vision, he began to proselytize. The Cubans, for their part, expected him to be interested in the progress they had made since the revolution—thousands of schools and hospitals built, the fight against illiteracy, the rise in the percentage of live births—but Allen's interest was in individual freedom, not in collective advance. Allen and the Cubans had two very different definitions of "revolution," forged from two very different viewpoints and virtually irreconcilable.

In Czechoslovakia, Allen could not have known that the Majalis parade would attract so many people, but since it was the first in twenty years, its student organizers should have anticipated its popularity. Unwisely, after his fears about his Cuban notebooks, he nonetheless continued to record compromising details in Czechoslovakia, which ultimately led to his expulsion. He behaved as he would have in San Francisco or New York, but in Prague, as Hajek said, his behavior was seen as provocative and therefore insulting. In this, Allen played straight into the hands of the Stalinists, who were using any excuse to stem the tide of liberalism. Although Allen was acclaimed for his chutzpah—no one else would have *dared* to behave as he did—for his friends and acquaintances in those countries, his visits were not a conspicuous success.

On the plane to London, Allen wrote his version of events in Prague. The words flowed easily onto the pages of his notebook, and by the time he landed at Heathrow he had a complete poem, requiring no tightening or changes, a perfect distillation of his feelings and experiences. He called it "Kral Majalis": "And I am the King of May, tho' paranoid, for the Kingdom of May is too beautiful to last for more than a month."

FOURTEEN | INTO THE VORTEX

When I tell any Truth it is not for the sake of convincing those who do not know it but the sake of defending those who do.

—William Blake

ALTHOUGH IT WOULD BE ANOTHER YEAR BEFORE THE COVER OF *TIME* magazine would proclaim "Swinging London," the city was already the center of a vibrant fashion and pop music scene. Allen arrived— *1965* on May 8, and the next night he found himself sitting in Bob Dylan's opulent suite at the Savoy, along with Joan Baez, Albert Grossman, and Don Pennebaker, whose three-man crew were filming every aspect of Dylan's tour. Dylan himself was looking sharp in Beatle boots, narrow black pants, and trendy London shirt with high-rolled collar. His hair was fashionably tousled. Joan Baez's hair was still long and center parted, but she wore the latest short skirt and puff-sleeved top. Though Dylan had not yet "gone electric" in public, the folk-singing Bob Dylan of the early sixties was now years behind him.

That night Dylan played the first of two concerts at the Royal Albert Hall. Allen was detailed by Dylan to escort the English pop singer Marianne Faithfull, and they traveled to and from the concert in a private black limousine. Afterward a large party gathered in Grossman's suite at the hotel. Dylan was in his own suite, entertaining the Beatles, and everyone else was forbidden to go in. Then Allen received a summons to the presence. The Beatles and their wives were there, with their two personal roadies, Mal Evans and

Neil Aspinall. The room was completely silent. "Just totally frozen, not knowing what to talk about:" Allen sat down on the arm of Dylan's chair. "Why don't you sit a little closer," mocked John Lennon. Allen responded by falling forward into Lennon's lap. Looking up into his face, laughing, a little drunk, Allen asked, "Have you ever read William Blake?"

"No, never heard of him," snapped Lennon.

"Oh, John, stop lying," said Cynthia, his wife, and everyone laughed.

Allen asked if they were aware of the relationship between "Beatles" and "Beats" and if they knew what the Beat Generation was. He told them about Kerouac, Cassady, and the others. Dylan had had a friendly meeting with the Beatles the previous year in America, when he had turned them on to pot for the first time. But now he was on their territory. Ginsberg remembered the evening well: "Dylan wasn't giving anything and they weren't giving anything. Dylan was laconic with them too; they were all uptight." Dylan must have realized that Allen was the only person capable of breaking the ice and summoned him.

The next day, Allen went to the American Embassy to begin negotiations to retrieve his notebook from the Prague police. Afterward he took a bus to the Savoy to visit with Dylan, then walked up through the charming clutter of the Covent Garden fruit and vegetable markets. The streets were filled with fashionably dressed long-haired young people, as London emerged in color for the first time since the war. He spent the afternoon in the National Gallery, revisiting his favorite pictures, then returned to the Savoy to join Dylan's party going to the Royal Albert for their second concert. After the performance, they all ate together at a trattoria in Soho, seated at a large round table. "How lovely to be back again in England," he wrote in his journal.

It was the first time Allen had been in Britain during the summer, and he took advantage of the good weather to explore the country, visiting poets and giving small readings in Worcester, Bristol, and Cambridge. In Newcastle he met the Imagist poet Basil Bunting, a friend of William Carlos Williams and Ezra Pound. Bunting had recently been "discovered" working at a local newspaper by the Newcastle poet Tom Pickard. From Liverpool, Allen wrote Peter: "I spent all week in Liverpool home of the Beatles and heard all the new rock bands and gave a little reading and had a ball with longhair boys—it's like San Francisco in Liverpool except the weather is greyer—lovely city, *mad* music, electronic hits your guts centers." The basements of the warehouses were alive with rock 'n' roll in sweaty, red-brick-arched clubs. He was so moved by the new dancing and music that he proclaimed, "Liverpool is at the present time the center of the consciousness of the human universe," a line still used by the city fathers.

Back in London, Allen found that he knew an enormous number of people. John Ashbery gave a reading at the American Embassy, which was followed by a cocktail party at which Tom Maschler of Jonathan Cape introduced Allen to the London literati. The poet Pablo Fernández, cultural attaché at the Cuban Embassy, was there and was intrigued to hear about Allen's experiences in Havana. Allen saw the gallery owner Robert Fraser, Andy Warhol's London dealer, and finally, after years of correspondence, he met the Finnish poet and translator Anselm Hollo, who was living in London. London was the place to be, and Americans were flocking across the Atlantic to join in the action. Among them were Lawrence Ferlinghetti and Allen's sometime girlfriend Barbara Rubin.

Allen used Better Books, London's main literary bookshop, as his headquarters and went to stay with the shop's manager in nearby Fitzrovia. He celebrated his birthday on June 3 with a classic sixties party, with Beatles and Stones records, Tamla Motown and Stax playing full volume, and girls in see-through lace and miniskirts dancing with long-haired youths.

John and Cynthia Lennon arrived with George Harrison and Patti Boyd. Allen rushed to embrace them, but by the time they arrived he was completely drunk and had removed all his clothing except his Jockey shorts, which were balanced on his head. A "Please do not disturb" hotel sign hung around his penis. John and George shrank back, making sure that no photographers were present. They talked a little, and John told Allen that he had once produced a magazine at Liverpool College of Art called the *Daily Howl*, but the Beatles, nervous at Allen's nakedness, soon left for another party. Asked why they were going so soon, Lennon hissed, "You don't do that in front of the birds!" Allen's arms had to be wrapped around a lamppost for support while a cab was found to take him home. Once in the cab, he lay on the floor, and was only able to make it up the stairs to the third-floor apartment by crawling on his hands and knees.

With Allen and Lawrence Ferlinghetti in town, Gregory Corso just over in Paris, and Andrei Voznesensky due to arrive any day, there was naturally talk of a reading. Barbara Rubin, never one to think small, hired the largest venue in London—the Royal Albert Hall. Although the reading itself was something of a flop—a succession of bad local poets monopolized the time—the event served as a model for the big international poetry festivals that were to become commonplace in Europe, occurring every summer from Amsterdam to Rome. The reading was also a catalyst for the burgeoning London arts community, and such diverse organizations as Europe's first underground newspaper, *International Times*, and the Arts Lab, a multimedia arts center for experimental films, avant-garde theater, and performance work, both traced their origins to the Albert Hall event. It was one of the reasons Ginsberg was held in such high esteem by that generation of English young people; his presence in London during the summer of 1965 primed the pump of the London "underground" and galvanized everyone into action. For Allen himself, his European trip was complete, and on June 29, after half a year away, he flew back to America on his still valid Cuban air ticket.

Throughout the sixties, Allen's fame continued to grow, until by 1967 he was a national figure; featured on talk shows, interviewed by *Playboy*, the subject of personality posters, he was a celebrity, famous for being famous. He had been abroad when the media first showed interest in the Beats over the trial of *Howl* and Kerouac's best-selling *On the Road*. The press had quickly developed their own stereotype beatnik, using the classic French bohemian, with beard, beret, and sandals, as their model. Allen's notion of the Beat Generation was more concerned with sensitivity, sensuality, and lack of hypocrisy than with the fashionable coolness, lack of visible emotion, and studied existential pose of the beatnik; the press, however, lumped them all together. With the Kennedy era, things had loosened up and the sixties really began: rock 'n' roll blossomed, birth control became truly feasible, a hundred different threads came together in the youth movement. Allen found himself one of its spokesmen.

He was obviously flattered by the media attention, but his primary motive was to get his various messages across, by all and any means. His years of market research training gave him a canny eye for presenting his ideas to the general population in the best possible light. He became expert at manipulating talk-show hosts, twisting questions in order to speak out against the war or in favor of legalizing pot, and he used his massive address book to connect up scholars and researchers, activists and journalists. Ten years before, he had spent his time putting together editors and poets; now his book of names became the central directory of what became known as the underground.

As Allen's legend grew, so did Peter's dependence on drugs. He had taken a great deal of Methedrine on the Lower East Side in 1959 and heroin in France in 1961. In India he was addicted to morphine, which was one of the reasons he didn't want to return to the United States with Allen. Faced with Allen's new role as guru to the burgeoning youth movement, Peter retreated into the false self-confidence of amphetamine, presenting a speedy, funny, distracted face to the world. His relationship with Allen grew more complex. Peter now had regular girlfriends, but his life was nevertheless dominated by Allen. He acted as Allen's chauffeur. He was Allen's secretary, answering the endlessly ringing telephone, fielding visitors, and looking after the apartment during Allen's frequent absences. And he was still Allen's lover. They were both living life very quickly, storing up problems for the future.

Peter was sometimes deeply depressed about his brothers or about his own life, but Allen was often too busy visiting, being Bob Dylan's confidant, or acting as guru of the youth movement to notice Peter's troubles and drug taking. "I didn't realize that it was a chronic problem that had distorted our relationship and distorted my whole behavior toward him and his toward me," Ginsberg later said. "I just wasn't facing it. It went on for twenty years."

When Allen arrived at U.S. customs after his flight from London, *1965* he was taken into a side room and stripped down to his underwear. Agents examined the lint in his pockets with a magnifying glass but found only tobacco crumbs. He managed to get a look at their documents, which had negligently been left face upward on the desk, and read: "Allen Ginsberg (reactivated) and Peter Orlovsky (continued)—These persons are reported to be engaged in smuggling narcotics."

While Allen was away in Eastern Europe, his East Fifth Street building had deteriorated. The water and heat had been shut off, and the city had given each tenant one hundred dollars to relocate. Peter had found a third-floor walk-up at 408 East 10th Street, in a dangerous, run-down block between avenues C and D. Allen arrived home to find that addicts had already broken in and stolen his typewriter and Peter's Indian harmonium. He didn't have much time to settle into his new quarters, because no sooner had he visited his family and recovered from jet lag than he and Peter headed out to California, where the Berkeley Poetry Conference would begin on July 12.

1965

The conference went down in history as a showcase of the most important younger poets working in America at that time: Gary Snyder, Robert Creeley, Robert Duncan, LeRoi Jones, John Wieners, Jack Spicer, and Ginsberg. Charles Olson made one of his rare public appearances. Allen wrote: "He got drunk and high on pot and bennies, and instead of reading, talked his head off for four hours to 700 people in the audience, concluding leaning over the podium with his huge bulk and growling out like a lion, '*I love POWER!*' Duncan got so scared that he fled in the middle. But it was a great night. I read drunk, but well, thank God."

To the delight of his family, Allen received a Guggenheim Foundation grant. He used the money to buy a Volkswagen camper equipped with a refrigerator, a bed, and a desk. In mid-August, Peter stayed behind in San Francisco with his girlfriend Stella, while Allen, Gary Snyder, and Gary's girlfriend Martine took off up the Pacific Highway to Oregon, camping on beaches and at riversides in forests. Once they reached the Oregon border, they turned inland to the Cascades and Crater Lake National Park, where they camped at the foot of Mount Scott. They spent two days backpacking on the Wonderland Trail in Mount Rainier National Park, looking down into foggy chasms, eating wild berries, tramping through the snow around the 14,400-foot peak, and developing tremendous appetites. Every morning they read aloud from the Tibetan classic *100,000 Songs of Milarepa*.

One morning, Allen and Gary got up at four and climbed the ten-thousand-foot Glacier Peak, into the thin air above the treeline. They climbed solidly until 2 P.M., crossing the giant glaciers and snowfield roped up and using crampons and ice axes, then sat looking through the perfectly transparent air at the nearby mountains. Below them, they could see every detail of the rocky crags, dotted with the tiny conical outlines of hemlock and the thin sticks of firs. Allen found a fly preserved in the ice on a crag, and the white skeletal remains of a mountain goat on the edge of a glacier. A few cirrus clouds stretched across the sky. They bounded down the snowy slopes to the meadows and paths and the welcoming curl of smoke from the chimney of their camp, which they reached at seven-thirty. "I've finally found a climbing companion," said Gary, which made Allen very happy.

They had been away a month, and Allen was delighted to see Peter again. He wrote in his journal: "Slept last night between Peter and Stella, naked, and turned this and that way, one to another on sofa bed, content." On October 1, with Peter at the wheel, his long *1965* hair tucked up under a woolly hat like a Rastafarian, Allen, his young friend Steven Bornstein, Julius, Neal Cassady, and his girlfriend Anne Murphy left San Francisco in the Volkswagen for a week of camping and driving around to visit friends. They saw Ken Kesey in La Honda and Carolyn Cassady in Los Gatos and drove all around the Salinas and Monterey area before finishing up in Big Sur, where they spent a few days at Lawrence Ferlinghetti's cabin in Bixby Canyon.

The cabin stood next to a small stream at the foot of the steep canyon walls, where the mist rarely burned off before midday. A path led down through the trees and mossy cliffs to a small white beach, spanned by the Bixby Canyon Bridge, one thousand feet above. One day, Allen took an acid trip, sitting on the warm sand at the foot of the cliffs where Bixby Creek trickled into the sea. Afterward he wrote Charles Olson: "I took some LSD at Big Sur . . . and felt great—finally—no horrors or worries—just titanic ocean and terrific cliffs and Blakean planet—sunshine and beautiful Wordsworthian kelp."

LSD had been giving Allen the same terrifying visions he experienced on ayahuasca in Peru, so he was very relieved. "No monster vibrations, no snake universe hallucinations. Many tiny jeweled violet flowers along the path of a living brook that looked like Blake's illustration for a canal in grassy Eden: huge Pacific watery shore. Orlovsky dancing naked like Shiva, long-haired before giant green waves, titanic cliffs that Wordsworth mentioned in his own horizon. No harm."

It seemed a long way from the real world, where the forceful Texan Lyndon Johnson dominated the political scene and had become a prime target for antiwar protesters. That day, President Johnson underwent a gallbladder operation, and despite Johnson's escalation of the Vietnam War, Allen felt compassion. He wrote: "Realizing that more vile words from me would send out physical vibrations into the atmosphere that might curse poor Johnson's flesh and further unbalance his soul, I knelt on the sand, surrounded by masses of green bulb-headed kelp vegetable-snake undersea beings washed up by last night's tempest, and prayed for the President's tranquil health."

Back in San Francisco, Allen, Peter, Julius, and Steven Bornstein all stayed at first with their old friend Shig Murao from City Lights, in his two-room North Beach apartment. Steven had a bad habit of inviting everyone he met to come and stay, so Shig would sometimes find his living room filled with people no one knew. They would all go out to eat, and Allen would invariably pick up the tab.

When Allen met Steven, on the street in New York, he was living in a juvenile home on St. Mark's Place. Steven began to visit Allen regularly at East Tenth Street, so Allen invited him out to San Francisco with them. Steven made a hundred-foot-long scroll illustrating the Tibetan Book of the Dead, drawing the various Tibetan deities with intense attention to detail. Allen wrote Huncke: "He doth take too much speed and *is* not in best (nor worst) of health."

Peter was also taking speed, and he spent a great deal of time scrubbing and dusting Shig's apartment. Although Shig was happy to have his toilet washed, he was less pleased when Peter cleaned his wok. "You have to season a wok, and the patina is what gives it the flavor. He spent a whole day cleaning that thing and scouring it. He didn't know. Peter one day took a toothbrush and he scrubbed the whole sidewalk. It was like a Happening. He knew that everyone was watching him, he was trying to be funny, toothbrush and cleanser."

They moved to a bigger place, where Neal and Anne often stayed with them, using Julius's bed. Allen described Neal in a letter to Huncke, who hadn't seen Neal in years: "Neal had entered a new space age dimension—all his old energy still full steam but after 13 years railroad, 2½ years jail and now divorced and years of intensive pot . . . several years of obsession with the racetrack where he lost $10,000 and now several years omnivorous absorption of amphets by mouth ('jumpers' he says) and company with huge crowds of Zonk-minded admirers, lovers of his legend, like, devotees of his energy and speed—he's become a sort of fantastic continuously talking (on 7 or 8 levels of simultaneous association) teacher, plus the fact that for 2 or 3 years he's gone into LSD mind too, also omnivorously, more even than Barbara Rubin and friends did."

Neal's home base was Ken Kesey's psychedelic community in the peninsula backwoods at La Honda, near Palo Alto, where a continuous LSD acid test was going on beneath the redwoods, with films and tapes and huge speakers cranked up to full volume and dozens of kids smoking pot and tripping, wandering among the trees. Neal, of course, drove the psychedelic bus, which now had a microphone slung above his head to broadcast his acid-crazed travelogue as he hallucinated that the gas pedal had turned to spaghetti or that he was being attacked by phantom cockroaches. On acid, he drove through a forest fire and all the way to Idaho and back, with no brakes, clutch, or reverse gear; seven or eight kids lay on a mattress on the roof, high on acid, while the huge roof-mounted speakers blasted rock 'n' roll at startled passersby.

Allen found the chaos at Kesey's hard to handle and dealt with it by just being quiet and looking around, speaking when spoken to and trying to say something sensible. He usually stuck with Neal but occasionally had "manly conversations" with Kesey. Peter's way of dealing with the acid madness was to chop wood.

In 1965, American involvement in Vietnam deepened. President Johnson sent in the first ground troops in March, bringing the number to 27,000. By September, it had risen to 125,000, and as winter set in, there were 175,000 American troops and a further 40,000 men in American naval units in the South China Sea. By the time 1965 was over, 1,365 of these men were dead, 145 missing or captured, and over 5,000 wounded. Domestic opposition to the war grew almost proportionally. On November 28, Saul Bellow, Norman Thomas, Arthur Miller, Alexander Calder, Dr. Benjamin Spock, John Hersey, and fifty thousand others marched in Washington in a demonstration organized by SANE, the Committee for a Sane Nuclear Policy.

In Berkeley, following the wake of the Free Speech Movement demonstrations, an antiwar march was organized by the Vietnam Day Committee, to go from the Berkeley campus, through the black district of Oakland, to the Oakland Army Terminal. It was the height of the black power movement, and since many disadvantaged blacks were against the war, the march organizers thought they would pick up more protesters that way. At the Oakland city line, they were stopped by police wearing full riot gear, with gas masks and guns. Everybody sat down in the street, while speeches were broadcast from the sound truck. At this point, a Hell's Angel named Tiny, who had been behind the police lines, rushed out with seven other Angels and tore down the "Peace in Vietnam" banner that had led the march. Then he ran to the sound truck and cut the wires. The Hell's Angels—motorcyclists who modeled themselves on Marlon Brando in *The Wild One*—inspired fear whenever they rode into town on their Harley-Davidsons. They were right-wing and patriotic in a populist sense. The police stood by and watched them disrupt the march.

Many of the marchers had been involved with the Free Speech Movement and were determined to exercise their constitutional rights, so another march was planned for November. There was a mass meeting to decide policy, during which the Angels were compared to Hitler's brownshirts and a proposal was made that all the men on the march carry long sticks to defend themselves. Allen proposed just the opposite: The march should be led by grandmothers carrying flowers, young women with babies in arms, and girls dressed in pretty costumes. He printed up a leaflet entitled "How to Make a March / Spectacle," suggesting that there be old-fashioned floats with big papier-mâché caricatures to dramatize the issues: a Vietnamese girl attacked by American soldiers in robotic battle gear or Lyndon Johnson with his pants down, surrounded by garlands of flowers and clowns and people playing music.

The Hell's Angels, for their part, threatened to beat up anyone who marched. Clearly something had to be done to avert a confrontation, so Ken Kesey proposed a meeting between the two sides, to be held at Ralph ("Sonny") Barger's house in Oakland. Barger was the president of the Oakland chapter of the Hell's Angels, the most powerful of the outlaw gangs operating on the Coast. Ginsberg, Cassady, Kesey, some Merry Pranksters in costume, and one or two people from the Vietnam Day Committee arrived, to be met by about twenty Angels, also in costume. The first thing they all did was drop acid, with the exception of Allen, who was certain that he would have a horrific trip. At first, the conversation did not go well. Kesey tried to explain to Barger that it was not a Communist plot, whereas the Angels said, "We gotta fight 'em here or there." The Angels thought a Communist victory in Vietnam would lead to a Communist police state in America. Kesey and Allen's argument was why fight them at all: America invaded Vietnam, Vietnam didn't invade America. The discussion began to get acrimonious.

Allen pulled out his harmonium and began to chant the Prajnaparamita, or "Highest Perfect Wisdom," sutra, singing in a deep-voiced monotone. After a few minutes, Tiny, the Angel who had torn up the "Peace in Vietnam" banner, sang, "Om, om, zoom, zoom, zoom, om!" Gradually the other Hell's Angels began to join in, followed by Cassady and Kesey, until, in the end, the whole room was chanting. "I was absolutely astounded," Ginsberg later said. "I knew it was history being made. It was the first time in a tense, tight, situation that I relied totally on pure mantric vocalization, breath-chant, to alleviate my own paranoia and anxiety." In the end, Barger put Dylan's "Gates of Eden" on the record player and confessed to Allen that he liked Joan Baez. By the time the meeting broke up, the tension had been dispelled. Kesey said he was on the side of the Angels and knew they were all blessed. Barger insisted that they had been inaccurately reported and had already made American flags for their own, peaceful, pro-American counterdemonstration.

Several days later, the Angels issued their Newspaper Edict, printed in the San Francisco *Examiner*, saying that it would demean them to attack the filthy Communist marchers and that they had sent a telegram to President Johnson offering to fight the Communists in South Vietnam as "Gorilla" soldiers. The Angels had found a way to save face, and the march was safe from attack.

Shortly after the march, there was a party at Ken Kesey's huge house in the woods, to which the Hell's Angels were invited. Allen, Peter, Julius, and Steven drove down to La Honda in the camper, and it was there, in early December 1965, that Allen wrote the poem *1965* "First Party at Ken Kesey's with Hell's Angels" at 3 A.M., while the huge loudspeakers blasted out Ray Charles, the Beatles, and the Rolling Stones, and four police cars waited outside, their red lights revolving in the leafy night.

> *Cool black night thru the redwoods*
> *cars parked outside in shade*
> *behind the gate, stars dim above*
> *the ravine, a fire burning by the side*
> *porch and a few tired souls hunched over*
> *in black leather jackets.*

Bob Dylan arrived to play some concerts in the Bay Area, and Allen saw him every day. They talked about poetry and fame, and again discussed the idea of doing something together, Dylan producing a record of Allen's mantras or their appearing in a movie or TV show. They had been discussing the idea for some time. In February, Dylan had referred to it on the Les Crane TV talk show:

Les Crane: "Have you ever given any thought to acting; think you might enjoy acting?"

Bob Dylan: "Well, I'm gonna try to make a movie this summer. Which Allen Ginsberg is writing. I'm rewriting."

LC: "Allen Ginsberg the poet?"

BD: "Yeah. Yeah."

LC: "He was on this program, you know."

BD: "Yeah."

LC: "Extolling the virtues of marijuana one night."

BD: "Really? Allen?" (Surprised) (Audience laughs) "Sounds like a lie to me." (Audience laughter)

LC: "That's really—you think I'm lying?"

BD: "No, I didn't mean that."

LC: "Allen Ginsberg was sitting in that chair where Caterina Valente is sitting right now and he said that he thought we ought to legalize pot."

BD: "He said that?"

LC: "Right on the television!"

BD: "Phhewwww!"

LC: "Can you imagine that?"

BD: "Nah. Allen is a little funny sometimes." (Audience roars with laughter)

LC: "Allen's a little funny sometimes, huh? Yes. What's this movie going to be about?"

BD: "Oh it's a, sort of a horror cowboy movie." (Audience laughs) "Takes place on the New York Thruway. I play my mother."

Dylan gave Allen thirty tickets for his concert at the Berkeley Community Center and asked him to spread them around. Allen invited McClure, Duncan, Snyder, LaVigne, Murao, Kesey, and other friends, and gave half the tickets to the Hell's Angels. At the concert, Sonny Barger, Terry the Tramp, and the other Angels sat quietly in the front row, together with Joan Baez, who sang along with Dylan from her seat. When Dylan reached the line in "Gates of Eden" about the motorcycle black madonna two-wheel gypsy queen, Allen screamed it out in unison. Afterward Allen took Sonny Barger backstage and Barger produced a huge bag of pot, putting Dylan on edge, since he did not want to be seen around drugs in a public situation.

There was a big party afterward at Robert LaVigne's studio in the Mission district, and Dylan, Joan Baez, the members of the Hawks (Dylan's musicians, who later changed their name to the Band), Ken

Kesey, Michael McClure, people from the Vietnam Day Committee, Sonny Barger, Freewheelin' Frank, Terry the Tramp, Tiny, and the other Hell's Angels all danced to an all-woman rock band, their differences forgotten.

Feeling generous, Dylan gave Allen six hundred dollars to buy himself a top-of-the-line portable reel-to-reel Uher tape recorder, which would run for ten hours on batteries and could be plugged into a socket to recharge. Dylan also bought an amplifier for Peter and an autoharp for Michael McClure. Allen and McClure spent a lot of time with Dylan, and at a party in his motel after a concert at the Masonic Auditorium, Joan Baez told Allen and Michael that they should be "Dylan's conscience." Since he had left the civil rights movement, Dylan's politics had shifted to the right. McClure recalled, "On some level Dylan's politics were like first strike capability politics. If the Chinese are building the hydrogen bomb, maybe it wouldn't be a bad idea to go in there and take it out. It's macho politics. It's young man politics, and it's not incompatible with 'Blowin' in the Wind.' Dylan is not a bleeding heart liberal. . . . I heard him bare his heart a couple of times and my blood ran a little cold, but it was nothing worse than Kennedy."

Allen, McClure, and most of all Joan Baez were trying to loosen him up, broaden his outlook a little, but Dylan could not be persuaded to speak out directly against the Vietnam War, despite the fact that he was staying with Baez in her house in Carmel and was still associated, in the public mind, with antiwar songs.

On December 15, Allen, Peter, Julius, and Steven left San Francisco to drive slowly across the U.S.A. They began by staying a week with Lawrence Ferlinghetti at his Big Sur cabin. Allen had got a prescription for morphine to relieve kidney stones, and he spent a lot of time sitting, high, on the beach, mumbling into his new tape recorder, getting to know it as a writing tool: "A new ax for composition," as he described it to Gregory. There was a big rock in the middle of the white sand beach, and he sat there and made a number of recordings of mantras, accompanying himself on his finger cymbals, while the sea sighed in the background. He practiced deep "Om"s, which blended in with the waves, and began to use the machine to record his impressions. When they were transcribed, they gave his journals a conversational tone. He described the walk from the cabin, following the creek down to the beach:

"The mossy rockface . . . many colors of green and yellow, tendrils of vines . . . reddish brown. Velvet moss. The brightness of the sun . . . all the little twinkling branches at the end of the path trembling in the wind, and the gurgling of the stream . . . weeds in the surface brown ground like animal hair—Camel hair weeds— tender little green creepers crawling up a tree. All the trees looking like St. Francis in Ecstasy—Snaky Reptilian Dinosaur tracks in the mud . . . Blue snout tip of ocean thru the rock path . . . God it's beautiful here now—a few birds flutter down the path—a robin?— Here you are little birdy . . . Oh, there's Steven perching and look- ing in his solitude and smiling—Hello Steven!"

In the evenings, they sat around the big stone fireplace, putting on logs and talking quietly. Allen reread Kerouac's *Big Sur*, written in the same cabin when Jack was having D.T.'s and thought that the canyon walls were going to close in and crush him. Kerouac's graffiti were still on the wall of the outhouse. At night, they could hear the shifting of the ashes in the fireplace and the tinkling of the stream by the side of the house.

On Christmas Eve, they cleaned the cabin, put fresh kindling and small logs under the porch, piled chopped wood by the fireplace, and set off south down the Coast Highway, intending to spend a month in Los Angeles. Christmas Day, they camped in the Santa Lucia Range. Allen wrote Gregory: "I'm heading down to L.A. . . . Hang around Wally Berman's Canyon home there and drive around to parties in the camper and play my tape recorder by my pillow and fuck Peter and Steven and tell Julius to wash the dishes."

Wally Berman, a friend of Allen's from North Beach, was an artist and the editor of *Semina* magazine. He was living with his wife, Shirley, and their son high in the Santa Monica Mountains. There, Allen and the others quickly settled into the strangely beau- tiful world of canyon living, with coyotes howling at night and the glittering web of lights spread out below. Allen did a couple of television debates about narcotics laws, met Laura Huxley, and had a brief visit with Christopher Isherwood. On January 10, 1966, he did a reading at Riverside University and sent the check to Ed Sanders, copies of whose *Fuck You / A Magazine of the Arts* had just been seized by the police in New York. Allen advised Sanders to contact the ACLU and organized a benefit reading in Los Ange- les, which brought in another three hundred dollars for the defense fund.

It was impossible not to get involved with the music scene in L.A. Through Dylan's manager, Albert Grossman, Allen met the Byrds, the rock group who took Dylan's acoustic "Mr. Tambourine Man" and recorded a sweetly harmonized rock 'n' roll version with a jangly twelve-string electric guitar. It was released in May and inspired Dylan to "go electric" himself. Allen mentioned in a letter to Ed Sanders that he was also seeing a lot of a "Teenage Rock King kid named Phil Spector." Spector was the creator of the famous "Wall of Sound," the genius behind the Ronettes, the Crystals, the Righteous Brothers, and many other acts. When Spector heard Allen's mantra-chanting, he offered to produce him singing the Prajnaparamita sutra as a jukebox record. Regrettably, this was one of the "little symphonies for the kids"—Spector's term—that he never got around to making.

On January 26, the Volkswagen bus set off to discover America. *1966* Peter drove, Julius and Steven sat in the back, while Allen, in the front, held his microphone and recorded impressions as they traveled. They headed east for San Bernardino, with Nelson Eddy singing "Oh, What a Beautiful Morning" on the tinny car radio, followed by news of the war. The poetry notations taped on the trip became "Hiway Poesy: L.A.–Albuquerque–Texas–Wichita," published in *The Fall of America*. Their first destination was Albuquerque, to visit Robert Creeley. They spent the night camped in snow in the vast empty Arizona desert. Peter drove steadily: through the Painted Desert, past the Meteor Crater to the Petrified Forest, through the lands of the Navajo and the Hopi, past gas flares and oil refineries emitting smoke and steam—"high aluminum tubes winking red lights over space ship runways"—till they finally crested a hill and saw nighttime Albuquerque sparkling below in the black desert.

Creeley taught at the University of New Mexico in Placitas, a few miles to the north. They had an enjoyable but short visit, and the Volkswagen was soon rolling along Route 66 again, this time toward Kansas, "Center of the Birchite Vortex" as Allen described it in a letter to Lucien Carr. They dropped off a pair of hitchhikers at Tucumcari and drove on into Texas. They were in the Bible Belt:

"On Radio entering Texas / Please For Jesus! / Grunts & Screams & Shouts / Shouts for the Poison Redeemer, / Shouts for the Venomous Jesus of Kansas. / Onward to Wichita! / Onward to the Vortex! / To the Birchite Hate Riddles, / cock-detesting, pussy-smearing / dry ladies and evil Police / of Central Plains State . . ."

They entered Kansas at Liberal, past radio towers with red blinking beacons, transmitting the "Hebrew-Christian Hour" and *Lifeline*. They passed a small herd of buffalo, their backs shining in the sun, slowly cropping the frosty grass at the edge of the Ninnescah River. The radio picked up nothing but religious broadcasting or news of the war. After the annual Tet truce, the United States launched Operation Rolling Thunder, bombing to within four miles of the center of Hanoi in a still undeclared war. American casualties were running at 100 dead, 600 wounded each week. This was to be the year when Johnson more than doubled U.S. troop numbers, from 181,000 in January to 400,000 by December. The United States dropped as many bombs on Vietnam as had been dropped in the whole Pacific theater during World War II, and by the end of 1966 another 4,800 Americans were dead and 335 American planes shot down.

"Martial music filling airwaves— / only the last few weeks / waves of military music / drum taps drum beats trumpets / pulsing thru radiostations / not even sad . . . / What Patriot wrote that shit?" The music was Sergeant Barry Sadler's "The Ballad of the Green Berets," a patriotic novelty song, which was climbing the charts. It reached number one on March 5, 1966, and stayed there for five weeks, such was the mood of the country.

They gave readings, which were sold out, and there were big parties with local poets, professors, and young people. Allen was at the height of his fame. All the newspapers wanted interviews, and *Life* magazine reporter Barry Farrell followed Allen around as if reporting on a royal tour, writing a huge story entitled "Guru Comes to Kansas." Robert Frank flew out and filmed the Kansas City reading and also shot footage of Allen and Peter in a Kansas wheat field. "It was a very romantic time and a very creative time," Ginsberg recalled. "It really dazzled me because there was so much going on."

In Wichita, Allen found the Chances R club, where the "fairy boys of the plains" danced to the Rolling Stones' "(I Can't Get No) Satisfaction" and Nancy Sinatra's "These Boots Are Made for Walking." His poem "Chances 'R' " later appeared in *Planet News*. They drove to Topeka to give a reading at the Menninger Clinic before an audience of psychologists and psychiatrists. Peter built up high hopes that the renowned clinic might be able to help Julius and might even take him on, but they didn't have anything new to suggest. Peter, on amphetamine, let his anger and frustration show. Ginsberg remembered his reaction: "So Peter took off all his clothes at this gathering of psychiatrists and showed 'em his asshole standing on a table, angrily. And then, driving back to Lawrence with me and Julius, he was very drunk and was driving very fast and suicidally. I got really scared and that was the one and only time I have been totally frightened [by Peter]."

As their Volkswagen circled Wichita, driving through McPherson and Emporia, straying north to Lincoln, Nebraska, the radio crackling with news of the war dead and cattle prices, Allen filtered the images of the winter farms, the advertising signs, the newspaper headlines—"Vietnam War Brings Prosperity"—the endless highways through the flatlands, the continual chatter of the car radio, into a series of spoken stanzas, two or three long lines at a time, murmured directly into the microphone of his Uher as they sped along.

". . . the triangle-roofed Farmer's Grain Elevator / sat quietly by the side of the road / along the railroad track / American Eagle beating its wings over Asia / million dollar helicopters / a billion dollars worth of Marines / who loved *Aunt Betty* / Drawn from the shores and farms shaking / from the high schools to the landing barge / blowing the air thru their cheeks with fear / in *Life* on Television."

He was dictating the lines that became "Wichita Vortex Sutra," possibly his best-known poem of the sixties and regarded as one of his finest. He collected Midwestern images, glimpses of the snow-covered farms and silent afternoon small towns, and collaged them with the hysterical headlines, reactionary radio editorials, quotes from political speeches, books, and articles, until the poem reached its climax when Ginsberg summoned all the powers of his imagination and, calling upon the various gods and gurus at his command, from Krishna to Blake, to empower him, he proclaimed the end of the war.

> *I lift my voice aloud*
> *make Mantra of American language now,*
> *I here declare the end of the War!*

He wrote Gregory: "I wrote huge 17 page 'Wichita Vortex Sutra' *1966* big Shelleyan poem ending Vietnam War—wrote it on tape machine betwixt Lincoln and Wichita." In print the poem came out at twenty-three pages, twice as long as "Howl." It was instantly recognized as the strongest, most heartfelt artistic response to the horror of the Vietnam War and the wanton destruction in Southeast Asia, as well as its effect on the United States.

The *Village Voice* published it on April 28, 1966. It was quickly picked up by the burgeoning underground press and appeared in the *L.A. Free Press*, the *Berkeley Barb*, the *Fifth Estate*, and *Ramparts*, among others. In England, *Peace News* ran it across their centerfold and issued it as a pamphlet. Coyote Books in the States also released it as a pamphlet, distributed by City Lights. *Life* magazine used a large section of it at the end of Barry Farrell's profile, and after "Howl" and "Kaddish," "Wichita Vortex Sutra" soon became one of Ginsberg's best-known works.

Despite the quotations and topical references, it was completely lacking in slogans and in the hectoring, self-righteous tone that flawed so many antiwar statements. Because it was not topical in that sense, the poem did not date, and it would come to be highly regarded for capturing, perhaps more than any other work, the precise atmosphere of the country at the height of the war.

They stayed in the Midwest for a month, traveling in Kansas, Nebraska, and Indiana. They were stopped by the vice squad in Wichita, visited by the police after a reading in Lincoln, and in Bloomington, where they had visited Dr. Kinsey's Sex Institute, they were threatened with investigation by the Indiana state legislature because Peter had read one of his transcribed "Sex Experiments" from Tangier. But they escaped without being arrested and continued on east, heading to New York City.

The most pressing item on Allen's desk when he returned was the case of Dr. Timothy Leary. On December 23, 1965, Leary, his son, Jack, and daughter, Susan, together with two members of his Castalia Foundation staff, were stopped at International Bridge in Laredo, Texas, where a Mexican secret service agent prohibited them from entering Mexico. The car and its five occupants were then searched by American customs officials, who found a half ounce of marijuana on Susan Leary, which Tim promptly claimed was his. Tim and Susan were tried in Laredo on three counts: smuggling, transportation, and failure to pay tax on marijuana. Both pleaded not guilty. The smuggling charge was dropped, since they never actually reached Mexico, but on March 11, Leary was convicted of transporting and tax avoidance and given the maximum sentence on both counts, a total of thirty years in prison and a fine of thirty thousand dollars, and was committed to a hospital for psychiatric observation. This draconian sentence was immediately appealed to a higher court, but the heat was on, and for the next decade Leary was hounded by the authorities, unable to pursue his research and forced to devote most of his time to defending himself from legal harassment.

Allen immediately got involved in the Timothy Leary Defense Fund and began gathering signatures and money for an advertisement in the *New York Times* condemning the sentence and calling for changes in the law. The advertisement was signed by Leslie Fiedler, Richard Alpert, Charles Olson, Robert Lowell, Norman Mailer, Jules Feiffer, Susan Sontag, Jonas Mekas, Kenneth Koch, Albert Grossman, Laura Huxley, Peter Fonda, and even Norman Podhoretz.

Allen continued his flirtation with the world of rock 'n' roll. Phil Spector's idea of recording mantras stuck with him. He wanted to make records and be a star, but his recording career got off to a slow start, and it was not until 1969 that he cut his first album. Thereafter he managed to record more albums than the average rock band.

Allen's girlfriend Barbara Rubin had become deeply involved with a new underground rock band managed by Andy Warhol, the Velvet Underground. Warhol superstar Edie Sedgwick and Warhol's assistant, the poet Gerard Malanga, danced in front of the group. Malanga wore black leather and cracked a whip, while slides and Warhol's films were projected over the dancers. The full mixed-media performance was known as the Exploding Plastic Inevitable, three words Paul Morrissey picked out of Dylan's amphetamine babble on the sleeve of his album *Bringing It All Back Home*.

In April 1966, Warhol and Morrissey hired an old Polish dance hall, the Dom, on St. Mark's Place, and began a series of public performances. Allen went along and danced to exhaustion with Barbara and her girlfriends, to the music of the Stones and the Beatles. "I Want to Hold Your Hand" was a great favorite at the club. Barbara arranged for Allen to sing with the Velvets, and he climbed onstage and sang "Hare Krishna" while Malanga danced around, cracking his whip, and the group provided appropriate backing. "I was trying to introduce a big serious note of spiritual materialism in the middle of all that!" joked Ginsberg. His role as spiritual adviser to the underground scene was becoming more defined.

When Allen was in London in 1965, he had made arrangements to have his collected poems published there by Jonathan Cape; Penguin would issue the paperback edition. This naturally brought up the possibility of a similar volume in the United States. The problem was that City Lights was still very much a small press, with correspondingly poor distribution. Allen enjoyed his relationship with City Lights because he was dealing with friends and was able to use them as an informal office to send out books to people and handle all the messy details of foreign editions and anthologies. They took a percentage for this service, of course, but it did relieve Allen's desk load. The mid to late sixties was a period of enormous success for Beat writers and writers influenced by the Beats. Richard Brautigan sold over two million copies of *Trout Fishing in America*, Lawrence Ferlinghetti's *Coney Island of the Mind* sold close to one million, and his publisher, New Directions, constantly reprinted his other books and those of Gregory Corso and Gary Snyder. Though it must have been galling for Ginsberg to see rows of Ferlinghetti's books in the stores and rarely any of his own, he stayed with City Lights. One of his reasons for doing so was that he was easily their best-selling author, and without him the press might have had to close.

The idea of a hardcover version of his collected poems, therefore, posed something of a problem. He had just returned from the Midwest, where, despite his tremendous fame and sold-out readings, he was unable to find any of his books in the stores. He wrote Ferlinghetti and suggested the idea of a joint imprint: Doubleday/ City Lights or Grove/City Lights, with the New York publisher handling the distribution and City Lights taking a share of the profits. "I wd give the book to City Lights to do hardcover," he wrote, "but having been in Lincoln, Nebraska, and Wichita, etc., I don't think it's possible in next few years for City Lights alone to compete with Grove etc. for distribution. I wanna big mass distribution if I can."

Allen had been offered a ten-thousand-dollar advance on a hardcover edition, and he proposed to forgo this if City Lights could be brought in as a profit-sharing copublisher. "Please say OK," he begged Ferlinghetti, "unless you have a groovier alternative." City Lights was naturally unwilling to lose its cash cow, and in the end Allen was persuaded to stay with it, largely because he could not face the unpleasantness of a break. He was at the peak of his fame, he could command enormous sums for poetry readings, and with proper distribution, he would certainly have been America's bestselling poet. With a good literary agent and a New York publisher, he could have sold at least four times as many books. In 1970, he was offered a $100,000 advance by a New York publisher, but it would have meant leaving City Lights altogether, and he turned it down. As it was, while Ferlinghetti and Snyder were buying beautiful houses for themselves, Ginsberg remained in the slums of the Lower East Side.

Most of the money he made from his readings he gave away to other poets, and to avoid paying tax on these funds, some of which would go toward the Vietnam War, Allen, with the legal assistance of his brother, set up a charitable foundation. On April 12, 1966, the paperwork was completed and the nonprofit Committee On Poetry came into being, making Ginsberg probably the first poet in America, possibly the world, with his own charitable foundation. Over the years, COP was to distribute tens of thousands of dollars to small presses, underground newspapers, impoverished poets, and other projects, to further the cause of poetry.

Shortly after Allen had been strip searched as a "narcotics trafficker" on his return to New York from Europe in 1965, there was another attempt by the authorities to curtail his activities as a marijuana advocate. A jazz musician named Jack Martin was arrested for possession of pot, and four narcotics agents, including the supervisor of the New York Bureau of Narcotics, had a private meeting with him, during which they told him that his bail would be raised from five to ten thousand dollars and that additional charges would be added to his indictment, unless he helped them out.

Agent Bruce Jensen acted as their spokesman. "We want Ginsberg," he said. "How would you like to see your wife in jail? . . . We don't want you, we want the guy you get it from. . . . Do you know Ginsberg? . . . Can you get him for us? . . . Can you set up Allen Ginsberg?" To the enforcers, it was inconceivable that Ginsberg would campaign for marijuana unless he was somehow involved with its sale and trafficking.

Jack Martin had been arrested with a friend of his, George Wilbourn, and on August 11, 1965, there had been a benefit to raise money for Wilbourn's bail. Though Martin had never met Ginsberg, he got up and gave a brief speech in which he described how Jensen had tried to get him to set Ginsberg up. At this point, three undercover agents in the audience came forward, and after a shouting match and a brief scuffle, Martin was arrested for a second time. Arrested with him were filmmakers Jack Smith and Piero Heliczer, who were charged with assault and resisting arrest. The narcotics agents had shown no identification, nor did they have arrest warrants. Smith and Heliczer thought that Martin was being attacked by thugs, which was why they intervened. They were all taken to the Fifth Precinct station, where Jack Smith was brutally beaten by a Detective Imp, who seemed quite unconcerned that many people were witnesses to his actions. Allen Ginsberg, meanwhile, was in California, quite unaware of what was going on.

Martin and Wilbourn pleaded guilty in the original marijuana case and received two-year suspended sentences. The cases of assault and resisting arrest didn't reach court until April 11, 1966, when the jury was selected. By this time, Ginsberg had been informed, and he turned up in court. He told the *New York Times*: "I feel like the noose of the police state is closing in on me. I've had experience of police states in Prague and it's very similar here." On April 13, Narcotics Agent Bruce Jensen testified that he had asked Martin if he knew whether Ginsberg ever possessed or sold narcotics in New York and that he had once asked Martin "if he would assist the Bureau of Narcotics as an informant." On April 15, Martin, Smith, and Heliczer were all found guilty of assault and resisting arrest.

Meanwhile, Tim Leary's case was slowly winding its way through the appeal courts, taking up much of his time and costing a huge amount in legal fees. Among his supporters were Billy and Peggy Hitchcock, heirs to the Mellon fortune, who placed at his disposal a mansion set in a 2,500-acre estate in Millbrook, New York. On April 17, at 1:30 A.M. the Dutchess County police raided it. Among the twenty-nine guests there that night were four medical and psychological doctors, three physical scientists, five journalists on assignments, and three photographers. There were twelve children. The police swept through the house, entering all the bedrooms without knocking and body searching all the adults. They searched all sixty-four rooms in the house, and though they found no drugs on Leary, he was arrested along with three of his guests for drug possession. It was a straightforward case of police harassment. Allen wrote to Ferlinghetti: "Shit's hit the fan on Leary and LSD in New York and phone's ringing in every direction."

1966

On June 14, attired in a new Brooks Brothers suit, Ginsberg flew to Washington to testify at the congressional hearings on LSD before Senator Edward Kennedy, Senator Jacob Javits, and others. Allen had prepared his presentation very carefully. It was one of his most persuasive appeals and also a superb piece of scholarship, basically proposing government-funded research into the safety of the drug, but none of his suggestions were heeded, and predictably, LSD was made illegal.

The next day, still in his new suit, he flew to San Francisco. This was to become the pattern of Allen's life, logging more airtime than most businessmen as he flew around the country and the world attending readings, conferences, workshops, and arts festivals, giving interviews, and appearing on television talk shows.

In the early hours of July 24, 1966, the young poet Frank O'Hara was hit by a dune taxi on Fire Island in a freak accident; he died the next evening. Allen had first met O'Hara in the early fifties, but it was when he returned to New York from San Francisco in 1956 that he got to know O'Hara's poetry. Later, O'Hara and Ginsberg both lived on the Lower East Side, and they would often visit each other. The two men had a lot in common: they were the same age, both homosexual, both poets who moved in circles that were not strictly defined by their literary work. O'Hara was an assistant curator at the Museum of Modern Art, and Allen admired the way he dealt with that uptown world. "Frank taught me to really see New York for the first time, by making of the giant style of Midtown his intimate cocktail environment. It's like having Catullus change your view of the Forum in Rome."

They dedicated poems to each other. Ginsberg's "My Sad Self" was to Frank O'Hara, and O'Hara wrote a poem called "Fantasy/ dedicated to the health of Allen Ginsberg." O'Hara's death was a shock, and Allen went out to Springs, Long Island, with Larry Rivers for the funeral. Two days later, late at night, Allen took some heroin, and as Peter stared out of the apartment window, distracted by amphetamine and the noisy nighttime Lower East Side clamor, Allen sat and wrote a poem for Frank O'Hara, "City Midnight Junk Strains."

> *I stare into my head   & look for your / broken roman*
> *nose*
> *your wet mouth-smell of martinis*
> *& a big artistic tipsy kiss.*

Allen awoke to the news that Bob Dylan had been thrown from *1966* his motorcycle near his home in Woodstock and broken his neck. Dylan had various internal injuries as well, and it was more than a week before he was allowed to return home from the hospital; he was nursed in bed for a further five weeks. After three weeks, he was permitted to have a few visitors, and on August 19, Allen went to spend the afternoon with him, taking a pile of poetry for him to read: Rimbaud, Blake, Shelley, and Emily Dickinson.

Dylan later telephoned from his bed in Woodstock and asked, "What's *your* poetry like now?" As for himself, he told Allen, "What I'm trying to do now is not too many words. There's no line that you can stick your finger through, there's no hole in any of the stanzas. There's no blank filler. Each line has something." Dylan had stopped his amphetamine babble and now seemed mostly interested in country music. He was writing *John Wesley Harding*.

1966

On October 23, Allen gave a reading with his father at the Paterson YMHA. It was Allen's first reading in his hometown and something of an occasion, with a heavy turnout of family members and press. Afterward there was some casual questioning from reporters, and Allen revealed that earlier that day he had gone to the falls on the Passaic River and smoked some marijuana. The mayor of Paterson promptly swore out a warrant for his arrest. Allen wrote Gregory: "My first reading in Paterson! With my pappa! ye Gods!" He was unable to return to New Jersey to see his family until the matter was cleared up.

His itinerary for November involved a three-day trip to Kansas, a trip to Toronto, and five readings in five days in Boston, where he made a speech in favor of LSD at the Arlington Church, which was widely reprinted in the underground press. He gave TV and press interviews and attended several peace marches and rallies. He appeared on Mike Wallace's show on CBS and was on NBC the next night. There was, in addition, his paperwork: That month he wrote an introduction to a book of poems by Charley Plymell and transcribed most of his "auto poesy" tapes, filling hundreds of pages of his notebooks with an almost indecipherable scrawl, which he would later cut and edit, then type up. He wrote ten or more letters a day and fired off Committee On Poetry checks to the needy—from an underground newspaper in trouble with the police in London to sending Gregory Corso $350 to get back to New York from Athens. "Just about keeping my head above water by furious energy at desk," he wrote Ferlinghetti. "But it's not natural. Something got to give."

1967

The Arts Council of Great Britain, in a surprise move, invited Allen to attend an international poetry festival planned for the summer of 1967. He was also invited to London by the "anti-psychiatrist" R. D. Laing, who was organizing a conference on the subject of the Dialectics of Liberation. Allen decided to accept the Arts Council offer and stay on for the conference. Since he was now bringing in two to three hundred dollars for each reading, he could afford to take Louis and Edith to Europe. He made plans for them to join him in London after the conference and to continue on from there to Paris, Venice, and Rome. Louis was now seventy-two, and Allen wanted to show him the sights before he was too old to travel.

Allen himself was forty-one, and his life seemed to be falling into a pattern. His enormous appetite for work and travel was, if anything, growing, but as a celebrity, he was spending much of his time presenting his message to the world not only in words but in person.

At the beginning of 1967, Allen, Peter, and Allen's mantrachanting girlfriend, Maretta Greer, flew to San Francisco. Allen took part in a round table discussion with Tim Leary, Gary Snyder, and Alan Watts organized by the *San Francisco Oracle*, the local underground newspaper, which was distinguished by its rainbow printing and psychedelic designs. The *Oracle* came from the Haight-Ashbury area, which was rapidly becoming the center of the hippie universe. In 1966, there had been a dozen or so hippie communes and a few crash pads in the area; now there were hundreds.

The youth of America, in distancing themselves from the mainstream, had established their own newspapers, their own music, cafés, bookshops, and in areas where there was a large hippie community, they set up crash pads, centers that provided legal advice, food, and medical care, and even job-finding centers run by hippie capitalists. Large communes in the country grew organic produce to be sold by the burgeoning health food shops. Allen, recognizing the hippies as literal descendants of the Beats, saw them as the hope of America. He thought they would transform society, fulfilling the prophecy of Walt Whitman and bringing a new spirituality and a new sexuality to the nation. He identified with their freewheeling sexuality, their use of psychedelics and soft drugs, their mysticism and rejection of middle-class mores; it was precisely their ideas about sex, drugs, ecology, and the Vietnam War that divided them from middle-class America.

The tentative experiments with psychedelic drugs conducted by Allen and Leary had mushroomed so that now over one million Americans had taken them. A large number of kids had gone further; following Tim Leary's dictum "Turn On, Tune In, Drop Out," they dropped out of college or jobs and headed for the Lower East

Side, Haight-Ashbury, or country communes. Acting as a central switchboard for the scene, Allen gave enormous assistance to the underground newspapers, doing benefits and interviews and providing contacts with like-minded people throughout America and the world. Everywhere he went, he spoke of legalizing pot and the benefits of LSD. With his luxuriant black beard and huge calm eyes, his beads and finger cymbals, he became almost symbolic of the movement itself, even though he was of a different generation. He assumed the role of elder statesman of the counterculture, one of the few older people the hippies felt they could trust.

All the Beats were highly regarded. Snyder was pleased by the widespread interest in American Indians, ecology, and tribalism. McClure delighted in his new role as anarchist prince, and both he and Snyder participated in be-ins and love-ins and wrote for the underground press. William Burroughs, living in London, followed the scene with great interest and wrote for the British underground paper *International Times*. Neal Cassady had found his niche as driver of the Merry Pranksters bus. Only Kerouac remained apart, trapped in a fifties cold war sensibility, along with his mother. Kerouac was convinced that anyone who demonstrated against the Vietnam War was a Communist. Peter Orlovsky said, "Over and over again he got drunk. He had a vision that he would go up in a treetop with a gun, ready to pop us off. He wanted to shoot the red Communists because we were demonstrating against our country. When it came time to come out and demonstrate, when it came time to write and talk in public, he wouldn't do it."

On January 19, 1967, Allen, Maretta, Gary Snyder, Tim Leary, and many others were onstage to chant mantras at the Human Be-In held at Golden Gate Park, San Francisco, where thirty thousand people assembled for what was advertised as a "Gathering of the Tribes." The Grateful Dead, Jefferson Airplane, and the Quicksilver Messenger Service all played, using a PA system guarded by the Hell's Angels. The Diggers distributed thousands of free turkey sandwiches laced with LSD, Leary told the audience to "Turn On, Tune In, Drop Out," antiwar activist Jerry Rubin said things like "Our smiles are our political banners and our nakedness is our picket sign," and the audience itself took up the mantra "We Are One! We Are One!" Someone parachuted from a light aircraft and floated gently down to the middle of the meadow, causing many people to think that they had just seen God. Gary Snyder ended the gathering by blowing a long note on a conch shell, as everyone turned to see the sun sink into the Pacific. Thousands of people walked to the beach to sit and watch the gathering dusk, and thousands more answered Allen's call for "kitchen yoga" and cleaned up. The memorable day was marred for Allen by an argument with Peter, who was high on amphetamine and refused to join them at the event.

It was the last innocent, idealistic hippie event. That night the police swept down Haight Street; all soft-drug dealers were driven off the scene or arrested, and within weeks the area was flooded with amphetamine and heroin. The communal nature of soft drugs —pot and acid—as demonstrated by the cleaning up of the park, was destroyed and replaced by the amphetamine culture, which would produce Charles Manson.

Poet Larry Fagin regarded Allen's appearance at the Be-In as the occasion that finally made him a household name. "Allen really became the Allen that we know in 1967. He got out into the public and could never really withdraw completely again. The Be-In skyrocketed the whole Ginsberg cottage industry into outer space. It was the highest visibility that he had up to that point." There had been Ginsberg jokes and cartoons in the press as far back as 1959, but now his picture cropped up everywhere as a pictorial shorthand representing the counterculture and hippie movement. Many of the kids who had a poster of him on their wall had probably never read his poetry.

Allen attended the 1967 Spoleto Festival, where he met Ezra Pound, who shook his hand but remained silent, and the Italian poet Giuseppe Ungaretti. Afterward he flew to London for an Arts Council poetry festival. The night Allen arrived, a big party was held at James McNeill Whistler's old house on Cheyne Walk, which had recently been used by Michelangelo Antonioni for the orgy scene in his film *Blow-Up*. Many of the same people were there for the party: young women in velvet and lace and diaphanous scarves, and men like dandies from a Beardsley drawing, with long hair and ruffles at neck and cuffs—the London style that year. The eighteenth-century paneling was hung with medieval tapestries, softly illuminated by a huge Moroccan chandelier. *Sgt. Pepper* played quietly in the background, and the butler offered brownies on a silver tray. Unfortunately, there had been some confusion about just how much hashish Alice Toklas's celebrated recipe for brownies actually called for, and half the people at the party succumbed to cannabis poisoning. Allen was talking with Mick Jagger, the lead singer and composer with the Rolling Stones, and his girlfriend, Marianne Faithfull, when it dawned on Mick and Marianne that the drug had been too powerful. They ran vigorously up and down Cheyne Walk; on returning, Marianne pronounced herself "high but cool." People began to panic; some members of Parliament telephoned their doctors and were taken away to have their stomachs pumped. "Groovy scene here," Allen wrote Peter the next day.

His first reading was on July 12. The evening began with W. H. Auden, who shuffled onstage in his carpet slippers and read familiar material. He was followed by Stephen Spender, and the first part concluded with Charles Olson, who was living in London. Allen led Giuseppe Ungaretti onstage for the second half and remained at his side to read English translations after Ungaretti read in Italian. Allen finished the evening with mantras and recent poems. He had more time to stretch out three days later, when he did a solo reading as part of the same festival. He attempted to dispel the formal atmosphere by laying out bananas and incense on the stage, and opened with his usual mantras, but though he read well, the reading was strained and not a great success. "Horrible. So much like an opera singer's performance," he said later. "I worked at it instead of just letting it come." After the reading, friends took him to Cavendish Avenue, in Saint John's Wood, to visit Paul McCartney.

All the other Beatles had bought country mansions, but McCartney lived in town, with the actress Jane Asher, in a large but unostentatious Regency house. The living room had French windows leading out to a patio. Two paintings by René Magritte hung on the wall, next to one of the versions of the drum skins painted by Peter Blake for the *Sgt. Pepper* album sleeve. A sculpture by Takis stood blinking in a corner next to an Indian sarod. Mick Jagger and Marianne Faithfull were already there, Mick in a rocking chair, his long white silk scarf trailing on the carpet. Paul and Allen sat on the floor. There was a slight nervousness at first, but everyone worked hard to dispel it. Allen sang a few mantras, accompanied by his finger cymbals, and tea was served.

They discussed acid, which Paul had taken, and William Burroughs, whose face appeared on the sleeve of *Sgt. Pepper* and who was making recordings in a small studio Paul had provided for poets and experimental musicians, but mostly McCartney preferred to tell stories about the old days in Liverpool and about his family. He tried to explain to Allen the nature of British eccentricity and said that most of the exploits of the Beat Generation would have been regarded as perfectly normal in Liverpool. They spoke at cross-purposes some of the time, but it was a friendly visit.

As they talked. Paul had been idly opening boxes of gifts from fans. In one he found a bright red satin shirt and began to draw paisley patterns, eyes, and psychedelic designs on the front of it, using Magic Markers. When it was time to leave, Paul reached over and gave the shirt to Allen. "A souvenir of swinging London," he said.

The next day, there was a rally in Hyde Park to demand the legalization of marijuana. Brian Patten and Adrian Henri read their poems, but no one heard them. Allen arrived late with friends, wearing his McCartney satin shirt, which was much too tight for him, and carrying a flower. Walter Cronkite immediately appeared with a camera crew and got in a quick interview before Allen reached the podium. Allen began chanting, accompanying himself on the harmonium. A young policeman came forward and informed him that the playing of music was not permitted in a royal park. Allen stopped playing and gave the policeman his flower. The policeman blushed.

A few people smoked joints, and members of the Balls Pond Road commune danced and sang, their bodies and faces painted with psychedelic colors, but it was a small gathering and most people drifted away early, leaving Allen sitting on the grass surrounded by a group of friends and admirers, all chanting the Hare Krishna mantra. That evening, BBC television's national news carried the music, and the announcer made a *namaste* hand gesture as he said good night, a new degree of levity for the BBC.

The month before Allen arrived in London, Rolling Stone Keith Richards had been found guilty of permitting his house to be used for the smoking of marijuana and sentenced to one year in jail and a fine of five hundred pounds. Mick Jagger, found guilty of the illegal possession of amphetamine on the same occasion, was sentenced to three months in jail and a three-hundred-pound fine. Now free on bail, pending an appeal, both had spent one night in jail. They wished to record their experience in a song. Allen was invited to the recording session.

Through the thick glass of the control room window, Allen saw not only the Stones, dressed in their flowing scarves and ruffled shirts, but John Lennon and Paul McCartney, who had come to sing in the chorus as a gesture of support. Allen was ecstatic. "It was wonderful," he told friends the next day. "They all looked like little angels." The song they recorded was "We Love You," which opened with the sound of footsteps and a prison door slamming. Allen wrote Peter: "Last night I spent at recording studio with Mick Jagger, Paul McCartney and John Lennon looking like Botticelli Graces singing together for the first time. I conducted through the window with Shiva Beads and Tibetan oracle ring."

Allen was an invited speaker at the Dialectics of Liberation conference, organized by R. D. Laing at London's Roundhouse. Laing's controversial views, that reality as experienced by a schizophrenic is just as real as any "normal" person's reality and that the mind-altering drugs and regimentation at mental hospitals were not the correct way to treat mental illness, had quickly made him a countercultural hero.

The conference was soon dominated by Stokely Carmichael, a leader of the American black power movement, whose plans for a separate black nation in the United States gave rise to many late-night arguments. The distinguished group of speakers also included Paul Goodman, John Gerassi, Gregory Bateson, Mircea Eliade, Ernest Mandel, and Paul Sweezy. Allen's theme was "Consciousness and Practical Action," which he began by quoting at length from Burroughs's *Nova Express,* as an example of what happens when a planet goes out of control. He was responding to Gregory Bateson's exposition on the greenhouse effect, which he accurately predicted would manifest itself within ten to thirty years. The entire conference was tape-recorded, to be released as a set of albums. Subsequently, a woman at the pressing plant, listening to a test pressing of Allen's speech to check for faults, was so upset by the quotes from *Nova Express* that she became ill and had to be sent home. The plant refused to press the record, and other means had to be found, holding up the release of the entire series.

On July 28, Allen drove to Wales with publisher Tom Maschler to spend the weekend at his country cottage in Llanthony Valley in the Black Mountains. They stopped en route at the magnificent ruins of Tintern Abbey, the inspiration for Wordsworth's ode. That afternoon, feeling relaxed in the tranquil setting, Allen took an acid trip, during which he wrote "Wales Visitation," a nature poem:

I lay down mixing my beard with the wet hair of the mountainside,
*   smelling the brown vagina-moist ground, harmless,*

> *tasting the violet thistle-hair, sweetness—*
> *One being so balanced, so vast, that its softest breath*
> *moves every floweret in the stillness on the valley floor . . .*

Allen's idyllic summer was interrupted by news of Peter. Overuse of Methedrine had caused him, on one occasion, to hallucinate that the house was on fire and, on another, that the window moldings were smoking, bugged, or electrified; he began to dismantle them. He was taken to Bellevue to calm down. Allen was worried, not just for Peter's health but for his own manuscripts and papers. He wrote to Peter, "I wish you would quit playing with meth: completely, you've seen it in others, it's always created sensory or ideal quirks that you didn't like from the outside. There's now so much chaos and craziness on all sides that I wish we two could be calm and not swept into violence. I say, fix up the house, fix windows fast, quit all needles and all meth, clean up and come over here to England. . . . If you get in such a state that you lose weight, are obsessed with spy-bugging, call fire-dept. for imaginary fires, wind up with police in house and yourself temporarily in Bellevue—things is gone too far."

It was a pattern that would continue for many years, whenever Allen left Peter alone for any length of time. In their correspondence that summer, they had been analyzing their relationship and clearing up some of the misunderstandings that had grown between them. Peter felt that Allen needed young boys like Steven Bornstein and was dissatisfied with him. Allen wrote:

"Well, I'm happy making it with you alone as long as we make it. I just chase after boys as a substitute when I get the idea that you don't want to be stuck with me and that I'm generally too old and repulsive to you now after so much familiarity. I mean, I really got the idea, the last year especially, that you basically don't dig making it with me, and so as not to lay my needs on you, I diverted sex lovemaking to others and accepted the situation cheerfully rather than getting hung up on it and laying guilt on you or me. I don't in any case want to monopolize all yr sex imagination and don't fantasize monogamy for you or me. If you've been at all avoiding lovemaking with me because you think I need or deserve younger various cats, well stop that thought and let's make it more again. I'd rather stick with you, if it were still pleasant to you. But basically —I think you've told me—that I'm getting physically too unappealing—which is no betrayal or fault of yours, that's nature—so I've not wanted to force myself on you lest I seem even more unappealing in the cold light of detached awareness. I have need for love touch and sex come but I'm not so nuts as to think that you or anybody has to find me sexy—so I've just been taking what comes to me, without my having to force the situation by willpower. . . .

"The worst thing has been the meth—I never know who you are or where you are in the universe—and yet as long as there are practical attachments, as long as there are sex attachments of some kind also, there has to be some reliable meeting place. Otherwise I get scared my mss will disappear or you'll change your mind in the middle of a trip and denounce me for being an old stinking fink."

After touring Europe with his parents, Allen went to stay with his translator Fernanda Pivano and her husband, designer Ettore Sottsass, in their beautiful Milan apartment. They spent a weekend with Nanda's mother, who lived at the seaside near Genoa. Nanda knew Olga Rudge and Ezra Pound, and she arranged a drive down to have lunch with them that Saturday, September 23. Olga Rudge, an American violinist, had been Pound's companion since the 1920s. They had a small terraced apartment in a large red house in Sant' Ambrogio, near Rapallo. The house was high on the mountainside and had a magnificent view out over Torquello Bay to Portofino on the promontory below.

Eighty-one-year-old Pound, who had been virtually silent for many years, said little during the meal. Allen asked him if he had ever met Céline. Olga Rudge said that he had not, so Allen described the visit that he and Burroughs made in 1958. Allen recounted that he had asked Céline which French prose writers he liked, and Céline had mentioned three: C. F. Ramuz, Henri Barbusse, and Paul Morand. While Allen tried to remember which of Morand's books Céline liked, Olga Rudge asked Pound, who was still digging into his plate of pasta, "Ezra, what was the name of that book by Morand you liked so much? You didn't like what he did later."

Pound looked up, and said in crisp French, *"Ouvert à la Nuit."*

Allen had brought along his harmonium, and before lunch he had sung Hare Krishna and the Prajnaparamita sutra. Nanda said afterward that Pound looked startled and a little scared when Allen began singing vigorous, loud "Om"s, but Olga Rudge said that he enjoyed it or else he would not have stayed in the room.

They returned to Milan and the next day resumed their translation work. A few weeks later, Nanda left for London, after making arrangements for Allen to visit Pound in Venice, his winter quarters.

Allen checked into the Pensione Cici, not far from the Salute, where Pound frequently ate his midday meals. As he stood in the lobby consulting a wall map of Venice, Olga Rudge and Pound emerged from the dining room. They all had coffee together and Rudge told Allen that if he had any trouble finding the pensione, "Oftentimes Venetians will walk half a mile to show you a tiny alley."

Pound suddenly broke his silence. "Forty years since I've seen anybody do that."

"Do what, Ezra?" she asked.

"Take the trouble to walk you along to show you the way."

Arrangements were made for Allen to come to luncheon the next day. On October 22, he stood before the lion-faced doorbell of the narrow three-floor house on Calle Querini that Olga Rudge had owned since 1928. Pound was silent throughout the visit. Allen had brought some records for Pound to hear, so they went to the top floor of the house, where the record player was. Allen recorded in his journals: "He had come upstairs swiftly when I asked him to listen, and folded self in chair, silent hands crossed on lap, picking at skin, absorbed." Allen put on the Beatles' "Eleanor Rigby" and "Yellow Submarine." Pound smiled lightly at the line "no one was saved." Allen next played Dylan's "Sad-Eyed Lady of the Lowlands" and "Gates of Eden," sometimes repeating words aloud for Pound to hear clearly. Allen had even brought along Donovan's "Sunshine Superman." "Is this all too much electric noise?" he asked. Pound smiled and sat still. "Sat there all along," Allen wrote. "I drunk, he impassive, earnest, attentive, asmile." Allen continued the concert by chanting mantras to Krishna, Tara, and Manjusri. Hearing the Manjusri mantra, Olga Rudge came to the top floor and joined them, saying, "It sounded beautiful down there." Pound said nothing. That evening, Allen went to Harry's Bar and got very drunk.

On October 28, Allen was seated in the dining room of the pensione with the English poet Peter Russell, the critic Michael Reck, and Reck's six-year-old son, waiting for Pound to arrive. An Italian crew making a film about Pound waited outside, cables trailing across the floor. Rudge and Pound eventually appeared, and Pound seated himself on Allen's right. Allen had spent the previous week reading the "Cantos" and walking around Venice, trying to find the places mentioned in the poems. He had heard that Pound would respond to specific textual inquiries. "I found the 'Place of Carpaccio's skulls,' " said Allen, "but where's the place where, 'in the font to the right as you enter / are all the gold domes of San Marco'?"

Pound looked up from his fish. "Yes, when the font was filled, now they've changed it, it used to be like that."

"I walked half a mile yesterday, looking for the spot in Dei Greci, in San Giorgio. Finally looked in San Marco."

"It used to be like that," continued Pound. "The center was filled with water and the reflection had the domes." Olga Rudge added that the font in San Giorgio Dei Greci had been fitted with a copper rim, which they now filled with water; the center was no longer filled.

After getting replies to a number of specific questions, Allen decided to try some of his own work on Pound. He looked through his notebook for a phrase. "I've been trying to find language equivalent for that light on water. Yesterday I arrived at this: Leaped on Vaporetto, / sun yellow in white haze, Salute's / silver light, crooked-mirrored on the glassy surface."

Pound looked Allen in the eye as he repeated the line "light, crooked-mirrored on the glassy surface." Allen smiled at him. "You approve of that?"

"That's good," said Pound, and returned Allen's smile.

"The phrasing of your poems has had a very concrete value for me as reference points for my own perception," Allen said. "Am I making sense?"

"Yes," said Pound, but after a pause mumbled, "But my own work does not make sense." Both Allen and Michael Reck assured him that it made sense to them. "A lot of double talk," said Pound. He seemed to search for words, then said, "Basil Bunting told me that there was too little presentation and too much reference."

Allen replied that the year before, the poet Basil Bunting had told him to look at Pound because Allen had too many words. Bunting showed Pound as a model for economy in the presentation of sensory phenomena via words.

Michael Reck told Pound that reading his poetry, one was struck by how real the descriptions were, even if one hadn't experienced the thing oneself. "Reading your poetry, I often feel this myself," he told Pound. "Your poetry is often shockingly direct."

Pound sat silent, rubbing his hands, then said, "At seventy I realized that instead of being a lunatic, I was a moron."

Both Allen and Reck protested, but Pound insisted. "My writing. Stupid and ignorant all the way through. Stupid and ignorant."

Reck said, "In your poetry, you have an *ear*. That's the most important thing for writing poetry. So it's hard for you to write a bad line."

"It's hard for me to write at *all*," Pound answered with a faint smile.

The conversation continued, and Allen asked if he would like to give a reading in the United States, in Buffalo, maybe, or San Francisco.

"Too late," said Pound.

"Too late for what?" Allen laughed. "For us, or for your voice?" Allen told him that it was never too late; that he had shown the way and that the more of Pound's work he read, the more convinced he was that it was the best of its time.

"The intention was bad," replied Pound, "that's the trouble. Anything I've done has been an accident. Any good has been spoiled by my intentions. The preoccupation with irrelevant and stupid things." Then, speaking slowly and with emphasis, he said, "But the worst mistake I made was the stupid suburban prejudice of anti-Semitism. All along, that spoiled everything."

"Ah, it's lovely to hear you say that," Allen said. It was Pound's first public expression of regret for the anti-Semitism of his wartime broadcasts for Radio Roma. Just as Allen had appeased Kerouac's anti-Semitism, so he had accepted all sides of Pound's character. "Anyone with any sense can see it as a humour," said Allen, "in that sense part of the drama. You manifest the process of thoughts, make a model of the consciousness, and anti-Semitism is your fuck-up, like not liking Buddhists, but it's part of the model as it proceeds. The great accomplishment was to make a working model of your mind. Nobody cares if it's Ezra Pound's mind, but it's a mind like everybody else's."

Allen leaned over to Pound, who was staring straight ahead, and told him, "But you must go on working, to record the last scenes of the drama. You still have a great deal to say. After all, now you have nothing to lose. You *are* working, aren't you?" But now Pound remained silent. Allen continued, "Ah, well. What I came here for, all this time, was to give you my blessing, then. Because despite your disillusion, unless you *want* to be a Messiah, then you'll have to be a Buddhist." Pound smiled.

"But I'm a Buddhist Jew," Allen continued. "Perceptions have been strengthened by the series of practical exact language models which are scattered throughout the 'Cantos' like stepping-stones. Ground for *me* to occupy, walk on. So that, despite your intentions, the practical effect has been to clarify my perceptions. And anyway, do you now accept my blessing?"

Pound hesitated, opening his mouth for a moment before speaking. "I do."

They all walked Pound and Olga Rudge to their doorway, where Allen took Pound by the shoulders and looked him straight in the eyes for a long moment before saying, "I have told you what I came here to tell you, and I also came here for your blessing. And now may I have it, sir?"

"Yes"—he nodded—"for whatever it's worth."

Allen stood talking with Olga Rudge as the others said their good-byes to Pound. "But if you wait," she told Allen, "and have patience, he needs to talk. He thinks all his work so bad, whereas when he reads it into tape, you can tell he reads with enthusiasm, some parts. Other parts of course he dislikes, but that's natural, after years to be self-critical, anyone would."

Then Allen turned to Pound and kissed him respectfully on his right cheek. Pound held Allen's hand and said, "I should have been able to do better."

"It was perfect," said Allen. "I haven't properly yet sung Hare Krishna to you either. I'll be around a few days more anyway, maybe. . . . See you." Pound stood at his doorway, hesitating, waving everyone down the alley.

The next evening at nine, Allen was waiting for the vaporetto at the Salute boat station, a floating platform on the Grand Canal. Pound and Olga Rudge appeared, on their way to the Carmini Church, where a woman friend of theirs was singing in a Vivaldi concert. Allen asked if he could accompany them, and Olga Rudge said, "Certainly." They climbed aboard the vaporetto, and Allen sat behind the others, leaning forward to speak between the backs of their heads so that both could hear him. He told them the story of Julius Orlovsky as a Manichaean who would not speak for fourteen years because he believed that all the evil in the universe came from his body and mouth. Olga Rudge laughed and asked, "Are you a Manichaean, Ezra?" but he would not answer.

Allen sat behind them in the ornate seventeenth-century candlelit nave and wrote a small poem-sketch of the scene: "Old man sat before me, / brown canvas shoes, one heel raised alert, / hat and cane in hand / Smooth woodslab resting / under a fold in his coat-back— / white cheek beard dyed red by / velvet light, / black not entirely faded from / back of his skull, / fringed with grey hair, / candle gleam through white web."

A delicate theme played on the violin began, and Olga Rudge rose, closely followed by Pound, and walked along the north aisle of the church to stand closer to their friend. When the piece was over, they left without waiting to hear any further music and began walking home through the alleyways. Allen spoke to Pound about the "Cantos" and Pound's apparent inability to finish them, saying that the work was not a static crystalline idealized structure but an open-ended one, "that is, epic, 'including history,' of movement of your mind and record of focused perceptions existing in *time*, and changing in time. Anything you write now will refer back to the beginnings and alter all that went before, like turning a Venetian blind. So *anything* you do now is okay and will be proper, appropriate, as means of altering preceding thought-flow by hindsight. Am I making sense?"

"It's all tags and patches," replied Pound.

Allen spoke more about the "Cantos" and finally asked, "Is your problem one of physical depression that keeps you from recording and registering these final perceptions—whatever you are *now*?"

"The depression's more mental than physical," Pound answered. They reached the house, and Allen went in with them and sat down while Olga Rudge lit a fire. Allen talked more about the "Cantos," but Pound remained silent. Then Allen asked, "Do you know the enormous influence you've had?"

"I'd be surprised if there was any," Pound replied dubiously, but he looked interested.

Allen recited a few short poems by Robert Creeley, then spoke of Charles Olson and John Wieners. He asked Pound if he was at all familiar with Allen's own work, and Pound shook his head. "Well, oddly, it might even please you," Allen told him. He asked if Pound understood that his own writing had been a model for a whole generation of younger poets in the United States, including himself, who at forty-one was exactly half Pound's age.

"It would be ingenious to see any influence," replied Pound.

Olga Rudge brought in cups of Ovaltine and a copy of "Canto CX." "Has Mr. Ginsberg seen this?" she asked. Allen said that he would return it, but she asked Pound to inscribe it to him.

Pound hesitated a long time, then said, "Oh, he doesn't *want* it."

"Well, yes. Sure, I do," said Allen. "If you want to check your perceptions. I absolutely do."

Pound took the small volume and signed, "Alan Ginsberg—dall'autore—Oct 29, 1967. Ezra Pound."

Olga Rudge invited Allen to come the next day and sing to Pound on the night of his eighty-second birthday. Allen arrived at 10 P.M., wearing the red satin shirt given to him by Paul McCartney, a large Buddhist trikaya emblem around his neck. He carried his harmonium. Pound was sitting in the downstairs room, warming himself before the fire. Allen ran through the Prajnaparamita sutra in both English and Japanese, then followed it with a rousing version of the Hare Krishna mantra. There was a break for some birthday cake and champagne, then Allen chanted the Three Buddhist Vows. He recorded the events in his journal:

"Then in silence till, to illustrate effect of his composition on mine, read—with indifferent voice alas—few pages of 'Middle Section of Long Poem On These States.' Oops! Silence. Eek! Put that down fast after asking, do you see the relationship in method of composition? Silence. So picked up harmonium and chanted 50 verses of 'Gopala Gopala Devaka Nandina Gopala'—high and sweet, and low solemn. Then explained 'Gopala means Krishna cowboy,' and said goodnight and 'Happy Birthday Krishna.' He smiled at that. Leaving from door I demanded, 'Well, say *Goodnight!*' He nodded amiably, said 'Goodnight.' So I left."

Allen saw Ezra Pound a few more times, and once they met at lunch at the Pensione Cici. The elderly waitress carefully boned Pound's grilled trout. He did not look well, and though he shook Allen's hand when Allen said goodbye, he did not speak throughout the meal or when he left.

The season was over. Many of the pensiones had closed up, and few tourists braved the wind and rain to walk on the Piazza San Marco. The outdoor cafés had taken in their chairs and potted palm trees. The orchestras had all gone home.

FIFTEEN | PATERFAMILIAS

I have to put up with a lot to please the sensitive race of poets!

—Horace, *Ars Poetica*

ALLEN DID NOT FULLY ACCEPT HIS MIDDLE AGE; HE WORRIED ABOUT AP-
proaching old age and ill health, about his deteriorating appearance
and childless future. On the plus side, at forty-one he now had a
sufficient body of solid work behind him, enough to guarantee his
place in American letters. He was easily the most famous poet in
America. He was witnessing the widespread application of many of
his ideas about free love and the use of consciousness-expanding
drugs. Hundreds of underground newspapers mixed anti–Vietnam
War news with esoteric discussions of the philosophies of Eastern
mystics previously unheard of in America; there was extensive interest in meditation, mantras, the occult, astrology, and every possible kind of spiritual quest, from shamanism to Aleister Crowley.
Allen had seen the initial tentative ideas of the "New Vision," which
he first discussed with Lucien Carr, Bill Burroughs, and Jack Kerouac back in 1944, blossom into nothing less than a movement that
involved possibly millions of people worldwide.

Other movements and rebellions took root and blossomed in the
sixties: women's liberation and the struggle for black civil rights.
Of the three, the youth movement was the most fragile, containing
within it the seeds of potential tragedy. But the sixties were not yet
over. Woodstock was still to come, in 1969, but so, too, were the

assassinations of Martin Luther King and Robert Kennedy, and the brutal clashes between authority and the counterculture at Kent State and in the streets of Chicago.

Allen came back to New York on November 15, 1967. Peter was in San Francisco, and Allen wrote him to stay out there as long as he wanted but warned him to stay off Methedrine. He added: "I want to live with you but I can't live with meth, things are so chaotic outside the house I need calm in the house. And I know that what I want to do is live quietly, stay at home a lot and work on Poetry. I did that in Europe and it makes me feel good. No meth and maybe even no phone."

Peter arrived in town a week later, calm and off speed. Allen was relieved of the guilt he always felt when Peter was taking a lot of meth. "In the late sixties, Peter started going crazy, partly because of his speed trips, perhaps. I felt I was to blame, that this was the result of my demands on him," he said. But now the atmosphere in East Tenth Street was relaxed, and Allen slowly eased his way back into the New York scene, dispensing advice, contacts, and money. His poetry foundation continued to distribute thousands of dollars each year to needy poets, and Allen himself gave endless benefit readings for pacifist groups, war resisters, deserters, little magazines, underground newspapers, small presses, and the inevitable legal defense campaigns.

Ever since the Beatles had begun to extol the virtues of Maharishi Mahesh Yogi in August 1967, Allen had wanted to meet him. With the Beatles' endorsement, the Maharishi was attracting an enormous number of young followers, including other rock musicians such as the Beach Boys. The Beatles had even announced their intention of going to India to study at his ashram (they did in fact go, in April 1968). In January 1968, the Maharishi came to New York. Allen had telephoned for tickets, and on the return phone call he was invited to meet the Maharishi in his suite at the Plaza Hotel.

The room was filled with flowers, and Allen sat on the floor along with dozens of devotees, who were listening to every word spoken in the Maharishi's high-pitched, squeaky voice. Allen had heard reports of the Maharishi's saying outlandish things at recent press conferences, such as "Poverty is laziness" and "Communism equals weakism," so he had a number of questions to ask him. Hippies were particularly vulnerable to this type of teaching since, having rejected their own culture and changed their perceptions of reality with acid, they were wide open to exploitation.

Allen had no arguments with the dictum that everyone should meditate for half an hour each morning and evening, and he remained open-minded about the Maharishi's claims that his special mantra form was more effective than any other, since Allen hadn't tried it. Allen even thought that the Maharishi's high-powered, highly organized method of advertising meditation and setting up what were in fact pyramid clubs of people meditating would tend toward a more general peacefulness in the land if they caught on. It was his political statements that worried Allen as being "definitely dim-witted and a bit out of place." Allen described the meeting:

"After I was introduced, I sat at his feet and literally started yelling at him—spent half an hour almost, challenging, arguing— all in good humor tho his business managers and devotees gasped with horror occasionally, but I never got impolite and he stayed calm and rather sweet, so no harm." The Maharishi had been discussing American "dissatisfaction," a word of President Johnson's that someone had quoted to him earlier. Allen said that specific dissatisfaction was among young people over the Vietnam War and that it was a problem troubling everyone in his audience that day, certainly all the young people there. Allen said that though, as the Maharishi had said, the United States was "creative," its creations were massively negative ones, as in Vietnam, and that was why people were restless and looked to persons such as Mick Jagger and the Beatles for spiritual guidance. It was because young people were "bugged by war." He said that the Maharishi had not confronted the problem satisfactorily.

The Maharishi replied, "Johnson and his secret police have more information than you, so they know what they are doing."

"Ah," said Allen, "they're a bunch of dumbbells. Don't you know that your implicit support of authoritarianism is making a lot of people wonder if you're not some kind of CIA agent?"

"CIA?" The Maharishi giggled. His devotees began muttering.

"It's a common question," Allen explained, "so it should be proposed. You shouldn't stand around silent and fearful to talk." Allen asked, "What about the kids who have resisted the draft? Should they go to war and murder people?"

"Either way," the Maharishi said, "meditate." Allen asked him about the Hare Krishna mantra, and the Maharishi said that one mantra does not fit everybody. Since everyone is different, everybody needs a different mantra. Allen thought that made sense, so he went on to ask about drugs, since the Maharishi had condemned drug usage.

"There wouldn't be anyone to see you today if it hadn't been for LSD!" Allen told him. The devotees gasped.

"Well," said the Maharishi, "LSD has done its thing. Now forget it. Just let it drop." He said that meditation was stronger.

"Excellent," said Allen. "If it works, why not? If it works." He said that he would be glad to try it and that it couldn't do anything but good. But then the Maharishi said that acid damaged hippies' nervous systems.

"I had six hippies visit me in a room in Los Angeles and had to take them into the garden because they smelled so bad."

"What?" Allen yelled. "Don't you realize that acid hippies were the largest part of your audience today?"

But the Maharishi was adamant. He would not be moved from his conviction that hippies smelled. As for a final judgment on the war, he didn't want to get into that. He only wanted to emphasize, "Meditation, meditation, meditation."

"That's fine," said Allen. "I'll meditate."

It was early on a cold February morning. Peter was lying on his bed with a girl who had spent the night. Allen was in his room with Louis Cartwright, a friend of about six months. The phone rang, and a friendly voice with a Denver accent, someone Allen didn't know, asked, "Have you heard the news from the West?"

Expecting to hear of yet another arrest, Allen replied, "No. Been away all week."

"You haven't heard the news from the West? Neal Cassady is dead."

Peter, on the other line, gasped, "Oh!"

On February 2, 1968, Neal had taken a train down to Celaya, a town in the mountains just north of Mexico City, and from there had gone by taxi to San Miguel de Allende, where Janice Brown, known to everyone as JB, was waiting for him. At noon on February 3, Neal left JB's house to return to Celaya and pick up his "magic bag," which he had left there. He told JB that he would walk the two and a half miles from her place to the railroad station at San Miguel, and would then walk all the way down the tracks to Celaya, about fifteen miles, counting the ties as he went. JB thought that he was kidding.

He got to San Miguel by midafternoon, but got caught up in a Mexican wedding party, where he washed down a handful of Seconals with a large quantity of pulque, the sacred Aztec drink made from the fermented sap of the maguey plant. The next morning, a group of Indians found him lying beside the railroad tracks a mile and a half outside San Miguel. He had apparently been trying to make good his word to walk to Celaya. He had passed out from the drink and drugs, wearing only a T-shirt and jeans as protection against the cold mountain rain, and had died of exposure; the death certificate said "generalized congestion."

Allen's first thought on hearing the news was, "Sir Spirit's now home in Spirit," an idea he was to use in "Elegy for Neal Cassady," a tearful poem written a few days later:

> Tender Spirit, thank you for touching me with tender hands
> When you were young, in a beautiful body,
>   Such a pure touch it was Hope beyond Maya-meat . . .
>
> After friendship fades from flesh forms—
> heavy happiness hangs in heart,
>   I could talk to you forever,
>   The pleasure inexhaustible,
>   discourse of spirit to spirit,
>   O Spirit.

The poem ends, "Sir Spirit, an' I drift alone: / Oh deep sigh."

As the sixties drew to a close, there was a great movement within the youth counterculture to leave the cities and establish communes. In the country, they could grow organic vegetables, build tepees or geodesic domes, live in whatever sexual combination they favored, have children, and be free from the pressure of police, drug addicts, rape, and street crime, which had begun to plague the hippie enclaves in the cities. Ginsberg was not immune from the trend. Ever since Gary Snyder set up house on land that he and Allen owned in the Sierra Nevadas, Allen had been thinking about getting a place outside New York, where, away from the pressure of the Lower East Side, Peter could kick drugs—something like a health farm where poets could dry out.

As the stresses of the Vietnam War tore deeper into the fabric of American life, and the pressure of the constantly ringing telephone and the mountains of unanswered mail on his desk became even greater, Allen thought more seriously of getting a place in the country. He asked his friend Barbara Rubin to look around for a place in upstate New York. She found one five miles outside Cherry Valley, a sleepy little village of clapboard houses, about eighty miles west of Albany. The farm consisted of a tumbledown farmhouse, a barn, and outbuildings set in ninety acres of well-drained land with a creek running through it. The land was surrounded by state forest. It seemed ideally private.

The house had four bedrooms and a vast attic. A big kitchen leading directly off the porch had a large range and a sink with an old hand pump. The foundations were made from huge slabs of stone, crudely piled but very strong, built by the original settler of the land. Allen bought the farm and hired the underground filmmaker Gordon Ball as manager.

Barbara had taken Allen's request that she scout for a farmhouse for them all to live in to mean that she and Allen were going to marry. Although she told a number of friends in New York, she knew better than to mention this to Allen, perhaps fearful that he would shatter her dreams or, more likely, waiting for the right moment to maneuver him into it. Allen and Barbara arrived in Cherry Valley in mid-March 1968.

Allen's main motivation in setting up the farm was to get Peter out of the city and away from Methedrine. That spring, Peter was still seriously addicted and was repeating his street-cleaning act, crawling about in the gutter on East Tenth Street with its overflowing garbage cans, scrubbing the filthy sidewalk as Puerto Rican street kids watched him suspiciously from their stoops. It was almost impossible for Allen to communicate with him. Allen also had it in mind to get Kerouac to the farm to dry out, rather like Allen Tate taking Hart Crane to the country, but Jack would not leave his mother.

In the fall of 1966, Gabrielle Kerouac had suffered a stroke, which paralyzed her, confining her to bed. Needing a nurse for Mémère, Jack married Stella Sampas in November 1966. The sister of an old school friend from Lowell, Charles Sampas, Stella was older than Jack and had never married. She was a reliable, efficient woman who had known Jack all his life. He knew he could trust her to nurse his mother, which she did. Jack bought a house in Lowell for the three of them, and Gabrielle's health began to improve. Jack spent his time at the bar owned by his new brother-in-law, Nick. He had no wish to live on a farm.

Peter, clearly in a bad way, arrived at the farm with his brother Julius. It soon became apparent that it was going to be hard to get him off Methedrine; he had hidden supplies all over the farm. In his "leper voice," so called by Allen for its gruffness and despair, Peter would sometimes go off on long "Shakespearean" monologues, which were quite poetic; but he could also be frightening. On one occasion, as Allen and Barbara pulled up at the farm in the VW bus, Peter ran out wrapped in heavy chains, brandishing a machete. While Gordon and the others froze in horror, Allen walked straight toward him and took him into the house.

Peter was not the only problem; Allen and Barbara argued constantly. Barbara, a terrible driver, would proceed down the middle of the road and even on the wrong side, because she always looked at the person she was talking to, and she was always talking. She and Allen never had much of a sexual relationship, but now her megalomania began seriously to impinge on Allen's life. Many of the arguments concerned religion. Barbara was becoming more and more involved with Judaism and thought Allen should follow suit. Gordon remembered one terrifying car ride on the way to Cooperstown: "I was holding on for my life in the back seat and . . . Allen finally got fist-shaking angry and said, 'I'm a Buddhist Jew!' and kept resisting her. . . . She was beginning to realize obviously that he wasn't going to come around."

People began to visit, and in April, Gregory Corso and his girlfriend Belle moved into the front bedroom, vacated by Allen, as the first official Committee On Poetry residents.

It turned out that the house was not as isolated as they had thought. Living on a patch of land adjacent to a corner of Allen's land was Ed the Hermit. Ed Urich had escaped to the country from Greenwich Village many years before. He lived in a small shack and kept a few goats for milk. He wore bib overalls and an Agway peaked cap. For a hermit, he had an enormous amount to say and would visit the farm every day to make predictions about the weather and advise on what to plant and when. He was lonely, and the poetry farm was a godsend to him, particularly in the summer, when the girls walked about naked. Allen and Ed soon struck up a friendship, and Allen would usually find Ed pottering about in the yard when he came down in the morning and went out onto the frosty grass to urinate, wrapped in an old coat.

In February 1968, the antiwar activist Abbie Hoffman had been to see Ginsberg in his Tenth Street apartment. It was the height of the Tet offensive in Vietnam, which was to kill over two thousand American troops. Hoffman said he and Jerry Rubin wanted to hold a Festival of Life in Chicago in August, the same time as the Democratic Party Convention, as an example of a life-style alternative to the one being promoted by the assembled politicians. To this end, they planned to launch a Youth International Party—called Yippies—and run their own candidate, a pig named Pigasus. The idea was to emulate the Human Be-In in San Francisco, with a similar lineup of teachers, yogis, poets, musicians, and antiwar speakers. Like everyone who had an idea for a festival, Abbie wanted Allen to contact the Beatles and Bob Dylan.

Allen, interested in the general idea, called Jerry Rubin. Allen had known Abbie only a few months, whereas his acquaintance with Rubin dated from the 1965 antiwar marches in Berkeley and the organization of the 1967 Be-In. Rubin had run for mayor of Berkeley in 1967, and Allen had supported him. Jerry told him that they would go soon to Chicago to apply for a permit and try to arrange for thousands of kids to camp out. Allen, inundated with work, could not take a central role, but he did subscribe his name to the project and on March 7 took part in a nationally televised press conference with Abbie and Jerry and the folksingers Phil Ochs and Arlo Guthrie. Allen outlined the purpose of the gathering as a manifestation of "a desire for the preservation of the planet," then sang the Hare Krishna mantra for ten minutes before the cameras.

The country was in great turmoil. A Gallup poll published on March 31 showed that only 36 percent of Americans approved of LBJ and only 23 percent approved of his handling of the war. On April 4, 1968, Martin Luther King, Jr., was assassinated, provoking widespread rioting. In Chicago, Mayor Richard Daley gave riot police his infamous instructions to "Shoot to kill," an ominous warning of what was to come that summer. On April 23, students at Columbia University barricaded the offices of the dean, sparking off a wave of college protests against the Vietnam War that affected nearly every campus in the nation. On June 3, Valerie Solanas attempted to murder Andy Warhol, and the next day, Sirhan Sirhan killed Robert Kennedy. Everywhere, people seemed to be turning to violence to redress their grievances.

Mayor Daley's office refused to give the Yippies a permit to hold their Festival of Life. Allen met with Abbie Hoffman in Chicago to discuss the situation. Even if they canceled the festival, thousands of people would come. Allen felt obliged to attend, since he had associated himself with the event from the beginning and felt a responsibility to make sure it was as peaceful as possible.

President Johnson's decision to withdraw from the presidential race caused the antiwar groups to rethink their tactics. Many had been going to Chicago specifically to protest against LBJ. A large coalition of antiwar groups was formed, headed by David Dellinger, Rennie Davis, and Tom Hayden, and a series of marches and demonstrations was planned. The Yippies coordinated their festival with the coalition.

Mayor Daley's response was to put his 11,500 police on twelve-hour shifts, mobilize 5,500 national guardsmen, and airlift in 7,500 troops under LBJ's command from Fort Hood, Texas. The police were armed with heavy wooden clubs and tear gas canisters. It was becoming clear that a Festival of Life, with dancing, poetry, and music, was very unlikely, so Rennie Davis and Tom Hayden began courses in karate and other forms of self-defense for their people. About a week before the convention, Allen went to them to advocate that they teach meditation and chanting instead. In Allen's view, "It was an invitation to violence rather than preparing for a real festival. My role was of chanting 'Om' and I thought the chanting of 'Pigs' was the wrong mantra."

Allen returned to Chicago on Saturday, August 24, and met the Yippie "leaders," Abbie Hoffman, Jerry Rubin, Ed Sanders, Paul Krassner, and others. Thousands of young people, invited by Hoffman and Rubin, were converging on the city and heading for Lincoln Park. The police said that the park was to close at 11 P.M. The Yippies had no permit and no contingency plans. Violent confrontation was inevitable, but as it turned out, this was what Jerry Rubin had wanted all along.

One of the editors at *Esquire* magazine decided to get a different angle on the convention; instead of sending a regular reporter, he commissioned Bill Burroughs, Terry Southern, and Jean Genet to write their impressions of it. It was the first time Burroughs had been in Chicago in twenty-six years, and he didn't like it. That evening, Allen had the chance to test the power of mantra in calming a violent situation. At ten-thirty, he and Ed Sanders were walking through Lincoln Park. It was very dark, and people had lit bonfires in garbage cans. There was a sudden burst of lights, and a wave of police moved in fast to clear the park. Allen was surprised and said to Ed, "They are not supposed to be here until eleven!" He began to chant "Om!" He and Sanders slowly walked out of the park, gathering a group of people, until fifteen or twenty of them were uttering a solid deep vibrational chant as they walked toward the Lincoln Park Hotel. It took about twenty minutes to reach the road dividing the park from the hotel, by which time they had attracted about a hundred people, all calm and unharmed by the police.

The next day, Sunday, Allen went to Lincoln Park, where a PA system had been set up and John Sinclair and the MC5 were playing. Allen asked if he could do a bit of chanting, and they gave him the microphone. He chanted Hare Krishna for about fifteen minutes, then sang William Blake's "The Grey Monk" to try and calm the crowd, still excited by MC5's "Up Against the Wall" rhetoric. The rock music resumed, and Allen walked away, surrounded by a group of young people.

Suddenly they saw a mass of police sweep through the center of the park toward the PA system. Allen felt an adrenaline flash and, following his own precepts, sat down and began chanting "Om!" He had originally intended to chant for twenty minutes to calm himself, but when a crowd gathered, he continued—for seven hours. Many people joined in, some staying for a short period, others for an hour or so. At dusk the crowd grew to several hundred. A core group of about fifty remained the whole time. At one point, someone passed Allen a note from an Indian: "Will you please stop playing with the mantra and do it seriously by pronouncing the 'M' in OM properly for at least five minutes? See how it develops." Allen realized that he had been using the mantra as a song instead of as a means of concentration, so he started to do it the Indian's way. He explained what happened in a *Playboy* magazine interview:

"After about 15 minutes, my breathing became more regular, even, steady, as if I were breathing the air of heaven into myself and then circulating it back out into heaven. After a while the air inside and outside became the same—what the Indians call *prajna*, the vital silvery, evanescent air. Then I began to feel a funny tingling in my feet that spread until my whole body was one rigid electrical tingling—a solid mass of lights." By this time it was 8 P.M., and Allen had been chanting for more than four hours. He sat facing the John Hancock Building, which was beginning to light up. "I felt like the building, except I realized it wasn't alive and I was. I felt a rigidity inside my body, almost like a muscle armor plating. With all this electric going up and down and this rigid muscle thing, I had to straighten my back to make a clear passage for whatever flow there was: my hands began vibrating. Five or six people were touching them. Suddenly I realized that I was going through some kind of weird trance thing like I read about in books. But it wasn't mystical. It was the product of six continuous hours of chanting 'Om,' regularized breathing and altering body chemistry."

He put his legs up into the full lotus position, something he could rarely do, and it felt good. "I realized that it was possible through chanting to make advances on the body and literally to alter states of consciousness. I'd got to euphorias, ecstasies of pleasure, years before; but this was the first time I'd gotten neurological body sensations, cellular extensions of some kind of cosmic consciousness within my body. I was able to look at the Hancock Building and see it as a tiny little tower of electrical lights—a very superficial toy compared with the power, grandeur and immensity of one human body."

He had never chanted that long before and was amazed at the effect it was having upon him. "It felt like grace. It felt harmoniously right that some psychophysical rarity should be happening on that political occasion as dusk fell on Lincoln Park and the Hancock Building lit up on the horizon. If there'd been panic and police clubs I don't think I would have minded the damage. Clubbing would have seemed a curiously impertinent intrusion from skeleton phantoms—unreal compared with the natural omnipresent electric universe I was in. This was the most interesting thing that happened, for me, in Chicago."

The next night, Allen was walking in Lincoln Park with Burroughs and Genet. They came upon a crude barricade made from picnic tables, trash cans, and police crash barriers. The police could easily have encircled it and pinned down the demonstrators. There were a lot of young people there, yelling and banging on metal trash cans. It seemed to Allen that they were looking for a confrontation with the police, since it was 11 P.M. He began chanting "Om!" and was joined by more and more people, until almost everybody at the barricades was doing it. After about fifteen minutes, a police car came rolling down the hill behind them and crashed straight into the barricade, with a tremendous sound of breaking glass. People scattered. Allen retained his composure and, still chanting, removed himself from the scene. People shrieked and screamed as the police attacked them. On this occasion, "Om!" was no protection.

Leaving the park, Allen, Bill, and Genet saw a mob of police burst out of the trees in pursuit, not of kids, but of news photographers. The police had taken off their badges and name plates, and some had even removed their unit patches. The club-swinging mob advanced on the crowd, and at the end of the incident, seventeen media people—pressmen from the Washington *Post*, the Chicago *American*, the Chicago *Sun-Times*, *Life*, and *Newsweek*, and cameramen from ABC, CBS, and NBC—had to be taken to Henrotin Hospital for emergency treatment.

The next evening, Allen, Bill, Genet, Terry Southern, and Dick Seaver from Grove Press made their way to Lincoln Park. A large crowd lined the outskirts of the park, ready to make a quick getaway, and an even larger one was moving toward the center of the park, where a group of about four hundred clergy and local people, horrified by the police brutality of recent days, had set up a ten-foot-high cross under one of the park lights to support the members of Students for a Democratic Society and the National Mobilization Committee, and the Yippies, in their fight for the privilege of staying in the park at night. The congregation was exhorted to join in a nonviolent vigil and sing "We Shall Overcome," "Onward Christian Soldiers," and various pacifist songs and hymns.

The police began to set up their lines, and the clergy lifted the cross and carried it away from the crowd to erect it facing the spotlights that marked the police lines, interposing the cross between police and demonstrators. Allen and his companions sat on a small hill overlooking the scene. Suddenly huge tear gas canisters came raining down on the cross, crashing through the branches of the trees. Gas filled the air, a great white plume in the police spotlights, enveloping the crowd. People ran in panic, screaming, their eyes streaming with tears. The police fired a second volley, this time into the crowd. The ministers took up their cross and retreated. Allen grasped Bill's hand and Genet's, and they walked slowly toward the edge of the park, away from the scene of carnage, as police advanced into the crowd, clubbing stragglers to the ground. Huge street-cleaning trucks, specially adapted, advanced on the demonstrators, spraying tear gas. Some of the crowd fought back vainly, ripping up the sidewalk to throw at the truck windows. A dozen patrol cars were engulfed and trashed as the kids broke up into mobs, roaming the streets, vandalizing everything in sight. Hundreds of people were arrested and hundreds more badly beaten by the club-wielding police.

The thousands of kids thrown out of Lincoln Park moved on to

Grant Park, where they continued to sing "We Shall Not Be Moved," hymns, and antiwar songs. The police tried to teargas them out, but the wind blew most of the gas into the air-conditioning ducts of the giant Hilton Hotel overlooking the park, where most of the delegates and press members were staying. The kids chanted all night, and many of the lights in the hotel stayed on as press and delegates watched the extraordinary spectacle below. In the middle of the night, the national guard was brought in. Armed troops in battle dress arrived all through the night in jeeps and military transport, as tear gas swirled through the hotel lobby and the noise of the trucks and the kids' loudspeakers ensured that everyone in the Hilton knew what was going on. By this time, many of the press and delegates shared Genet's opinion of Chicago. He told Burroughs, "I can't wait for this city to rot. I can't wait to see weeds growing through empty streets."

The main battle of Chicago occurred outside the Hilton Hotel on August 28. The National Mobilization Committee had organized a pacifist rally and march, starting at the band shell in Grant Park. Police and troops had sealed off the park, but Allen, Bill, Genet, and Terry Southern found a way in by climbing over some trestles. They reached the stage area, and Dellinger invited them onstage to address the crowd. Allen was unable to speak and just managed to croak "Om!" The others said their bit and moved to the back of the stage as the speeches continued.

The peace march began assembling, and Dellinger asked Allen to march with his companions at the front. The march moved off, preceded by a man carrying a portable PA system. Then came David Dellinger, followed by a group of marshals. The march itself was led by Allen Ginsberg, William Burroughs, Jean Genet, Terry Southern, Richard Seaver, and the British photographer Michael Cooper, their arms linked, all holding flowers—an obvious target for press photographers, who swarmed around, delighted by the lineup. The march progressed for a couple of blocks until it reached the edge of the park, where national guardsmen blocked the way with machine guns and jeeps equipped with barbed-wire shields.

The march was not allowed onto the city streets. Dellinger asked Allen to calm the crowd and the troops by chanting. "There was this long line behind us, there was this great mass of armed people in front of us. It was a tricky, scary moment," Allen said later. He took the microphone, and with the tattered remains of his voice, he began chanting "Om Sri Maitreya." People sat down, expecting a long wait, and quite a few began to chant along with him. When Allen's voice finally gave out, everybody just sat quietly.

In the end, David Dellinger announced that the march was over; the government had forced them to abandon their citizens' right to have a peaceable assembly for redress of grievances. The march broke up, but it was impossible for anyone to get out of the park because the troops were still blocking all the bridges, which were the only exits. The police, however, tried to clear the park by firing tear gas at the marchers. Allen and Bill finally found an unmanned bridge and escaped. Meanwhile, a huge group had managed to force a lightly guarded bridge and get back to the city across Michigan Avenue, only to run straight into the Reverend Ralph Abernathy's Poor People's Campaign march, complete with mules and wagons, which was just then progressing up the avenue. The police had had no choice but to grant the reverend a permit for his march, unless they wanted the press and cameras to focus on a full-scale riot in Chicago's black South Side as well. It was like an episode in a science fiction book, the mules in contrast to the troops in battle dress and gas masks, and the thousands of ragged long-haired kids breaking through the armor to join in.

Just before the Hilton Hotel, the mules and wagons were allowed across the intersection, then, as the Poor People's Campaign marched out of sight, the others found themselves surrounded on three sides by rows of angry cops. The police, moving in arcs of twenty or thirty men, sliced into the crowd with their clubs and with Mace, beating people indiscriminately. Tourists, newsmen, people on their way home from work, were all attacked and beaten. The *New York Times* reported: "Even elderly bystanders were caught by the police onslaught. At one point the police turned on several dozen persons standing quietly behind police barriers in front of the Conrad Hilton Hotel watching the demonstrators across the street. For no reason that could be immediately determined, the blue-helmeted policemen charged the barriers, crushing the spectators against the windows of the Haymarket Inn, a restaurant in the hotel. Finally the window gave way, sending screaming middle-aged women and children backward through the broken shards of glass. The police then ran into the restaurant and beat some of the victims who had fallen through the windows and arrested them."

So many people were injured that the Eugene McCarthy campaign headquarters on the fifteenth floor was turned into a make-shift hospital, but the police even burst into that and swept through, clubbing people, leaving great pools of blood on the floor. Ginsberg, with some poetic license, described the scene in his poem "Grant Park: August 28, 1968":

> *The teargas drifted up to the Vice*
>   *President naked in the bathroom*
> *—naked on the toilet taking a shit weeping?*
> *Who wants to be President of the*
>   *Garden of Eden?*

Even those taking part in the convention had to acknowledge the blood in the streets after the siege of the Hilton, and it was Connecticut Senator Abraham Ribicoff who did it, in his nominating speech. He told the assembled delegates, "With George McGovern as President of the United States we wouldn't have Gestapo tactics in the streets of Chicago." Mayor Richard Daley rose up from his seat, shaking his fist at Ribicoff and mouthing anti-Semitic obscenities, but the gray-haired Ribicoff stood his ground and simply said, "How hard it is to accept the truth."

The convention went on to nominate Hubert Humphrey. He would lose the November election to Richard Nixon, and the war in Vietnam would drag on.

Allen was only confirmed in his view that the United States was becoming a police state. He said in *Playboy*: "I think everybody who watched television during the convention experienced a widening of consciousness because . . . outright police brutality was shown so clearly that even TV and radio commentators were saying, 'This is a police state!' Before Chicago, that would have been considered an impropriety, even though many already felt it was true, secretly. To make it official like that turns things over in people's minds; suddenly they wake up in a different country from where they thought they were. But it was there all along!"

When Allen had first told Kerouac—in one of their recent telephone conversations—that he was going to Chicago, they quickly got into an argument. "Kerouac thought that Dave Dellinger, the leader of the antiwar movement, was Jewish," Ginsberg said. But when Kerouac attacked Hoffman and Rubin—"Ginsberg, what are you hanging around with all those dirty Jew Communists for, anyway?"—Allen realized what the key was. "I said, 'What the fuck, is that what your mother put in your mouth? Tell your mother she's got a dirty cunt! And I'm gonna shove a Coke bottle in it and put some gasoline in it and explode it!' and he started laughing. All of a sudden got friendly and pleasant and began talking common sense instead of the usual contentious macho trading of ego pinpricking. So I found what he was actually doing was just seeing how much ego I got, and how much attached to it I was, and if I could be upset still, until I finally just laid it back on him, realizing that he was just being playful with me rather than really mean."

Clearly the idea that he and Kerouac still had some sort of friendship was so important to Allen that he would go to almost any length to maintain it, even if it meant explaining away years of anti-Semitic insults as playfulness. He recognized that Kerouac was sick and made the same allowances for him as he had for Naomi. "How do you draw the line between complete honesty and disillusionment?" he asked a class of poetry students. "I never solved the problem because when I read his books I realize he was enormously brooding, vaster of mind and heart than myself, and that my irritation was jejune and egoistic and self-defensive and contributed to his death and disillusionment, so I always feel guilty. On the other hand, occasionally I'd come up against him when I would realize he was full of shit. And *vain!* Totally vain! That whole thing wasn't wisdom at all, it was like some kind of complete paranoic vanity! That's why it rubbed so badly."

After a few days in New York with Burroughs, who was writing up his Chicago article for *Esquire*, before going home to London, Allen returned to the farm, where Herbert Huncke had joined the others. Encouraged by Allen and by a grant from a wealthy patron, Huncke was assembling more of his occasional writings and essays for a book. His first, *Huncke's Journal*, had been published by Diane di Prima in 1965. The farm was in full swing, with a menagerie that included a horse and chickens. Barbara had bought some African geese, which shit all over the front porch and bit everybody. They kept them for a while because they were as good as guard dogs. Allen learned how to milk Bessie, the cow, and the goats, and helped pick young cucumbers for the pickle barrel. Two acres that Peter and Gordon had planted on strictly organic principles yielded an enormous amount of fresh, tasty vegetables, and they began to think about self-sufficiency. A row of old maples grew alongside the patch of grass next to the house, and Allen liked to sit in their shade at a small table, working on his proofs and notebooks.

Allen's success with chanting had furthered his interest in music. He had already set Blake's "The Grey Monk" to music and performed it in Chicago. Now he began work on the whole of *Songs of Innocence and Experience,* which Blake had originally sung but for which no musical notation survives, if there ever was any. "Finding right melodies for a dozen or more songs and taping them—lovely extension of my mantra practice," Ginsberg wrote.

Allen bought a dusty old upright pump organ at a barn sale, cleaned it up, and installed it in the living room. In the evenings, with his Aladdin lamp burning, Allen sat and painfully picked out the melodies of his Blake songs, working on them over and over again, until he was able to get the melody in his head recorded on tape. The old organ whistled and groaned, the lamp flickered, and moths flew around its bright globe like a scene from the previous century. Lee Crabtree, a musician who had played with the Fugs, came to the farm and taught Allen basic musical notation.

Barbara was getting more involved in the Jewish religion and began to spend a lot of time at a yeshiva in nearby Sharon Springs. She now realized that her master plan of marrying Ginsberg and converting him to Judaism was not going to work. By this time she had distanced herself from the other people on the farm, and in September she left to go and live at the yeshiva.

The nights got chilly, and Peter began cutting and stacking wood for the winter. He was in good health, ruddy and tanned from spending his days outdoors. It seemed that the farm was working.

Winter came early to that part of upper New York State, but they were prepared. By the time the last of the leaves had blazed scarlet and fallen, they had more or less finished work on the house. Though it was not yet completely winterized, the house now had insulation in the attic, and the walls of all the bedrooms were paneled in raw pine. The cellar was filled with Ball jars of home-grown tomatoes, beans, beets, and squash. Apples stood in rows on the wooden shelves, alongside jars of cloudy home-pressed apple juice. They had picked all the cucumbers and harvested all the crops. The barn had been fixed up to provide shelter for the cow and the horse, and plenty of hay and fodder was laid in. The chicken coop and the goat house were both weatherproofed, and thick waterproof winter boots and warm woolly socks and hats had been bought. They achieved a remarkable amount during that first season, and things seemed to be going well.

In November, Allen fractured his hip and cracked four ribs in a car crash after taking Lawrence Ferlinghetti to the airport. He spent several weeks in the hospital in Albany, then returned to the farm for an enforced period of rest. He hobbled around on crutches and spent his time reading, composing Blake songs, and answering his mail. He wrote Ferlinghetti: "It's been a sort of pleasure to go through, I never had a broken bone before in 42 years."

In January 1969, Maretta Greer arrived on the farm unexpectedly, having been deported from India. Gordon remembered her arrival: "It was an average cool winter day, overcast, temperature about zero. And here was this woman with short hair, with a blanket wrapped around her, getting out of a car and walking barefoot through the snow toward the house. I thought, Terrific! Wonderful!"

Maretta was installed in the attic, where she set up a little altar and spent a lot of time crying and complaining how uncivilized the United States was. She expected to be treated as an honored guest and made no effort to help with the cooking or cleaning. Since Allen was leaving on a four-month reading tour at the end of February, Gordon requested that he ask Maretta to do a little of the work.

Allen broached the subject with her as he was coming down the stairs. Three or four steps from the bottom, he asked, "Say, Maretta, while I'm gone, can you pitch in and do a little work around the place?" Maretta was outraged. "I'll never tell you the secrets of the seven mysteries!" she screamed, and knocked the crutches out from under his arms.

"Keep on!" said Allen, encouraging her to let it all out. Her voice grew shrill. She was insulted that he should be leaving so soon after her arrival. "[She thought] I was leaving her there like in a mental hospital or a retirement farm," said Ginsberg; "she was very demanding."

On February 18, back briefly in New York City, Allen gave the first public performance of his Blake songs, accompanied by Lee Crabtree on piano and Cyril Caster on guitar. It was the beginning of Ginsberg's practice of using musicians as an integral part of his act. That June he went into the recording studio.

Rather than have a small combo play all the tunes, each song was treated individually: "The Garden of Love" was arranged as a country and western number, whereas "The Blossom" came out like a minuet. This meant that specialist musicians were needed for some of the tracks, to achieve special effects. At the suggestion of

Charles Mingus, they used Herman Wright on bass and Julius Watkins, famous for his work with the Thelonious Monk Quintet, to play French horn.

To get the appropriate sonorous drum rolls on "The Grey Monk," Blake's powerful cry against tyranny, Elvin Jones was brought in. He arrived looking very sharp, accompanied by his Japanese wife, Keiko, who carried his drum kit and then assembled it. Jones listened carefully to the song, played exactly what was needed, collected his five hundred dollars, and disappeared. It would be fifteen years before Allen played with him again. Percussionist and trumpet player Don Cherry added the finishing touches to many of the tracks. The whole project was recorded and mixed for ten thousand dollars. Though originally intended for the Beatles' Apple Records, it was released on MGM in 1970.

Allen was able to spend most of the summer of 1969 on the farm. There was a new calf and kittens, and an expensive new water system was being installed, which used the force of gravity to pump water up to the house. With a 50 percent state grant, they constructed a pond below the barn and stocked it with fish. It rapidly attracted frogs and all the wildlife associated with ponds, and soon looked as though it had been there forever. Allen actually had time to relax. He walked around the fields a lot, knee deep in wildflowers and grasses, listening to the birds and insects. He communed with the goats, the horse, and the cows, kept up his gigantic correspondence, and helped bring in the harvest.

That summer, Jane Kramer's biography *Allen Ginsberg in America* was published by Random House, to generally favorable reviews. Even *Time* recognized his fame and influence: "Ginsberg has also come to be legitimized by a wide public (*Life*, *Playboy*, TV talk shows) and all but officially designated as a peculiar national treasure of sorts." Of the book itself, which was based on a two-part *New Yorker* profile, Ginsberg told *Publishers Weekly*, "I wish Miss Kramer had been more realistic about homosexual situations."

Recognition in another form came earlier in the year, when Ginsberg received a grant of five thousand dollars from the National Institute of Arts and Letters, "In recognition of his creative work in literature."

On the evening of October 21, there was a phone call from journalist Al Aronowitz. Gregory took the call, turned to Allen, and cried, "Al! Jack died."

The next morning, they rose early and dressed warmly. Allen and Gregory took a walk through the snow to the row of trees at the top of the property, and there, near Ed the Hermit's cabin, they carved Jack's name in a tree.

Kerouac died the classic drunkard's death, from cirrhosis of the liver. At the end of 1968, he had moved his wife and mother to St. Petersburg, hoping the Florida sun would speed Gabrielle's recovery. Although Jack sometimes typed all night, he spent most of his time watching television, alternating beers with sips of whiskey. His mother lay bedridden in the back room, tended by Stella. On October 20, after a sleepless night, he was watching *The Galloping Gourmet* on TV when his liver finally collapsed. He dragged himself to the bathroom, where Stella found him vomiting blood. He was given emergency surgery but never regained consciousness.

Allen had a reading at Yale that day. The students had stretched a twelve-foot paper banner across the stage, which read, "In Memoriam: Jack Kerouac, 1922–1969," and on the line below, "Neal Cassady, 1927–1968." Peter and Allen climbed onstage. Allen arranged his papers, books, and harmonium, then said, "We'll begin with a prayer." He and Peter chanted the Diamond Sutra, Jack's favorite. When it was over, there was scattered applause, but Allen quietly told them, "You don't applaud a prayer." He read a number of choruses from Jack's *Mexico City Blues*, repeating the final lines of the "211th Chorus" three times, to make sure the youthful audience got it:

> Poor! *I wish I was free*
> *of that slaving meat wheel*
> *and safe in heaven dead.*

He ended his reading of Kerouac with the "242nd Chorus," the last in the book, and stressed the final stanza:

> *Stop the murder and the suicide!*
> *All's well!*
> *I am the Guard.*

Allen read his own work, and then there was the usual question period. Someone asked why Kerouac was so important and why he had turned so right-wing in his last decade. Allen waited almost a minute before venturing a reply. Finally, he said, "Well, he was the first one to make a new crack in the consciousness." He told them that pot, rock, "doing your own thing," "making a new Jerusalem," etc., had all come out of that crack.

"He broke open the fantastic solidity in America, as solid as the Empire State Building, that turned out not to be solid at all. His vision was what the universe as we will experience it is—golden ash, blissful emptiness, a product of our own grasping speed." Allen said that Kerouac had tried to follow the implications of his sad-comic view of things to the bottom of his own nature, and transcribe it in its own onrushing spontaneous flow, and leave it there for others. "So he drank himself to death," Allen said bluntly. "Which is only another way of living, of handling the pain and foolishness that it's all a dream, a great baffling silly emptiness, after all." Allen ended it there.

The next day was crisp and cold as Allen and Peter, Gregory and John Clellon Holmes, drove to the funeral in Jack's hometown. Lowell was then an ugly mill town, with empty factories sprawled along the banks of the Merrimack, its miraculous self-renewal still many years away. They found the bar owned by Nick Sampas, Jack's brother-in-law, and sat reading the funeral announcement in the Lowell *Sun*. The bartender said that Nick had gone to the airport to pick up Stella, and that Jack's body had arrived in Lowell on an earlier flight. The funeral was to be held the next morning at eleven in Saint John the Baptist Church, where Jack had been an altar boy thirty-five years before.

Nick and Stella arrived, and tearful introductions were made. Jack had told countless stories about them all, but Allen was the only one Stella had ever met, because when Kerouac went into town to see his friends he refused to allow her to accompany him. The Sampas family insisted on putting them all up and feeding them, and they suddenly found themselves in another world, that of a close-knit Greek-American family, sharing their food and wine and their bereavement. They were plied with lobster, shrimp, and steaks; bottles of retsina were produced. Suddenly they remembered that they had made no arrangements for flowers.

Gregory sketched an elaborate design of a heart on a lotus, but at that time of night the florist could manage only a simple heart of red roses with their names on the ribbons: Allen, Peter, Gregory, John, Bill, Lucien, and Robert (Creeley). Across the center was a ribbon reading "Guard the heart."

At the funeral parlor, Jack lay surrounded by flowers, a rosary entwined around his fingers. He wore a yellow shirt, a houndstooth sports jacket, and a red bow tie with white dots. Allen reached over and touched his forehead. "Touch him," he said. "There's really nothing inside." He quoted a few stanzas from *Mexico City Blues*, while Peter fought back tears. Gregory knelt at the side of the coffin, weeping openly. Allen described the scene in a letter to Carolyn Cassady:

"Jack in coffin looked large headed, grim lipped, tiny bald spot top of skull begun but hair still black and soft, cold skin makeup chill to finger touch on his brow, fingers wrinkled, hairy hands protruding from sports jacket holding rosary, flower masses around coffin and shaped wrinkle-furrow familiar at his brow, eyes closed, mid-aged heavy looked like his father had become from earlier dream decades—shock first seeing him there in theatric-lit coffin room as if a Buddha in Paranirvana pose, come here left his message of Illusion-wink and left the body behind."

Jack was given a high requiem mass, complete with priest circling the coffin with a swinging censer. Allen, in beads and beard, was a pallbearer. There were many cameras and reporters, and Allen was interviewed next to the hearse. At the cemetery, after a priest said final prayers, they all took roses from a wreath and placed them on the coffin before it was lowered. Allen was asked to throw the first handful of dirt. He did, and the others followed suit. The TV people packed up their equipment, and the gravediggers began to shovel the October earth.

The next day, Allen gave a teach-in at Columbia University. Nineteen sixty-nine was an angry year, a time when much of the idealism of the mid-sixties began to sour. In May, during the battle for People's Park in Berkeley, an unarmed student was shot from a rooftop by police as he watched a demonstration. At Altamont, the Hell's Angels murdered a member of the audience and roughed up the performers at a rock concert. Moratorium Day, on October 15, brought tens of thousands of people to the streets nationwide to protest the war, and on November 15, in Washington, D.C., a quarter of a million marched against the war. By the end of the year, 31,000 American troops had been killed in Vietnam. There seemed no end to the slaughter.

On the farm, the telephone rang continually, and Allen would hurry to answer it, sitting on a little child's chair by the front door, where he spent hours receiving horror stories from New York, Newark, San Francisco, and Seattle. He sat, brow furrowed, his address book open before him, fingers dialing lawyers, the Civil Liberties Union, his father; he called the *New York Times* to complain angrily about distortion in their news coverage of demonstrations or arrests.

Allen's fall tour took him all through New England and Canada. Then, in Chicago on December 7, he delivered his testimony for the defense in the so-called Chicago Conspiracy Trial. David Dellinger, Rennie Davis, Abbie Hoffman, Jerry Rubin, Tom Hayden, Lee Weiner, John Froines, and Bobby Seale were all charged with conspiring to incite a riot at the 1968 Democratic Party Convention. Bobby Seale's trial was quickly separated off, much of it occurring with him bound, gagged, and shackled to his chair, in full view of the jury, which found him guilty. On appeal, he was acquitted of all charges. The lumping together of the antiwar organizers with media freaks Hoffman and Rubin was also unfair, but they decided to fight it together, with William Kunstler and Leonard Weinglass as their defense lawyers.

Judge Julius Hoffman presided, and his encounter with Allen manifested a total lack of communication. The large court doors swung open, and Allen strode down the carpeted aisle, paused, and gave Judge Hoffman a Hindu *namaste* greeting, holding his hands in prayer before his beard. The tiny, seventy-four-year-old judge peered down at him from his high perch, then sank even deeper into his leather chair, his eyes half closed.

Leonard Weinglass, for the defense, led Allen through a description of his profession: teaching, lecturing, writing, and reciting poetry. Allen explained in some detail his studies in India and Japan and carefully spelled the names of all the swamis he met there, so that the court reporter could list them accurately. He pointed out that all his studies involved chanting and praying, "praying out loud and in community." The judge looked puzzled.

Allen described his role in the February 1968 news conference in which plans for the Yippie Festival of Life were announced, and he told the judge the contents of his speech, trying to show that the plan had been to hold a peaceful festival, like the San Francisco Be-In, not a riot. He said that he had concluded his speech by chanting the Hare Krishna mantra for ten minutes for the television cameras. Then, to demonstrate, Allen launched into the mantra: "Hare Krishna, Hare Krishna, Krishna Krishna, Hare Hare, Hare Rama, Hare Rama, Hare Hare, Rama Rama."

Prosecutor Thomas Foran, among others in the court, laughed.

William Kunstler objected, saying that the chanting had been a serious presentation of a religious concept. "I don't understand it," said Judge Hoffman. "The language of the United States District Court is English."

"I know," said Kunstler, "but you don't laugh at all languages."

"I didn't laugh, I didn't laugh," protested the judge. "I didn't laugh at all. I wish I could tell you how I feel. Laugh—I didn't even smile." Allen pointed out, helpfully, that the language was Sanskrit. "That's why I didn't understand it," Hoffman said, and he told Kunstler, "You may use an interpreter for the remainder of this witness's testimony."

Hoffman could not see what the mantra had to do with the case, and the prosecution agreed, saying, "He is talking about things that have no conceivable materiality to this case."

"It adds spirituality to the case, sir," Allen offered. But Judge Hoffman had had enough.

"Will you remain quiet, sir!" he yelled at Allen, who murmured an apology.

Next, Allen's harmonium was presented in court, and Allen was asked to identify it.

"It is an instrument known as the harmonium, which I used at the press conference at the Americana Hotel," said Allen, happily playing several ascending chords.

"All you were asked was what it is, and instead you played a tune on it," snapped Hoffman, but as Allen tried to explain, the judge cut him off and adjourned the case until the next morning.

Allen testified for the whole of the next day, during which time he was able to deliver a spirited reading of Blake's "The Grey Monk" and his own poems "Going to Chicago," "The Night Apple," "In Society," and "Love Poem on a Theme by Whitman," which the prosecution asked him to read, hoping that their homosexual themes would discredit him as a witness. At the close of his day on the stand, he was asked to read "Howl." He did not have a copy with him but recited as much as he could remember, which was quite a lot. For the most part, he was questioned on his recollections of the days in Chicago and of specific meetings with the defendants, many of which he was able to recall in great detail. The defense was trying to show that the intent was peaceful and that mantra chanting, as a way of calming crowds, had been planned from the very beginning, but most of the attempts to prove this were rejected by the judge, who sustained constant prosecution objections to the testimony. Some of Allen's testimony did genuinely seem to surprise the court, particularly the fact that he had chanted "Om!" for seven hours straight.

The case had a predictable outcome. The academics, Lee Weiner and John Froines, were acquitted of all charges; all the defendants were absolved of conspiracy; Hoffman, Rubin, Dellinger, Hayden, and Davis were individually convicted of crossing state lines to incite a riot. Judge Hoffman then spent two days giving 175 contempt-of-court citations, totaling nineteen years in prison, to the eight defendants and their attorneys, Weinglass and Kunstler. Bobby Seale and Kunstler both received more than four years for contempt.

It was to be two years before the U.S. Court of Appeals overturned the verdict and most of the contempt citations, finding that "the demeanor of the judge and the prosecutors would require reversal if other errors did not." Once all the jail time had been voided and the citations reversed, Jerry Rubin confessed, "We *wanted* disruption. We *planned* it. We *were not* innocent victims. Guilty as hell! Guilty as charged!" Allen, who had accepted all along that the Youth International Party was planning a nonviolent festival of youth, was as annoyed as everyone else to find that the original good intentions had been undermined. "Jerry Rubin covering our karma with shame, disgrace," Allen wrote. "I alibied for him in Chicago, now he says peace was a lie, we meant to start a war. Guilty 1968."

By 1970, five people were living on the farm: Allen, Gordon, Julius, Peter, and Denise Mercedes. Denise, a guitar player from New York, had moved to the farm at the end of 1969 to be with Peter. Peter bought a banjo, and they spent hours together in their room off the porch, making music. In the spring of 1970, the poet Ray Bremser, his wife, Bonnie, and their three-year-old daughter, Georgia, moved into the attic.

June came, and Peter's behavior was still erratic. He was taking amphetamines from time to time, his gravelly voice giving him away. Naturally strong and energetic, he was almost superhuman on speed. He and Gordon built a foxproof fence to protect the chickens. Peter fenced in several acres of garden land to keep out deer, then he and Denise planted an acre of soybeans. He embarked on the ambitious task of posting the entire land, all ninety acres of it, and early each day he and Julius would disappear and only return at dusk, their bare chests burned a deep tan by the sun.

Since Julius did only what he was told, he sometimes spent all day standing in the hot sun in the middle of the soybean patch, because Peter had forgotten about him. If he was not told to go to bed, Julius would sit all night on the settee, his big boots arranged neatly at his side; he was always waiting in the upstairs corridor in the morning for someone to tell him to make himself some breakfast. Sometimes several people would tell him, so Julius had several breakfasts.

Peter went through a phase of speedy good humor, when he was fun to be with, but it was impossible to talk seriously with him. Then, at the end of June, he and Allen finally sat down and talked. Allen noted in his journal: "Sad conversation with Peter. He'd secretly spent all his bank money on great stores of amphetamine. Plastic packages later burned in guilt in trashcan. So no money more in hiding though his checkbook said full." The thousands of dollars spent on speed had originally been obtained by Peter's selling his letters from Allen, Jack, and other friends. Although he told Allen he had destroyed the speed, he had clearly not destroyed all of it. It was hidden all over the farm, and Allen and Gordon had already discovered some of it in the barn. It was a very difficult time for everyone.

The speed made Peter very paranoid. He was convinced that the young redneck farmers from Cherry Valley were going to come and kill everyone on the farm, and he watched the lane suspiciously for lights. He and Denise had a small black-and-white television, which Peter thought was watching him. He destroyed it with an iron bar and threw it out into the yard, following it with the remains of the two car batteries that had powered it. He gave careful consideration to Allen's views on sex and decided that Flash, the horse, was not safe from Allen. "That Ginzy, he'd fuck anything," he muttered, and slept in the barn to protect Flash.

His withdrawal, when it came, was anguished. He lay outside the house, banging his head on a rock until he bled, crying, moaning, and cursing himself. "Why do I do it? It's poison, it's fucking poison!" Allen hovered over him, helpless, offering advice, knowing that Peter had more speed hidden away.

"Let's chant together," suggested Allen. "Maybe that'll ease the pain."

"That stuff doesn't work," Peter retorted angrily. "You don't really believe in all that chanting, do you?"

Allen looked sorrowful. He sat next to Peter and wiped the sweat away as Peter writhed and burned up on the damp evening grass. The windy darkness was punctuated with the green neon flashes of fireflies. Peter pulled through.

One day, Peter and Ray Bremser got drunk, and Allen yelled angrily at them. The purpose of the farm was for them to dry out, he told them; alcohol and drugs were banned. The problem was that the ban was very difficult to enforce, since he did not feel that he could extend it to all his visitors, or even to other members of the farm, like Gordon or Bonnie. It was a constant problem for him. Allen himself used drugs rarely: the occasional joint at a party or LSD in special circumstances, such as Big Sur or the Welsh countryside. It was also only sensible to keep the farm as clean as possible from drugs in case the police raided.

Shortly after Memorial Day, 1970, Peter and Denise bought a baby pig. Allen's face dropped as the piglet exploded from the sack it was in and ran in confused circles in the front yard. The farm already had a horse that no one rode or groomed, a billy goat that did nothing but smell and eat; there were dogs, cats, geese, and even a gerbil in a cage in the kitchen, but none of them did anything but consume food. The piglet was named Don't Bite Me, and it lived in Denise and Peter's room. It followed them everywhere, rooting in the garden, digging up the lawn, and would come running whenever they whistled. It grew rapidly, but they still kept it in their room, even when it weighed more than Denise.

More people arrived, and in July, Gregory moved in. Trouble began almost immediately. He deeply resented not being allowed to drink and followed Allen around, telling him that the only reason he had come there was to kill him. "You, you're dead already. And Peter! He's just a parasite on you!" he yelled at Allen, who sat under the maples, trying to read the manuscript of the French translation of *Planet News* that his translators had brought up to the farm to work on with him. "This is Gregory, Allen. Your oldest friend. I have to kill you to save you from all this!"

Allen gave up trying to work and went inside, while Gregory tagged along, stamping his feet and shouting abuse. Allen flopped exhausted in a chair and said, "You know, though I've known you for so many years, I don't think I like you so much anymore. It's been a long time since there was any friendship. It's all been unpleasantness." The implications of this remark kept Gregory quiet for the rest of the day.

A few days later, beer cans were found floating on the pond.

Everyone trooped down to look at them, and a full-scale investigation began at once, with all eyes on Gregory and Ray as the culprits. Allen wrote: "Beercans found in the pond, and their smiling faces turned snarling and screaming at each other at dusk—Peter drunk also screaming in garage. Second day, all calm and a wave of happiness passed through tranquil grassy yard—yesterday more vodka's swearing and threats of death."

Gregory made life as unpleasant for Peter as he could, calling him "Allen's little bum boy," abusing his poetry, and accusing him of being a leech on Allen. Peter kept out of his way as much as possible because sometimes, when Gregory really provoked him, Peter had to hit him, which he always regretted afterward. Gregory could also be violent when drunk, and on one occasion gave Gordon a black eye because he refused to buy beer for him in Cherry Valley.

Allen wrote Ferlinghetti: "Gregory's here. Several wild screaming drunk explosions. Quiet today. We'll kick his ass if he starts again." A few days later, Gregory returned to Buffalo, where he immediately wrote to ask Allen for an allowance of a hundred dollars a week.

Allen replied: "It's maybe not practical supporting 13 people, 1 horse, 2 cows, 10 ducks, 30 chickens, 1 pig, 3 dogs, 3 cats, 1 gerbil and now one big white rabbit here and promising to support you at $100 a week in Buffalo—take it easy on me." He told Gregory that he had set up the farm as a refuge, suggesting that the farm was where Gregory should be if he wanted Allen to support him, "but since you don't live peaceably with others, or relatively peaceably, it makes domestic situation too tough to live with when you take such perverse pride in putting down everyone and attacking people when drunk. It's too hard to live with. If you really want to stop off here, you'll have to come to some kind of peaceably sober understanding with the household outside of me. Which basically means no lushing and exacerbation from fire-engine mouth and fists. I'm tired and just wanna get my desk work done."

There was a constant stream of visitors that summer, with sometimes as many as two dozen people on a weekend. Poets Robert Creeley and Allen DeLoach were both teaching at Buffalo, so the farm was a convenient halfway stop on the drive to and from New York City. Artist Wynn Chamberlain and poet John Giorno came, dressed in flowing Indian cotton and chiffon. The poet Paul Blackburn arrived, looking thin and wan. He joked about lung cancer as he chain-smoked the Gitanes that later killed him.

Carl Solomon spent a few days on the farm after Allen reassured
his mother that he would be safe there and told her how good for
his health the trip would be. He arrived on a Greyhound bus and
immediately called his mother from the drugstore. That evening,
Carl and Allen lounged in the living room. "We're not young and
pretty anymore," said Allen.

"No, but we can still be old and bestial," replied Carl, and they
laughed. Carl was very relaxed, but when the conversation took a
political turn, he said that he could not discuss such things because
his uncle would not approve and it made him nervous.

Elsa Dorfman, Herbert Huncke, and a friend came to stay. "Man,
we got such boss wheels outside," said Huncke, entering the
kitchen as if it were a Times Square bar. "Dig the threads," he told
Allen, grabbing his hand to make him feel the quality of his clothes.
"We've brought pink gin," he said happily. "Where shall we put
it?" Allen, flustered, tried to explain that they must not give any to
Ray and Peter, because they were supposed to be drying out.
Among other visitors that summer were the translators Claude Pelieu and Mary Beach, come to work on the French edition of *Planet
News*, and Ann Charters, who came to interview Allen for her
ground-breaking biography of Kerouac, published in 1973, which
she dedicated to Allen.

Allen spent the summer evenings tootling away at the pump organ
beneath the kerosene lamp. He often slipped into Denise and
Peter's room to watch the news of the war on the flickering blue
screen (they had replaced the TV). Leaving their room, he would
stand in the yard and look up at the thick band of the Milky Way,
imagining the destruction taking place half the world away. The
news that September was grim: The United States was bombing
Cambodia, Laos, and Vietnam from bases in Thailand.

Allen felt impotent in the face of the U.S. war machine, but using
his skill at "reading between the lines in the *New York Times*," he
found an area where his special knowledge of drugs and his antiwar
efforts could be combined: he began a massive project to investigate
the role of the CIA in opium smuggling in Southeast Asia. He already had extensive files, which he now added to by gaining access
to the files of Time-Life. His spring 1971 reading tour opened with
a week in Washington, D.C., and he used this time to visit Les
Whitten in the office of columnist Jack Anderson, in search of a
vital letter that had mysteriously disappeared from the files of a
Senate government operations committee. Both the *New York Times*
and *Ramparts* were researching the story (at Ginsberg's instigation),

but whereas they had only telephoned Anderson's office to see if he had a copy of the letter, Allen appeared in person.

"To our surprise, his detailed files and probing questions were thoroughly professional," Anderson's "Washington Merry-Go-Round" column reported. "The poet's theory is that the CIA has been compelled to help the opium farmers in the mountains of northern Laos in order to keep them fighting the communists. The CIA has raised a 10,000 man army from the Meo tribesmen. Without their opium trade, they might require massive US economic aid." The letter Allen was looking for was written by a former CIA employee, S. M. Mustard, and addressed to former senator Ernest Gruening of Alaska. It charged that South Vietnamese Vice President Nguyen Cao Ky "took advantage of [the] situation to fly opium from Laos to Saigon." With a copy of the letter in his folder, Allen went off to interview Walter Pincus, a former Senate Foreign Relations Committee investigator with a lot of inside information on Indochina.

Ginsberg established that 80 percent of the heroin on the streets of America came from Southeast Asia via Saigon (20 percent was the official line). In charge of the opium traffic were Nguyen Van Thieu, the head of the U.S. puppet government in South Vietnam, Madame Nhu, Marshal Ky, and other top politicians, all aided and abetted by the CIA, which provided the air transport. Allen's point was that the misery and violence in the streets of American cities was directly related to U.S. policy in Southeast Asia.

On March 4, Allen and Louis Ginsberg gave a joint reading at the Corcoran Gallery in Washington. The audience was filled with society hostesses and government top brass. Richard Helms, the head of the CIA, sat in the front row, and Allen delivered an impassioned version of "Pentagon Exorcism," looking straight at him. He had met Helms at a reception before the reading and immediately quizzed him about the CIA's role in smuggling opium. Helms, of course, denied that CIA-owned airlines had anything to do with it, and the discussion finished with a wager. Allen bet his bronze dorje (Tibetan thunderbolt) that he would prove that the secret CIA-Meo airbase at Long Cheng was used as a depot for transshipment of Golden Triangle opiates to Saigon. Helms accepted the wager and agreed to meditate for one hour each day if he was proved wrong. (Senate hearings later proved Ginsberg right. It is not known if Helms began to meditate.)

SIXTEEN | THE LION OF DHARMA

Allen is a rabbinic *sadhu* who can at need transform himself into
an astute and hardheaded lawyer, and only this combination of
fearless holiness, blazing compassion, and clear intellect has
prevented him from being jailed or shot long ago.

—Alan Watts, *In My Own Way*

IN APRIL 1971, THERE WAS AN IMPORTANT EXCHANGE OF LETTERS IN THE
New York Times Book Review between Ginsberg and Richard Howard. Along with Carolyn Kizer and W. D. Snodgrass, both had been
judges on the National Book Award poetry panel. The panel had
chosen in favor of Mona Van Duyn, but Allen disagreed with the
verdict and disassociated himself from it. In his closely argued
2,500-word letter, Allen spelled out why he thought that Gregory
Corso should have been awarded the prize. "So what are you proposing," he wrote, "that Mona Van Duyn has a better EAR than
Gregory Corso, a greater juxtapositional economy, a more fertile
sense of invention, a greater grasp of history, a greater involvement
of person with poetics, a superior shrewdness in phrasing, a loftier
metaphysics, even a more practical hand? Are you all mad? Have
you no sense of modesty or proportion to your dreadful ambition to
reduce all poetic judgments to domesticated mediocrity? There is
nothing wrong with Van Duyn's book except that it is not the work
of Genius, and there is nothing right about Corso's book except that
it is the work of Genius."

Allen then went on to extol the "poetic genius" of McClure, Lamantia, Whalen, Snyder, and Kerouac, and as much as claimed
that there was still a conspiracy against them all. He signed his

letter, "Your disobedient servant." Richard Howard's reply began by querying the "persistent association by you of Kerouac-McClure-Lamantia-Whalen-Corso in a pentad of 'experimentalism' to which no other name has been added, not Merwin, not Ashbery, since you began to haunt these States."

Allen was very widely read and had assembled an enormous poetry library, but though he recognized the high quality and degree of achievement of many other poets, he remained convinced that his poet friends from the mid-fifties—Howard's "pentad," to which a dozen or so others working in the "open form" Williams tradition, such as Creeley and Snyder, could be added—were the only "prophetic" poets in the United States of world stature. Such loyalty was perhaps to be expected from the members of any literary movement, but it was his insistence that his friends were "geniuses" that rankled writers and critics outside of his circle.

In the years to come, this sometimes resulted in accusations of nepotism, as Ginsberg's influence in literary society grew stronger and universities looking for writers in residence or organizers of foreign poetry festivals assembling an American contingent turned to him for advice and suggestions.

In his *New York Times* correspondence with Howard, Ginsberg distinguished between "open breath poetry" and the traditional academic style of the time. That the "Open Breath School" was possessed of genius was disputed by Howard. "I wish I could come to terms with this Genius business, Allen," he wrote, "but I cannot. It seems to me you use the word the way hardhats use the word 'American' and it seems to me that if 'Genius' does not include Shakespeare's Sonnets and Milton and Wallace Stevens, it means merely madness, and that is what you want it to mean." He went on to complain that Allen drew a line between art and genius, "between excellence and ecstasy—as if the one had to, or could, preclude the other. You make out that if it's bad enough, it's got to be good, and that indeed is the parting between us." Over the years, Allen's continuing preference for the Whitman-Williams lineage of "mad scribblers," as McClure called them, was often to place him in conflict with the literary establishment—though less so in succeeding decades as the academic tradition itself shifted to a more open form.

In the early seventies, the youth movement began to drift apart. The antiwar groups fragmented, with some factions becoming more strident and others, like the Weathermen, going underground. As

the war in Vietnam intensified, so did the war at home, with a rash
of terrorist bombings and bloody confrontations between demonstrators and police.

Meanwhile, from another side of the youth movement, the human
potential movement and New Age Consciousness was emerging.
This was accompanied by an increasing interest in Oriental religions, particularly Buddhism, which was first popularized in the late
fifties by the works of D. T. Suzuki, Alan Watts, and, to a certain
extent, Kerouac's *Dharma Bums*. The widespread use of LSD had
given large numbers of young people quasi-mystical or in some
cases genuine religious experiences. Many had taken trips aided by
Timothy Leary's *The Psychedelic Experience*, a text based upon the
Tibetan Book of the Dead, and went on to study Tibetan Buddhism
itself.

In the sixties, Allen had been a longtime public advocate of LSD,
marijuana, mantra chanting, and spiritual exploration as a means of
expanding consciousness. During the seventies he concentrated
more on mantra chanting and meditation, and was proclaimed by
the Luce press as the guru of the youth movement. His readings
became more like seminars, consisting of poetry, mantra chanting,
and often an exposition of his current political preoccupations: the
CIA role in dope smuggling in Southeast Asia, FBI infiltration of the
antiwar movement, or support for a worthy local cause. His stage
props included incense, a Tibetan bell and brass thunderbolt
(dorje), his ever-present harmonium, and, on one occasion, a large
brass statue of Vajrasattva. To the incomprehension of some audience members, he began his readings by chanting mantras, often
accompanied with explications of the poetic symbolism of the syllables. It was as if T. S. Eliot, at a poetry reading, were to sing
plainsong.

Ginsberg, playing the role of teacher, had a limited practitioner's
knowledge of the mantras he sang with such devotion. He had never
taken a teacher in Hinduism and Buddhism and had only recently
begun to meditate, though he had chanted mantras for half the
previous decade, encouraged by Swami Bhaktivedanta and various
other gurus. In 1970, Swami Muktananda Paramahansa invited him
to Dallas, where, for a week, Allen sat alone in his hotel room,
meditating Hindu style, repeating the Guru Om mantra with each
breath, as instructed. Each midday and evening, Muktananda
would come to see how he was getting on and to correct his posture.
Back on the farm, Allen continued to meditate an hour each morning before work.

Over the years, he had met a large number of Zen masters, swamis, and lamas, many of whom gave him teachings, particularly in India. Allen learned a good many mantras from Maretta Greer, though her explanations of their meaning were not informed by religious practice under a single teacher. Some of Allen's friends were concerned by his new preoccupation with chanting, thinking that it was distracting him from his poetry. Then he took Chögyam Trungpa as a teacher, and he dropped all but a few of the mantras from his performances, in favor of explaining basic Tibetan-style meditation practice to his audiences.

Allen first met the Venerable Chögyam Trungpa, Rinpoche, on the street in New York in late summer 1970. Allen was with his father, who was feeling weak from the heat. Trungpa had just hailed a cab, and Allen asked, "Can I steal your vehicle?" explaining that his father was sick. Trungpa's assistant, Kunga Dawa, recognized him, and addresses were exchanged. Ginsberg saluted Trungpa Indian style and recited the common Padma Sambhava mantra: "Om Ah Hum Vajra Guru Padma Siddi Hum." Trungpa later told Ginsberg that he wondered if the poet knew its full significance. Not long afterward, Trungpa invited him to critique his poetic Buddhist ritual text, the Sadhana of Mahamudra, which Dawa had translated into English.

In the spring of 1971, Ginsberg moved to Berkeley to supervise the final stages of the assembly of a sixteen-hour tape of his best recorded readings. That May, Chögyam Trungpa arrived in Berkeley and Allen visited him. Trungpa had already been to the bar across the street from his hotel and was drunk. Helped back to his room by two of his students, he had fallen on the stairs and torn his pants. When he bent over his son, his wife yelled at him for breathing vodka all over the baby. "Aren't you drinking too much?" Allen asked.

Down in the hotel restaurant, Trungpa looked at Allen. "Why do you wear a beard?" he challenged. "You're attached to your beard, aren't you? I want to see your face!" Allen sped to the hotel pharmacy and then into the men's room with a new pair of scissors. He reappeared five minutes later at the cocktail table where Trungpa was sipping his third Bloody Mary. "You didn't shave it! All you did was cut it off two inches!" Trungpa teased.

"It's eight o'clock, and you've got a lecture to give at eight-thirty," said Allen. "I'll shave there."

"They know me," said Trungpa. "They expect me to be late. You can shave now. Order another drink." But Allen insisted they go.

Backstage at the lecture hall, halfway through shaving, Allen realized that he was free of his familiar bearded media image and could now walk anonymously down Telegraph Avenue. He appeared from the men's room clean-shaven, and Trungpa exclaimed, "He took off his mask!"

Allen was staying at a commune on Woolsey Street in Berkeley, and when he returned, for a moment no one recognized him. He enjoyed his new invisibility. In an interview with Irving Rosenthal at the time, he said: "Several nights later I closed the Capri invisible and went to the Basket dressed in my Salvation Army $3.50 Montgomery Street suit and porkpie hat, white shirt and tie and close-cropped hair. I stood around watching everybody dance all night, got beat for a buck by a halfdrunk speedfreak kid I picked up in front of Finocchio's, and wound up taxiing alone to Pam-Pam's at 6 A.M. Great gathering of beautiful varied lads and queens at table, so I walked up hat in hand and said, 'Can I sit with you? I'm lonely.' They said, '*No!* No room here, we're expecting more people.' And suddenly I was on the outside of gay hippie culture looking in and realized I'd stumbled on a new karma yoga treasure: anonymity."

During his talk with Trungpa at the hotel, Allen had complained that he was fatigued by his endless cross-country poetry readings and the extended air travel. "That's because you don't like your poetry," said Trungpa.

"What do you know about poetry?" exclaimed Allen, struck but amused.

"Why do you need to depend on a piece of paper when you recite your poetry?" continued Trungpa. "Don't you trust your own mind? Why don't you do like the great poets, like Milarepa—improvise spontaneously on the spot."

That evening, at Trungpa's lecture, Allen improvised a silly ditty, rhyming "moon" and "June," "beer" and "dear"; it was surprisingly easy. His father's example and all Allen's youthful years of writing rhymed couplets came to fruition. The next night, at a benefit for Tarthang Tulku's Tibetan Buddhist meditation center in Berkeley, Ginsberg tested Trungpa's suggestion; he took no books or texts onstage. He chanted Tarthang Tulku's melody for the Padma Sambhava mantra for more than an hour, then, using the same two harmonium chords, he made the transition to a twenty-minute bittersweet improvised lament, beginning, "How sweet to be born here in America."

"It was the first time I ever got onstage without a text," he said,

"and had to improvise it out of the whole cloth of what I was thinking at the moment. And it was really awkward and unfinished, but
it was so profound . . . and so liberating when I realized I didn't
have to worry if I lost a poem anymore, because I was the poet, I
could just make it up."

Allen was deeply impressed by Trungpa, who, by quiet suggestion over the short time he had known him, had inspired changes in
his approach to poetry and his appearance. He began to realize that
in Trungpa he had found his teacher.

Chögyam Trungpa, the eleventh Trungpa Tulku, was from the
northern Chinese province of Tsinghai, a rugged, primitive area of
mountains between the upper reaches of the Yangtse and Mekong
rivers. The plateau was divided into the territories of twenty-five
tribes, each with its own hereditary chief; it was at the outer rim of
influence of the Tibetan religion.

Trungpa was born in Geje, a tent village that moved according to
season, following its livestock from pasture to pasture. His parents
owned a little land, but his mother was abandoned by his father,
and she had remarried by the time he was born, in February 1939.
At the age of thirteen months, the young Chögyam was selected as
the reincarnation of the tenth Trungpa Tulku, supreme abbot of the
Surmang group of monasteries in Jye Kundo (now Yushu), the most
important city in the region. He was the leader of over a thousand
monks and the countless peasants and serfs who worked the land.
In 1959, the Communist government began to institute reforms in
the feudal land system (many of the peasants were indentured to
the monasteries, and there was still slavery in some parts of the
region). This was strenuously opposed by the local rulers, particularly in Kham—a situation that was seized upon by the CIA. In a
massive operation, hundreds of Khampa tribesmen were transported out of Tibet to a secret base in Colorado, where they were
trained in guerrilla warfare to harass the Red Army.

As resistance to the Chinese reforms began, many landowners
and top religious leaders, including the Dalai Lama, decided that it
would be advisable to flee the country, and as part of the general
exodus, nineteen-year-old Trungpa left for the West, walking from
Kham to Arunachal Pradesh in India with a group of attendants and
followers. In the years that followed, many tens of thousands of
Tibetans fled the country.

It was a prescient move, given the near-complete destruction of
the traditional Tibetan religion and the apparatus of the theocratic

state. During the violence of the Cultural Revolution between 1965 and 1968, the army and the Red Guards leveled temples to the ground, humiliated and tortured monks, and sent thousands to detention camps. A disastrous bureaucratic attempt to cultivate wheat instead of barley on the high plateau resulted in widespread famine. Years later, the Chinese apologized and rebuilt a few of the temples, mostly where tourists could see them.

Trungpa learned English, studied comparative religion, philosophy, and fine arts at Oxford University, and became the first Tibetan to hold a British passport. He attracted a group of Western followers and set up the Samye Ling monastery in Scotland, but as he absorbed the influence of the West he developed a fondness for wine, women, and fast cars. In May 1969, he crashed his sports car into a novelty shop, paralyzing his left side. He gave up his monastic robes and in January 1970 married a young woman, Diana Pybus; they moved to the United States with several of his followers. "I'm sure he will be much happier there," said the secretary of the sedate Buddhist Society in London. "His style of Buddhism is much more suited to the Americans, I think."

This proved to be the case. Stories quickly spread about this amazing new teacher of "Wild Wisdom," who drank beer all through his lectures, occasionally fell asleep during meditation sessions, was always at least an hour late, and was known to creep up on students who were too comfortable in meditation, blasting them with his water pistol. On one famous occasion, he drunkenly insulted a redneck truckdriver in a roadhouse, and when it came time for him to leave, he and his attendant, Kunga Dawa, found the door barred by the trucker, who was fuming with anger and leveling a double-barreled shotgun at Trungpa's head. Not to be outdone, Trungpa pulled out his water pistol and squirted the man. The trucker left in a squeal of wheels.

His religious lineage was that of the Kagyü sect, but the Venerable Trungpa, Rinpoche, was also empowered to teach the N'yingma, the oldest of the Tibetan Buddhist schools. Since the time of the Buddha, all the major schools of Buddhism comprised three types of practitioners: the lay community; strictly disciplined monastic communities devoted to scholarship; and nonmonastic "wild wisdom" yogins, known as the mahasiddhas, some of whom retreated to solitary caves or forests, while others lived secular lives as butchers, courtesans, or householders. All placed great value on meditation under the tutelage of a personal teacher. They drank a lot, often exhibited "divine madness," and were known as the "mishap lineage." They were reputed to be great meditation instructors, and their teachings were handed down through the centuries by written and oral tradition from guru to disciple. It was the Kagyü and N'yingma sects of Tibetan Buddhism that embodied the mahasiddhas' lineage. Trungpa's "Wild Wisdom" was in a classic tradition of Tibetan teachers going back to the yogi poet Milarepa. Allen found this method very attractive, combining, as it did, many of the traits of the Beat Generation: the emphasis on the "sacredness" of immediate experience, sexual candor, and absence of censoriousness. Trungpa's alcoholism, which paralleled that of Kerouac and many of Allen's other friends, did not put him off. Trungpa became a major influence on Allen throughout the seventies and into the eighties.

Allen involved himself in the gay liberation movement from the beginning. The day after the famous riot in 1969, he had visited the Stonewall Bar, hoping to calm any further violence and to give his seal of approval to the gays who had finally stood up against police harassment. When he arrived, he was applauded by the crowd and allowed through the police line into the club; one police officer even asked for his autograph.

In the summer of 1971, Allen gave a very frank interview to the *Berkeley Barb*, in which he spoke at length about his homosexuality. "I'm very shy," he said. "I've always found it difficult to proposition people on the street or in urinals or anything like that. It's not my scene exactly. Although I have all sorts of heartbeats and heart throbs and longing desires walking up and down the streets for practically half the young cats I see, it's really hard to communicate it. I'm also so busy I hardly have time for romantic dalliance, even if I could break through my shyness. I'm at liberty in case anybody wants to know," he said. (Peter had stayed behind in New York with Denise.) "I'm almost at the level of putting an ad in the *Berkeley Barb* for something like that: 'Wanted: one young man, secretary, companion, body servant, who can drive, take shorthand, competent in business matters and correspondence, can cook, camp, good carpenter, a forest hippy.' "

Back in New York after a brief visit to India, Allen received a flurry of telegrams and phone messages from Yoko Ono, asking him to join her and John Lennon in Syracuse for the opening of a show of their sculpture. John and Yoko first met in 1966 and had been inseparable since 1968, with Yoko even sitting in on Beatles record-ing sessions. It was October 9, 1971, John Lennon's thirty-first birthday, and a number of people had gathered in his Syracuse hotel suite to celebrate. There was a giant birthday cake, and toys and telegrams littered the room.

John sat on the bed wearing his little round eyeglasses, his hair very long, parted in the middle. Record producer Phil Spector was there, completely drunk, and insisted on holding Allen's hand. Ringo reminisced about the old days with the Beatles, who had formally broken up the previous year, but had not toured since 1966. John talked at length, attacking the concept of "God," as he had done on his *Imagine* album. Allen seated himself in a half lotus on the carpet and, arranging his Tibetan bell and dorje, incense, and harmonium around him, began to chant the Padma Sambhava mantra: "Om Ah Hum . . ."

John jumped up and said, "Wait a minute. I'll get my guitar." Ringo borrowed Allen's finger cymbals and upturned a wastebasket to make a drum. Someone gave Spector a guitar, and he took it upon himself to sing harmony with Allen. In the first hour or so, Allen led with mantras—Om Ah Hum, Om Namah Sivaye, and Om Mani Padme Hum—all taken very slowly. He also did Blake's "Nurse's Song," but he couldn't get the timing right. It didn't mat-ter, and they all began to improvise blues.

They strummed their way through "Yellow Submarine" and "Give Peace a Chance," both of which had good choruses to join in on. They jammed for about six hours. "Lovely day," wrote Allen.

Afterward Allen found himself in a limousine with John Lennon and a drunk Phil Spector. The car was surrounded by screaming teenagers, and Allen got some sense of what it must have been like to be a Beatle. "Just like in 'Help,' " he said. "I think probably relations with Lennon and others easier in future. This is first time we really got together on art vibration."

Peter and Denise wanted to spend the winter in New York, so Allen closed down the farm for the season. The animals were all given away, with great care taken in selecting their new owners. They even found a farmer who would take their three-hundred-pound pig, Don't Bite Me, as a pet. Julius was sent to the Binghamton Hospital, still not talking but in good physical shape after his work outdoors.

• • •

Trungpa asked Allen to come and stay at his house in Boulder for a week, to appear with Gary Snyder and Robert Bly at a poetry reading to raise money for Vajradhatu, Trungpa's religious organization. Allen already regarded Trungpa as his teacher, but now he took the formal vows of Buddhism. On May 6, 1972, he underwent the traditional Buddhist Three Refuges ceremony at Dharmadhatu meditation center, with Gary Snyder in the congregation. Allen committed himself: to take refuge in the Buddha (either the historical Buddha or simply a state of "awakened mind"); to take refuge in the dharma (the teachings, the cumulative body of Buddhist knowledge); to take refuge in the sangha (the Buddhist community or congregation; all sentient beings). Allen repeated the vows three times and accepted as his refuge name Lion of Dharma. Trungpa had already given him a new mantra for meditation.

Although not required to, he also took the Bodhisattva Vows. "I was doing Trungpa's instruction so it seemed natural," he said, "but the Bodhisattva was the one which was most interesting." The four vows began: "Sentient beings are numberless. I vow to liberate them all," which Allen interpreted as meaning: "Enlighten all, help all or get on with, which is the same thing I took on the Columbia ferry boat. I felt I was already on my road and this was merely like a formulation, in classical terms, of what was already my intuitive desire." The vows continued: "Obstacles are inexhaustible. I vow to cut through them," explained as: "One's own aggression is inexhaustible, yet one vows to relate to it, to acknowledge it and work on it." The third vow was: "The gates of the Dharma are countless. I vow to enter every gate," which Allen described as: "The notion of relating to any situation and not boycotting any situations. Not avoiding, but trying to alchemize every situation, by skillful means to turn it to advantage . . . To turn it from shit to roses." The final vow was: "The Buddha Path (of awakened mind) is endless. I vow to follow through."

It is easy to see why Ginsberg should be attracted to the Bodhisattva ideal, since one of his great strengths was always his willingness to take a difficult or painful situation and try to salvage something from it, whether it was dealing with his mother's madness, becoming involved with the lepers and dying beggars in India, or talking amiably with street people and bag ladies. He would intervene in street arguments, talk to belligerent drunks and spaced-out junkies. If someone had a bad skin condition or disfigurement,

Ginsberg would immediately ask about it rather than pretend it was not there. His enormous inquisitiveness and almost complete lack of embarrassment sometimes led him to quiz complete strangers about their income or sex life and volunteer the same, uncalled for information about himself.

For two years, Allen had been devoting more and more of his time onstage to singing lengthy versions of the Om Ah Hum and Om Mani Padme Hum mantras, often to the irritation of those members of the audience who had paid their money to hear him read poetry. Although most of the audience was prepared to go along with it, many were clearly bored, others were puzzled, and some simply regarded the whole thing as a massive ego trip. Trungpa suggested that he stop using the mantras at his readings. "It was rousing an expectation in the audience, getting them high," said Ginsberg, "but I had no further instruction to give. So it was just a trip, a buzz, which it was, but what good would it do unless I was aiming to provide something further. I can't deliver a teaching." Allen's friends were much relieved.

Throughout 1972, Allen and Peter were deeply involved in the antiwar movement. Allen used press interviews and television talk shows as vehicles for his message, sometimes angering TV hosts by twisting their questions to his purposes. His position was that the United States had split Vietnam unnaturally in two, and he often quoted Eisenhower, who had said that 80 percent of the Vietnamese would have voted for Ho Chi Minh if the United States had allowed elections at the end of the Indochinese war with France. The statistics of the war filled him with horror, and he used every possible opportunity to protest. "The thing that struck me," he said, "was that though there were big mobilizations, and although the majority of the country was against the war, there was no dialogue between the government and the people organizing the antiwar movement. They weren't communicating."

In 1972, Allen spent ten days with Gary Snyder in the Sierras. Gary had no telephone, but while visiting a friend nearby, Allen phoned the White House and got through to Henry Kissinger, Richard Nixon's chief adviser on the war. "This is Allen Ginsberg—the poet," he introduced himself.

"I know," said Kissinger.

Allen suggested that Kissinger get together with David Dellinger and the leaders of the peace movement and try to open a dialogue. Kissinger said that he was agreeable to a meeting, in principle. Allen told Dellinger, who approved of the idea. Senator Eugene McCarthy offered his place for a meeting, but there was no reply from the White House when he left a message to this effect for Kissinger.

Shortly afterward, at a huge demonstration outside the White House, Allen found himself onstage, singing Blake, as tear gas swirled about him yet again. He was often arrested and teargassed at demonstrations. One such occasion occurred in Miami during the 1972 Democratic and Republican conventions. The peace movement planned huge demonstrations and took great care to ensure that Miami 1972 was not a repeat of Chicago 1968. Given the strength of the antiwar movement in the country, the administration did not relish the thought of the media coverage that massive peace demonstrations would get and used every means to disrupt them. Even before the Chicago riots, the FBI had infiltrated the Yippies with agents. When the Yippies went to Miami, both they and the breakaway Zippies had agents provocateurs in their midst, whose job was to disrupt peaceful demonstrations and cause violent scenes; the media were bound to concentrate on them and ignore the much larger number of people engaged in peaceful protest marches and rallies. The tactic worked well, and as predicted, the press ran a number of editorials denouncing the peace movement for violent behavior.

The Vietnam Vets had also been infiltrated by the FBI, and Allen was particularly incensed when a peaceful march of about two hundred mantra-chanting people, which he had helped organize, was disrupted by large numbers of veterans. The march had begun very peacefully. "Walking down Collins Avenue, everybody was very pleased, chanting 'Ah!' which sounded great, good vibration, people were being friendly. And the old folks in Miami Beach were on our side. All of a sudden, a block behind us bursting into the street, are all these Vietnam Veterans coming to join us, digging what we were doing, I thought. They scattered in our ranks and began overturning garbage cans, stopping cars, pulling out the spark plugs, totally wrecking the scene and creating a traffic jam. So immediately the police arrived, apparently notified in advance that this was the tactic of the FBI, because these were Vietnam Vets who were FBI agents."

At first, Allen couldn't understand why the Vietnam Vets would behave like that, then it became obvious that they were trying to get everyone arrested. "So we kept our group together and went back, cleaning up the garbage cans and putting them right and trying to create order, but by that time the police had gathered about five blocks down and formed a line to stop us." When they got there, the police ordered them to disband the march or be arrested for disturbing the peace. "So we all sat down in the middle of the street and the police surrounded us and slowly rounded us up and one by one threw us into meat trucks that they hired for the occasion to take us to jail." It took him three days to get out. Peter had also been arrested but was in a different cell.

Allen described the event: "It was a real bitter political experience because it was the total sabotage of every possible good natured attempt to do a peaceful festival of life. And it was overt. . . . The press said we had rioted. The wool was pulled over the public's eyes completely in that way. It was difficult enough to realize that we had been that much infiltrated but then to explain it, and on top of that, how could we prove it until years later when the Vietnam Veterans [the Gainesville Eight] won their case." It took five years for the proof slowly to emerge through the Freedom of Information Act—"By which time nobody remembers it. But I remember it!"

> *A mass of idiots whopping out mass murder*
> *Cowards with billion dollar guns*
> *Calling it patriotic, the president to the janitor*
> *Hypocrite infanticides, mangrove swamps biocided.*
>
> *We are a mass of idiots, we are a mass of idiots*
> *The world will never forgive, the world will maybe forgive*
> *   The world will have to forgive*

Allen's desk was still filled with appeals for help. That year, Timothy Leary and Abbie Hoffman both found themselves in deep trouble with the authorities in ways far beyond any aid Allen could give. Leary had escaped from jail with the aid of the Weathermen and gone to live in exile. He had been serving twenty years for two pot convictions: ten years for possession of two roaches weighing only a few grams, imposed in Orange County, California; and ten years imposed in Houston for his original conviction in Texas for possession of a half ounce four years before. So desperate was the FBI to get Leary back that American agents snatched his passport at the Kabul airport and bundled him onto a plane for the United States. Leary was placed in solitary confinement and his bail set at five million dollars, the highest in American history. In a remarkable display of erudition, Allen responded by setting out the complicated facts surrounding the case in the form of a sestina—a lyric fixed form consisting of six stanzas, each comprising six lines, in which the end words of the first stanza recur as end words of the following five stanzas, and as the middle and end words of the concluding tercet. The end words should rotate in order, but in Allen's poem they didn't, so he called it "Mock Sestina: The Conspiracy Against Dr. Tim Leary." It was distributed as a flier in May 1973.

Equally imaginative, perhaps, was Allen's attempt to defend Abbie Hoffman, who was arrested while trying to sell more than three pounds of cocaine to undercover narcotics agents. Unable to deny that Hoffman was involved in a large-scale drug deal, Allen wrote: "In time of communal Apathy synchronous with Abbie Hoffman's recent disillusioned withdrawal to private life (after crises of his public affairs to confound Government police bureaucracy and war led him to be attacked left and right), Mr. Hoffman is now to be congratulated on an arrest which by its very surprise, its simultaneous whimsicality and seriousness, re-unites many of his fellow workers once again to resist the steamroller of police state power crushing another live citizen's body." Allen concluded his open letter: "I pray with body speech and mind OM AH HUM for courts and government and public to recognize the strange delicacy and historical charm of the situation in which they are placed together with peace poet Abbie Hoffman, and myself, sincerely yours, recommending Hare Krishna to one and all, Allen Ginsberg."

That fall, Allen spent a few weeks on the farm, where Peter and Denise were bringing in the harvest, boiling beets for canning, gathering apples to store in the cellar, and bottling giant zucchinis. He spent long hours in his room with its hissing gas mantle, answering letters and preparing to attend Trungpa's three-month Vajrayana seminary in Teton Village, a ski resort in Jackson Hole, Wyoming. Trungpa intended to take eighty advanced students through the three *yanas* of Buddhism, devoting a month to the study of each. He wanted very much to get Allen involved with his organization and asked him if he would teach poetics at the seminary. "[In] 1973 he flattered me by inviting me to come out to the Vajrayana seminary in Teton Village and teach poetry in the Teton mountains,"

Allen said. "So I thought I was going there as a teacher, and I got there and I found out, yes, I was teaching, but I was being treated like everybody else. As a student, if I chose to be a student, or a recluse, if I chose to be a recluse. He was teaching a full course on Hinayana, Mahayana, Vajrayana, so I could either take the position of student or pursue my own universe, and it seemed I'd learn more by being a student and not making a scene over my deflated ambition to be a teacher, though I was teaching."

Before this, in New York, Trungpa had asked Allen to be his poetry guru, which puzzled Allen. "I couldn't figure on what level he meant it. Somewhat mockingly but also very serious . . . So I said, 'Sure, I'll be your poetry guru. Please be my meditation guru.' So we made a little deal. 'You teach me meditation, I'll teach you poetry.' Obviously somewhat playful, and he was being very courteous to me." The deal is an interesting reversal of the "vows" Ginsberg had taken with Neal Cassady and Peter Orlovsky. With Neal and Peter, Allen offered to teach spiritual and intellectual skills in exchange for physical love and practical help. In this case, it was Trungpa offering the spiritual advice and Allen the practical skill.

In Jackson Hole, Allen found the experience of intensive sitting "painful and changing and rapturous and boring, like some kind of flattened out acid trip extending through time. Lovely." Bearded again, he sat nine hours a day, staring through a giant plate-glass window, watching the dawn break pink on the powdered snow of the mountain peaks and the shadows move imperceptibly throughout the day, until dusk fell and the light faded. He repeated his A Ah Sha Sa Ma Ha mantra silently in his head, using it to measure his breath. His mind raced with thoughts, chatter and anger, frustrations and erotic fantasies, until each one was played out, and he was still sitting there in bib overalls, with balding head and graying beard, feeling calm and strangely high.

After nine days, Trungpa told him just to watch his breath moving out, otherwise he would get "entangled in a body trip too heavily." Allen would do this simple samatha meditation—no mantra, eyes open—for the next decade or so, and he incorporated instructions on how to do it into his reading program. He described it in detail:

"Specifically, samatha—as distinct from Zen style—is paying attention to the breath leaving the nostril and dissolving into the space in front of the face. . . . I've heard it described as touch and let go, touch and let go—or attention to the breath going out, and then dropping it as the breath ceases, and then attention again to the breath when it goes out. So it's practice in *re*-directing your attention constantly to the space in front of your face, outside of your body. In that sense, almost by definition, it's practice of egolessness because you're meditating on the empty space into which your breath dissolves, rather than into any psychological or sensational phenomena going on inside the body. Then there is constant daydreaming and drifting away from that attention to the space. You're constantly waking up—mindfully waking up to the actual space around you, into which you're breathing. You use the breath as a handle to get back into that space."

This type of meditation was referred to time and time again in his poetry and was the subject of the title poem of his City Lights book *Mind Breaths*. He continued the intensive sitting, "eye fixed on glittering tremble of gold aspen leaves all day, glittering like buds."

It was the time of the CIA-sponsored overthrow of Salvador Allende's democratic government in Chile, and Allen's thoughts were dominated by despair, anger, and confusion over the role of the United States in toppling a legally elected government. He worried over the fate of Nicanor Parra and his other Chilean friends and vowed that if they were harmed he would somehow find a way to throw Kissinger in jail. He read in the Denver *Post* that Pablo Neruda had died of cancer but the military regime would not allow him a public funeral. Allen wrote several small poems for Neruda during his breaks from meditation:

> *Your poetry long as Chile*
> *epics, verses, sonnets,*
> *line by line lie empty . . .*

On September 30, he learned of the death of W. H. Auden and that afternoon sat weeping, remembering how he first met Auden in 1946, in Earl Hall at Columbia, and how he had ridden the subway with Auden all the way down to Sheridan Square, just to talk to him. He remembered Auden's apartment on Cornelia Street, which had seemed so glamorous at the time, and his loft on Twenty-first Street, where Auden had read the manuscript of Allen's *Empty Mirror* and recommended that he study David Jones as a model for open verse. He recalled their shouted argument on the isle of Ischia in 1957 and later, in the sixties, sitting on his couch at St. Marks

Place, New York, offering to sing Blake for him, and Auden's reply: "Oh no! I get so embarrassed when people sing to me alone. That's for the concert hall." It had been only two months since Allen had read with him in London and he had explained Welsh verse forms to Allen, counting the syllables. As he wrote his journal, Allen turned his thoughts to Auden's lover, Chester Kallman, weeping in Bavaria, to Christopher Isherwood mourning his old friend in Hollywood, and to the sadness at Oxford, Harvard, and Columbia. He wrote: "The aspen grove lost its yellow leaft roof, 'tis end of September, kind Auden's gone away forever."

The second two-week session in Teton Village went better than the first. Allen was more relaxed, and his sexual fantasies began to lose some of their power: "less intensely hot and horny lov'd—and less painful to repeat phantom mind fucks o'er—sexual spectres more transparent than before, almost invisible asses and cocks, couldn't maybe even get a hard-on over real ruddy ass meat—all in my mind!" he wrote. On his last day there, he talked with Trungpa about sex and asked if maybe they should sleep together.

"I think that would be interesting," said Trungpa, "if there's ever time—and space—to explore those feelings."

Allen's intensive meditation was interrupted by the beginning of his fall reading tour, but he managed to rearrange his schedule so that he could spend a further two weeks at Teton Village, midway through the tour.

Most of January 1974 Allen spent on the farm, meditating in the attic. He began by sitting for five hours a day, then slowly increased this to eight, "staring open eye at horizon hill woods dawn and dusk west over the State land, snow all over pond fields and red barn roof, flies born buzzing in the sunny window."

Back in New York City, he got caught up in the excitement surrounding Burroughs's return to the States to teach at City College from February until May, two hours a week—a position Allen had engineered for him, thinking that he was stagnating in London. Bill still dressed in the same conservative suit and tie, which made the subject matter of his readings seem even more outrageous. He did a number of readings and found, to his surprise, that he was a natural performer. His dry, sardonic reading style delighted audiences, and he was given a rapturous reception. "One standing ovation is enough," Bill commented. Many people thought he was dead, so his return to live in New York was much like that of the prodigal son and was the cause of a great round of parties, drinks, and dinners. Allen saw a lot of Bill and taught him Trungpa's meditation system, which, to Allen's astonishment, Bill approved of completely. Allen had been seeing Yoko Ono, and on Valentine's Day he took her to visit Burroughs at his loft at 452 Broadway. Yoko, wearing a big floppy hat, sat holding hands with Burroughs, who was so drunk that the next day he had no memory whatsoever of their visit.

Allen made another rock 'n' roll connection that month, with James Taylor and Carly Simon, whom he visited one evening at their apartment in the East Forties. He also spent time with Gregory, who had had a breakdown and been admitted to the Bronx State Mental Hospital on February 20.

Allen's 1974 spring tour finished in California, and Allen, Peter, and Denise left for the Sierras, to start building a house on the land Allen owned with Gary Snyder. Allen's journal happily recorded: "May 28. Kitkitdizze Poets' Hermitage, Ponderosa Pine Circle Site —birds chirrping and titting. 5am dawn bell from Hindu ashram uphill bonging the morn." The ashram was near Gary Snyder's Zendo, where Allen, Peter, and Denise were staying. Another journal entry read: "I wake up, Snyder with flashlights at his porch shelf in the pre-dawn rain in the Sierra foothill summer dark"; the feeling is that caught by Kerouac in *The Dharma Bums*.

The land was not far from Nevada City, a small town in the foothills of the Sierra Nevadas near Donner Pass, on the Truckee wagon train route to California. The whole area, studded with abandoned mines from the gold rush days, was thick with oak and fast-growing ponderosa pine. Peter worked naked, huffing and sweating, helped by Denise and a number of young "Buddhist striplings living out their forest manhood with Indian headbands and leather carpenter aprons," as Allen described them. They poured concrete, dug up bedrock, sawed and shaped wood. Allen learned to cut wood and hammer nails. They were working from an architect's drawing designed to their specifications, which included a proper kitchen and a sun deck. Gradually the house began to take form.

Allen and the poet Anne Waldman both gave readings and poetry workshops at Chögyam Trungpa's newly formed Naropa Institute in Boulder that summer, and when the sessions came to an end,

Trungpa asked them to start a poetry school there. Anne was an obvious choice to codirect the school, as she had years of experience in running the St. Mark's Church Poetry Project. Trungpa had already planned a "national poetry conference" to be held at Naropa the next year, and the poet Lewis MacAdams had prepared a list of some sixty poets for Trungpa to choose from. Allen felt himself becoming inexorably entangled in Trungpa's world. As he frequently did, he expressed his worries in his journal as a "worst-case scenario," writing: "I am caught in whirlpool of Ego Desire Ambition Power, to run the school and be elder poet host to such a large company of bards fighting for recognition and fame." Allen seemed not to have considered the fact that dozens of established universities would have been pleased and honored to offer him a similar position and would even have offered him money, something that was very scarce around Naropa. The attraction of Naropa was the association with Trungpa. Allen agreed.

Allen was sharing an apartment in Boulder with Anne Waldman, and they began to discuss names for the school. Anne suggested "Gertrude Stein School," but Allen wanted to honor his old friend. "Jack Kerouac School" was kicked around for a while, and then Anne came up with "Jack Kerouac School of Disembodied Poetics," which it became. A student later asked why "disembodied" poetics, when the emphasis was on getting back into the body. "That's a joke," Allen replied, "because he's dead, so he's disembodied, so to speak. Also because we were fools and didn't know what we were getting into. We didn't realize it would be such a serious body. Also because of beatnik poetic inspiration that made it sound funny. I objected to Anne, saying 'Wait a minute, this is contrary to all the basic principles enunciated by Pound and Williams and the Imagists,' but Trungpa said, 'Ah, it's pretty funny. Why don't you use it? It's too late to change it. Too late!' "

By mid-August 1974, Allen was back at Ponderosa Pine Circle, helping Peter build the cabin. The structure was not habitable yet, so they slept outside in sleeping bags. By mid-September, the roof was on and the windows were being hung. It looked like a tiny wooden castle amid the blue oak and ponderosa pine. Allen filled a journal with images from the four months of living deep in the woods: Peter yodeling as he worked, the Milky Way through the pinetops, the mosquitoes at sunset, the time he found a rattlesnake curled up under a stone, how the helpers sat around in the evenings playing guitars by the light of the kerosene lamp, swimming in the cold pool. . . . By October, the house was finished, and it was time to leave.

Allen returned to San Francisco on his way to New York, where he had several upstate readings lined up. One evening, he and Anne Waldman attended a concert by jazz pianist Cecil Taylor at a San Francisco nightclub. Sitting there, he noted in his journal: "I want to be known as the most brilliant man in America." Allen said later, "I was so ashamed of what I wrote down that I wouldn't let her see it. I hid my notebook from her with my hand. Within a month I realized that the poem was funny. It's obviously a great burlesque, a take-off on myself, shameful, shocking." He added to it, and it became "Ego Confession," which appeared in *Mind Breaths*.

Allen had reason to feel confidence in his position. The Vietnam War was finally over, ended when the last helicopter left the roof of the American embassy as the victorious Vietcong swept through Saigon. At home, Allen's deep suspicions about the Nixon administration were all vindicated by the Watergate affair, in which Nixon was forced to resign and many of his top aides were jailed for lying to Congress.

No major pastoral poems came from Allen's period in the woods. Instead, he proved once again that he was the master of the urban landscape, managing to turn a mugging into a successful poem. On November 2, he left his East Tenth Street apartment and walked past the usual throngs of youths lounging on the stoops and leaning on wrecked cars. One block from his house, two youths tripped him and immediately dragged him into the basement of a burned-out store, where they relieved him of his week's seventy dollars spending money. Allen kept up a continuous chant of "Om Ah Hum," thinking that this would calm them, until they yelled, "Shut up or we'll murder you!"

"Om Ah Hum," replied Allen. "Take it easy."

They pulled down his socks, looking for hidden hundred-dollar bills, while a third youth tore off his wristwatch. "Shut up and we'll get out of here," they said, and left.

". . . I rose from the cardboard mattress thinking Om Ah Hum didn't stop em enough, / the tone of voice too loud," he wrote, "—my shoulder bag with 10,000 dollars full of poetry left on the broken floor . . ."

He stood up and found his eyeglasses on the edge of the step where he had thoughtfully placed them as he was dragged to the basement. Emerging into the half-gutted street, he called the police from a nearby bodega. He and a policeman examined the basement to see if his wallet had been discarded there before the muggers left. The neighborhood kids had seen nothing. Still a little shaken, Allen walked along East Tenth Street and crossed Avenue C to his own block, realizing that he had lived there for ten years and didn't know anyone more than half a block away. He sold the resulting poem, "Mugging," to the *New York Times* for seven times the amount that the kids had stolen from him.

In March 1975, Allen and Peter moved into a much larger apartment, on East Twelfth Street between First Avenue and Avenue A. It had six rooms, two of which were very small, and had been created by knocking together two small apartments, an arrangement that led, somewhat incongruously, to Allen's having a sink right next to his desk in his office. There were three south-facing front rooms, and Allen and Peter each took one, with the third becoming Allen's office. When Allen woke in the morning, all he could see from the window was the top of the church opposite, which, in the gray winter light, reminded him of his days in Paris. Denise had a small room of her own off the kitchen, where she practiced her guitar. They painted the walls white, tacked their picture of the young Rimbaud on the wall, and were home.

Allen's reading on April 17, 1975, in New York was a historic occasion. Allen, Peter, and Gregory returned to McMillin Theatre at Columbia University for a benefit for Naropa Institute, billed as "Another Night at Columbia." The first night had been the historic reading of February 5, 1959, the subject of Diana Trilling's infamous essay. This time they had William Burroughs with them onstage; it was the first time they had all appeared together since their informal reading at George Whitman's Paris bookshop in 1958. Allen announced that he would read the best poems he had written since he was last there, sixteen years before. His choice was "Kral Majalis," a section from "Wichita Vortex Sutra," "Wales Visitation," "Please Master" (during which a few people in the audience groaned at the painfully explicit sexual revelations), "On Neal's Ashes," and "Ego Confession." At the line "I want to be known as the most brilliant man in America," the audience erupted into a great wave of applause and laughter.

· · ·

After the summer sessions at Naropa that year, Allen spent two weeks in solitary meditation at Trungpa's Rocky Mountain Dharma Center, in Livermore, Colorado, attending lectures and catching up on his prostrations in a little cabin in the mountains. It was standard Tibetan Buddhist practice that in order to qualify to receive the higher level of teachings from the guru, the disciple had to first complete 100,000 prostrations. With each prostration, the disciple committed himself to his guru, the Buddha, the dharma, and the sangha. Trungpa had said, "Surrender to prostrations as you surrender to toilet bowl. You're a poet, so have some humor." It was not until October 1975 that Allen got back to New York.

That spring, Bob Dylan had returned to New York, leaving his wife and family in Malibu. He looked his old self from his early sixties days as a folksinger, with a scruffy leather jacket, dark glasses, and several days' growth of beard. His marriage appeared to be breaking up, and he was lean and anxious to do something new. He began hanging out at the late-night rock and folk clubs in the Village, often taking part in jam sessions. After a summer break, he was ready to go out on the road in a tour bus with a few friends and play small halls. He put bass player Rob Stoner in charge of getting the band together and asked Joan Baez if she would like to come along. Dylan's original idea soon grew into an elaborate project calling for a large road crew, a lighting crew, an advance party to oversee hotels, ticket sales, and posters, a management team of bookkeepers and luggage handlers, and a security team. Then he decided to make a movie of the tour, which added two film crews, with their own sound men and their equipment and lighting handlers.

So many celebrities were interested in doing guest spots or in joining the tour for a few days that Dylan thought it would be a pity to gather all that creative talent and just make a concert movie, so he decided to intercut the live footage with improvised scenes using the musicians as actors. Dylan phoned Allen one morning at 4 A.M., asking him to join the tour to help set up suitable scenarios. It was the first time they had spoken in four years. "What're you writing?" Dylan asked. "Sing it to me on the phone." Allen did. Dylan said, "Okay, let's get out on the road."

Allen was delighted, particularly when Dylan told him, at a party a few days later, that his improvised songs "have everything. They are understandable at every level." Dylan told Allen, "You're the

King, you're the King, but you haven't found your kingdom. But you've always been the King. . . . People get off on your energy."

Allen was not sure what was expected of him, since Dylan had also roped in the playwright Sam Shepard to write spontaneous scripts. At the rehearsal studio, Allen asked, "Bob, what do you want of me? What's your fantasy? Your idea?"

"Well, it's up to you to decide," said Dylan, characteristically. "You're the King. Whatever you want to do, get it together. I'm presenting you. It's about time. This country has been asleep. It's time it woke up." Dylan asked who else should come along, and Allen immediately suggested Burroughs; but Bill wasn't happy with the idea of constantly changing hotel rooms and the chaos of a rock 'n' roll tour, and he declined. Allen suggested Anne Waldman, Peter, and Denise, and Dylan agreed. Peter came along as a luggage handler, and Denise's job was to provide fresh flowers and fruit for Dylan's hat before each show.

The tour, named the Rolling Thunder Revue, was organized under conditions of extreme secrecy. So that it would be able to play small halls, not even the musicians knew which town they would be playing in until the day of the concert. Dylan had not forgotten the last time he announced a tour: there were six million applications for tickets.

They began shooting the film before they even got out on the road. In one scene, Allen was supposed to be filmed from an Eighth Street balcony while he stood in the street and read his poems. Behind the balcony, everyone in the room was high on grass, and the film crew was shooting close-ups of Dylan's twitching face while Phil Ochs tried incoherently to explain the plot of "Hard Times" to him. Allen, in the street, kept calling up that he was ready, but no one seemed to hear. This standard of professionalism persisted throughout the tour, leading eventually to Sam Shepard's premature departure.

The touring band now consisted of Rob Stoner; his friend the drummer Howie Wyeth, whom nothing could faze, not even Dylan's bad timing; Luther Rix on drums and percussion; and Scarlet Rivera on violin. David Mansfield, described by Ginsberg as "a boy with a Botticelli face," doubled on violin as well as dobro, steel guitar, and mandolin. There were now four guitarists, not counting Dylan and Joan Baez: Roger McGuinn, Steve Soles, Mick Ronson, and Bobby Neuwirth. Ronee Blakely played piano and sang. It was clear that so many performers could not play at once, and the show was organized in segments, with everyone but the rhythm section doing a small set, sometimes joining one another on songs, with all coming together for the finale. They rehearsed for three days in New York, during which, to Allen's disappointment, his idea of ending the show with a mantra was dropped. This meant that his only appearance onstage was in the chorus of "This Land Is Your Land," which was chosen as the finale. To see if it worked on location, they booked the Seacrest, a resort hotel in Falmouth, Massachusetts, and did a run-through of some of the numbers in the lounge.

It was out of season, and the only other occupants of the hotel were a party of 165 elderly Jewish ladies gathered for a fund-raising mah-jongg championship. To their great surprise, late one evening the hotel manager rose to announce, in best Las Vegas fashion, that there would be a poetry reading by "one of America's foremost poets, Mr. Allen Ginsberg!" Allen shuffled to the podium, wearing a brown suit, rabbinical curls, and a beard. He sat on a stool, hunched over the microphone, and announced that he would read "Kaddish." The ladies smiled encouragingly. Dylan filmed the reading and included a large segment of it in the final film. The camera team captured the tension perfectly. Sam Shepard, in his book of the tour, *Rolling Thunder Logbook*, described how he saw it:

"The mothers go from patient acquiescence to giggled embarrassment to downright disgust as Allen keeps rolling away at them. . . . Since I was raised a Protestant, there's something in the air here that I can't quite touch, but it feels close to being volcanic. Something of generations, of mothers, of being Jewish, of being raised Jewish, of *Kaddish*, of prayer, of America even, of poets and language. . . . The ladies sit through it, captured in their own seaside resort. A place they've all come to escape to, and there they are, caught." Shepard was surprised at the burst of applause Allen received; evidently no one could fail to be moved by the poem. It was as if Allen was finally reading it to Naomi herself. Dylan sat silently throughout, absorbing the whole performance.

Joan Baez followed and charmed the ladies with "Swing Low, Sweet Chariot." Dave Mansfield played some fancy classical guitar, then Dylan set things jumping with "Simple Twist of Fate," accompanying himself on the piano. He was soon joined by the rest of the band, and the Seacrest was transformed into a late-night Greenwich Village rock club. The mah-jongg ladies appeared to enjoy every bit of it.

The first concert was on October 30, 1975, in Plymouth, just around Cape Cod Bay from the Seacrest. Anticipating the bicentennial year, they could not overlook a chance to film a few scenes at Plymouth Rock, and a great deal of time was devoted to trying to lower Allen down from the granite portico that protects it from vandals. Allen was to sit on the rock while Dylan, at the helm of a rubber dinghy that also contained Bobby Neuwirth, Ramblin' Jack Elliott, and Peter Orlovsky, landed on the beach and set foot in America. As the dinghy crew, shivering with cold, dragged their craft up the beach to prevent its being swept away by the winter tide, Allen busied himself chanting and ringing his finger cymbals, much to the amazement of tourists visiting the historic spot, who stood gaping at him through the railings.

That evening, Allen asked Dylan, "Well, how do you like your party?"

"It's *your* party, it's not mine."

"Well, is it giving you pleasure?"

"Pleasure? Pleasure? No, not at all. I wouldn't want that, would you? That's too dangerous. I do what I do without thinking of pleasure."

"And when did you come to that state?" asked Allen.

"Couple of years back," said Dylan. "I mean, at one time I went out for a lot of pleasure, all I could get, because, see, there was a lot of pain before that. But I found that the more pleasure I got, subtly there was as much pain. And I begun to notice a correspondence, the same frame. I began to experiment and saw it was a balance. So now I do what I do without wanting pleasure. Or pain. Everything in moderation."

Allen asked if he believed in God.

"God? You mean God? Yes, I do. I mean, I know because where I am I get the contact with—it's a certain vibration—in the midst of—you know, I've been up the mountain, and—yes, I've been up the mountain and I had a choice. Should I come down? So I came down. God said, 'Okay, you've been up on the mountain, now you go down. You're on your own, free. Check in later, but now you're on your own. Other business to do, so check back in sometime. Later.' "

"I *used* to believe in God," said Allen.

"You don't now?" said Dylan, surprised.

"No, I *used* to believe in God."

"Well, I used to believe in God too," said Dylan. "Yes, I *used* to believe in God. If you believed in God now you'd write deeper poetry now. I mean, there's no question I didn't get any answers. He's too busy to answer. I understand that—making elephants. Anyone who can make camels go through needles' eyes is too busy to answer my questions. I'm on my own."

"Did you study Kabala?"

"Well, yeah, but it's complicated, and not satisfactory."

"Any good teachers?"

"Yeah, lots of good teachers, but . . ."

"So you said the other day that you had your own practice. What is it?"

"Oh, I'm not going to give away any secrets! Be sure! I'll cover for God, I'll alibi for God anytime. I'll cover for him. Sure. Absolutely! You don't want me to give him away, do you?"

Allen obviously did, but he tried another approach. "Well, then, how do you get on the mountain? Or where does the road to the mountain begin?"

"Oh, I can't tell you that. But I can take you there. I promise I'll take you there! You wanna go?"

"I'll come following you." Allen sang one of Dylan's own lines.

Despite the enormous cost of keeping an ever-changing touring party of forty or more people on the road, Dylan stuck to the idea of playing small halls, though in most places they did two performances a night to bring in more money. Dylan was quoted in *Time*: "We were all very close. We had this fire going ten years ago and now we've got it burning again." The concert schedule accommodated the needs of the film crew; in fact, the cost of the film soon became so high that Dylan had to introduce some larger venues into the itinerary to help break even. The caravan of two touring buses, several cars, equipment trucks, and Dylan's personal luxury mobile home slowly wound its way across New England, traveling in great secrecy, always staying twenty or thirty miles from the concert site, in small, out-of-the-way hotels.

Allen's first idea for the film was, perhaps predictably, that he and Dylan should sleep together, and their subsequent conversation in bed should be filmed. When he addressed himself seriously to the problem of the film, he came up with a scheme that was nothing if not ambitious. The film, he thought, should "wrap up all questions" on ecology, capitalism, communism, God, poetry, meditation, and America "as best we can." He also thought it should present their thoughts on acid, grass, and sexual liberation and have dramatic cameos on the atomic bomb and war, and Jerusalem and the Jews. His notebook brimmed with ideas: a meditation sequence with Burroughs and Trungpa; a dialogue on God between himself and Dylan; Dylan's wife, Sara (who was on the tour), as a mother goddess; a dialogue between Dylan and LeRoi Jones on black and white working together; "whole cast and crew, Mick to Andy, Chris to Sara, lined up family naked for portrait perhaps by swimming pool"; Dylan giving Allen guitar lessons; Allen reading from Sacco and Vanzetti's speech. . . . They shot several scenes at the Seacrest before the tour began, as well as one improvised dialogue in a diner on November 1, with Allen playing the Emperor and Dylan the Alchemist:

Allen: "I've heard through the grapevine that you have certain powers."

Dylan (evasive as ever): "Oh, that's not me. But I know who you mean."

One of the most successful early scenes they shot, and one of the most poignant in the finished film, was a visit to Jack Kerouac's grave. Lowell was the third town on the itinerary, and as soon as they got to town, Allen and Sam Shepard drove to Nick's Lounge. Kerouac's brother-in-law, Nick Sampas, and his brother Tony were delighted to see Allen again, and Tony drove them out to the cemetery so that Sam could examine the location and make plans for the next day's filming there.

At noon on November 3, Allen, Dylan, Sam, and Peter, accompanied by the camera crew and the sound man holding his Nagra, drove through the black iron gates of the graveyard. Allen and Dylan approached the spot where Kerouac lay and read the inscription on the small marble plaque set in the earth, half covered by grass and autumn leaves:

> "TI JEAN" JOHN L. KEROUAC
> MAR. 12, 1922–OCT. 21, 1969
> HE HONORED LIFE

Allen quoted Jack's favorite lines from Shakespeare: "How like a winter hath my absence been . . . What freezings have I felt, what dark days have seen! What old December's bareness everywhere!" Allen and Dylan settled themselves cross-legged on the grass before the plaque. Dylan tuned his Martin guitar, and Allen unpacked his harmonium and quoted a few lines from *Mexico City Blues*, then

Dylan borrowed the harmonium and they began to improvise a slow blues, trading verses back and forth, to Jack Kerouac beneath them, under the grass. Allen described the scene in a letter to Gregory: "Then Dylan took guitar and played slow blues while I composed celestial triplet-rhyme lines, Jack looking down from clouds over trees weeping a big tear—Dylan stopped playing to stuff an autumn leaf in his breast pocket, I continued a capella on the beat, when he picked up the guitar hit chord in time to end my line in proper measure—like old time blues licks—then we walked harmonium and guitar together down vista of gravestones and November bare trees—bright . . . leaves blowing in our path in Graveyard."

Ramblin' Jack Elliott told Dylan about a friend of his, a Cherokee medicine man called Chief Rolling Thunder. The coincidence of the name was too much for Dylan to resist, and Chief Rolling Thunder, his wife, Spotted Fawn, and one of his assistants were flown to Newport, Rhode Island, from their reservation in Nevada. It was decided to film a traditional Indian sunrise ceremony, so at 4 A.M. on November 5, a bedraggled collection of about twenty musicians and tour members, many of whom had not yet been to bed, assembled in the lobby of the Newport Sheraton. They squeezed into three cars and followed Dylan's camper to the grounds of a restored mansion on Rhode Island Sound. There they found an isolated spot at the water's edge, and as the horizon grew light, Rolling Thunder and his assistant began to build a fire. The medicine man had taken the precaution of calling the coast guard to find the exact time of daybreak. Once the fire was burning, he had everyone form a circle around it, and his assistant circulated with a tobacco pouch. As the dawn broke, Rolling Thunder explained the symbolic meaning of the sunrise in terms of renewal and the generosity of the Great Spirit, and asked everyone to toss tobacco into the fire and make a prayer. He then asked Allen to read a poem.

Allen, wearing a denim jacket and a scarf in the chilly air, a red bandanna wrapped around his head, produced his Australian aboriginal song sticks from his shoulder bag and began to improvise a sunrise ceremony poem, based on the traditional mode of repeated line verses he had been taught in Adelaide by an aboriginal during a reading tour of Australia in 1971.

> *When Music was needed Music sounded*
> *When a Ceremony was needed a Teacher appeared*

> *When Students were needed Telephones rang*
> *When Cars were needed Wheels rolled in*
> *When a Place was needed a Mansion appeared*
> *When a Fire was needed Wood appeared*
> *When an Ocean was needed Waters rippled waves*
> *When Shore was needed Shore met ocean*
> *When People were needed People arrived*
> *When a Circle was needed a Circle was formed.*

As the Rolling Thunder Revue continued, Allen's onstage role increased. He was allowed to play finger cymbals on one of Rick Danko's solo numbers and sing in the chorus on another, but he spent most of his time working on the film scenario. He and Ramblin' Jack Elliott discussed the old days and reminisced about the time, twenty-five years before, when Elliott had gone off with Helen Parker, Allen's first girlfriend, leaving Allen frustrated and broken-hearted. Allen composed a song to her.

> *Here's to Helen Parker*
> *wherever she may be*
> *Cape Cod or on 14th Street*
> *in New York City*
>
> *She took old Allen's cherry*
> *his first radiant lay*
> *She stole Jack's ramblin' heart*
> *practically the same day.*

Although he was delighted by the communalism and creative energy of the Rolling Thunder Revue, Allen told Dylan that he couldn't stay on for the whole tour because his father was dying and he had to spend time with him.

"Bring your father," said Dylan.

"What about me, when I'm dying?" asked Allen.

"We'll take care of you when you're dying," replied Dylan.

But as Allen said later, "The next morning he was glum and he didn't remember. And I went up thinking that he was going to take care of me for the rest of my life! I didn't realize that his munificence was engorged with snow."

It was the first time Allen had been on a big rock tour, and the amount of cocaine being used disturbed him; he wrote a triplet about it for the daily tour newspaper:

> *Nobody saves America by sniffing cocaine*
> *Jiggling yr knees blankeyed in the rain*
> *When it snows in yr nose you catch cold in yr brain.*

Dylan had become convinced of the innocence of the black boxer Hurricane Carter, in jail for murder, and in order to raise money for his appeal fund, they took the Rolling Thunder Revue to Madison Square Garden. The "Night of the Hurricane" was December 8, 1975, and tickets sold out in five hours. Louis and Edith attended their first rock concert, to see Allen onstage, in suit and tie and sneakers, not only with Bob Dylan, Joan Baez, Joni Mitchell, and Roberta Flack, but with Muhammad Ali, who came to introduce the show. The concert raised $100,000 toward Carter's appeal, and after the Christmas break they did another at the Houston Astrodome. Many years later, Dylan's support for Carter was vindicated when his conviction was reversed.

Allen saw the poet W. S. Merwin in New York and got a firsthand report of the incident at Trungpa's Vajrayana seminary the previous fall that had become an exciting source of gossip in Buddhist and poetry circles. The event occurred at the three-month intensive seminar that Trungpa organized each year. Allen had attended the first one in 1973 and subsequently went to several more with Peter. In 1975, the seminar had been held at the Eldorado Ski Lodge in Snowmass, Colorado, which Vajradhatu had taken over completely from the beginning of September until Thanksgiving; sessions cost $550.

Merwin had given a lecture on Dante and a poetry reading at Naropa and was spending the summer there with Dana Naone. He asked Trungpa if they could attend the seminary. At first, Trungpa refused his request. Only a quarter of those who applied had been accepted, and the enrollment was complete. The usual requirement was that the applicant had previously sat a *dathun* (a thirty-day sitting period) and taken various preseminar training courses in Boulder or Vermont. Merwin and Naone were not students of Trungpa's and had no retreat experience, though they were long familiar with Zen sitting practice. Merwin strongly wanted to attend, and Trungpa finally agreed. They were told to say nothing about it to anyone until they got to the seminary, because they had been given preference over a long waiting list.

The curriculum was rigorous. Approximately one month apiece was devoted to Hinayana, Mahayana, and Vajrayana study, each involving two weeks of lectures and courses with examinations, followed by two weeks of intensive sitting. Attendance at each of the six daily sitting sessions was posted at the shrine room door, recording how many hours each person sat. Merwin's background was intellectual, monastic, contemplative, and peaceful, and as a pacifist, he refused to participate in the chants dedicated to "Wrathful Deities" (defined by Ginsberg as deities "which represent insight into human passion, aggression and ignorance, the traditional 'three poisons' "). At lines such as "You enjoy drinking the hot blood of ego" or "As night falls, you cut the aorta of the perverters of the teachings," Merwin put down his chant sheet, which was in English translated from the Tibetan, and kept silent until the passage was over. The "bloodthirsty" references in the chants made Merwin and Naone less and less keen to take vows with Trungpa, and they told him so in a private meeting. They were not prepared to surrender to the guru and were uncomfortable with the outer forms of Tibetan Buddhism as well.

October 31 occurred in the middle of a period of sitting, and Trungpa declared a Halloween party to celebrate the start of the Vajrayana teaching. At the party, Merwin and Dana danced to records for an hour or so with the other students. Trungpa arrived drunk at about ten-thirty, held up by the attendants who usually assisted him to his seat, his left side having been paralyzed in the auto crash seven years earlier. They had already caught him twice as he fell entering the shrine room. Earlier that evening, he told one of the older women students that he intended to take off people's clothes as a form of Halloween demasking. She was the first one he had stripped. She went along with it but afterward said she felt "trashed out." Then Trungpa himself stripped, and when he was naked, two students, one of them also naked, lifted him onto their shoulders and paraded him around the room. Dressed again, Trungpa pointed from one person to another, instructing his guards to "Chop 'em up"—strip off their clothing.

Trungpa announced a lecture on Vajrayana. Learning that Merwin and Dana had left the shrine room before he arrived, Trungpa sent a student, William McKeever, to get them. They dressed and came to the dining room door, but not approving of the atmosphere at the party, they decided to drive into Aspen for the night. As they were preparing to leave, McKeever came to their room with a command from Trungpa that they attend. They explained they had already been back once and were not going again.

According to Merwin's account, he saw heads peering around the end of the corridor and locked the door as a precaution. When McKeever returned yet again, he had orders from Trungpa to escort them to the party. Merwin reiterated their refusal and locked the large glass door on the balcony against the people outside. A threatening crowd had now gathered in the hall, the telephone line had been cut, and someone tried to use the passkey to get in. As the mob began kicking the door, Merwin pushed a large chest of drawers against it. He turned off the lights so that it was harder for the people on the balcony to see inside.

Then someone announced, with great satisfaction, that Trungpa had sent an ultimatum that they be brought down "at any cost." Hearing that Merwin had barricaded the door, Trungpa had suggested smashing the window. His guards planned a simultaneous attack on door and window. As they began breaking down the door, Merwin warned that he would hurt the first ones in.

The door gave way and Merwin struck out with a bottle in the darkness as his attackers came pushing through the splinters. The bottle broke and several people were cut. Grabbing another bottle, he hit out again; that bottle broke too. Merwin described what happened next: "At that point Dana shrieked and there was a loud crashing as the big glass balcony door was smashed by McKeever. . . . I crossed the room and started to beat the remnants of the glass door outward onto the balcony, pushing with broken bottles, but meantime the crowd forced its way into the room behind us from the hall. Dana was shouting, 'Police! Why doesn't somebody call the police?' but they laughed at her, women too, and Trungpa later mocked her, for that, in one of his lectures."

Merwin and Dana were surrounded. She was backed into a corner and he was keeping the mob away with broken bottles. Then he saw blood streaming down the face of his friend Loring Palmer and put his arms out to let them take the bottles. The guards immediately jumped on him and pinned his arms back. Dana managed to give one guard a black eye before she, too, was subdued. The hallway was crowded with onlookers, and Dana again pleaded, "Why doesn't someone call the police?" One of the women insulted her, and a man threw a glass of wine in her face.

Trungpa was sitting in a chair surrounded by his disciples, who sat in a ring on the floor. Merwin's account continued: "Trungpa called us to come over in front of him, looked up at me, and said, 'I hear you've been making a lot of trouble.' Grabbed my free hand to try and force me down, saying, 'Sit down.' (The other hand had been bleeding a lot and was wrapped in a towel.) When he let go, we sat down on the floor. He said we hadn't accepted his invitation. I said that if we *had* to accept, it wasn't an invitation. An invitation, I said, allowed the other person the privilege of declining. We pushed that around a bit. The way he saw it, no force seemed to have been used, except by us. I reminded him that we never promised to obey him. He said, 'Ah, but you asked to come.' Then, dramatically, 'Into the lion's mouth.' I said that they'd developed big corkscrews, now, for forcing coyotes out of their burrows, and that maybe he ought to get one, to do his job more easily."

During one of their exchanges, Trungpa threw a glass of wine in Merwin's face. "That's sake," Trungpa told him, then turned to Dana Naone. "You're Oriental," he said, "you're smarter than this. You might be playing slave to this white man, but you and I know where it's at. We're both Oriental . . . we know where it's at." He began talking about "my country being ripped out from under me, and it was the Chinese Communists who did it. . . . If there's one thing I want to see in my lifetime, it's to see my country back. Only one Oriental to another can understand that." According to Jack Niland, one of Trungpa's students, "He kept doing this superracist thing . . . very cutting, and her only response was, 'You're a Nazi, you're a Nazi' and 'Someone call the police.' She was completely freaking out." Then Trungpa asked them to join in the dance and celebration and take their clothes off. They both refused.

"Why *not*?" asked Trungpa. "What's your *secret*? Why don't you *want* to undress?" and to Dana he said, "Are you afraid to show your pubic hair?" Trungpa said that if they wouldn't undress, they would be stripped. Merwin described the stripping: "He ordered his guards to do the job. They dragged us apart, and it was then that Dana started screaming. Several of them on each of us, holding us down. Only two men, Dennis White and Bill King, both of whom were married, with small children there at the seminary, said a word to try and stop it, on Dana's behalf. Trungpa stood up and punched Bill King in the face, called him a son of a bitch, and told him not to interfere. The guards grabbed Bill King and got him out of there. One of the guards, who'd stayed out of it, went out and vomited, as we heard later. When I was let go I got up and lunged at Trungpa. But there were three guards in between, and all I could swing at him through the crowd was a left, which was wrapped in the towel and scarcely reached his mouth. It didn't amount to much, and I was dragged off, of course."

As the guards reached for Dana, she tried to hang on to Merwin; they were pulled apart. She tried to get at Trungpa, but he was too well protected. "Guards dragged me off and pinned me to the floor," she wrote in her account of the incident. "I could see William struggling a few feet away from me. I fought and called to friends, men and women whose faces I saw in the crowd, to call the police. No one did. . . . Richard Assaly was stripping me while others held me down. Trungpa was punching Assaly in the head, urging him to do it faster. The rest of my clothes were torn off."

"See?" said Trungpa. "It's not so bad, is it?" Merwin and Dana stood naked, holding each other, Dana sobbing.

After meeting with Trungpa the next day for tea, Merwin and Naone elected to stay on at the seminary to attend Trungpa's climactic Vajrayana lectures, which took place as scheduled for the next two weeks. They made no public statements about their humiliating experiences, but rumor and gossip soon spread throughout the Buddhist and poetry communities. Many Buddhists felt misgivings about Trungpa's methods, while Merwin's friends, outraged at the treatment he and Naone had received, felt an apology, at least, was in order. None came, and the affair tarnished Trungpa's reputation, particularly among critics suspicious of or hostile to Tibetan Buddhism. To supporters of the Chinese revolution, it was further proof that change in Tibet was long overdue.

Louis Ginsberg's health was slowly deteriorating. In his eighties, he was now too tired to go out for a walk or even to reach down and take off his shoes. He needed help to rise from his velvet armchair, where he sat looking out over the rooftops. Allen and Peter spent as much time as possible in Paterson, looking after him. "Don't get old," he advised Peter. Louis was diagnosed as having a tumor of the pancreas and spots on his lungs. Against the wishes of the family, Allen asked the doctor to tell Louis what was wrong. "Thank God," said Louis. "I thought it was cancer of the brain."

One evening, Allen took a walk through the old downtown section of Paterson. Entire blocks had been torn down, and new buildings and malls stood near Fair Street, where he grew up. The site of their old house now lay beneath the newly built Hamilton Plaza. "Massive poured concrete building sites and walkways, all downtown changed," he wrote, "ghostly and empty streeted."

Louis and Edith's apartment on Park Avenue was so quiet that Allen was able to complete his first ten thousand prostrations, but he was still way behind everyone else in his group. Although Louis was very sick, the doctor thought that he would live for some time yet, so at the end of March 1976, Allen left to teach at Naropa. "Off to see that Trungpo-Mumpo?" Louis complained.

Allen wrote to Gregory: "Louis is dying in Paterson, wasted thin arms, wrinkled breasts, big belly, skull nose speckled feet thin legs, can't stand up out of bathtub . . . I may have to leave Naropa to help him out of bed to die."

Returning to New York briefly in early May, Allen was walking down Central Park West and found himself at the Dakota Apartments at Seventy-second Street. He telephoned upstairs and visited John Lennon and Yoko Ono for an hour. In a bizarre arrangement, Yoko Ono had set Lennon up with a Chinese-American woman, May Pang, and encouraged them to have an affair. Ono controlled the situation by telephone—sometimes as many as twenty calls a day. The liaison lasted for eighteen months and became much more serious than she had expected. Lennon and Pang moved to Los Angeles, where Lennon cut two albums and produced a third with Harry Nilsson. The cocaine and madness of the L.A. music scene brought out the worst in Lennon, and he eventually returned home to Ono, dumping May Pang in a rather callous manner en route. Now he and Ono had a child, Sean, and Lennon was devoting his time to bringing him up. Lennon told Allen that he and Ono had gone on a forty-day fast after Sean's birth and were practicing a very clean and healthy diet. Lennon baked all the bread.

He said that he had been lying sleepless one night, listening to WBAI on headphones, when he heard someone reading a long poem. He thought at first that it was Bob Dylan and was surprised when the announcer said that it was Allen Ginsberg reading "Howl." He admitted that he had never read it or understood it before. Although he had a copy, "my eyes saw the page, but I can't read anything. I can't get anything from print." Now, hearing "Howl," he understood why Dylan had mentioned Allen so often, how much Allen had influenced Dylan, and how close to Dylan's his style was.

· · ·

In the middle of May, Allen flew to Wichita to rejoin the Rolling Thunder Revue, which had been touring Florida and the southern states. The film had completed shooting in January, and Allen, who spent a week hanging out with Dylan, decided to ask him for fifteen thousand dollars for acting in it and setting up the scenes and dialogue. He wanted a car and a stereo set and to give some money to Ray Bremser. The mention of Bremser, whom Dylan had heard read in New York in 1961, did the trick, and the money came through. Dylan took 120 hours of film into the Sound Factory in Hollywood and emerged twenty months later with a four-hour film called *Renaldo and Clara*, in which Allen played a major dramatic role.

Allen continued to spend as much time as he could with his father. On June 4, Louis felt strong enough to talk to a reporter from the *Village Voice*. He said that he didn't believe in life after death. "I'll tell you what my attitude is. It's full of awe and wonder, because when you think about a galaxy with billions of stars, and you think of billions of galaxies sweeping through the universe, you wonder, why this prodigious display of energy?"

Allen returned to Boulder to teach his summer classes. A telephone call early in the morning of July 8, 1976, informed him that Louis had died peacefully in his sleep. Allen was on the first plane out of Denver for New York. As he flew over Lake Michigan in the morning sun, the poem "Father Death Blues" came to him in rhyming triplets, complete with a tune:

> *Hey Father Death, I'm flying home*
> *Hey poor man, you're all alone*
> *Hey old daddy, I know where I'm going*
>
> *Father Death, Don't cry any more*
> *Mama's there, underneath the floor*
> *Brother Death, please mind the store*

The next day, the *New York Times* devoted sixteen column inches to an obituary headed: "Louis Ginsberg, Traditional Poet." The subhead read: "Gave Readings with His Son, Allen, in Last Years." The obituary quoted from Louis's poem "The Fly," which concluded: "All material / Things depart / Now all the world / Is hinged on the heart."

Not long after his father's death, Allen joined Peter at an intensive meditation seminary held at Land O'Lakes, Wisconsin. Allen and Peter sat looking out over the snow-powdered flatland day after day. Allen needed the solitude of meditation to come to terms with his father's death and with the reflected significance of his own middle age. He wrote Gregory: "I'm finished as a poet, no more magic, nobody left out there to yell at, nobody left to curse out, to take revenge on or feel superior to! Not even Rockefeller! God knows where you are! My book 'Mind Breaths' ends up in my father's grave. Take care."

Ginsberg had three important books published in the fall of 1977: *As Ever: The Collected Correspondence of Allen Ginsberg and Neal Cassady,* published by Creative Arts in Berkeley with a foreword by Carolyn Cassady; *Mind Breaths,* his new City Lights collection, which appeared at the beginning of December; and his first hardback, *Journals Early Fifties Early Sixties,* edited by Gordon Ball and published by Grove Press. The journals drew a lot of press attention, including a long review from Allen's old Columbia classmate Louis Simpson in the *New York Times Book Review.* Simpson regretted the "acres" of dreams in the book but also said: "There are some entertaining 'political ravings' in these 'Journals,' including insults to some people at Columbia who did not pay sufficient attention to his poems when they first came out. As I was one of those people, I am happy to have this opportunity to say that I was wrong—not merely wrong, obtuse." A remarkable—and an honorable—volte-face from Allen's old opponent.

As winter began, Allen still worried continuously about the Merwin-Trungpa conflict. A journal entry for November 28, in his habitual "worst case" stylization of transient anxieties, noted that he felt "trapped 'like smoke going down bamboo tube' between poesy and Dharma, Merwin and Trungpa, in their ghost war. Hypocrite, I take rides with each. I haven't pursued my prostrations, I push and preach Dharma and poetry in public. I *can't* face Merwin, I get angry at my boyfriends and students, I am a hairy loss." He spent much of January 1978 on the farm with Peter, then fitted in a short reading tour before returning to Naropa in March to teach his students William Blake's *Urizen*—a project that became a four-term course, a line-by-line discussion of Blake's works from early poems through the prophetic books to the Seventh Night of "Vala, or the Four Zoas."

Among the administrative problems facing him as codirector of
the Jack Kerouac School was the rejection of two grant applications
by the National Endowment for the Arts, which had learned about
Merwin's treatment by the president of Naropa. Allen's argument
was that "while the Naropa Institute and its Poetics Department
was certainly Buddhist-oriented, in its secular interface to the public, the school was independent of the traditional procedures of a
formal and specialized Vajrayana seminary attended by old and
close practitioners." Although the Poetics Department did have
complete independence in its teaching, it was still criticized by
some for being a department of the institute of which Trungpa was
chief director. Naropa also had a $35,000 grant from the Rockefeller
Foundation to protect.

Naropa grew chronically short of funds; in 1977, many of the
teaching staff did not receive their salaries on time. Allen donated
most of his salary to Naropa, as did many of the staff who could
afford to, and raised money with many benefit readings.

Members of the poetry community began to align themselves for
or against Trungpa, but it was not until the spring of 1977 that Allen
was first involved in the controversy on a personal level. Among the
most vocal in his outrage at the treatment of Merwin and Naone
was the poet Robert Bly, who was using the term "Buddhist fascism" to describe Trungpa's behavior. This was a serious criticism,
because Bly had been a student of Trungpa's and had even helped
him edit his first book, *Meditation in Action*.

As Bly interpreted the situation, Allen, despite being in charge of
the poetry school that had presented Merwin's lecture and reading,
had sided with his teacher against the poetry community that he
was supposed to be encouraging and protecting, poets he had devoted his whole life to promoting and nurturing. "So what is this
community of poets I was talking to you about?" he asked Allen.
"What happened to that? . . . You're sacrificing that, for what?
That teacher? You can't sacrifice human beings and poets you've
been associated with your whole life!" It was this basic charge that
Allen had to consider seriously, particularly when the Merwin affair
resurfaced at Naropa that summer.

Ed Sanders had been invited to teach a course on "Investigative
Poetics" and had expected his students to choose a subject such as
the strike against compulsory lie detector tests at the nearby Coors
Brewery or an investigation into the local Rocky Flats plutonium
factory, south of Boulder. To his surprise, the class voted overwhelmingly to investigate the circumstances of the infamous Hal-

loween party at the Vajradhatu seminary. Twenty-four students worked on the project, sometimes until dawn, intending to interview everyone even remotely connected with the incident and to reconstruct the events leading to the final stripping. Trungpa was the only person who declined to be interviewed, though he urged those who assented to speak freely but without sensationalism. The 179-page report was finished in less than a month, but to the relief of the Poetics Department and the Naropa administration, the students voted not to publish their findings for the time being, considering the controversy a private matter.

Trungpa's style had gradually changed, prompted by the visit in 1974 of the karmapa, the head of his lineage; he now advocated short hair and neat dress as a secular form of monks' robes among his followers. Suits and ties slowly supplanted the casual hippie outfits of many of his original followers, and alcohol became the drug of choice. Trungpa was chauffeured around in an old blue Mercedes-Benz, purchased for him by one of his students, and his home was staffed by students dressed as English butlers and maids; they were required to call Trungpa and his wife "Sir" and "Lady Diana." He was protected by bodyguards known as the Vajra Guard, who wore blue blazers and received specialized training that included haiku composition and flower arranging. On one occasion, to test a student guard's alertness, Trungpa hurled himself from a staircase, expecting to be caught. The guard was inattentive, and Trungpa landed on his head, requiring a brief visit to the hospital.

Allen's involvement with Naropa was paralleled with other interests and campaigns. Twelve miles from Boulder, in Rocky Flats, the Rockwell Corporation made nuclear triggers for hydrogen bombs. In 1975, Allen had gone on a group tour of the plant with W. S. Merwin, among others, and he had also been involved in various antinuclear demonstrations directed against the factory. On June 10, 1978, he began work on a long poem, his own version of Corso's "Bomb," and two days later, after one of his typical all-night marathon writing sessions, he had the completed manuscript of "Plutonian Ode." The poem began: "What new element before us unborn in nature? Is there / a new thing under the Sun?"

The next day, he and Peter were arrested along with other demonstrators as they sat meditating on the railroad tracks, blocking the passage of a trainload of nuclear waste labeled "Fissile Materials," which was being transported out of the Rocky Flats precincts.

"Plutonian Ode" became the title poem of his next City Lights book and appeared in numerous underground newspapers and magazines. Ginsberg wrote: "Title poem combines scientific info on 24,000-year cycle of the Great Year compared with equal half-life of Plutonium waste, accounting Homeric formula for appeasing underground millionaire Pluto Lord of Death, jack in the gnostic box of Aeons, and Adamantine Truth of ordinary mind inspiration, unhexing Nuclear ministry of fear." The poem was a good example of Ginsberg's mature style—"glittering thoughtful galaxies, whirlpools of starspume silver-thin as hairs of Einstein!"—and he delivered the polemic by addressing himself directly to the strange new transuranic substance and detailing its manufacture, describing the apparatus that his bardic chant was meant to penetrate: "My voice resounds through robot glove boxes & ingot cans and echoes in electric vaults inert of atmosphere . . ."

Throughout the summer, a frequent subject of conversation was the Merwin affair. Of particular concern was whether Trungpa could do no wrong, since as lineage holder of the Dharma, his every action was a teaching and could be learned from. "If you make a mistake, you learn from it, therefore there are no mistakes," said Ginsberg, referring to Trungpa's position as a member of the "Mishap Lineage." The opposing view was that Trungpa had been an alcoholic ever since the late sixties and was certainly capable of making mistakes. It appeared, particularly to outsiders, that Trungpa was intent on recreating the situation he had in Kham. The apparent drift of his teachings was toward the "mandala-concept" of the Kingdom of Shambala, a nondemocratic kingdom using terms drawn in part from the Tibetan secular epic *Gesar of Ling*, and his inner circle became more and more like a court, complete with court intrigue and rivalry.

Though Ed Sanders's investigative poetics team had voted not to publish their report on the Merwin incident, photocopies were circulating in the poetry community. Sanders had given poet Ed Dorn permission to distribute copies as he saw fit, and Dorn had mailed out fifty of them, mostly to other poets. There was widespread interest in the report, and Ferlinghetti asked Allen for a copy so that he could consider it for publication by City Lights; Allen refused. Poet Tom Clark, now the senior writer on the local *Boulder Monthly*, also asked Sanders for permission to publish the report, since he thought that Boulder residents should be better informed of the activities of the large Buddhist community in their midst.

Sanders told Clark that the poetry class had been canvassed earlier that year and still voted against publication.

On September 13, Ed Sanders informed Dorn that a majority of the class were now in favor of publication. He added: "Report came in yesterday that the Vajra Guards were recently training wearing Canadian mountie uniforms and that the word 'democracy' is now being used apparently at Naropa as a catch-all word for the ills of the world." Still, Ed was hesitant to publish, because it would mean a "sure or probable break" with many of his old poet colleagues.

All this changed when the news broke of the events of November 18, 1978, when the Reverend Jim Jones led a mass suicide of 911 members of his People's Temple in Guyana. Horrific photographs of bloated bodies heaped in the temple compound filled the press and television screens, and religious cults became a national topic of conversation. Ed Sanders's investigative poetics group immediately voted overwhelmingly to publish their report.

Inevitably comparisons were made: Jones, like Trungpa, had forced men and women to strip in public and had sex with many of his female followers. When he ordered the mass suicide, not all of his followers had acquiesced, and it was his armed guards who forced many of them to drink the cyanide-laced Kool-Aid. Trungpa's students did not consider that a Jonestown was a possibility in Boulder or at a seminary, but people further removed from Tibetan Buddhist studies and meditation practice were less sure. Allen realized that fear of Vajradhatu stemmed largely from the traditionally hermetic nature of such teachings, and he began to wonder if the inner workings of Vajradhatu ought not to be made public. Ten days after the Jonestown massacre, he wrote: "Also I had in mind the question of the worth of secrecy of Vajrayana practice and guru-disciple wedding and vows and samya (or wedding vows), with the news of mass suicides by members of the church of a disaffected priest / teacher / revolutionary, Mr. Jones, in Guyana." Allen still gave Trungpa his general support, considering the real heat of the controversy to be an aspect of cultural xenophobia.

The first articles about the Merwin affair began appearing in the press, with the publication in the February 1979 *Harper's* of "Spiritual Obedience" by Peter Marin, a writer who had taught two courses in literature at Naropa in 1977. The local newspaper, the *Daily Camera*, asked at Vajradhatu for any comment on the *Harper's* article and ran a piece about Trungpa. In a follow-up, the *Camera* carried an editorial headlined: "To Avoid the Name, Shed the Disguise," which commented on the *Harper's* piece and briefly described the Merwin incident. Regarding the charge that Trungpa was operating a Jim Jones type cult, the *Camera* mentioned the guards, the limousine, and the drinking, and suggested: "To avoid being called a cult, it might help not to act like one."

Tom Clark asked if he could interview Allen about the affair for *Boulder Monthly*. Allen had reservations about the magazine and about talking about the incident, since he had not been there. Though he knew Clark regarded Oriental meditation practice as a cultural anachronism and disapproved of Trungpa, he was confident of Clark's good intentions because their *Paris Review* interview in 1965 had worked out so well. As codirector of the poetry school, Allen agreed, assuming he would have a chance to edit his interview as he had done for the *Paris Review*.

The interview took place on January 12, 1979, with Ed Dorn and a student present. The first question put by Clark regarded the effect on Allen and the Buddhist community of Peter Marin's article. "Universal paranoia, I think," said Allen. "Also some clarification of complexities that everybody feels within the Buddhist community. It brings to the surface a lot of thoughts that people have had anyway and discussed among themselves, but just didn't discuss publicly: fear of Buddhist fascism, paranoia about submission to a guru, the apparent incomprehensibility of the Merwin thing . . . It's like reading your marriage troubles in the newspaper."

Tom Clark was a skilled interviewer, and he almost immediately steered Allen to the heart of the matter: the political implications of the submissive relationship between disciple and guru. Allen demurred. "You know you're talking about my love life," he said. "My extremely delicate love life. My relations with my teacher."

Clark pointed out that people were interested in the subject more for its implications than just regarding the rights or wrongs of the Merwin incident itself. "If you turn this around and say it takes two to make a master," stated Clark, "you're not necessarily saying that one or the other's culpable."

"*I* feel culpable," said Ginsberg. "It's my paranoia that I'm expressing."

"I don't think that you personally were ever accused by anybody of anything in this regard," said Clark.

"I accuse myself, all the time, of seducing the entire poetry scene and Merwin into this impossible submission to some spiritual dictatorship which they'll never get out of again, and which will ruin

American culture forever. Anything might happen," Allen joked. "We might get taken over and eaten by the Tibetan monsters. All the monsters of the Tibetan Book of the Dead might come out and get everybody to take LSD! . . . The Pandora's Box of the Bardo Thodol has been opened by the arrival in America of one of the masters of the secrets of the Tibetan Book of the Dead."

Allen said he trusted and had faith in Trungpa's intelligence and thought that there had been no sexual motive in Trungpa's approach to Dana Naone. Clark pointed out that it was only natural, in the light of Jonestown, to be concerned when a large group of people appeared to condone the assault on two others by not helping, even when one of them was pleading with them to call the police. At this Allen grew passionate: "In the middle of that scene, to yell 'Call the police'—do you realize how *vulgar* that was? The Wisdom of the East was being unveiled, and she's going 'Call the police!' I mean, shit! Fuck that shit! Strip 'em naked, break down the door! Anything—symbolically. I mentioned privacy before—the entrance into Vajrayana is the abandonment of all privacy. And the entry onto the Bodhisattva path is totally— You're saying, 'I no longer have any privacy ever again.' "

Clark pointed out, "You only make that sacrifice if you *want* to."

"Only if you want to," Allen agreed.

"What if they didn't want to?"

"Then what were they doing at this Vajrayana seminary?"

To Allen, much of this seemed hypocritical. He complained that all poets demanded poetic license, the divine "right to shit on anybody *they* want to . . . Burroughs commits murder, Gregory Corso borrows money from everybody and shoots up drugs for twenty years but he's 'divine Gregory' but poor old Trungpa, who's been suffering since he was two years old to teach the dharma, isn't allowed to wave *his* frankfurter! And if he does, the poets get real mad that their territory is being invaded!"

The interview with Tom Clark was ill-advised in every way. Until that point, as Clark said, no one had blamed Allen for the Merwin affair, or even for encouraging members of the poetry community to get mixed up with Tibetan Buddhism and learn to meditate. Allen asked to see a copy of the transcript to approve the editing and accuracy of it. Clark had a deadline to meet, and as Allen was about to fly to New York to receive a poetry prize, he decided to trust Clark's editorial judgment. He asked him to show the edited transcript to Anne Waldman instead. Allen had regarded the interview as a chance to present his ideas on this much discussed subject to Dorn and Clark, two literate and sophisticated friends from the poetry world. He did not suspect that his interview was designed by Clark to be used as part of a highly critical attack on Trungpa and the Buddhist community. When he returned from New York in February, Tom Clark dropped off a copy of the complete transcript. Allen read it through and wrote Clark: "My intemperate comments on Merwin's poetry should not be printed as they were only abusive inaccurate and would only escalate enmity and not bring reconciliation."

Clark had edited the transcript prejudicially to retain all of Allen's most critical references to Merwin and to leave out his major compliments—particularly Trungpa's comment that he thought Merwin had behaved, all in all, in gentlemanly fashion in maintaining the privacy of the episode. Meanwhile, Allen corrected the transcript himself. "For my opinion," he wrote in the covering letter to Clark, "I was more interested in talking to you and Ed [Dorn] as friend poets than publishing my thoughts lest I escalate mis-understanding and continue foolish gossip trend. What Merwin had left alone I should & you should, so I'd rather this not be printed. However use your own best judgement." It was too late. When he and Peter arrived at the offices of *Boulder Monthly* to give Clark the revised version of the transcript, they were horrified to find the office piled high with cartons of the March 1979 issue, waiting to be shipped out. It contained Allen's interview, a section of the Sanders report, and an extremely unflattering flash photo of Trungpa on the cover. Allen was enraged. He complained about the secrecy of editing his interview to deliberately offend Merwin and exacerbate the controversy. Ed Dorn, who was in the *Boulder Monthly* office, replied laconically that Merwin deserved to be attacked for his overpraised poetic stature and that Allen was to be congratulated for doing so.

Meanwhile, all over town, the magazine was selling out, as Buddhists bought four or five copies at a time. Sanders flew in from California and picked up a bundle of the magazine to distribute, and Dorn happily sent copies to poet friends around the country.

The article provoked some strong reactions, including one from Bob Callahan, the publisher of Turtle Island Press, who was so concerned that he circulated a petition requesting the members of the poetry community to suspend any participation in the activities of the Jack Kerouac School of Disembodied Poetics until the Vajra Guards had been disbanded and efforts made to guarantee that such a thing could not occur again. It demanded that the "rights of individuals to dissent according to conscience be at all times respected." Callahan received between forty and forty-five signatures, with the Bay Area poets split roughly down the middle. Those not already connected to Naropa were usually happy to sign. Native American poets such as Jim Pepper, Leslie Silko, and Simon Ortiz all signed, as did black or third world poets, such as Ishmael Reed, Victor Hernandez Cruz, and Allen's friend David Henderson. Many of the poets with Buddhist connections agreed in private with Callahan but were not prepared to put their name on anything in public. Michael McClure telephoned Callahan and told him, "Those wimps at Naropa are no threat to *you*. I've told Allen for years, privately, to get out of that scene. Still, Allen believes in it. It's his family. You can't attack him for it. You're trying to ruin Allen Ginsberg. You can't do that!" McClure then began a telephone campaign to stop people from signing the petition.

Gary Snyder telephoned Callahan and said, "Your response isn't generous enough." Two weeks previously, Snyder had told Callahan that he had "grave doubts" about Trungpa's behavior, but now he said, "Take off my clothes? Sure, I'd do it. It's a big joke to me. Just don't criticize Allen in public." One of the strongest attacks on Trungpa came from Kenneth Rexroth, a longtime student of Buddhism and translator from the Chinese and Japanese, who said, "Many believe Chögyam Trungpa has unquestionably done more harm to Buddhism in the United States than any man living." Few defended Trungpa, but few would criticize Allen or the Jack Kerouac School of Disembodied Poetics, which had, after all, engendered the original Sanders Class Report.

Allen was, as usual, his own severest critic. In an apologetic letter he later wrote to Merwin, he described his reaction when he learned that the unauthorized version of his interview had been printed: "I was freaked out and yelled at Tom, thinking he had betrayed my trust and purposely got me into hot water. My main worry was that indiscreet put downs of your poetry, hyperbolic fantasies of Buddhist fascism, low grade gossipy opinions about scenes where I wasn't present, distorted paraphrases of conversations with Trungpa . . . would not only reveal my own basic hypocrisy, but also confuse the public issue (if there was one) with my un-edited, private, and hysteric or irritable conversation with friends. I'd thought I'd have a chance to correct the interview or Clark have the friendly common sense to edit and clean up my solecisms.

"I stopped yelling at Tom when I realized it was a fait-accompli irreversible," Allen continued, "and he thought he was doing it (aside from pressure from the magazine) as the rare bold action of an honest reporter, and that my yelling was only making the situation worse by solidifying my own and Tom's self-righteousness. I also breathed a sigh of relief, that I had hit bottom and my own hypocrisies were unmasked to fellow poets and fellow Buddhists, and that was almost a service rather than a stumbling block."

SEVENTEEN | EMINENCE GRISE

> Poet, but sick of writing about myself / Homosexual role model,
> noted for stable relationship, but separating out from companion
> & now worried about lacklove who's going to take care of me in
> deathbed senility / Buddhist agitator, but bad meditator with high
> blood pressure / Scholar but hardly read books no patience
> anymore / Peacenik Protestor but coward and bored with
> confrontation / Left wing but suspicious of communism &
> revolutions including American revolution / Anti-bourgeois, but
> want a house & garden & car / Musician, but haven't written new
> songs in years / Democrat but following guru leader / Anarchist
> individualist but involved in sangha
>
> —A. G., Journal, September 1, 1984

BY THE END OF THE 1970s, GINSBERG, NOW IN HIS FIFTIES, HAD ESTAB-
lished what his friends often referred to as the "Ginsberg cottage
industry," a team of people engaged to further Allen's projects and
campaigns: a secretary, a file clerk, a booking agent, a bibliographer, teams of students to transcribe his journals, translators in
dozens of languages, teaching assistants, lawyers specializing in the
Freedom of Information Act, lawyers good at civil rights, lawyers
knowledgeable about drug laws, accountants specializing in nonprofit foundations. In addition to this, a limitless supply of editors
of little literary magazines and small presses remained anxious to
publish his texts. The amount of paperwork generated grew to staggering proportions and became itself a subject for poems. Thousands of pages of transcribed journals sat unread, great files on the
CIA, drug busts, censorship, and dozens of other projects packed
the file cabinets in the apartment on Twelfth Street, all kept in some

semblance of order by Bob Rosenthal, who had been Allen's secretary since 1978.

Allen had now reached an age where his fame and notoriety were such that the establishment was forced to recognize his achievements. His pioneering work in promoting open-form poetry and the work of his friends in the Beat Generation had created a whole new genre of American letters. Recognition had first come in April 1974, when he was given the National Book Award in Poetry for *The Fall of America*. Next came the National Arts Club gold medal, and acceptance into that establishment on February 22, 1979, at the club's Gramercy Park South headquarters. The principal speaker was the commissioner of cultural affairs for the City of New York, Henry Geldzahler, who, to everyone's astonishment, chose this august occasion to come out of the closet. He announced, "It is easier and more palatable for me to be an American and to be a homosexual because Allen has stood and spoken out. His eloquence allows us to share his victory." After speeches by Norman Mailer, the previous year's recipient, William Burroughs, John Ashbery, and Ted Berrigan, Allen remarked how pleased he was to have "the stamp of the City's approval on cocksucking by the commissioner of cultural affairs," which drew roars of laughter. Afterward Allen examined the medal and found the word "distinction" misspelled on its obverse. "And these were the people we were fighting against!" he commented.

Following hot on the heels of the National Arts Club came the American Academy and Institute of Arts and Letters, which also inducted him as a member. He even received the Medal of Honor from the Commune of Rimini in Italy. Allen was now an official decorated member of the establishment. None of these honors, however, loosened his writer's block or relieved his preoccupation with his role in the Merwin affair. In his journals, he mused: "I've difficulty knowing whether I'm lying to myself to cover Trungpa's hierarchical secrecy, or lying to Clark in not openly and continuously confronting him in his journalistic spitefulness and intrigue. . . . This inhibits my writing altogether since I don't want to waste my poesy and readers' time on gossip and spite, or exhibit my own confusion." Ranged against him in his defense of Trungpa were his old friends Clark, Dorn, and Sanders, as well as Merwin himself. At a meeting of the American Academy of Arts and Letters, Allen had run into Merwin, who looked at him calmly and said, "I don't trust you, Ginsberg!"

In December 1979, *The Great Naropa Poetry Wars* by Tom Clark was published, closely followed in March 1980 by Ed Sanders's Naropa Class Report, *The Party: A Chronological Perspective on a Confrontation at a Buddhist Seminary.* Clark's book provoked a spate of critical articles in the underground, from the *Berkeley Barb* to the New York *SoHo Weekly News,* reviving all Allen's fears. But despite his private reservations, he campaigned to limit the damage caused by Clark's book, taking it upon himself to correct every minor factual error and innuendo, of which there were many. Talking about the Vajra Guards, Clark wrote: "The rumor is, they're armed with M-16s. Others say it's submachine guns." Naturally, the local press was interested in a private Buddhist army in training, and Allen spent weeks anxiously following up on the story, until he found its source: someone on the other side of a valley who saw the guards practicing bowing and thought they were doing bayonet practice. He tape-recorded all his telephone calls and drove himself so hard that he almost lost his voice, but he was finally able to assure the local *Rocky Mountain News* that there were no guns.

The book caused more than a temporary rift between friends. On the last page, Clark ran an appendix entitled "The Big Payoff," which listed fifteen recipients of $10,000 National Endowment for the Arts awards for November 1979 who had been staff instructors or faculty members of the Jack Kerouac School and who, in Clark's words, "therefore are at least implicit proponents of what Allen Ginsberg has called the 'experiment in monarchy' of Chögyam Trungpa." He pointed out that the Literature Advisory Panel included Ron Padgett, a former Naropa poetics instructor. Clark said that he had suggested to David Wilk, the Literature Program Director of the NEA, that awarding $150,000 in fellowships to that one small identifiable group of writers amounted to wholesale federal subsidy of an avowedly antidemocratic literary movement. "Personally, I'm upset about it," Wilk responded, "but publicly I can't say a word."

Some, but not all, of the poets listed in the book were Buddhists, yet as Allen and many others pointed out, the same group was more closely identified with the St. Mark's Poetry Project in New York, but that did not make them Christians. Many of the people who had read or taught at Naropa—William Burroughs and Gregory Corso, for instance—were not Buddhists and did not agree with Trungpa's philosophy or politics.

This was no longer an internecine dispute among poets. Clark had handed the ultraconservative Heritage Foundation and those who styled themselves "neoconservatives" a weapon with which they could attack, not just Naropa, but the NEA itself. Ginsberg said, "It seemed to me an enormous mistake to make a political issue out of an aesthetic issue. . . . Ron Padgett went through a horror scene after getting money for all those poet friends of his who were worthy, like Ted Berrigan and Alice Notley. That led to a round of critiques in *Coda*, saying we were a clique. And it was just the opposite. This was the first time there was ever *any* money given to the bohemian group. It was like a nightmare, them announcing they were anti-fascist and then aligning themselves with the Heritage Foundation."

A series of articles appeared in *West Coast Book Review* and elsewhere, all attacking Naropa, Allen, Peter, and Anne Waldman for garnering NEA grants or for claiming that Naropa was the "center of American poetry" (a line, in fact, taken from *Time* magazine). The articles led to the Heritage Foundation's denouncing Allen and the grants, which in turn led to the diminishing of NEA grants to magazines and a cutoff of funds for autonomous community organizations like the St. Mark's Poetry Project, the Detroit Institute of Arts program, Beyond Baroque in Los Angeles, and other poetry projects. A trend began that would still be visible in September 1985, in an attempt by a group of Republican congressmen to withdraw funding from work that was thought to be "obscene, and contrary to the taste of the public," a reference to Peter Orlovsky's book *Clean Asshole Poems and Smiling Vegetable Songs*.

Throughout the seventies, Allen's reading tours had taken him to many of the European summer arts festivals. He developed a very accomplished performance style, which combined poetry with music—usually provided by guitarist Steven Taylor, Allen's arranger and accompanist since 1976. In 1980, Allen, Peter, and Steven made their first visit to Eastern Europe, performing in Yugoslavia and Hungary before making a grueling six-week tour of Austria and Germany.

They flew home from Frankfurt on December 15, to find Peter's eighty-one-year-old father mortally ill. Oleg was hospitalized in New York, and Peter took over some of his nursing care. Allen also learned that Barbara Rubin had died from a postnatal infection in October 1980. Having finally accepted that Allen would not marry her, she had become a Hasidic Jew, married, and eventually moved to an Orthodox community in southern France, where she had five children.

The European tour had exhausted Allen, and he spent a week in bed with flu, depressed about the political situation. "Cold war fear in my head, rueful of red, capitalist and bohemian Buddhist military police hierarchies," he wrote. He set up a low altar next to the window in his bedroom and covered it with red cloth. On it he placed a smiling Thai statue of the Buddha and arranged his bell, dorje, mantra beads, and prostration-counter, a Chinese ceramic incense holder, and a red box of Japanese temple incense. A Catholic lectern held a Vajradhara tanka that Allen had bought in Benares. His room had been freshly painted white by Lucien Carr's son, Caleb, and was very bright. Through the slatted blinds Allen could see the cornice of the Catholic church opposite and a Tibetan banner, now little more than a sooty rag after five years in the New York air, flapping from his rusty fire escape.

Above the bed was a large framed example of Trungpa's calligraphy: Allen's mantra, "Ah!" At the foot of the bed was Louis's desk, upon which stood Allen's battered typewriter, with its red dust cover. The desk was piled with mail and manuscripts overflowing from his office. Below the window was a silver-painted radiator, on which Allen dried his socks and which whispered and clanked while he was meditating.

Above the altar hung a framed illustration of the Kagyu lineage tree, used in visualizing during prostrations. These he did on a sheet of shiny composition board laid on the wood floor. Stacked against the wall was a brown *zabutan* meditation mat and a brightly colored *zafu* cushion for sitting meditation. One wall was covered to the ceiling with books. Another whole room was filled floor to ceiling with books, and twice a year, those no longer in use were shipped to join Allen's archives on deposit at Columbia University.

Soon after the new year began, Allen lay ill, preoccupied with the inflated accounts of the celebration of the return of the American hostages from captivity in Iran. In the *New York Times*, ex–Nixon speechwriter William Safire thundered that the barbarians must be punished. From his sickbed, Allen improvised another of his East-West songs, including lines about the hostages:

CIA's Col Roosevelt overthrew Mossadegh
They wanted oil, now they got Ayatollah's dreck

They put in the Shah and trained the police, the Savak
All Iran was our hostage quarter century, that's right Jack

The release of the hostages seemed suspiciously well timed to coincide with the inauguration of Ronald Reagan. "Reagan inaugurated with Hollywood pomp and Mafia banquets," Allen noted gloomily. "The Right Wing strong jawed movie star on the path of Supreme Power." In El Salvador, right-wing death squads were murdering people with impunity while the regime received massive grants of American military aid, whereas Nicaragua's application for aid was summarily turned down, forcing the Sandinistas to look elsewhere for development money. Allen's journals from December 1980 to February 1981 were filled with long catalog poems of atrocities committed by the United States and the USSR. He felt paralyzed into inaction by the world situation, which he thought was heading toward another Vietnam, this time in Central America.

When Allen complained to Burroughs about world problems, Bill told him, "No problem can be solved. When a situation becomes a problem, it becomes insoluble. Problems are by definition insoluble. No problems can be solved, and all solutions lead to more problems."

Intrigued, Allen asked, "Who wrote that?"

"I did," said Bill's flat voice over the telephone.

When Allen returned to Boulder for the beginning of the 1981 Naropa term, he moved into 425 Varsity Manor, in the Swiss-style Varsity Townhouses complex. His two-room apartment faced an inner courtyard, across the hall from where Bill Burroughs had lived from 1977 to 1979, during the tragic years of his son's illness.

Billy Burroughs had grown up virtually acting out his father's books; he even stole his grandmother's opium suppositories. After his mother's death, he was brought up by his grandparents in Florida. He rarely saw his father, who lived in Europe throughout most of the boy's childhood. Bill summoned him to Tangier when he was sixteen, but he found living with Mikey Portman and Ian Sommerville difficult and was disturbed by the homosexuality and drugs. Unable to establish a rapport with his father, he soon returned to Florida. He became an amphetamine addict in New York, and, like his father, was arrested; he recorded these experiences in a book, *Speed*, for which Allen wrote an introduction. Amphetamine and alcohol were in Billy's blood even before he was born. He led the life of a derelict hippie, and in the spring of 1976, after he left a detoxification clinic in Santa Cruz, Allen found him a job as a teaching assistant at Naropa and sponsored a few readings for him. Although he was difficult to be around, Allen and the Naropa staff helped him as best they could. Not long after he arrived, his drinking led him to the hospital emergency room, where he was diagnosed as having cirrhosis of the liver. On August 21, 1976, at a party in Allen's apartment, he began to vomit blood. The local hospital diagnosed his condition as critical and referred him to the Colorado General Hospital in Denver, which had the only surgical team in the world able to perform a liver transplant. Eight days later, during a fourteen-hour operation, a surgeon and two assistants replaced his liver with that of a young woman.

The years that followed were difficult for Billy and everyone surrounding him. His father flew back and forth between Boulder and New York as Billy resumed his heavy drinking and became a morphine addict. He returned frequently to the transplant ward, suffering from complications. Then he moved to Florida, where, on March 3, 1981, he was found in a roadside ditch, dead from severe internal bleeding caused by cirrhosis. He was thirty-three years old.

Billy had been separated from his wife for many years, but she did not want his ashes to go to his father, whom she blamed for his self-destructiveness. She asked Allen to handle Billy's burial, and since Billy had been one of Trungpa's followers, he suggested that Billy's ashes be interred at the Rocky Mountain Dharma Center. She agreed, telling Allen, "Billy loved you."

Allen took the ashes to the Karma Dzong shrine room and placed them in their tin urn on the altar, where they were to remain for the traditional forty-nine-day purification period. That morning he had opened the urn and crumbled a few of the dry black grains in his fingers. He sat in the shrine room meditating for an hour, then took a small card and wrote: "WSB Jr. Born July 21, 1947—Died March 3, 1981," and placed it beside the urn on the altar.

Allen contacted John Galbraith, Billy's flatmate during his time in Boulder, and the two of them sorted through Billy's belongings that had been left in storage in Galbraith's closet. They pulled out the clothing, much of it ornamented with feathers or bone, and separated out knickknacks, walking canes, and toys from the books and manuscripts. Allen took all the papers back to his apartment to examine and preserve. There were notebooks filled in Billy's neat hand, essays about his liver transplant, suicide poems, scraps of writing on napkins and torn pieces of paper. Allen engaged a poetry student to sort and type up the fragments, and what emerged was a full-length book manuscript.

On May 3, it was raining heavily as Allen and Billy's few friends drove up the mountainside from the Rocky Mountain Dharma Center to the side of Marpa Point. They reached the grave of Cyrus, the eldest member of the Boulder Buddhist community, who had been buried there the previous day, and dug a hole nearby, covering the urn containing Billy's ashes with dirt and setting a small cairn of stone above it. They stood in the rain holding incense and copies of Vajrayana prayers covered with plastic and chanted the Heart Sutra—"Form is emptiness, emptiness is form"—for final burial. Allen's thoughts returned to the apartment on 115th Street where he had lived with Billy's parents and his half sister in 1945, half a lifetime before. Billy's father did not attend the ceremony.

Allen was alone in Boulder when Peter returned to Cherry Valley to fix the porch and tend the fruit trees. Allen's course that term was a second series of lectures on "The Literary History of the Beat Generation." Despite the "Naropa Poetry Wars," Allen had managed to do an enormous amount of work during his decade in Boulder. He had taught five terms of William Blake, doing a line-by-line analysis from the earliest poem to the "Four Zoas," and from tapes of these classes he had developed a number of lectures and texts on Blake, the first of which would be published in 1988. He taught the work of William Carlos Williams and two terms on English lyric poetry, and he had assembled a massive teaching anthology, *Twentieth Century International Heroic Verse*, from Rimbaud to the younger modern poets such as William Antler. At one point, he had five teaching assistants, all typing up his voluminous journals and putting his manuscripts in order.

Istvan Eorsi, a Hungarian poet with whom Allen became friends on his 1980 trip to Budapest, spent four nights at Allen's apartment en route to Chicago. During a walk in Chautauqua Park, a wide meadow overlooking Boulder, Allen asked him what criticisms he had of his work.

Taking Allen seriously, Eorsi said he had three points to make: That Allen in his older age seemed to have substituted Buddhism for all the enthusiasm and energy he once had for creating an open-hearted society. That, like many great poets, he wrote too much and published too many "dead" poems. ("Time will edit them out for me," Allen rejoined.) That the repetition of certain homosexual details was sometimes compulsive or too self-conscious or programmatic. Other than that, Eorsi said, he thought that Allen was the greatest poet in the world.

His judgment saddened Allen, who said that he was neither here nor there, with either meditation or revolution. Eorsi pointed out that unlike Mayakovsky, who had to live with the revolution that he prophesied and helped to create, Allen had to live with the fact that the revolution he helped to create did not win but lost. By this he meant the Beat, hippie, anarchic, flower-power, LSD-using, pot-smoking, sexual-freedom movement of the sixties, which was being swamped by the neoconservatism of the late seventies and early eighties. Eorsi thought that Allen had used Oriental meditation as a substitute for his failed revolution and that, important as it was to him, meditation did not serve as a total inspiration and did not have an all-inclusive poetic intensity. Allen felt that this was appropriate criticism from a Middle European standpoint, which did not take into account American concerns with self-awareness and ecology.

In New York once again, Allen went to the rock club Bonds on June 10, 1981. The British punk band the Clash was in residence. The Clash, together with their friends the Sex Pistols, had startled and horrified the British press and recording industry in 1976 with their strident music, aggressive energy, bad language, and outrageous clothes. Their lyrics, when they could be heard through the buzz-saw guitars, had a strong left-wing populist slant; anti-racist, anti-elitist, and pro–working class. Allen went backstage to meet them, and as he walked into their dressing room, Joe Strummer, the lead singer, greeted him: "Well, Ginsberg, when you gonna run for President?"

"Never, or I'll wind up in Diamond Hell"—a Tibetan Buddhist allusion.

"You got any poems you can read to our audience?" Strummer asked. "We had somebody get up to lecture about El Salvador, and they were throwing tomatoes."

Seeing his chance to play with the Clash, Allen said, "Well, I got a poem that has chord changes. You want to try that?" So for the next ten minutes, with the audience screaming for the band to appear, Allen and the Clash rehearsed the changes of "Capitol Air." Then they went out onstage and performed it in front of the violent crowd of three thousand rowdy punks. Everybody liked it, including Strummer. "I think they were surprised that I was able to get up and belt out a song," Ginsberg said later. "They're all good musicians, Mick Jones particularly, and they're very sensitive and very literate underneath all the album-cover roughneck appear-

ance. I don't know of any other band that would, in the middle of a
big heavy concert, be willing to go on with a big middle-age goose
like me, who might or might not be able to sing in tune, for all they
know."

He found the hard-rock crowd very different from his usual audiences. "The real challenge is to be so clear and definite and so
courageous and so authoritative as to lay down a story in front of
three thousand screaming new-wave heads that they actually listen
to because it makes sense."

Again Allen was able to transcend the generation gap. He wrote
"Howl" just after rock 'n' roll was invented, but a decade later was
able to relate to Lennon, McCartney, Jagger, Dylan, and the other
sixties musicians. Now there was a new wave of rock musicians,
who saw the previous generation as boring, lifeless, and irrelevant,
yet they regarded Ginsberg as a source of inspiration and as someone who would understand exactly what they were doing—as he
did.

Medals and memberships aside, there were still many areas
where Allen's views contrasted sharply with those of the establishment, in particular his views regarding sex. That summer, as a
roving teacher, he had a number of students to whom he was attracted, and to his delight, some of them reciprocated. Allen's belief
that a sexual relationship between student and teacher was not only
permissible but salutary shocked a number of people, particularly
educators. The issue came up during an interview for the Washington *Post*, when Nancy Bunge asked him how he got his poetry
students to locate their own perceptions rather than just imitate his.
He gave her many examples, ending with: "Check out the students'
own writing. In personal conversation and contact, or by lovemaking with the students in bed where appropriate."

"Are you serious?" she asked.

"I'm totally serious," Allen said. "I believe the best teaching is
done in bed, and I am informed that's the classical tradition. That
the present prohibitive and unnatural separation between student
and teacher may be some twentieth-century Wowser, Moral Majority, un-American obsession. The great example of teaching was
Socrates, and if you remember 'The Symposium,' the teaching
method involved Eros. So Eros is the great condition for teaching.
It's healthy and appropriate for the student and teacher to have a
love relationship whenever possible. Obviously the teacher can't
have a love relationship with everyone in the class and the student

can't have a love relationship with every one of the teachers, because this is a strictly human business where some people are attracted to others, but where there is that possibility, I think it should be institutionally encouraged."

He went on to discuss the danger of exploitation of the student by the teacher and vice versa, but suggested that problems arise in any love relationship. He didn't see why they should arise more in a student-teacher relationship than in any other. "My own experience is that a certain kind of genius among students is best brought out in bed," he told Bunge. "Things having to do with tolerance, humor, grounding, humanization, recognition of the body, recognition of ordinary mind, recognition of impulse, recognition of diversity. Given some basic honesty, some vulnerability on the part of teacher and student, then trust can arise."

Although some people have claimed that this was a self-seeking argument to legitimize Ginsberg's desire for his young male students, it did follow quite naturally from his ideas of sexual freedom, which began in the forties and which he promoted most actively in the sixties. It was, in fact, the attitude people expected from him, whether it was practiced or not. For the purpose of the interview, Allen was indulging in hyperbole in citing Socrates and his active recommendation of teacher-student love, just to shock Bunge. However, during his years of teaching and traveling, he had had many relationships with young men, who may have derived some good from this special attention. On the obverse side, women had often complained that Allen was inclined to pay less attention to females in his classes. There were, of course, no women among Socrates' students.

Allen traveled extensively during his 1981 summer break from Naropa, going first to Mexico City, in August, where he attended a writers conference along with Günter Grass, Andrei Voznesensky, Octavio Paz, Jorge Luis Borges, and others. After one of the day's proceedings, he helped Borges to his car. "Ginsberg," said Borges, trying to place the name. "Ah yes, I read a book by a man of that name. *The Cabala*, 1911, edited by—" Allen protested that this could not possibly have been by him and again told Borges his name. Borges was sure he had read such a text, long ago.

"Maybe by my father, Louis Ginsberg?" Allen suggested.

"Perhaps," agreed Borges, "on the Cabala!" It was a classic circular Borges conversation.

Another day, after Allen had read a number of his poems, including "Capitol Air," he took Borges's arm to help him offstage. "Did you understand the English stanzas?" asked Allen.

"Of course," he replied. "I am Borges." Later, in the dressing room, he complained about a line in "Capitol Air": "I don't like police assassinating Argentine Jews." It wasn't true, he said. "Nonetheless," he continued, still referring to the poem, "in the main I agree with your opinions." Although blind, he told Allen that he saw lights and shadows, mostly at night, and a luminous sunset. He said that he did not like the poetry of Ezra Pound, whereupon Allen quoted "Canto XIV" to him. "He didn't write that in verse properly," Borges complained. Allen explained that it was the quantitative aspect of Pound's prosody that he admired, and Borges allowed that he perhaps liked some of the early work but not the "Cantos."

"I'll consider your opinions," said Allen.

"Because I'm eighty-two doesn't mean my opinions are to be respected," Borges replied.

After Mexico City, Allen visited Toronto to see a stage version of "Kaddish." From New York he flew to Rome, initiating one of his frequent Italian tours. On October 7, after having made a grueling twenty-three-hour flight from Naples to San Francisco to work on the proofs of *Plutonian Ode* at City Lights, he finally found himself back in Boulder and spent his first night at 2141 Bluff Street, where he was to live for the next few years. It was a large house, set on a bluff, with a fine view out over the Flatirons, which he would describe in many poems during the coming years. Since 1978, he had lived at the Boulderado Hotel or taken one of the Varsity Townhouse apartments, and were it not for the Poetry Wars, he would not have moved full time to Boulder at all, for despite the attraction of Trungpa and the Buddhist teachings available, he regarded the town as "a honky paradise . . . with all the advantages and disadvantages that that implies. The lack of racial mix makes it bland, lacking color." However, as coadministrator of the Poetics Department, he felt a duty: "I moved to Boulder in response to Clark and Dorn's attacks. I felt Naropa needed my help." Ginsberg always considered his helping to introduce Buddhism to the United States as one of his highest achievements, and he never regretted the move, which would keep him away from his New York office for five years.

He still had a crowded schedule of readings, the most important of which was the highly publicized twenty-fifth-anniversary reading of "Howl" at Columbia's McMillin Theatre on November 14, 1981. The event was a complete sellout, with people clamoring to get in. During the two-hour program, he sang Blake, read "Birdbrain!" and "Capitol Air," and finally gave a twenty-seven-minute rendition of "Howl." The poem used to take him twenty to twenty-two minutes to read, but he no longer had the long breath of his youth. The slower delivery enabled him to emphasize the irony and humor of the poem, and the audience frequently roared with laughter. The reading was a great triumph, and even Allen's old adversary *Time* magazine gave him a full-page review, headed: "Howl Becomes a Hoot." They still disliked "Howl," but Ginsberg himself was acceptable now.

That winter, the Clash returned to New York to cut their next album; they called Allen in Boulder to invite him to join the sessions. A few days into January 1982, Allen was in New York for a reading, and he stopped by Electric Ladyland, Jimi Hendrix's old studio on West Eighth Street, to see them. Joe Strummer greeted him in his usual gruff yet friendly way: "You're the greatest poet in America—can you improve on these lyrics?" Strummer handed him "Ghetto Defendant," and Allen began tinkering with the words, much as he corrected his students' poems at Naropa.

For "the admiral lies asleep," he wrote, "the admiral snores command," and instead of saying "lines cross oceans," Allen wrote, "submarines boil oceans." Strummer liked all the suggestions and used them. Then they needed something on the track that sounded like the voice of God, so Allen wrote something appropriate and also sang in a deep bass in the studio; when the recording was mixed, his voice appeared beneath Strummer's main vocal on the track.

He spent about seven nights with the Clash, sometimes working through until 9 A.M. Strummer would hand him a Xerox copy of lyrics written out in his notebook, Allen would change a phrase or two and make other suggestions, then Strummer would go out in the studio and sing it. Maybe an hour later, Allen would have another idea about how to change a phrase to make it more pronounceable. He would join Strummer in the studio and show him his suggestion. Strummer would try it on a separate vocal track, and if it worked, would select all or part of it for the final mix.

In this way, Allen worked on three or four of their numbers. And during the time it took to get microphone levels and headphone volume levels and to set up equipment, he just kept them company, helping them smoke a large amount of very strong pot. He began to take books in to show them, including Gregory's new book, *Herald of the Autochthonic Spirit*, and Peter's new City Lights title, *Clean Asshole Poems and Smiling Vegetable Songs*. The album was released as *Combat Rock*, with all of Allen's contributions on it, including his duet with Strummer. Allen was pleased to see it rise in the charts but, characteristically, asked for no payment.

Allen's next major trip was to Managua, Nicaragua, where his old friend the poet Ernesto Cardenal was now the minister of culture. Cardenal had organized a poetry festival to bring together "poets of national liberation" from all over Latin America to honor the centenary of Nicaragua's great national poet, Rubén Darío. The exiled Argentinian poet José Antonio Cedrón was there, as was Roberto Sosa from Honduras, but most of the press attention was focused on the poets of the two superpowers: Ginsberg and Yevgeny Yevtushenko.

Allen and Peter arrived on January 21, 1982, and checked into the Hotel Intercontinental, where they had a fine view of Lake Managua and the dramatic volcanoes ringing the city. It seemed as if the great earthquake of 1972 had occurred only weeks before; large buildings with their insides reduced to rubble still stood all over the city, their shattered remains used by squatters. President Anastasio Somoza, the U.S.-backed dictator, had done nothing to repair the ruins after the earthquake and had caused even more damage himself when, during the final offensive against his regime, he ordered his air force to bomb those areas of downtown Managua controlled by the Sandinistas. Many of the Chevrolet taxis were still riddled with bullet holes from those final days. The victorious junta was composed of leading businessmen as well as leftists and Marxists, and they pledged themselves to a free society and a mixed economy, but the scale of the problem they faced meant that it would be years before Managua looked like anything other than a war zone, particularly with an American economic blockade in force.

Allen and Peter went straight to a reception, and after pleasantries, Allen approached Comandante Daniel Ortega and asked for a minute of his time. Allen said that he didn't want to be a problem to Nicaragua, but that some of his texts might be regarded as controversial; he went on to explain what had happened to him in Cuba and Czechoslovakia in 1965. In reply, Ortega asked him to try to understand the situation from their point of view in the face of threats being made against them by the United States government. He said that they were dependent on their friends. "You are free to do what you want, but please remember that we are up against the wall. My main task in the next few weeks is to deal with the threat of an American invasion. Anything you say critical of the Nicaraguans and their allies, the Russians and the Chinese, will be used in America and *La Prensa* as propaganda." Ortega explained that no matter how well intentioned Allen was, even if in a friendly critical spirit, statements would be taken out of context and exaggerated and abused.

Allen understood that, but he said that for "propaganda," it would be to the Nicaraguans' advantage to have him speak freely. He told Ortega that the majority of Americans in a recent Gallup poll disapproved of U.S. violence or war in Central America and that it would look good if he could read the same texts in Nicaragua that he usually read at home. They talked at length, with Yevtushenko listening in and taking photographs. Ernesto Cardenal explained to Ortega that Allen had done benefit readings in the States to raise money for the fight against Somoza and to help the Sandinista cause. Before the revolution, Cardenal had translated Allen's poetry into Spanish; now he was presenting it to the people.

At the dinner following the reception, Allen spoke with Yevtushenko, who complained that as long as his novel had remained unpublished in Russia, he had had big money offers for it from American publishers, which he had refused because he wanted to publish it first in his homeland. Now that the book was out in the USSR, however, American publishers would not touch it. They had wanted it for propaganda.

The next day, Allen met with the American poet Margaret Randall, who had been living in Managua since the revolution. He and Peter spent the day sightseeing and preparing for their reading, which was held at the Teatro Nacional. Allen opened with the first page of "Howl," followed by "Howl," Part II, then "America," "Elegy Che Guevara," "Don't Grow Old," "Father Death Blues," "Homework," "Birdbrain!" and "Meditation Blues." The poems were all translated simultaneously, except for the final blues. It was "Birdbrain!" that the American press picked up, and it was quoted in several reports.

> *Birdbrain runs the World!*
> *Birdbrain is the ultimate product of Capitalism*

> *Birdbrain chief bureaucrat of Russia, yawning*
> *Birdbrain ran FBI 30 years appointed by F. D. Roose-*
> *velt and never chased Cosa Nostra!*
> *Birdbrain apportions wheat to be burned, keep prices*
> *up on the world market!*
> *Birdbrain lends money to developing Nation police-*
> *states thru the International Monetary Fund!*

Allen was pleased by his reception; a lot of people had laughed and only a few got up and left. Afterward he went drinking with Yevtushenko and various members of the American press, Russians and Nicaraguans. "Some Russians came to your reading, but no Americans came to my reading," complained Yevtushenko, "which tells you something about the nature of our countries' relationship. But do you know, Allen, the translator, he made one very big mistake, because he mixed up 'hippie' and 'beatnik,' and the only one who caught the difference was one Russian technician. This is because when the beatnik era was born in your country, there was a parallel time in Russia, an echo across the oceans, the same moment with some awareness of cultural differences."

"I didn't know that," said one of the Americans.

"But now things between us are culturally fucked up," Yevtushenko continued angrily. "We are separated by an ocean of *shit! Oceans of shit!*" He raised his glass. "A toast! May our two shit countries not go to war!" Yevtushenko was in good form, and many empty rum bottles already littered the table. The waiters refused to serve them any more, so the party moved to Yevtushenko's room, where he could order rum through room service. There Allen told him that Ezra Pound and William Carlos Williams were a big influence in Latin America, largely because of Cardenal. "You know," said Yevtushenko, "Pound is not published in the Soviet Union because he is so much connected with fascism."

"Then you should start with publishing his late poems," Allen suggested, "where he renounced fascism."

"Yes, we should publish him," Yevtushenko agreed, "but you know, we lost twenty millions [to fascism]. I was asked to read one of his poems, and I like some of his poems, but I could not do it. I could not read Pound."

The next morning, all the poets assembled for an outing to León, fifty miles northwest of Managua. On arrival, Allen, Yevtushenko, and various reporters gathered at a sidewalk café outside the cathedral, and by 11 A.M. the drinking had begun, except for Allen. One of the American reporters asked Yevtushenko if he thought Managua was heading toward a totalitarian state that would not tolerate intellectual freedom. "Maybe not totally," he said, ambiguously.

Allen was more sanguine. "Intellectual freedom can flourish here if the U.S. doesn't continue putting pressure on them," he told reporters. "But the U.S. is fast making a situation where someone who wants to be open and liberal is put in the position where the Sandinista hard liners say, 'Look, you're threatening the security of our revolution.' . . . In a situation where the U.S. puts them in a totally defensive military posture, they're going to put all the energies of the society toward militarization of the society."

In Managua, Allen, Yevtushenko, and Cardenal sat down and wrote an appeal for the liberty of Nicaragua, which they addressed to the world's writers and presented at a press conference. They called it "The Declaration of Three," and it said in part: "We call the world's writers to come to Nicaragua to see with their own eyes the reality of Nicaragua, and lift their voices in defense of this country, small but inspired. They'll be welcome and can acquaint themselves directly with the true character of this revolution, of the efforts of the people to create a just society exempt from violence, a revolution whose image is being consciously distorted by those who have an interest in destroying the alternative which it proposes.

"The Damocles' sword of aggression now hangs in the air above these people.

"We trust that if the writers of the world get together, their pens will be mightier than any sword of Damocles."

As a member of PEN, the international writers' organization, Allen had voted to denounce the Sandinista government for the repeated closings of the antigovernment newspaper *La Prensa*, but now he began to think the shutdowns might have been justified, given the strong likelihood that *La Prensa* had been infiltrated by the CIA. The strongest evidence for this was the parallels in form and style between *La Prensa* and *El Mercurio*, the Chilean newspaper that the Church Committee of the U.S. Senate proved had been infiltrated by the CIA and that had whipped up anti-Allende hysteria prior to the CIA overthrow of the government. In a very short time, *La Prensa* had gone from being what Allen called "a respectable *NY Times*-type newspaper to a *National Enquirer* scandal sheet," filled with horror stories of murders, car accidents, and food shortages. The change was so dramatic that on his return home, Allen wrote to the State Department to ask whether the CIA had in fact infiltrated the newspaper. Assistant Secretary of State Thomas Enders responded: ". . . the aspirations of the Nicaraguan people are being progressively betrayed by an anti-democratic vanguard mortgaging their country and their revolution to Havana and Moscow."

Allen was impressed by what he saw in Nicaragua and by the great changes that had been made in the short time since the revolution. The Sandinistas had abolished the death penalty. The child mortality rate had decreased dramatically. The literacy rate had risen from 20 percent to more than 50 percent, thanks partly to the Cubans. Many of the Cuban technicians in the country, whom President Reagan and his secretary of state, General Alexander Haig, were fulminating against, were literacy workers, who had accomplished a similar improvement in their own country after the overthrow of the dictator Batista.

Ginsberg's visit to Nicaragua revealed an enormous change in his political attitude. During his visit to Cuba in 1965, when it was under the same economic pressure and threat of invasion from the United States, he was obsessed with the twin problems of the persecution of homosexuals and the legalization of pot, to the virtual exclusion of all else. He showed no interest in the revolution or its achievements and did not take advantage of the situation to meet any of the revolutionary leaders. In Nicaragua, his primary concern was the revolution. Questioned by reporters on his return home about his opposition to U.S. political interference, he said: "It's a self-fulfilling prophecy. We're forcing them into Soviet hands to mortgage their revolution as we forced Castro. They want a pluralistic society. They're just as aware of the abuses of Socialism in the Soviet Union and Cuba as we are." In another interview, Allen stated: "Castro came to Nicaragua and said, 'Don't make the mistake we did of being dependent on the Soviet Union,' and Haig recently called the Nicaraguans pawns of Russia. American strategy, in sum, is to make it hard for them, make them look bad and starve them economically."

Ginsberg's views were backed up by the announcement of a $17 million CIA destabilization plan. "The United States has run Central and South America for the last century," Allen said. "We had our chance but we drove them into the ground with dictatorships so painful, so unbearable, the people had to rebel. The rebellions were popular and influenced by Marxist theory." He told the *Colorado*

Daily that the real problem, as he saw it, was that the U.S. military was "so completely interconnected" with the militaries in Latin America that "we can't let anybody go."

Allen spent less than a week at home before he was off on yet another tour of Italy with Peter and Steven Taylor, which was followed by a short tour of California before he returned to Boulder. Peter had been in Cherry Valley, and in May he arrived at the house in Boulder in a very strange state of mind. He unloaded the car in silence, then carried a beautiful dead pheasant into his room, which he knelt over, pursing his lips, making a high-pitched moaning sound. The bird remained in the center of his room for two days, carefully arranged on a cloth. One night, Allen came downstairs at 1 A.M. to find Peter crouched over three bags of garbage, separating out the paper from the cans. "What are you doing?" Allen asked nonchalantly.

Peter did not reply, then a few minutes later, he whispered, "Compost." He would make coffee in the middle of the night and tiptoe about the house, replying to questions in a whisper. Then one morning Allen looked out of the window and saw him cleaning the blue Volvo with his bare hands. Allen tried to talk with him, but Peter replied, "I have no time, gotta do my prostrations."

Allen meanwhile was suffering from a bad kidney stone attack. He lay in bed delirious with the pain and from the opiate painkillers his doctor had prescribed. He did not have the energy to do anything except occasionally read a fragment from Kerouac's *Book of Dreams*. Thoughts, visions, and poems passed before his eyes, and he talked to himself in his sleep. The stones showed clearly on x-rays taken at Boulder Hospital, and it was a week before he recovered. Peter also recovered after a week, and life on Bluff Street returned to normal.

That spring, the Poetics Department at Naropa was in a constant flurry of activity, planning a Jack Kerouac conference, an idea sparked by the success of the 1976 anniversary reading of "Howl" at Columbia, which had raised enough money to keep the Poetics Department going for a year. Since the school was named after Kerouac, it seemed appropriate to mark the twenty-fifth anniversary of the publication of *On the Road*. From the very beginning, it was seen as a fund-raising media event rather than a scholarly conference, more concerned with the cult of personality than with academic study of Kerouac's texts. The original list of "VIPs," as

Allen called them, at the preliminary planning meeting, in July 1981, included Bob Dylan, Tom Waits, William Buckley, Jr., Abbie Hoffman, and Ken Kesey, but made no mention of Kerouac's widow or his two ex-wives, whose contributions to a serious study would have been of value. Basically, Allen was presenting *his* Kerouac: the sensitive footballer, intimate friend, and confidant from the forties, the great genius writer who had "heart," not the anti-Semitic Kerouac who abandoned his daughter to a life as a drug addict and prostitute, and who wanted to shoot all antiwar protesters. It was an idealized, sanitized Kerouac, the greatest writer in America, the Kerouac Allen always wanted him to be.

The conference was to be held during the second summer session of 1982, and Allen had sensibly decided to repeat his "Literary History of the Beat Generation" lectures during the first summer session so that he could devote more time to the conference. Naropa did not have the facilities for large gatherings, so most of the events were held on the University of Colorado campus. The conferees stayed at the Columbine Lodge in Chautauqua Park, overlooking the city; Robert Creeley, Gregory Corso, Ann and Sam Charters, Ray Bremser, Carl Solomon, Diane di Prima, Herbert Huncke, Joyce Johnson, Michael and Joanna McClure, Jack Micheline, Lawrence Ferlinghetti, and others flew into town. The front porch of the lodge became the unofficial meeting place for everyone and was the scene of many reunions and introductions. Huncke had not seen Edie Parker Kerouac since the forties; Carolyn Cassady had never before met John Clellon Holmes. Many of the conferees had never been with Burroughs, who had spent so much of his time out of the States and played no part in the San Francisco scene of the mid-fifties. Rather than film the conference itself, Robert Frank chose to set up his camera outside the lodge and simply filmed people gossiping on the porch. Also at the conference were Ken Kesey and his friend Ken Babbs, Paul Krassner, Timothy Leary, Abbie Hoffman, and other sixties people who regarded themselves as keepers of the flame, as well as Beat critics and translators such as Dennis McNally and Nanda Pivano.

The proceedings took place before a twenty-foot-high backdrop of Kerouac shown as a gentle, suffering saint with a large cross at his neck. Allen had written across the painting: "O Jack of Light, here's Your Cross of Tenderness." Between three and four hundred people had enrolled for the conference, paying $160, or $240 if they wished to attend the writing workshops being given by Burroughs, Ginsberg, Herbert Huncke, and others.

The conferees were virtually outnumbered by the press. Allen's publicity machine was almost too good, and in the end there were more than 130 accredited reporters from over 100 organizations to witness the historic reunion. There were representatives from the *New York Times,* the Washington *Post,* the Miami *Herald, Newsweek,* Swedish radio, and Swiss television; two NET television crews and three documentary film crews were on hand, as well as reporters from the three networks, AP, and UPI. The perspective and composition of the conference had changed somewhat during the planning stages, and the list of people invited grew to include practically all of Kerouac's old friends.

There was a series of well-received readings by all the principal writers and poets present, but the workshops and panel discussions were given a more critical reception from the press and public. As the Miami *Herald* reported: "Amid the conference's obsession with celebrity, [Kerouac's writing] was exempt from much measured assessment." For the speakers, however, the entire event consisted of what Allen called "delicious orgies of nostalgia."

The conference was a success, a memorable reunion for the generations of the forties, fifties, and sixties. It provided the press with a ready-made story and numerous photo opportunities. It made money for Naropa (they did not pay back the few thousand dollars of start-up costs that came from Ginsberg's own pocket), and it was great fun for all who attended. It had little to do with Kerouac's work and a lot to do with his personality. Allen summed it up in his journal: "No great revelations re Jack K. None of us brought up any big scandals, last letters, etc., just praised his heart and prose."

It was also a tribute to Ginsberg's genius for organization and publicity. All through the conference, he ran around frantically, sleeping a bare five hours a night. When it was over, he collapsed with food poisoning and spent three days vomiting.

On a visit to New York in late August 1982, Allen went backstage at a Clash concert at Pier 84 to wait for them to finish their set. The band brought him onstage for "Ghetto Defendant," their second encore, and in front of eight thousand ratty-looking New York punks, Joe Strummer, in a fierce Mohawk haircut, announced, "Mr. Allen Ginsberg," pointed his finger at Allen, and began to sing the verses. Feeling completely relaxed, Allen chanted his own verses in response, as he had done on their *Combat Rock* album.

On the evening of November 12, Peter's father died of cancer. Peter had been with him until the end of hospital visiting hours.

Peter had become a Tibetan Buddhist, so Allen, in Boulder, called Naropa to get meditation instruction for him. He was told to breathe in the confusion and pain of the dead, and breathe out friendliness and willingness to help, as prescribed by the Tibetan Book of the Dead. Oleg's death exacerbated Peter's feelings of responsibility for his family; he had worried about their welfare ever since the fifties, when he returned home from Paris to care for them. He felt "married to my crazy brothers," and with Oleg gone, he now faced the possibility of having to look after his mother, sister, and three brothers.

Allen had a three-month European winter tour through France, Italy, Holland, Denmark, Sweden, Norway, and Finland. On December 6, he and Steven Taylor left New York for Paris, to appear at War On War, the first of a series of readings organized by Jean-Jacques Lebel for UNESCO; it featured nineteen poets from five continents. This was followed by a One World Poetry tour of Holland, which extended into the new year. Whenever practical, Allen and Steven stayed in Amsterdam, at Simon Vinkenoog's book-lined house on the bank of the Amstel River, and Simon often accompanied them to readings, acting as interpreter if needed. They spent Christmas with the Vinkenoogs. Peter had remained behind to care for his family but made arrangements to join them in Amsterdam at the end of the year.

He flew in on the morning of December 29, seeming calm and in good shape. He slept all day, but that evening, at an important reading with Andrei Voznesensky at the Paradiso, he began to act strange. Allen sang, Voznesensky read his first group of poems, then came Peter's turn. First he delayed, drinking vodka and chortling to himself. Then he read "You Have to Stop and Think This Thing Out, Peter," smacking himself hard on the head with his fist after each line.

Allen grew nervous, knowing that Voznesensky did not like to be associated with anything that might jeopardize his freedom to travel. Peter was stopping after each word to ask Simon Vinkenoog to translate and spell it in Dutch, beginning with the word "shit," until Simon finally objected. He explained to the audience that Peter had just flown in and that his father had recently died. Peter gurgled and guffawed, drank and yelled at Simon, "You want 'em clean or dirty? Dirty? I'll give you dirty!" Allen was eventually able to coax him offstage, then he read an abbreviated program very self-consciously, anxious about what Peter might do.

The next day, Peter stood in the kitchen from midnight until 9 A.M., practicing a single short Jimmie Rodgers riff on his banjo, bare-chested, eyes closed, while everyone else attended a New Year party next door. "Don't wreck your voice," Allen cautioned him when he returned. Peter slept two hours, then began to clean the house. He cleaned all day, until they left that evening for Vlissingen, a resort town on the southwest coast of Zeeland. Peter read there with deliberate care, but the next morning he was up early and standing barefoot in the fog at the ocean's edge, strumming the same short riff over and over on his banjo. When Allen approached him, he snapped, "Fuck you. Don't talk to me. Leave me alone."

He was the same later in the morning, when Allen couldn't get a sensible answer out of him about breakfast. "At that moment I recognized that it seemed finally a thread of communication had snapped, and he was refusing simple information," Allen wrote later. The ride back from Vlissingen was a nightmare. Peter laughed, wheezed, and cursed at Allen all the way through a pea-soup fog. "Three hours like that in the car is too much," Vinkenoog told Allen when they got home. "You're a saint!"

John Lennon had suggested that Allen perform "Jessore Road" with a string quartet, as the Beatles had done with "Eleanor Rigby." In Vlissingen, Steven Taylor had completed the last violin part of an arrangement for two violins, viola, and cello. The tour promoter, Ben Posset, arranged for them to use the recording equipment at the Milky Way concert hall in Amsterdam and hired the Mondrian String Quartet. They worked until 1 A.M. and got two good recordings. Allen's vocals were steady, only slightly wanting on the melody line.

When they returned to the Vinkenoogs', enthusiastic over the recording, Peter was scrubbing the kitchen sink. Wearing only his bathing shorts, which sagged below his potbelly, he was sweating, eyes closed as if in a trance, repeating, "Fuck Reagan, Fuck Reagan," like a mantra.

"I don't think I could stand a week of this," said Vinkenoog.

Steven wondered whether Peter should continue the tour.

Allen remembered that the previous February, Peter had driven from the Vajrayana seminary in Pennsylvania to Cherry Valley and had so frightened the poet Andy Clausen and his family, who were staying at the farm, that they telephoned Allen for advice. When Peter had returned to Boulder that summer, he had been in the same trance state, talking and moaning to himself for several days after he arrived. He told Allen later that he had been in terror, thinking that the police and the CIA were following him and that Richard Helms himself was at the wheel of the car behind. Several people from the seminary were riding back to Boulder with him, and Peter imagined that they were watching him. The only way he had been able to ward off an attack was to control them by singing in a high-pitched voice all the way to Colorado.

Peter's crisis came a few days later, in the office at the Milky Way. He raged and yelled, shrieked and yodeled. Screaming "Kill Reagan! Shit!" he smashed his banjo to pieces and broke his glasses. Allen considered calling the police to prevent him from hurting himself. Steven and the Vinkenoogs commented that Peter's anger and frustration might be related to Allen's overdominating paternal role: "always ordering him around, constantly commenting on his behavior, his readings—on being far too long a time over-interfering with his every common social moves, behavior, gestures."

Dominating Peter was almost second nature to Allen, and he found taking their advice extremely difficult, but he made some progress, and Peter calmed down as the tour continued. In Copenhagen, they stayed with Rosebud Felieu, an old friend of Allen's from the early sixties, who had been Barbara Rubin's closest friend. The promoter had arranged readings in every major town in Denmark. The comic aspect of the trip appealed to Allen's sense of the ridiculous, as he and Peter appeared in towns they had never heard of and preached Buddhist meditation to people whose lives they knew nothing about. He wrote: "Peter meanwhile daily waves his copy of Naropa at audiences, preaches Buddhist guru information, imitates Aula-Rega's cotton clad nakedness, and carries around his gomden [square sitting pillow] everywhere, while I hypocritically sing 'Do the Meditation' as a rock song. What a mess, mentally." Allen hadn't meditated for months.

In Stockholm, they stayed with Ann Charters, Kerouac's biographer, and her husband, the record producer Sam Charters. Sam asked Allen why he was getting so involved with music. "I love to sing," said Allen, detecting a note of disapproval.

"Everybody is waiting for you to write the Final Poem," Charters said.

" 'Plutonian Ode' is quite strong," Allen offered. "Why? Do you think it's draining energy away from my writing?"

Charters didn't answer him directly, and Allen felt depressed and wondered if it was true. Certainly a number of his friends thought so.

The tour continued to Helsinki, where they were only two hundred miles from Leningrad, which, to Peter's frustration, they had no time to visit. Allen was relieved, imagining dreadful consequences if Peter went crazy in the Soviet Union. They returned to tour Norway and Germany, where the final performance, on February 16, 1983, at Friedrich Engels Haus in Wuppertal, was filmed; it was released as a commercial video, *Allen Ginsberg on Tour*. It was one of the most strenuous tours Allen had ever undertaken. Steven told Allen that he would never tour Europe with Peter again.

While they were in Europe, record producer John Hammond had released the double album *First Blues*, containing twenty-four Ginsberg performances. Allen had barely recovered from jet lag in New York before he was on the road again, this time to promote his record. For the album notes, Hammond had written: "Allen Ginsberg is not only one of the world's best poets but one of its finest citizens as well. Long impressed with his musical abilities, I recorded Allen in 1976 but CBS refused to issue the results, considering the songs obscene and disrespectful. I am thrilled to finally be able to present Allen on my own label; not only the 1976 sessions but those from 1971 and 1981 as well. I will present 'disrespectful' music like this as often as possible."

The album gathered together the best of Ginsberg's various musical sessions, including three tracks improvised with Bob Dylan in 1971. Allen had suggested that Hammond talk with "a photographer friend" about the jacket. He turned out to be Robert Frank, who produced a montage of photographs that made the album look a little like his jacket for the Rolling Stones' *Exile on Main Street*. As befitted a rock star, the launch party was held at Studio 54. Allen performed many of the songs from the album with a five-piece combo, surrounded by high-tech glitz.

He toured all through the spring of 1983, this time doing more television appearances than usual and including a four-day trip to Palermo, Italy, for another UNESCO War On War reading. Keeping one foot in the rock 'n' roll world, he did a benefit for Naropa at the Peppermint Lounge in New York. He hadn't spent time at his New York desk for months and was dogged by a mountain of paperwork and letters, which fortunately he approached with a sense of humor. He wrote:

I'm a prisoner of Allen Ginsberg
Who is this slave master that makes me answer letters
in his name
Write poetry year after year to keep up appearances
Pays a dumb secretary Jewish boy to answer phone pay
bills shuffle papers
Who is this egoist whose file cabinets leave no more
room for pictures of me?
I want to escape his clutches, his life, his bank ac-
counts, his Master Charge debts.
Who is this politician who has my life hypnotized by his
favors . . .

Allen arrived in Boulder in late spring 1983. He opened up the house on Bluff Street after a six-month absence and hired someone to clean it from top to bottom so that when Peter arrived he would not go on a cleaning jag. Allen had decided to leave Boulder, having co-administered the Poetics Department for a decade. He wanted to depart with no bad feelings, particularly any residual gripes from the Poetry Wars and made a point of contacting all his old adversaries. As usual, he had not had time to prepare himself properly for the course he was teaching. His classes were on Poe, Melville, and Whitman, and he rushed to read their biographies and writings.

Allen found himself divided between envy of those students who had started with him and were now far along in their Buddhist studies, and the pull of the "poetry rock 'n' roll world TV newspapers politics fame." He also knew that he was growing older and that as things stood, he did not make enough money from poetry to live. His City Lights royalties were only seven thousand dollars a year, not much for a lifetime's work. Though he made considerably more than that at readings, seminars, and workshops and for television appearances, almost all his money went toward supporting Peter, paying his musicians, and running his office, or else into the Committee On Poetry, which was still giving grants to poets. "Maybe I'm getting too old to go out fight the world with new wave rock and roll and platform oratory poetry," he mused, wondering what his next move should be.

Peter arrived in Boulder and cleaned the whole clean house. There was snow in May as Allen began a poetry workshop, instructing his students to use meditation breathing techniques, pay attention to the sound of one word at a time in their heads with each inhalation of breath, and write it down with each exhalation. His goal was to teach concentration and economy of breath. Like Burroughs, Allen was always able to see the possibilities of new techniques.

He was concerned about the future of the Poetics Department. Anne Waldman was away, so Allen was the sole director, but there were precious few students and even fewer faculty. One of the staff, Michael Brownstein, told him that there was little he could do about it and that he should leave as he planned. "You shouldn't feel guilty," he said. "Trungpa doesn't feel guilty."

Not long afterward, on June 3, Allen celebrated his fifty-seventh birthday with his brother on Long Island. Eugene was sixty-two the same day. Allen blew out the ring of candles, and they both composed haiku. Allen's read:

> Two brothers at table on their birthday
> Each his own thoughts, writing—
> think of our mother in the grave

On July 15, Allen went on a month's retreat at the Rocky Mountain Dharma Center. His tent was set at the edge of a meadow thick with wildflowers beneath pines, where the scent of lilacs filled the air. He looked at the surrounding peaks and remembered his travels through other mountains long ago, in Bolivia, Peru, India. "Another life," he thought. "What did I see, will I ever go back? I'm glad I kept a record or else even the memory of everything be gone." He remembered his first trip to Mexico and the bougainvillea in the square by the mayor's house in Yajalon, Chiapas. "God, what naïveté, my behavior then," he wrote in his journal. "Wiring New York thinking I'd discovered a giant earthquake and cave. On that basis I inadvertently conned the folks of that village to put me up for a week, doing nothing but wandering around emptyheaded and lost."

Many of Allen's old friends came to teach the summer writing program at Naropa that August, including Bill Burroughs, Gary Snyder, and Timothy Leary. This was the first time that Burroughs and Snyder had met (Snyder had diplomatically bowed out of the Kerouac conference). Snyder gave a major reading in Boulder, but Bill left it before the end in search of a drink, as Gary spoke lovingly about making an ax handle. It was not Bill's scene at all.

That August, a friend persuaded Allen to get a literary agent to handle his affairs and recommended Andrew Wylie in New York.

Though this was something Allen had shied away from all his life, he finally recognized that his business affairs were a mess, with books coming out from myriad publishers all over the world, which he couldn't keep track of. He decided to work with Wylie, and within a few months a deal had been struck with Harper & Row to produce a uniform edition of his work, beginning with *Collected Poems* and continuing with an annotated edition of "Howl," based on the Faber facsimile of "The Waste Land"; a volume of new poems, 1980–1985; and volumes of letters, essays, and journals. The advance on this multibook contract took care of his immediate financial worries.

He also no longer had to worry about Naropa's financial straits, because that September they received an anonymous million-dollar endowment, and another donor gave them one and a half acres of land and buildings adjoining the school, valued at over $650,000.

In February 1984, the United States Information Agency "blacklist" of speakers surfaced in Washington; it was published by the *New York Times* on March 15. The people banned from government-sponsored overseas speaking engagements numbered eighty-four; Ginsberg was among them. The list included James Baldwin, David Brinkley, Representative Jack Brooks, McGeorge Bundy, Shirley Chisholm, Walter Cronkite, Representative Thomas Downey, Betty Friedan, John Kenneth Galbraith, Senator Gary Hart, Coretta Scott King, Ralph Nader, and Tom Wicker. A USIA official explained that most of them were liberals whose views were thought to be inconsistent with administration policy, a clear indication that in the Reagan administration, even the cultural agencies had a political bias. Allen felt proud to be in such august company.

In 1984, after two short European tours, Allen began a three-week teaching course at the Atlantic Center for the Arts in New Smyrna Beach, Florida. Allen's secretary was booking him into more workshops, seminars, and courses, which paid well and enabled him to stay in one place for a few days and not be continually zigzagging across the country from reading to reading. On this occasion, he was given a luxurious wooden cabin set among scrub palmetto and live oak filled with squawking tropical birds. The campus buildings were connected by elevated boardwalks, which passed between the palm fronds and branches. Allen felt slightly guilty about his accommodation and wrote: "Gold in the sky, cool as an icebox in my giant wooden cabin. How many poems have I written denouncing air conditioning? I thought I locked myself out in the moist heat on the porch and got scared among the palmetto bird chirps. . . . It's an anxiety attack, well deserved. Haven't finished the long delayed preface to 'Collected Poems.' "

Despite his idyllic surroundings, Allen felt depressed. He filled his journal with his usual doubts and fears, but there was still an edge of irony and humor in his entries: "I haven't sat in a year. Taken vows I can't remember for a lifetime devotions and saddhanas. Took a vow of sainthood 40 years ago, now potbellied my life's slipped by. . . ." He questioned his role as a teacher: "Students in front of me for three weeks. What are their names? What do they need?" A decade before, when he began to teach at Naropa, Lucien Carr had asked him, "What have you to teach my children?" Allen did not reply. Now he remembered Lucien's question and wondered: "Why must I teach anyone? Where'd I assume that guruship? That's not poetry."

It was not his only worry. He was growing concerned about the effect his work might have, in particular his mythmaking about his homosexual marriage to Peter. It had been years since they had made love, and now Peter was drinking heavily and Allen was fearful, yet in his poems he paraded their model of gay love. "How many people will go the wrong way," he asked himself, "defy their parents and die in hovels alone, childless, because they read, 'I will be home in two months & look you in the eye'?" As usual in his journals, he played out his ideas to the full in order to explore them, but there was a kernel of truth in his fears.

That summer, the Atlantic Center for the Arts also featured courses by photographer Robert Frank and jazz drummer Elvin Jones, who had worked on Allen's 1969 recording of Blake songs. Allen was pleased to see Jones again, and they made another recording together. The first take of "Big Fish, Little Fish" was perfect, except for the guitar part, played by one of Jones's students. By the third take, the musicians were finally together, but Allen spoiled it by hesitating at one line and getting the order of the lines wrong in the second stanza. He was too ashamed to tell them, so they moved on and wound up the session with a recording of Allen's explosive "Hum Bomb!" in one flawless take. "We all felt good," he wrote, "because the quality of the music cooked." Jones told Allen that it was the sanctified church beat that made it cook. "At the bottom it's got to be religious," he explained. "It's all religious or it doesn't count."

Allen noted in his journal: "Sanctified church beat! And I flubbed the lyric!"

Allen had given up his Bluff Street house and shipped his library and belongings back to New York, so he spent that summer in Boulder in the Varsity Townhouses. There he maintained a tight schedule in order to complete his *Collected Poems*, working through the nights, when there were fewer distractions. He finished the last batch of three hundred pages of manuscript on July 19 and sent them to his editor with a feeling of great relief. He had been thinking about a Collected Poems since 1965, and as the culmination of his life's work he wanted it to be right. The 837-page volume included 88 pages of notes on the poems, photographs, an index of titles and first lines, and an index of proper names; it reprinted the original cover blurbs, dedications, and introductions, and opened with an "Author's Preface, Reader's Manual," in which Allen listed his best poems for the reader's convenience, an audacious move which would cause comment by reviewers.

In the fall of 1984, Allen returned to New York in good health. He had quit smoking, was practicing t'ai chi, and had been swimming regularly in Boulder Creek. He was getting himself in shape for a visit to China. The trip was organized by Norman Cousins, the former editor of the *Saturday Review,* and Robert Rees, a poet; both were on the faculty of UCLA, the venue of the first meeting between Chinese and American writers, two years before. Both Allen and Gary Snyder had been very eager and active participants in the earlier meeting, presenting the Chinese delegation with a list of "100 Questions That American Poets Would Like To Ask Chinese Poets." The leader of the Chinese delegation said that they could answer some of them, that they could write and send back the information on others, but that for some of them, they would just have to come to China and see the answers for themselves— which was, of course, the idea. It was therefore not too much of a surprise when Cousins and Rees chose Allen and Snyder as members of the American delegation to China for a reciprocal visit. The delegation, which landed in Beijing on October 18, 1984, also included Leslie Marmon Silko, William Least Heat Moon, Toni Morrison, Maxine Hong Kingston, William Gass, and Harrison Salisbury, most of them accompanied by their wives or husbands. Snyder brought along his wife, Masa, who was born in Beijing.

Gary Snyder, Michael McClure, Ginsberg and Maretta Greer at the "Gathering of the Tribes for a Human Be-In," a protest against the escalating war in Vietnam, and a celebration of Love and Peace, held in San Francisco's Golden Gate Park, January 14, 1967. [LISA LAW]

Burroughs, Terry Southern, Jean Genet and Ginsberg led demonstrations against the war at the Democratic Party Convention in Chicago in 1968, where peaceful protest erupted into brutality and violence. [MICHAEL COOPER: GINSBERG COLLECTION]

Timothy Leary, drug guru of the 1960s, who introduced Allen to LSD and whose phrase "Turn On, Tune In, Drop Out" became the motto of the hippie movement. [JOHN GRISSOM]

In 1968, Allen joined the hippie exodus and set up his own poetry commune on a farm in upstate New York. Standing (l. to r.): Peter Orlovsky, Denise Mercedes, Julius Orlovsky and Gordon Ball. Seated (l. to r.): Allen, Bonnie and Ray Bremser, and Gregory Corso.

[GINSBERG COLLECTION]

Allen found his own guru in Chögyam Trungpa Rinpoche, the colorful and controversial teacher of Tibetan Buddhism, whose followers gathered at Naropa, his retreat in Boulder, Colorado. They appeared onstage together in May of 1972, on the day Allen took his Buddhist vows and assumed the name Lion of Dharma. [GINSBERG COLLECTION]

Allen joined Bob Dylan and his Rolling Thunder Review in the last months of 1975, reading his poetry and appearing in improvised dramatic scenes filmed as they toured New England. [ELSA DORFMAN]

Allen and Peter were arrested on June 13, 1978, for demonstrating outside the Rockwell Corporation's nuclear trigger factory at Rocky Flats, Colorado.

In January 1982, Allen worked with Joe Strummer (center) and Mick Jones (r.) of the British punk rock band The Clash. His poetry of personal freedom and social protest easily spanned changing musical styles and still attracted enthusiastic young crowds.

A reunion at the Arts Center in Madison, Wisconsin, in the early 1980s, of the original Beat writers: Corso, Ginsberg, and Burroughs. Kerouac had died, an alcoholic and a recluse, in 1969. [GINSBERG COLLECTION]

Steven Taylor, Allen and Peter in Denmark during a 1984 European poetry-reading tour. Allen's relationship with Peter, through fair weather and foul, had lasted almost thirty years.
[SAUL SHAPIRO: GINSBERG COLLECTION]

A teacher of poetry and tireless champion of the literature of the Beats, Allen, with Anne Waldman, administered the Jack Kerouac School of Disembodied Poetics at Naropa for a decade. [RAYMOND FOYE]

In concert.

[JOHN MUREO]

In Boulder, 1985,
in the eye of his
camera.

In his New York
apartment with Bob
Rosenthal, 1988.

[LISA LAW]

In his own eyes.

Allen Ginsberg, distinguished poet and professor, winner of the National Book Award, member in good standing of the literary establishment, performer, photographer, world traveler, crusader for the right of free expression and the cause of social justice. "Perhaps the good outweighs the bad," he said. "I'll never know. Still I feel guilty I haven't done more." [LISA LAW]

The subject of the conference was "The Source of Inspiration," a tricky title designed to dodge the doctrine of art as revolutionary propaganda and allow the Chinese writers, as well as the Americans, to discuss their real motivation and reasons for writing. "The Chinese are heartbreakingly in love with the Americans," Allen would tell the Boulder *Daily Camera* when he returned. "They look to America for technology and know-how and those who learn English get a thorough background in American literature." Allen had been surprised to find that extracts from *On the Road* and Mailer's *The Executioner's Song* were among the required reading for every technician who wanted to study in the United States. His own "Howl" was also widely read among intellectuals, who could relate immediately to the opening line, "I saw the best minds of my generation destroyed by madness." The reference for them was the persecution of intellectuals during the Cultural Revolution.

China was in the throes of self-examination in the wake of the excesses of the Cultural Revolution and the Gang of Four, and the Americans were there, in part, as a sounding board for the Chinese writers. In a report written for UPI, Allen said: "In conversation, the Chinese express different emotions about the decade of upheaval. They feel bewilderment that China, which was the greatest civilization in the world, went through this period of self-degradation."

The four-day conference was wide-ranging, but one of the questions asked repeatedly was how contemporary Chinese literature could be introduced to American readers. The Chinese were publishing many American books, from Richard Nixon's memoirs to *Jonathan Livingston Seagull*. When the poet Yuan Kejia was asked about his literary influences, he named Walt Whitman, the works of T. S. Eliot, and Allen Ginsberg. He had also recently read, in translation, works by John Cheever, James Joyce, Bernard Malamud, and Saul Bellow. This surprised the Americans, who were expecting to be told about Marx, Lenin, and Mao, but none of the Chinese writers mentioned them. Some did, however, refer to China's glorious past, particularly the Tang dynasty (A.D. 618–907), which had produced such poets as Li Po, Tu Fu, and Han Yü, and several mentioned the classic novel *The Dream of the Red Chamber*, which interested Allen because homosexuality was spoken of in the novel and he had decided not to discuss the subject unless the occasion seemed suitable.

With the conference over, the delegates set off on a ten-day sightseeing tour, beginning at Xi'an, where the amazing Han army of life-size clay figures cast in full military regalia had been buried with the emperor. Most of the soldiers had been uncovered and restored, "stepping forward silent motionless underground," as Allen described them.

In Shanghai, they saw the Temple of the Jade Buddha, the Bund, and the waterfront of the Huangpu River, with its rows of British colonial hotels. They took an excursion to the beautiful old city of Suzhou and visited the Cold Mountain temple, where the Tang dynasty poet Han Shan (whose name means Cold Mountain) once lived beside the Grand Canal. Gary Snyder had published transla-tions of twenty-four of Han Shan's poems in 1958, and he presented them to the Buddhist monk who now looked after the temple, im-provising a new poem as he did so, which he called "At Maple Bridge." Robert Rees, moved by the occasion, improvised a poem about Snyder improvising a poem. The local people began to gather to watch this display of poetics.

The official tour ended in Canton on November 5, and the dele-gates returned to the United States. All except Allen, who always tried to take advantage of conferences as a departure point for his explorations, as he had done in Chile, Australia, England, and other countries. Before leaving for China, he had arranged to extend his stay, teaching at Beijing and Hebei universities.

Before returning to Beijing, he spent a week exploring the inte-rior, notably on an unaccompanied trip through the famous Yangtze River Gorges. At the Beijing School of Foreign Languages, he gave morning lectures on Williams, Creeley, Corso, Kerouac, and Orlov-sky. He found the people open, friendly, and inquisitive. The Cul-tural Revolution had cut everyone off from the outside world for a decade, and now they wanted to know what Allen and the Beats had been doing during that time. "People now hopeful and cheerful and disillusioned with dogma," he wrote.

In his UPI report, Allen said: "Everybody had a story about the Cultural Revolution, about how they were sent to the country as a Red Guard, or how their parents were fired from their jobs as trans-lators or physicists, or their mothers sent off to the countryside or how they themselves were exiled to jobs cleaning latrines. Elderly physicians were forced to stand bowed over, wearing dunce caps, answering questions from a bowed position day and night."

At Hebei University in Baoding, eighty miles southwest of Bei-jing, Allen had his own apartment, three concrete rooms in the Foreign Teachers apartment block. The electricity was not very reliable, and Allen sometimes found himself writing his journal by candlelight after the lights had flickered out. It was cold, and he had had bronchitis for three weeks. Finally, he was able to get a hot plate, for heating water and humidifying the room, which received only a few hours' heat and hot water. The boiling water plus herbal medicine from the university infirmary eventually cured him.

At the university, he taught Williams's short poems, as well as work by Reznikoff, Creeley, Corso, Orlovsky, and Kerouac. He mimeographed a sheaf of work by Philip Whalen, Philip Lamantia, and Bill Burroughs, and also taught the work of Walt Whitman. Rereading "Leaves of Grass," he felt a surge of affection that inspired him to write the poem "I Love Old Whitman So":

> *I skim thru the book beginning to end, again and again,*
> *this year in China again and marvel over his swimmers*
> *huffing naked on the wave*
> *and weep at his desperado farewell, "Who touches this*
> *book touches a man."*

Allen's chill kept him indoors most of the time, wrapped in blankets, sleeping or reading in bed. Now that he was settled in his own rooms, and the guided tours were over, he began to write. Previously, every moment had been filled with talk and sightseeing. In Baoding, he had time to poke about in the markets and shopping streets, jotting down observations, eating food from street vendors, and absorbing everyday life. Baoding was not an open city, so there were no facilities for tourists. Allen was seeing the "real" China. In late November he wrote:

> *One morning I took a walk in China*
> *students danced with wooden silver painted swords,*
> *twirling on hard pathed muddy earth*
> *as I walked to Hebei University's concrete north gate,*
> *crossed the street, a blue capped man sold fried sweet*
> *dough-sticks, brown as new boiled donuts . . .*

Allen taught Whitman to the older students in a special class of advanced semiprofessionals who had been displaced by the Cultural Revolution or who were middle-school teachers coming in for continuing education. Allen explained references in Whitman to prostitutes, orgies, and revolution, and watched his class carefully. There were many smiling faces and nods, but the students asked very few questions except technical ones. A student told Allen that anyone who asked too much, or was too curious, would stand out, and it might be noted in his dossier. They were also inhibited by cultural timidity and a traditional Chinese Confucian respect for authority.

After one class, Allen went downtown to buy some traditional Chinese ink and calligraphy brushes, accompanied by a student. As they waited for a bus, Allen asked him what unmarried men did for love. "They must live pure lives," his student told him.

"Why?" asked Allen.

"If their behavior was loose, they would be considered trouble-makers."

"You're married and have a place to live and a job, so you can talk," said Allen. "But what right have you or anyone to tell those without wives or jobs or station to live loveless the rest of their lives? What kind of communist community is that? What kind of equality? It's barbaric exploitation! You expect to have those people dig your trenches and plant your rice and live without love?"

The student smiled. "I really agree," he said. "That's what I think too."

It was the first time since he had arrived that Allen was able to make intimate contact with a Chinese. Knowing that this world of secret personal views must exist, he had not been able to penetrate it. The longer he stayed, the more often this occurred, and he was eventually able to get the viewpoint of the individual Chinese, or at least those attached to the foreign language departments of the universities.

On December 1, he finished his two-week course of lectures. The faculty held a farewell banquet for him and for another American who was leaving. An old cadre member at the dinner, whom Allen had always been suspicious of, thinking he was a police spy, revealed that in the mid-fifties he had managed a Chinese opera company. He sang to the gathering and then sentimentally recited a famous heroic poem by Mao Tse-tung:

> *The mountains are dancing silver serpents*
> *The hills on the plain are shining elephants*
> *I desire to compare our height with the skies.*

The old man wanted to show the departing Americans his great depth of feeling for China. "Our farewell was warm with tipsy embraces," Allen wrote.

Two days later, he took the train back to Shanghai, where he was to teach at Fudan University. There he stayed in the guest room of the old President's House, carpeted and furnished with a shining armoire and two comfortable sofas beside a tea table. Above his bed hung a mosquito net, tied in a giant white knot when not in use. The heat came from a noisy ventilator grille set high in the wall above his desk. The north wall was composed entirely of French windows, which were curtained at night, and in the garden below his balcony were a stone table and chairs. Nurses and children gathered in the garden beneath the trees in the daytime. Each morning, he awoke to the sound of music playing over the campus loudspeakers as staff and students did their morning exercises.

He spent the first two days at Fudan resting, recovering from his virus, but he had many visitors and was soon conversant with the latest Shanghai gossip. Whenever it was appropriate, he asked about sex, and he always received the same answer: premarital sex, except if the couple was intending to marry, was considered immoral, and love between men was unheard of. One day after class, a professor asked Allen if he had a family. Allen told him that he was homosexual, and the professor asked if he would explain that to him. He said that he had asked other American visitors, but they said it was something disgusting.

One of his students had translated a number of Allen's erotic poems. Allen was surprised and asked him whom he would show them to. "My girlfriend," he replied.

"What's your pleasure in that?" Allen asked.

"I'm young and I enjoy love," he replied. "I'm interested in love." But he added that he would not be able to show the translations to very many people, just one or two friends. In his UPI report, Allen wrote: "There's an ambiguousness among the Chinese. The people are trying to sort out how much of the sexual repression, how much of the travel limitations, how much of the hyper-organization is really a support system for keeping the whole society together and how much is a control system to keep power at the top."

He finished teaching on December 20 and prepared to leave China. Christmas Day he spent in Yunnan province, just above the Vietnam border, where he lectured at the National Minorities School and was given a Christmas meal by the faculty. He arrived in San Francisco on December 28, 1984, just in time for the publication of his *Collected Poems*.

· · ·

Collected Poems 1947–1980 was published on February 2, 1985, to considerable critical attention, beginning with *Time* magazine, which ran a full-page interview, with a color photograph. The article, written by R. Z. Sheppard, took the standard *Time* line; "Howl," which the magazine had put down in the fifties, was called "once effective as a counter-culture manifesto . . . now an unconvincing historical oddity." "Kaddish," however, which *Time* had ignored when it was published, could now be safely described as "a masterpiece of candor and emotional persuasion." In its reference to "Howl," the article quoted a line from the "Moloch!" section, leaving out the last four words: "granite cocks! monstrous bombs!" Allen, interviewed for the Detroit *Jewish News*, protested: "By leaving out 'monstrous bombs!' which is a contemporary problem, they can declare it obsolete and archaic. They amputated the line in order to try and prove their point. That really is unfair journalism as well as being unethical and anti-literate to doctor my verse to fit their view. The one line which they quoted, they bowdlerized politically."

It was not the only objection Allen had to the piece, which he must have known would be a hatchet job when he agreed to do the interview. *Time* was more interested in how much money his new book contract was worth than in the poetry, and the very title of their piece, "Mainstreaming Allen Ginsberg," suggested that Allen had somehow gone commercial. "It requires vision and careful work to make a life, let alone leave a literary legacy. This follower in Whitman's footsteps has shown that he is capable of both. One can see it in his eyes: one wide and innocent, gazing at eternity; the other narrowed and scrutinizing, looking for his market share."

"That was rather cruel," said Allen. "Look at my face. I have Bell's palsy, so one eye and one part of my mouth is a little distorted. Paralyzed. So 'one eye narrowed and looking for his market share' is a little like kicking a cripple."

Allen for his part was clearly delighted with the book. When asked by the Philadelphia *Inquirer* what he would like to leave as his legacy, he laughed and said, "A great big book of poems, a big fat book of poems. I just hope somebody will sit down and read it, beginning to end, familiar with the whole thing. It will be like reading through Yeats. It will actually alter slightly perceptions of the world and open up space and tolerance and humor. For one thing, the realization that you don't have to be right, all you have to do is be candid . . . I don't think any poet will be able to get around it.

It's like a big roadblock. They're gonna have to talk about something real, about their phenomenal world."

Seeing the poems presented in true chronological order for the first time invited comparisons with Pound's "Cantos," Whitman's "Leaves of Grass," and Williams's "Paterson" (what the Washington *Post* called "the garrulous side to American poetry"). Allen said that all along his intention had been to make "a graph or a picture of my mind over the seasons, months, years, decade"—the quantitative verse of Pound. He accepted that he did not always succeed, and told the Washington *Post*: "My intention was to make a picture of my mind, mistakes and all. Of course, I learned I'm an idiot, a complete idiot who wasn't as prophetic as I thought I was. The crazy angry philippic sometimes got in the way of clear perception."

His intentions were recognized by some of the critics. Stephen Salisbury wrote in the *Inquirer*: "by turns funny, personal, public, boring and quirky, the poems offer a record of life in postwar America, a map of his slowly evolving spiritual awareness and a frame-by-frame picaresque documentary starring the gamboling self in modern society."

Even his enemies on the right had to recognize the seriousness of his undertaking. Robert Richman devoted six pages to attacking him in *Commentary*, and Roger Rosenblatt, senior writer for *Time*, gave him a three-page review in the *New Republic*, saying: "What these 800 pages prove is that Ginsberg has always been a minor poet; that is, a poet who has produced a few remarkable pieces, but the bulk of whose work shows no philosophical growth (despite its ostentatiously philosophical preoccupations) and rarely any depth. It is no small thing to be a minor poet; few make the list in any century."

It must be left to history to determine Ginsberg's literary rank. Certainly he was preeminent among the poets of the postwar generations, their loudest and most influential voice. For Ginsberg, poetry, philosophy, political action, and personal expression go hand in hand. His biggest battles have been with society and with himself. His entire career, as lived in public and documented in his poetry and journals, has been a struggle to explore and express his own awareness, and to protect the right of others to do the same. His is a fight for life, for individual freedom, against the incursions of social forces. As he told the Washington *Post*: "The condition of society is one of homogeneity and hyperindustrialism, so the individual perceptions of body and mind are not valued. Poetry is not an expression of the party line. It's that time of night, lying in bed, thinking what you really think, making the private world public, that's what the poet does."

AFTERWORD

Most poets, on reaching their sixties and having seen the successful publication of a doorstop tome of their collected poems, would think it time for a rest, to slow down and reap the benefits of long service to literature. Not so Ginsberg. After *Collected Poems* came more trips, books, records, and readings: a writers conference in the Soviet Union, a return trip to Nicaragua, a reading and lecture tour in Israel, a reading tour of Japan, a trip to receive the Golden Wreath for Poetry in Struga, Yugoslavia (the previous recipient was W. H. Auden), benefit readings for Solidarity in Krakow and Warsaw. If anything, Ginsberg's work load increased. Signed with Harper & Row, he faced publisher's deadlines for the first time; his all-night work marathons were now undertaken to get manuscripts in on time as well as to keep abreast of his massive correspondence. He still crisscrossed the country for readings, although less frequently now that Bob Rosenthal concentrated on booking him into colleges for week-long workshops. The problem was solved in 1986, when Brooklyn College appointed him distinguished professor; teaching one day a week, he made money enough so that he did not have to tour unless he wanted to.

Meanwhile, the Beat Generation industry continued to grow. Two fan magazines kept track of Kerouac lore, international conferences were held in Jack's name, documentaries were made and more books published about him than he himself wrote. His widow, Stella, has consistently refused access to his papers and unpublished manuscripts, but if they do ever become available, they will clearly provoke a new spate of biographies and critical studies.

William Burroughs was also the subject of documentaries, a biography, a number of critical works and conferences. He bought himself a small house in Lawrence, Kansas, with an acre of ground for his cats and his target practice. After the completion of his trilogy, *Cities of the Red Night, The Place of Dead Roads,* and *The Western Lands,* Bill concentrated largely on painting. His work, which began as "shotgun art," plywood panels, splintered by Bill's gunfire, received critical acclaim, and he had successful shows across the United States and Europe.

Ginsberg also discovered a new art form—photography. Throughout the years, he had always taken pictures of his friends: Neal buying a car in San Francisco in 1955; Peter posing before Robert LaVigne's huge portrait of him; Bill reclining on Allen's floor in New York in 1953; Gary Snyder pissing off a mountain; Kerouac on the beach in Tangiers in 1961. Allen described his approach to photography in terms of the original Beat sensibility: "It's like looking through a telescope back into time at people who were really interesting in the period of their greatest creativity," he told a Miami *Herald* reporter. "I'm not a photographer, but I was aware of the sacredness and the poignance of the pictures. It's kind of a poignance of the moment, like an appreciation of the color of the sky, the blue of the blue and the face of the face and the Jack Kerouac of the Jack Kerouac."

His photographs were the most utilized section of his archives on deposit at Columbia University and had appeared in many books on Kerouac or the Beats. Ann Charters chose the best of them in her photo-essay book, *Scenes Along the Road,* but many of the shots were not in the archives. Originally processed by labs that serviced corner drugstores, many of the prints had been given away to friends over the years.

Photographs were disappearing and negatives being roughly handled at Columbia, so Ginsberg asked art curator Raymond Foye to organize and catalog the collection. Foye printed up thousands of negatives on contact sheets, and the wide range and extent of the collection became visible for the first time. Allen asked Brian Graham, Robert Frank's printer, to print a few professionally and was surprised by the results. It was obvious that there was enough good material for an exhibition.

"It was like a whole other career going on that I didn't know was there," said Ginsberg. "I had always enjoyed taking pictures of my friends, but I hadn't thought about it. Without knowing, I had made a record over the years, a chronicle of the scene." His first show, "Hideous Human Angels," was presented at the Holly Solomon Gallery on Fifty-seventh Street in January 1985. The New York Public Library bought a number of his photographs and showed them in their "New Acquisitions" group show the next month. Ginsberg's office swung into action; one of his assistants spent her entire time organizing the developing, printing, and cataloging of his photographs. Brian Graham found his work load dramatically increased, and Ginsberg had shows at the Middendorf Gallery in Washington, D.C., the Dallas Museum of Art, Galerie Watari in Tokyo, the Fogg Museum in Boston, and many other museums and galleries around the world.

He took advice from photographers like Berenice Abbot and Robert Frank, and he bought a new camera, which he began to carry everywhere, using it constantly. He was absolutely unabashed about taking photographs: Julian Beck of the Living Theater smiled weakly for Allen's camera from his deathbed; Allen's uncle Abe managed a wave from his, days before he died. As the police carried a struggling Peter Orlovsky away to Bellevue after he smashed up the janitor's apartment in a drunken rage, Allen clicked away, recording everything for posterity.

He was just as uninhibited about pictures of himself, as Richard Avedon's famous nude shots of Allen and Peter demonstrate. Now he proudly showed visitors a new picture of himself, taken by a boyfriend: Allen reclining naked, a Modigliani odalisque, smiling sweetly for the camera. His technique improved rapidly, and soon at least half of the photographs in his shows were recent work. He took great pride in seeing his work in the photography journal *Aperture* and popular magazines such as *Vanity Fair*.

As part of a project with John Cage, he took a series of views of the four seasons from his kitchen window, which were widely exhibited. When Sony gave him a video camera, he made a twenty-minute video film of scenes around the house: Julius Orlovsky talking guardedly over breakfast, Harry Smith—filmmaker, sound archivist, occult bibliophile—delivering a monologue, a Russian poet who spoke no English smiling at the camera, fleeting appearances by Bob Rosenthal and the stream of visitors who fill the apartment at all hours of the day.

White Shroud, "a mellow sampler of Ginsberg in his prime," as Ann Charters described it in the Los Angeles *Times,* was published in December 1986. One of the most considered reviews came in a syndicated column by Allen's old adversary Tom Clark, who generously allowed: "If Ginsberg isn't the world's first truly international poet, he'll do until one comes along." Although, like many reviewers, he had reservations about the political "list" poems in the book, Clark thought the title poem, a dream apparition of Naomi, more than made up for them. "This memorable poem has a way of bathing the rest of Ginsberg's new work in its calm light, to some extent relieving the black-and-white, stencilled-in spareness of 'political' vision in the surrounding pieces."

When Elise Cowen finished typing a fair copy of the original manuscript of "Kaddish," she had told Allen, "You haven't finished with her yet." "White Shroud" is an epilogue to "Kaddish." In a dream, Allen returned to the Bronx, scene of his earliest memories, and saw Naomi in an alley, living like a bag lady. "I / was looking for a house, I thought, she has one, in poor / Bronx, needs someone to help her shop and cook, needs her children now." He and Naomi were at last reconciled in his dream. "My breast rejoiced, all my troubles over, she was / content, too old to care or yell her grudge, only complaining / her bad teeth. What long-sought peace!" He awoke before dawn and looked out over the rooftops of Boulder.

> *. . . I returned*
> *from the Land of the Dead to living Poesy, and wrote*
> *this tale of long lost joy, to have seen my mother again!*
> *And when the ink ran out of my pen, and rosy violet*
> *illumined city treetop skies above the Flatiron Front*
>   *Range,*
> *I went downstairs to the shady living room, where Peter*
>   *Orlovsky*
> *sat with long hair lit by television glow to watch*
> *the sunrise weather news, I kissed him & filled my pen*
>   *and wept.*

Chögyam Trungpa died of a heart attack on April 4, 1987, in Halifax, Nova Scotia, having spent the previous year and a half in a semicoma. Allen went to see him a few weeks before he died. "In a sense he made himself unnecessary for the continuation of this particular meditative development he was teaching," Ginsberg said. "It's almost as if he lingered there while everybody picked up their own responsibilities. He empowered everybody in that sense, very directly said, 'You've got to do it now.' So when he died, everybody began appreciating how good a job he did despite all the drunkenness."

According to Tibetan Buddhist custom, his body was embalmed in salt and arranged in the sitting meditation position inside an upright closed wooden box. The cremation was held at Karme-Choling, the 540-acre estate in the Green Mountains near Barnet, Vermont, that had been Trungpa's first center in the United States. On May 26, early in the day, Trungpa's body was carried in procession to a meadow in which there had been erected a two-story-high brick stupa—a domelike structure surrounded by banners and prayer flags. A crowd of fifty visiting Tibetan lamas and two thousand students and friends had gathered there for the rites. After three hours of meditation and prayer, a cannon was fired, somewhere bagpipes skirled, and a fire was kindled beneath the stupa, which now held his remains.

As the flames consumed his body, Tibetans in traditional robes and hats played the prescribed funeral music on long Tibetan horns, bells, drums, and cymbals, while Trungpa's students threw rice, butter, wheat, and barley into the fire and four Zen archers enacted a choreographed ritual around the fiery stupa.

"Nobody here is crying, 'Oh, dear Guru, don't go away,' " Allen told a *New York Times* reporter. "His teaching is part of our minds now. In a sense we look through his eyes as some look through Hemingway's or Dostoevsky's eyes." Trungpa's death, he said later, made him understand the notion of the guru's mind being everywhere: "Certain perceptions and understandings are permanent and affect your perspective on things. In this case, the notion of emptiness, interrupting the build up of anxiety and conceptual thought by some trick of emptying the mind, either by thinking of his [Trungpa's] face, or by stopping and meditating a moment, one breath, or looking out at the sky. Any number of mind tricks. Cutting through the build up of superficial anxiety, or illusory consciousness, so the final resting place really is just open empty mind. That's his mind, but also my mind, so space itself. I began appreciating how helpful he had been in establishing that."

Trungpa's long illness came not long after Allen moved back to New York. Trungpa had told him, "Take more space. Go to New York and make some money." Allen's day-to-day involvement with Naropa ended, though he still taught there during the summer.

While Allen was in China in 1984, Peter had gone through a crisis. He stayed up for two days, drinking sake, then scared Allen's staff by appearing naked in the apartment with a machete, threatening to cut his own head off. Exhausted from lack of sleep and overcome by alcohol, he was impossible to reason with. He waved around a pair of sharp scissors and offered Bob Rosenthal a haircut, then began hacking off hanks of his own long hair. When he began to stab the scissors into his arm, Rosenthal called the police.

When policemen arrived to take him to Bellevue, Peter got permission to go next door to his apartment to dress. At the door, he wrenched out of their grip and locked himself in. Only when he had nothing left to drink was he eventually coaxed out by a friend from Dharmadhatu, who offered him sake. By this time, a crowd had gathered and a row of police cars stood along Twelfth Street; a television news unit was on hand to film Peter's being carried from the building, tied to a chair.

When Allen returned from China, he began attending the family service program at Bellevue with Peter, seeing an analyst once or twice a week at low cost. A year later, the analyst went into private practice; her rates went up considerably, but Allen continued to see her. Peter was in Bellevue only a few weeks, but following his discharge he began to drink again, and increasingly difficult scenes ensued. After several violent episodes, he and Allen were advised by their psychiatrists not to see or contact each other for a year. That was particularly hard for Allen, because for the first few months, Peter's then girlfriend, Juanita Lieberman, worked as Bob Rosenthal's assistant and was a constant reminder of Peter.

Since Peter could hardly remain in his apartment without constantly encountering Allen, he spent much of their enforced separation at Trungpa's new center in Nova Scotia. Reports from Trungpa's followers said that Peter continued to drink and that his behavior was "strange" or "peculiar." One of the conditions of the separation was that Peter should become economically self-sufficient and break his thirty-year dependency on Allen, which was the root of much of the problem. This caused more arguments at the end of their year apart, in 1986, because Peter believed that

Allen should sell his archives and use the money to relocate himself, Peter, and Peter's mother, sister, and brothers, in Nova Scotia, as Trungpa had suggested that his followers do.

After more difficult episodes, Allen attempted to get Peter to attend the family service course at Hazelden Hospital in Minneapolis, the home hospital of Alcoholics Anonymous. Peter refused to go, so Allen went with Beverly Isis, Peter's current girlfriend. The family service program at Hazelden was based on the notion that alcoholism is a family disease: the family becomes codependent with the alcoholic, in the sense that it attempts to keep order while the alcoholic causes disorder. Ginsberg said, "It was very similar to my situation with Naomi. . . . The key neurosis that all the co-dependents have, and the alcoholics, is a feeling of worthlessness, of not being able to correct the situation and feeling that it's their fault, a feeling of guilt, that if I can't stop Peter from drinking I must have been treating him wrong all these years and it must be my fault."

Allen was told to go about his own life and stop taking on the burden of guilt, which came from trying to control the situation and constantly failing. "That was very much my own situation with Peter and my mother," Ginsberg said. "Peter repeating my mother and the chaos she created." Allen had to realize that Peter was the only one who could make up his mind to stop drinking; all Allen could do was try to offer a supportive situation. His talks at Hazelden and with his psychiatrist were revelatory. He had spent his adolescence trying to control and contain the chaos caused by Naomi's madness: "My father rejected me if I didn't believe him, and if I didn't believe her stories, she would reject me. So in order to win *her* affection, I would have to believe her delusions. It's a double bind that leaves a permanent sense of guilt."

Allen identified this as the cause of his assuming a massive work load. "Certainly the reason for my workaholism is a low sense of self-esteem and a constant need to produce something to feel that I've done something that people will accept me for." On leaving Hazelden, he was supposed to make a resolution. He tried, with some success, to stop working at eight each evening. "That was my resolution—take it easy, meet friends or go to a movie or have some human contact, instead of working until five in the morning." It was only then that he realized he didn't have a real living room. Most visitors were destined for the office or the bedroom; a set of uncomfortable chairs in the kitchen did duty for everyone else. Allen bought a television and a video recorder for the living room and began entertaining there. When he purchased a new dish rack and an electric clock for the kitchen, Bob Rosenthal accused him of becoming a yuppie.

It was not easy to give up habits of a lifetime, but he now felt he had a better understanding of his own motivations. His duties at Brooklyn College consisted of one three-hour writing seminar a week, but characteristically, he stayed on afterward to give tutorials until about nine in the evening. "I had to do extra work to prove to them it was worthwhile having me there," Allen said. "I could've rested on my laurels."

Allen was not lonely in the apartment. Harry Smith came to visit, hurt his leg, and, as in *The Man Who Came to Dinner*, stayed almost a year. It was a stormy interlude; Harry's health was poor, and he was a difficult, stubborn guest unused to sharing a dwelling. He took a perverse enjoyment in antagonizing Allen, who was once reduced to slapping him in frustration. On one occasion, Bob Dylan came to meet him; many of the songs Dylan performed in the early days of his career he had taken from the Folkways *Anthology of American Folk Music* which Harry had compiled. To Allen's annoyance, Harry refused to get up. In the end, Allen's psychiatrist stepped in and told him that Harry had to go; he was raising Allen's blood pressure.

In January 1988, Ginsberg went to Israel, where he read poetry at a huge demonstration in Tel Aviv protesting the treatment of Palestinians in the occupied territories. A crowd estimated at sixty thousand gave him the loudest applause of the day for his 1974 poem "Jaweh and Allah Battle," an attack on the role of the two religions in the Arab-Israeli conflict. In an interview, Ginsberg said he had come because he wanted to be "a calm voice among a lot of ranting voices, polarized voices." On his return to New York, he began attending informal weekly meetings with Arthur Miller, Norman Mailer, Erica Jong, Susan Sontag, Roy Lichtenstein, and a hundred other Jewish artists and writers, to organize a stand against Israel's treatment of Palestinians. At the end of February, the group sent a telegram to express solidarity with an association of Israeli artists and writers protesting Israel's conduct on the occupied West Bank.

While in Israel, Allen had compiled a dossier of information on censorship in that country for the PEN Freedom-to-Write Committee. In June, the committee sent a letter to the Israeli government, urging it "to cease its practice of censorship" of Palestinian writers and journalists in the occupied West Bank and Gaza Strip. The letter, the result of months of heated discussion that divided some of the leading writers in the United States, called on Israel "to end its policy of arrests of Palestinian and Israeli journalists, to reopen censored Palestinian newspapers, to reopen the Palestinian Press Service, and to cease its practice of censorship of books, school reading materials, newspapers and literary texts circulated in the West Bank and the Gaza Territories."

In addition to Ginsberg, its initiator, the letter was signed by Susan Sontag, president of the PEN American Center; Faith Sale and Rose Styron, the cochairwomen of the Freedom-to-Write Committee; William Styron, and Grace Paley. Faith Sale said, "The letter is not a political statement. It's a statement about censorship —and that is PEN's mandate."

As expected, the letter was opposed by Israel's supporters at PEN. Cynthia Ozick said in an interview: "Criticism of Israel must have credentials and I feel no one on the Freedom-to-Write Committee has such credentials." Yet the letter went into considerable detail, listing specific charges of censorship, including the detention of thirty-five Palestinian journalists without trial or charges and the forced closure of several Palestinian newspapers and magazines, as well as the Gaza Press Service and the Palestinian News Service.

Allen had been a member of the Freedom-to-Write Committee since 1966 and had long used it as the vehicle for his various campaigns, beginning with LeRoi Jones's trial in Newark, where his writing was used as evidence against him in an assault case, and continuing with cases involving Timothy Leary, John Lennon, and FBI and CIA sabotage of the underground press. He was a very active committee member and was eventually asked to become a vice president.

Ginsberg would have achieved very little in taking on the powerful Israeli lobby alone, but his new position in the establishment gave him the ability to campaign on a much higher level, dealing with international affairs. The views of the committee members made headlines in the *New York Times* and were given serious consideration.

Ginsberg and the Beats had been an inspiration for a number of younger artists, many of whom had now reached the peaks of their

careers. The Italian painter Francesco Clemente had great success
working in New York and collaborated with Allen on an illustrated
edition of *White Shroud*. At the New York Shubert Theatre benefit
for Vietnam Veterans in February 1988, Allen and Philip Glass
performed "Wichita Vortex," Allen's poem set to music by Glass.
Allen had also been approached by Robert Wilson, Glass's longtime
collaborator, who was working on a performance called *Cosmopoli-
tan Greetings*, based on the life of Bessie Smith. Allen was originally
asked for a new text, but instead of overloading himself with yet
more work, he offered old material, which they accepted. "I would
normally have been flattered at working with these famous names,"
he said, pleased that his antiworkaholic resolution was bearing
fruit.

On June 25, 1988, an event dear to Allen's heart occurred: the
opening of the Jack Kerouac Commemorative in the new $3.5 mil-
lion Eastern Canal Park in Lowell, Massachusetts. It featured fifteen passages from Kerouac's books cut into the sides of eight
three-sided granite columns arranged in a rough mandala.

When the news was first announced that Lowell's City Council
had decided to approve a new park in Kerouac's memory, Kerouac's
old enemy Norman Podhoretz used the occasion to attack the Beats
yet again. In the New York *Post*, under the headline "Strange
Honor for a False Prophet," he once more fulminated against
"Howl": "In its glorification of madness, drugs and homosexuality,
and in its contempt and hatred for anything and everything generally deemed healthy, normal or decent, Ginsberg's poem simultaneously foreshadowed and helped to propagate the values of the
youth culture of the 1960's. . . . Kerouac and Ginsberg once played
a part in ruining a great many young people who were influenced by
their 'distaste for normal life and common decency.' "

But Allen no longer rose to the bait. In an interview in *New Letters*, he said: "Good old Norman Podhoretz. If he weren't there like
a wall I can butt my head against, I wouldn't have anybody to hate.
And why hate him? He's part of my world, and he's sort of like the
character the Blue Meanie . . . did I ever really hate him or was I
just sort of fascinated by him? I saw him as a sort of sacred personage in my life, in a way; someone whose vision is so opposite from
mine that it's provocative and interesting—just as my vision is interesting and provocative enough for him to write columns against
it in the newspaper. In fact, maybe he's more honest than I am

because he attacks me openly. So I should really respect him as one of the sacred personae in the drama of my own transitory existence."

That Norman Podhoretz should still seethe with indignation over the Beats thirty years later is some measure of their impact. How great that impact really was is a matter of debate. Much has been claimed, but it is in literature that the most obvious effects are to be found. "There was some conscious intention to make a cultural breakthrough, to talk in public as we talked in private," Ginsberg said. "How we behave in private is actually the ultimate politics. So the original literary inspiration was to behave in public as we do in private." The naked, confessional statement became one of the most influential aspects of the Beats' literary heritage. Together with Henry Miller and Jean Genet, they are responsible for the "confessional" work of Charles Bukowski, Hubert Selby, John Rechy, Alexander Trocchi, Leonard Cohen, Stephen Schneck, Irving Rosenthal, and more recent writers such as Tom Robbins, Jay McInerney, Paul Rudnick, Jim Carroll, Tama Janowitz, Bret Easton Ellis, and Kathy Acker. Critics have even detected their influence on Philip Roth (*Portnoy's Complaint*) and Erica Jong (*Fear of Flying*). The so-called New Journalism of Tom Wolfe, Hunter S. Thompson, Gay Talese, and Michael Herr had its roots in the Beats. Their impact, however, has been less significant outside the United States.

Since the publication of Don Allen's 1960 anthology, *New American Poetry 1945–1960*, there has been a revolution in American poetry. The San Francisco Renaissance poets: Gary Snyder, Michael McClure, John Wieners, Lawrence Ferlinghetti, Philip Lamantia; the Black Mountain school: Robert Creeley, Ed Dorn, Charles Olson; the New York school: Frank O'Hara, LeRoi Jones, Diane di Prima, John Ashbery, Anne Waldman, Ed Sanders, and Ted Berrigan, have all taken their places in the pantheon of American letters. Thanks to the pioneering publishing of City Lights Books, Grove Press, Don Allen, Corinth, New Directions, and a multitude of small presses, open-form poetry has now been placed alongside "establishment" verse. The reputations of William Carlos Williams, Basil Bunting, Charles Reznikoff, Lorine Niedecker, Louis Zukofsky, and other open-form poets from an earlier generation have been secured, and a new post-Beat generation of younger poets is emerging. Ginsberg's proselytizing role in all this has been substantial, and aside from his own work, it is probably his biggest contribution to changing the direction of American culture.

The Beats shook up American life in ways other than literature. With their free-and-easy ways, their belief in love and visions and openness, they made the first cracks in the armor and gave America some breathing room after the claustrophobia of the postwar decade. Ginsberg has claimed that the Beat Generation influenced everything from gay liberation, black liberation, and women's liberation to liberation of the word from censorship, the demystification and/or decriminalization of some laws against marijuana and other drugs, and the spread of ecological consciousness.

Some of these claims have been dismissed by critics. The Beats had no obvious connection with the civil rights movement, and most feminist historians are critical of the Beats for their misogyny; it would be ingenious to find the origins of the women's movement among Beat Generation literary activity, except perhaps as a reaction against it.

The gay movement, however, has clear roots in the kind of open-minded comradeship and male bonding found among the early Beats, particularly between Ginsberg and Kerouac, or Kerouac and Cassady. It was a kind of masculine tenderness out of Walt Whitman, virtually unknown in the late forties and early fifties, which later became a prototype in the gay community, what Ginsberg called a "co-operative tender heart."

The bravery of Ginsberg's confessions in *Howl*—"America, I'm putting my queer shoulder to the wheel" or "who let themselves be fucked in the ass by saintly motorcyclists, and screamed with joy" —revelations of homosexuality in the middle of the McCarthy period, made without guilt or shame, was inspirational to homosexuals across the country and heralded the beginnings of the gay liberation movement. Ginsberg held up his gay "marriage" to Peter as exemplary, although he later worried about the harm that may have caused to anyone copying him and was later criticized by sectors of the movement for simply reproducing role stereotypes. He gave dozens of benefit readings for gay causes and championed the cause in interviews and the media. In the history of the struggle to achieve acceptance for homosexuals in American society, Ginsberg was a central figure.

The Beats and their publishers, notably Barney Rosset at Grove Press, played an important role in ending literary censorship, through the trials of *Howl* and *Naked Lunch*. Ginsberg was always willing to put himself on the line, whether testifying on behalf of Jack Smith's film *Flaming Creatures,* which had been seized as obscene, or opposing 1988 FCC regulations that prohibited "Howl" from being read aloud on the radio except after midnight. Although Ginsberg often claims the Beat Generation as the genesis of the ideas of sixties youth culture, in most instances, where some lasting influence on society can be shown, it was caused not by the Beat Generation but by Ginsberg himself in his tireless campaigning for what he regards as a better world.

The one continuous thread throughout his life has been to fulfill the vow he made as a teenager, standing on the windswept prow of the Hoboken ferry on his way to take the Columbia University entrance examinations: to devote his life to helping mankind. He became the poet advocate of the underdog, and this has always been his greatest theme. To paraphrase Richard Ellmann on Oscar Wilde, Ginsberg's greatness as a writer is partly the result of the enlargement of sympathy that he demands for society's victims.

It was not an easy ride. Ginsberg's sincerity has been doubted, his methods have often been criticized, his poetry has been ridiculed. Despite that, he has become the most famous living poet on earth, one of America's best-known cultural ambassadors, his poetry translated into virtually every language, from Chinese to Serbo-Croatian. He changed the world a little.

"I'm famous, / my poems have done some men good / and a few women ill, perhaps the good / outweighs the bad, I'll never know. / Still I feel guilty I haven't done more."

ACKNOWLEDGMENTS

In the course of my research for this book, I played back all the recordings I could find in Ginsberg's tape archives of conversations between Allen and his father, Louis. It came as a shock to find my own voice on a cassette from 1970, interviewing Louis about the Ginsberg family history in Newark before Allen was born. I was staying on Allen's farm in upstate New York, engaged in cataloging his tape archives, when Louis, and Allen's stepmother, Edith, came for a vacation. It had seemed only natural to record Louis's memories. In a sense, then, I began researching this book almost two decades ago.

My acquaintance with Allen Ginsberg goes back even further. In 1965, he walked in to the London bookshop I was managing. He needed a place to stay, so my wife and I put him up. Since then, he and I have worked together on a number of projects. I produced spoken-word albums of two of his poetry readings in 1965, and later in the sixties I produced his *William Blake's Songs of Innocence and Experience Tuned by Allen Ginsberg*, which was released by MGM Records.

In 1970–71, I spent eighteen months cataloging his tape archives and produced a sixteen-hour program of the best available recording of each of his published poems. In the years I lived in New York

City, I saw a lot of Allen, and later in the seventies, he often stayed with me when he passed through London. During the winter of 1985–86, we worked together in New York, preparing the annotated edition of *Howl*, published by Harper & Row. Over the years, I have come to know many of his friends and members of his family. I therefore cannot claim complete impartiality, since I was present at many of the events I have written about in this book and have been described in print as "Ginsberg's advocate in Britain." I have, however, attempted to give as objective a view as possible, which means that Allen and I do not always see eye to eye on what happened.

My thanks to Allen for agreeing to the project. He gave me complete access to his private papers and archives and allowed me to interview him at length—a rare situation between biographer and subject. Not only has Ginsberg kept all the sixty thousand–plus letters he has received throughout his life, but he has saved his manuscripts, journals, notebooks, and doodles. For the last two decades, he has frequently taped his lectures, his conversations with relatives and friends, and, on occasion, his telephone conversations. In addition to his voluminous correspondence over the years, from the mid-sixties onward he has been one of the most interviewed men on earth.

Once I had established a rough draft of the book, Allen allowed me to question him about specifics that were unclear from his correspondence or from other people's recollections. He spent hours researching his own files to provide me with documents and photographs, wrote to friends and relatives, answered my questions in planes, cabs, buses, and on the Brooklyn Bridge, until at last he cried, "I feel like I'm a robot being deprogrammed!" The main sources for the book, then, were threefold: Ginsberg's three hundred or so largely unpublished journals, his extensive correspondence with friends and family, and my interviews with him and his friends.

His criterion in authorizing the book was that I could say what I wanted about him. He did, however, want to review my remarks about his friends for accuracy and in fear of invading their privacy, since much of my information about them was taken from his unpublished journals. I readily agreed. It is a tribute to his belief in the freedom of expression that he did not ask for a final veto over the book's contents. He read the final draft manuscript and made numerous suggestions. He corrected my chronology of his childhood, suggested new approaches to his relationship with his mother, disagreed with my interpretation of his visit to Cuba in 1965, and offered a great deal of new material on his relationship with his Tibetan guru. I used many of his suggestions, mostly as additions, and corrected the factual errors he identified. My debt to him extends far beyond this book, which is, of course, but one view of his life. I hope he finds something of value in it.

In the five years it has taken to write this book, an enormous number of people have helped me by granting interviews, locating documents and photographs, extending hospitality, and suggesting ideas. I wish to thank: Simon Albury, Tsultrim Allioni, Jerry Aronson, Gordon Ball, Annabel Bartlett, Mary Beach, Julian Beck, Hazel Bennington, Ann Biderman, Peggy Biderman, Rick Blume, Eugene Brooks, Pete Brown, Michael Brownstein, William S. Burroughs, Lucien Carr, Carolyn Cassady, Simon Caulkin, Chris Challis, Ann Charters, Ira Cohen, Gregory Corso, Raymond Danowski, David Dawson, Ellie Dorfman, Valerie Estes, Larry Fagin, Mick Farren, Lawrence Ferlinghetti, Rick Fields, James Fox, Raymond Foye, Robert Frank, Edith Ginsberg, the late Louis Ginsberg, John Giorno, Jeff Goldberg, Albert Goldman, James Grauerholz, Theo Green, the late Brion Gysin, Igor Hajek, Anthony Harwood, Michael Henshaw, John Herman, Stellan Holm, Michael Horovitz, Jerry Howard, Robert Jackson, Kathy John, Ted Joans, Terry Karten, Tony Lacey, Jay Landesman, Charles Landry, Timothy Leary, Edith Levy, Juanita Lieberman, Leo and Hannah Litzky, Colin McCabe, Michael McClure, Patrick MacMullen, Legs McNeil, Gerard Malanga, Judith Malina, Mark and Anita Mannes, Pearce Marchbank, Felicity Mason, Steve Mass, Laury and Elizabeth Minard, Adrian Mitchell, Marko Modiano, Stuart Montgomery, Ted Morgan, Sterling Morrison, Eric Mottram, Shig Murao, Hank O'Neal, Julius Orlovsky, Edie Parker-Kerouac, Claude Pelieu, Jim Perrizo, Nancy Peters, Rosebud Pettet, Tom Pickard, Fernanda Pivano, Joyce Ravid, Randy Roark, Aram and Gailyn Saroyan, Michael Schumacher, Gavin Selerie, Josef Skvorecky, Harry Smith, Gary Snyder, Carl Solomon, Vicki Stanbury, John Steinbeck, Jr., Bernard Stone, Steven Taylor, Lionel Tiger, Simon Vinkenoog, Jeffrey Vogel, Anne Waldman, Barry Wallenstein, Regina Weinreich, Philip Whalen, and Peter Wollen.

Ginsberg's correspondence has been preserved in libraries across the United States. I would like to thank the following for their valuable assistance: Mary Angelotti at the Beinecke Rare Book and Manuscript Library of Yale University; Michael Davidson, director of the Archive for New Poetry at the University of California, San Diego; James Davis, rare books librarian, University of California, Los Angeles; Robert J. Bertholf, curator, The Poetry/Rare Books Collection, State University of New York at Buffalo; Barbara A. Filipac, Manuscripts Division, Brown University Library; Timothy D. Murray, curator of manuscripts, Washington University in St. Louis; Anthony S. Bliss, rare book librarian, Bancroft Library, University of California, Berkeley; Robert A. Hull, Manuscripts Department, University of Virginia Library; Saundra Taylor, curator of manuscripts, Indiana University; J. Fraser Cocks, curator, Special Collections, Miller Library, Colby College; Kevin F. McKelvey, Special Collections, Mugar Library, Boston University; George Butterick, curator, Literary Archives, University of Connecticut; Alexandra Mason, Department of Special Collections, Kenneth Spencer Research Library, University of Kansas. Special thanks are due to the staff of the Fales Library of New York University; the staff of the Harry Ransom Humanities Research Center, University of Texas at Austin; and particularly to Kenneth A. Lohf, director of manuscripts and rare books, Bernard Crystal, assistant director, and their staff at the Special Collections Division, Butler Library, Columbia University.

I owe an enormous debt to my friend Victor Bockris for his limitless hospitality; to Bobbie Bristol for her editorial suggestions and friendship; to Felix Dennis for being a stalwart friend; to Ginsberg's bibliographer, Bill Morgan, for his archive research and his many useful suggestions; to Peter Orlovsky for his helpful assistance over the years; to Ginsberg's secretary, Bob Rosenthal, for hours of valuable research and conversation; to my friend and agent, Andrew Wylie, for first suggesting the book and then seeing it through; to my wonderful companion, Rosemary Bailey, whose expert editorial eye read every draft, for her unstinting support throughout; to Winston J. Dong, Jr., to Marge Horvitz, copy editor, and to my editors at Simon and Schuster, Fred Hills and Burton Beals.

CHAPTER NOTES

ABBREVIATIONS

AG: Allen Ginsberg
BM: Barry Miles
EB: Eugene Brooks
GC: Gregory Corso
HH: Herbert Huncke
JK: Jack Kerouac
LC: Lucien Carr

LF: Lawrence Ferlinghetti
LG: Louis Ginsberg
LHBG: Literary History of the
   Beat Generation
PO: Peter Orlovsky
WCW: William Carlos Williams
WSB: William S. Burroughs

NOTE: Bibliographic details are given only if the book cited does not appear in the Bibliography.

ONE: CHILDHOOD, PATERSON

The opening quote is from an unpublished MS.

AG describes the writing of "Kaddish" in "How Kaddish Happened," Allen and Tallman, *The Poetics of the New American Poetry*.

My interviews with AG, Jan. 28, 1971, and Aug. 15, 1983, were principally about his family and childhood; also my interviews with AG's brother, Eugene Brooks, Feb. 11, 1986, and with his paternal aunt, Hannah Litzky, Jan. 29, 1986. The Brooks and Litzky interviews provided material for the whole chapter. Other material comes from AG to BM, Feb. 20, 1987, and conversations with AG, 1983–88.

I used the original MS of "Kaddish" in the Fales Library, New York University, the 1964 "Kaddish" film script by AG and Robert Frank, and

AG's dramatization of "Kaddish" for the Chelsea Theater Center, Brooklyn, in Feb. 1972, as well as the published version.

The description of the CP meeting is from AG, "America" (*Collected Poems 1947–1980*).

His family background was established from notes and tape recordings of conversations between AG and his maternal aunt Edie Leegant. Also Edie Leegant to AG, Mar. 26, 1986; Gene Berlin to AG, Feb. 28, 1987. AG's recorded conversation with Louis Ginsberg, Jan. 12, 1976 [76D1/035], is about LG's youth, as was my interview with LG, June 25, 1970.

Details of Russia came from Jesse D. Clarkson, *A History of Russia* (New York: Random House, 1969); Louis Greenberg, *The Jews in Russia: The Struggle for Emancipation*, 2 vols. (New Haven: Yale University Press, 1944, 1951); David Philipson, *Old European Jewries* (Philadelphia: Jewish Publication Society of America, 1894); Israel Friedlander, *The Jews of Russia and Poland* (New York: G. P. Putnam, 1915); Sidney Alexander, *Marc Chagall* (London: Cassell, 1979); Robert Brym, *The Jewish Intelligentsia and Russian Marxism* (London: Macmillan, 1978); Basil Dmytryshyn, *A History of Russia* (Englewood Cliffs, N.J.: Prentice-Hall, 1977); *Glavnoye Upravleniye Geodezii i Kartografii Atlas Belorusskoi Sovetskoi Sotzialisticheskoi Respubliki* (Moscow, 1958).

The Kay Boyle reference is in Robert McAlmon and Kay Boyle, *Being Geniuses Together: 1920–1930* (San Francisco: North Point Press, 1984), p. 18. The Untermeyer and Wheelock quotes are from Louis Ginsberg, *The Everlasting Minute* (New York: Liveright, 1937). See also Alfred Kreymborg, *Troubadour: An Autobiography* (New York: Liveright, 1925).

AG's relationship with his parents comes from AG, unpublished journals and MSS as well as Eugene Brooks, "Allen Ginsberg: Parents' Influence on Poetry and Politics" (unpublished, n.d.); Elenore Lester, "Allen Ginsberg Remembers Mama," *New York Times*, Feb. 6, 1972. AG's sexual relationship with LG dealt with in my interviews with AG, Aug. 15, 1983, Jan. 5, 1988. Other material comes from my conversations with LG in 1967, 1970 onward.

The episode with Morton is from AG, unpublished journals.

AG's discovery of Whitman is described in "The School Day I Remember Most," *Instructor* magazine, May 1979.

Taking Naomi to Lakewood is from "Kaddish," poem and film script versions, plus my interview with AG, Aug. 15, 1983.

Paul Roth to AG, May 9, 1943; AG, *Indian Journals*, pp. 127, 173–4.

TWO: A COLUMBIA EDUCATION
THE ORIGINS OF THE BEAT GENERATION

My interview with AG, June 6, 1985, specifically covered his first spell at Columbia. This was augmented by my conversation with AG, Feb. 21, 1984. AG: The LHBG lectures (delivered at Naropa Institute) deal with this period in depth. The dialogue with Carr comes from AG, unpublished prose, c. 1944 (a fictional re-creation of their meeting).

The description of Trilling is taken from my interviews with AG. Mark

Krupnick, *Lionel Trilling and the Fate of Cultural Criticism* (Evanston, Ill.: Northwestern University Press, 1986), and my conversation with AG, Nov. 1983. Van Doren: My interviews with AG; also AG, LHBG lectures. George Hendrick, ed., *The Selected Letters of Mark Van Doren* (Baton Rouge: Louisiana State University Press, 1987). Weaver: My interviews with AG. AG describes all three professors in the LHBG lectures.

AG's term papers, reading lists, and journals were consulted at the Butler Library, Columbia University.

Lucien Carr: My interview with LC, Mar. 9, 1986; unpublished transcription of a conversation among LC, Barry Gifford, Lawrence Lee, and James Grauerholz. JK, *Vanity of Duluoz*. AG, LHBG lectures.

Kammerer: My interview with AG. AG, LHBG lectures. Kammerer's room from unpublished prose by AG and AG to JK, [Sept.] 1944.

AG's meeting with WSB: The Shakespeare quote is from *Troilus and Cressida*, I, 1 (Troilus speaking). Howard Brookner's film *William Burroughs, Current Biography* 32, no. 10 (Nov. 1971). WSB, interview, *Paris Review* 35 (Fall 1965). My conversations with WSB, London 1973–74. AG, LHBG lectures. JK, *Vanity of Duluoz*.

Friendship with LC: My interview with AG; my interview with LC, Mar. 9, 1986, used throughout this chapter.

West End: AG, "West End Bar," unpublished prose, c. 1944. JK, *Visions of Cody; Vanity of Duluoz*.

AG's meeting with JK: JK, *Vanity of Duluoz; Visions of Cody*. JK, interview, *Paris Review* 43 (Summer 1968). AG to EB, Dec. 1943. John Tytell interview with WSB in *The Beat Book*. Aaron Latham interview with AG, Aug. 31, 1972, unpublished. AG, LHBG lectures, deal with meeting in great detail.

Leaving Theological Seminary: My conversation with AG, Mar. 1984, at the location. Aaron Latham interview with AG, Aug. 31, 1972, unpublished. AG, LHBG lectures.

Visit to WSB: AG, "Burroughs Memorabilia," unpublished prose. My interview. AG, LHBG lectures. AG to WSB, telephone, Oct. 4, 1988.

Death of Kammerer: LC to AG, Sept. 21, 1944. LC to AG, Sept. 30, 1944. LC to AG, Aug. 13, 1944. Celine Young to JK, Oct. 1, 1944. Celine Young to AG, Sept. 15, 1944. Celine Young to JK, Oct. 8, 1944. Three undated letters: Celine Young to AG [1944]; JK to AG, [Aug.?] 1944; AG to EB, Oct. 1944. AG, LHBG lectures. AG to LG [late 1944–early 1945]. AG to JK, Aug. 1944. AG to JK [Sept. 1944]. AG to EB, Sept. 1944. AG, unpublished prose. AG, unpublished journals. JK, *The Town and the City; Vanity of Duluoz*.

Columbia: N. M. McKnight to AG, Nov. 13, 1944. AG, "The Village Jade," unpublished prose [1944]. AG, "Work in Progress," unpublished prose [1944]. AG, journals and notebooks for the period.

AG as poet: Edward C. Norton, "Louis Ginsberg & Son, Poets," *Ave Maria* (Catholic Weekly; Notre Dame, Ind.), Sept. 6, 1969.

WSB "dangerous": LG to AG [Jan. 1945].

Columbia suspension: N. M. McKnight to LG, Jan. 2, 1945; Mar. 17, 1945; Mar. 30, 1945. N. M. McKnight to AG, Mar. 17, 1945. Louis-Ferdinand Céline, *Journey to the End of the Night* (Paris, 1932). AG, LHBG lectures. AG interview with Paul Geneson, 1974.

THREE: A STREET EDUCATION

My interview with AG, June 6, 1985, covers this period.

Bar lists are among Ginsberg's papers at Columbia.

WSB and HH: HH, *The Evening Sky Turned Crimson*. WSB, *Junky*. JK, *Vanity of Duluoz; The Town and the City*. AG, LHBG lectures. John Tytell interview with WSB in *The Beat Book*.

115th St.: WSB, in Howard Brookner film *William Burroughs*. AG, LHBG lectures. My conversation with AG, Feb. 21, 1984. JK to AG, Nov. 13, 1945. EB to AG, Apr. 29, 1945. My interview with AG, June 6, 1985. Feldman and Mitchell interview with AG, *Red Hand 3* (Jan. 20, 1982).

AG's sex life is from my interviews of Mar. 28, 1985, Jan. 5, 1988.

Maritime service: LG to AG, Aug. 8, 1945; Oct. 29, 1945. AG to EB, Sept. 3, 1945. AG to JK [1945]. AG to JK, Aug. 12, 1945; Aug. 22, 1945; Sept. 4, 1945; [Sept. 1945]. AG to Lionel Trilling, Aug. 27, 1945. JK to AG, Aug. 17, 1945; Aug. 23, 1945; Sept. 6, 1945. Aaron Latham interview with AG, Aug. 31, 1972, unpublished. WSB to JK, July 24, 1945. WSB to AG, July 24, 1945. Celine Young to AG, Aug. 3, 1945. Four undated letters from Celine Young to AG [1945]. Background: Aaron Bates, "Eversoft at the Everard," *The Best of Gay*, Jan. 24, 1972. AG, LHBG lectures.

WSB with Joan: Howard Brookner film *William Burroughs*. JK, *Vanity of Duluoz; The Town and the City; Visions of Cody*.

Maritime service: U.S. Coast Guard to AG, May 23, 1951.

Night of the Wolfeans: My interview with AG. AG, *Indian Journals*, p. 175. AG, unpublished journals. AG, LHBG lectures. Howard Brookner film *William Burroughs*. JK, *Vanity of Duluoz*, AG, unpublished journals. My interview with AG.

The Herbert Huncke story is told in the special Huncke issue of *The Unspeakable Visions of the Individual* 3, nos. 1–2 (1973). See also background in HH: *The Evening Sky Turned Crimson; Huncke's Journal; Guilty of Everything*.

Naomi in N.Y.C.: "Kaddish." Three undated letters from Naomi to AG. My interviews with AG. AG, unpublished journals. "Kaddish" film script, 1964. My interview with Eugene Brooks, Feb. 11, 1986.

AG return to Columbia: My interview with AG, Columbia. N. M. McKnight to AG, July 10, 1946. Hans Wassing, M.D., to N. M. McKnight, July 31, 1946.

Joan's hearing: My interview with AG. My conversation with AG, Feb. 21, 1984. Her use of amphetamine: HH interview, *Newave* 1, no. 5 (April 1981).

WSB in Texas: WSB to AG, Sept. 1, 1946; [late Sept. 1946]; Oct. 10, 1946. HH to Joan Vollmer, Oct. 8, 1946. HH to AG, Sept. 23, 1946. My conversation with AG, Feb. 21, 1984. JK, *Vanity of Duluoz*. WSB, *Junky*. Three letters, AG to JK [Fall 1946].

First marijuana: AG narration for film *Fried Shoes, Cooked Diamonds*, Feb. 1979. My interview with AG.

Naomi: "Kaddish." My interview with EB, Feb. 11, 1986. AG, unpublished journals.

AG and Neal Cassady: NC, *The First Third*. AG, "Many Loves," JK, *The Town and the City*; *Vanity of Duluoz*; *On the Road*. John C. Holmes, *Go*. AG, LHBG lectures. AG, unpublished journals and *Journals*. The complete correspondence between Neal Cassady and AG is published in *As Ever*; however, I consulted the originals at the University of Texas, Austin, since there are minor errors of transcription in the published versions. LG to AG, July 23, 1948; Oct. 6, 1948. Neal as "sexual sadist," Carolyn Cassady interview with Gina Berriault, *Rolling Stone*, Oct. 12, 1972.

Denver: AG, *Journals*. LG to AG, July 1947; Aug. 13, 1947; Aug. 18, 1947; Sept. 15, 1947. EB to AG, Sept. 4, 1947. Becker and Drew, interview with AG, Sunday Denver *Post*, Aug. 12, 1979.

Texas visit: HH to AG, Mar. 26, 1947. AG to LG, Sept. 3, 1947; Sept. 12, 1947. AG, LHBG lectures. AG to JK [Fall 1947]. AG to HH, Oct. 1947 (from a notebook draft). WSB to AG, Feb. 19, 1947; [1947]; July 10, 1947. JK to WSB, July 14, 1947. AG, "The Green Automobile." AG, "The Monster of Dakar," unpublished story. The bed: HH, *The Evening Sky Turned Crimson*. JK, *Visions of Cody*.

Naomi: "Kaddish," poem and film script. My interview with AG.

AG to Wilhelm Reich, Mar. 11, 1947.

Cézanne: AG interview, *Paris Review* 37 (Spring 1966). Paul Cézanne to Émile Bernard, Apr. 15, 1904. Quoted in Émile Bernard, *Souvenirs sur Paul Cézanne* (Paris: Chez Michel, 1939). AG, term paper on Cézanne in Columbia deposit.

N.Y.C. 1948–49: WSB to AG, Feb. 20, 1948; Mar. 3, 1948. JK to AG [Apr. 1948]; May 18, 1948. WSB to AG, June 5, 1948. JK to AG, May 23, 1949.

The Blake vision is described in great detail in Tom Clark's interview with AG, *Paris Review* 37 (Spring 1966); also in Paul Portugés, *The Visionary Poetics of Allen Ginsberg*. AG, *Journals*.

The episode of Huncke stealing Durgin's books was given fictional treatment in Holmes's *Go*, where Durgin appears as Verger, Huncke is Ancke, and Ginsberg is Stofsky. WSB to AG, Oct. 14, 1948. HH to AG [Feb. 1948?]. The original MS of "Howl" gives long list of Durgin's books. Description of 121st St.: Herbert Gold, "My Last Two Thousand Years," *The Unspeakable Visions of the Individual* 3, nos. 1–2 (1973).

Alan Ansen: Dorothy J. Franan, *Auden in Love* (New York: Simon & Schuster, 1984).

The story of Huncke, Little Jack, and Vickie Russell is taken from AG's "The Fall," a 147-page unpublished account of the entire period written 1949 for his lawyer after his arrest. John C. Holmes, *Nothing More to Declare; Go*. AG, LHBG lectures. Rick Fields, interview with AG, *Open Secret* (Boulder: Naropa, 1974). Larry Sloman, interview with AG, *High Times* 86 (1982). AG, *Journals* and unpublished journals.

WSB in New Orleans: WSB to AG, Oct. 14, 1948; Nov. 4, 1948; Nov. 30, 1948. WSB to JK, Nov. 30, 1948. WSB to AG, Dec. 2, 1948. NC, *As*

Ever. WSB to AG, Jan. 10, 1949; Jan. 16, 1949; Jan. 17, 1949; Jan. 30, 1949. WSB to JK, Mar. 15, 1949. WSB to AG, Mar. 16, 1949; Mar. 26, 1949. WSB to JK, May 27, 1949. WSB to AG, Apr. 16, 1949. JK: *On the Road*. WSB to JK, June 24, 1949.

Other background: JK, "The Origins of the Beat Generation," *Playboy*, June 1959. JK to AG, Sept. 18, 1948; Dec. 15, 1948.

Arrest: N.Y. *Daily Mirror*, Apr. 23, 1949. N.Y. *Herald Tribune*, Apr. 23, 1949. N.Y. *World-Telegram*, Apr. 23, 1949. *New York Times*, Apr. 23, 1949. N.Y. *Daily News*, Apr. 23, 1949. Long account by AG in Jane Kramer, *Allen Ginsberg in America*.

FOUR: THE SUBTERRANEANS

Psychiatric Institute: A 1984 study conducted by UCLA at Oxford University between 1982 and 1983 concluded that artists, writers, and poets are 35 times more likely to seek treatment for serious mood disorders than the average person, and of these three groups, poets suffered the severest forms of disturbance. The poets in the study were limited only to those who had received the Queen's Gold Medal for poetry, a very conservative group compared to the poets of Ginsberg's milieu, yet even of these, nearly 20 percent had suffered at least one manic-depressive episode serious enough to require hospitalization, and more than 50 percent had received some form of medical treatment for mania or depression. Clearly Ginsberg was in a dangerous profession. Of American poets, one thinks of Lowell, Roethke, Berryman, Jarrell, and Plath. Ginsberg's IQ test at the P.I. showed him to be near genius level.

P.I.: JK to AG, June 10, 1949; July 5, 1949; July [26], 1949. John C. Holmes to AG, June 14, 1949; July 6, 1949. WSB to JK, Sept. 26, 1949. WSB to AG, Oct. 13, 1949. WSB to JK, Nov. 2, 1949. WSB to AG, Nov. 8, 1949. WSB to AG, Dec. 24, 1949. AG to JK, June 15, 1949; June 17, 1949. JK to AG, Jan. 13, 1950. WSB to JK, Jan. 1, 1950. JK to AG, Jan. 13, 1950. WSB to JK, Jan. 22, 1950; Jan. 28, 1950. JK to AG, Feb. 1950. WSB to JK, Mar. 1950. WSB to AG, May 1, 1950. AG, LHBG lectures. AG to PO, Apr. 1, 1958. AG, unpublished journals. My interview with AG, June 6, 1986, covered the period of this chapter. AG's letters to NC in *As Ever* also cover the period. Carl Solomon, *Mishaps Perhaps*. Interview with Carl Solomon in *The Beat Book*. AG, "The Fall," MS.

William Carlos Williams reprinted most of the letter in Part Four of his poem "Paterson." See also Paul Mariani, *William Carlos Williams: A New World Naked* (New York: McGraw-Hill, 1981), pp. 604, 621.

San Remo: Jay Landesman, *Rebel Without Applause*. John Gruen, *The Party's Over Now*. Fred McDarrah, *Kerouac & Friends*. Judith Malina, *Diaries of Judith Malina: 1947–1957*. AG, LHBG lectures. AG to JK, [Mar.] 1950. WSB to AG, May 1, 1950. JK, *The Subterraneans*. Alan Ansen to AG, June 5, 1950; June 17, 1950. JK to AG, June 1950; Oct. 1950.

Helen Parker: AG, LHBG lectures. My interview with AG. WSB to JK, Sept. 18, 1950. Helen Parker to AG, July 7, 1950, plus five undated letters from same period. WSB to AG [summer 1950]. John C. Holmes to AG, Aug. 9, 1950.

Ribbon factory: AG, "How Come He Got Canned at the Ribbon Factory."

Bill Cannastra: Alan Harrington, *The Secret Swinger* (New York: Knopf, 1966). Cannastra appears as Bill Genovese. In John C. Holmes, *Get Home Free* and *Go*, he appears as Bill Agatson. In JK, *Visions of Cody*, he appears as Finistra. AG, LHBG lectures. Cannastra's death: N.Y. *Herald Tribune*, Oct. 13, 1950. N.Y. *Daily News*, Oct. 13, 1950. N.Y. *Daily Mirror*, Oct. 13, 1950.

GC: *The Riverside Interviews 3: Gregory Corso* (London: Binnacle Press, 1982) gives GC's family history. AG, LHBG lectures. Dom Moraes, *My Son's Father* (New York: Macmillan, 1968), p. 202. My interview with AG. Interview in *The Beat Book*.

WSB in Mexico: WSB to JK, Sept. 18, 1950; Dec. 26, 1950. AG to JK, May 15, 1952.

Mexican trip: My interview with LC, Mar. 9, 1986. Howard Brookner's film *William Burroughs*. My interview with AG, Mar. 28, 1985.

Joan's death: N.Y. *Daily News*, Sept. 8, 1951. *New York Times*, Sept. 8, 1951. N.Y. *World-Telegram & Sun*, Sept. 7, 1951; Sept. 11, 1951. *Journal-American*, Sept. 9, 1951. WSB to AG, Nov. 5, 1951. Howard Brookner's film *William Burroughs*. WSB, *Queer*.

FIVE: ON THE ROAD TO CALIFORNIA

My interview with AG, Mar. 28, 1985, covers this period. AG was involved in a very heavy correspondence with Neal Cassady for most of the period. See *As Ever*. WSB, *Letters to Allen Ginsberg: 1953–1957*, also covers much of this period.

West 15th St.: AG, unpublished journals and poems. WSB to AG, Jan. 1, 1951; Jan. 11, 1951. WSB to LC, Mar. 5, 1951. JK to AG [Mar. 1951]. WSB to JK, Apr. 24, 1951. AG to JK [1951]. WSB to AG, May 5, 1951. JK to AG, July 1951. WSB to AG, Nov. 1951; Dec. 20, 1951. AG, LHBG lectures. AG to JK, Feb. 15, 1952.

AG writes about Dusty Moreland in his correspondence with Neal Cassady (*As Ever*). Also, GC, *The Riverside Interviews 3: Gregory Corso*. AG, unpublished journals. AG: LHBG lectures. My interview with LC.

Death of Phil ("The Sailor") White: AG to NC, Feb. 15, 1952. WSB to AG, Jan. 19, 1952.

Peyote: AG, *Journals*. AG, LHBG lectures.

Jan Kerouac: Jan Kerouac, *Baby Driver*.

Publication of *Go*: MS of Holmes's *Nothing More to Declare* in Ginsberg deposit at Columbia.

WSB in Mexico re *Junky*: WSB to JK, Mar. 26, 1952; [1952]. JK, *On the Road*. WSB to AG, Feb. 20, 1952. WSB to JK, Apr. 3, 1952. WSB to AG, Mar. 20, 1952; Apr. 5, 1952; Apr. 9, 1952; Apr. 14, 1952; Apr. 26, 1952; May 15, 1952; June 4, 1952. AG to WSB, June 12, 1952. WSB to AG, June 15, 1952; June 23, 1952; June 27, 1952; July 1, 1952; July 6, 1952; July 10, 1952; July 13, 1952; Aug. 20, 1952; Oct. 6, 1952, Nov. 1952; Nov. 5, 1952; Nov. 6, 1952; Dec. 23, 1952; Dec. 24, 1952; Jan. 10, 1953; Jan. 19, 1953. WSB goes to South America in search of yage: WSB to AG,

Jan. 25, 1953; Mar. 1, 1953; Apr. 12, 1953; Apr. 22, 1953; Apr. 30, 1953; May 4, 1953; May 5, 1953; May 12, 1953; May 15, 1953; May 23, 1953; May 30, 1953; June 6, 1953; June 8, 1953; June 18, 1953; July 8, 1953; July 21, 1953; Aug. 17, 1953.

AG's new "sketching" style: Transcript of AG talk at Warwick University, Nov. 6, 1979. AG to JK and NC, Feb. 1952. AG to JK, Mar. 8, 1952. JK to AG, Mar. 12, 1952; Mar. 15, 1952. AG to JK and NC: Feb. 1952. Aaron Latham interview with AG, Aug. 31, 1972, unpublished. AG to JK, May 15, 1952. JK to AG, Apr. 8, 1952; May 18, 1952. WSB to JK, Apr. 8, 1952. AG to Ezra Pound, May 30, 1952.

WCW: AG, *Journals* and unpublished journals. WCW to AG, Feb. 27, 1952. AG to JK, Apr. 1952. AG, *Journals*, Mar. 12, 1952. AG to WCW, Mar. 9, 1952. WCW to AG, May 24, 1952. AG to WCW, June 6, 1952; Aug. 10, 1952. AG interview in *Monmouth Letters*, Spring 1961. Linda Wagner, ed., *Interviews with William Carlos Williams* (New York: New Directions, 1976).

JK in Mexico City: AG, LHBG lectures. AG to JK, May 15, 1952. JK to AG, May 10, 1952; May 17, 1952; May 18, 1952. AG to JK and WSB, June 12, 1952. JK to AG, June 20, 1952; July 28, 1952 (from North Carolina).

AG and Dusty Moreland: AG's letters to NC (*As Ever*). JK to Dusty Moreland [1952]. JK to AG, 1951.

JK's attack on his friends: Oct. 8, 1952. JK to AG, Nov. 8, 1952; Dec. 29, 1952. JK's objection to name on *Junkie*: JK to AG, Feb. 21, 1953. AG to JK, Feb. 24, 1953. Friends again: JK to AG, May 7, 1953. AG to JK, May 1953; July 13, 1953.

Naomi: "Kaddish." Naomi to AG, Jan. 5, 1953. AG, unpublished journal, Jan. 18, 1953. Naomi to EB [1955].

Three Graces: AG, Annotated edition of *Howl*. My interview with AG. Elise Cowen: Joyce Johnson, *Minor Characters*.

Ending to *Dr. Sax*: AG, LHBG lectures. JK to AG, May 7, 1953.

WSB in N.Y.C.: My interview with AG. AG, LHBG lectures. AG, unpublished journal, transcribes long conversations. Terry Wilson and Brion Gysin, *Here to Go: Planet R-101*. WSB to JK, Dec. 14, 1952. Howard Brookner's film *William Burroughs*.

Orgone accumulator: A device designed by Wilhelm Reich to gather "orgone energy," the natural life force in the atmosphere, and concentrate it in a box. By sitting in the box, one was supposed to become energized. See Wilhelm Reich, *The Orgone Energy Accumulator: Its Scientific and Medical Uses* (Maine: Wilhelm Reich Institute, 1951).

Mexico trip: AG, *Journals* and unpublished journals. AG to JK, NC, and Carolyn Cassady, Jan. 9, 1953. Karena Shields, *The Changing Wind* (London: John Murray, 1960). The spelling "Xibalba" is taken from Shields. Ginsberg misspells it in his poem "Siesta in Xbalba." AG to LC, Jan. 18, 1954; Feb. 18, 1954; Mar. 29, 1954 [cable]; Mar. 31, 1954; Apr. 1, 1954. WSB to JK, Apr. 22, 1954. AG to LC, May 21, 1954. WSB to JK, May 24, 1954. AG to JK, June 18, 1954.

AG at the Cassady household: AG, unpublished journals. AG, LHBG lectures. Carolyn Cassady, *Heart Beat*. William Plummer, *Holy Goof*. JK to Carolyn Cassady, May 17, 1954. JK to AG [May 1954]; July 30, 1954. AG to EB, Aug. 14, 1954. JK to AG, Aug. 23, 1954. Several undated letters from JK to AG.

Sheila Williams: AG to JK, Sept. 7, 1954; Nov. 26, 1954. NC to AG, Nov. 27, 1954. AG to JK, Nov. 9, 1954. AG, unpublished journals.

Kenneth Rexroth: Ann Charters, *The Beats: Literary Bohemians in Postwar America*, Part 2. My conversations with Rexroth, 1966.

Robert Duncan: Ekbert Fass, *Young Robert Duncan: Portrait of the Poet as Homosexual in Society* (Santa Barbara: Black Sparrow, 1983).

Life with Sheila: AG to JK, Sept. 7, 1954; [Oct. 1954]; Oct. 9, 1954; Nov. 26, 1954; Dec. 29, 1954.

Problems with WSB: WSB to JK, Apr. 22, 1954; May 4, 1954; May 24, 1954; July 17, 1954; [July? 1954]; Sept. 3, 1954. JK to AG, Oct. 26, 1954; Dec. 7, 1954. WSB to JK, Dec. 7, 1954. JK to AG, Dec. 7, 1954.

Peter Orlovsky: Ann Charters, *The Beats: Literary Bohemians in Postwar America*, Part 2. My conversations with PO, particularly in Cherry Valley, 1970–71. PO interview, *Gay Sunshine*. AG interview, *Gay Sunshine*. AG, unpublished journals.

City Lights Books: My interview with LF, Mar. 20, 21, 1986. My interview with Shigeyoshi Murao, Mar. 22, 1986.

LF: Neeli Cherkovski, *Ferlinghetti: A Biography*. Larry Smith, *Lawrence Ferlinghetti: Poet at Large*.

Montgomery St.: AG, unpublished journals. Photographs of interior in annotated *Howl*. "Howl" text from first-draft MS. AG, LHBG lectures. WSB to AG, Jan. 6, 1955. AG to JK, [Jan.] 1955. WSB to AG, Jan. 9, 1955. AG to JK, Jan. 12, 1955; Jan. 14, 1955. WSB to AG, Jan. 15, 1955. JK to AG, Jan. 18–20, 1955; Feb. 10, 1955. AG to JK, Feb. 11, 1955. WSB to JK, Feb. 12, 1955. JK to AG, Mar. 4, 1955. AG to JK, Mar. 13, 1955; Apr. 22, 1955; Apr. 25, 1955; May 10, 1955. JK to WSB [May 1955]. JK to AG, May 11, 1955. AG to JK, May 27, 1955. JK to AG, May 27, 1955; June 1, 1955. AG to JK, June 1, 1955; June 5, 1955. WSB to JK, June 9, 1955. JK to AG, June 29, 1955. AG to JK [July 1955]; July 5, 1955. JK to AG, July 14, 1955. AG to LG, July 28, 1955. Bob LaVigne to AG, Aug. 6, 1955. JK to AG, Aug. 7, 1955.

SIX: "HOWL" AND THE SAN FRANCISCO RENAISSANCE

My interview with AG, Mar. 28, 1985, covers this period. AG, LHBG lectures. AG, unpublished journals.

AG has given a number of full descriptions of writing "Howl," the most detailed being in the annotated *Howl* and the liner notes to the album, reprinted in Thomas Parkinson, ed., *Casebook on the Beat*. See also AG interview, *Paris Review* 37 (Spring 1966). The quotes are from the first draft of the MS and differ from the final version. JK to AG, Aug. 19, 1955. AG to JK, Aug. 25, 1955; Aug. 30, 1955.

Montgomery St.: Robert LaVigne to AG, Aug. 16, 1955. AG to EB, Aug. 16, 1955. AG to JK [Aug. 1955].

Berkeley Cottage: Robert LaVigne to AG, Sept. 6, 1955. WSB to AG,

Sept. 21, 1955. Robert LaVigne to AG, Sept. 21, 1955. AG to Robert LaVigne, Sept. 26, 1955. WSB to AG [Oct. 1955]. LG to AG, Dec. 12, 1955. AG to EB, Dec. 27, 1955. AG to PO, June 21, 1958. AG to LC, Jan. 16, 1956. AG to LG, Apr. 26, 1956; [May 1956]. AG to EB, May 18, 1956.

An anthology of articles about the Six Gallery reading is in the annotated *Howl*. See also Michael McClure, *Scratching the Beat Surface*. Gary Snyder to AG, Feb. 24, 1956.

Gary Snyder: JK, *The Dharma Bums*. David Kherdian, *Six San Francisco Poets*; *A Biographical Sketch and Descriptive Checklist of Gary Snyder*. Bert Almon, *Gary Snyder*. Katherine McNeil, *Gary Snyder: A Bibliography*. Gary Snyder, *The Real Work: Interviews and Talks, 1964–1979*.

Philip Whalen: JK, *The Dharma Bums*. David Kherdian, *Six San Francisco Poets*. Ann Charters, *The Beats: Literary Bohemians in Postwar America*, Part 2.

"Howl," Part III: Christopher Smart, *Selected Poems* (Manchester: Carncanet, 1979). Henry Allen, "The Poet's Poet: Stanley Kunitz at the Library of Congress," Washington *Post*, *Potomac* magazine. Jan. 5, 1975.

"Yabyum": JK, *The Dharma Bums*. Diane di Prima, *Memoirs of a Beatnik*.

Nudity: My interview with Philip Whalen, Mar. 16, 1986. AG, interviewed by Al Aronowitz, N.Y. *Post*, 12-part series, "The Beat Generation," March 9–22, 1959.

Natalie's death: AG poem, unpublished.

San Francisco renaissance. My interview with Philip Whalen, Mar. 16, 1986, covered this period, as did my interviews with Michael McClure, Mar. 19, 1986, and with Lawrence Ferlinghetti, Mar. 20–21, 1986. LG to AG, Feb. 29, 1956. AG to EB, May 26, 1956. LG to AG, Aug. 4, 1956; Aug. 13, 1956. GC to AG, Aug. 23, 1956. LG to AG, Sept. 11, 1956. AG to EB, Sept. 19, 1956. Aaron Latham interview with AG, Aug. 31, 1972, unpublished.

Naomi's death: AG, unpublished MSS. EB to AG, June 9, 1956 (telegram); June 11, 1956. LG to AG, June 20, 1956. AG to Rebecca Ginsberg (Buba), Aug. 11, 1956.

The Arctic Circle: AG, unpublished journals. AG to EB, July 10, 1956. AG to Hannah Litzky, Aug. 11, 1956. AG to JK, Aug. 12, 1956. AG to PO, Mar. 16, 1956; [1956]. My interview with LF, Mar. 20–21, 1986.

Publication of "Howl": AG to Richard Eberhart, May 18, 1956.

JK in Mexico: AG to JK, Mar. 10, 1956. JK to AG, Sept. 26, 1956. AG to JK, Oct. 10, 1956.

WSB in Tangier: WSB to AG, Mar. 9, 1956. Alan Ansen to AG, June 18, 1956; Aug. 24, 1956. WSB to AG, Sept. 16, 1956. JK to AG, Sept. 26, 1956. WSB to AG, Oct. 13, 1956; Oct. 29, 1956. Alan Ansen, "William Burroughs: A Personal View," *Review of Contemporary Fiction* 4, no. 1 (Spring 1984). Alan Ansen, *William Burroughs* (Sudbury: Water Row, 1986).

Los Angeles visit: WSB to AG, Dec. 20, 1956. AG to Anaïs Nin [1956]. Lawrence Lipton, *The Holy Barbarians*. Anaïs Nin, *The Journals of Anaïs Nin*, vol. 6 (London: Peter Owen, 1977). AG to LG, Oct. 31, 1956.

Mexico: JK, *Desolation Angels*. AG to JK, Jan. 4, 1957.

N.Y.C.: Diane di Prima described the orgy with JK and AG in *Memoirs of a Beatnik*. AG on orgies: AG narration for film *Skeletons Rolling on the Noble Road*, Boulder, Feb. 1979. Robert LaVigne to AG: Jan. 25, 1957; Mar. 31, 1957. Joyce Johnson, *Minor Characters*. Harvey Breit, "En Garde," *New York Times*, Jan. 20, 1957. Howard Klausner, "Paterson Man's Poems Draw Attention of Major Critics," Paterson *Herald-News*, Feb. 25, 1957. AG to Robert LaVigne, Jan. 15, 1957. AG to Charles Olson, Feb. 18, 1956. AG to LF, two undated letters [Jan.–Feb. 1957]; Jan. 15, 1957; Mar. 3, 1957.

Dali: AG, unpublished journals.

WCW: AG, unpublished journals. Paul Mariani, *William Carlos Williams: A New World Naked* (New York: McGraw-Hill, 1981).

SEVEN: "THE CLASSIC STATIONS OF THE EARTH"

My interview with AG, Mar. 28, 1985, covers this period.

WSB in Tangier: Paul Bowles, "Burroughs in Tangier," *Big Table* 2 (Summer 1959). WSB to AG, Aug. 18, 1954; Sept. 16, 1956. WSB, interview in *The Beat Diary*. Bowles on WSB, Harold Norse interview, *Gay Sunshine*. WSB to AG, Feb. 14, 1957. JK to AG, Jan. 21, 1958.

JK in Tangier: JK, *Desolation Angels*. JK interview, *Paris Review* 43 (Summer 1968). JK to Alan Ansen, Aug. 20, 1957.

AG and PO in Tangier: AG, unpublished journals. JK, *Desolation Angels*. PO to Robert LaVigne, May 3, 1957. PO to Ron Lowenstein, May 3, 1957. PO to Robert LaVigne, May 29, 1957. PO to JK, May 31, 1957. Millicent Dillon, *A Little Original Sin: The Life and Work of Jane Bowles* (New York: Holt, Rinehart & Winston, 1981), p. 347. Millicent Dillon, ed., *Out in the World: Selected Letters of Jane Bowles* (Santa Barbara: Black Sparrow, 1985). AG to LF, Apr. 3, 1957. AG to LC, Apr. 4, 1957. AG to NC, Apr. 24, 1957. WCW to AG, Apr. 29, 1957. AG to LF, May 10, 1957. AG to JK, May 31, 1957. AG to LC [late May 1957]. AG to LF, May 31, 1957. JK to AG and WSB [June 1957]. JK to AG, June 7, 1957. AG to GC, June 8, 1957. AG to LG, June 1957. AG to WCW, Aug. 22, 1957. AG, unpublished journals.

AG and PO in Spain: PO to Robert LaVigne, June 21, 1957. AG to EB, June 20, 1957. PO to AG, June 26, 1958. AG, unpublished journals.

AG and PO in Venice: My conversation with AG and Alan Ansen, 1986. AG to LG, June 26, 1957. PO to AG, Feb. 10, 1958. AG to LG, July 9, 1957. AG to LF, July 10, 1957. AG to EB, July 15, 1957. PO to Robert LaVigne, July 25, 1957. AG to EB, Aug. 10, 1957. AG to LG, Aug. 10, 1957. AG to JK, Aug. 13, 1957. JK to Alan Ansen, Aug. 20, 1957. AG to LF, Aug. 21, 1957. LG to AG, Aug. 26, 1957. AG to LF, Sept. 3, 1957. PO to Henry Schlachler, Sept. 4, 1957. AG to LG, Sept. 4, 1957. AG to EB, Sept. 6, 1957. WSB to AG, Sept. 6, 1957; Sept. 11, 1957. AG to LG, Sept. 1957. WSB to AG, Sept. 20, 1957; [Sept.? 1957]. AG, unpublished journals.

Howl trial: "Statement of facts," City Lights Books, San Francisco, Apr. 11, 1957. JK to AG, June 7, 1957. AG to LF, June 10, 1957.

Travels in Italy: AG to LG, Aug. 10, 1957. AG to PO and Alan Ansen,

Aug. 26, 1957. AG to PO, Aug. 27, 1957. AG to PO and Alan Ansen, Aug. 29, 1957.

AG and Auden: Charles H. Miller, *Auden: An American Friendship* (New York: Scribner's, 1983), p. 146. AG to LG, Sept. 1, 1957.

AG and PO in Paris: My interview with Larry Fagin, Jan. 23, 1986.

On the Road review: *New York Times*, Sept. 5, 1957. AG to JK, Sept. 1957; Oct. 9, 1957; Oct. 16, 1957.

Howl trial: J. W. Ehrlich, *Howl of the Censor: The Four Letter Word on Trial* (San Carlos, Cal.: Mourse, 1961). Neeli Cherkovski, *Ferlinghetti: A Biography.* Norman Podhoretz, "A Howl of Protest in San Francisco," *New Republic*, Sept. 16, 1957. John Roberts, "Juvenile Police Head Raids Bookshop in San Francisco," *National Guardian*, Aug. 5, 1957. John Roberts, "West Coast Censorship Trial Draws Big Audiences in Support of Poem," *National Guardian*, Sept. 9, 1957. San Francisco *Chronicle*, Oct. 7, 1957. Francis O'Gara, " 'Howl' Ruled Not Obscene; 2 Acquitted," San Francisco *Examiner*, Oct. 4, 1957. JK to AG, Oct. 18, 1957.

Rue Git le Coeur: Michael Zwerin, "Brion Gysin: The Dreamer and His Dream Machine," *Paris Metro*, Aug. 16, 1978. Maxine Feifer, "Times Past at the Beat Hotel," *Paris Metro*, Aug. 16, 1978. WSB foreword to Harold Norse, *Beat Hotel.* Harold Norse, "The Death of 9, rue Git le Coeur," *City Lights Journal* 1 (1963). Howard Chapman, *The Beat Hotel.* My conversations with Ian Sommerville, 1965–70. Geoffrey Wolff, *Black Sun: The Brief Transit and Violent Eclipse of Harry Crosby* (New York: Random House, 1976). Brion Gysin, *Here to Go: Planet R-101.* AG to LG, Sept. 18, 1957. AG to LF, Sept. 23, 1957. AG to JK, Sept. 28, 1957. AG to LG, Sept. 30, 1957. JK to AG, Oct. 1, 1957. AG to JK, Oct. 9, 1957. AG to LF, Oct. 10, 1957. WSB to AG, Oct. 14, 1957. AG to JK, Oct. 16, 1957. AG to LG, Oct. 19, 1957. PO to Ron Lowenstein, Oct. 19, 1957. WSB to AG, Oct. 19, 1957; Oct. 28, 1957; Oct. 31, 1957. PO to Robert LaVigne, Nov. 2, 1957. WSB to AG, Nov. 10, 1957. AG to JK, Nov. 13, 1957. WSB to AG, Nov. 26, 1957. AG to LG, Nov. 30, 1957. JK to AG, Nov. 30, 1957. WSB to JK, Dec. 4, 1957. WSB to AG, Dec. 4, 1957. PO to JK, Dec. 5, 1957. PO to Robert LaVigne, Dec. 7, 1957. WSB to AG, Dec. 8, 1957. JK to AG, PO and GC, Dec. 10, 1957. AG to LC, Dec. 11, 1957. AG to Edith Ginsberg, Dec. 15, 1957. AG to JK, Jan. 4, 1958. AG to LG, Jan. 14, 1958. AG to JK, Jan. 11, 1958. AG to LG, Jan. 14, 1958. AG to PO, Jan. 20, 1958. JK to AG, Jan. 21, 1958. AG to EB, Jan. 23, 1958. AG to LG, Jan. 23, 1958. AG to PO, Jan. 23, 1958; Jan. 28, 1958. AG to LG, Feb. 2, 1958. AG to PO, Feb. 3, 1958; Feb. 15, 1958; Feb. 24, 1958. AG to LG, Mar. 2, 1958. AG to EB, Mar. 12, 1958. AG to LG, Mar. 15, 1958. AG to PO, Mar. 16, 1958. AG and WSB to JK, Mar. 29, 1958.

AG begins "Kaddish": AG to JK, Nov. 13, 1957.

Françoise: My interview with AG.

LeRoi Jones: AG to LG, Nov. 30, 1957. LeRoi Jones, *The Autobiography of LeRoi Jones / Amiri Baraka.*

PO returns to N.Y.C.: Joyce Johnson, *Minor Characters*, pp. 184–6. Lafcadio Orlovsky to PO, July 16, 1957. PO to JK, Oct. 18, 1957.

WSB in Paris: WSB to AG, Jan. 9, 1958; Jan. 13, 1958. AG to LF,

Jan. 18, 1958. WSB to AG, Feb. 2, 1958. AG to LF, Feb. 2, 1958. WSB to AG, Feb. 10, 1958. WSB to AG, Feb. 16, 1958.

First U.K. trip: AG to LG, Feb. 2, 1958. AG to PO, Feb. 3, 1958. WSB to AG, Feb. 3, 1957. GC to AG, Feb. 7, 1957. AG to PO, Feb. 13, 1958. AG to PO, Feb. 15, 1958. WSB to AG [1957]. AG to PO, Feb. 24, 1958.

Spring in Paris: Art Buchwald, "Two Poets in Paris," N.Y. *Herald Tribune*, June 26, 1958. AG to PO, Apr. 1, 1958; Apr. 9, 1958. AG to LF, Apr. 15, 1958. Philip Whalen to AG, Apr. 17, 1957. AG to LF [April 1958]. Gary Snyder to AG, Apr. 22, 1958. AG to LG, May 24, 1958. AG to LF, May 24, 1958. AG to Jack Micheline, May 25, 1958. AG to LC, May 30, 1958. AG to PO, May 30, 1958; June 3, 1958. AG to LG, June 4, 1958. AG to PO, June 8, 1958; June 15, 1958. AG to Hannah Litzky, June 20, 1958. AG to LF, June 20, 1958. AG to PO, June 21, 1958. AG to JK, June 26, 1958. JK to AG, July 2, 1958. AG to EB [Spring 1958]. AG to EB, July 9, 1958. AG to PO, July 16, 1958.

Second U.K. trip: Dom Moraes, *My Son's Father* (New York: Macmillan, 1968). LG to AG, Mar. 5, 1958; Apr. 10, 1958. David Widgery interview with AG, *U* magazine, Summer 1965. AG to PO, May 12, 1958. AG to LG, May 24, 1958. AG to PO, May 30, 1958.

Edith Sitwell: "The Only Rebellion Around," *Life*, Nov. 30, 1959. Letter from Edith Sitwell, *Life*, Feb. 8. 1960. AG to PO, May 30, 1958. Elizabeth Salter, *The Last Years of a Rebel: A Memoir of Edith Sitwell* (Boston: Houghton Mifflin, 1967). Edith Sitwell to James Purdy, July 25, 1958, in Edith Sitwell, *Selected Letters* (New York: Vanguard, 1970); Sitwell clearly believed that both Ginsberg and Corso were addicted to heroin.

Céline: My interview with AG. My conversation with WSB, Feb. 1974. AG to PO, July 11, 1958. AG to NC, July 7, 1958.

Michaux: AG on Michaux for *Cahiers l'Herne* (written December 1965). GC to AG, Nov. 28, 1958.

EIGHT: "KADDISH"

My interview with AG, Mar. 28, 1985, covers this period.

N.Y.C.: AG to JK, Aug. 20, 1958. AG to GC, Aug. 27, 1958; Nov. 1958. AG to JK, Nov. 1958. AG to Robert LaVigne, Sept. 10, 1958. AG to JK, Sept. 10, 1958. Joe Hyams, "Good-by to the Beatniks!" *This Week* magazine, Sept. 28, 1958. Norman Podhoretz, "Where Is the Beat Generation Going?" *Esquire*, Dec. 1958. Marc Schleifer, "Here to Save Us, but Not Sure from What," *Village Voice* Oct. 15, 1958. "Beat Generation and the Angry Young Men," *Time*, June 9, 1958. Luther Nichols, "Kerouac as the Savant of the Religious Beat," San Francisco *Chronicle*, Oct. 5, 1958. Marc Schleifer, "The Beat Debated—Is It or Is It Not?" *Village Voice*, Nov. 19, 1958. AG, "The Dharma Bums," *Village Voice*, Nov. 12, 1958. Series of five undated letters. AG to LF, Mar. 6, 1959. Fred McDarrah, *Kerouac & Friends: A Beat Generation Album*.

JK's mother: JK to AG, July 2, 1958. Gabrielle Kerouac to AG, July

13, 1958. WSB to AG, July 15, 1958. WSB to AG, July 24, 1958. JK to AG, Aug. 11, 1958.

Thelonious Monk: AG, unpublished journals. AG to JK, Sept. 16, 1958.

JK's publishing career: AG to JK, Oct. 29, 1958; Nov. 17, 1958.

AG as agent: AG to LF, Aug. 20, 1958; Sept. 4, 1958; Sept. 10, 1958; Sept. 30, 1958; Jan. 23, 1959. Gary Snyder to AG, Feb. 2, 1959. AG to WSB, Aug. 27, 1959; Dec. 12, 1959. AG to JK, May 12, 1959. AG to GC, May 1959.

Laughing Gas: AG to JK; also AG, unpublished journals.

Writing "Kaddish": Original MS in Fales Library, NYU. AG to Charles Olson, Nov. 1958. AG to WCW, Jan. 23, 1959. AG to LF, Mar. 19, 1959. AG to WCW, May 30, 1959. AG, LHBG lectures.

P.I. patient: AG to Charles Olson, Nov. 26, 1958.

"Pull My Daisy": JK, *Pull My Daisy*. David Amram, *Vibrations*.

Chicago visit: AG, PO, and GC to *Time*, Feb. 17. 1959. AG to JK, Feb. 6, 1959.

Columbia reading: AG to LF, Feb. 12, 1959. Diana Trilling, "The Other Night at Columbia," *Partisan Review*, Spring 1959.

San Francisco: "Poetry in the Bay Area," AG to *Chronicle*, in San Francisco *Chronicle*, May 27, 1959. AG to LG, May 12, 1959.

"Kaddish": AG to LG, [May] 20, 1959.

Beatitude magazine: John Kelly, ed., *Beatitude Anthology*. AG to LF, Aug. 15, 1960.

Lower East Side: My conversations with Alexander Trocchi, 1965–70. AG, LHBG lectures.

Reading tours: Elsa Dorfman, *Elsa's Housebook: A Woman's Photo-journal* (Boston: David R. Godine, 1974).

"Hairy loss": AG, unpublished journals. AG, LHBG lectures.

NINE: ADVENTURES IN PSYCHEDELIA

Virtually all the material about South America is taken from AG's unpublished South American journals. See also AG, "Aether," "Magic Psalm," and "The Reply." AG to LF, Mar. 14, 1960; Apr. 6, 1960. AG to EB, June 2, 1960. AG to WSB, June 2, 1960. AG to JK, June 6, 1960. AG to WSB, June 10, 1960. AG to LF, Aug. 15, 1960.

WSB's search for yage is detailed in AG and WSB, *The Yage Letters*. My interview with Burroughs, May 28, 1988.

Machu Picchu: "The Might of Machu Picchu," *New York Times*, June 9, 1985.

N.Y.C.: AG, unpublished journals.

Completion of "Kaddish": AG to LF, July 5, 1960; Sept. 16, 1960. AG to JK, Sept. 19, 1960. AG to LF, Oct. 5, 1960; Oct. 11, 1960; Oct. 1960; Oct. 24, 1960.

Cubans: Carlos Franqui, *Family Portrait with Fidel* (New York: Random House, 1984). AG to GC, Sept. 25, 1960.

Mailer: Peter Manso, *Mailer* (New York: Simon & Schuster, 1985). Hilary Mills, *Mailer: A Biography* (New York: Empire, 1982).

AG with Leary at Harvard: Timothy Leary, *Flashbacks: An Autobiography* (Los Angeles: J. P. Tarcher, 1983). Timothy Leary, *High Priest* (New York: World, 1968). Timothy Leary, *The Politics of Ecstasy* (London: MacGibbon & Kee, 1970). Kerouac dialogue: AG to GC, Dec. 8, 1960. My interview with AG. My conversations with Leary, 1967, 1969, 1983. John Bryan, *Whatever Happened to Timothy Leary?* (San Francisco: Renaissance, 1980). Peter Whitmer, *Aquarius Revisited.*

Sessions with JK, Lowell: AG, unpublished journals. AG, "Journal Night Thoughts."

N.Y.C.: My interview with Lucien Carr.

Methedrine madness: AG, LHBG lectures.

TEN: CUT-UPS

My interview with AG, Mar. 28, 1985, covers this period.

Departing N.Y.C.: AG to JK, May 11, 1962. AG, *Journals Early Fifties Early Sixties*, p. 191. AG to LF, Jan. 30, 1961; Feb. 17, 1961.

Cut-ups: Brion Gysin to BM, Feb. 13, 1984. Brion Gysin, *Here to Go: Planet R-101.* AG to Howard Schulman, Oct. 1961. WSB, GC, Brion Gysin, and Sinclair Beiles, *Minutes to Go.* WSB and Brion Gysin, *The Exterminator*; *The Third Mind.*

Paris: PO, unpublished journals, Apr. 22–May 22, 1961 (in U. of Texas, Austin, coll.). AG, unpublished journals. AG to LF [April 1961].

WSB's application of cut-ups to life: AG, LHBG lectures. AG to LeRoi Jones, Mar. 3, 1961.

AG and PO in Tangier: Note that Ginsberg always uses the French spelling, Tanger. AG, unpublished MS, "A wooden table on an Arab roof." AG, *Journals Early Fifties Early Sixties.* Paul Bowles, "A Résumé," *The Beat Book.* Paul Bowles, *Without Stopping.* AG to Ted Wilentz, June 12, 1961.

Ian Sommerville: My talks with Sommerville, 1965–70. My talks with Brion Gysin, 1964–84. AG, LHBG lectures.

Michael Portman: AG, LHBG lectures. AG to LC, July [June] 28, 1961.

Teasing PO: My talk with AG, Feb. 21, 1984.

Conflict between PO and WSB: AG to Howard Schulman, Oct. 1961. AG to LF [Oct. 1961]. AG, LHBG lectures.

PO's transcriptions: Ernie Barry, "A Conversation with Allen Ginsberg," *City Lights Journal* 2 (1964). Transcription no. 2 was made July 12, 1961; transcription no. 3, July 16, 1961. AG and PO, *Straight Heart's Delight.*

PO leaves: PO to JK, May 11, 1961. AG to LF [1961]. AG to Howard Schulman, Oct. 1961. AG to PO, Aug. 2, 1961.

Leary in Tangier: Timothy Leary, *High Priest*; *Flashbacks.*

Greece: AG, *Journals Early Fifties Early Sixties.* AG to Hannah Litzky, Oct. 13, 1961. AG to LF [Oct. 1961]. AG to Charles Olson, Aug. 14, 1961. AG to GC, Aug. 30, 1961; Aug. 31, 1961. AG to LG, Nov. 12, 1961.

Tel Aviv: GC to AG, Nov. 14, 1961. AG to LF, Dec. 20, 1961. AG to

Diane di Prima, Nov. 30, 1961. AG to LG, Nov. 2, 1961. AG to LG [Nov. 1961]. AG to LG, Nov. 29, 1961. AG to JK, May 11, 1962.

PO's family problems: EB to AG, Dec. 3, 1961. AG to EB, Dec. 20, 1961.

Martin Buber: AG, *Journals Early Fifties Early Sixties*, p. 191.

ELEVEN: INDIA

Opening quote adapted from Gary Snyder, *Passage Through India* (San Francisco: Grey Fox, 1983), p. 61.

India: AG, *Indian Journals*. Joanne Kyger, *The Japan & India Journals: 1960–1964* (Bolinas: Tombouctou Books, 1981). Gary Snyder, *Passage Through India*. My interview with AG, Mar. 28, 1985. My conversations with PO, particularly 1970. My conversations with Manjula Mitra, 1965–66. David Widgery interview with AG, *U* magazine, Summer 1965. Alice Glaser, "Back on the Open Road for Boys," *Esquire* 60, no. 1 (July 1963). AG, "The Rain on Dasaswamedh," *Illustrated Weekly of India*, Mar. 4, 1984. Lafcadio in trouble: PO to Kate and Marie Orlovsky [1962].

Bombay and Calcutta: AG to LF, Feb. 25, 1962. GC to AG, Mar. 9, 1962. AG to GC, Apr. 19, 1962. AG to Ted Wilentz, Apr. 24, 1962. AG to LF, Apr. 24, 1962. AG to JK, May 11, 1962. PO to LC, May 29, 1962. AG to PO, June 6, 1962. AG to Paul Bowles, June 28, 1962. AG to Robert LaVigne, June 30, 1962. AG to JK, July 29, 1962; Sept. 9, 1962. AG to LC, Oct. 6, 1962. AG to LG, Oct. 11, 1962. AG to LF [1962]. PO to Ted Wilentz, Oct. 25, 1962. AG to LF, Nov. 2, 1962. AG to Paul Bowles [1962]. AG to WCW, Nov. 19, 1962.

Benares: AG, unpublished journals. AG to LG, Jan. 10, 1963. AG to LF, Jan. 10, 1963. AG to LC [1963]. AG to LF, Feb. 1, 1963. AG to Ted Wilentz, Mar. 2, 1963. AG to Paul Bowles [Mar. 1963]. AG to LF, Mar. 15, 1963. AG to GC, Mar. 21, 1963. AG to Ted Wilentz, Mar. 21, 1963. AG to GC, May 5, 1963. AG to JK, May 8, 1963. AG to PO, May 25, 1963. AG to LG, June 14, 1963.

TWELVE: THE CHANGE

My interview with AG, Mar. 28, 1985, covers this period.

Southeast Asia: AG, unpublished journals. AG, "The Change" (original in journals). Joanne Kyger, *The Japan & India Journals*. AG interview, *Paris Review* 37 (Spring 1966). AG in Saigon: David Halberstam, "Buddhists Find a Beatnik Spy," *New York Times*, June 6, 1963. AG interview with Ernie Barry, *City Lights Journal* 2 (1964). JK to AG, June 29, 1963.

Bangkok: AG to PO, May 31, 1963; June 4, 1963.

Thailand: AG to PO, June 6, 1963; June 11, 1963.

Japan: AG to LF, June 14, 1963. AG to PO, June 16, 1963; June 27, 1963; June 28, 1963; July 1, 1963; July 9, 1963; July 14, 1963.

Vancouver: AG, unpublished journals. AG to LF, Aug. 5, 1963. AG to John Wieners, Aug. 16, 1963. AG to LF, Aug. 19, 1963. AG to LC, Aug. 19, 1963.

San Francisco: AG, unpublished journals. Andrew T. Weil, "The Strange Case of the Harvard Drug Scandal," *Look*, Nov. 5, 1963. CIA memorandum, Nov. 1, 1963, re Richard Alpert and Tim Leary. AG, "Statement to the Burning Bush," *Burning Bush* II (1963). My interview with Lucien Carr, Mar. 9, 1986. My interview with Lawrence Ferlinghetti, Mar. 20, 1986. My interview with Michael McClure, Mar. 19, 1986. My interview with Shigeyoshi Murao, Mar. 22, 1986. My interview with Philip Whalen, Mar. 16, 1986. AG to PO, Aug. 17, 1963; Aug. 29, 1963; Sept. 18, 1963 (telegram). AG to JK, Oct. 6, 1963. AG to Charles Olson, Oct. 6, 1963. AG to PO, Oct. 10, 1963; Nov. 1, 1963; Nov. 20, 1963. AG to LC, Nov. 22, 1963. AG to PO, Nov. 29, 1963.

New York: Taylor Mead interview, *Gay Sunshine Interviews* 1. AG, introduction to JK: *Visions of Cody*. Bob Dylan, sleeve, *Bringing It All Back Home*. Nat Freedland, "Allen Ginsberg and the Law," N.Y. *Herald Tribune*, May 24, 1964. AG to PO, Oct. 6, 1963; Aug. 29, 1963. Alan Ansen to AG, Oct. 1, 1963. AG, unpublished journals. AG interview, N.Y. *Post*, Mar. 5, 1964. AG to LF, Mar. 14, 1964; Apr. 4, 1964; Aug. 10, 1964; Aug. 12, 1964; Sept. 30, 1964. AG to Charles Olson, Oct. 21, 1964.

Underground movies: AG, unpublished journals. My conversations with Gerard Malanga, 1984–86. AG to LF, Jan. 13, 1964.

Kerista community: Rose Pettet, "Thinking of Allen," Morgan and Rosenthal *Best Minds*.

Orgies: My conversations with Ann Buchanan, 1971–79. My conversations with Gerard Malanga, 1965–87. My conversations with Peter Orlovsky, 1970–71. My interview with AG. AG, interview with Bruce Kawin, Oct. 1964, for WKCR-FM (Columbia University).

JK: AG to JK [1964]; Feb. 26, 1964; June 10, 1964. Problems with JK: AG to JK, Apr. 1964; June 20, 1964.

LeMar: N.Y. *Herald Tribune*, Dec. 28, 1984. My conversations with Michael Aldrich in 1969. *The Marijuana Review* 1–6. *The Marijuana Newsletter* 1–2.

Cambridge, Mass.: AG to LF, Dec. 3, 1964.

THIRTEEN: THE KING OF MAY

Cuba: Virtually all the material on Cuba comes from the three volumes of Ginsberg's unpublished Cuban journals. *El Mundo*, Jan. 20, 1965. *Bohemia*, Feb. 5, 1965. *El Mundo*, Feb. 7, 1965. *Hoy*, Feb. 18, 1965.

El Puente group: No charges were brought against the boys, but eight years later, on Aug. 23, 1973, Manuel Ballagas was arrested and charged with writing poems and other literature critical of Cuba and of sending "social information" to the U.S. agent Allen Ginsberg. They had maintained a correspondence over the years, some of which must have been intercepted. Ballagas was jailed for four years and he eventually moved to the U.S., paid for, in part, by Ginsberg. See "When Police Took Poems, They Took His Heart, Too," Miami *Herald*, Aug. 16, 1980. AG to LC, Jan. 17, 1965. AG to LF, Jan. 18, 1965. AG to PO, Feb. 4, 1965; Feb. 5, 1965; Feb. 15, 1965. AG to Nicanor Parra, Aug. 20, 1965.

Prague: My interview with Josef Skvorecky, Sept. 20, 1984. *Literarni noviny*, Mar. 6, 1965. Josef Skvorecky entry, *Contemporary Authors, Autobiography Series*, vol. 1. Igor Hajek to BM [Oct. 1984]. AG to PO, Feb. 26, 1965. AG to LF, n.d. AG to PO, Mar. 1, 1965; Mar. 12, 1965.

Moscow: AG, unpublished journals. AG to PO, Mar. 17. 1965; Mar. 27, 1965. AG to Ed Sanders, Mar. 28, 1965. AG to LC, Mar. 28, 1965. AG to PO, Mar. 31, 1965; Apr. 5, 1965. AG to Charles Olson, Apr. 6, 1965.

Prague (second visit): AG to PO, May 4, 1965.

FOURTEEN: INTO THE VORTEX

My interview with AG, Feb. 17, 1986, covers this period.

London: Tom McGrath, "Ginsberg in London," *Peace News*, May 28, 1965. AG to Nicanor Parra, Aug. 20, 1965. GC to AG, n.d. David Widgery interview with AG in *U* magazine, Summer 1965. D. A. Pennebaker, *Bob Dylan: Don't Look Back* (New York: Ballantine, 1968). My conversation with George Harrison, June 1987. Richard Kostelanetz, "Ginsberg Makes the World Scene," *New York Times Magazine*, July 11, 1965. My notes made at the time. AG to PO, May 25, 1965; June 10, 1965; n.d. [p./c.]. AG to editor of the London *Times*, June 19, 1965.

Berkeley: *The Berkeley Poetry Conference*, July 12–24, program. AG, unpublished journals. "Allen Ginsberg's suggestions for November 20: Demonstration or Spectacle As Example, As Communication" [unpub.]. Frank Reynolds (with Michael McClure): *Freewheelin' Frank*. Dylan: *Les Crane Show*, Feb. 1965. KQED-TV press conference, Dec. 1965. My interview with Michael McClure, Mar. 19, 1986. AG to PO, Aug. 18, 1965. AG to BM, Aug. 20, 1965. AG to PO, Aug. 28, 1965; Sept. 1, 1965. AG to GC, n.d. AG to PO, Sept. 9, 1965; Sept. 10, 1965. AG to GC, Sept. 29, 1965.

Midwest: Conversations with Ann Buchanan, 1970–77. Auto-poesy tapes in Ginsberg archive.

New York: AG, LHBG lectures. Leary ad, *New York Times*, Apr. 3, 1966. The details of the Martin-Wilbourn case are in *Little Caesar 9* (1979), pp. 382–92. See also "U.S. Plot to 'Set Up' Ginsberg for Arrest Is Described to Jury," *New York Times*, Apr. 14, 1966; and Jay Levin, "Jazzman Who Accused Feds Is Convicted," N.Y. *Post*, Apr. 15, 1966.

LSD hearings: *The Narcotics Rehabilitation Act of 1966*. AG interview, *Paris Review* 37 (Spring 1966). "Seminar on Marihuana and LSD Controls," AG and James H. Fox, M.D., National Student Association Convention, University of Illinois, Aug. 24, 1966, published transcript.

San Francisco: My interview with Larry Fagin, Jan. 23, 1986. I have also referred to issues of *San Francisco Oracle* and *Berkeley Barb* for the period. AG, LHBG lectures. AG to BM. Sept. 29, 1965. AG, NC, Carolyn Cassady, and PO to JK, Oct. 1, 1965. AG to Charles Olson, Oct. 26, 1965. AG to LG, Nov. 6, 1965. AG to Ted Wilentz, Nov. 23, 1965. AG to LG, Nov. 29, 1965. AG to HH, Dec. 5, 1965. AG to LF, Dec. 24, 1965. "The Hippies, Philosophy of a Subculture," *Time*, July 7, 1967.

PO breakdown: AG to EB, Aug. 7, 1967. AG to PO, Aug. 10, 1967; Oct. 7, 1967; Nov. 16, 1967.

Ginsberg in London: Emmett Grogan, *Ringolevio*. AG, unpublished journals. Iain Sinclair, *The Kodak Mantra Diaries*. AG to PO, July 12, 1967; July 18, 1967; July 26, 1967.

Record pressing plant problems: Joe Berke to BM, Oct. 23, 1968.

AG with Ezra Pound: AG, "Encounters with Ezra Pound," *Composed on the Tongue*. Michael Reck, *Ezra Pound: A Close Up* (New York: McGraw-Hill, 1973), pp. 150–59. Alan Levy, *Ezra Pound: The Voice of Silence* (Sag Harbor, N.Y.: Permanent Press, 1983). AG interview with Robert Kramer, Antioch, 1967 (unpublished?). AG to LF, Sept. 29, 1967. AG to PO, Oct. 25, 1967; Nov. 2, 1967. AG to LF, Nov. 11, 1967; Nov. 26, 1967. AG to BM, Dec. 19, 1967.

FIFTEEN: PATERFAMILIAS

I made much use of AG's unpublished journals for this period. The period is also covered by my interviews with AG of March 28, 1985, Feb. 17, 18, 1986.

Peter's Methedrine addiction: Notes made during visits to the farm in 1969 and when I moved there in 1970.

The meeting of AG and the Maharishi is taken from AG to BM, Oct. 13, 1967. AG to BM, Dec. 29, 1967. All dialogue from AG to BM, Jan. 24, 1968. Neal's death: Louis Cartwright, "Message from Mexico," *The Beat Diary*. Note: The facts of this article are disputed by Ginsberg. I have used his own recollection of first hearing of the death of NC. See also AG: "Elegy for Neal Cassady," *Collected Poems*. Notes from my conversations with Janice Brown, 1970.

Buying Cherry Valley farm: Gordon Ball to AG, Jan. 19, 1969. July 2, 1968, given as date for down payment in COP records. My interview with Gordon Ball, Nov. 26, 1984. AG to BM, Aug. 31, 1969. AG to LF, Sept. 9, 1969.

Barbara Rubin: My interview with Gordon Ball, Nov. 26, 1984. My interview with AG, Feb. 18, 1986.

Days of unrest: PO at Salem State College Symposium, April 1973.

Chicago 1968: List of delegates to National Peace Convention made by 113th Military Intelligence Group, Fort Sheridan, Ill. (obtained by AG using the Freedom of Information Act). FBI memorandums of Sept. 27, 1968; Sept. 30, 1968; Oct. 1, 1968, Oct. 7, 1968, show how intense the FBI surveillance of AG was following the convention. AG interview in *Playboy*, Apr. 1969. AG, *Chicago Trial Testimony*. AG, LHBG lectures. "Scruffy Vagabonds Who Shook Up America," *National Observer*, Dec. 9, 1968.

Kerouac's anti-Semitism: AG, LHBG lectures.

I observed AG composing the Blake songs while I stayed on the farm in 1969. See also AG interviewed by Alison Colbert and Anita Box, *West End* 1, 1971. AG to BM, Nov. 19, 1968. Ann Charters, *Beats and Company*.

Car crash: AG to LF, Dec. 7, 1968. AG to Charles Olson, Dec. 7, 1969. AG to Shigeyoshi Murao, Dec. 7, 1969. AG, unpublished journals.

Maretta Greer: My interview with Gordon Ball, Nov. 26, 1984. AG, unpublished journals.

I was the producer of *William Blake's Songs of Innocence and Experience Tuned by Allen Ginsberg*, released on Verve FTS 3083. Reviewed in detail in *Blake Newsletter* 4, no. 3 (Winter 1971).

Jack Kerouac's death: Eric Ehrmann and Stephen Davis, "There Really Is Nothing Inside," *Rolling Stone*, Nov. 29, 1969. John Clellon

Holmes, "Gone in October," *Cambridge Phoenix* 1, no. 4 (Oct. 30, 1969).
AG to Carolyn Cassady, Feb. 19, 1970. Also described in all the biographies of JK.

Chicago trial: *The Chicago Conspiracy vs. the Washington Kangaroos: Official Pogrom* (New York: Grove Press, 1969). Official trial transcript. *New York Times*, Dec. 12, 1969. Nicholas von Hoffman, "The Chicago Conspiracy Circus," *Playboy*, Dec. 1970.

Rubin's intentions are described in Abe Peck, *Uncovering the Sixties*. Also AG, LHBG lectures. AG, unpublished journals.

I lived on the Cherry Valley farm Mar.–Oct. 1970, and the descriptions of Gregory Corso, Ray Bremser, Julius Orlovsky, Peter Orlovsky's speed problem, etc., are taken from my journals. Also BM to WSB, Aug. 4, 1970. PO on speed: AG, unpublished journals, June 28, 1970. Also archive tape 70 D1/011 [June 20, 1970?]. Ray Bremser to AG, Oct. 29, 1969. AG to LF, July 13, 1970. AG to GC, Aug. 14, 1970.

CIA smuggling drugs: See *Allen Verbatim*. Steve Levine, "All of Us Have a Stake in Allen Ginsberg's Bet," Denver *Post*, June 6, 1971. Flora Lewis, "CIA and Drugs," L.A. *Times* Syndicate column, May 6, 1971. *New York Times*, Aug. 11, 1971. Jack Anderson, Washington *Post*, Mar. 22, 1971.

Poem "What Was the Vietnam War" from AG, unpublished journals.

SIXTEEN: THE LION OF DHARMA

My interview with AG, Apr. 20, 1986, covers this period.

Richard Howard–AG: *New York Times*, Apr. 4, 1971.

Muktananda: My interview with AG, Apr. 20, 1986.

Trungpa: Meeting Trungpa is covered in detail in an interview by James Harris, Aug. 21, 1971 (unpublished?). AG interviewed by Rick Fields, Boulder, 1971 (unpublished?). AG interviewed by Peter Chowka in *New Age* [date unknown]. AG interviewed by Irving Rosenthal in *Kaliflower* 3, no. 17 (Aug. 26, 1971).

AG shaves beard: AG, unpublished journals.

Homosexual rights: The Stonewall riot was June 27, 1969. "Allen's Barb Ad" leaflet issued by *The Effeminist* [Berkeley, 1971].

John Lennon: AG, unpublished journal entries. AG to BM, Oct. 13, 1971.

Buddhist vows: My interviews with AG. AG to George Dowden, July 21, 1972. AG to BM, July 31, 1972.

Bly, Snyder, AG, Trungpa reading: Ed Sanders, *The Party*. Tom Clark, *The Great Naropa Poetry Wars*. My interview with Bob Rosenthal, Apr. 3, 1986.

Kissinger: My interview with Gordon Ball, Nov. 26, 1984.

Vietnam Vets at Miami: AG, "Television Address, 1972," MS. See Geoffrey Rips, *Unamerican Activities*, for details of the FBI Counterintelligence Program against the New Left; see particularly the 12-point program of July 5, 1968, recommending "misinformation."

Tim Leary: AG to Leary's judge, telegram, Feb. 25, 1970. Also AG, "Declaration of Independence for Dr. Timothy Leary." "Mock Sestina:

The Conspiracy Against Dr. Tim Leary," issued as a flier for *Rallying Point*, May 16, 1973.

Abbie Hoffman as cocaine dealer: AG letter to *Liberation*, Sept. 1973.

Meditation: PO to BM, May 20, 1972. "Jackson Hole Meditation Sessions," MS. AG to BM and Ann Buchanan, Sept. 24, 1973. AG to BM, Sept. 14, 1974.

CIA overthrows Allende: AG, unpublished journals.

W. H. Auden's death: AG, unpublished journals.

WSB and meditation: AG to BM, Feb. 14, 1974.

Building house in Calif.: Conversations with PO, 1977. AG, unpublished journals. My interview with AG.

I attended the Ram Dass–Trungpa shoot-out in Vermont and reported it for the *Village Voice*.

Kerouac school: 42-page untitled transcript of an interview (c. 1975) with AG from AG archives gives detailed description of meeting Trungpa, starting Kerouac School, etc. "General Practice of Kerouac School of Disembodied Poetics at Naropa Institute," MS from AG archives.

"Ego Confession": AG, *Collected Poems*. Details in AG, unpublished journals.

Mugging: *New York Times*, Jan. 5, 1975. And in AG, *Collected Poems*.

Details of the Columbia reading are from a transcript made by Victor Bockris.

Boulder: AG conversation with BM, summer 1983.

Rolling Thunder tour: *NME* (London), Dec. 6, 1975. My interviews with Rob Stoner and Howie Wyeth, 1976 (for *NME*). On the road with Dylan: AG, unpublished journals. Cocaine: "AG and Andrei Voznesensky in Conversation," *Paris Review* 78 (Summer 1980). Sam Shepard, *Rolling Thunder Logbook*. Rolling Thunder dawn ceremony: Larry Sloman, *On the Road with Bob Dylan*. All conversation with Dylan taken from AG, unpublished journals. Other details are from my conversations with Denise Mercedes and PO after the tour and from the Rolling Thunder tour daily newsletter. See the four-hour version of Bob Dylan's film *Renaldo and Clara* for AG reading "Kaddish," sitting with Dylan at Kerouac's grave, and other scenes. AG to GC, [1975]. AG to BM, Nov. 17, 1975.

The assault on Merwin is taken from Ed Sanders, *The Party*, and Tom Clark, *The Great Naropa Poetry Wars*. AG and Jacqueline (?) from Naropa both read through the sections of the MS on Trungpa and made various suggestions, correcting errors in Clark's book and clarifying certain points. I have used much of the new material provided by them. Material is also taken from my interviews with AG on Sept. 23, 1988; Sept. 24, 1988; Sept. 30, 1988; Oct. 2, 1988; Oct. 4, 1988. Other details of Tibetan practices here and later are taken from my own library of Tibetan studies. The principal works consulted were: Shashibhusan Dasgupta, *Obscure Religious Cults* (Calcutta: Mukhopadhyay, 1969); Robert Ekvall, *Religious Observances in Tibet* (Chicago: University of Chicago, 1964); R. P. Anuruddha, *An Introduction to Lamaism* (Hoshiarpur: Vishveshvaranand Vedic Research Institution, 1959); Helmut Hoffmann, *The Religions of Tibet* (London: George Allen & Unwin, 1961); Pedro Carrasco, *Land*

and Polity in Tibet (Seattle: University of Washington, 1959); Thubten Jigme Norbu and Colin Turnbull, *Tibet: Its History, Religion and People* (London: Chatto & Windus, 1969). I also drew on conversations with Trungpa in the late sixties in London, 1970 in New York, and 1971 in Berkeley. I visited Tail of the Tiger and the Maitri Center with AG in 1973. AG interviewed by Peter Chowka for *New Age Journal*, April 1976. AG interviewed by Paul Portuges, July 1976, published in *Boston University Journal* 125, no. 1 (1977). Robert Coe, "Dharma Matter," *Village Voice*, Nov. 20, 1978.

AG and John Lennon: AG, unpublished journals, and my interview with AG, Apr. 20, 1986.

"Father Death Blues": AG, *Collected Poems*.

Louis Simpson review of *Journals*: *New York Times Book Review*, Oct. 23, 1977.

Further details on Merwin affair from Ed Sanders, *The Party*, and Tom Clark, *The Great Naropa Poetry Wars*. AG quote on Guyana from AG, unpublished journals. Robert Wood [Tom Clark], "Buddha Gate: Scandal and Cover-up at Naropa Revealed," *Berkeley Barb*, Mar. 29, 1979.

SEVENTEEN: EMINENCE GRISE

My interviews with AG, Apr. 20, 1986; Sept. 23, 1988; Sept. 24, 1988; Sept. 30, 1988; Oct. 2, 1988; Oct. 4, 1988, cover this period.

I am grateful to Victor Bockris, who provided me with a transcript of the National Book Awards ceremony. AG commented on the misspelling in a telephone call to the author a few weeks after the event.

Heritage Foundation and neoconservative reaction to Clark's book from my interview with AG, Apr. 20, 1986, and from his extensive document files on the subject. The Republican attempt to withdraw NEA poetry funding was reported in the *New York Times*, Sept. 10, 1985.

East European trip: My interview with Steven Taylor, Apr. 21, 1986. Details of Barbara Rubin's death reported to me by Rosebud Pettet and AG in conversation at the time.

WSB Jr.'s death: AG, unpublished journals. AG, LHBG lectures. Ted Morgan, *Literary Outlaw: The Life and Times of William Burroughs* details Billy's illness and death.

AG and the Clash: My interviews with AG. AG, unpublished journals. AG interviewed by Michael Schumacher, Mar. 11, 1982; Mar. 23, 1982 (unpublished?). AG interviewed by Katharyn Machan Aal at Cornell University, June 20, 1981 (transcript of a broadcast on college radio?). AG interview with Michael Feldman, Feb. 20, 1982, for *Red Hand* 3. AG interview with Will Doherty, Mar. 8, 1982, for *Link* 3.

AG's teaching methods: Explained to Nancy Bunge at Michigan State University, Feb. 1981; published in Washington *Post*, July 29, 1984.

AG's meeting with Borges: AG, unpublished journals, and my interview with AG, Apr. 20, 1986.

Peter's trip to Boulder: AG, unpublished journals.

Kerouac Conference: AG, unpublished journals. Henry Allen, "25

Years Later," Washington *Post* "Style," Aug. 2, 1982. William Schmidt, "Beat Generation Elders Meet to Praise Kerouac," *New York Times*, July 30, 1982. William Robertson, "On the Road Again," Miami *Herald*, Oct. 24, 1982. "Celebrating the Beat Spirit," *Naropa Institute Bulletin*, Feb. 1982. "Beatnik Gurus Look Ahead and the Young Look Askance," Philadelphia *Inquirer* (date unknown).

Nicaragua: "Ordinary Mind," AG interview with Jay Rubin, *The Sun* 77, Mar. 1982. "Ginsberg on Ginsberg," *Up the Creek*, Denver, May 28, 1982. "A Moveable Fiesta," AG interview with Ewan Courage, *SoHo Weekly News*, Feb. 16, 1982. "East Meets West over a Bottle of Rum in Nicaragua," AG interview with Rod Norland, San Francisco *Examiner*, Feb. 13, 1982. AG interview with S. K. Levin, *Colorado Daily*, May 7, 1982. AG interview with Jay Murphy and Mary Jane Ryals, *Red Bass* 7, 1984. AG interview with Leif Owen Klein, *Talking Heads* 2 (Spring 1982). AG interview with Mark Kingsley, *Reporter*, Feb. 10, 1984. AG interview, *Dartmouth Review*, Apr. 8, 1984 (also discussed censorship).

Death of Oleg Orlovsky: AG, unpublished journals.

Scandinavian tour: AG, unpublished journals. My conversation with Simon Vinkenoog, Amsterdam, summer 1987.

USIA blacklist: Joel Brinkley, "USIA's 'Blacklist,' " *New York Times*, Mar. 15, 1984.

"White Shroud," *New York Times Magazine*, Nov. 11, 1984.

China: AG, "China Notebook" (unpublished). Harrison E. Salisbury, "On the Literary Road: American Writers in China," *New York Times Book Review*, Jan. 30, 1985. AG, "China Through a Poet's Eyes," San Jose *Mercury News*, Feb. 20, 1985 (released through UPI; appeared in a number of other papers, including San Francisco *Examiner*).

Collected Poems reviews: Roger Rosenblatt, "A Major Minor Poet," *New Republic*, Mar. 4, 1985. Robert Richman, "Allen Ginsberg Then and Now," *Commentary* 80, no. 1 (July 1985). *City Limits*, May 24, 1985. Philadelphia *Inquirer*, Mar. 15, 1985. Sam Maddox, "Allen Ginsberg: Portrait of a Popular Poet," Boulder *Camera*, Apr. 14, 1985. David Remnick, "The World & Allen Ginsberg," Washington *Post*, Mar. 17, 1985. Garry Abrams, "Allen Ginsberg Still Controversial," Los Angeles *Times*, Apr. 18, 1985. Chicago *Tribune*, Feb. 10, 1985. *USA Today*, Jan. 4, 1985. Ed McCormack, "A Real Howl," N.Y. *Daily News Magazine*, May 19, 1985. Bruce Cook, "Allen Ginsberg: The Beat Goes On," *Washington Post Book World*, Jan. 13, 1985. Tom Valeo, "Ginsberg: He's Indignant as Ever and Proud of It," Chicago *Daily Herald*, Apr. 18, 1985. *Los Angeles Times Book Review*, Jan. 20, 1985. Ken Tucker, "Power Of Babble," *Village Voice*, Jan. 29, 1985. R. Z. Sheppard, "Mainstreaming Allen Ginsberg," *Time*, Feb. 4, 1985. Alan Abrams, "Still Making Poetic Waves," Detroit *Jewish News*, Mar. 1, 1985. *Cherwell*, May 10, 1985. *Melody Maker*, May 11, 1985. Detroit *Free Press*, Feb. 13, 1985. Milwaukee *Journal*, Mar. 4, 1985. *New Musical Express*, June 1, 1985.

AG's photographic shows: Washington *Post*, Jan. 8, 1985; Apr. 13, 1985.

AFTERWORD

Photography: Miami *Herald*, Feb. 2, 1987.

White Shroud: Los Angeles *Times*, Feb. 15, 1987.

Kerouac Memorial: Podhoretz column, *N.Y. Post*, Jan. 6, 1987. AG response, *New Letters*, Fall 1987.

Ginsberg's list of Beat Generation effects: "A Definition of the Beat Generation," *Friction* 2/3 (Winter 1982).

BIBLIOGRAPHY

NOTE: Cited are the editions used, which are not always the first editions.

BOOKS BY ALLEN GINSBERG

Airplane Dreams: Compositions from Journals. Toronto: Anansi, 1968.

Allen Ginsberg on Tour. Wuppertal, Ger.: Lichtblick, 1983.

Allen Verbatim: Lectures on Poetry, Politics, Consciousness. New York: McGraw-Hill, 1974.

Angkor Wat. London: Fulcrum, 1968.

Bixby Canyon Ocean Path Word Breeze. New York: Gotham Book Mart, 1972.

The Change. London: Writers' Forum, 1963.

Chicago Trial Testimony. San Francisco: City Lights, 1975.

Collected Poems 1947–1980. New York: Harper & Row, 1985.

Composed on the Tongue. Bolinas, Cal.: Grey Fox, 1980.

Declaration of Independence for Dr. Timothy Leary: July 4, 1971. San Francisco: Hermes Free Press, 1971.

Documents on Police Bureaucracy's Conspiracy . . . . New York, 1970 (self-published).

Empty Mirror. New York: Totem/Corinth, 1961.

The Fall of America: Poems of These States 1965–1971. San Francisco: City Lights, 1973.

First Blues, Rags, Ballads & Harmonium Songs 1971–74. New York: Full Court, 1975.

The Gates of Wrath. Bolinas, Cal.: Grey Fox, 1972.

Gay Sunshine Interview (with Allen Young). Bolinas, Cal.: Grey Fox, 1974.

Howl and Other Poems. San Francisco: City Lights, 1956.

Howl; Original Draft Facsimile. New York: Harper & Row, 1986.

Improvised Poetics. San Fransisco: Anonym, 1972.

Indian Journals. San Francisco: City Lights, 1970.

Iron Horse. Toronto: Coach House, 1972.

Journals Early Fifties Early Sixties. New York: Grove, 1977.

Kaddish and Other Poems. San Francisco: City Lights, 1961.

Many Loves. New York: Pequod, 1984.

Mostly Sitting Haiku. Paterson, N.J.: From Here, 1978.

Mystery in the Universe (interview by Edward Lucie-Smith). London: Turret, 1965.

Planet News. San Francisco: City Lights, 1968.

Plutonian Ode. San Francisco: City Lights, 1982.

Poems All Over the Place, Mostly Seventies. Cherry Valley, N.Y.: Cherry Valley, 1978.

Reality Sandwiches. San Francisco: City Lights, 1963.

The Riverside Interviews 1: Allen Ginsberg. London: Binnacle, 1980.

Sad Dust Glories. Berkeley: Workingman's Press, 1975.

To Eberhart from Ginsberg. Lincoln, Mass.: Penmaen, 1976.

TV Baby Poems. London: Cape Goliard, 1967.

The Visions of the Great Rememberer. Amherst, Mass.: Mulch, 1974.

Wales: A Visitation. London: Cape Goliard, 1968.

White Shroud: Poems 1980–1985. New York: Harper & Row, 1986.

Wichita Vortex Sutra. London: Peace News, 1966.

(With Cassady, Neal) *As Ever: The Collected Correspondence*. Berkeley: Creative Arts, 1977.

(With Orlovsky, Peter) *Straight Heart's Delight: Love Poems & Selected Letters*. San Francisco: Gay Sunshine, 1980.

BOOKS BY WILLIAM S. BURROUGHS

The Adding Machine: Collected Essays. London: John Calder, 1985.

The Burroughs File. San Francisco: City Lights, 1984.

The Job. New York: Grove, 1972, 1974 (rev.).

Junkie. New York: Ace, 1953.

Junky. New York: Penguin, 1977.

Letters to Allen Ginsberg. Geneva: Claude Givaudan, 1978.

Naked Lunch. Paris: Olympia, 1959.

Queer. New York: Viking, 1985.

Roosevelt After Inauguration. New York: Fuck Press, 1964.

The Soft Machine. Paris: Olympia, 1960.

(With Ginsberg, Allen) *The Yage Letters*. San Francisco: City Lights, 1960.

(With Gysin, Brion) *The Exterminator*. San Francisco: Auerhahn, 1960.

(With Gysin, Brion) *The Third Mind*. New York: Seaver, 1978.
(With Corso, Gregory; Gysin, Brion; Beiles, Sinclair) *Minutes to Go*. Paris: Two Cities, 1960.

BOOKS BY JACK KEROUAC
Big Sur. New York: Bantam, 1963.
The Book of Dreams. San Francisco: City Lights, 1961.
Dear Carolyn: Letters to Carolyn Cassady. California, Pa.: Unspeakable Visions of the Individual, 1983.
Desolation Angels. London: Granada, 1972.
The Dharma Bums. London: Granada, 1972.
Doctor Sax. New York: Grove, 1959.
Heaven & Other Poems. San Francisco: Grey Fox, 1977.
Lonesome Traveller. London: Andre Deutsch, 1962.
The Mexican Girl. [Brighton, Eng.] Pacific Car Press, n.d.
Mexico City Blues. New York: Grove, 1959.
On the Road. Harmondsworth, Eng.: Penguin, 1972.
Pull My Daisy. New York: Grove, 1960.
Satori in Paris. New York: Grove, 1966.
Scattered Poems. San Francisco: City Lights, 1971.
The Scripture of the Golden Eternity. New York: Totem/Corinth, 1960.
The Subterraneans. London: Andre Deutsch, 1960.
The Town and the City. New York: Grosset & Dunlap, n.d.
Tristessa. New York: Avon, 1960.
Vanity of Duluoz. New York: Paragon, 1979.
Visions of Cody. New York: McGraw-Hill, 1978.

BOHEMIA
Easton, Malcolm. *Artists and Writers in Paris: The Bohemian Idea*, 1803–1867. London: Edward Arnold, 1964.
Émile-Bayard, Jean. *Montmartre Past and Present*. New York: Brentano, n.d.
Miller, Richard. *Bohemia: The Protoculture Then and Now*. Chicago: Nelson-Hall, 1977.
Murger, Henri. *The Bohemians of the Latin Quarter (Scènes de la Vie de Bohême)*. Paris: Société des Beaux-Arts, 1915.
Parry, Alfred. *Garrets and Pretenders: A History of Bohemianism in America*. New York: Dover, 1960 (rev.).
Richardson, Joanna. *The Bohemians*. South Brunswick, N.J.: A. S. Barnes, 1971.

THE BEATS
Allen, Donald, ed. *The New American Poetry, 1945–1960*. New York: Grove, 1960.

Allen, Donald, and George F. Butterick, eds. *The Postmoderns*. New York: Grove, 1982.

Allen, Donald, and Warren Tallman, eds. *The Poetics of the New American Poetry*. New York: Grove, 1973.

Bartlett, Lee. *The Beats: Essays in Criticism*. Jefferson, N.C.: McFarland, 1981.

Charters, Ann. *Beats and Company*. Garden City, N.Y.: Doubleday, 1986.

Charters, Ann. *The Beats: Literary Bohemians in Postwar America*, Parts 1 and 2. Ann Arbor: Gale Research, 1983.

Charters, Ann. *Scenes Along the Road*. New York: Portents/Gotham Book Mart, 1970.

Clay, Mel. *Jazz, Jail and God: Bob Kaufman*. San Francisco: Androgyne, 1987.

Cook, Bruce. *The Beat Generation*. New York: Scribner, 1971.

Di Prima, Diane. *Memoirs of a Beatnik*. New York: Olympia, 1969.

Di Prima, Diane, and LeRoi Jones, eds. *The Floating Bear: A Newsletter*, 1–37. La Jolla: Laurence McGilvery, 1973.

Fass, Ekbert. *Towards a New American Poetics: Essays and Interviews*. Santa Barbara: Black Sparrow, 1979.

Feldman, Gene, and Max Gartenberg, eds. *The Beat Generation and the Angry Young Men*. New York: Citadel, 1958.

Ferlinghetti, Lawrence, and Nancy Peters. *Literary San Francisco*. New York: Harper & Row, 1980.

Girodias, Maurice, ed. *The Olympia Reader*. New York: Grove, 1965.

Holmes, John Clellon. *Get Home Free*. New York: Dutton, 1964.

Holmes, John Clellon. *Go*. New York: New American Library, 1980.

Holmes, John Clellon. *Nothing More to Declare*. New York: Dutton, 1967.

Honan, Park, ed. *The Beats: An Anthology of "Beat" Writing*. London: J. M. Dent, 1987.

Horemans, Rudi, ed. *Beat Indeed!* Antwerp: EXA, 1985.

Huncke, Herbert. *Huncke's Journal*. New York: Poets Press, 1965.

Huncke, Herbert. *The Evening Sun Turned Crimson*. Cherry Valley, N.Y.: Cherry Valley, 1980.

Johnson, Joyce. *Minor Characters*. London: Picador, 1983.

Jones, LeRoi. *The Autobiography of LeRoi Jones/Amiri Baraka*. New York: Freundlich, 1984.

Kelly, John, ed. *Beatitude Anthology*. San Francisco: City Lights, 1960.

Kherdian, David. *Six San Francisco Poets*. Fresno: Giligia, 1969.

Knight, Arthur and Glee, eds. *Herbert Huncke*. California, Pa.: Unspeakable Visions of the Individual, 1973.

Knight, Arthur and Glee, eds. *The Beat Book*. California, Pa.: Unspeakable Visions of the Individual, 1974.

Knight, Arthur and Kit, eds. *Beat Angels*. California, Pa.: Unspeakable Visions of the Individual, 1982.

Knight, Arthur and Kit, eds. *The Beat Diary*. California, Pa.: Unspeakable Visions of the Individual, 1977.

Knight, Arthur and Kit, eds. *The Beat Journey*. California, Pa.: Unspeakable Visions of the Individual, 1978.

Knight, Arthur and Kit, eds. *The Beat Road*. California, Pa.: Unspeakable Visions of the Individual, 1984.

Knight, Arthur and Kit, eds. *The Beat Vision*. New York: Paragon House, 1977.

Krim, Seymour. *Views of a Nearsighted Cannoneer*. London: Alan Ross, 1969.

Lipton, Lawrence. *The Holy Barbarians*. London: W. H. Allen, 1960.

McClure, Michael. *Scratching the Beat Surface*. San Francisco: North Point, 1982.

McDarrah, Fred. *Kerouac & Friends: A Beat Generation Album*. New York: William Morrow, 1985.

Malina, Judith. *The Diaries of Judith Malina, 1947–1957*. New York: Grove, 1984.

Norse, Harold. *Beat Hotel*. San Diego: Atticus, 1983.

Ossman, David. *The Sullen Art*. New York: Corinth, 1963.

Parkinson, Thomas, ed. *Casebook on the Beat*. New York: Crowell, 1961.

Perloff, Marjorie. *Frank O'Hara, Poet Among Painters*. Austin: University of Texas, 1977.

Rigney, Francis J., and L. Douglas Smith. *The Real Bohemia*. New York: Basic, 1961.

Rosset, Barney, ed. *The Evergreen Review Reader, 1957–1961*. New York: Grove, 1979.

Saroyan, Aram. *Genesis Angels: The Saga of Lew Welch and the Beat Generation*. New York: William Morrow, 1979.

Seaver, Richard, Terry Southern, and Alexander Trocchi, eds. *Writers in Revolt: An Anthology*. New York: Frederick Fell, 1963.

Simpson, Louis. *A Revolution in Taste*. New York: Macmillan, 1978.

Snyder, Gary. *The Real Work: Interviews and Talks, 1964–1979*. New York: New Directions, 1980.

Solomon, Carl. *Mishaps Perhaps*. San Francisco: Beach Books, Texts & Documents, 1966.

Solomon, Carl. *More Mishaps*. San Francisco: Beach Books, Texts & Documents, 1968.

Tytell, John. *Naked Angels*. New York: McGraw-Hill, 1976.

Watts, Alan W. *Beat Zen Square Zen & Zen*. San Francisco: City Lights, 1959.

Whalen, Philip. *Off the Wall: Interviews with Philip Whalen*. Bolinas, Cal.: Four Seasons, 1978.

Wilentz, Elias, ed. *The Beat Scene*. New York: Corinth, 1960.

THE FIFTIES

Amram, David. *Vibrations*. New York: Macmillan, 1968.

Cassady, Carolyn. *Heart Beat: My Life with Jack and Neal*. Berkeley: Creative Arts, 1976.

Chapman, Howard. *The Beat Hotel*. Montpellier, Fr.: Gris Banal, 1984.

Duberman, Martin. *Black Mountain: An Exploration in Community*. London: Wildwood, 1974.

Ebin, David, ed. *The Drug Experience*. New York: Orion, 1961.

Edinger, Claudio. *Chelsea Hotel*. New York: Abbeville, 1984.

Gruen, John. *The Party's Over Now*. New York: Viking, 1972.

Podhoretz, Norman. *Making It*. New York: Random House, 1967.

Rexroth, Kenneth. *An Autobiographical Novel*. Weybridge, Eng.: Whittet, 1977.

Richards, Janet. *Common Soldiers*. San Francisco: Archer, 1979.

Rosenthal, Irving. *Sheeper*. New York: Grove, 1967.

Watts, Alan W. *In My Own Way*. New York: Random House, 1972.

Wolf, Daniel, and Ed Fancher, eds. *The Village Voice Reader*. Garden City, N.Y.: Doubleday, 1962.

THE SIXTIES

Alpert, Jane. *Growing Up Underground*. New York: William Morrow, 1983.

Anthony, Gene. *The Summer of Love: Haight-Ashbury at Its Highest*. Millbrae, Cal.: Celestial Arts, 1980.

Benton, Ralph. *Psychedelic Sex*. Canoga Park, Cal.: Viceroy, 1968.

Berke, Joseph, ed. *Counter Culture*. London: Peter Owen, 1968.

Bremser, Bonnie. *Troia: Mexican Memoirs*. New York: Croton, 1969.

Burroughs, William, Jr. *Kentucky Ham*. London: Picador, 1975.

Burroughs, William, Jr. *Speed*. New York: Olympia, 1970.

Clark, Tom. *Who Is Sylvia?* (novel). Berkeley: Blue Wind, 1979.

(Congress of the U.S.) *The Narcotics Rehabilitation Act of 1966. Hearings Before a Special Subcommittee of the Committee on the Judiciary United States Senate 89th Congress, Second Session*. Washington, D.C. 1966.

Davidson, Sara. *Loose Change*. New York: Doubleday, 1977.

Goldman, Albert. *Grass Roots*. New York: Harper & Row, 1979.

Goldman, Albert. *Freakshow*. New York: Atheneum, 1971.

Goodman, Mitchell. *The Movement Toward a New America*. New York: Knopf, 1970.

Grogan, Emmett. *Ringolevio*. London: William Heinemann, 1972.

Gruen, John. *The New Bohemia*. New York: Shorecrest, 1966.

Gutman, Walter. *The Gutman Letter*. New York: Something Else, 1969.

Hayes, Harold, ed. *Smiling Through the Apocalypse*. New York: McCall, 1970.

Hewison, Robert. *Too Much: Art and Society in the Sixties, 1960–1975.* London: Methuen, 1986.

Hoffman, Abbie. *Revolution for the Hell of It.* New York: Dial, 1968.

Hoffman, Abbie. *Soon to Be a Major Motion Picture.* New York: Putnam, 1980.

Hoffman, Abbie. *Steal This Book.* New York: Pirate, 1971.

Hoffman, Abbie. *Woodstock Nation.* New York: Vintage, 1969.

Hoffman, Abbie and Anita. *To America with Love.* New York: Stonehill, 1976.

Hoffman, Abbie, Jerry Rubin, and Ed Sanders. *Vote!* New York: Warner, 1972.

Hoffman, Abbie, et al. *The Chicago 8 Speak Out! Conspiracy.* New York: Dell, 1969.

Hoffman, Anita (as Ann Fettamen). *Trashing.* San Francisco: Straight Arrow, 1970.

Hollingshead, Michael. *The Man Who Turned On the World.* New York: Abelard-Schuman, 1973.

Holmquist, Anders. *The Free People.* New York: Outerbridge & Dienstfrey, 1969.

Hopkins, Jerry, ed. *The Hippie Papers.* New York: Signet, 1968.

Howard, Mel, and Thomas K. Forcade, eds. *The Underground Reader.* New York: New American Library, 1972.

Jamer, Ronard. *Hippie Sex Communes.* Los Angeles: Impact, 1970.

Katzman, Allen, ed. *Our Time: Interviews from the* East Village Other. New York: Dial, 1972.

Kerouac, Jan. *Baby Driver.* New York: Holt, Rinehart & Winston, 1981.

Kleps, Art. *Millbrook.* Oakland: Bench, 1977.

Kornbluth, Jesse, ed. *Notes from the New Underground.* New York: Viking, 1968.

Kostelanetz, Richard. *Master Minds.* New York: Macmillan, 1969.

Krassner, Paul. *How a Satirical Editor Became a Yippie Conspirator.* New York: Putnam, 1971.

Lee, Martin, and Bruce Shlain. *Acid Dreams.* New York: Grove, 1985.

Lennon, John. *Skywriting by Word of Mouth.* New York: Harper & Row, 1986.

Lewis, Roger. *Outlaws of America: The Underground Press and Its Context.* London: Heinrich Hanau, 1972.

Leyland, Winston, ed. *Gay Sunshine Interviews, Vol. 1.* San Francisco: Gay Sunshine, 1978.

McNeill, Don. *Moving Through Here.* New York: Knopf, 1970.

McReynolds, David. *We Have Been Invaded by the 21st Century.* New York: Praeger, 1970.

Peck, Abe. *Uncovering the Sixties: Life and Times of the Underground Press.* New York: Pantheon, 1985.

Raskin, Jonah. *Out of the Whale: An Autobiography.* New York: Links, 1974.

Rips, Geoffrey. *Unamerican Activities: The Campaign Against the Underground Press.* San Francisco: City Lights, 1981.

Rodman, Selden. *Tongues of Fallen Angels: Conversations with Ginsberg* (et al.). New York: New Directions, 1974.

Rolling Stone Editors. *The Age of Paranoia: How the Sixties Ended.* New York: Pocket Books, 1972.

Roszak, Theodore. *The Making of a Counter Culture.* London: Faber, 1970.

Rubin, Jerry. *Do It!* New York: Simon & Schuster, 1970.

Rubin, Jerry. *We Are Everywhere.* New York: Harper & Row, 1971.

Sanders, Ed. *Investigative Poetry.* San Francisco: City Lights, 1976.

Sanders, Ed. *Shards of God.* New York: Grove, 1970.

Sanders, Ed. *Tales of Beatnik Glory.* New York: Stonehill, 1975.

Snyder, Don. *Aquarian Odyssey.* New York: Liveright, 1979.

Solomon, David, ed. *The Marihuana Papers.* Indianapolis: Bobbs-Merrill, 1966.

Spitz, Robert. *Barefoot in Babylon: The Creation of the Woodstock Festival.* New York: Viking, 1979.

Stafford, Peter. *Psychedelic Baby Reaches Puberty.* New York: Praeger, 1971.

Stansill, Peter, and David Mairowitz. *Bamn: Outlaw Manifestos.* Harmondsworth, Eng.: Penguin, 1971.

Taylor, Derek. *It Was 20 Years Ago Today.* London: Bantam, 1987.

Turner, Florence. *At the Chelsea.* London: Hamish Hamilton, 1986.

Warhol, Andy, and Pat Hackett. *POPism: The Warhol 60s.* New York: Harcourt Brace Jovanovich, 1980.

Whitehead, Peter. *Wholly Communion.* London: Lorrimer, 1965.

Whitmer, Peter. *Aquarius Revisited.* New York: Macmillan, 1987.

Willett, John, ed. *Astronauts of Inner-Space.* San Francisco: Stolen Paper, 1966.

Williams, Paul. *Pushing Upwards.* New York: Links, 1973.

Wolfe, Burton. *The Hippies.* New York: Signet, 1968.

Wolfe, Tom. *The Electric Kool-Aid Acid Test.* New York: Farrar, Straus & Giroux, 1968.

Youth International Party. *Blacklisted News: Secret History, Chicago to 1984.* New York: Bleecker, 1983.

Zaroulis, Nancy, and Gerald Sullivan. *Who Spoke Up?* New York: Holt, Rinehart & Winston, 1984.

THE SEVENTIES AND EIGHTIES

Clark, Tom. *The Great Naropa Poetry Wars.* Santa Barbara: Cadmus, 1980.

Fields, Rick. *How the Swans Came to the Lake* (rev. ed.). Boston: Shambala, 1986.

Goldman, Albert. *The Lives of John Lennon.* London: Bantam, 1988.

Sanders, Edward, ed. *The Party: A Chronological Perspective on a Confrontation at a Buddhist Seminary.* Woodstock, N.Y.: Poetry, Crime and Culture, 1977.

Shepard, Sam. *Rolling Thunder Logbook.* New York: Viking, 1977.

Sloman, Larry. *On the Road with Bob Dylan.* New York: Bantam, 1978.

Trungpa, Chögyam. *Born in Tibet.* London: George Allen & Unwin, 1966.

Trungpa, Chögyam. *First Thought Best Thought.* Boulder: Shambala, 1983.

Wiener, Jon. *Come Together: John Lennon in His Time.* New York: Random House, 1984.

BIOGRAPHIES AND MONOGRAPHS

William Seward Burroughs

Ansen, Alan. *William Burroughs.* Sudbury, Mass.: Water Row, 1986.

Bockris, Victor. *With William Burroughs: A Report from the Bunker.* New York: Seaver, 1981.

Goodman, Michael. *William S. Burroughs: An Annotated Bibliography.* New York: Garland, 1975.

Gysin, Brion (with Terry Wilson). *Here to Go: Planet R-101.* San Francisco: Re/Search, 1982.

Gysin, Brion. *Brion Gysin Let the Mice In.* West Glover, Vt.: Something Else, 1973.

Lydenberg, Robin. *Word Cultures: Radical Theory and Practice in William S. Burroughs' Fiction.* Urbana: University of Illinois, 1987.

Maynard, Joe, and Barry Miles. *William S. Burroughs: A Bibliography 1953–1973.* Charlottesville: University of Virginia, 1978.

Miles, Barry. *A Catalogue of the William S. Burroughs Archive.* Ollon, Switz., and London: Am Here and Covent Garden, 1973.

Morgan, Ted. *Literary Outlaw: The Life and Times of William S. Burroughs.* New York: Henry Holt, 1988.

Mottram, Eric. *William Burroughs: The Algebra of Need.* London: Marion Boyars, 1977.

Skerl, Jennie. *William S. Burroughs.* Boston: Twayne, 1985.

Neal Cassady

Cassady, Neal. *The First Third.* San Francisco: City Lights, 1971, 1981 (expanded).

Plummer, William. *The Holy Goof: A Biography of Neal Cassady.* Englewood Cliffs, N.J.: Prentice-Hall, 1981.

Stephenson, Gregory. *Friendly & Flowing Savage.* Clarence Center, N. Y.: Textile Bridge, 1987.

Gregory Corso
The Riverside Interviews 3: *Gregory Corso*. London: Binnacle, 1983.
Wilson, Robert. *A Bibliography of Works by Gregory Corso*. New York: Phoenix, 1966.

Lawrence Ferlinghetti
Cherkovski, Neeli. *Ferlinghetti: A Biography*. Garden City, N.Y.: Doubleday, 1979.
Smith, Larry. *Lawrence Ferlinghetti, Poet at Large*. Carbondale: Southern Illinois University, 1983.

Allen Ginsberg
Dowden, George. *A Bibliography of Works by Allen Ginsberg: October, 1943 to July 1, 1967*. San Francisco: City Lights, 1971.
Hyde, Lewis, ed. *On the Poetry of Allen Ginsberg*. Ann Arbor: University of Michigan Press, 1984.
Kramer, Jane. *Allen Ginsberg in America*. New York: Random House, 1969.
Kraus, Michelle P. *Allen Ginsberg: An Annotated Bibliography 1969–1977*. Metuchen, N.J.: Scarecrow, 1980.
McBride, Dick. *Cometh with Clouds (Memory: Allen Ginsberg)*. Cherry Valley, N.Y.: Cherry Valley, 1982.
Morgan, Bill, and Bob Rosenthal, eds. *Best Minds: A Tribute to Allen Ginsberg*. New York: Lospecchio, 1986.
Morgan, Bill, and Bob Rosenthal, eds. *Kanreki: A Tribute to Allen Ginsberg*, Part 2. New York: Lospecchio, 1986.
Mottram, Eric. *Allen Ginsberg in the Sixties*. Brighton, Eng.: Unicorn [1972].
Mottram, Eric. *The Wild Good and the Heart Ultimately: Ginsberg's Art of Persuasion*. London: Spanner, 1978 (*Spanner* 2, no. 5).
Portugés, Paul. *The Visionary Poetics of Allen Ginsberg*. Santa Barbara: Ross-Erikson, 1978.
Sinclair, Iain. *The Kodak Mantra Diaries*. London: Albion Village, 1971.

Jack Kerouac
Beaulieu, Victor-Levy. *Jack Kerouac: A Chicken Essay*. Toronto: Coach House, 1979.
Challis, Chris. *Quest for Kerouac*. London: Faber & Faber, 1984.
Charters, Ann. *A Bibliography of Works by Jack Kerouac*. New York: Phoenix, 1967, 1975 (rev.).
Charters, Ann. *Kerouac*. New York: Warner, 1973, 1974 (rev.).
Clark, Tom. *Jack Kerouac*. New York: Harcourt Brace Jovanovich, 1984.
Eaton, V. J., ed. *Catching Up with Kerouac*. Mesa, Ariz.: The Literary Denim, 1984.
Gifford, Barry, and Lawrence Lee. *Jack's Book*. New York: St. Martin's, 1978.

Hipkiss, Robert A. *Jack Kerouac: Prophet of the New Romanticism*. Lawrence, Kan.: Regents Press, 1976.

Holmes, John Clellon. *Gone in October*. Hailey, Idaho: Limberlost, 1985.

Holmes, John Clellon. *Visitor: Jack Kerouac in Old Saybrook*. California, Pa.: Unspeakable Visions of the Individual, 1981.

Hunt, Tim. *Kerouac's Crooked Road*. Hamden, Conn.: Shoe String, 1981.

Jarvis, Charles E. *Visions of Kerouac*. Lowell, Mass.: Ithaca, 1973.

McNally, Dennis. *Desolate Angel: A Biography of Jack Kerouac*. New York: Random House, 1979.

Montgomery, John, ed. *Kerouac at the "Wild Boar."* San Anselmo, Cal.: Fels & Firn, 1986.

Nicosia, Gerald. *Memory Babe: A Critical Biography of Jack Kerouac*. New York: Grove, 1983.

Weinreich, Regina. *The Spontaneous Poetics of Jack Kerouac*. Carbondale: Southern Illinois University, 1987.

Gary Snyder

Almon, Bert. *Gary Snyder*. Boise, Idaho: Boise State University, 1979.

Kherdian, David. *A Biographical Sketch and Descriptive Checklist of Gary Snyder*. Berkeley: Oyez, 1965.

McNeil, Katherine. *Gary Snyder: A Bibliography*. New York: Phoenix, 1983.

INDEX

Abbot, Berenice, 523
Abernathy, Ralph, 420
Ace Books, 143, 144, 148, 151–52
ACLU (American Civil Liberties Union),
    227, 336, 382, 429
Adams, Darryl, 240
Adams, Walter, 56, 80–81, 106
"After Whitman & Reznikoff"
    (Ginsberg), 25–26
Allen, Donald, 218, 233, 252, 254, 334,
    531
Allen Ginsberg in America (Kramer),
    425
Allen Ginsberg on Tour, 507
Almendres, Maria Rosa, 343, 346, 347
Alpert, Richard, 387
"America" (Ginsberg), 19, 202, 211, 497
American Civil Liberties Union (ACLU),
    227, 336, 382, 429
Amram, David, 257
Anderson, Jack, 435–36
Angelico, Fra, 225
Angkor Wat (Ginsberg), 324
Ansen, Alan, 106, 127–28, 139, 141, 148,
    293
Antonioni, Michelangelo, 395
Arab-Israeli conflict, 528–29
Archer, David, 242
Aronowitz, Al, 333, 425
Artaud, Antonin, 118, 123, 124, 242, 255,
    291
As Ever (Ginsberg and Cassady), 473
Ashbery, John, 371, 438, 484, 531
Asher, Jane, 396
Aspinall, Neil, 370
Assaly, Richard, 470
Atlantic Center for the Arts, 510, 511
Atlantic Records, 339
Auden, W. H. 183, 210, 229, 230–31,
    242–43, 396, 452–53, 521
Australia, 464, 514
Austria, 486
Avedon, Richard, 523
ayahuasca (yage), Ginsberg's use of, 266,
    269–73, 274, 279, 289, 375

Babbs, Ken, 502
Baez, Joan, 333, 369, 379, 380, 381, 458,
    459, 460, 466
Balf, John, 241
Ball, Gordon, 412, 413, 422, 424, 433,
    434, 473
Ballagas, Manuel, 343, 345

Barger, Ralph ("Sonny"), 378–79, 380,
    381
Barker, George, 242
Barney, Natalie, 210
Barron, Frank, 277–78, 279
Bateson, Gregory, 260, 398
Battaglia, Basil, 28
Beach, Mary, 435
Beat Generation:
    Ginsberg as spokesman for, 248, 372–
        373, 394
    Ginsberg's literary promotion of, 212–
        213, 215, 262, 264, 437–38
    hippie movement started by, 239, 240–
        241, 393
    Holmes's article on, 128
    impact of, 531–33
    New Vision of, 47, 54, 58, 62, 65, 407
    origin of, 128
    publicity for, 128, 234, 259, 263, 333,
        372, 388, 503, 521–22
    public misconception of, 248–49, 372
Beat Generation, The (Kerouac), 257
Beatitude, 262
Beatles, 349–50, 369–70, 371, 379, 387,
    396, 401, 408, 409, 414, 425, 445, 505
beatniks, 240–41, 245, 248–49, 263, 372
Beat Scene, The, 333, 354
Beck, Julian, 127, 523
Behari, Bankey, 314
Beiles, Sinclair, 285
Bellamy, Richard, 257
Bellow, Saul, 377, 513
Belmaure, Odette, 118
Berkeley:
    antiwar demonstrations in, 377–78
    Poetry Conference in, 374
Berman, Wally, 382
Berrigan, Ted, 484, 486, 531
Bhaktivedanta, Sri, 301, 439
Big Sur (Kerouac), 382
Big Table, 259, 261, 263, 264
"Birdbrain!" (Ginsberg), 495, 497–98
Bisland family, 184
Blackburn, Paul, 434
Blake, William, 48, 183, 239, 240, 241,
    281, 314, 318, 369, 370, 375, 385,
    392, 473
    Ginsberg's songs of, 416, 423, 424–25,
        445, 448, 453, 495, 511
    Ginsberg's vision of, 99–105, 117, 121,
        142, 143, 189, 271, 308, 309, 325,
        326–27, 358

Bly, Robert, 446, 474
Bodenheim, Maxwell, 15, 25
Bogan, Louise, 210, 217, 227
Bolivia, 264, 268, 509
"Bomb"; (Corso), 9–10, 243, 252, 267, 475
Borges, Jorge Luis, 493–94
Bornstein, Steven, 375, 376, 379, 381, 382, 383
Boucher, Sheila Williams, 170–71, 172, 173, 175–77, 178, 185, 252, 253
Bowles, Paul, 287, 308, 314, 320
Boyd, Patti, 371
Boyle, Kay, 15
Brandenberg, Bob, 63–65
Brautigan, Richard, 262, 388
Breit, Harvey, 217
Bremser, Ray, 260, 431, 433, 434, 435, 472, 502
"Bricklayer's Lunch Hour, The" (Ginsberg), 88, 146
Brody, Iris, 150–51
Brooks, Alan Eugene, 204–5
Brooks, Connie Herbert, 177, 204–5, 206, 333
Brooks, Eugene, 16, 17, 19, 22, 24, 26, 27, 28, 30, 31, 34, 35, 39, 58, 69, 114, 115, 141, 165, 217, 249, 332–33, 357, 509
    Ginsberg's letters to, 53, 56, 67, 208, 225, 244, 245
    marriage of, 177–78, 205
    Naomi Ginsberg and, 76, 81, 95
    Orlovsky advised by, 297
Brown, Janice, 410
Buber, Martin, 296
Buddhism, 104, 153, 167, 174–75, 176, 193–94, 199, 200, 253, 299, 306, 309–310, 324, 403, 406, 439, 440, 442–44, 446, 450–51, 458, 467, 470, 474, 477, 478, 479, 480, 481, 490, 494, 525
Bunge, Nancy, 492, 493
Bunting, Basil, 370, 402, 531
Burroughs, Joan Vollmer, 43, 57, 62, 73, 112, 285
    Burroughs and, 69, 88, 89–90, 91, 99, 111, 130, 137–38, 186, 285
    children of, 62, 89–90, 91, 135, 136, 138
    death of, 137–38, 186, 285
    drug addiction of, 65, 77–79, 135
    Huncke and, 67, 77–79
Burroughs, William Jr., 89, 135, 136, 138, 488–90
Burroughs, William S., 9, 41, 46–49, 51, 52, 54, 58, 68, 86, 120, 134, 141, 189, 394, 396, 407, 422, 453–54, 457, 459, 463, 479, 484, 502, 509, 522
    arrests of, 78, 112, 135, 138
    background of, 48–50, 63–64
    Céline and, 245–46, 400
    Chicago riots and, 415, 417–18, 419, 420
    cut-ups of, 284–87, 288, 290, 291, 295, 296, 302, 327, 348
    drugs used by, 64–65, 70, 77, 148, 222, 235, 240, 246, 269
    Gabrielle Kerouac and, 249–51
    Ginsberg advised by, 48, 63, 106, 108, 130, 192, 271–72, 488
    Ginsberg influenced by, 47–49, 58, 63, 75, 291, 509
    Ginsberg psychoanalyzed by, 70–71, 72–73, 79, 96, 122
    Ginsberg's love affair with, 155–56, 164, 165–66, 169–70, 172–73, 174, 222–23, 237–39
    Ginsberg's promotion of works by, 143–44, 148, 151–52, 175–76, 182, 207, 212, 213–14, 217, 224, 237, 253–254, 264, 336, 340
    Ginsberg's rejection of, 121–22, 123, 173, 174
    Kerouac and, 48, 57, 59, 71, 72, 143, 165, 169–70, 172, 174, 214–15, 221–223, 427
    Leary and, 291, 292
    "Love bliss" vision of, 238–39
    in Mexico City, 135, 136, 137–38, 144, 147–48, 154
    Orlovsky and, 224–25, 288–89, 308
    in Paris, 237–39, 240–41, 245–47, 248, 282
    "routines" of, 71–72, 155, 174, 175
    "schlupping" and, 155–56, 180, 239
    in Tangier, 214–15, 216, 221–25, 284–293
    Texas farming of, 79–80, 89–91, 93
    Vollmer shot by, 137–38, 186
    weapons used by, 49, 137–38, 221–22, 223
Butler, Nicholas Murray, 60

Caen, Herb, 244, 245
"Café in Warsaw" (Ginsberg), 361
Cage, John, 127, 523
Calder, Alexander, 377
California, University of, 186, 199, 260, 512
Callahan, Bob, 480–81
Cambodia, 323–24
Cannastra, Bill, 106, 127, 131–32, 192, 285, 359
Cannes Film Festival, 286, 293
"Cantos" (Pound), 402, 405, 494, 519

"Capitol Air" (Ginsberg), 494, 495
Cardenal, Ernesto, 496, 497, 499
Carmichael, Stokely, 398
Carr, Lucien, 38, 39, 46, 54–55, 56, 75,
    80, 109, 112, 113, 127, 131, 132, 134,
    139, 140, 141, 147, 151, 165, 174,
    210–11, 249, 283, 407, 511
  background of, 39–40
  Ginsberg's letters to, 123, 224, 237,
    287, 314, 327, 383
  Ginsberg's relationship with, 36–37,
    41–42, 43, 46–47, 252
  Joan Burroughs and, 135–37
  Kammerer and, 40, 42, 50, 51, 52, 53,
    262
  Kerouac and, 43–44, 47, 50–52, 142,
    149, 262, 427
  Lois and, 328–29
  on New Vision, 47
  trial and imprisonment of, 53
Carroll, Paul, 258, 259
Carter, Hurricane, 466
Cartwright, Louis, 410
Cassady, Carolyn Robinson, 86, 87, 93,
    97, 105, 107, 123, 130, 142, 166–67,
    168, 169, 170, 175, 200, 201, 257,
    279, 329, 375, 428, 473, 502
Cassady, LuAnne, 82, 84, 87, 88, 107
Cassady, Neal, 78, 87, 88, 123, 130, 189,
    200, 201, 211, 257, 279, 329–30, 331,
    338–39, 375, 376–77, 378–79, 394
  arrest of, 244, 329
  background of, 82–83
  Cayce and, 166–68, 175
  death of, 410–11
  Ginsberg's love affair with, 83–88, 90–
    92, 93, 95, 97–98, 105, 140, 153–54,
    165, 167–69, 171, 173, 214, 451
  imprisonment of, 244, 250, 329
  Jackson and, 177, 178, 179, 185, 200,
    201
  Kerouac and, 142–43, 148, 244, 250,
    339, 532
Caster, Cyril, 424
Castro, Fidel, 266, 274–75, 331, 341, 342,
    343, 344, 346, 500
Castro, Raul, 347, 350
Cayce, Edgar, 166, 167, 168, 175
Cedrón, José Antonio, 496
Céline, Louis-Ferdinand, 48, 60, 190,
    245–46, 400
Cendrars, Blaise, 172
Central Intelligence Agency, *see* CIA
Cerepkova, Vladimira, 354
Chamberlain, Wynn, 434
"Change, The" (Ginsberg), 326
Charters, Ann, 435, 502, 506, 522, 524

Charters, Sam, 502, 506–7
Chase, Hal, 62, 69, 70, 72, 78, 80, 82
Cherry, Don, 425
Chicago, University of, 9, 40, 258–59
Chicago Conspiracy Trial, 429–31
Chicago Daily News, 258
Chicago Review, 9, 258–59
Chicago riots, 408, 414–21, 448
Chile, 264, 266–68, 452, 499, 514
China, People's Republic of, 442–43,
    512–17
CIA (Central Intelligence Agency), 286,
    304, 367, 409, 435–36, 439, 442, 452,
    483, 487, 499–500, 506, 529
Ciardi, John, 340
City Lights Books, 183–84, 192, 193, 207,
    209, 227, 252, 253, 289, 328, 376,
    386, 388, 452, 473, 475, 476, 494,
    496, 508, 531
"City Midnight Junk Strains" (Ginsberg),
    391
Clark, Tom, 301, 476–77, 478–80, 481–
    82, 484, 485, 486, 494, 524
Clash (punk band), 491–92, 495–96, 503
Clausen, Andy, 505
*Clean Asshole Poems and Smiling
    Vegetable Songs* (Orlovsky), 486, 496
Clemente, Francesco, 530
coffeehouses, legal campaign for, 336
Collected Poems (Ginsberg), 510, 511,
    512, 517, 518–19, 521
Columbia Presbyterian Psychiatric
    Institute, 117–18, 119, 120–24, 256
Columbia Review, 79, 85
Columbia University, 35–61, 77, 95, 119,
    184, 414, 428, 452, 453, 473, 487,
    522, 533
  English Department of, 37–38
  Ginsberg disciplined by, 57, 59–61
  Ginsberg's poetry readings at, 259–60,
    457, 494, 501
  Kammerer's death and, 52, 54, 57
Committee on Poetry, 389, 392, 408, 413,
    508
Communism, 10, 12, 14, 343, 357, 359,
    365, 378, 408
Communist Party, 15, 18–19, 27, 118
Concepción, University of, 266–67
Cooper, Michael, 419
Corso, Gregory, 9, 140, 154, 155, 191,
    211–12, 213, 215–17, 219, 257, 259,
    260, 335, 337, 338, 388, 413, 437,
    438, 454, 457, 479, 496
  background of, 133–34
  in Europe, 220, 234, 236–37, 238, 241–
    243, 245–47, 248, 254, 261–62, 267,
    282, 285

Corso, Gregory (cont.)
  gambling habit of, 262, 293
  Ginsberg's financial support of, 261–
    262, 293, 392, 433, 434
  Ginsberg's letters to, 294, 306–7, 318,
    319, 381, 382, 385, 392, 464, 471, 473
  Kerouac's death and, 425, 426, 427,
    428, 502
  in Tangier, 286, 287, 288, 289
Cott, Allan, 96–97, 120
Cousins, Norman, 512
Cowen, Elise, 151, 217, 218, 220, 282,
    283, 306, 308, 524
Cowley, Malcolm, 15, 232
Crabtree, Lee, 423, 424
Crane, Hart, 48, 67, 255, 412
Crane, Les, 379–80
Creeley, Robert, 203, 217, 240, 321, 327,
    350, 374, 383, 405, 427, 434, 438,
    502, 531
Cronkite, Walter, 397, 510
Cuba, 266, 267, 275, 338, 341–52, 356,
    496, 500
  Ginsberg's deportation from, 351–52,
    367–68
  Ginsberg's misunderstanding of
    revolution in, 344–46, 347, 349–50,
    367–68
  Lacra Social crackdown in, 342, 343,
    344–45, 350
cummings, e. e. 210, 244
cut-ups, 285–87, 288, 295, 302, 348
Czechoslovakia, 353–55, 362–68, 496

Dada, 118, 245
Dahlberg, Edward, 258–59
Daily Camera, 477–78, 513
Daimler, Harriet, 241
Dalai Lama, 303–5, 442
Daley, Richard, 414, 421
Dali, Gala, 218–19
Dali, Salvador, 218–19, 245
Darío, Rubén, 496
David-Neel, Alexandra, 274
Davis, Rennie, 415, 429, 431
Dawa, Kunga, 440, 443
"Death News" (Ginsberg), 319
Debs, Eugene Victor, 13, 14, 19
Decline of the West, The (Spengler), 48,
    73
de Gaulle, Charles, 244
de Kooning, Willem, 177, 252, 267, 280
Delhi, India, 298–300
Dellinger, David, 415, 419, 420, 421, 429,
    431, 447–48
DeLoach, Allen, 434

Dempsey, David, 152
Denmark, 504, 506
De Ropp, Robert, 274
Desolation Angels (Kerouac), 223
Dharma Bums, The (Kerouac), 194, 254,
    439, 454
Dialectics of Liberation, 393, 398
di Prima, Diane, 218, 333, 422, 502, 531
Doctor Sax (Kerouac), 120, 148, 149, 152,
    254–55, 262
"Don't Grow Old" (Ginsberg), 96
Doolittle, Hilda, 125
Dorfman, Elsa, 264, 435
Dorn, Ed, 217, 476, 477, 478, 480, 484,
    494, 531
Doyle, Kirby, 260
"Dream Record" (Ginsberg), 186
"Drive All Blames into One" (Ginsberg),
    20
drugs:
  Ginsberg's rejection of, 325–26
  Ginsberg's use of, 80–81, 93, 95, 97,
    103–104, 141–42, 192, 235, 255–56,
    260, 262, 263, 269–74, 276–83, 348,
    375, 398, 433
  lobby for legalization of, 274, 279–82,
    340, 390, 392, 394, 397, 439, 532
  psychedelic revolution through, 274,
    279–82, 393–94
Duchamp, Marcel, 245
Dudjom Rinpoche, 104, 309, 325–26
Duncan, Robert, 171, 183, 203, 212, 213,
    217, 227, 327, 374, 380
Dupee, F. W., 259
DuPeru, Peter, 171–72, 176, 189
Durbin, Frances, 30
Durgin, Russell, 98, 99, 105–6, 127, 189
Dylan, Bob, 333–34, 369–70, 373, 379–
    380, 381, 382–83, 387, 391–92, 401,
    414, 458–59, 460, 461–62, 463–64,
    465, 466, 471, 502, 507, 528

Eberhart, Richard, 203, 211, 213, 217,
    219
"Ego Confession" (Ginsberg), 456, 457
Ehrlich, J. W. K., 227
Eisenhower, Dwight D., 323, 327, 447
"Elegy for Neal Cassady" (Ginsberg), 411
Eliade, Mircea, 398
Eliot, T. S., 48, 125, 203, 210, 259, 263–
    264, 439, 513
Elliot, Ramblin' Jack, 133, 241, 461, 464,
    465
El Salvador, 488, 491
Elvins, Kells, 79–80, 89·
Empty Mirror (Ginsberg), 112, 121, 139–

140, 147, 149, 154, 164, 171, 193,
  252, 333, 452
Enders, Thomas, 500
Eorsi, Istvan, 490–91
Espin, Yves, 350
Esquire, 217, 315, 316, 415, 422
Evans, Mal, 369
Evening Sky Turned Crimson, The
  (Huncke), 91
Evergreen Review, 218, 233, 234, 264,
  343, 359
Exploding Plastic Inevitable, 387

Fagin, Larry, 328, 395
Fainlight, Harry, 338
Faithful, Marianne, 369, 396
Fall of America, The (Ginsberg), 172,
  382, 484
Fantasy Records, 203, 234, 259
Farrell, Barry, 384, 386
"Father Death Blues" (Ginsberg), 472, 497
FBI (Federal Bureau of Investigation),
  286, 436, 448, 449, 529
Federn, Louis, 71
Feiffer, Jules, 387
Feitlowitz, Danny, 17
Felieu, Rosebud, 337–38, 506
Ferlinghetti, Lawrence, 193, 195, 197,
  203, 209, 227, 237, 253–54, 255, 261,
  262, 264, 266, 288, 289, 298, 328,
  329, 371, 375, 381, 389, 424, 476,
  502, 531
  background of, 183–85
  Ginsberg's letters to, 207, 258, 259–60,
    274, 291, 335, 353, 390, 392, 434
Fernández, Pablo, 371
Fiedler, Leslie, 294, 387
Finland, 504, 507
"First Party at Ken Kesey's with Hell's
  Angels" (Ginsberg), 379
Fonda, Peter, 387
Foran, Thomas, 429
"For the Death of 100 Whales"
  (McClure), 195
Foye, Raymond, 522
Frank, Robert, 257, 258, 335, 384, 502,
  507, 511, 522, 523
Fraser, Robert, 371
Frere, Nate González, 344
Frohman, Edie and Max, 94
Froines, John, 429, 431
Fulcrum Press, 324
Furman, Dean, 60

Galbraith, John Kenneth, 489, 510
García Lorca, Federico, 218, 255

Garcia Villa, Jose, 244
"Garden State" (Ginsberg), 22, 23
Garver, Bill, 74, 93, 112, 140, 189, 235
Gascoyne, David, 242
Gaslight Café, 260
Gasoline (Corso), 246
Gates of Wrath (Ginsberg), 104, 112, 334
Geldzahler, Henry, 484
Genet, Jean, 123–24, 148, 226, 236, 336,
  415, 417–18, 419, 531
Gerassi, John, 398
Gide, André, 48, 118, 235
Gillespie, Dizzy, 280
Ginsberg, Allen:
  anti-Catholicism of, 228, 229
  anti-Semitism and, 23, 59, 61, 336, 403,
    421–22
  arrest of, 113–16
  artistic influences on, 36, 48, 50, 97,
    109, 190, 225–26, 228, 235, 306, 359–
    360
  "auto poesy" tapes of, 381–82, 383,
    392
  death feared by, 272–73
  early poems of, 29, 58, 79, 85, 88, 90,
    92–93, 97, 112, 126, 129, 139, 497
  early sexual experiences of, 19, 23–24,
    28, 65–66
  East Village apartments of, 251–53,
    274, 282–83, 334–35, 373–74, 408,
    456, 457, 487, 527–28
  employment of, 62, 77, 105, 110–11,
    124, 127, 130–31, 134–35, 139, 148–
    149, 154, 171, 185, 190
  exhibitionism of, 20, 24, 199–200, 215–
    216, 371
  fame of, 372–73, 388–89, 407, 425, 455,
    473, 484, 533
  farm owned by, 411–13, 422–24, 425,
    428, 431–35, 439, 445, 450, 453, 473,
    490
  Harlem vision of, *see* Blake, William,
    Ginsberg's vision of
  heterosexuality of, 124–25, 129–30,
    133, 134, 140, 170–71, 172, 236, 266,
    272, 279, 289
  homosexuality of, 24, 65–66, 96, 444,
    511
  hostility of, 314–15, 317, 318, 343, 344
  humiliation of, 18, 20–21, 168–69
  illnesses of, 109, 423–24, 501, 503, 515,
    518
  Jewish heritage of, 210, 332, 403, 413,
    423, 460
  as literary agent, 143–44, 148, 151–52,
    175–76, 182, 183, 207, 212–13, 216,

Ginsberg, Allen: as literary agent (cont.)
217–18, 232, 237, 250, 253–55, 258,
264, 336
literary influences on, 38, 48, 58, 67,
99, 101, 123–24, 144–46, 171–72,
186, 187, 190, 198, 236, 255, 307
literature taught by, 145, 146, 321,
327–28, 350, 422, 428, 450–51, 454,
472, 473, 490, 492–93, 508–9, 510,
511, 514–16, 517, 521, 526, 528
love idea of, 326, 327, 328, 332, 407
madness feared by, 271–72, 309
madness understood by, 25–26, 37, 75,
149, 337, 422, 446–47
meditation practiced by, 324, 415–17,
419–20, 431, 439–40, 446, 447, 451–
452, 453, 458, 472–73, 491, 506, 508,
509
middle age as viewed by, 407, 483–84,
506–7, 511
movies as influence on, 26–27, 29, 245,
334, 335
movies created by, 257–58, 335, 364–
365, 379–80, 462–64, 472
musical influences on, 29, 35, 36, 64,
75, 106, 160, 185, 255, 276, 279, 345,
354, 371, 379, 383, 384, 387, 401
musical performances of, 447, 448,
466, 486, 491–92, 503
musical recordings of, 387, 424–25,
495–96, 505, 506, 507, 511
naval duty of, 66–67, 68–69, 205, 207–
210
notebook poems of, 145–46
photography by, 522–24
poetic improvisation by, 441–42
on poetry, 11, 144–45, 164, 201, 261,
291–92, 295, 317, 347–48, 360, 381–
382, 520, 531
police harassment of, 373, 389–90
political influences on, 28, 29, 30, 176,
244, 267
political involvement of, 275–76, 330–
331, 447–49, 450, 475, 528–29
political opinions of, 275, 330–31, 332,
487–88, 500–501, 531
Psychiatric Institute tenure of, 117–18,
119, 120–24, 256
radio experience of, 19, 239, 240, 313
Reichian analysis of, 95–97
school performance of, 17, 19–20, 23,
28–30, 57, 79, 98
spiritual quest of, 210, 229, 301–2,
304–5, 308–9, 314, 317, 325–27
visions of, 99–105, 117, 121, 142, 143,
189, 228–29

visions renounced by, 325–26
vows taken by, 35, 43, 90, 123, 267,
446, 451, 533
writer's blocks of, 291, 295, 309, 484
Ginsberg, Edith, 119, 125, 141, 211, 333,
393, 466, 471
Ginsberg, Eugene, see Brooks, Eugene
Ginsberg, Louis, 10, 12, 20, 23, 31, 33,
34, 38–39, 56, 60, 94, 95, 114, 122,
141, 142, 206, 207, 246, 260, 261,
262, 333, 357, 393
background of, 13–16
Burroughs and, 58–59, 75, 165
debt of, 17, 21, 22, 24, 39
Ginsberg's homosexuality and, 26, 96
on Ginsberg's writing, 204, 208, 211,
261
old age of, 440, 465, 470–71, 472
poetry and, 15–16, 27, 28, 29, 58, 125,
392, 436, 441, 472
Socialism of, 13–14, 18, 19
as worried about Ginsberg, 58–59, 75,
105, 109, 119, 202
Ginsberg, Naomi, 18–19, 28, 38–39, 75,
76, 94, 178, 205, 208, 357, 524
background of, 11–13, 14–15
Communism of, 13–14, 18–19, 27–28,
244
death of, 205–7, 208
funeral of, 10, 206, 207
mental illness of, 14, 16, 17, 21–23, 24–
26, 30–34, 38–39, 81, 93–95, 150,
185, 205, 527
nudism of, 21, 81
Giorno, John, 434
Girodias, Maurice, 263
Giroux, Robert, 110
Glaser, Alice, 316
Glassman, Joyce, 151
Go (Holmes), 128, 143, 152
Goddard, Dwight, 167
Gold, Herbert, 38
Gold, Ronnie, 118
Goldenberg, Ruth, 151, 189
Goodman, Paul, 127, 398
Gould, Joe, 15
Graham, Brian, 522, 523
"Grant Park: August 28, 1968"
(Ginsberg), 421
Grass, Günter, 493
Great Britain, 239–40, 241–44, 369–72,
386, 387, 392, 395–99, 514
Greece, Ginsberg's stay in, 293–96
"Green Automobile, The" (Ginsberg), 90,
153–54, 174
Greer, Maretta, 338, 393, 394, 424, 440

Grey Fox Press, 334
"Greyhound" (Ginsberg), 209
Grossman, Albert, 333, 369, 382, 387
Grove Press, 218, 227, 234, 254–55, 264,
    282, 340, 388, 418, 473, 531, 532
Gruening, Ernest, 436
Grunes, Leni, 118
Guerrero, Reglo, 344
Guevara, Che, 347, 497
Guthrie, Arlo, 414
Guthrie, Woody, 333
Gysin, Brion, 137, 284–85, 287

Haig, Alexander, 500
Hajek, Igor, 354–55, 366, 367, 368
Halberstam, Dan, 361
Hall, Donald, 218
Hammond, John, 507
Hanrahan, William, 227
Hansen, Diana, 123, 130
Hardwick, Elizabeth, 281
Harper & Row, 510, 521, 536
Harper's, 477–78
Harrington, Alan, 106
Harvard University, 49, 273, 276, 280,
    286, 291, 305, 339, 340, 453
Haverty, Joan, *see* Kerouac, Joan Haverty
Hayden, Tom, 415, 429, 431
Healy, John, 138
Heine, Bill, 283
Helbrant, Maurice, 152
Heliczer, Piero, 389, 390
Hell's Angels, 377–79, 380, 381, 394, 428
Helms, Richard, 436, 506
Hendrych, Jiri, 364
Henri, Adrian, 397
Herbert, Connie, *see* Brooks, Connie
    Herbert
Heritage Foundation, 486
Hersey, John, 377
Hicks, Philip, 175, 179–80
Hinkle, Al, 107, 176, 178, 185
hippie movement, 239, 241, 393–94, 407–
    409, 411, 438–39
"History of Visions—A List" (Ginsberg),
    228–29
Hitchcock, Billy and Peggy, 390
Hitler, Adolf, 28, 29, 350, 378
"Hiway Poesy: L.A.-Albuquerque-
    Texas–Wichita" (Ginsberg), 383
Ho Chi Minh, 322, 323, 447
Hoffenberg, Mason, 241
Hoffman, Abbie, 413–14, 415, 421, 429,
    431, 449, 450, 502
Hoffman, John, 195
Hoffman, Julius, 429, 430, 431

Hoffman, Ted, 56
Holland, 504–5
Hollander, Ann, 141
Hollander, John, 141, 147
Hollo, Anselm, 371
Holmes, John Clellon, 106, 114, 128, 143,
    144, 149, 152, 191, 217, 427, 502
Horn, W. J. Clayton, 232
Howard, Richard, 141, 437, 438
"Howl" (Ginsberg), 48, 79, 97, 99, 107–8,
    118, 122, 123, 127, 131, 139, 151,
    172, 186, 187–204, 237, 353, 385,
    386, 492, 510, 513, 518, 530, 532, 533
  censorship trial over, 10, 227–28, 232–
    233, 234, 372, 532
  composition of, 187–91, 192, 197–99
  Eberhart's review of, 211, 217, 227
  Footnote to, 198–99, 232
  Kerouac on, 191
  Part II, 192, 197, 202, 232, 360, 497
  Part III, 197–98, 232, 256, 360
  public readings of, 195–97, 202, 215–
    216, 240, 242, 259, 354, 430, 471,
    495, 497, 501
  Williams's Introduction to, 204, 227
Howl and Other Poems (Ginsberg), 207,
    209, 210–11, 217, 227–28, 232–33,
    234, 246, 254, 315, 317
"How to Make a March/Spectacle"
    (Ginsberg), 378
Humphrey, Hubert, 421
Huncke, Herbert, 63–64, 66, 73, 79, 80,
    81, 89–90, 91, 92, 119, 120, 128, 140,
    141, 144, 147, 189, 264, 267, 282,
    283, 336, 376, 422, 435, 502
  Ginsberg imposed on by, 93, 105, 107–
    109, 110–116, 154
  Joan Burroughs and, 67, 77–79
Hungary, 486, 490
Huxley, Aldous, 215, 244
Huxley, Laura, 382, 387

"In Back of the Real" (Ginsberg), 186
India, 298–321, 444, 509
  funeral pyres in, 310–12, 313, 318
  Ginsberg on religion in, 299–300, 310
  Ginsberg's assistance to beggars in,
    319–21
  Ginberg's harassment in, 315–17
  Ginsberg's lessons from, 325–27
  Kumbh Mela in, 302–3
  Shivananda's ashram in, 300–302
Information Agency, U.S., 510
"In Vesuvio's Waiting for Sheila"
    (Ginsberg), 171
Iran, 487–88

Iron Horse (Ginsberg), 172
Isherwood, Christopher, 215, 382, 453
Isis, Beverly, 527
Israel, 296, 521, 528-29
Italy, 226–27, 228–31, 395, 400–406, 484, 494, 501, 504, 507

Jack Kerouac School of Disembodied Poetics, 455, 474, 480, 481
Jackson, Natalie, 177, 178, 179, 185, 200–201, 329
Jagger, Mick, 396, 397–98, 409, 492
Jarrell, Randall, 227
Javits, Jacob, 390
"Jaweh and Allah Battle" (Ginsberg), 528
Jayakar, Radhika, 306, 309
Jeffers, Robinson, 210, 211
Jennison, Keith, 232
Jensen, Bruce, 389, 390
"Jessore Road" (Ginsberg), 505
Johnson, Joyce, 151, 502
Johnson, Lyndon Baines, 344, 375–76, 377, 378, 379, 384, 409, 414, 415
Jonathan Cape, 349, 371, 387
Jones, Elvin, 425, 511
Jones, Keiko, 425
Jones, LeRoi, 237, 252, 260, 275, 280, 284, 333, 374, 463, 529, 531
Jones, Mick, 491
Jonestown massacre, 477, 478, 479
Jong, Erica, 528, 531
Journals Early Fifties Early Sixties (Ginsberg), 294, 473
Joyce, James, 232, 279, 513
Junky (Burroughs), 63, 143, 144, 151–52, 155, 246
Jurado, Bernabé, 138, 154

"Kaddish" (Ginsberg), 11, 14, 18, 22, 25, 27, 28, 30, 32, 34, 35, 76, 81, 94, 150, 205, 207, 261, 335, 342–43, 386, 518, 524
    composition of, 235–36, 256–57, 274
    public readings of, 259, 260–61, 307, 339, 460
Kaddish and Other Poems (Ginsberg), 270, 274
Kallman, Chester, 127, 242, 453
Kammerer, David, 40, 41, 42, 43, 50, 51, 52, 53, 56, 57, 65, 262, 285
Karmapa, Gyalwa, 309–10
Kazi, Sonam, 304
Keck, Bill, 141, 192
Kennedy, Edward M., 390
Kennedy, John F., 275, 323, 327, 331–32, 372, 381

Kennedy, Robert F., 408, 414
Kerista collective, 337
Kerouac, Edie Parker, 43, 44, 50, 51, 52–53, 55, 57, 59, 62, 65, 69, 502
Kerouac, Gabrielle, 44, 249–51, 264, 333, 412, 426
Kerouac, Jack, 9, 40, 48, 52–53, 54, 57, 60, 65, 123, 127, 128, 131, 132–33, 142–43, 152, 183, 189, 200–201, 202, 207, 213, 218, 219, 252, 278–79, 283, 335, 407, 432, 435, 521–22
    alcoholism of, 248, 249, 264, 275, 283, 307, 426, 444
    background of, 44–45
    Buddhism and, 167, 174–75, 176, 200, 250, 265
    Burroughs and, 48, 57, 59, 71, 72, 143, 165, 169–70, 172, 174, 214–15, 221–223, 427
    Carr and, 43–44, 47, 50–52, 142, 149, 262, 427
    Cassady and, 142–43, 148, 244, 250, 339, 532
    death and funeral of, 425–26, 427–28
    frustration of, 148, 149–50
    Ginsberg on writing of, 98, 154, 188, 426–27
    Ginsberg's friendship with, 44, 45–46, 47, 55–56, 58, 59, 61, 110, 124, 140, 149–50, 182–83, 251, 265, 283, 336–337, 403, 421–22, 532
    Ginsberg's letters to, from Europe, 226, 231–32, 244, 246, 296
    Ginsberg's letters to, from India, 299, 301, 305–6, 308–9, 317
    Ginsberg's letters to, from Mexico, 163, 164, 165
    Ginsberg's love affair with, 66, 67–68, 74–75, 95, 214
    Ginsberg's promotion of works by, 143–44, 148, 149, 152, 182, 183, 207, 212, 232, 237, 250, 253–55, 437, 438
    Ginsberg's Psychiatric Institute correspondence with, 117, 119, 120, 121
    Holmes and, 106, 114
    homosexual tendencies of, 68, 95
    memorials for, 455, 463–64, 501–3, 509, 530
    mother and, 44, 132, 248, 249–51, 333, 412
    parsimony of, 143, 147–48, 235, 237, 246, 262, 264
    political conservatism of, 176, 248, 249, 394, 421–22, 426
    at Six Gallery, 194, 195, 196

in Tangier, 220, 221–23, 224
writing style of, 56, 88, 145, 188, 191, 200, 359
Kerouac, Joan Haverty, 131, 132–33, 142–43
Kerouac, Stella Sampas, 412, 426, 427
Kesey, Ken, 329, 338–39, 376–77, 378–379, 380–81, 502
King, Bill, 469
King, Martin Luther, Jr., 408, 414
Kingsland, John, 56, 69, 127
Kinsey, Alfred, 73, 386
Kissinger, Henry, 447–48, 452
Kizer, Carolyn, 437
Kline, Franz, 177, 252, 280
Koch, Kenneth, 387
Korda, Zoltán, 51
"Kral Majalis" (Ginsberg), 368, 457
Kramer, Jane, 425
Krasner, Paul, 415, 502
Krim, Seymour, 275
Krishnaji, Srimata, 314
Kunstler, William, 429, 430, 431
Kupferberg, Tuli, 189
Kyger, Joanne, see Snyder, Joanne Kyger

Laing, R. D., 393, 398
Lamantia, Philip, 127, 195, 217, 262, 267, 437, 438, 515, 531
Lancaster, William Woart, 57, 58, 60–61
Landesman, Jay, 128–29
Lansky, Meyer, 341
"Laughing Gas" (Ginsberg), 255
Laughlin, James, 217, 227, 253
LaVigne, Robert, 177, 178–79, 180, 182, 199, 202, 219, 249, 253, 329, 337, 380
Lazarus, Arthur, 39, 56
Leary, Timothy, 276–82, 291, 292, 293, 305, 350, 386–87, 390, 393, 394, 439, 449–50, 502, 509, 529
Lebel, Jean-Jacques, 504
Lennon, John, 349, 370, 371, 397–98, 444–445, 471, 492, 505, 529
Leonard, Donna, 42
Leslie, Alfred, 257, 258
Levertov, Denise, 212, 216, 217, 240, 327
Levitt, Al, 241
Levy, Anne, 357
Levy, Joe, 356–57
Liang Kai, 153
Lichtenstein, Roy, 528
Lieberman, Juanita, 526
Life, 10, 217, 234, 244, 259, 285, 384, 385, 425
"Lion for Real, The" (Ginsberg), 259
Lipton, Lawrence, 213, 215, 216

Livergant, Eleanor, 12, 13, 16, 39, 75, 81, 94, 120, 206, 244, 357
Livergant, Isser, 12, 357
Livergant, Mendel, 11–12, 357
Living Theater, 127, 258, 523
Lord, Sterling, 255, 264
Los Angeles Times, 524
"Love Poem on a Theme by Whitman" (Ginsberg), 167–68, 430
Lowell, Robert, 280, 281–82, 387
LSD, 376–77
congressional hearings on, 390
Ginsberg's use of, 260, 262, 271, 274, 375, 398, 433
Luria, Leon, 39, 76, 81, 95
Lurie, Frieda, 355–56, 358

Mabley, Jack, 258
MacAdams, Lewis, 455
McCarthy, Eugene, 448
McCarthyism, 176, 249, 332, 532
McCartney, Paul, 396–98, 406, 492
McClure, Michael, 183, 193, 195–96, 211, 212–13, 217, 262, 264, 328, 380, 381, 394, 437, 438, 481, 502, 531
McDarrah, Fred, 354
McGovern, George, 421
McIntosh, Ralph, 227
McKeever, William, 467–68
McKnight, Nicholas, 57, 60–61, 77
McNally, Dennis, 502
Maggie Cassady (Kerouac), 152
"Magic Psalm" (Ginsberg), 270
Maharishi Mahesh Yogi, 408–10
Mailer, Norman, 263, 275–76, 340, 387, 484, 513, 528
Malanga, Gerard, 335, 387
"Malest Cornifici Tuo Catullo" (Ginsberg), 179
Mandel, Ernest, 398
Manhattan Project, 49
Man Ray, 245
Mansfield, Dave, 459, 460
Manson, Charles, 395
"Many Loves" (Ginsberg), 83
Many Loves (Williams), 258
Mao Tse-tung, 330, 516
Marin, Peter, 477, 478, 480
Mario, José, 343
Marker, Lewis, 135, 137–38
Markfield, Wallace, 118
Martin, Jack, 389–90
Martin, Peter, 183
Martinelli, Sheri, 150
Maschler, Tom, 349, 371, 398
Matthiessen, Peter, 269

Mekas, Jonas, 258, 334, 336, 387
Melody, Little Jack, 109–10, 111–16, 119, 140
Melville, Herman, 38, 48, 508
Mercedes, Denise, 431, 432, 433, 435, 444, 445, 450, 454, 457, 459
Merry Pranksters, 338–39, 378
Merwin, W. S., 438, 466–70, 473–75, 476–82, 484
"Message" (Ginsberg), 354
"Message II" (Ginsberg), 353, 354
Methedrine University, 263
Mexico, Ginsberg's visits to, 135–37, 156–66, 493, 509
Mexico City Blues (Kerouac), 237, 253, 254, 426, 428, 463
Meyerzove, Leland, 332
MGM, 258, 425, 535
Michaux, Henri, 124, 246–47
Micheline, Jack, 502
Miller, Arthur, 377, 528
Miller, Charles H., 242
Miller, Henry, 210, 236, 294, 531
Millstein, Gilbert, 231, 283
Mind Breaths (Ginsberg), 452, 456, 473
Mingus, Charles, 425
Minutes to Go (Burroughs et al.), 285
Mondrian String Quartet, 505
Monk, Thelonius, 252–53, 280, 425
Montgomery, John, 200, 254
Moore, Marianne, 15, 210, 244
Moraes, Dom, 241, 242
Moreland, Dusty, 127, 133, 134, 140, 141, 147, 148, 149
Morrissey, Paul, 387
Motherwell, Robert, 245
"Mugging" (Ginsberg), 457
Muktananda Paramahansa, Swami, 439
Murao, Shigeyoshi, 183, 227, 376, 380
Murphy, Anne, 329, 375, 376
Mustard, S. M., 436
"My Sad Self" (Ginsberg), 391

Naked Lunch (Burroughs), 9, 64, 72, 155, 175, 207, 222, 258, 263, 264, 340, 532
Naone, Dana, 466–70, 479
Naropa Institute, 454–55, 457, 458, 466–470, 473–75, 476–82, 484–86, 488, 490, 494, 501, 502, 503, 504, 507, 508, 509, 510, 526
National Book Awards, 437–38, 484
Nearing, Scott, 19
Nehru, Pandit, 317
Neruda, Pablo, 452
Neuwirth, Bobby, 459, 461

New American Poetry, 1945–60 (Allen), 252, 531
New Directions, 145, 147, 176, 217, 253, 254, 388
New Letters, 530
Newman, Mr. and Mrs. Albert A., 259
New Republic, 519
New World Writing, 232
New York Daily News, 52, 109
New Yorker, 106, 217, 425
New York Herald Tribune, 38, 340
New York Post, 530
New York Times, 9, 16, 28, 29, 38, 52, 58, 128, 211, 217, 227, 231, 283, 323, 387, 390, 420, 429, 435–36, 437–38, 457, 472, 473, 487, 503, 510, 525, 529
New York World-Telegram, 154, 165, 217
Ngo Dinh Diem, 323, 330
Ngo Dinh Nhu, 330
Nguyen Cao Ky, 436
Nguyen Van Thieu, 436
Nhu, Madame, 330, 436
Nicaragua, 488, 496–501, 521
Niland, Jack, 469
Nilsson, Harry, 471
Nin, Anaïs, 215, 216
Nixon, Richard M., 275, 421, 447, 456, 487, 513
Norse, Harold, 127, 221
Norway, 504, 507
Notley, Alice, 486
Nova Express (Burroughs), 398
Novotny, Anton, 367

O'Brien, Professor, 314
Ochs, Phil, 414, 459
O'Hara, Frank, 391, 531
"Old Angel Midnight" (Kerouac), 258
Olson, Charles, 217, 327, 338, 374, 375, 387, 396, 405, 531
Olympia Press, 236, 241, 263
"One Day" (Ginsberg), 104
Ono, Yoko, 444, 454, 471
On the Road (Kerouac), 9, 82, 107, 132, 143–44, 148, 149, 191, 231–32, 234, 235, 244, 246, 254, 283, 372, 501, 513
Oppenheimer, Joel, 212, 252
Orlovsky, Julius, 235, 249, 250, 337, 375, 376, 379, 381, 382, 383, 384–85, 404, 413, 431, 432, 445, 523
Orlovsky, Lafcadio, 186, 191–92, 215, 216, 217, 234, 249, 251, 253, 276, 282, 283, 284, 296–97, 307
Orlovsky, Marie, 264, 283, 296, 297
Orlovsky, Oleg, 249, 486, 503–4
Orlovsky, Peter, 11, 177, 205, 207, 211,

212, 213, 216, 217, 218, 219, 253,
    262, 275, 296, 329, 339, 375, 377,
    379, 381, 383, 386, 393, 394, 426,
    427, 428, 447, 449, 451, 454, 455,
    459, 461, 463, 470, 475, 486, 496, 523
background of, 181–82
in Boston, 276, 277, 278, 281, 339–40
Burroughs and, 224–25, 288–89, 308
drug addiction of, 321, 373, 376, 399,
    408, 412, 413, 431–33, 434
East Village apartments of, 251–53,
    282, 283, 334, 336, 373–74, 408, 410,
    444, 457
family cared for by, 186, 191–92, 217,
    234–35, 249, 296–97, 307, 337, 384–
    385, 503–4
Ginsberg's farm and, 413, 422, 423,
    431–33, 434, 435, 445, 450, 473, 490
Ginsberg's letters to, 239, 240, 267,
    291–93, 322, 323, 325, 327, 353, 354,
    359, 370, 396, 398, 399
Ginsberg's love affair with, 178–81,
    182, 185, 186, 199, 214, 288–93, 373,
    399–400, 526, 527, 532
India visited by, 298–321
Italy visited by, 226, 228–31
Morocco visited by, 223–25, 286–90
in Paris, 231, 233–34, 236–38, 284–86
poetry readings by, 259, 260, 457
Pull My Daisy and, 257, 258
strange behavior of, 501, 504–7, 508,
    526–27
Orlovsky family, 217, 234–35, 249, 251,
    296–97, 307, 333, 503–4
Ortega, Daniel, 496–97
Oswald, Lee Harvey, 331
Owens, Iris, 241
Ozick, Cynthia, 529

Padgett, Ron, 486
Palestinian territories, 528–29
Paley, Grace, 529
Pang, May, 471
Paris, Ginsberg's stay in, 231, 233–34,
    236–39, 240–41, 244–47, 284–86, 457
Paris Review, 232, 234, 301
Parker, Edie, *see* Kerouac, Edie Parker
Parker, Helen, 129, 130, 131, 132–33,
    241, 465
Parkinson, Thomas, 239, 240, 260, 261
Parmentel, Noel, Jr., 275
Parra, Nicanor, 364, 452
Partisan Review, 124, 147, 212, 217, 259
Patchen, Kenneth, 172, 210, 211, 212,
    345
Paterson (Williams), 125, 126, 253, 519

Patten, Brian, 397
Paz, Octavio, 493
Pegler, Westbrook, 123
Pelieu, Claude, 435
PEN, 499, 528–29
Pennebaker, Don, 369
Peret, Benjamin, 245
Perlis, Leo, 28
Peru, 154, 264, 266, 268–73, 375, 509
Phipps, Harry, 307
Pickard, Tom, 370
Pincus, Walter, 436
Pivano, Fernanda, 267, 400, 401, 502
Planet News, 309, 433, 435
Plant, Sheila, 253, 262
Playboy, 372, 416, 421, 425
"Please Master" (Ginsberg), 20–21, 457
Plutonian Ode (Ginsberg), 475, 494
Plymell, Charley, 392
Podhoretz, Norman, 9, 387, 530–31
Poland, 361–62, 521
Portman, Michael, 287, 288, 292, 293,
    488
Posset, Ben, 505
Pound, Ezra, 15, 79, 125, 150, 203, 204,
    210, 253, 370, 395, 400–406, 455,
    494, 498
psilocybin, 274, 276–83
Puente, 341, 342, 346, 347, 351
Pull My Daisy (film title), 258
"Pull My Daisy" (Ginsberg poem), 128–
    129
Putnam, Samuel, 124
Putterman, Zev, 9, 10, 255–56
Pybus, Diana, 443

Ramparts, 386, 435
Randall, Margaret, 497
Random House, 147, 425
Rauch, Jerry, 37
Reagan, Ronald, 488, 500, 505, 506,
    510
Reality Sandwiches (Ginsberg), 274
Reck, Michael, 401, 402–3
Rees, Robert, 512, 514
Reich, Wilhelm, 10, 95
Rexroth, Kenneth, 147, 171, 176, 183,
    186, 193, 195, 196, 202–3, 211, 212,
    227, 244, 354, 481
Ribicoff, Abraham, 421
Richards, Keith, 397
Richman, Robert, 519
Ridge, Lola, 15
Rimbaud, Arthur, 36, 43, 48, 58, 74, 118,
    191, 237, 285, 392, 457, 490
Rivers, Larry, 127, 177, 241, 257, 258

Robinson, Carolyn, *see* Cassady, Carolyn Robinson
Roethke, Theodore, 219
Rolling Stones, 379, 387, 396, 397, 507
Rolling Thunder, Chief, 464
Rolling Thunder Revue, 458–66, 472
Rolling Thunder Logbook (Shepard), 460
Romanova, Ylena, 355, 360
Roosevelt Routine (Burroughs), 336
Rosa, Blas, 343
Rosenblatt, Roger, 519
Rosenthal, Bob, 26, 484, 521, 524, 526, 528
Rosenthal, Irving, 258, 259, 441
Rosset, Barney, 233, 261, 282, 532
Roth, Paul, 35
Roy, Kali Pada Guha, 317
Rubin, Barbara, 334, 335, 371, 372, 376, 387, 412, 413, 422, 423, 486–87, 506
Rubin, Jerry, 394, 414, 415, 421, 429, 431
Rudge, Olga, 400, 401, 402, 404, 405, 406
Russell, Peter, 401
Russell, Vickie, 65, 69, 81, 82, 109–10, 111–16, 119
Ruz, Alberto, 157, 158

Sabbah, Hassan i, 272
Safire, William, 487
Sahl, Mort, 342
Sale, Faith, 529
Salter, Elizabeth, 243
Sampas, Stella, *see* Kerouac, Stella Sampas
Sampas family, 412, 427, 463
Sanders, Ed, 340, 382, 383, 415–16, 474, 476–77, 480, 481, 484, 485, 531
San Francisco Human Be-In, 394–95, 414, 429
San Francisco Poetry Renaissance, 193–197, 199–200, 202–3, 210–13, 262, 531
San Remo bar, 127–28, 131, 133, 141, 150, 151, 189, 195, 252
Santamaria, Haydée, 338, 344, 346, 347, 348–50, 351, 352
Savage, Hope, 220
Schapiro, Meyer, 97, 119, 151, 203
Schechtman, Rebecca, 13, 14, 24, 30, 31, 38, 39, 81, 94, 178
Schoen, Steven, 175
Schulman, Howard, 294, 295
Schwarten, Katherine, 181
Scribner's, 128, 217
Scripture of the Golden Eternity (Kerouac), 333
Seale, Bobby, 429, 431

Seaver, Richard, 418, 419
Sedgwick, Edie, 387
Shapiro, Karl, 203
Sheehan, Neal, 323
Shelley, Percy Bysshe, 10, 58, 228, 230, 242, 255, 256, 385, 392
Shepard, Sam, 459, 460, 463
Sheppard, R. Z., 518
Shields, Karena, 159–60, 163, 164, 165, 166, 209
Shivananda, Swami, 300–301, 325
"Siesta in Xbalba" (Ginsberg), 105, 164, 209
Simon, Carly, 454
Simpson, Louis, 189, 217, 473
Singh, Mr., 315–17
Sirhan, Sirhan, 414
Sitwell, Edith, 243–44
Six Gallery, 193, 195–97, 202
Skvorecky, Josef, 353, 354, 362
Smart, Christopher, 198, 255
Smith, Grover, 56
Smith, Harry, 523, 528
Smith, Jack, 336, 389–90, 533
Smith, Seldon Kirby, 184
Snodgrass, W. D., 437
Snyder, Gary, 193–94, 195, 197, 199, 200, 202, 211, 212, 213, 217, 252, 253, 254, 255, 258, 291, 293, 298, 321, 324, 333, 374, 380, 388, 389, 393, 394, 438, 446, 481, 509, 512, 514, 531
in India, 300–307
Sierra Nevadas land of, 411, 447, 454, 455–56
Zen and, 302, 305–6, 324
Snyder, Joanne Kyger, 300–307, 321, 324
on Ginsberg, 303, 305, 326
on Orlovsky, 303
Socialism, 11, 12, 13, 14, 500
Soft Machine, The (Burroughs), 64, 287
Solanas, Valerie, 414
Solomon, Carl, 122, 123–24, 127, 128, 141, 148, 195, 210, 253, 263, 284, 435, 502
Ace Books edited by, 143–44, 148, 149, 232
background of, 117–18
"Howl" and, 118, 189, 190–91
Solomon, Olive, 141, 148
Sommerville, Ian, 285–86, 287, 293, 488
Songs of Innocence and Songs of Experience (Blake), 99–102
Sontag, Susan, 336, 387, 528, 529
Sosa, Roberto, 496
Sottsass, Ettore, 400

Southern, Terry, 241, 415, 418, 419
Soviet Union, 355–61, 488, 497, 500, 521
Spain, 28, 225–26
Spector, Phil, 383, 384, 445
Spellman, Cardinal, 323
Spender, Stephen, 261, 396
Spengler, Oswald, 48, 73, 109, 210
Spicer, Jack, 171, 328, 374
Spock, Benjamin, 377
Stalinism, 357, 359, 366, 368, 498
State Department, U.S., 338
Steeves, Harrison, 57
Stein, Gertrude, 199
Steloff, Frances, 62
Stern, Fritz, 57
Stevenson, Quentin, 243
Stoner, Rob, 458, 459
"Stotras to Kali Destroyer of Illusions"
    (Ginsberg), 309
"Strange New Cottage in Berkeley, A"
    (Ginsberg), 193, 201
Stringham, Ed, 106
Strummer, Joe, 491, 495, 503
Styron, Rose, 529
Styron, William, 529
Sublette, Al, 170, 175, 176
Subterraneans, The (Kerouac), 254
"Sunflower Sutra" (Ginsberg), 200, 201,
    202, 211, 216
"Supermarket in California" (Ginsberg),
    193, 201, 216, 240
Suzuki, D. T., 153, 439
Sweden, 504, 506
Sweezy, Paul, 398
Szabo, 338

Tangier, 214–15, 216, 221–25, 284–93
    Ginsberg's visits to, 223–25, 286–93
Taylor, Cecil, 456
Taylor, James, 454
Taylor, Steven, 486, 501, 504, 505, 506,
    507
Temko, Alan, 83
Thakur, Citaram Onkar Das, 317
Thomas, Dylan, 242, 255
Thomas, Norman, 19, 377
Three Graces, 150–51
Tibet, 303–4, 442
Tibetan Book of the Dead, The, 274, 439,
    504
Time, 217, 229, 230, 259, 285, 286, 318,
    323, 369, 425, 462, 495, 518, 519
Toklas, Alice, 395
Town and the City, The (Kerouac), 62, 74,
    80, 98, 110, 145, 152
Tresca, Carlo, 183

Trilling, Diana, 61, 120, 259, 457
Trilling, Lionel, 37–38, 58, 61, 79, 98,
    103, 111, 119, 120, 184, 203, 212,
    259, 287
Tristessa (Kerouac), 216
Trocchi, Alexander, 263, 283, 531
Trungpa, Chögyam, 440–44, 446, 447,
    450–51, 453, 454, 455, 458, 463, 471,
    487, 489, 494, 509, 524–26, 527
    Merwin affair and, 466–70, 473–75,
    476–81, 484–86
Turner, Pete, 315
Tzara, Tristan, 245

Ugly Spirit, 137, 138
"Understand That This Is a Dream"
    (Ginsberg), 20
Ungaretti, Guiseppe, 395, 396
Ungerer, Joy, 236
Untermeyer, Louis, 15, 16, 48
Urich, Ed, 413

Van Doren, Mark, 37, 38, 61, 79, 97, 103,
    110, 119, 120, 122, 147, 184, 203
Van Duyn, Mona, 437
Van Hartz, Francesca, 140
Vanity of Duluoz (Kerouac), 40, 44, 69,
    262
Varona, Carlos, 352
Vietnam:
    Ginsberg's visit to, 20, 322–23
    religious repression in, 323, 330
    war in, 322–23, 375–76, 377, 381, 383,
        384, 385, 389, 393, 409, 411, 414,
        421, 428, 435, 447, 448, 456
Village Voice, 217, 262, 386, 472
Villa Muniriya, 221, 222, 287, 293
Villiers Press, 207
Vinkenoog, Simon, 504, 505, 506, 507
"Vision 1948" (Ginsberg), 104
Visions of Cody (Kerouac), 78, 91, 141,
    182–83, 254
Vitebsk, 12, 361
Vollmer, Joan, *see* Burroughs, Joan
    Vollmer
Voznesensky, Andrei, 343, 360–62, 371,
    493, 504

Walberg, Leo, 71
Waldman, Anne, 454–55, 456, 459, 479,
    486, 531
"Wales Visitation" (Ginsberg), 398–99,
    457
Wallace, Mike, 392
Warhol, Andy, 258, 335–36, 371, 387, 414
Washington Post, 492, 503

Wassing, Hans, 31, 77
Watkins, Julius, 425
Watts, Alan, 393, 438, 439
Weaver, Raymond, 37, 38, 79
Wechsler, Herbert, 119
Weiner, Lee, 429, 431
Weinglass, Leonard, 429, 431
Welch, Lew, 194
West End Bar, 42, 43, 47, 54, 63, 82, 98
Wexler, Jerry, 339
Whalen, Philip, 44, 194–95, 199, 200,
    205, 208, 211, 212, 217, 237, 240,
    252, 253, 255, 258, 260, 262, 264,
    327, 328, 333, 437, 438
Wheelock, John Hall, 16, 143
White, Dennis, 469
White, Ed, 145
White, Phil ("The Sailor"), 63–65, 78,
    140–41, 144, 285
White Shroud (Ginsberg), 524, 530
Whitman, Walt, 30, 79, 124, 125, 190,
    197, 211, 218, 230, 231, 393, 438,
    508, 513, 515, 518, 532
Whitten, Les, 435
"Wichita Vortex Sutra" (Ginsberg), 385–
    386, 457
Wieners, John, 267, 374, 405, 531
Wilbourn, George, 389–90
Wilentz, Ted, 333
Williams, William Carlos, 79, 88, 125–27,

    139, 142, 144, 145–47, 171, 186, 190,
    194, 195, 199, 201, 204, 212, 219,
    227, 253, 256, 279, 318–19, 344, 350,
    370, 438, 455, 490, 498, 515, 519, 531
Witt-Diamant, Ruth, 183, 196, 203, 227,
    244, 260
Wolfe, Thomas, 70
Woods, Dick, 167
Woods, Ed, 138
Wright, Herman, 425
Writers Union, 342, 343, 350, 353, 355,
    358, 360, 361, 366
Wylie, Andrew, 509–10
Wyse, Seymour, 240, 283

yage (ayahuasca), Ginsberg's use of, 266,
    269–73, 274, 279, 289, 375
Yage Letters, The (Burroughs), 336
Yeats, W. B., 36, 58, 518
Yevtushenko, Yevgeny, 358–59, 496, 497,
    498–99
Yippies, 414, 415, 418, 429, 430, 448
Young, Celine, 42, 43, 51, 53–54, 66, 69
Yuan Kejia, 513
Yugen, 237, 252, 261, 264
Yugoslavia, 486, 521

Zabrana, Jan, 353, 362
Zen, *see* Buddhism
Zukofsky, Louis, 210, 212